AN MMY MONOGRAPH

Publications of
THE INSTITUTE OF MENTAL MEASUREMENTS
Edited by Oscar Krisen Buros

EDUCATIONAL, PSYCHOLOGICAL, AND PERSONALITY TESTS OF 1933 AND 1934

EDUCATIONAL, PSYCHOLOGICAL, AND PERSONALITY TESTS OF 1933, 1934, AND 1935

EDUCATIONAL, PSYCHOLOGICAL, AND PERSONALITY TESTS OF 1936

THE NINETEEN THIRTY-EIGHT MENTAL MEASUREMENTS YEARBOOK

THE NINETEEN FORTY MENTAL MEASUREMENTS YEARBOOK

THE THIRD MENTAL MEASUREMENTS YEARBOOK

THE FOURTH MENTAL MEASUREMENTS YEARBOOK

THE FIFTH MENTAL MEASUREMENTS YEARBOOK

TESTS IN PRINT

THE SIXTH MENTAL MEASUREMENTS YEARBOOK

READING TESTS AND REVIEWS

PERSONALITY TESTS AND REVIEWS

THE SEVENTH MENTAL MEASUREMENTS YEARBOOK

TESTS IN PRINT II

ENGLISH TESTS AND REVIEWS

FOREIGN LANGUAGE TESTS AND REVIEWS

INTELLIGENCE TESTS AND REVIEWS

MATHEMATICS TESTS AND REVIEWS

PERSONALITY TESTS AND REVIEWS II

READING TESTS AND REVIEWS II

SCIENCE TESTS AND REVIEWS

SOCIAL STUDIES TESTS AND REVIEWS

VOCATIONAL TESTS AND REVIEWS

READING

TESTS AND REVIEWS II

READING
TESTS AND REVIEWS II

A Monograph
Consisting of the Reading Sections of the
SEVENTH MENTAL MEASUREMENTS YEARBOOK (1972)
and
TESTS IN PRINT II (1974)

Edited by
OSCAR KRISEN BUROS
Director, The Institute of Mental Measurements

THE GRYPHON PRESS
HIGHLAND PARK · NEW JERSEY
1975

DESIGNED BY LUELLA BUROS

COPYRIGHT 1975 BY OSCAR KRISEN BUROS, PUBLISHED BY THE GRYPHON PRESS,
220 MONTGOMERY STREET, HIGHLAND PARK, NEW JERSEY 08904. No part of this publication may
be reproduced in any form, nor may any of the contents be used in an informational storage,
retrieval, or transmission system without the prior written permission of the publisher.

LC 70-13495, ISBN 910674-20-5

MANUFACTURED BY QUINN & BODEN COMPANY, INC., RAHWAY, NEW JERSEY
PRINTED IN THE UNITED STATES OF AMERICA

To the memory of
Lenora

TABLE OF CONTENTS

MMY TEST REVIEWERS

Ira E. Aaron	6:830, 6:831
	6:834, 7:720, 7:721
Georgia S. Adams	7:711
Janet G. Afflerbach	5:693
Lois G. Afflerbach	5:693
Nicholas Anastasiow	7:766
Irving H. Anderson	1:1095, 1:1097
	1:1104, 3:514, 3:518, 3:519, 3:521
Mary C. Austin	6:848
Warren R. Baller	4:583
Rebecca C. Barr	7:717, 7:754, 7:758
Thomas C. Barrett	6:795, 6:814
Robert H. Bauernfeind	7:707
Robert M. Bear	3:497
	3:509, 4:575, 4:586
Paul Conrad Berg	7:749, 7:752
Allen Berger	7:686, 7:709
Emmett A. Betts	6:810, 6:831
L. B. Birch	6:833
Donald B. Black	7:688, 7:704
Emery P. Bliesmer	6:826, 6:832, 6:842
Paul J. Blommers	3:530
Joan Bollenbacher	5:675, 5:679
Guy L. Bond	2:1533, 2:1548
Ivan A. Booker	1:1105, 1:1110, 2:1547
	2:1581, 3:505, 3:532, 3:534, 4:544, 4:558
John R. Bormuth	7:728
M. Alan Brimer	6:843, 7:774
M. Eustace Broom	2:1534
Charles M. Brown	6:829, 6:834
N. Dale Bryant	5:649
	5:676, 6:821, 6:824, 7:722
Carolyn L. Burke	7:689
Guy T. Buswell	2:1559
Thorsten R. Carlson	7:700, 7:701
Harold D. Carter	4:559
Stella Center	1:1108
W. V. Clemans	6:806
William E. Coffman	6:786, 7:713
S. Alan Cohen	7:759
Thomas E. Culliton, Jr.	6:820, 6:836
Reginald R. Dale	5:652
Frederick B. Davis	1:1107, 1:1114
	2:1529, 2:1563, 3:480
	3:489, 3:507, 4:531, 7:697
Robert A. Davis	3:536
Stanley E. Davis	6:865
James Deese	5:688, 5:697
Gabriel M. Della-Piana	6:824
Dennis J. Deloria	7:742, 7:762
Evelyn Deno	7:764
Clarence Derrick	5:649, 6:815
Joseph C. Dewey	1:1105
	1:1110, 1:1115, 2:1539
Jerome E. Doppelt	5:644
Gerald G. Duffy	7:721, 7:745
Lydia A. Duggins	5:671, 5:672
S. S. Dunn	5:631, 5:677, 5:679
Henry S. Dyer	5:621
Robert Dykstra	7:749, 7:757
Robert L. Ebel	4:582, 5:696, 5:698
William Eller	6:792, 6:836
Alvin C. Eurich	2:1578
Roger Farr	7:682, 7:744
Ethel M. Feagley	3:536, 3:543
Leonard S. Feldt	5:687

Henry D. Rinsland   2:1535, 4:585
Holland Roberts   2:1547, 3:477, 4:536
H. Alan Robinson   6:797
                 6:802, 7:707, 7:723
Helen M. Robinson   4:561
                 4:562, 5:656, 5:675
Benjamin Rosner   5:625
Jerome Rosner   7:747, 7:760
David H. Russell   2:1570, 3:513
        3:515, 3:517, 3:520, 4:551, 4:572
Roger A. Ruth   7:767
Richard Rystrom   7:684
Rachel Salisbury   2:1580
Douglas E. Scates   3:538, 3:540, 3:542
Fred J. Schonell   4:566, 5:616, 5:617
Virginia Seavey   3:484, 3:493
Spencer Shank   1:1114
Carleton B. Shay   7:782
William D. Sheldon   4:545, 4:553
Louis Shores   4:578, 4:585
Harry Singer   7:757, 7:758
Edward R. Sipay   7:753, 7:754
Donald E. P. Smith   5:621
                 5:666, 6:840, 6:857
Henry P. Smith   4:529, 4:541
Kenneth J. Smith   7:737, 7:744
Nila Banton Smith   4:539, 4:542, 4:565
George D. Spache   3:484, 3:485
                 3:486, 5:660, 5:662
        6:793, 6:829, 6:838, 7:726, 7:728
Herbert F. Spitzer   3:485, 3:487
Russell G. Stauffer   5:620, 5:650, 6:814
Harry L. Stein   5:619
Clarence R. Stone 2:1548, 2:1570, 2:1571
Ruth M. Strang   1:1106
                 1:1107, 5:696, 5:698

J. B. Stroud   3:480, 3:497, 3:524
Edward A. Tenney   2:1561
Edith I. M. Thomson   3:499
Robert H. Thouless   3:544
Joseph Tiffin   1:1108
Miles A. Tinker   1:1108, 2:1533
        2:1579, 3:524, 3:539, 4:660
T. L. Torgerson   3:485, 3:510
Agatha Townsend   5:620, 5:656
                 6:787, 6:798, 6:800, 6:822
Marion R. Trabue   1:1171
Arthur E. Traxler   5:650
                 6:791, 7:697, 7:708
Frances O. Triggs   3:502
William W. Turnbull   3:477
                 3:489, 4:531, 4:550
Robert E. Valett   7:759
Byron H. Van Roekel   5:659, 5:667
        6:823, 6:830, 7:689, 7:692
Magdalen D. Vernon   5:619
                 5:636, 5:637, 6:812, 6:843
Verna L. Vickery   5:659, 5:665
Guy W. Wagner   1:1097
Morey J. Wantman   6:793, 6:859
David M. Wark   7:733
David P. Weikart   7:739, 7:759
Henry Weitz   4:531
Carolyn M. Welch   3:509, 3:512
Frederick L. Westover   4:557
D. K. Wheeler   5:617, 5:674
Stephen Wiseman   5:652, 5:653
Paul A. Witty   3:513, 3:514, 3:516
D. A. Worcester   2:1551
C. Gilbert Wrenn   1:1166, 2:1578, 5:688
J. Wayne Wrightstone   2:1581
                 3:535, 3:537, 3:545, 5:693

PREFACE

IT IS my considered belief that most standardized tests are poorly constructed, of questionable or unknown validity, pretentious in their claims, and likely to be misused more often than not. This conviction began to form 48 to 50 years ago when I was taking courses in testing at the University of Minnesota. I vividly recall presenting a paper entitled "Common Fallacies in the Use of Standardized Tests" in an advanced educational psychology class taught by Professor W. S. Miller, a paper in which I criticized some of the views of my instructors. Shortly thereafter, I had the good fortune to read a book which was a landmark in the consumer movement—*Your Money's Worth* by Stuart Chase and F. J. Schlink. It was this book which led to the founding of Consumers' Research, Inc., an organization which tests and evaluates commonly used commercial products. This book and the establishment of Consumers' Research stimulated me to begin thinking about a test users' research organization to evaluate tests.

After failing to secure financial support for the initiation of a test users' research organization, I scaled down my objectives to the establishment of a cooperative test reviewing service which would report on and evaluate standardized tests used in education, industry, and psychology. One hundred thirty-three specialists in a wide variety of disciplines cooperated by contributing "frankly critical reviews" for *The 1938 Mental Measurements Yearbook* (also called *The First Yearbook*). Later yearbooks (each volume supplementing earlier volumes) were published in 1941, 1949, 1953, 1959, 1965, and 1972.

The objectives of the *Mental Measurements Yearbooks* (MMY's) have remained essentially the same since they were first presented in detail in *The 1940 Mental Measurements Yearbook* (also called *The Second Yearbook*): (*a*) to provide information about tests published as separates throughout the English-speaking world; (*b*) to present frankly critical test reviews written by testing and subject specialists representing various viewpoints; (*c*) to provide extensive bibliographies of verified references on the construction, use, and validity of specific tests; (*d*) to make readily available the critical portions of test reviews appearing in professional journals; and (*e*) to present fairly exhaustive listings of new and revised books on testing along with evaluative excerpts from representative reviews in professional journals.

As important as the above objectives are, I place even greater importance on these less tangible objectives: (*f*) to impel test authors and publishers to publish better tests and to provide test users with detailed information on the validity and limitations of these tests; (*g*) to inculcate in test users a keener awareness of the values and limitations of standardized tests; (*h*) to stimulate contributing reviewers to think through more carefully their own beliefs and values relevant to testing; (*i*) to suggest to test users better methods of appraising tests in light of their own particular needs; and (*j*) to impress upon test users the need to suspect all tests unaccompanied by detailed data on their construction, validity, uses, and limitations—

even when products of distinguished authors and reputable publishers.

As the number of published tests and, especially, the related literature increased tremendously over the years, the MMY's became increasingly more encyclopedic in scope. Many test users, however, are interested in only one or two areas of testing. To meet their needs, we announced in 1941 plans for publishing monographs in English, foreign languages, intelligence, mathematics, personality, reading, science, social studies, and vocations. Unfortunately, we were too optimistic; it was over a quarter of a century before we were able to finance the publication of the first monograph, *Reading Tests and Reviews* (RTR I), published in 1968.

The next monograph, *Personality Tests and Reviews* (PTR I), was published in 1970. The core of these two monographs, RTR I and PTR I, consists of a reprinting of the reading and personality sections, respectively, of the first six MMY's and a new section listing both in print and out of print tests in the area represented by the monograph.

Despite the use of a large amount of reprinted material, the preparation and publication of these two monographs turned out to be very costly. Since sales later proved insufficient to finance similar monographs in other areas, we temporarily abandoned our plans for additional monographs.

Following the publication of *The Seventh Yearbook* in early 1972, we began devoting all of our time to the completion of *Tests in Print II: An Index to Tests, Test Reviews, and the Literature on Specific Tests* (TIP II). In mid-1974, while TIP II was in press, it suddenly occurred to me that up-to-date monographs could be prepared at a manageable cost by re-printing a given section of TIP II along with the corresponding sections of the seven MMY's. As a consequence, we are now publishing monographs in nine areas: second monographs in personality and reading, and first monographs in English, foreign languages, intelligence, mathematics, science, social studies, and vocations. Hopefully, the publication of these monographs will make our material available to many test users who might otherwise not consult the MMY's and TIP II. Broadening the readership of our test reviews will bring us closer to achieving our objectives.

This monograph, *Reading Tests and Reviews II* (RTR II), supplements the 1968 RTR I. The indexing in this volume is cumulative, covering the contents of both reading monographs.

It has been particularly hectic preparing nine MMY monographs simultaneously. Fortunately, I have been assisted by a dedicated staff. Although other people worked for shorter periods of time, there are seven whom I would like to name for special recognition: Mary Anne Miller Becker, Sandra Boxer Discenza, Doris Greene McCan, Barbara Ruis Martko, Mary T. Mooney, Joan Stein Paszamant, and Natalie J. Rosenthal Turton. I am greatly indebted to my staff colleagues for their assistance in producing these nine derivative monographs.

We plan to publish *The Eighth Mental Measurements Yearbook* in 1977, followed by *Tests in Print III* in 1978. The reading sections of these volumes will supplement and update the material in RTR I and RTR II.

OSCAR KRISEN BUROS

Highland Park, New Jersey
February 24, 1975

INTRODUCTION

OR THE past 40 years we have been providing test users in education, industry, and psychology with a series of publications designed to assist them in the selection and use of tests which best meet their needs. We maintained an annual production schedule for our first four volumes (1935–38); since then, however, the intervals between books have been quite irregular with publication dates 1941, 1949, 1953, 1959, 1961, 1965, 1968, 1970, 1972, and 1974. Our publications through 1974 include three test bibliographies, seven *Mental Measurements Yearbooks,* two monographs, and two *Tests in Print.*[1] Nine derivative monographs—this volume and eight others—are being published in 1975. A brief description of our first fourteen publications follows.

FIRST THREE PUBLICATIONS

Although the earliest three publications are noncritical bibliographies, the original intent had been to prepare an annual critical review of new tests for journal publication. It soon became apparent, however, that this was far beyond the capacity of a single individual. A more modest goal was substituted, the publication of an annual bibliography of tests, as described in the Introduction to the first one:

To locate the standard tests recently published in specific areas is a laborious task. The usual bibliographic aids for locating periodical, monograph, and book publications are of little value in locating standard tests. New tests are being published so rapidly that the test technicians themselves find it difficult to locate the test titles of the past year without an inordinate amount of searching. For these reasons, the writer has undertaken the task of preparing a bibliography of psychological, achievement, character, and personality tests published in 1933 and 1934. This bibliography will be the first of a series to be published annually by the School of Education, Rutgers University.[2]

This 44-page bibliography lists 257 tests that were new, revised, or supplemented in 1933 and 1934. Many of these tests, usually revised editions, are still in print today.

Similar test bibliographies[3] were published in 1936 and 1937. During this time, attempts were being made to obtain a grant to initiate a

---

1 The first fourteen publications (1935–1974), edited by Oscar K. Buros and now published by The Gryphon Press, are listed from the most recent to the oldest:
a) Tests in Print II: An Index to Tests, Test Reviews, and the Literature on Specific Tests, December 1974. Pp. xxxix, 1107. $70.
b) The Seventh Mental Measurements Yearbook, Vols. I and II, 1972. Pp. xl, 935; vi, 937–1986. $70 per set.
c) Personality Tests and Reviews: Including an Index to The Mental Measurements Yearbooks, 1970. Pp. xxxi, 1659. $45. For reviews, see 7:B120.
d) Reading Tests and Reviews: Including a Classified Index to The Mental Measurements Yearbooks, 1968. Pp. xxii, 520. $20. For reviews, see 7:B121.
e) The Sixth Mental Measurements Yearbook, 1965. Pp. xxxvii, 1714. $45. (Reprinted 1971) For reviews, see 7:B122.
f) Tests in Print: A Comprehensive Bibliography of Tests for Use in Education, Psychology, and Industry, 1961. Pp. xxix, 479. $15. (Reprinted 1974) For reviews, see 6:B105.
g) The Fifth Mental Measurements Yearbook, 1959. Pp. xxix, 1292. $35. (Reprinted 1961) For reviews, see 6:B104.
h) The Fourth Mental Measurements Yearbook, 1953. Pp. xxv, 1163. $30. (Reprinted 1974) For reviews, see 5:B84.
i) The Third Mental Measurements Yearbook, 1949. Pp. xv, 1047. $25. (Reprinted 1974) For reviews, see 4:B71.
j) The Nineteen Forty Mental Measurements Yearbook, 1941. Pp. xxv, 674. $20. (Reissued 1972) For reviews, see 3:788 and 4:B70.
k) The Nineteen Thirty Eight Mental Measurements Yearbook, 1938. Pp. xv, 415. $17.50. (Reissued 1972) For reviews, see 2:B858.
l) Educational, Psychological, and Personality Tests of 1936: Including a Bibliography and Book Review Digest of Measurement Books and Monographs of 1933–36, 1937. Pp. 141. Out of print. For reviews, see 1:B326.
m) Educational, Psychological, and Personality Tests of 1933, 1934, and 1935, 1936. Pp. 83. Out of print. For reviews, see 36:B46.
n) Educational, Psychological, and Personality Tests of 1933 and 1934, 1935. Pp. 44. Out of print. For a review, see 36:B45.

2 *Educational, Psychological, and Personality Tests of 1933 and 1934,* p. 5.
3 *Educational, Psychological, and Personality Tests of 1933, 1934, and 1935.*
Educational, Psychological, and Personality Tests of 1936.

research organization which would serve as a bureau of standards for the evaluation of educational and psychological tests. It was only after we despaired of raising such funds that we decided to set up a test reviewing service.

THE SEVEN MMY'S

Since tests, unlike books, were rarely reviewed in professional journals, it was a revolutionary step forward when we published *The 1938 Mental Measurements Yearbook* 37 years ago. In his Foreword, Clarence E. Partch's comments reflect our excitement and mood in those early days:

The publication of *The 1938 Mental Measurements Yearbook of the School of Education, Rutgers University* is likely to prove a landmark of considerable importance in the history of tests and measurements. Heretofore, despite the obvious need of test users for frank evaluations of tests by competent reviewers, few standardized tests have been critically appraised in the professional journals and textbooks for students of education and psychology. Now, for the first time, a large number of frankly evaluative reviews by able test technicians, subject-matter specialists, and psychologists are available to assist test users in making more discriminating selections from among the hundreds of tests on the market.[4]

Except for a few test authors and publishers who objected to unfavorable reviews, *The 1938 Yearbook* (also referred to as *The First Yearbook*) was enthusiastically acclaimed in this country and abroad. It took some time, however, before most of the protesting publishers were able to accept unfavorable test reviews with equanimity.

Before *The 1938 Yearbook* was off the press, we began sending out invitations to review tests for a 1939 yearbook. Unfortunately, because of financing and production problems, we were unable to maintain our annual production schedule. It took us over two years to publish the next volume, *The 1940 Mental Measurements Yearbook*.

Much enlarged and greatly improved over its predecessor, *The 1940 Yearbook* (also referred to as *The Second Yearbook*) has been the prototype for all later yearbooks. In addition to the increased number of tests, reviews, and references, there were many qualitative changes: (*a*) The objectives which have characterized all MMY's were presented in detail for the first time. (*b*) The format was standardized. (*c*) The classification of tests was

4 *The 1938 Mental Measurements Yearbook*, p. xi.

changed from 40 specific categories to 12 broad categories. (*d*) The practice of including very short reviews of 100 words or less was discontinued. (*e*) The review coverage was extended to old tests and to tests previously reviewed as well as new tests. (*f*) The instructions given to reviewers concerning the preparation of their test reviews were presented. (*g*) The reactions of test authors and publishers—most of them objecting strenuously to unfavorable reviews—were reprinted for the first and last time.

In the Preface of *The 1940 Yearbook* we announced that the yearbooks would be published every two years. Because of World War II, however, *The Third Mental Measurements Yearbook* was not published until 1949. Except for its larger size and more thorough preparation, *The Third Yearbook*—like all later yearbooks—is very similar in its coverage, format, indexing, and organization to *The 1940 Yearbook*. There were, however, several improvements: (*a*) The "Classified Index of Tests," an expanded table of contents, was introduced. (*b*) Stars and asterisks were used preceding test titles to indicate, respectively, tests listed in a yearbook for the first time and tests revised or supplemented since last listed. (*c*) Asterisks were used at the end of a reference to indicate that the reference had been examined personally for accuracy and relevance. (*d*) Whenever possible, the abstract in *Psychological Abstracts* was cited for each reference. (*e*) Two improvements were made in the name index. Previously authors of references for specific tests had been indexed merely by citing the test for which the reference appears. After locating the test, one then had to search through the references to find those by that author. The new index eliminated this searching by citing each reference both to the test number and the reference number. Secondly, the index was converted into an "analytic index" in which *"test," "rev," "exc," "bk,"* and *"ref"* were used to indicate whether a citation referred to authorship of a test, review, excerpted review, book, or reference. These five features have been included in all later yearbooks.

In *The Fourth Mental Measurements Yearbook,* published in 1953, our review coverage was extended for the first time to many tests restricted to testing programs administered by organizations such as the College Entrance Examination Board. Six years later, in 1959, *The Fifth Yearbook* was published. Upon the completion of that volume, we were concerned that some cutbacks would be necessary to stem the phenomenal growth of production costs, as well as the ever increasing length of each MMY. As a result, we decided to discontinue specific test bibliographies and almost all reviews of foreign tests. The appreciative reviews *The Fifth Yearbook* received, however, especially those mentioning the value of the specific bibliographies to students of testing, caused us to reconsider. Consequently, despite the expanding literature on specific tests, we decided to continue all features of the earlier volumes. As a result, it took us six years to publish in 1965 *The Sixth Mental Measurements Yearbook,* a 1,751-page volume, approximately one-third larger than the previous yearbook. In addition to its more extensive coverage, *The Sixth Yearbook* presents a comprehensive listing of all tests in print as of mid-1964. The latest yearbook to date, *The Seventh Yearbook,* was published in 1972. This massive two-volume work of 2,032 pages may well be considered the zenith of the MMY's.

Like all other volumes published since 1938, *The Seventh Yearbook* supplements rather than supplants earlier yearbooks. For complete coverage, therefore, a reader must have access to all seven MMY's. A person using only the latest, *The Seventh Yearbook,* will miss a tremendous amount of valuable information in the six earlier volumes. Although the more recent yearbooks—especially the last three—are of greatest value, the third and fourth yearbooks also contain much useful information on many in print tests. Even though the first two yearbooks are mainly of historical interest, they also include some critical information on currently used tests. Our faith in the value of the first four MMY's, published between 1938 and 1953, is attested to by our reissuing of the first and second yearbooks in 1972 and reprinting of the third and fourth in 1974. Consequently, all seven yearbooks are now in print.

EARLIER MMY MONOGRAPHS

It is with amusement and wonder that we look back at some of the dreams of our youth.

The 1940 Mental Measurements Yearbook was the first yearbook published by my wife and myself. In those depression days, money was scarce but printing was cheap and penny postcards could be used for advertising. Borrowed capital of $3,500 was sufficient to launch us into book publishing. Even before our first book was off the press we were planning to publish not only a new MMY every two years, but also a series of derivative monographs. Our plans were confidently announced in the Preface of *The 1940 Yearbook* thus:

In order to make the material in the yearbooks more easily accessible to individuals who are interested in only a small part of each volume, a new series of monographs is being planned. If the first two or three monographs prove successful, others will eventually be prepared to cover tests in each of the following fields: business education, English and reading, fine arts, foreign languages, health and physical education, home economics, industrial arts, intelligence, mathematics, sciences, social studies, and vocational aptitudes. The first publication in each field will include: a comprehensive bibliography of all standard tests in print in that area; a reprinting, in part or in full, of all reviews of these tests which have appeared in previous yearbooks or in the journal literature; new reviews written especially for the monograph (to be, in turn, reprinted, in part or in full, in the following yearbook); and an extensive list of references on the construction, validation, use, and limitations of the tests. Separates in each field will be issued every four, six, or eight years depending upon the frequency of test publication. These monographs will range in size from fifty to two hundred pages. This new series will make it possible for an individual to purchase, at a nominal cost, every four, six, or eight years a monograph devoted solely to the tests and reviews of most interest to him.[5]

However, the publishing of the MMY's alone, even at intervals of 4 to 8 years, proved to be so time consuming and difficult that initiating the monograph series had to be continually postponed. But the dreams were never abandoned.

In 1968, 27 years after the monograph series was initially announced, the first monograph, *Reading Tests and Reviews* (RTR I), was published. (Further information on RTR I is given in subsequent paragraphs.) A second monograph, *Personality Tests and Reviews* (PTR I), was published two years later. This 1,695-page volume lists all personality tests as of June 1969 and provides a reprinting of the personality sections of the first six MMY's. The preparation of these two monographs turned out to be too costly and time consuming to justify working on monographs in other areas.

[5] *The 1940 Mental Measurements Yearbook,* p. xx.

TIP I AND TIP II

In 1961, we published the ninth volume in the MMY series: *Tests in Print: A Comprehensive Bibliography of Tests for Use in Education, Psychology, and Industry.* The objectives and nature of *Tests in Print* (hereafter called *Tests in Print I* or TIP I) are described in its Introduction as follows:

The objectives of *Tests in Print* are threefold: first, to present a comprehensive bibliography of tests—achievement, aptitude, intelligence, personality, and certain sensory-motor skills—published as separates and currently available in English-speaking countries; second, to serve as a classified index and supplement to the volumes of the *Mental Measurements Yearbook* series published to date; third, to give a wider distribution to the excellent recommendations for improving test manuals made by committees of the American Psychological Association, the American Educational Research Association, and the National Council on Measurements Used in Education.[6]

TIP I lists 2,967 tests—2,126 in print and 841 out of print as of early 1961, and also serves as a master index to the contents of the first five MMY's. Originally, we had planned to publish a new edition of TIP shortly after the publication of each new MMY, but poor sales of TIP I caused these plans to be abandoned. *The Sixth Yearbook,* in effect, served as a new edition of *Tests in Print* by referring to the tests in TIP I which were still in print as of mid-1964. Surprisingly, however, sales of the 1961 *Tests in Print* began to pick up after publication of *The Sixth Yearbook* in 1965. This unexpected upturn encouraged us to begin devoting all of our time to the preparation of a new edition of TIP immediately after approving the last proofs for *The Seventh Yearbook.*

Tests in Print II: An Index to Tests, Test Reviews, and the Literature on Specific Tests (TIP II) was published in December 1974. Like the 1961 volume, *Tests in Print II* presents: (*a*) a comprehensive bibliography of all known tests published as separates for use with English-speaking subjects; (*b*) a classified index to the contents of the test sections of the seven *Mental Measurements Yearbooks* published to date; and (*c*) a reprinting of the 1974 APA-AERA-NCME *Standards for Educational and Psychological Tests.*

In addition, TIP II introduces the following new features: (*d*) comprehensive bibliographies through 1971 on the construction, use,

and validity of specific tests; (*e*) a classified list of tests which have gone out of print since TIP I; (*f*) a cumulative name index for each test with references; (*g*) a title index covering in print and out of print tests, as well as inverted, series, and superseded titles in the MMY's and monographs; (*h*) an analytic name index covering all authors of tests, reviews, excerpts, and references in the MMY's and monographs; (*i*) a publishers directory with a complete listing of each publisher's test titles; (*j*) a classified scanning index which describes the population for which each test is intended; (*k*) identification of foreign tests and journals by presenting the country of origin in brackets immediately after a test entry or journal title; (*l*) inclusions of factual statements implying criticism such as "1971 tests identical with tests copyrighted 1961 except for format," and "no manual"; (*m*) listing of test titles at the foot of each page to permit immediate identification of pages consisting only of references or names; and (*n*) directions on how to use the book and an expanded table of contents printed on the endpages to greatly facilitate its use.

TIP II contains 2,467 in print test entries, 16.0 percent more than in TIP I. Table 1 presents a breakdown of the number of tests and new references in TIP II by classification. Personality—the area in which we know the least about testing—has, as it did in 1961, the greatest number of tests. Although the percentage of personality tests is 17.9, 44.9 percent of the TIP II references are for personality tests. Three categories—intelligence, personality, and

6 *Tests in Print*, p. xv.

TABLE 1
Tests and New References in Tests in Print II

Classification	Tests		References	
	Number	Percent	Number	Percent
Achievement Batteries	50	2.0	438	2.6
English	131	5.3	220	1.3
Fine Arts	35	1.4	229	1.4
Foreign Languages	105	4.3	81	.5
Intelligence	274	11.1	4,039	24.4
Mathematics	168	6.8	166	1.0
Miscellaneous	291	11.8	866	5.2
Multi-Aptitude	26	1.1	235	1.4
Personality	441	17.9	7,443	44.9
Reading	248	10.1	837	5.1
Science	97	3.9	72	.4
Sensory-Motor	62	2.5	382	2.3
Social Studies	85	3.4	49	.3
Speech and Hearing	79	3.2	216	1.3
Vocations	375	15.2	1,301	7.8
Total	2,467	100.0	16,574	99.9

vocations—make up 44.2 percent of tests and 77.1 percent of the references in TIP II.

RTR I AND RTR II

Inasmuch as the first *Reading Tests and Reviews* should be used in conjunction with this volume, *Reading Tests and Reviews II,* a brief description of the earlier volume seems desirable. The 542-page RTR I includes: (*a*) a bibliography of 209 in print and 83 out of print reading tests as of May 1, 1968; (*b*) a reprinting of the reading sections of the first six *Mental Measurements Yearbooks;* (*c*) a classified listing of all tests (including nonreading tests) in the first six MMY's with cross references to reviews, excerpts, and references in the relevant yearbooks; (*d*) a directory of 86 publishers of reading tests; and title, name, and scanning indexes.

RTR II presents: (*a*) a bibliography of in print reading tests as of early 1974; (*b*) 1,812 new references on the construction, use, and validity of specific tests; (*c*) cumulative name indexes for each test with references in the reading monographs; (*d*) a reprinting of the reading section of *The Seventh Yearbook;* (*e*) a scanning index of all tests (including nonreading tests) listed in *Tests in Print II;* (*f*) a directory of 112 publishers of reading tests; (*g*) cumulative title and name indexes covering both reading monographs; and (*h*) an end-of-the-book scanning index for reading tests.

TIP II TESTS REPRINT

The section of this volume reprinted from *Tests in Print II,* TIP II Tests, contains a bibliography of in print reading tests, references for specific tests, cumulative name indexes for specific tests with references, and lists of tests which have gone out of print since TIP I. (The out of print tests are listed alphabetically at the end of each of the eight classifications of reading tests.) The first three of these categories will be described in more detail.

READING TESTS

The TIP II reprint section lists 248 reading tests in print as of early 1974—18.7 percent more tests than were listed in RTR I. The numbers and percentages of tests in the various classifications are shown in Table 2 for both

TABLE 2
IN PRINT READING TESTS
IN RTR II AND RTR I

Classification	RTR II		RTR I	
	Number	Percent	Number	Percent
General	88	35.5	89	42.6
Diagnostic	40	16.1	27	12.9
Miscellaneous	20	8.1	13	6.2
Oral	14	5.6	11	5.3
Readiness	44	17.7	29	13.9
Special Fields	13	5.2	18	8.6
Speed	2	.8	2	1.0
Study Skills	27	10.9	20	9.6
Total	248	99.9	209	100.1

reading monographs. Since RTR I there have been marked increases in the number of tests in four categories of reading tests: miscellaneous tests, 53.8 percent; reading readiness, 51.7 percent; diagnostic tests, 48.1 percent; and study skills tests, 35.0 percent.

Table 3 contains statistics on the number of tests new or revised (or supplemented) since RTR I. Of the 248 reading tests, 32.7 percent are new since RTR I and 13.7 percent have been revised or supplemented.

Unlike the long test entries in the *Mental Measurements Yearbooks,* the TIP II test entries in this volume are short entries supplying the following information:

a) TITLE. Test titles are printed in boldface type. Secondary or series titles are set off from main titles by a colon. Titles are always presented exactly as reported in the test materials. Stars precede titles of tests listed for the first time in TIP II; asterisks precede titles of tests which have been revised or supplemented since last listed.

b) TEST POPULATION. The grade, chronological age, or semester range, or the employment category is usually given. Commas are used to indicate separate grade levels. "Grades 1.5–2.5, 2–3, 4–12, 13–17" means that there are four test booklets: a booklet for the middle of the first grade through the middle of the second grade, a booklet for the beginning of the second grade through the end of the third grade, a booklet for grades 4 through 12 inclusive, and a

TABLE 3
IN PRINT READING TESTS
NEW OR REVISED (OR SUPPLEMENTED) SINCE RTR I

Classification	Tests In Print	Percent		
		New	Revised	Total
General	88	21.6	14.8	36.4
Diagnostic	40	37.5	20.0	57.5
Miscellaneous	20	40.0	10.0	50.0
Oral	14	28.6	21.4	50.0
Readiness	44	45.5	6.8	52.3
Special Fields	13	15.4	15.4	30.8
Speed	2		50.0	50.0
Study Skills	27	48.1	7.4	55.6
Total	248	32.7	13.7	46.4

booklet for undergraduate and graduate students in colleges and universities. "First, second semester" means that there are two test booklets: one covering the work of the first semester, the other covering the work of the second semester. "1, 2 semesters" indicates that the second booklet covers the work of the two semesters. "Ages 10-2 to 11-11" means ages 10 years 2 months to 11 years 11 months and "Grades 4-6 to 5-9" means the sixth month in the fourth grade through the ninth month in the fifth grade. "High school and college" denotes a single test booklet for both levels; "High school, college" denotes two test booklets, one for high school and one for college.

c) COPYRIGHT DATE. The range of copyright dates (or publication dates if not copyrighted) includes the various forms, accessories, and editions of a test. When the publication date differs from the copyright date, both dates are given; e.g., "1971, c1965–68" means that the test materials were copyrighted between 1965 and 1968 but were not published until 1971. Publication or copyright dates enclosed in brackets do not appear on the test materials but were obtained from other sources.

d) ACRONYM. An acronym is given for many tests.

e) SPECIAL COMMENTS. Some entries contain special notations, such as: "for research use only"; "revision of the ABC Test"; "tests administered monthly at centers throughout the United States"; "subtests available as separates"; and "verbal creativity." "For research use only" should be interpreted to mean that the only use of the test should be in research designed to assess its usefulness; contrary to what the implications seem to be, "for research use only" does not mean that a test has any use, whatsoever, as a research instrument. Tests used in research studies should have demonstrated validity before being selected as research tools. A statement such as "verbal creativity" is intended to further describe what the test claims to measure.

f) PART SCORES. The number and description of part scores is presented.

g) FACTUAL STATEMENTS IMPLYING CRITICISM. Some of the test entries include factual statements which imply criticism of the test, such as "1970 test identical with test copyrighted 1960" and "no manual."

h) AUTHOR. For most tests, all authors are reported. In the case of tests which appear in a new form each year, only authors of the most recent forms are listed. Names are reported exactly as printed on test materials. Names of editors are generally not reported.

i) PUBLISHER. The name of the publisher or distributor is reported for each test. Foreign publishers are identified by listing the country in brackets immediately following the name of the publisher. The Publishers Directory and Index must be consulted for a publisher's address.

j) FOREIGN ADAPTATIONS. Revisions and adaptations of tests for foreign use are listed in parentheses following the description of the original edition.

k) CLOSING ASTERISK. An asterisk following the publisher's name indicates that the entry was prepared from a first-hand examination of the test materials.

l) SUBLISTINGS. Levels, editions, subtests, or parts of a test which are available in separate booklets are sometimes presented as sublistings with titles set in small capitals. Sub-sublistings are indented with titles set in italic type.

m) CROSS REFERENCES. Except for tests being listed for the first time, a test entry includes a second paragraph with cross references to relevant material which may be found in the MMY reprint sections in RTR I and RTR II, or, in rare cases, to material in a non-reading section of one of the seven MMY's. These cross references may be to "additional information" reported in longer entries, or to reviews, excerpts, and references for specific tests.

REFERENCES

The specific test bibliographies in the two reading monographs together contain 1,940 references—1,812 of these references are for tests in print (Table 4). Reading test references have been increasing steadily over the past 18 years reaching an average of 171 references per year in the triennium 1969–71. Over half (53.5 percent) of all references reported in the two reading monographs were published in the years 1963–71. Table 5 reports reference counts for the 23 tests with 20 or more references through 1971 together with their statistics for the triennium 1969–71. Five tests are responsible for 38.6 percent of the references: *Metropolitan Readiness Tests* (10.9 percent), *Watson-Glaser Critical Thinking Appraisal* (7.9 percent), *Survey of Study Habits and Attitudes* (7.1 percent), *Reading Comprehension: Cooperative English Tests* (6.7 percent), and *Iowa Silent Reading Tests* (6.0 percent). The 23 tests in Table 5 account for 73.3 percent of all the references for in print reading tests.

The 1,812 references for in print tests have also been broken down by reading subclassifications. General reading tests, the category with the largest number of tests, generated 673 references, followed by readiness with 399 references. The category with the third largest reference count, study skills, with 336, is the fourth largest category as far as number of tests. Diagnostic tests drew 196 references. The

TABLE 4
READING TEST REFERENCES IN RTR I AND RTR II BY TRIENNIUMS

Years	In Print	Out of Print	Total	Percent
1969–71	511	1	512	26.4
1966–68	309		309	15.9
1963–65	216	1	217	11.2
1960–62	137	7	144	7.4
1957–59	112	9	121	6.2
1954–56	88	6	94	4.9
1951–53	53	5	58	3.0
1948–50	65	5	70	3.6
1945–47	48	13	61	3.2
1942–44	49	13	62	3.2
1939–41	79	28	107	5.5
1936–38	46	13	59	3.0
1933–35	21	6	27	1.4
Earlier	78	21	99	5.1
Total	1,812	128	1,940	100.0

TABLE 5
READING TESTS
WITH 20 OR MORE REFERENCES THROUGH 1971

Test (Rank)	References	
	Total	1969–71
Metropolitan Readiness Tests (1)	197	80
Watson-Glaser Critical Thinking Appraisal (2)	144	51
Survey of Study Habits and Attitudes (3)	128	43
Reading Comprehension: Cooperative English Tests (4)	121	6
Iowa Silent Reading Tests (5)	109	8
Nelson-Denny Reading Test (6)	82	18
California Achievement Tests: Reading (7)	74	20
Diagnostic Reading Tests (8)	61	4
Stanford Achievement Test: Reading Tests (9)	53	20
Lee-Clark Reading Readiness Test (10)	37	10
Metropolitan Achievement Tests: Reading Tests (11.5)	32	17
Monroe's Standardized Silent Reading Test (11.5)	32	
Sequential Tests of Educational Progress: Reading (13)	31	8
Gates-MacGinitie Reading Tests: Readiness Skills (14)	29	3
Standardized Oral Reading Paragraphs (15)	26	1
Schonell Reading Tests (16)	25	6
Gilmore Oral Reading Test (17.5)	22	10
Study Habits Inventory (17.5)	22	2
Durrell-Sullivan Reading Capacity and Achievement Tests (20)	21	2
Murphy-Durrell Reading Readiness Analysis (20)	21	9
Reading Aptitude Tests (20)	21	4
Davis Reading Test (22.5)	20	8
Durrell Analysis of Reading Difficulty (22.5)	20	4
Total for 23 in print tests	1,328	330
Total for remaining 225 in print tests	484	181
Grand Total	1,812	511

remaining classifications with their respective reference counts are: oral, 95; miscellaneous, 79; special fields, 19; and speed, 15.

These specific test bibliographies cover not only the literature of the English-speaking world, but also the literature in English published in non-English-speaking countries. Our goal has been to include all published material—articles, books, chapters, and research monographs—as well as unpublished theses. We do not list as references research reports prepared for internal organizational use, prepublication reports, ERIC material, or abstracts of documents which are reproduced only on receipt of a purchase order (e.g., JSAS manuscripts). Secondary sources (e.g., *Psychological Abstracts*) may provide leads, but if the original publication cannot be located and examined, the reference is not used. We do, however, rely on secondary sources (primarily *Dissertation Abstracts International*) for unpublished theses. Except for doctoral dissertations abstracted in DAI, in recent years all thesis entries have been checked for accuracy by the degree-granting institutions.

References for a given test immediately fol-

low the test entry. They are numbered consecutively for each test as they appear in the first through the seventh MMY and TIP II. References which appeared in earlier volumes are referred to but not repeated; e.g., "19–142. *See* 7:757" indicates that references 19–142 can be found directly following test 757 in the section Seventh MMY Reviews in this volume. Citations to the first six MMY's (e.g., "*See* 6:823" and "*See* 3:510") will be found in the respective yearbook reprint sections in RTR I.

References are arranged in chronological order by year of publication and alphabetically by authors within years. No references later than 1971 have been included. Supplementary bibliographies will be provided in the forthcoming 8th MMY for those tests which are listed again in that volume; the bibliographies for other tests will be brought up to date in *Tests in Print III*, scheduled for publication after the 8th MMY.

CUMULATIVE NAME INDEXES

A cumulative name index has been provided for every in print test having references to facilitate the search for an author's writings relevant to that test. To simplify indexing, forenames were reduced to initials. Authors not consistent in reporting their names will find their publications listed under two or more citations. On the other hand, a given name may represent two or more persons. In all cases, however, the references present names exactly as they appear in the publication referenced.

SEVENTH MMY REVIEWS REPRINT

This 148-page reprint is the reading section of *The Seventh Mental Measurements Yearbook*. It contains long entries for 102 reading tests, 104 test reviews of 72 tests by 66 specialists, 16 excerpted reviews of 11 tests, and 518 references. Of the 102 tests listed, 70.6 percent were reviewed, 30.4 percent by two or more reviewers.

The contributing reviewers represent a wide range of interests and viewpoints. Every effort was made to select reviewers who would be considered highly competent by a sizable group of test users. Our practice of publishing multiple reviews of given tests makes it possible to give representation to differing viewpoints among reviewers. The test reviews in a given yearbook are not limited to new and revised tests; old tests, especially those generating considerable research and writing, are frequently reviewed in successive yearbooks.

In order to make sure that persons invited to review would know what was expected of them, a sheet entitled "Suggestions to MMY Reviewers" was enclosed with each letter of invitation. The suggestions follow:

1. Reviews should be written with the following major objectives in mind:
a) To provide test users with carefully prepared appraisals of tests for their guidance in selecting and using tests.
b) To stimulate progress toward higher professional standards in the construction of tests by commending good work, by censuring poor work, and by suggesting improvements.
c) To impel test authors and publishers to present more detailed information on the construction, validity, reliability, uses, and possible misuses of their tests.
2. Reviews should be concise, the average review running from 600 to 1,200 words in length. The average length of the reviews written by one person generally should not exceed 1,000 words. Except for reviews of achievement batteries, multi-factor batteries, and tests for which a literature review is made, longer reviews should be prepared only with the approval of the Editor.
3. Reviews should be frankly critical, with both strengths and weaknesses pointed out in a judicious manner. Descriptive comments should be kept to the minimum necessary to support the critical portions of the review. Criticism should be as specific as possible; implied criticisms meaningful only to testing specialists should be avoided. Reviews should be written primarily for the rank and file of test users. An indication of the relative importance and value of a test with respect to competing tests should be presented whenever possible. If a reviewer considers a competing test better than the one being reviewed, the competing test should be specifically named.
4. If a test manual gives insufficient, contradictory, or ambiguous information regarding the construction, validity, and use of a test, reviewers are urged to write directly to authors and publishers for further information. Test authors and publishers should, however, be held responsible for presenting adequate data in test manuals—failure to do so should be pointed out. For comments made by reviewers based upon unpublished information received personally from test authors or publishers, the source of the unpublished information should be clearly indicated.
5. Reviewers will be furnished with the test entries which will precede their reviews. Information presented in the entry should not be repeated in reviews unless needed for evaluative purposes.
6. The use of sideheads is optional with reviewers.
7. Each review should conclude with a paragraph presenting a concise summary of the reviewer's overall evaluation of the test. The summary should be as explicit as possible. Is the test the best of its kind? Is it recommended for use? If other tests are better, which of the competing tests is best?
8. A separate review should be prepared for each test. Each review should begin on a new sheet. The test and forms reviewed should be clearly indicated. Your name, title, position, and address should precede

each review, e.g.: John Doe, Professor of Education and Psychology, University of Maryland, College Park, Maryland. The review should begin a new paragraph immediately after the address.
9. All reviews should be typed double spaced and in triplicate. Two copies of each review should be submitted to the Editor; one copy should be retained by the reviewer.
10. If for any reason a reviewer thinks he is not in a position to write a frankly critical review in a scholarly and unbiased manner, he should request the Editor to substitute other tests for review.
11. Reviewers may not invite others to collaborate with them in writing reviews unless permission is secured from the Editor.
12. Most tests will be reviewed by two or more persons in order to secure better representation of various viewpoints. Noncritical content which excessively overlaps similar materials presented by another reviewer may be deleted. Reviews will be carefully edited, but no important changes will be made without the consent of the reviewer. Galley proofs (unaccompanied by copy) will be submitted to reviewers for checking.
13. The Editor reserves the right to reject any review which does not meet the minimum standards of the MMY series.
14. Each reviewer will receive a complimentary copy of *The Seventh Mental Measurements Yearbook*.

The long test entries in the section Seventh MMY Reviews contain all the information in the short TIP II entries plus the following:

a) INDIVIDUAL OR GROUP TEST. All tests are group tests unless otherwise indicated.
b) FORMS, PARTS, AND LEVELS. All available forms, parts, and levels are listed with copyright dates.
c) PAGES. The number of pages on which print occurs is reported for test booklets, manuals, technical reports, profiles, and other nonapparatus accessories.
d) FACTUAL STATEMENTS IMPLYING CRITICISM. Much more so than short entries, the long entries include factual statements implying criticism of the following type: "no data on reliability," "no data on validity," "no norms," "norms for grade 5 only," "no description of the normative population," "no norms for difference scores," "test copyrighted in 1970 identical with test copyrighted in 1960," and "statistical data based on earlier forms."
e) MACHINE SCORABLE ANSWER SHEETS. All types of machine scorable answer sheets available for use with a specific test are reported: Digitek (OpScan Test Scoring and Document Scanning System), IBM 805 (IBM Test Scoring Machine), IBM 1230 (IBM Optical Mark Reader), MRC (MRC Scoring and Reporting Service), NCS (NCS Scoring and Reporting Service), and NCS Sentry/70, and a few other answer sheets less widely used.
f) COST. Price information is reported for test packages (usually 20 to 35 tests), answer sheets, all other accessories, and specimen sets. The statement "$5.20 per 35 tests" means that all accessories are included unless separate prices are given for accessories. The statement also means 35 tests of one level, one edition, or one part unless stated otherwise. Quantity discounts and special discounts are not reported. Specimen set prices include copies of each level and part—but not all forms—unless otherwise indicated. Since 1970 prices are reported, the latest catalog of a test publisher should be consulted for current prices.
g) SCORING AND REPORTING SERVICES. Scoring and reporting services provided by publishers are reported along with information on costs. Special computerized scoring and interpretation services are sometimes given

in separate entries immediately following the test entry.

h) TIME. The number of minutes of actual working time allowed examinees and the approximate length of time needed for administering a test are provided whenever obtainable. The latter figure is always enclosed in parentheses. Thus, "50(60) minutes" indicates that the examinees are allowed 50 minutes of working time and that a total of 60 minutes is needed to administer the test. When the time necessary to administer a test has been obtained through correspondence with the test publisher or author, the time is enclosed in brackets.

RUNNING HEADS AND FEET

To use this volume most efficiently, it is important to take advantage of the information given at the top and bottom of each page in the test and review sections. Both test entry and page numbers are given in the running heads. However, since all citations in the indexes and cross references are to entry numbers, these numbers, found next to the outside margins on facing pages, can be used as guide numbers in locating a particular test. The entry number on the left-hand page corresponds to the test embodying the first line of type on that page; the entry number on the right-hand page refers to the test containing the last line of type on that page. The test titles corresponding to these guide numbers are given in the running feet at the bottom of the page. Thus, the reader can quickly identify the first and last test discussed on each pair of facing pages.

The first reprint section, from *Tests in Print II,* has guide numbers in the range 1529 to 1776; the second reprint section, from *The Seventh Mental Measurements Yearbook,* 7:682 to 7:783.

TIP II SCANNING INDEX

The complete TIP II Scanning Index, a classified listing of all tests in TIP II, has been reprinted to provide readers with an overview of tests available in areas other than reading. The 2,467 tests are divided into the 15 classifications listed in Table 1 of this Introduction. Since the reading section of the TIP II Scanning Index will be of most interest to readers of this monograph, we have reprinted that section (entitled Reading Scanning Index) at the end of this volume for convenient reference. This end-of-the-book index is especially useful for locating reading tests suitable for a given population, since descriptions of these popula-

tions are reported immediately following the test titles.

PUBLISHERS DIRECTORY AND INDEX

Instead of citing only the entry numbers of the tests of a given publisher, as in our earlier publications, this Publishers Directory and Index provides test titles as well as entry numbers. Stars denote the 29 publishers with test catalogs listing 10 or more tests (not necessarily reading tests). Tests not originating in the country of publication are identified by listing in brackets the country in which the test was originally prepared and published.

All addresses have been checked by the publishers (except for one publisher who did not reply to our four requests for verification), and are accurate through 1973. However, with such a large number of publishers (including many author-publishers), some address changes must be expected.

The directory lists 112 publishers of reading tests—56.3 percent of which publish only one reading test. Eleven publishers offer five or more reading tests: Bobbs-Merrill Co., Inc., 14 tests; Harcourt Brace Jovanovich, Inc., 12; CTB/McGraw-Hill, 10; Science Research Associates, Inc., 9; Australian Council for Educational Research, 8; Houghton Mifflin Co., 7; Psychometric Affiliates, 7; Teachers College Press, 7; University of London Press Ltd., 7; Cooperative Tests and Services, 5; and Van Wagenen Psycho-Educational Research Laboratories, 5. The geographical distribution of reading test publishers covers seven countries: United States, 91 publishers; Great Britain, 11; Canada, 4; Australia, 3; New Zealand, 1; Republic of South Africa, 1; and Sweden, 1.

INDEX OF TITLES

This cumulative title index includes (*a*) reading tests in print as separates as of February 1, 1974; (*b*) out of print or status unknown reading tests; and (*c*) tests reclassified since last listed in RTR I or in the reading section of the 7th MMY.

Citations are to test entry numbers, not to pages. Numbers without colons refer to in print tests listed in the first reprint section (TIP II Tests) in this volume; numbers with colons refer to tests out of print, status unknown, or reclassified since last listed with reading tests. Unless preceded by the word "consult," all numbers containing colons refer either to tests in this volume in the Seventh MMY Reviews section (when the digit 7 precedes the colon) or to tests in RTR I (when the letter R or a digit from 1 through 6 precedes the colon). To obtain the latest information on a test no longer classified with reading tests, the reader is directed to consult either TIP II (if the test is in print) or an MMY (if the test is out of print). For example, "Meeting Street School Screening Test, 7:756; reclassified, *consult* T2:984" indicates that the test is 7:756 in the Seventh MMY Reviews section in this volume but has been reclassified and, for the latest information, test 984 in TIP II must be consulted. Superseded titles are listed with cross references to the current titles. Tests which are parts of series are listed under their individual titles and also their series titles.

INDEX OF NAMES

This cumulative index is an analytical index distinguishing between authorship of a test, test review, excerpted review, or reference dealing with a specific test. Furthermore the index indicates whether the relevant test is in print or out of print. Numbers with colons refer to out of print or status unknown tests. Unless preceded by the word "consult," all numbers containing colons refer either to tests in this volume (reprinted from the 7th MMY) or to tests in RTR I (reprinted from the first six MMY's or a new listing in RTR I).

Forenames have been reduced to initials to lower the cost of indexing. Since authors are not always consistent in how they list their names, two or more listings may refer to the same person. On the other hand, the use of initials sometimes results in one name representing two or more persons. Reference to the cited material in the text will resolve these difficulties in almost all cases.

Except in the case of authors of in print tests, the use of the Index of Names is a two-step process. For example, if the name index reports *"rev, 1611"* for M. A. Tinker, the reader must look at the cross reference for test 1611 to learn in which yearbook Tinker's review of that test may be found. Similarly, if the name index cites *"ref, 1690"* for W. S. Gray, the reader must look at the Cumulative Name Index for test 1690 to learn where, in this volume or RTR I, Gray's reference or references on that test may be found. For example, in the main Index of Names, a reference listed for F. J. Schonell is *"ref, 1646."* Looking next in the Cumulative Name Index for test 1646, the reader will find that Schonell is the author of six references for this test, each cited by number, so the reader can quickly locate them in the list of references under the test entry.

READING

TESTS AND REVIEWS II

Reprinted from *Tests in Print II*

READING – TIP II

[1529]
A.C.E.R. Lower Grades Reading Test: Level 1, Second Edition. Grade 1; 1962–64; for schools in New South Wales; M. L. Clark, N. E. Morison, and J. L. A. Russell; Australian Council for Educational Research [Australia]. *

[1530]

★**ACER Primary Reading Survey Tests.** Grades 3, 4, 5, 6; 1971–72; 2 parts: word knowledge, comprehension; interim manual prepared by G. P. Withers in collaboration with M. L. Clark, W. T. Renehan, and B. Rechter; Australian Council for Educational Research [Australia]. *

[1531]

A.C.E.R. Silent Reading Tests: Standardized for Use in New Zealand. Ages 9–12; 1955; 3 parts; tests identical with corresponding parts of Form B (Part 2) and Form C (Parts 1 and 3) of *A.C.E.R. Silent Reading Tests;* A. E. Fieldhouse (manual); New Zealand Council for Educational Research [New Zealand]. *
a) PART 1, WORD KNOWLEDGE.
b) PART 2, SPEED OF READING.
c) PART 3, READING FOR MEANING.
For additional information, see 5:618.

REFERENCES THROUGH 1971
1. FOSTER, MARION E. "A Comparison of Reading Achievement of Christchurch, New Zealand and Edmonton Alberta Public School Students of the Same Age and Number of Years of Schooling." *Alberta J Ed Res* (Canada) 11:21–31 Mr '65. * (*PA* 39:16455)
2. McCREARY, J. R. "Reading Tests With Maori Children." *N Zeal J Ed Studies* 1(1–2):40–50 '66. *

CUMULATIVE NAME INDEX
Foster, M. E.: 1   McCreary, J. R.: 2

[1532]

American School Achievement Tests: Part 1, Reading. Grades 2–3, 4–6, 7–9; 1941–63; 3 scores: sentence and word meaning, paragraph meaning, total; 1955–57 tests essentially the same as tests copyrighted 1941–43; Willis E. Pratt, Robert V. Young, and Clara E. Cockerille; Bobbs-Merrill Co., Inc. * For the complete battery entry, see 4.
For additional information, see 6:783; for reviews by Russell G. Stauffer and Agatha Townsend, see 5:620. For reviews of the complete battery, see 6:2 (2 reviews), 5:1 (2 reviews), 4:1 (1 review), and 3:1 (2 reviews).

[1533]

American School Reading Tests. Grades 10–13; 1955; 3 scores: vocabulary, reading rate, comprehension; Willis E. Pratt and Stanley W. Lore; Bobbs-Merrill Co., Inc. *
For additional information and reviews by Henry S. Dyer and Donald E. P. Smith, see 5:621.

[1534]

Buffalo Reading Test for Speed and Comprehension. Grades 9–16; 1933–41; 3 scores: speed, comprehension, total; 1965 tests identical with tests copyrighted 1941; 1965 manual reprinted from 1936 manual; Mazie Earle Wagner and Daniel S. P. Schubert (1965 manual); Mazie Earle Wagner. *
For additional information and reviews by Holland Roberts and William W. Turnbull, see 3:477.

REFERENCES THROUGH 1971
1. GREENWOOD, ROBERT LEROY. *The Prediction of Academic Success in the Technical Curricula of Community Colleges: An Investigation of the Prediction of Academic Success in the Chemical, Electrical, and Mechanical Curricula of Three Community Colleges in New York State.* Doctor's thesis, New York University (New York, N.Y.), 1962. (*DA* 23:898)

CUMULATIVE NAME INDEX
Greenwood, R. L.: 1   Turnbull, W. W.: *rev,* 3:477
Roberts, H.: *rev,* 3:477

[1535]

Burnett Reading Series: Survey Test. Grades 1.5–2.4, 2.5–3.9, 4.0–6.9, 7.0–9.9, 10.0–12.9; 1966–70; 5

levels; Richard W. Burnett; Scholastic Testing Service, Inc. *
a) PRIMARY 1. Grades 1.5–2.4; 1966–69; 4 scores: word identification, word meaning, comprehension, total.
b) PRIMARY 2. Grades 2.5–3.9; 1966–69; scores same as for Primary 1; 1967 test identical with test published 1966.
c) INTERMEDIATE. Grades 4.0–6.9; 1966–69; scores same as for Primary 1; 1967 test identical with test published 1966.
d) ADVANCED. Grades 7.0–9.9; 1967; 4 scores: vocabulary, comprehension, total, rate and accuracy.
e) SENIOR. Grades 10.0–12.9; 1968–70; scores same as for Advanced.
For additional information and a review by Roger Farr, see 7:682.

[1536]

＊**California Achievement Tests: Reading.** Grades 1–14; 1933–72; earlier editions called *Progressive Reading Tests;* 3 scores: vocabulary, comprehension, total; 2 editions; Ernest W. Tiegs and Willis W. Clark; CTB/McGraw-Hill. * For the complete battery entry, see 7.
a) 1957 EDITION WITH 1963 NORMS. Grades 1–2, 2.5–4.5, 4–6, 7–9, 9–14; 1933–63; test booklet title is *California Reading Test;* 1963 tests identical with tests copyrighted 1957 except for profile and revision of Form X (grades 7–9).
b) 1970 EDITION. Grades 1.5–2.5, 2.5–4.5, 4–6, 6–9, 9–12; 1933–72.
For additional information concerning the 1970 edition, see 7:683 (29 references); see also 6:784 (13 references) and 5:622 (5 references); for reviews by John C. Flanagan and James R. Hobson and an excerpted review by Laurance F. Shaffer of an earlier edition, see 4:530; for a review by Frederick B. Davis, see 2:1563; for reviews by Ivan A. Booker and Joseph C. Dewey, see 1:1110. For reviews of the complete battery, see 6:3 (2 reviews), 5:2 (1 review), 4:2 (3 reviews), 3:15 (1 review), 2:1193 (2 reviews), and 1:876 (1 review, 1 excerpt).

REFERENCES THROUGH 1971
1–5. See 5:622.
6–18. See 6:784.
19–47. See 7:683.
48. WILSON, FRANK Y.; BURKE, AGNES; AND FLEMMING, CECILE WHITE. "Sex Differences in Beginning Reading in a Progressive School." *J Ed Res* 32:570–82 Ap '39. * (*PA* 13:4386)
49. AUKERMAN, ROBERT C., JR. "Differences in the Reading Status of Good and Poor Eleventh Grade Students." *J Ed Res* 41:498–515 Mr '48. * (*PA* 22:4599)
50. SCHUBERT, DELWYN G. "A Comparative Study of the Hearing and Reading Vocabularies of Retarded College Readers." *J Ed Res* 46:555–8 Mr '53. * (*PA* 28:3219)
51. MORRISON, IDA E., AND PERRY, IDA F. "Spelling and Reading Relationships With Incidence of Retardation and Acceleration." *J Ed Res* 52:222–7 F '59. * (*PA* 34:2012)
52. McBEE, GEORGE, AND DUKE, RALPH L. "Relationship Between Intelligence, Scholastic Motivation, and Academic Achievement." *Psychol Rep* 6:3–8 F '60. * (*PA* 34:8404)
53. POWELL, MARVIN, AND BERGEM, JERRY. "An Investigation of the Differences Between Tenth-, Eleventh-, and Twelfth-Grade 'Conforming' and 'Nonconforming' Boys." *J Ed Res* 56:184–90 D '62. *
54. KITTELL, JACK E. "Intelligence-Test Performance of Children From Bilingual Environments." *El Sch J* 64:76–83 N '63. *
55. PARSLEY, KENNETH M., JR.; POWELL, MARVIN; O'CONNOR, HENRY A.; AND DEUTSCH, MURRAY. "Are There Really Sex Differences in Achievement?" *J Ed Res* 57:210–2 D '63. *
56. SCHNEIDERHAN, ROSEMARY MALMGREN. *A Correlation of Individual and Group Reading Tests.* Master's thesis, St. Cloud State College (St. Cloud, Minn.), 1963.
57. KATZ, STANLEY S. "Selection and Evaluation of Students in Medical Technology Degree Programs." *Am J Med Technol* 30:51–63 Ja '64. *
58. NEVILLE, MARY H., AND FROST, BARRY P. "Differential Achievement in Reading and Arithmetic." *Alberta J Ed Res* (Canada) 10:192–200 D '64. *

59. FOSTER, MARION E. "A Comparison of Reading Achievement of Christchurch, New Zealand and Edmonton Alberta Public School Students of the Same Age and Number of Years of Schooling." *Alberta J Ed Res* (Canada) 11:21–31 Mr '65. * (*PA* 39:16455)

60. SINKS, NAOMI B., AND POWELL, MARVIN. "Sex and Intelligence as Factors in Achievement in Reading in Grades 4 Through 8." *J Genetic Psychol* 106:67–79 Mr '65. * (*PA* 39: 12952)

61. THOMPSON, EVA LUCILE. *Relationship of Standardized Reading Test Findings for Primary Grade Children.* Master's thesis, Illinois State University (Normal, Ill.), 1965.

62. KNIGHT, DAVID, AND ALCORN, JOHN D. "Comparisons of the Performance of Educationally Disadvantaged Adults and Elementary Children on Selected Measures of Reading Performance." *South J Ed Res* 4(4):262–72 O '70. *

63. SMITH, I. MACFARLANE. "The Use of Diagnostic Tests for Assessing the Abilities of Overseas Students Attending Institutions of Further Education, Part I." *Voc Aspect Ed* (England) 22(51):1–8 Mr '70. *

64. BURKE, LEE A. *Reading Habits and Reading Background and How They Effect a Student's Performance on the Interpretative Section of the California Reading Test.* Master's thesis, Jersey City State College (Jersey City, N.J.), 1971.

65. DAVIS, BOBBIE, AND MCNINCH, GEORGE. "A Comparison of Three Standardized Reading Tests in a Fifth Grade Sample." *South J Ed Res* 5(2):101–12 Ap '71. *

66. FARR, ROGER, AND ROELKE, PATRICIA. "Measuring Subskills of Reading: Intercorrelations Between Standardized Reading Tests, Teachers' Ratings, and Reading Specialists' Ratings." *J Ed Meas* 8(1):27–32 sp '71. * (*PA* 46:5464)

67. KNIGHT, DAVID, AND ALCORN, JOHN D. "Comparisons of the Performance of Educationally Disadvantaged Adults and Elementary Children on Selected Measures of Reading Performance." *Yearb Nat Read Conf* 19(2):113–7 '71. *

68. MICHAEL, WILLIAM B.; HANEY, RUSSELL; LEE, YOUNG B.; AND MICHAEL, JOAN J. "The Criterion-Related Validities of Cognitive and Noncognitive Predictors in a Training Program for Nursing Candidates." *Ed & Psychol Meas* 31(4):983–7 w '71. * (*PA* 48:1866)

69. PARKER, DEWEY L. *Relationships Among the Keystone Visual Survey Telebinocular With Reading Achievement and the Diagnoses of a Vision Clinic.* Doctor's thesis, University of Oklahoma (Norman, Okla.), 1971. (*DAI* 32:2316A)

70. PURCELL, ELIZABETH WELLS. *The Relationship of Personality to Achievement in Reading Comprehension.* Doctor's thesis, St. Louis University (St. Louis, Mo.), 1971. (*DAI* 33:906A)

71. SEITHER, FRANCES GARDNER. *An Investigation of the Predictive Validity of Selected Admission Screening Measures Relative to Success in Practical Nursing.* Doctor's thesis, University of Maryland (College Park, Md.), 1971. (*DAI* 32:5890B)

72. SMITH, I. MACFARLANE. "The Use of Diagnostic Tests for Assessing the Abilities of Overseas Students Attending Institutions of Further Education, Part II." *Voc Aspect Ed* (England) 23(54):39–48 Ap '71. *

73. WETHERELL, RICHARD H. *A Study of the Relationship Between Visual Perception and School Achievement.* Doctor's thesis, University of Southern Mississippi (Hattiesburg, Miss.), 1971. (*DAI* 32:2324A)

74. WINEMAN, JOHN H. "Cognitive Style and Reading Ability." *Calif J Ed Res* 22(2):74–9 Mr '71. * (*PA* 46:9762)

CUMULATIVE NAME INDEX

[1537]

*The Carver-Darby Chunked Reading Test. Grades 9–16 and adults; 1970–72; CDCRT; 3 scores: efficiency, accuracy, rate; Ronald P. Carver and Charles A. Darby, Jr.; American Institutes for Research; distributed by Revrac Publications. *

For additional information and reviews by Arlen R. Gullickson and Richard Rystrom, see 7:684.

REFERENCES THROUGH 1971

1. CARVER, RONALD P. "Criterion Referenced Aspects of the Carver-Darby Chunked Reading Test." *Yearb Nat Read Conf* 20:182–6 '71. *
2. CARVER, RONALD P. "What Is Reading Comprehension and How Should It Be Measured?" *Yearb Nat Read Conf* 19(1): 99–106 '71. *
3. CARVER, RONALD P., AND DARBY, C. A. "Development and Evaluation of a Test of Information Storage During Reading." *J Ed Meas* 8(1):33–44 sp '71. * (*PA* 46:5461)
4. SWALLOW, ROSE-MARIE. *Automatic Processing of Perceptual-Linguistic Stimuli in Second Grade Achieving and Non-Achieving Readers.* Doctor's thesis, University of Southern California (Los Angeles, Calif.), 1971. (*DAI* 32:3827A)

CUMULATIVE NAME INDEX

[1538]

Commerce Reading Comprehension Test. Grades 12–16 and adults; 1956–58; Irma T. Halfter and Raymond J. McCall; Department of Psychological Testing, DePaul University. *

For additional information, see 5:624.

REFERENCES THROUGH 1971

1. HALFTER, IRMA T., AND DOUGLASS, FRANCES M. "Measurement of College Level Reading Competence in a Content Area." *J Ed Res* 53:223–30 F '60. *

CUMULATIVE NAME INDEX

[1539]

Comprehension Test for Training College Students. Training college students and applicants for admission; 1962; E. L. Black; distributed by NFER Publishing Co. Ltd. [England]. *

For additional information, see 6:785.

[1540]

Comprehensive Primary Reading Scales. Grade 1; 1956–60; 4 parts; M. J. Van Wagenen, Mary A. Van Wagenen (Part 1), and Maximilian L. G. Klaeger (Part 2); Van Wagenen Psycho-Educational Research Laboratories. *

a) PART 1, READING COMPREHENSION SCALE.
b) PART 2, PICTURE READING VOCABULARY SCALE.
c) PART 3, MEANING READING VOCABULARY SCALE.
d) PART 4, WORD RECOGNITION VOCABULARY SCALE.

[1541]

Comprehensive Reading Scales. Grades 4, 5, 6, 7, 8, 9–10, 11–12; 1948–53; M. J. Van Wagenen; Van Wagenen Psycho-Educational Research Laboratories. *

[1542]

*Comprehensive Tests of Basic Skills: Reading.
Grades kgn–12; 1968–73; 2 editions; CTB/McGraw-
Hill. * For the complete battery entry, see 11.
a) FORMS Q AND R. Grades 2.5–4, 4–6, 6–8, 8–12; 1968–
71; 3 scores: vocabulary, comprehension, total.
b) EXPANDED EDITION, FORM S. Grades kgn.5–1.9,
1.5–2.9, 2.5–4.9, 4.5–6.9, 6.5–8.9, 8.5–12.9; 1968–73; 2
tests.
  1) *Reading*. Grades kgn.5–1.9, 1.5–2.9; 2 levels.
    (a) Level B. Grades kgn.5–1.9; 5 scores: letter
    sounds, word recognition (2 scores), reading com-
    prehension, total.
    (b) Level C. Grades 1.5–2.9; 4 scores: vocab-
    ulary, sentences, passages, total.
  2) *Reading and Reference Skills*. Grades 2.5–4.9,
  4.5–6.9, 6.5–8.9, 8.5–12.9; 4 scores: reading (vocabulary, comprehension, total), reference skills.
For additional information and a review by Earl F.
Rankin of a, see 7:685. For reviews of the complete
battery, see 7:9 (2 reviews, 3 excerpts).

REFERENCES THROUGH 1971
  1. KIDD, LOR RHEBA R. *A Comparison of the Wide Range
Achievement Test With the Stanford Achievement Test and
Comprehensive Tests of Basic Skills as a Measurement of Read-
ing Achievement.* Master's thesis, California State College (Hay-
ward, Calif.), 1970.
  2. DAVIS, BOBBIE, AND McNINCH, GEORGE. "A Comparison of
Three Standardized Reading Tests in a Fifth Grade Sample."
South J Ed Res 5(2):101–12 Ap '71. *
  3. DAVIS, BOBBIE SUE. *A Comparative Analysis of Three
Widely Used Standardized Reading Achievement Tests for a
Selected Group of Elementary School Children.* Doctor's thesis,
University of Southern Mississippi (Hattiesburg, Miss.), 1971.
(*DAI* 32:4831A)

CUMULATIVE NAME INDEX
Davis, B.: 2   McNinch, G.: 2
Davis, B. S.: 3   Rankin, E. F.: *rev*, 7:685
Kidd, L. R. R.: 1

[1543]

Cooperative Primary Tests: Reading. Grades
1.5–2.5, 2.5–3; 1965–67; Cooperative Tests and Services. * For the complete battery entry, see 12.
For reviews of the complete battery see 7:10 (2
excerpts).

[1544]

**Cooperative Reading Comprehension Test, Form
Y.** Secondary forms 5–6 and university; 1948–64
(Australian edition, 1960–64); Australian adaptation
(spelling only) of Form Y of *Reading Comprehension:
Cooperative English Test, Higher Level C2;* 4 scores:
vocabulary, speed of comprehension, level of comprehension, total; Frederick B. Davis, Clarence Derrick,
Jeanne M. Bradford, and Geraldine Spaulding; Australian Council for Educational Research [Australia]. *

REFERENCES THROUGH 1971
  1. ANDERSON, A. W. "Personality Traits in Reading Ability
of Western Australian University Freshmen." *J Ed Res* 54:234–
7 F '61. *
  2. LEE, STUART E.; WITH THE ASSISTANCE OF COLETTE M.
ROSEN AND DOUGLAS McNALLY. "Report on the Administration
and Standardization of the Co-operative Reading Comprehension
Test Higher Level C2 Form Y." *Forum Ed* (Australia) 22:90–
117 S '63. *
  3. ANDERSON, A. W. "Reading and English Scores of a Group
of Foreign Students Entering the University of Western Australia in 1964." *Austral J Higher Ed* 2:84–90 N '64. *
  4. POND, L. "A Study of High-Achieving and Low-Achieving
University Freshmen." *Austral J Higher Ed* 2:73–8 N '64. *
  5. ANDERSON, A. W. "Intelligence and Reading Scores of
Entrants to the University of Western Australia 1954–65."
Austral J Higher Ed 2:177–82 N '65. *
  6. SILCOCK, ANNE. "An Investigation Into Possible Relationships Between Reading Ability Scores and University First Year
Examination Results." *Austral J Higher Ed* 2:113–8 N '65. *

CUMULATIVE NAME INDEX
Anderson, A. W.: 1, 3, 5   Pond, L.: 4
Lee, S. E.: 2   Rosen, C. M.: 2
McNally, D.: 2   Silcock, A.: 6

Comprehensive Tests of Basic Skills: Reading

[1545]

**Cooperative Reading Comprehension Test,
Forms L and M.** Secondary forms 2–4 (ages 14–16);
1960–67 (Australian edition, 1964–73); Australian
adaptations (spelling only) of Forms 2A, 2B, and 2C
of *Reading Comprehension: Cooperative English Test,
1960 Revision;* 3 scores: vocabulary, level of comprehension, speed of comprehension; Clarence Derrick,
David P. Harris, and Biron Walker; Australian
Council for Educational Research [Australia]. *

[1546]

Davis Reading Test. Grades 8–11, 11–13; 1956–62;
2 scores: level of comprehension, speed of comprehension; Frederick B. Davis and Charlotte Croon Davis;
Psychological Corporation. *
For additional information and reviews by William
E. Coffman and Alton L. Raygor, see 6:786 (2 references); for a review by Benjamin Rosner of the
lower level, see 5:625.

REFERENCES THROUGH 1971
  1–2. See 6:786.
  3. ALSHAN, LEONARD M. *A Factor Analytic Study of Items
Used in the Measurement of Some Fundamental Factors of Reading Comprehension.* Doctor's thesis, Columbia University (New
York, N.Y.), 1964. (*DA* 25:5101)
  4. GLIDDEN, GEORGE WAYNE. *Factors That Influence Achievement in Senior High School American History.* Doctor's thesis,
University of Nebraska (Lincoln, Neb.), 1964. (*DA* 25:3429)
  5. McGUIRE, FREDERICK L., AND SCOTT, WYNELLE. "The Davis
Reading Test, Hr Scale, MCAT, and Undergraduate Grades as
Predictors of Success in Medical School." Abstract. *J Med Ed*
39:886 S '64. *
  6. RADCLIFFE, ROBERTA D. *An Analysis of Junior High School
Standardized Reading Tests Employing the Davis Reading Comprehension Scale.* Master's thesis, Glassboro State College (Glassboro, N.J.), 1965.
  7. ALEXAKOS, C. E. "Predictive Efficiency of Two Multivariate
Statistical Techniques in Comparison With Clinical Predictions."
J Ed Psychol 57:297–306 O '66. * (*PA* 40:12756)
  8. DAVIS, FREDERICK B. "Experimental Use of the Davis Reading Test in Independent Schools." *Ed Rec B* 89:46–50 F '66. *
(*PA* 40:7048, title only)
  9. GOLDEN, JAMES FRANKLIN. *Aspirations and Capabilities of
Rural Youth in Selected Areas of Arkansas in Relation to Present
and Projected Labor Market Requirements.* Doctor's thesis, University of Arkansas (Fayetteville, Ark.), 1966. (*DA* 27:1199A)
  10. CLAWAR, HARRY J. "A Comparison of the Davis Reading
Test and the Survey Section of the Diagnostic Reading Test
When Used With Independent-School Pupils." *Ed Rec B* 92:
39–42 Jl '67. * (*PA* 42:1126)
  11. HOLLENBECK, GEORGE P. "Predicting High School Biology
Achievement With the Differential Aptitude Tests and the Davis
Reading Test." *Ed & Psychol Meas* 27:439–42 su '67. * (*PA*
41:14218)
  12. HARDESTY, D. L., AND JONES, W. S. "Characteristics of
Judged High Potential Management Personnel—The Operations
of an Industrial Assessment Center." *Personnel Psychol* 21:85–
98 sp '68. * (*PA* 42:16197)
  13. FEUERS, STELLE. *The Relationship Between General Reading Skills and Junior College Academic Achievement.* Doctor's
thesis, University of California (Los Angeles, Calif.), 1969.
(*DAI* 30:3186A)
  14. WEAVER, WENDELL W.; KINGSTON, ALBERT J.; BICKLEY,
A. C.; AND WHITE, WILLIAM F. "Information-Flow Difficulty in
Relation to Reading Comprehension." *J Read Behav* 1(3):41–9
su '69. * (*PA* 45:2355)
  15. CARLETON, FREDERICK O. "Relationships Between Follow-
Up Evaluations and Information Developed in a Management
Assessment Center." Abstract. *Proc 78th Ann Conv Am Psychol
Assn* 5(2):565–6 '70. * (*PA* 44:19655)
  16. JOHNS, DANIEL JAY. *Correlates of Academic Success in a
Predominantly Black, Open-Door, Public, Urban Community
College.* Doctor's thesis, University of Virginia (Charlottesville,
Va.), 1970. (*DAI* 31:4464A)
  17. BRADLEY, RICHARD W., AND SANBORN, MARSHALL P.
"Using Tests to Predict Four-Year Patterns of College Grade
Point." *J Col Stud Personnel* 12(2):138–42 Mr '71. * (*PA* 46:
5699)
  18. HOLZMAN, PHILIP S., AND ROUSEY, CLYDE. "Disinhibition
of Communicated Thought: Generality and Role of Cognitive
Style." *J Abn Psychol* 77(3):263–74 Je '71. * (*PA* 46:6158)
  19. KLINDIENST, DAVID HARVEY. *Predicting the Accommoda-
tion and Progressive Retention of Selected Freshmen at Clarion
State College.* Doctor's thesis, Pennsylvania State University
(University Park, Pa.), 1971. (*DAI* 33:988A)
  20. SYKES, KIM CRISPIN. *A Comparison of the Effectiveness*

of Standard Print and Large Print in Facilitating the Reading Skills of Visually Impaired Students. Doctor's thesis, Michigan State University (East Lansing, Mich.), 1971. (*DAI* 32:3128A)

CUMULATIVE NAME INDEX

Alexakos, C. E.: 7
Alshan, L. M.: 3
Bickley, A. C.: 14
Bradley, R. W.: 17
Carleton, F. O.: 15
Clawar, H. J.: 10
Coffman, W. E.: *rev,* 6:786
Davis, F. B.: 8
Feuers, S.: 13
Glidden, G. W.: 4
Golden, J. F.: 9
Hardesty, D. L.: 12
Hollenbeck, G. P.: 11
Holzman, P. S.: 18
Johns, D. J.: 16

Jones, W. S.: 12
Ketcham, H. E. (Mrs.): 1
Kingston, A. J.: 2, 14
Klindienst, D. H.: 19
McGuire, F. L.: 5
Radcliffe, R. D.: 6
Raygor, A. L.: *rev,* 6:786
Rosner, B.: *rev,* 5:625
Rousey, C.: 18
Sanborn, M. P.: 17
Scott, W.: 5
Sykes, K. C.: 20
Weaver, W. W.: 2, 14
White, W. F.: 14

[1547]

Delaware County Silent Reading Test, Second Edition. Grades 1², 2¹, 2², 3¹, 3², 4, 5, 6, 7, 8; 1965; 5 scores: interpretation, organization, vocabulary, structural analysis, total; no manual; Judson E. Newburg and Nicholas A. Spennato; Delaware County Reading Council. *

For additional information and a review by Allen Berger, see 7:686.

[1548]

★Edinburgh Reading Tests. Ages 8.5–10.5, 10–12.5; 1972–73; ERT; 2 levels; University of London Press Ltd. [England]. *

a) STAGE 2. Ages 8.5–10.5; 7 scores: vocabulary, comprehension of sequences, retention of significant details, use of context, reading rate, comprehension of essential ideas, total; test by Godfrey Thomson Unit, University of Edinburgh, in association with Scottish Education Department and Educational Institute of Scotland; manual by M. J. Hutchings and E. M. J. Hutchings.

b) STAGE 3. Ages 10–12.5; 6 scores: reading for facts, comprehension of sequences, retention of main ideas, comprehension of points of view, vocabulary, total; test by Moray House College of Education in association with Scottish Education Department and Educational Institute of Scotland; manual by J. F. McBride and P. C. McNaught.

[1549]

Emporia Reading Tests. Grades 1, 2–3, 4–6, 7–8; 1962–64; first published in the Every Pupil Scholarship Test series; 4 tests; M. W. Sanders, Marjorie Barnett (*a–b*), Donald E. Carline (*c–d*), Ed. L. Eaton (*d*), Angie Seybold (*c*), and Stafford E. Studer (*d*); Bureau of Educational Measurements. *

a) EMPORIA PRIMARY READING TEST. I, 2 semesters grade 1.

b) EMPORIA ELEMENTARY READING TEST. I, 2 semesters grades 2–3.

c) EMPORIA INTERMEDIATE READING TEST. I, 2 semesters grades 4–6.

d) EMPORIA JUNIOR HIGH SCHOOL READING TEST. I, 2 semesters grades 7–8.

For additional information and a review by Ronald W. Mitchell, see 7:687.

[1550]

GAP Reading Comprehension Test. Grades 2–7; 1965–70; GAP; cloze technique with approximately every tenth word omitted; 2 editions; J. McLeod. *

a) AUSTRALIAN EDITION. 1965–67; for an upward extension, see 1551; Heinemann Educational Australia Pty Ltd. [Australia].

b) BRITISH EDITION. 1965–70; manual edited by Derick Unwin; Heinemann Educational Books Ltd. [England].

For additional information and reviews by Donald B. Black and Earl F. Rankin, see 7:688.

REFERENCES THROUGH 1971

1. McLEOD, J., AND ANDERSON, J. "Readability Assessment and Word Redundancy of Printed English." *Psychol Rep* 18:35–8 F '66. * (*PA* 40:7051)
2. COCHRANE, R. G.; ELKINS, J.; AND RICHMOND, DAWN M. "Analysis of Fourth Grade Testing." *Slow Learning Child* (Australia) 16(3):131–42 N '69. * (*PA* 44:18351)
3. ELKINS, J. "Some Recent Queensland Norms for Widely Used Standardized Tests." *Slow Learning Child* (Australia) 18(3):142–7 N '71. *

CUMULATIVE NAME INDEX

Anderson, J.: 1
Black, D. B.: *rev,* 7:688
Cochrane, R. G.: 2
Elkins, J.: 2–3

McLeod, J.: 1
Rankin, E. F.: *rev,* 7:688
Richmond, D. M.: 2

[1551]

★GAPADOL. Ages 10 and over; 1972; upward extension for "adolescent children" of *GAP Reading Comprehension Test;* cloze technique; J. McLeod and J. Anderson; Heinemann Educational Australia Pty Ltd. [Australia]. *

[1552]

***Gates-MacGinitie Reading Tests.** Grades 1, 2, 3, 2.5–3, 4–6, 7–9; 1926–72; GMRT; Primary A is a revision of *Gates Primary Reading Tests;* Primary B is a revision of *Gates Advanced Primary Reading Tests;* the other tests in this series are revisions of *Gates Reading Survey;* 6 levels; Arthur I. Gates and Walter H. MacGinitie; Teachers College Press. *

a) PRIMARY A. Grade 1; 1926–72; 2 scores: vocabulary, comprehension. (British adaptation of Form 1: Ages 6-10 to 8-0; 1971–73; norms supplement by. Peter Saville and Stephen Blinkhorn; NFER Publishing Co. Ltd. [England]).

b) PRIMARY B. Grade 2; 1926–72; 2 scores: same as for Primary A.

c) PRIMARY C. Grade 3; 1939–72; 2 scores: same as for Primary A.

d) PRIMARY CS. Grades 2.5–3; 1926–72; speed and accuracy.

e) SURVEY D. Grades 4–6; 1939–72; 3 scores: speed and accuracy, vocabulary, comprehension.

f) SURVEY E. Grades 7–9; 1939–72; 3 scores: same as for Survey D.

For additional information, reviews by Carolyn L. Burke and Byron H. Van Roekel, and an excerpted review by William R. Powell, see 7:689. For reviews by William Eller and Coleman Morrison of the *Gates Primary Reading Tests,* see 6:792 (1 reference); see also 5:632 (2 references); for reviews by William S. Gray and George D. Spache of an earlier edition, see 3:486 (7 references). For a review by Kenneth D. Hopkins of the *Gates Advanced Primary Reading Tests,* see 6:790 (1 reference); see also 5:630 (3 references); for reviews by Virginia Seavey and George D. Spache of an earlier edition, see 3:484. For reviews by George D. Spache and Morey J. Wantman of the *Gates Reading Survey,* see 6:793 (7 references); for reviews by Dorothy E. Holberg and Herbert F. Spitzer of an earlier edition, see 3:487.

REFERENCES THROUGH 1971

1. DAVIS, WILLIAM QUINBY. *A Study of Test Score Comparability Among Five Widely Used Reading Survey Tests.* Doctor's thesis, Southern Illinois University (Carbondale, Ill.), 1968. (*DA* 29:4370A)
2. BEYER, DONALD A. *A Comparative Study of the Reading Performance of Third Grade Children Measured by the Reading Eye Camera and the Gates MacGinitie Reading Tests.* Master's thesis, Cardinal Stritch College (Milwaukee, Wis.), 1969.

3. FARR, ROGER, AND ANASTASIOW, NICHOLAS. *Tests of Reading Readiness and Achievement: A Review and Evaluation*, pp. 30–4. Newark, Del.: International Reading Association, 1969. Pp. iv, 51. *

4. RODGERS, DENIS CYRIL. *An Investigation of the Auditory Memory Abilities of Grade 2 Retarded-Underachieving Readers and Competent-Achieving Readers Under Conditions of Reinforcement and Non-Reinforcement.* Doctor's thesis, University of Toronto (Toronto, Ont., Canada), 1969. (*DAI* 31:2196A)

5. ROELKE, PATRICIA LYNN. *Reading Comprehension as a Function of Three Dimensions of Word Meaning.* Doctor's thesis, Indiana University (Bloomington, Ind.), 1969. (*DAI* 30:5300A)

6. WALLACE, GERALD. *A Study of the Relationship of Selected Visual Perceptual Capabilities and Intelligence to Achievement in Reading of Educable Mentally Retarded Children.* Doctor's thesis, University of Oregon (Eugene, Ore.), 1969. (*DAI* 30: 3336A)

7. ALLEN, JOHN EDWARD. *A Survey of Third Grade Reading in the State of Utah.* Doctor's thesis, University of Utah (Salt Lake City, Utah), 1970. (*DAI* 31:2165A)

8. GAULKE, MARY FLORENCE. *A Longitudinal Two-Generation Study of Parent-Child Relationships on Selected Reading Skills and Aptitudes.* Doctor's thesis, University of Oregon (Eugene, Ore.), 1970. (*DAI* 31:3371A)

9. PAYNE, PATSY P. *A Comparison of the Performance of Third Grade Pupils Who Were Reading Below Grade Level on Two Test Formats of the Gates-MacGinitie Reading Test: Primary C Vocabulary and Comprehension.* Master's thesis, University of Texas (Austin, Tex.), 1970.

10. SMITH, CHARLES LEROY. *A Comparison of Selected Standardized Reading Test Scores and Informal Reading Inventory Results at Intermediate Grade Levels.* Doctor's thesis, University of Northern Colorado (Greeley, Colo.), 1970. (*DAI* 31:4046A)

11. CALVERT, KENNEITH CAROL HARBISON. *An Investigation of Relationships Between the Syntactic Maturity of Oral Language and Reading Comprehension Scores.* Doctor's thesis, University of Alabama (University, Ala.), 1971. (*DAI* 32:4828A)

12. COMPTON, MARY ELIZABETH. *A Study of the Relationship Between Oral Language Facility and Reading Achievement of Selected First-Grade Children.* Doctor's thesis, University of North Carolina (Chapel Hill, N.C.), 1971. (*DAI* 32:6848A)

13. FARR, ROGER, AND ROELKE, PATRICIA. "Measuring Subskills of Reading: Intercorrelations Between Standardized Reading Tests, Teachers' Ratings, and Reading Specialists' Ratings." *J Ed Meas* 8(1):27–32 sp '71. * (*PA* 46:5464)

14. GIRARD, JUDITH ANDERSON FUNK. *A Study of the Correlations Between the Gates-MacGinitie Reading Comprehension Test and Various Subtests From the Analysis of Learning Potential.* Doctor's thesis, University of Northern Colorado (Greeley, Colo.), 1971. (*DAI* 32:5468A)

15. GORMLY, JOHN, AND NITTOLI, MICHAEL J. "Rapid Improvement of the Reading Skills in Juvenile Delinquents." *J Exp Ed* 40(2):45–8 w '71. * (*PA* 48:1688)

16. JOHNSON, THEOLA GAE. *Influence of Selected Factors on the Ability of Fourth, Fifth, and Sixth Graders to Read Graphs.* Doctor's thesis, University of Southern California (Los Angeles, Calif.), 1971. (*DAI* 32:726A)

17. MYKLEBUST, HELMER R.; BANNOCHIE, MARGARET N.; AND KILLEN, JAMES R. Chap. 9, "Learning Disabilities and Cognitive Processes," pp. 213–51. In *Progress in Learning Disabilities, Vol. 2*. Edited by Helmer R. Myklebust. New York: Grune & Stratton, Inc., 1971. Pp. ix, 404. *

18. WADE, VERN JOSEPH. *A Comparison of Selected Standardized Reading Test Scores and Informal Reading Inventory Results at Eighth Grade Level.* Doctor's thesis, University of Northern Colorado (Greeley, Colo.), 1971. (*DAI* 32:3853A)

CUMULATIVE NAME INDEX

[1553]

Gates-MacGinitie Reading Tests: Survey F. Grades 10–12; 1969–70; 3 scores: speed and accuracy, vocabulary, comprehension; Arthur I. Gates and Walter H. MacGinitie; Teachers College Press. *

Gates-MacGinitie Reading Tests

For additional information and a review by Jason Millman, see 7:690.

[1554]

Group Reading Assessment. End of first year junior school; 1964, c1962–64; Frank A. Spooncer; University of London Press Ltd. [England]. *

[1555]

Group Reading Test. Ages 6–10; 1968–69; D. Young; University of London Press Ltd. [England]. *
For additional information, see 7:691.

[1556]

High School Reading Test: National Achievement Tests. Grades 7–12; 1939–52; 6 scores: vocabulary, word discrimination, sentence meaning, noting details, interpreting paragraphs, total; 1951–52 tests identical with tests copyrighted 1939–40 except for minor changes; Robert K. Speer and Samuel Smith; Psychometric Affiliates. *
For additional information and a review by Victor H. Noll, see 5:634; for a review by Holland Roberts, see 4:536; for a review by Robert L. McCaul, see 3:488.

[1557]

Individual Reading Test. Ages 6-0 to 9-9; 1935–36; 3 scores: oral word reading, comprehension, speed; L. W. Allen; Australian Council for Educational Research [Australia]. *
For additional information and a review by R. W. McCulloch, see 5:663.

[1558]

★**Informal Reading Assessment Tests.** Grades 1–3; 1971; IRAT; 7 nonstandardized tests which may be used with the publisher's reading program or independently; Margaret Gerrard and Elinor Beard; Thomas Nelson & Sons (Canada) Ltd. [Canada]. *
a) TEST 1. 6 scores: vocabulary, comprehension, phonics (consonants, rhyme), oral reading (vocabulary, comprehension).
b) TEST 2. 6 scores: vocabulary, comprehension, word attack (word structure, phonics), oral reading (vocabulary, comprehension).
c) TEST 3. 6 scores: same as for Test 2.
d) TEST 4. 6 scores: same as for Test 2.
e) TEST 5. 6 scores: same as for Test 2.
f) TEST 6. 6 scores: same as for Test 2.
g) TEST 7. 6 scores: same as for Test 2.

[1559]

★**Inventory-Survey Tests.** Grades 4–6, 7–8; 1968–69; IST; 6 scores: word meaning, sentence meaning, paragraph meaning, word analysis, dictionary skills, total; 2 levels; Marion Monroe; Scott, Foresman & Co. *
a) INVENTORY-SURVEY TEST FOR INTERMEDIATE GRADES. Grades 4–6.
b) INVENTORY-SURVEY TEST FOR UPPER GRADES. Grades 7–8.

[1560]

Iowa Silent Reading Tests. Grades 4–16; 1927–73; ISRT; 2 editions; Harcourt Brace Jovanovich, Inc. *
a) 1939–42 EDITION. Grades 4–8, 9–14; 1927–56; 2 levels; H. A. Greene, A. N. Jorgensen, and V. H. Kelley.
1) *Elementary Test.* Grades 4–8; 1933–56; 9 scores: rate, comprehension, directed reading, word meaning, paragraph comprehension, sentence meaning, alphabetizing, use of index, total.

2) *Advanced Test*. Grades 9–14; 1927–43; 10 scores: rate, comprehension, directed reading, poetry comprehension, word meaning, sentence meaning, paragraph comprehension, use of index, selection of key words, total.

b) 1973 EDITION. Grades 6–9, 9–14, 11–16; 1927–73; 3 levels; coordinating editor: Roger Farr.

1) *Level 1*. Grades 6–9; 5 scores: vocabulary, reading comprehension, total, directed reading, reading efficiency.

2) *Level 2*. Grades 9–14; 5 scores: same as for Level 1.

3) *Level 3*. Grades 11–16; 4 scores: vocabulary, reading comprehension, total, reading efficiency.

For additional information and a review by Worth R. Jones of *a*, see 6:794 (40 references); for reviews by Frederick B. Davis and William W. Turnbull and excerpted reviews by Earl R. Gabler and Margaret Pankaskie, see 3:489 (21 references); for reviews by Ivan A. Booker and Holland D. Roberts of an earlier edition, see 2:1547 (6 references).

REFERENCES THROUGH 1971

1-6. See 2:1547.
7-27. See 3:489.
28-67. See 6:794.
68. LITTERER, OSCAR F. "An Experimental Study of Visual Apprehension in Reading." *J Appl Psychol* 17:266-76 Je '33. * (*PA* 8:496)
69. ROBINSON, F. P., AND McCOLLOM, F. H. "Reading Rate and Comprehension Accuracy as Determinants of Reading Test Scores." *J Ed Psychol* 25:154-7 F '34. * (*PA* 8:2703)
70. KELLEY, VICTOR H. "The Reading Abilities of Spanish and English Speaking Pupils." *J Ed Res* 29:209-11 N '35. * (*PA* 10:1621)
71. ANDERSON, VERNA L., AND TINKER, MILES A. "The Speed Factor in Reading Performance." *J Ed Psychol* 27:621-4 N '36. * (*PA* 11:1386)
72. ANDERSON, IRVING H., AND SWANSON, DONALD E. "Common Factors in Eye Movements in Silent and Oral Reading." *Psychol Monogr* 48(3):61-9 '37. * (*PA* 11:3319)
73. FAIRBANKS, GRANT. "The Relation Between Eye Movements and Voice in the Oral Reading of Good and Poor Silent Readers." *Psychol Monogr* 48(3):78-107 '37. * (*PA* 11:3325)
74. KENNAH, CATHERINE J. *A Comparison of Reading Grades Made on the Iowa Silent Reading Test With Scores Made in the Final Examination by Pupils in the Albany Senior High School*. Master's thesis, New York State College for Teachers (Albany, N.Y.), 1937.
75. SCHMITZ, SYLVESTER B. "Predicting Success in College: A Study of Various Criteria." *J Ed Psychol* 28:465-73 S '37. * (*PA* 12:538)
76. SWANSON, DONALD E. "Common Elements in Silent and Oral Reading." *Psychol Monogr* 48(3):36-60 '37. * (*PA* 11:3369)
77. READ, CECIL B. "The Prediction of Scholastic Success in a Municipal University." *Sch & Soc* 48:187-8 Ag 6 '38. * (*PA* 12:6645)
78. SMITH, MARJORIE A. *The Correlation Between Intelligence and Reading Ability*. Master's thesis, Fordham University (New York, N.Y.), 1938.
79. BEAR, ROBERT M., AND IMUS, HENRY A. "Changes in Reading Performance During the Freshman Year of College." *J Ed Psychol* 30:667-73 D '39. * (*PA* 14:3190)
80. DOUGLASS, LOWELL N. "A Study of Certain Factors Influencing Academic Achievement With Special Reference to the Health Factor." *J Exp Ed* 7:235-44 Mr '39. * (*PA* 13:5911)
81. BEAR, ROBERT M., AND ODBERT, HENRY S. "Experimental Studies of the Relation Between Rate of Reading and Speed of Association." *J Psychol* 10:141-7 Jl '40. * (*PA* 14:6188)
82. POND, FREDERICK L. "Influence of Reading Abilities on School Success in Grade IX." *Sch R* 48:437-44 Je '40. *
83. OSBORNE, AGNES ELIZABETH. "The Relationship Between Certain Psychological Tests and Shorthand Achievement." *Teach Col Contrib Ed* 873:1-58 '43. *
84. JONES, MARY M. WILCOX. "Relationship Between Reading Deficiencies and Left-Handedness." *Sch & Soc* 60:238-9 O 7 '44. * (*PA* 19:1055)
85. BERRY, GEORGE S. "An Experiment in Self-Analysis." *J Ed Psychol* 37:111-24 F '46. * (*PA* 20:2061)
86. MOORE, CHARLES E. A. "Reading and Arithmetic Abilities Associated With Speech Defects." *J Speech Disorders* 12:85-6 Mr '47. * (*PA* 21:3582)
87. FREEBURNE, CECIL MAX. "A Study of the Relationship Between Figural After-Effect and Reading-Test Performance." *J Ed Psychol* 43:309-12 My '52. * (*PA* 27:3752)
88. ADAMS, SAM, AND GARRETT, H. L. "Scholastic Background

as Related to Success in College Physics." *J Ed Res* 47:545-9 Mr '54. * (*PA* 28:7951)
89. WHEELER, LESTER R., AND WHEELER, VIOLA D. "A Study of the Relationship of Auditory Discrimination to Silent Reading Abilities." *J Ed Res* 48:103-13 O '54. * (*PA* 29:6186)
90. MANN, HELENE POWNER. "Some Hypotheses on Perceptual and Learning Processes With Their Applications to the Process of Reading: A Preliminary Note." *J Genetic Psychol* 90:167-202 Je '57. * (*PA* 35:1187)
91. TURNER, DANIEL. *A Study of Speech Effectiveness and Personal and Social Adjustment Among Ninth Grade Pupils*. Doctor's thesis, Boston University (Boston, Mass.), 1957. (*DA* 17:2902)
92. OLANDER, HERBERT T., AND KLEYLE, HELEN M. "Differences in Personal and Professional Characteristics of a Selected Group of Elementary Teachers With Contrasting Success Records." *Ed Adm & Sup* 45:191-8 Jl '59. * (*PA* 34:6582)
93. SIMMONS, AUDREY ANN. "Factors Related to Lipreading." *J Speech & Hearing Res* 2:340-52 D '59. * (*PA* 34:6510)
94. DARTER, CLARENCE LESLIE, JR. *A Comparative Study of Over-Achieving and Under-Achieving Ninth-Grade Students*. Doctor's thesis, Texas Technological College (Lubbock, Tex.), 1961. (*DA* 22:1462)
95. ROTHMAN, ARTHUR I. *The Determination of Criteria for the Selection of Students for the PSSC Physics Course*. Master's thesis, University of Maine (Orono, Me.), 1965.
96. JENKINS, ALICE CRAWFORD. *The Relationship of Certain Measurable Factors to Academic Success in Freshman Biology*. Doctor's thesis, New York University (New York, N.Y.), 1966. (*DA* 27:2279A)
97. KARP, ROBERT EUGENE. *An Analysis of Aptitudes, Abilities, and High School Class Rank and Their Relation to the Academic Success of First-Year Private Business School Students*. Doctor's thesis, Northern Illinois University (DeKalb, Ill.), 1966. (*DA* 27:3289A)
98. WHITTEMORE, ROBERT G.; ECHEVERRIA, BEN P.; AND GRIFFIN, JOHN V. "Can We Use Existing Tests for Adult Basic Education?" *Adult Ed* 17:19-29 au '66. *
99. HUFF, BETTY. *The Predictive Value of Standardized Testing in Relation to Mathematical Achievement at Virginia High School*. Master's thesis, East Tennessee State University (Johnson City, Tenn.), 1967.
100. JANSEN, DAVID G. "Verbal and Reading Skills of Students Participating in a University Reading and Study Skills Program." *J Col Stud Personnel* 8:181-4 My '67. *
101. KUSHINKA, MICHAEL. *The Predictive Components of Pupil Performance in Senior High School*. Doctor's thesis, Yeshiva University (New York, N.Y.), 1967. (*DA* 28:434A)
102. FARR, ROGER, AND ANASTASIOW, NICHOLAS. *Tests of Reading Readiness and Achievement: A Review and Evaluation*, pp. 34-6. Newark, Del.: International Reading Association, 1969. Pp. iv, 51. *
103. HALL, LUCIEN TALMAGE, JR. *The Prediction of Success in Each of Six Four-Year Selections of Secondary Mathematics Courses*. Doctor's thesis, University of Virginia (Charlottesville, Va.), 1969. (*DAI* 30:4141A)
104. HAYES, EDWARD MAJELLA. *The Relationship of Race and Sex to Academic Achievement in Selected Rural Elementary and High Schools Before and After Desegregation*. Doctor's thesis, University of Virginia (Charlottesville, Va.), 1969. (*DAI* 31:149A)
105. SUTHERLAND, KELLEY. *The Predictive Value of School and College Ability Test, Sequential Test of Educational Progress, Differential Aptitude Test, Iowa Silent Reading Test, and California Test of Mental Maturity Scores at Clintwood High School, Clintwood, Virginia*. Master's thesis, East Tennessee State University (Johnson City, Tenn.), 1969.
106. HALL, LUCIEN T., JR. "The Prediction of Success in Each of Six Four-Year Selections of Secondary Mathematics Courses." *Sch Sci & Math* 71(8):693-6 N '71. *
107. HARRIS, JOHN A. *A Study of Selected Graduate Students' Performances on Graduate Record Examination, Iowa Silent Reading Test, and Grade-Point Average*. Master's thesis, Fort Valley State College (Ft. Valley, Ga.), 1971.
108. HAYNES, ELIZABETH FINGER. *An Analysis of the Relationships Between Pupil Performance in the Learning of Transformational Grammar and Intelligence Test Scores*. Doctor's thesis, University of Virginia (Charlottesville, Va.), 1971. (*DAI* 32:4591A)
109. TAYLOR, ALTON L. "Regression Analysis of Antecedent Measures of Slow Sections in High School Biology." *Sci Ed* 55(3):395-402 Jl-S '71. *

CUMULATIVE NAME INDEX

Davis, F. B.: *rev*, 3:489
Dearborn, W. F.: 3, 10
Donnelly, M. C.: 9
Douglass, L. N.: 80
Dungan, E. W.: 56
Eaton, M. T.: 20, 25
Echeverria, B. P.: 98
Fairbanks, G.: 73
Farr, R.: 102
Freeburne, C. M.: 87
Gabler, E. R.: *exc*, 3:489
Garrett, H. L.: 88
Garrett, W. S.: 64
Garrison, K. C.: 30
Giesecke, G. E.: 36
Gladfelter, M. E.: 40
Gores, H. B.: 3
Gowan, J. C.: 60
Greene, H. A.: 27
Griffin, J. V.: 98
Grilk, W.: 51
Hall, L. T.: 103, 106
Harris, J. A.: 107
Havighurst, R. J.: 37, 41
Hayes, E. M.: 104
Haynes, E. F.: 108
Holcomb, G. W.: 7
Huff, B.: 99
Humber, W. J.: 38
Imus, H. A.: 79
Janke, L. L.: 37, 41
Jansen, D. G.: 100
Jenkins, A. C.: 96
Jones, K. J.: 67
Jones, M. M. W.: 84
Jones, W. R.: *rev*, 6:794
Jorgensen, A. N.: 1
Karp, R. E.: 97
Kelley, V. H.: 27, 70
Kennah, C. J.: 74
Kilby, R. W.: 23
Kleyle, H. M.: 92
Kushinka, M.: 101
Landry, H.: 4
Langsam, R. S.: 11, 34
Larsen, R. P.: 36
Laslett, H. R.: 7
Lindquist, E. F.: 18
Litterer, O. F.: 68
McCollom, F. H.: 69
Madigan, M. E.: 14
Mann, H. P.: 90
Manson, W. Y.: 50
Miles, T. A.: 21

Moore, C. E. A.: 86
Moore, J. E.: 32
Morgan, C. L.: 16
Norton, D. P.: 63
Odbert, H. S.: 81
Olander, H. T.: 92
Osborne, A. E.: 83
Pankaskie, M.: 12; *exc*, 3:489
Pflieger, E. F.: 46
Pond, F. L.: 82
Preische, W. A.: 19
Preston, R. C.: 43, 52
Pugh, G. S.: 24
Rainier, R. N.: 14
Read, C. B.: 77
Rehfeld, F. W.: 14
Ridley, W. N.: 53
Roberts, H. D.: *rev*, 2:1547
Robinson, F. P.: 69
Rothman, A. I.: 95
Scarborough, R. L.: 65
Schmitz, S. B.: 75
Shaw, G. S.: 59
Sherman, O.: 31
Simmons, A. A.: 93
Slocum, R. L.: 33
Smith, F. F.: 42
Smith, H. L.: 20, 25
Smith, J. M.: 13
Smith, M. A.: 78
Solomon, L. E.: 39
Steinman, C. C.: 16
Strang, R.: 2
Stuit, D. B.: 8–9
Sullivan, B. A.: 48
Sutherland, K.: 105
Swanson, D. E.: 72, 76
Taylor, A. L.: 109
Terry, P. W.: 28
Tinker, M. A.: 21, 71
Townsend, A.: 22
Traxler, A. E.: 5–6, 29, 47, 49
Treumann, M. J.: 48
Tuft, E. N.: 43
Turnbull, W. W.: *rev*, 3:489
Turner, D.: 91
Wheeler, L. R.: 89
Wheeler, V. D.: 89
Whittemore, R. G.: 98
Wilking, S. V.: 15
Wittenborn, J. R.: 36

[1561]
Kelvin Measurement of Reading Ability. Ages 8–12; 1933; C. M. Fleming; Robert Gibson & Sons, Glasgow, Ltd. [Scotland]. *
For additional information, see 1:1103.

[1562]
The Kingston Test of Silent Reading. Ages 7–11; 1953–54; M. E. Hebron (formerly M. E. Highfield); George G. Harrap & Co. Ltd. [England]. *
For additional information and reviews by Neil Gourlay and Magdalen D. Vernon, see 5:637.

[1563]
Lee-Clark Reading Test. Grades 1, 1–2; 1931–65; 2 levels; J. Murray Lee and Willis W. Clark; CTB/McGraw-Hill. *
a) PRIMER. Grade 1; 1931–58; 4 scores: auditory stimuli, visual stimuli, following directions, total.
b) FIRST READER. Grades 1–2; 1931–65; 6 scores: auditory stimuli, visual stimuli, following directions, completion, inference, total.
For additional information and reviews by Thomas C. Barrett and Coleman Morrison, see 6:795; for a review by Ruth Lowes of an earlier edition of the primer level, see 3:490.

REFERENCES THROUGH 1971
1. DURKIN, DOLORES. "A Case-Study Approach Toward an Identification of Factors Associated With Success and Failure in Learning to Read." *Calif J Ed Res* 11:26–33 Ja '60. * (*PA* 34:8336)

Iowa Silent Reading Tests

2. MATTICK, WILLIAM E. "Predicting Success in the First Grade." *El Sch J* 63:273–6 F '63. *

CUMULATIVE NAME INDEX
Barrett, T. C.: *rev*, 6:795
Durkin, D.: 1
Lowes, R.: *rev*, 3:490
Mattick, W. E.: 2
Morrison, C.: *rev*, 6:795

[1564]
McGrath Test of Reading Skills, Second Edition. Grades 1–13; 1965–67; 4 scores: oral word recognition, oral paragraph reading, silent reading vocabulary, oral reading rate; Joseph E. McGrath; McGrath Publishing Co. *
For additional information and a review by Byron H. Van Roekel, see 7:692.

[1565]
McMenemy Measure of Reading Ability. Grades 3, 5–6, 7–8; 1964–68; Richard A. McMenemy; the Author. *
For additional information and reviews by Marvin D. Glock and Ronald W. Mitchell, see 7:693.

[1566]
Maintaining Reading Efficiency Tests. Grades 7–16 and adults; 1966–70; MRET; 3 scores: rate, comprehension accuracy, reading efficiency; 5 forms; no manual; Lyle L. Miller; Developmental Reading Distributors. *
a) TEST 1, HISTORY OF BRAZIL, 1970 REVISION. 1966–70.
b) TEST 2, HISTORY OF JAPAN, 1970 REVISION. 1966–70.
c) TEST 3, HISTORY OF INDIA. 1970.
d) TEST 4, HISTORY OF NEW ZEALAND. 1970.
e) TEST 5, HISTORY OF SWITZERLAND. 1970.
For additional information, see 7:694.

[1567]
*Metropolitan Achievement Tests: Reading Tests.** Grades 2–9; 1932–71; catalog uses the title *Metropolitan Reading Tests*; 2 editions; Walter N. Durost, Harold H. Bixler, J. Wayne Wrightstone, Gertrude H. Hildreth (*a*), Kenneth W. Lund (*a*), George A. Prescott (*b*), and Irving H. Balow (*b*); Harcourt Brace Jovanovich, Inc. * For the complete battery entry, see 22.
a) 1958 EDITION. Grades 2, 3–4, 5–6, 7–9; 1932–62; 2 or 3 scores: word knowledge, word discrimination (grade 2 only), reading.
b) 1970 EDITION. Grades 2.5–3.4, 3.5–4.9, 5.0–6.9, 7.0–9.5; 1932–71; 3 scores: word knowledge, reading, total.
For additional information concerning the 1970 edition, see 7:696 (16 references); for a review by H. Alan Robinson of the 1958 edition, see 6:797 (4 references); for reviews by James R. Hobson and Margaret G. McKim of an earlier edition, see 4:543; for a review by D. A. Worcester, see 2:1551; for reviews by Ivan A. Booker and Joseph C. Dewey, see 1:1105. For reviews of an earlier edition of the complete battery, see 6:15 (2 reviews), 4:18 (1 review), 2:1189 (2 reviews), and 1:874 (3 reviews).

REFERENCES THROUGH 1971
1–4. See 6:797.
5–20. See 7:696.
21. JUSTMAN, JOSEPH. "Academic Aptitude and Reading Test Scores of Disadvantaged Children Showing Varying Degrees of Mobility." *J Ed Meas* 2:151–5 D '65. * (*PA* 40:5943)
22. RAPHAEL, SHARON. *The Relationship of Intelligence and Personality on the Reading Achievement of Culturally Deprived Second-Grade Students.* Master's thesis, Central Connecticut State College (New Britain, Conn.), 1965.
23. SAMTUR, SUSAN JOY. "The Effects of Noise on a Complex Task." *Grad Res Ed & Related Discip* 4(2):63–81 sp '69. * (*PA* 46:11670)
24. FELDHUSEN, HAZEL J.; LAMB, POSE; AND FELDHUSEN, JOHN. "Prediction of Reading Achievement Under Programmed and Traditional Instruction." *Read Teach* 23(5):446–54 F '70. * (*PA* 45:1382)

25. BALOW, BRUCE; FULTON, HELEN; AND PEPLOE, ELLA. "Reading Comprehension Skills Among Hearing Impaired Adolescents." *Volta R* 73(2):113–9 F '71. *

26. CROWLEY, HARRY L., AND ELLIS, BESSIE. "Cross Validation of a Method for Selecting Children Requiring Special Services in Reading." *Read Teach* 24(4):312–9 Ja '71. *

27. DAVIS, BOBBIE SUE. *A Comparative Analysis of Three Widely Used Standardized Reading Achievement Tests for a Selected Group of Elementary School Children.* Doctor's thesis, University of Southern Mississippi (Hattiesburg, Miss.), 1971. (*DAI* 32:4831A)

28. FLEISCHMAN, HOWARD L.; ORR, DAVID B.; AND STRASEL, H. C. "Relationships Between the Subtests of Six Achievement Test Batteries." Abstract. *Proc 79th Ann Conv Am Psychol Assn* 6(1):109–10 '71. * (*PA* 46:3727)

29. FLEISCHMANN, LILLIAN S. *A Comparison of the Gilmore Oral Reading Test and the Metropolitan Achievement Test in Reading for Grade Placement.* Master's thesis, Sacramento State College (Sacramento, Calif.), 1971.

30. HOPKINS, KENNETH D., AND BRACHT, GLENN H. "A Longitudinal Study of Constancy of Reading Performance," pp. 103–12. In *Diagnostic Viewpoints in Reading.* Edited by Robert E. Leibert. Newark, Del.: International Reading Association, 1971. Pp. viii, 133. *

31. SMITH, CAROLYN M. "The Relationship of Reading Method and Reading Achievement to ITPA Sensory Modalities." *J Spec Ed* 5(2):143–9 su '71. * (*PA* 48:9854)

32. SOLOMON, ALAN. "The Effect of Answer Sheet Format on Test Performance by Culturally Disadvantaged Fourth Grade Elementary School Pupils." *J Ed Meas* 8(4):289–90 w '71. * (*PA* 47:11632)

CUMULATIVE NAME INDEX

Anastasiow, N.: 15
Arnold, R. D.: 11, 14
Aronow, M. S.: 4
Balow, B.: 25
Booker, I. A.: *rev*, 1:1105
Bracht, G. H.: 30
Brandinger, A. L.: 19
Brown, S. R.: 6
Bruininks, R. H.: 20
Crowley, H. L.: 26
Davis, B. S.: 27
Davis, W. Q.: 12
Dewey, J. C.: *rev*, 1:1105
Ellis, B.: 26
Farr, R.: 15
Feldhusen, H. J.: 24
Feldhusen, J.: 24
Fleischman, H. L.: 28
Fleischmann, L. S.: 29
Fulton, H.: 25
Furth, H. G.: 9
Gropper, R. L.: 16
Hanson, E.: 13
Hobson, J. R.: *rev*, 4:543
Hopkins, K. D.: 30

Justman, J.: 21
Kaufman, M.: 8
Lamb, P.: 24
Lloyd, C. J.: 3
Lucker, W. G.: 20
McKim, M. G.: *rev*, 4:543
Miceli, F.: 17
Moskowitz, S.: 4
Orr, D. B.: 28
Peploe, E.: 25
Raphael, S.: 22
Robinson, H. A.: 13; *rev*, 6:797
Roelke, P. L.: 18
Samtur, S. J.: 23
Sipay, E. R.: 5
Smith, C. M.: 31
Solomon, A.: 32
Spache, G.: 1
Stone, C. R.: 2
Strasel, H. C.: 28
Sutherland, S. P.: 10
Williams, J. L.: 7
Worcester, D. A.: *rev*, 2:1551
Wrightstone, J. W.: 4

[1568]
Minnesota Reading Examination for College Students.
Grades 9–16; 1930–35; 2 scores: vocabulary, paragraph reading; Melvin E. Haggerty and Alvin C. Eurich; University of Minnesota Press. *

For additional information and a review by James M. McCallister, see 3:491 (3 references); for a review by W. C. McCall, see 2:1554 (3 references); for a review by Ruth Strang, see 1:1106.

REFERENCES THROUGH 1971

1–3. See 2:1554.
4–6. See 3:491.
7. EURICH, ALVIN C. "The Relation of Speed of Reading to Comprehension." *Sch & Soc* 32:404–6 S 20 '30. * (*PA* 5:764)
8. LITTERER, OSCAR F. "An Experimental Study of Visual Apprehension in Reading." *J Appl Psychol* 17:266–76 Je '33. * (*PA* 8:496)
9. SORENSON, HERBERT. "Mental Ability Over a Wide Range of Adult Ages." *J Appl Psychol* 17:729–41 D '33. * (*PA* 8:3830)
10. RIZZO, NICHOLAS D. *The Predictive Value of the Minnesota Reading Examination.* Master's thesis, University of Kansas (Lawrence, Kan.), 1935.
11. PACE, C. ROBERT. "Handedness and Reading Ability in High School and College Students." *J Ed Res* 31:205–10 N '37. * (*PA* 12:952)
12. LANGSAM, ROSALIND STREEP. *A Factorial Analysis of Reading Ability.* Doctor's thesis, New York University (New York, N.Y.), 1941.
13. SOLOMON, LEWIS E. *Some Relationships Between Reading Ability and Degree of Academic Success in College.* Doctor's thesis, University of Colorado (Boulder, Colo.), 1944.

CUMULATIVE NAME INDEX

Eurich, A. C.: 1, 4–5, 7
Langsam, R. S.: 6, 12
Litterer, O. F.: 8
McCall, W. C.: *rev*, 2:1554
McCallister, J. M.: *rev*, 3:491
Pace, C. R.: 11
Paterson, D. G.: 3

Rizzo, N. D.: 10
Schneidler, G. G.: 3
Solomon, L. E.: 13
Sorenson, H.: 9
Strang, R.: 2; *rev*, 1:1106
Williamson, E. G.: 3

[1569]
Monroe's Standardized Silent Reading Test.
Grades 3–5, 6–8, 9–12; 1919–59; 2 scores: rate, comprehension; Walter S. Monroe; Bobbs-Merrill Co., Inc. *

For additional information and reviews by Charles R. Langmuir and Agatha Townsend, see 6:798 (5 references).

REFERENCES THROUGH 1971

1–5. See 6:798.
6. MONROE, WALTER SCOTT. *Measuring the Results of Teaching,* pp. 22–9, *passim.* Boston, Mass.: Houghton Mifflin Co., 1918. Pp. xviii, 297. *
7. WEBB, L. W. "Ability in Mental Tests in Relation to Reading Ability." *Sch & Soc* 11:567–70 My 8 '20. *
8. WILSON, G. M., AND HOKE, KREMER J. *How to Measure,* pp. 111–8. New York: Macmillan Co., 1920. Pp. vii, 285. *
9. GATES, ARTHUR I. "An Experimental and Statistical Study of Reading and Reading Tests." *J Ed Psychol* 12:303–14, 378–91, 445–64 S, O, N '21. *
10. MADSEN, I. N. "Some Results From a Testing Program in Idaho." *Sch & Soc* 13:668–71 Je 11 '21. *
11. MONROE, WALTER S. Chap. 2, "Tentative Grade Norms," pp. 19–24, 58–9. In his *Report of Division of Educational Tests for '19–20.* University of Illinois Bulletin, Vol. 18, No. 21; Bureau of Educational Research Bulletin No. 5. Urbana, Ill.: the Bureau, 1921. Pp. 64. *
12. MONROE, WALTER S. *The Illinois Examination.* University of Illinois Bulletin, Vol. 19, No. 9; Bureau of Educational Research Bulletin No. 6. Urbana, Ill.: the Bureau, 1921. Pp. 70. *
13. PRESSEY, L. W., AND PRESSEY, S. C. "A Critical Study of the Concept of Silent Reading." *J Ed Psychol* 12:25–32 Ja '21. *
14. WYMAN, J. BENSON, AND WENDLE, MIRIAM. "What Is Reading Ability?" *J Ed Psychol* 12:518–31 D '21. *
15. FRANZEN, RAYMOND. "Attempts at Test Validation." *J Ed Res* 6:145–58 S '22. *
16. HARLAN, CHAS. L. "The Age-Grade Status as an Index of School Achievement." *Ed Adm & Sup* 8:413–23 O '22. *
17. MADSEN, I. N. "Tests and Measurements in the Schools of Idaho." *J Ed Res* 5:175–8 F '22. *
18. BROOKS, FOWLER D. "The Reliability of Silent Reading Tests." *Sch & Soc* 19:652 My 31 '24. *
19. GATES, ARTHUR I. "A Critique of Methods of Estimating and Measuring the Transfer of Training." *J Ed Psychol* 15:545–58 D '24. *
20. HULTEN, C. E. "A Study of the Speed of Upper Grade Reading." *J Ed Res* 10:141–8 S '24. *
21. KATHLEEN, M. "A Comparative Study of Certain Silent Reading Tests." *Cath R* 22:589–95 D '24. *
22. MONROE, WALTER SCOTT; DEVOSS, JAMES CLARENCE; AND KELLY, FREDERICK JAMES. *Educational Tests and Measurements,* Revised Edition, pp. 99–106. Boston, Mass.: Houghton Mifflin Co., 1924. Pp. xxvii, 521. *
23. RITTER, B. T., AND LOFLAUD, W. T. "The Relation Between Reading Ability as Measured by Certain Standard Tests and the Ability Required in the Interpretation of Printed Matter Involving Reason." *El Sch J* 24:529–46 Mr '24. *
24. JONES, A. M. "An Analytical Study of One Hundred Twenty Superior Children." *Psychol Clinic* 16:19–76 Ja–F '25. * (*PA* 3:1656)
25. FORAN, T. G. "The Present Status of Silent Reading Tests: Part 1, The Measurement of Rate of Reading." *Cath Univ Am Ed Res B* 2(2):1–27 F '27. * (*PA* 2:2609)
26. MOSHER, RAYMOND M. "A Further Note on the Reliability of Reading Tests." *J Ed Psychol* 19:272–4 Ap '28. * (*PA* 2:2623)
27. SIMS, VERNER MARTIN. "The Relative Influence of Two Types of Motivation on Improvement." *J Ed Psychol* 19:480–4 O '28. * (*PA* 3:583)
28. EURICH, ALVIN C. "The Relation of Speed of Reading to Comprehension." *Sch & Soc* 32:404–6 S 20 '30. * (*PA* 5:764)
29. WERNER, OSCAR H. Chap. 2, "The Influence of the Study of Modern Foreign Languages on the Development of Desirable Abilities in English," pp. 97–145. (*PA* 4:2847) In *Studies in Modern Language Teaching.* By E. W. Bagster-Collins and Others. New York: Macmillan Co., 1930. Pp. xxxi, 491. *
30. HUDSON, ALVA. "Reading Achievement, Interests and Habits of Negro Women." *J Negro Ed* 1:367–73 O '32. * (*PA* 8:3590)
31. CROOKS, KENNETH B. M. "Entrance Examinations for Negro Colleges." *J Negro Ed* 3:593–7 O '34. * (*PA* 8:6093)
32. FEINBERG, HENRY, AND REED, CLYDE L. "Reading Level of a Group of Socially Maladjusted Boys." *J Social Psychol* 12:31–8 Ag '40. * (*PA* 15:424)

CUMULATIVE NAME INDEX

[1570]

N.B. Silent Reading Tests (Beginners): Reading Comprehension Test. Substandard B (grade 2); 1961; Human Sciences Research Council [South Africa]. *

For additional information, see 6:799.

[1571]

*National Teacher Examinations: Reading Specialist. College seniors and teachers; 1969–73; formerly entitled *National Teacher Examinations: Reading Specialist—Elementary School;* an inactive form (1969) entitled *Reading Specialist—Elementary School* is available to school systems for local use as part of the program entitled *School Personnel Research and Evaluation Services;* Educational Testing Service. *

For the testing program entry, see 869.

For additional information concerning earlier forms, see 7:731. For reviews of the testing program, see 7:582 (2 reviews), 6:700 (1 review), 5:538 (3 reviews), and 4:802 (1 review).

[1572]

The Nelson-Denny Reading Test. Grades 9–16 and adults; 1929–73; NDRT; 4 scores: vocabulary, comprehension, total, rate; original edition by M. J. Nelson and E. C. Denny; revision by James I. Brown; Houghton Mifflin Co. *

For additional information, reviews by David B. Orr and Agatha Townsend, and an excerpted review by John O. Crites, see 6:800 (13 references); for a review by Ivan A. Booker of an earlier edition, see 4:544 (17 references); for a review by Hans C. Gordon, see 2:1557 (6 references).

REFERENCES THROUGH 1971

1–6. See 2:1557.
7–23. See 4:544.
24–36. See 6:800.
37. NELSON, M. J. "Some Data From Freshman Tests." *Sch & Soc* 31:772–4 Je 7 '30. * (*PA* 4:3694)
38. JOHNSON, DONALD M., AND REYNOLDS, FLOYD. "A Factor Analysis of Verbal Ability." *Psychol Rec* 4:183–95 Ja '41. * (*PA* 15:3315)
39. SPOERL, DOROTHY TILDEN. "The Academic and Verbal Adjustment of College Age Bilingual Students." *J Genetic Psychol* 64:139–57 Mr '44. * (*PA* 18:2275)
40. WAGGONER, R. W., AND ZEIGLER, THORNTON WOODWARD. "Psychiatric Factors in Medical School Students Who Fail." *Am J Psychiatry* 103:369–76 N '46. * (*PA* 21:1671)
41. MCCLANAHAN, WALTER R., AND MORGAN, DAVID H. "Use of Standard Tests in Counseling Engineering Students in College." *J Ed Psychol* 39:491–501 D '48. * (*PA* 23:3448)
42. BELLOWS, CAROL S., AND RUSH, CARL H., JR. "Reading Abilities of Business Executives." *J Appl Psychol* 36:1–4 F '52. * (*PA* 26:7286)
43. MCCOLLUM, CLIFFORD G. "The Performance of Prospective Elementary School Teachers in a General Physical Science Course." *J Ed Res* 45:695–704 My '52. * (*PA* 27:2963)
44. OTTMAN, ROBERT WILLIAM. *A Statistical Investigation of the Influence of Selected Factors on the Skill of Sight-Singing.* Doctor's thesis, North Texas State College (Denton, Tex.), 1956. (*DA* 16:763)

45. CURRIE, CAROLINE. *The Relationship of Certain Selected Factors to Achievement in Freshman Composition.* Doctor's thesis, Northwestern University (Evanston, Ill.), 1957. (*DA* 18:884)
46. HAAS, MARY GERALDINE. *A Comparative Study of Critical Thinking, Flexibility of Thinking, and Reading Ability Involving Religious and Lay College Seniors.* Doctor's thesis, Fordham University (New York, N.Y.), 1963. (*DA* 24:622)
47. BLANTON, WINCIE L., AND PECK, ROBERT F. "College Student Motivation and Academic Performance." *Ed & Psychol Meas* 24:897–912 w '64. * (*PA* 39:8695)
48. PABST, ROBERT LEROY. *A Validation Study of the Relationship of Size of High School and Certain Intellective Factors to Academic Achievement in College.* Doctor's thesis, Indiana University (Bloomington, Ind.), 1965. (*DA* 27:331A)
49. TROY, ELIZABETH MCGOLDRICK. *A Study of the Predictive Value of Eleven Variables Used at King's College to Determine General Scholastic Achievement of Two Hundred Forty-Three Entering Students.* Master's thesis, Marywood College (Scranton, Pa.), 1965.
50. LINDLEY, MICHAEL R. *A Study of the Relationship Between Self-Concept and Reading Ability.* Master's thesis, Furman University (Greenville, S.C.), 1966.
51. MCCORMICK, ALBERT GRANT. *An Investigation of Reading Skills, General Mental Ability and Personality Variables Used in the Selection of Practical Nursing Students.* Doctor's thesis, Oklahoma State University (Stillwater, Okla.), 1966. (*DA* 27:4136A)
52. MOGHRABI, KAMEL M. *An Analysis of Factors That Influence the Degree of Success or Failure of Foreign Students at Texas A & M University.* Doctor's thesis, Texas A & M University (College Station, Tex.), 1966. (*DA* 27:3232A)
53. SHRADER, EDWARD FRANKLYN. *A Descriptive Study of Students in the Precollege Summer Session Program, the University of Maryland, 1964–1965.* Doctor's thesis, George Washington University (Washington, D.C.), 1966. (*DA* 27:4104A)
54. ADAMS, EFFIE KAYE. "Reading Performance of Elementary Student Teachers in a Developing Institution." *Yearb Nat Read Conf* 16:47–57 '67. *
55. WELCH, JOYCE. *The Effects of Timing on the Reliability and Validity of the Nelson-Denny Reading Test in Establishing Shasta Junior College Norms.* Master's thesis, Chico State College (Chico, Calif.), 1967.
56. BRADSHAW, OTTIE LEON. *The Relationship of Selected Measures of Aptitude, Interest, and Personality to Academic Achievement in Engineering and Engineering Technology.* Doctor's thesis, Oklahoma State University (Stillwater, Okla.), 1968. (*DAI* 30:979A)
57. FARR, ROGER. "The Convergent and Discriminant Validity of Several Upper Level Reading Tests." *Yearb Nat Read Conf* 17:181–91 '68. *
58. GREEN, JOHNNIE HENDERSON. *An Analysis of Academic Proficiency of the 1965–66 Beginning Freshman Class, School of Business, Texas Southern University, Houston, Texas.* Doctor's thesis, University of Houston (Houston, Tex.), 1968. (*DA* 29:3323A)
59. MARSHALL, JOSEPH JEMERSON. *Non-Cognitive Variables as a Predictor of Academic Achievement Among Freshmen, Sophomores, and Juniors at Abilene Christian College.* Doctor's thesis, Baylor University (Waco, Tex.), 1968. (*DA* 29:3833A)
60. MUNDAY, LEO. "Correlations Between ACT and Other Predictors of Academic Success in College." *Col & Univ* 44:67–76 f '68. *
61. REID, RONALD H. "Grammatical Complexity and Comprehension of Compressed Speech." *J Commun* 18:236–42 S '68. * (*PA* 43:3969)
62. REID, RONALD HENRY. *Comprehension of Compressed Speech as a Function of Difficulty of Material.* Doctor's thesis, Indiana University (Bloomington, Ind.), 1968. (*DA* 29:1689A)
63. SPURLIN, MELVIN DAVID. *A Study of the Relationship of Sex, Ability Level and Biology Preparation to Achievement in Freshman Biology at Metropolitan State College.* Doctor's thesis, University of Colorado (Boulder, Colo.), 1968. (*DA* 29:1173A)
64. STOUGH, KENNETH FRANCIS. *An Analysis of Selected Factors as Predictors of Success in Vocational Industrial Certification Courses.* Doctor's thesis, University of Maryland (College Park, Md.), 1968. (*DA* 29:2595A)
65. CLINE, RUTH K. J. "Reading Ability and Selection for Teacher Education Programs." *J Read* 12(8):634–8+ My '69. *
66. FEUERS, STELLE. *The Relationship Between General Reading Skills and Junior College Academic Achievement.* Doctor's thesis, University of California (Los Angeles, Calif.), 1969. (*DAI* 30:3186A)
67. JOHNSON, JOSEPH CARLTON, II, AND JACOBSON, MILTON D. "An Investigation of the Interrelationships Among Certain Specific Predictor Variables and Two College Bound High School Student Reading Enhancement Classes." *Yearb Nat Read Conf* 18:240–5 '69. *
68. PIERCE, DAVID RANDALL. *A Comparison of the Conventional, Printed-Programed and Audio-Programed Methods of Teaching Remediation-Oriented Mathematics.* Doctor's thesis, Purdue University (Lafayette, Ind.), 1969. (*DAI* 30:4692A)
69. TASCHOW, HORST GERARD. "A Comparison of Individual Reading Improvement Scores on a Group of Community College

Monroe's Standardized Silent Reading Test

Freshmen as Measured by the Crude Gain Method and the Residual Gain Method." *Yearb Nat Read Conf* 18:27–37 '69. *
70. WILLIAMS, VERNON. *A Multi-Predictive Measure to Predict Success at Two Levels in Freshman College Mathematics.* Doctor's thesis, Oklahoma State University (Stillwater, Okla.), 1969. (*DAI* 31:4026A)
71. CARVER, RONALD P. "Analysis of 'Chunked' Test Items as Measures of Reading and Listening Comprehension." *J Ed Meas* 7(3):141–50 f '70. * (*PA* 45:4913)
72. CREASER, JAMES; JACOBS, MITCHELL; ZACCARIA, LUCY; AND CARSELLO, CARMEN. "Effects of Shortened Time Limits on the Nelson-Denny Reading Test." *J Read* 14(3):167–70 D '70. * (*PA* 48:3667)
73. DEFRAIN, DAVID MURRAY. *The Effects of Self-Concept and Selected Personal and Educational Variables Upon Attrition in a Non-Credit College Reading Improvement Program.* Doctor's thesis, Oklahoma State University (Stillwater, Okla.), 1970. (*DAI* 31:5195A)
74. FOLLMAN, J. C.; LOWE, A. J.; AND BURLEY, W. W. "Relationship of Two Matching Item Test Formats to the Nelson-Denny Reading Test." *Fla J Ed Res* 12(1):103–8 Ja '70. *
75. RUSSELL, WENDELL PHILLIPS. *Intellectual and Non-Intellectual Factors Affecting the Attrition Rate of Students Entering Virginia Union University in 1965.* Doctor's thesis, University of Virginia (Charlottesville, Va.), 1970. (*DAI* 31:4474A)
76. CARVER, RONALD P., AND DARBY, CHARLES A., JR. "Development and Evaluation of a Test of Information Storage During Reading." *J Ed Meas* 8(1):33–44 sp '71. * (*PA* 46:5461)
77. FARR, ROGER, AND SMITH, CARL B. "The Effects of Test Item Validity on Total Test Reliability and Validity." *Yearb Nat Read Conf* 19(1):122–34 '71. *
78. FOLLMAN, JOHN; LOWE, A. J.; AND WILEY, RUSSELL. "Correlational and Factor Analysis of Critical Reading and Thinking Test Scores—Twelfth Grade." *Yearb Nat Read Conf* 20:128–36 '71. *
79. GIBSON, WALTER DANA. *Relationship Between Difficulty Levels of Assigned English Texts and Reading Ability of Community College Students.* Doctor's thesis, University of Southern California (Los Angeles, Calif.), 1971. (*DAI* 31:6362A)
80. JOHNSON, ROGER; FOLLMAN, JOHN; WILEY, RUSSELL; LOWE, A. J.; AND MILLER, WILLIAM. "Canonical and Partial Correlation of Critical Reading and Critical Thinking Test Scores—Twelfth Grade." *Yearb Nat Read Conf* 20:137–41 '71. *
81. KIRBY, BARBARA JANE. *An Analysis of the Relationships Between Academic Performance and Scores on Licensure Examinations of Mortuary Science Students at Miami-Dade Junior College 1966–1969.* Doctor's thesis, University of Miami (Coral Gables, Fla.), 1971. (*DAI* 32:3122A)
82. LOWE, A. J.; FOLLMAN, JOHN; BURLEY, WADE; AND FOLLMAN, JOHNNY. "Psychometric Analysis of Critical Reading and Critical Thinking Test Scores—Twelfth Grade." *Yearb Nat Read Conf* 20:142–7 '71. *

CUMULATIVE NAME INDEX

Adams, E. K.: 54
Anderson, I. H.: 13
Beamer, B. A.: 34
Bellows, C. S.: 42
Blanton, W. L.: 47
Booker, I. A.: *rev*, 4:544
Bradshaw, O. L.: 56
Burley, W.: 82
Burley, W. W.: 74
Carsello, C.: 72
Carver, R. P.: 71, 76
Cline, R. K. J.: 65
Creaser, J.: 72
Crider, B.: 16
Crites, J. O.: *exc*, 6:800
Currie, C.: 45
Darby, C. A.: 76
Davis, F. B.: 19
Davis, N. W.: 7
Dearborn, W. F.: 13
Defrain, D. M.: 73
Durnall, E. J.: 25
Edmonson, L. D.: 21
Farr, R.: 57, 77
Feuers, S.: 66
Fleming, W. G.: 28–30, 35
Follman, J.: 78, 80, 82
Follman, J. C.: 74
Freehill, M. F.: 24
Gentry, D. E.: 17
Gibson, W. D.: 79
Gordon, H. C.: *rev*, 2:1557
Green, J. H.: 58
Greene, P. C.: 14
Haas, M. G.: 46
Held, O. C.: 4
Horn, E.: 2
Jacobs, M.: 72
Jacobson, M. D.: 67
Johnson, D. M.: 38
Johnson, J. C.: 67

Johnson, R.: 80
Kirby, B. J.: 81
Langsam, R. S.: 15
Larsen, R. P.: 8
Lawrence, W. A.: 9
Lindley, M. R.: 50
Lott, H. V.: 10
Lowe, A. J.: 74, 78, 80, 82
McClanahan, W. R.: 41
McCollum, C. G.: 43
McCormick, A. G.: 51
MacDonald, G. L.: 22
Marshall, J. J.: 59
Massey, H. W.: 27
Miller, W.: 80
Moghrabi, K. M.: 52
Morgan, D. H.: 41
Munday, L.: 60
Munger, P. F.: 26
Murphy, H. D.: 19
Nelson, M. J.: 37
Orr, D. B.: *rev*, 6:800
Ottman, R. W.: 44
Pabst, R. L.: 48
Palacios, J. R.: 31
Peck, R. F.: 47
Pierce, D. R.: 68
Pipher, J. A.: 33
Portenier, L. G.: 18
Reid, R. H.: 61–2
Reynolds, F.: 38
Robinson, W.: 36
Roy, E. A.: 11
Rush, C. H.: 42
Russell, W. P.: 75
Shrader, E. F.: 53
Silvey, H. M.: 20, 23
Smith, C. B.: 77
Smith, D. D.: 32
Spoerl, D. T.: 39
Spurlin, M. D.: 63

Stough, K. F.: 64
Strang, R.: 3
Taschow, H. G.: 69
Thorndike, E. L.: 1
Townsend, A.: *rev*, 6:800
Traxler, A. E.: 5
Troy, E. M.: 49
Upshall, C. C.: 6

Varnado, G. R.: 12
Vineyard, E. E.: 27
Waggoner, R. W.: 40
Welch, J.: 55
Wiley, R.: 78, 80
Williams, V.: 70
Zaccaria, L.: 72
Zeigler, T. W.: 40

[1573]
The Nelson Reading Test, Revised Edition. Grades 3–9; 1931–62; revision of *The Nelson Silent Reading Test: Vocabulary and Paragraph;* 3 scores: vocabulary, paragraph comprehension, total; M. J. Nelson; Houghton Mifflin Co. *

For additional information and a review by H. Alan Robinson, see 6:802; for a review by William D. Sheldon of the original edition, see 4:545 (1 reference); for a review by Constance M. McCullough, see 3:492; for an excerpted review by Albert Grant, see 2:1558.

REFERENCES THROUGH 1971

1. See 4:545.
2. COLBY, ARCHIE N., AND TIFFIN, JOSEPH. "The Reading Ability of Industrial Supervisors." *Personnel* 27:156–9 S '50. * (*PA* 25:3437)
3. HALL, JODY C. "The Effect of Background Music on the Reading Comprehension of Eighth and Ninth Grade Students." *J Ed Res* 45:451–8 F '52. * (*PA* 27:2195)
4. FREEHILL, MAURICE F. "The Prediction of Teaching Competence." *J Exp Ed* 31:307–11 Mr '63. *
5. FARR, ROGER. "The Convergent and Discriminant Validity of Several Upper Level Reading Tests." *Yearb Nat Read Conf* 17:181–91 '68. *
6. GEESLIN, ROBERT H., AND YORK, PATRICIA W. "Literacy Skills as a Barrier to Inservice Training." *J Read Behav* 3(3):9–12 su '70–71 ['71]. *

CUMULATIVE NAME INDEX

Colby, A. N.: 2
Farr, R.: 5
Freehill, M. F.: 4
Geeslin, R. H.: 6
Grant, A.: 1; *exc*, 2:1558
Hall, J. C.: 3

McCullough, C. M.: *rev*, 3: 492
Robinson, H. A.: *rev*, 6:802
Sheldon, W. D.: *rev*, 4:545
Tiffin, J.: 2
York, P. W.: 6

[1574]
New Developmental Reading Tests. Grades 1–2.5, 2.5–3, 4–6; 1955–68; revision of *Developmental Reading Tests;* Guy L. Bond, Bruce Balow, and Cyril J. Hoyt; Lyons & Carnahan, Inc. *

a) PRIMARY TESTS. Grades 1–2.5, 2.5–3; 1955–65; 4 scores: word recognition, comprehending significant ideas, comprehending specific instructions, average grade score. *Out of print.*

b) INTERMEDIATE TESTS. Grades 4–6; 1959–68; 5 basic scores: (1) vocabulary, (2) reading for information, (3) reading for relationships, (4) reading for interpretation, (5) reading for appreciation, plus 3 combination scores—literal comprehension (2 and 3), creative comprehension (4 and 5), and general comprehension (2, 3, 4, and 5).

For additional information and reviews by Frederick B. Davis and Arthur E. Traxler, see 7:697 (4 references); for reviews by Edward B. Fry and Agatha Townsend of the original edition, see 6:787.

REFERENCES THROUGH 1971

1–4. See 7:697.
5. ROSEN, CARL L. "An Experimental Study of Visual Perceptual Training and Reading Achievement in First Grade." *Percept & Motor Skills* 22:979–86 Je '66. * (*PA* 40:11008)
6. BALOW, BRUCE; FULTON, HELEN; AND PEPLOE, ELLA. "Reading Comprehension Skills Among Hearing Impaired Adolescents." *Volta R* 73(2):113–9 F '71. *

CUMULATIVE NAME INDEX

Balow, B.: 6
Davis, F. B.: *rev*, 7:697
Fry, E. B.: *rev*, 6:787
Fulton, H.: 6
Lamb, G. S.: 1–2
Ohnmacht, F.: 3

Peploe, E.: 6
Rosen, C. L.: 3, 5
Townsend, A.: *rev*, 6:787
Traxler, A. E.: *rev*, 7:697
Wasson, J. B.: 4

New Developmental Reading Tests

[1575]
**OISE Achievement Tests in Silent Reading:
Advanced Primary Battery.** Grade 2; 1969–71; 5
scores: words in use, multiple word meanings, Part A
comprehension, Part B comprehension, total; Ontario
Institute for Studies in Education and Patricia Tracy
(handbook); distributed by Guidance Centre [Canada]. *
For additional information, see 7:698.

[1576]
Pressey Diagnostic Reading Tests. Grades 3–9;
1929; 4 scores: speed, vocabulary, paragraph meaning,
total; S. L. Pressey and L. C. Pressey; Bobbs-Merrill
Co., Inc. *

REFERENCES THROUGH 1971
1. FORAN, T. G., AND ROCK, ROBERT J., JR. "The Reliability of
Some Silent Reading Tests." *Cath Univ Am Ed Res B* 5(6):
1–23 Je '30. * (*PA* 5:2921)
2. BARNARD, WILLIAM H. "An Analysis of a Sixth Grade
Vocabulary Test." *Ed* 61:285–7 Ja '41. *
3. HARRIS, CHESTER W. "An Exploration of Language Skill
Patterns." *J Ed Psychol* 39:321–36 O '48. * (*PA* 23:1755)

CUMULATIVE NAME INDEX
Barnard, W. H.: 2   Harris, C. W.: 3
Foran, T. G.: 1   Rock, R. J.: 1

[1577]
★[**Primary Reading Survey Tests.**] Grades 2, 3;
1973; subtest of *Primary Survey Tests;* 2 levels;
Kenneth S. Goodman, John C. Manning, Marion Monroe, Andrew Schiller, Joseph M. Wepman, and E.
Glenadine Gibb (handbooks); Scott, Foresman &
Co. * For the complete battery entry, see 27.
a) EARLY PRIMARY READING SURVEY TEST. Grade 2.
b) LATE PRIMARY READING SURVEY TEST. Grade 3.

[1578]
**Primary Reading Test: Acorn Achievement
Tests.** Grades 2–3; 1943–57; 5 scores: word recognition, words-similar meaning, word meaning-opposites,
story-paragraph-sentence meaning, total; Winifred E.
Stayton, Frances C. Ranson, and Roland L. Beck;
Psychometric Affiliates. *
For additional information, see 5:642; for a review
by Alice N. Jameson, see 3:495.

[1579]
Progressive Achievement Tests of Reading.
Standards 2–4 and Forms I–IV (ages 8–14); 1969–70;
PATR; 2 tests; manual by Warwick B. Elley and
Neil A. Reid; New Zealand Council for Educational
Research [New Zealand]. (Australian edition: Grades
3–9; 1970–73; manual by M. L. Clark; Australian
Council for Educational Research [Australia].) *
a) READING COMPREHENSION.
b) READING VOCABULARY.
For additional information and excerpted reviews by
Milton L. Clark and J. Elkins, see 7:699.

REFERENCES THROUGH 1971
1. MARSH, R. W. "Notes on Sampling in the Standardization
of the Progressive Achievement Tests." *N Zeal J Ed Studies*
4(1):69–73 My '69. * (*PA* 46:11513)

CUMULATIVE NAME INDEX
Clark, M. L.: *exc*, 7:699   Marsh, R. W.: 1
Elkins, J.: *exc*, 7:699

[1580]
RBH Basic Reading and Word Test. Disadvantaged adults; 1968–69; Richardson, Bellows, Henry &
Co., Inc. *
For additional information and a review by Thorsten R. Carlson, see 7:700.

[1581]
RBH Test of Reading Comprehension. Business
and industry; 1951–63; Richardson, Bellows, Henry &
Co., Inc. *
For additional information and reviews by Thorsten R. Carlson and Willard A. Kerr, see 7:701.

[1582]
*✻Reading Comprehension: Canadian English
Achievement Test, Part 1.** Grades 8.5–9.0; 1959–
68; subtest of *Canadian Test Battery, Grades 8–9;*
Ontario Institute for Studies in Education; distributed
by Guidance Centre [Canada]. * For the complete
battery entry, see 1047.
For additional information and reviews of the
complete test, see 6:253 (2 reviews).

[1583]
**Reading Comprehension: Cooperative English
Tests.** Grades 9–12, 13–14; 1940–60; separate booklet
edition of reading subtest of *Cooperative English
Tests;* 4 scores: vocabulary, level of comprehension,
speed of comprehension, total; revision by Clarence
Derrick, David P. Harris, and Biron Walker; Cooperative Tests and Services. * For the complete
battery entry, see 69.
For additional information and reviews by W. V.
Clemans and W. G. Fleming, see 6:806 (12 references); see also 5:645 (21 references) and 4:547
(20 references); for reviews by Robert Murray Bear
and J. B. Stroud of an earlier edition, see 3:497 (15
references); see also 2:1564 (2 references). For
reviews of the complete battery, see 6:256 (2 reviews,
1 excerpt) and 3:120 (3 reviews).

REFERENCES THROUGH 1971
1–2. See 2:1564.
3–17. See 3:497.
18–37. See 4:547.
38–58. See 5:645.
59–70. See 6:806.
71. ARTLEY, A. S. "The Appraisal of Reading Comprehension." *J Ed Psychol* 34:55–60 Ja '43. * (*PA* 17:3236)
72. ARTLEY, A. STERL. "A Study of Certain Relationships
Existing Between General Reading Comprehension and Reading
Comprehension in a Specific Subject Matter Area." *J Ed Res*
37:464–73 F '44. * (*PA* 18:2556)
73. COOLEY, JOHN CHRISTOPHER. *A Study of the Relation
Between Certain Mental and Personality Traits and Ratings of
Musical Abilities.* Doctor's thesis, Michigan State College (East
Lansing, Mich.), 1952. (*DA* 13:240)
74. SOMMERFELD, ROY ELMER. *The Relationship of Reading
Ability to Measures of Perceptual Span With Special Reference
to Tachistoscopic Span for Digits.* Doctor's thesis, University of
Michigan (Ann Arbor, Mich.), 1952. (*DA* 12:527)
75. BREEN, LELWYN CLYDE. *The Relation of Reading Ability
to College Mortality of Certain Entering Freshmen at the University of Washington in the Year 1950–1951.* Doctor's thesis,
University of Washington (Seattle, Wash.), 1953. (*DA* 14:483)
76. BRUCE, WILLIAM JOHN. *The Contribution of Eleven Variables to the Prognosis of Academic Success in Eight Areas at
the University of Washington.* Doctor's thesis, University of
Washington (Seattle, Wash.), 1953. (*DA* 13:505)
77. HUNT, JACOB TATE. "The Relation Among Vocabulary,
Structural Analysis, and Reading." *J Ed Psychol* 44:193–202
Ap '53. * (*PA* 28:3205)
78. PHILLIPS, CLARENCE. "Achievement, Aptitude, and Background of Liberal Arts and Science Students (General Curriculum) Deficient in High School Mathematics." *J Ed Res* 47:
169–80 N '53. * (*PA* 28:6515)
79. SMITH, ALLAN B. *The Prediction of Scholastic Success for
Freshman Entrants to the University of Connecticut 1933–1951.*
Doctor's thesis, University of Connecticut (Storrs, Conn.),
1953. (*DA* 13:1121)
80. WHEELER, D. K. "Reading Ability of Students Entering
the University of Western Australia." *Educand* (Australia) 1:
37–46 N '53. *
81. HYMAN, SIDNEY ROBERT. *The Development of Criteria of
Research Competence in Psychology and Their Prediction From
Certain Intellectual and Achievement Measures.* Doctor's thesis,
University of Pittsburgh (Pittsburgh, Pa.), 1954. (*DA* 14:2395)
82. LA BUE, ANTHONY CHARLES. *An Analysis of Some Factors
Associated With Persistence of Interest in Teaching as a Voca-*

tional Choice. Doctor's thesis, Syracuse University (Syracuse, N.Y.), 1954. (*DA* 14:2001)

83. LEBSACK, JACOB ROBERT. *Specific Reading Ability as Associated With Subject Matter Achievement.* Doctor's thesis, University of Nebraska (Lincoln, Neb.), 1954. (*DA* 14:1995)

84. HAO, PETER TE YUAN. *An Analysis of Certain Learning Difficulties of Chinese Students in New York City.* Doctor's thesis, New York University (New York, N.Y.), 1955. (*DA* 15:1551)

85. LINS, L. J., AND PITT, H. "Comparison of Ability and Background of University of Wisconsin Freshmen According to Distance From Home to the University or Another College." *J Ed Res* 48:333–44 Ja '55. * (*PA* 29:8951)

86. SANDERS, WILLIAM B.; OSBORNE, R. TRAVIS; AND GREENE, J. E. "Intelligence and Academic Performance of College Students of Urban, Rural, and Mixed Backgrounds." *J Ed Res* 49:185–93 N '55. * (*PA* 30:7774)

87. CHAHBAZI, PARVIZ. "Use of Projective Tests in Predicting College Achievement." *Ed & Psychol Meas* 16:538–42 w '56. * (*PA* 32:939)

88. HENDRICKS, RICHARD. *Relationships Among Tests of Intelligibility, Word-Reception, and Other Measures of Symbolic Formulation.* Doctor's thesis, Ohio State University (Columbus, Ohio), 1956. (*DA* 16:2239)

89. ANDERSON, A. W. "Reading Ability and Intelligence of Students: A Study of New Admissions to the University of Western Australia in 1957." *Educand* (Australia) 3:108–12 Mr '57. *

90. FARNUM, HOLLIS B. "A Comparison of the Academic Aptitude of University Extension Degree Students and Campus Students." *J Appl Psychol* 41:63–5 F '57. * (*PA* 32:942)

91. MANN, HELENE POWNER. "Some Hypotheses on Perceptual and Learning Processes With Their Applications to the Process of Reading: A Preliminary Note." *J Genetic Psychol* 90:167–202 Je '57. * (*PA* 35:1187)

92. FLETCHER, JUNIOR EUGENE. *A Study of the Relationships Between Ability to Use Context as an Aid in Reading and Other Verbal Abilities.* Doctor's thesis, University of Washington (Seattle, Wash.), 1959. (*DA* 20:2675)

93. FREDERIKSEN, NORMAN, AND GILBERT, ARTHUR C. F. "Replication of a Study of Differential Predictability." *Ed & Psychol Meas* 20:759–67 w '60. * (*PA* 35:7953)

94. GUNDERSON, DORIS VIRGINIA. *The Influence of College Reading Instruction Upon Academic Achievement.* Doctor's thesis, University of Minnesota (Minneapolis, Minn.), 1960. (*DA* 21:1806)

95. ANDERSON, A. W. "School of Entry and First-Year Academic Performance in the University of Western Australia." *Austral J Higher Ed* 1:20–3 N '61. *

96. OBST, FRANCES. "A Study of Abilities of Women Students Entering the Colleges of Letters and Science and Applied Arts at the University of California, Los Angeles." *J Ed Res* 57: 84–6 O '63. *

97. RANKIN, EARL F., JR. "Reading Test Performance of Introverts and Extroverts." *Yearb Nat Read Conf* 12:158–66 '63. *

98. CALLIS, ROBERT, AND PREDIGER, DALE J. "Predictors of Achievement in Counseling and Guidance Graduate Study." *Counselor Ed & Sup* 3:63–9 w '64. *

99. CHANSKY, NORMAN M. "A Note on the Validity of Reading Test Scores." *J Ed Res* 58:90 O '64. *

100. HOGBEN, D. "School of Entry and First Year Performance of Medical Students in the University of Western Australia." *Austral J Higher Ed* 2:79–83 N '64. *

101. PRESTON, RALPH C. "Ability of Students to Identify Correct Responses Before Reading." *J Ed Res* 58:181–3 D '64. *

102. ANDERSON, A. W. "Intelligence and Reading Scores of Entrants to the University of Western Australia 1954–65." *Austral J Higher Ed* 2:177–82 N '65. *

103. CHASE, CLINTON I. *The University Freshman Dropout.* Indiana University, Monograph of the Bureau of Educational Studies and Testing. Indiana Studies in Prediction, No. 6. Bloomington, Ind.: the Bureau, 1965. Pp. 36. *

104. DAVIS, LUTHER EDWARD, JR. *A Study of Selected Traits of St. Petersburg Junior College Students and Their Value in Predicting Academic Success in Certain Courses of Study at the Senior College Level.* Doctor's thesis, Auburn University (Auburn, Ala.), 1965. (*DA* 26:791)

105. HOGBEN, D. "The Prediction of Academic Success in Relation to Student Selection in Medicine at the University of Western Australia." *Austral J Higher Ed* 2:152–60 N '65. *

106. ROULETTE, THOMAS GRIER. *An Investigation of Response Style Effects in an Objective Test of Achievement.* Doctor's thesis, Western Reserve University (Cleveland, Ohio), 1965. (*DA* 27:1611B)

107. CASHMAN, JEROME PATRICK. *A Study of the Relationship Between Organic Factors, Certain Selected Variables and Progress in a Reading Improvement Program.* Doctor's thesis, Fordham University (New York, N.Y.), 1966. (*DA* 27:1648A)

108. FRIEDMAN, STUART M. *Predicting Students' Success in a Comprehensive Junior College.* Doctor's thesis, University of Southern California (Los Angeles, Calif.), 1966. (*DA* 26:7112)

109. GUILLIAMS, CLARK IRVIN. *Predicting Creative Productivity in College Classes Where Creative Thinking Is Empha-*

sized. Doctor's thesis, University of Arkansas (Fayetteville, Ark.), 1966. (*DA* 27:675A)

110. LINS, L. JOSEPH; ABELL, ALLAN P.; AND HUTCHINS, H. CLIFTON. "Relative Usefulness in Predicting Academic Success of the ACT, the SAT, and Some Other Variables." *J Exp Ed* 35:1–29 w '66. *

111. HARTSOCK, WOODROW WILSON. *The Prediction of Academic Performance in a Seminary.* Master's thesis, Southern Methodist University (Dallas, Tex.), 1967.

112. RENGSTORFF, ROY H. "The Types and Incidence of Hand-Eye Preference and Its Relationship With Certain Reading Abilities." *Am J Optom* 44:233–8 Ap '67. * (*PA* 41:10908)

113. FARR, ROGER. "The Convergent and Discriminant Validity of Several Upper Level Reading Tests." *Yearb Nat Read Conf* 17:181–91 '68. *

114. McDONALD, ANDREW A. *Relationship Between Subtest Scores of Cooperative Reading and Grade Point Averages in Certain General Education Courses at Howard University.* Master's thesis, Howard University (Washington, D.C.), 1968.

115. THUMIN, FRED J. "Ability Scores as Related to Age Among Male Job Applicants." *J Gerontol* 23:390–2 Jl '68. *

116. HOWLETT, JOHN L. "A Study of Placement Methods for Entering College Freshmen in the Proper Mathematics Sequence at Michigan Technological University." *Math Teach* 62(8):651–9 D '69. *

117. BIGGS, J. B. "Personality Correlates of Certain Dimensions of Study Behaviour." *Austral J Psychol* 22(3):287–97 D '70. * (*PA* 46:1843)

118. SINGER, CARROLL ROSENFELD. *Eye Movements, Reading Comprehension, and Vocabulary as Effected by Varying Visual and Auditory Modalities in College Students.* Doctor's thesis, New Mexico State University (University Park, N.M.), 1970. (*DAI* 31:164A)

119. WILE, MARCIA ZISKIND. *Sex Knowledge and Reading Ability of Selected Graduate Professional School Students.* Doctor's thesis, Case Western Reserve University (Cleveland, Ohio), 1970. (*DAI* 31:3307A)

120. DIELMAN, T. E.; BARTON, K.; AND CATTELL, R. B. "The Prediction of Junior High School Achievement From Objective Motivation Tests." *Personality* 2(4):279–87 w '71. * (*PA* 48:7881)

121. ROSS, LOUIS. "Forecasting the Academic Achievement of Engineering Freshmen." *J Ed Res* 64(7):307–10 Mr '71. *

CUMULATIVE NAME INDEX

Stancik, E. J.: 62
Stroud, J. B.: *rev*, 3:497
Stucky, M. O.: 59–60
Thumin, F. J.: 115
Thurstone, L. L.: 14
Traxler, A.: 2

Traxler, A. E.: 15, 28, 34, 36
Van Der Jagt, E. R.: 54
Votaw, D. F.: 16
Wallace, W. L.: 37
Wheeler, D. K.: 80
Wile, M. Z.: 119

[1584]

Reading Comprehension Test. College entrants; 1963–68; William A. McCartney; the Author. *

[1585]

*Reading Comprehension Test DE. Ages 10–12.5; 1963–71; formerly called *Reading Comprehension Test 1*; E. L. Barnard; published for the National Foundation for Educational Research in England and Wales; Ginn & Co. Ltd. [England]. *
For additional information, see 7:702.

[1586]

Reading Comprehension Test: National Achievement Tests [Crow, Kuhlmann, and Crow]. Grades 4–9; 1953–57; 1957 test identical with test copyrighted 1953; Lester D. Crow, Martha J. Kuhlmann, and Alice Crow; Psychometric Affiliates. *
For additional information, see 5:647.

[1587]

Reading Comprehension Test: National Achievement Tests [Speer and Smith]. Grades 3–8; 1938–57; 4 scores: following directions, sentence meaning, paragraph meaning, total; 1957 test identical with test copyrighted 1938; Robert K. Speer and Samuel Smith; Psychometric Affiliates. *
For additional information, see 5:646; for a review by James R. Hobson, see 3:498.

[1588]

*Reading for Understanding Placement Test. Grades 3–8, 8–12, 5–16; 1959–69; designed for use with the self-teaching reading exercises prepared by the same author; 3 levels; Thelma Gwinn Thurstone; Science Research Associates, Inc. *
a) JUNIOR EDITION. Grades 3–8; 1963.
b) SENIOR EDITION. Grades 8–12; 1963–65.
c) GENERAL EDITION. Grades 5–16; 1959–69.

REFERENCES THROUGH 1971
1. FULLER, GERALD B., AND ENDE, RUSSELL. "The Effectiveness of Visual Perception, Intelligence and Reading Understanding in Predicting Reading Achievement in Junior High School Children." *J Ed Res* 60:280–2 F '67. *
2. ENDE, RUSSELL S. "Reading for Understanding in Grades 7, 8, and 9." *Ill Sch Res* 7(2):32–7 w '71. *

CUMULATIVE NAME INDEX
Ende, R.: 1   Fuller, G. B.: 1
Ende, R. S.: 2

[1589]

★The Reading Progress Scale. Grades 3–12; 1970–71; RPS; Ronald P. Carver; Revrac Publications. *

[1590]

Reading: Public School Achievement Tests. Grades 3–8; 1928–59; Jacob S. Orleans; Bobbs-Merrill Co., Inc. * For the complete battery entry, see 28.
For additional information, see 6:807. For reviews of the complete battery, see 2:1194 (2 reviews).

[1591]

Reading Test AD. Ages 7-6 to 11-1; 1956–70; formerly called *Sentence Reading Test 1*; 1960 test identical with test published 1956 except for format; 1970 manual identical with manual published 1956 except for title; A. F. Watts; published for the

National Foundation for Educational Research in England and Wales; Ginn & Co. Ltd. [England]. *
For additional information, see 7:703; for reviews by Reginald R. Dale and Stephen Wiseman, see 5:652.

REFERENCES THROUGH 1971
1. LOVELL, K.; SHAPTON, D.; AND WARREN, N. S. "A Study of Some Cognitive and Other Disabilities in Backward Readers of Average Intelligence as Assessed by a Non-Verbal Test." *Brit J Ed Psychol* 34:58–64 F '64. * (*PA* 38:9233)
2. YOUNG, J. A., AND JENKINSON, M. D. "An Objective Comparison of Achievement in the Basic Subjects for Matched Groups of Children in Manchester, England and Edmonton, Alberta." *Alberta J Ed Res* (Canada) 10:59–66 Je '64. * (*PA* 39:12096)
3. SAVAGE, R. D., AND O'CONNOR, D. J. "The Assessment of Reading and Arithmetic Retardation in the School." *Brit J Ed Psychol* 36:317–8 N '66. *

CUMULATIVE NAME INDEX
Dale, R. R.: *rev*, 5:652
Jenkinson, M. D.: 2
Lovell, K.: 1
O'Connor, D. J.: 3
Savage, R. D.: 3
Shapton, D. 1
Warren, N. S.: 1
Wiseman, S.: *rev*, 5:652
Young, J. A.: 2

[1592]

Reading Test (Comprehension and Speed): Municipal Tests: National Achievement Tests. Grades 3–6, 6–8; 1938–57; subtest of *Municipal Battery;* 5 scores: following directions, sentence meaning, paragraph meaning, reading speed, total; 1950–55 tests identical with tests copyrighted 1938–39; Robert K. Speer and Samuel Smith; Psychometric Affiliates. *
For additional information, see 5:648. For reviews of the complete battery, see 5:18 (1 review), 4:20 (1 review), and 2:1191 (2 reviews).

[1593]

Reading Test: McGraw-Hill Basic Skills System. Grades 11–14; 1970; also called *MHBSS Reading Test;* although designed for use with the MHBSS instructional program, the test may be used independently; 7 scores: 2 reading rates (recreational, study), flexibility, retention, skimming and scanning, paragraph comprehension, total; Alton L. Raygor; McGraw-Hill Book Co., Inc. *
For additional information and a review by Donald B. Black, see 7:704.

[1594]

*Reading Tests A and BD. 1, 2–4 years primary school; 1967–73; 2 levels; published for the National Foundation for Educational Research in England and Wales; Ginn & Co. Ltd. [England]. *
a) READING TEST A. 1 year primary school; 1968–73; formerly called *Primary Reading Test 1*.
b) READING TEST BD. 2–4 years primary school; 1967–69; formerly called *Primary Reading Test 2*.
For additional information, see 7:705.

[1595]

Reading Tests EH 1–3. First 4 years of secondary school; 1961–66; formerly called *Secondary Reading Tests 1–3;* 3 tests; S. M. Bate; published for the National Foundation for Educational Research in England and Wales; Ginn & Co. Ltd. [England]. *
a) TEST 1, VOCABULARY.
b) TEST 2, COMPREHENSION.
c) TEST 3, CONTINUOUS PROSE. Reading speed.

[1596]

SRA Achievement Series: Reading. Grades 1–2, 2–4, 4–9; 1954–69; Forms C and D; more recent Forms E and F are not available as separates; Louis P. Thorpe, D. Welty Lefever, and Robert A. Naslund; Science Research Associates, Inc. * For the complete battery entry, see 29.

a) HAND SCORED EDITION. Grades 1-2, 2-4; 1954-68; 2 levels. *Out of print.*

    1) *Grades 1-2.* 5 scores: verbal-pictorial association, language perception, comprehension, vocabulary, total.

    2) *Grades 2-4.* 3 scores: comprehension, vocabulary, total.

b) MULTILEVEL EDITION. Grades 4-9; 1963-69; 3 scores: comprehension, vocabulary, total.

For additional information and a review by John T. Guthrie, see 7:706 (6 references); for a review by Edward B. Fry of earlier forms, see 6:808; for a review by N. Dale Bryant and Clarence Derrick, see 5:649. For reviews of the complete battery, see 7:18 (2 reviews), 6:21 (1 review), and 5:21 (2 reviews).

REFERENCES THROUGH 1971

1-6. See 7:706.
7. BUSWELL, G. T. "The Relationship Between Rate of Thinking and Rate of Reading." *Sch R* 59:339-46 S '51. *
8. FLEISCHMAN, HOWARD L.; ORR, DAVID B.; AND STRASEL, H. C. "Relationships Between the Subtests of Six Achievement Test Batteries." Abstract. *Proc 79th Ann Conv Am Psychol Assn* 6(1):109-10 '71. * (*PA* 46:3727)

CUMULATIVE NAME INDEX

Anastasiow, N. J.: 5	Jolly, H.: 1
Bryant, N. D.: *rev,* 5:649	Karlin, R.: 1
Buswell, G. T.: 7	Orr, D. B.: 8
Davis, W. Q.: 4	Powell, K.: 6
Derrick, C.: *rev,* 5:649	Strasel, H. C.: 8
Fleischman, H. L.: 8	Sutherland, S. P.: 2
Fry, E. B.: *rev,* 6:808	Weaver, W. W.: 6
Guthrie, J. T.: *rev,* 7:706	Zeman, S. S.: 3
Hafner, L. E.: 6	

[1597]

SRA Reading Record. Grades 6-12; 1947-59; 5 scores: reading rate, comprehension, everyday reading skills, vocabulary, total; Guy T. Buswell; Science Research Associates, Inc. *

For additional information and a review by William W. Turnbull, see 4:550 (2 references); for a review by Frances Oralind Triggs and an excerpted review, see 3:502.

REFERENCES THROUGH 1971

1-2. See 4:550.
3. KERN, DONALD WARREN. *The Prediction of Academic Success of Freshmen in a Community College.* Doctor's thesis, New York University (New York, N.Y.), 1953. (*DA* 15:85)

CUMULATIVE NAME INDEX

Budrow, G. F.: 1	Triggs, F. O.: *rev,* 3:502
Kern, D. W.: 3	Turnbull, W. W.: *rev,* 4:550
Selders, G. R. W.: 2	

[1598]

Schrammel-Gray High School and College Reading Test. Grades 7-16; 1940-42; 3 scores: gross-comprehension, comprehension-efficiency, rate; H. E. Schrammel and W. H. Gray; Bobbs-Merrill Co., Inc. *

For additional information, reviews by James M. McCallister and Robert L. McCaul, and an excerpted review by William J. Jones, see 3:500.

REFERENCES THROUGH 1971

1. ANDERSON, MARY R., AND STEGMAN, ERWIN J. "Predictors of Freshman Achievement at Fort Hays Kansas State College." *Ed & Psychol Meas* 14:722-3 w '54. * (*PA* 29:7952)
2. YOUNG, LEIL L. "Comparisons Between Eighth Grade Students and a Select Group of Adult Males on a Standardized Reading Test." *Calif J Ed Res* 8:129 My '57. *

CUMULATIVE NAME INDEX

Anderson, M. R.: 1	McCaul, R. L.: *rev,* 3:500
Jones, W. J.: *exc,* 3:500	Stegman, E. J.: 1
McCallister, J. M.: *rev,* 3:500	Young, L. L.: 2

[1599]

*Sequential Tests of Educational Progress: Reading. Grades 4-6, 7-9, 10-12, 13-14; 1956-72;

2 editions; Cooperative Tests and Services. * For the complete battery entry, see 35.

a) ORIGINAL SERIES [70 MINUTE TESTS]. 1956-63; Braille and large type editions (grades 4-12) are available from American Printing House for the Blind, Inc.

b) SERIES 2 [45 MINUTE TESTS]. 1956-72.

For additional information and reviews by Emmett Albert Betts and Paul R. Lohnes of *a*, see 6:810 (6 references); for reviews by Eric F. Gardner, James R. Hobson, and Stephen Wiseman, see 5:653. For reviews of the original edition of the complete battery, see 6:25 (2 reviews) and 5:24 (2 reviews, 1 excerpt).

REFERENCES THROUGH 1971

1-6. See 6:810.
7. TRIMBLE, W. EUGENE. "A Study Using STEP Reading Scores to Predict Students Likely to Experience Academic Difficulty in the Freshman Year." *J Res Services* 3:9-12 D '63. *
8. MICHAEL, WILLIAM B.; CATHCART, ROBERT; AND ZIMMERMAN, WAYNE S. "Linguistic Factors in Various Measures of Communication Skills for College Students With Implications for Predictive Validity." *Ed & Psychol Meas* 24:363-7 su '64. * (*PA* 39:3192)
9. SCHECK, ROSE RAYNOR. *An Investigation of Children's Knowledge of Single and of Multiple Meanings of Words and Reading Comprehension.* Doctor's thesis, Temple University (Philadelphia, Pa.), 1964. (*DA* 25:6057)
10. ELLIOTT, MERLE H., AND BADAL, ALDEN W. "Achievement and Racial Composition of Schools." *Calif J Ed Res* 16:158-66 S '65. * (*PA* 40:1478)
11. MACGILLIVRAY, MARGARET C. *A Critical Analysis of the Item Content of the STEP Reading Test in Terms of Bloom's Taxonomy, Cognitive Domain.* Master's thesis, Catholic University of America (Washington, D.C.), 1965.
12. MILLER, DORIS KOTEEN. *A Study of Differences Between Auditory and Visual Learners in Respect to Extraversion-Introversion.* Doctor's thesis, New York University (New York, N.Y.), 1965. (*DA* 26:4078)
13. LUNDSTEEN, SARA W., AND MICHAEL, WILLIAM B. "Validation of Three Tests of Cognitive Style in Verbalization for the Third and Sixth Grades." *Ed & Psychol Meas* 26:449-61 su '66. * (*PA* 40:12763)
14. PHELPS, ARTHUR M. *Predicting First Semester Grades in the Junior College Two-Year Terminal Vocational-Technical Programs.* Master's thesis, Stetson University (DeLand, Fla.), 1966.
15. SUTHERLAND, SAMUEL PHILIP. *A Factor Analytic Study of Tests Designed to Measure Reading Ability.* Doctor's thesis, University of Southern California (Los Angeles, Calif.), 1966. (*DA* 27:414rA)
16. HAYWARD, PRISCILLA. "A Comparison of Test Performance on Three Answer Sheet Formats." *Ed & Psychol Meas* 27:997-1004 w '67. * (*PA* 42:9420)
17. HEATH, ROBERT W.; JANSSEN, DAVID R.; FORTNA, RICHARD O.; BIANCHINI, JOHN C.; AND YOUNG, MAURICE R. "The Use of Achievement and Ability Test Averages." *J Ed Meas* 4:81-6 su '67. *
18. LIOTTI, ANTHONY R. *A Factor Analytic Study of Items Measuring Reading Comprehension in the STEP Reading Test.* Master's thesis, City College (New York, N.Y.), 1967.
19. NICHOLLS, J. G. "Anxiety, Defensiveness, Self-Esteem, and Responsibility for Intellectual Achievement: Their Relation to Intelligence and Reading Achievement Test Score." *N Zeal J Ed Studies* 2:125-35 N '67. *
20. TENOPYR, MARY L. "Social Intelligence and Academic Success." *Ed & Psychol Meas* 27:961-5 w '67. * (*PA* 42:9509)
21. TRELA, THADDEUS M. "Comparing Achievement on Tests of General and Critical Reading." *J Read Specialist* 6:140-2 My '67. * (*PA* 41:14190)
22. ORR, DAVID B., AND GRAHAM, WARREN R. "Development of a Listening Comprehension Test to Identify Educational Potential Among Disadvantaged Junior High School Students." *Am Ed Res J* 5:167-80 Mr '68. *
23. STOREY, ARTHUR G. "The Versatile Multiple-Choice Item." *J Ed Res* 62:169-72 D '68. *
24. ANASTASIOW, NICHOLAS J. "Fourth Through Sixth Grade Student Performance Differences on STEP and SRA Achievement Tests." *Meas & Eval Guid* 2(3):149-52 f '69. * (*PA* 44:13276)
25. BOTEL, MORTON. "A Comparative Study of the Validity of the Botel Reading Inventory and Selected Standardized Tests." *Proc Ann Conv Int Read Assn* 13(1):721-7 '69. *
26. SARUK, ALEC, AND GULUTSAN, METRO. "Academic Performance of Students and the Cultural Orientation of Their Parents." *Alberta J Ed Res* (Canada) 16(3):189-95 S '70. * (*PA* 45:8988)
27. BRADLEY, RICHARD W., AND SANBORN, MARSHALL P. "Using Tests to Predict Four-Year Patterns of College Grade Point." *J Col Stud Personnel* 12(2):138-42 Mr '71. * (*PA* 46:5699)

28. FLEISCHMAN, HOWARD L.; ORR, DAVID B.; AND STRASEL, H. C. "Relationships Between the Subtests of Six Achievement Test Batteries." Abstract. *Proc 79th Ann Conv Am Psychol Assn* 6(1):109–10 '71. * (*PA* 46:3727)

29. JEFFERSON, GEORGE L., JR. "Lexical and Structural Items as Predictors of Readability for High and Low Ability Readers." *Yearb Nat Read Conf* 19(1):172–8 '71. *

30. SHAVER, JAMES P., AND NUHN, DEE. "The Effectiveness of Tutoring Underachievers in Reading and Writing." *J Ed Res* 65(3):107–12 N '71. * (*PA* 48:1878)

31. TUINMAN, J. JAAP. "Assessment of the Acquisition of Information From Reading Prose Passages." *Yearb Nat Read Conf* 20:198–205 '71. *

For additional references, see the bibliography for the series, 35.

CUMULATIVE NAME INDEX

Anastasiow, N. J.: 24	Michael, W. B.: 6, 8, 13
Badal, A. W.: 10	Milfs, M.: 6
Betts, E. A.: *rev,* 6:810	Miller, D. K.: 12
Bianchini, J. C.: 17	Nicholls, J. G.: 19
Botel, M.: 25	Nuhn, D.: 30
Bradley, R. W.: 27	Orr, D. B.: 22, 28
Cathcart, R.: 6, 8	O'Shaughnessy, M. M.: 2
Elliott, M. H.: 10	Phelps, A. M.: 14
Endler, N. S.: 5	Rudd, J. P.: 3
Fleischman, H. L.: 28	Sanborn, M. P.: 27
Fortna, R. O.: 17	Saruk, A.: 26
Gardner, E. F.: *rev,* 5:653	Scheck, R. R.: 9
Graham, W. R.: 22	Shaver, J. P.: 30
Gulutsan, M.: 26	Steinberg, D.: 5
Hayward, P.: 16	Storey, A. G.: 23
Heath, R. W.: 17	Strasel, H. C.: 28
Hobson, J. R.: *rev,* 5:653	Sutherland, S. P.: 15
Janssen, D. R.: 17	Tenopyr, M. L.: 20
Jefferson, G. L.: 29	Trela, T. M.: 4, 21
Liotti, A. R.: 18	Trimble, W. E.: 7
Lohnes, P. R.: *rev,* 6:810	Tuinman, J. J.: 31
Lundsteen, S. W.: 13	Wiseman, S.: *rev,* 5:653
MacGillivray, M. C.: 11	Young, M. R.: 17
Mayer, R. W.: 1	Zimmerman, W. S.: 6, 8

[1600]

Silent Reading Tests. Standards 1–3 (ages 7–10), 3–8 (ages 10–15), 6–10 (ages 13–17); 1947–63; 3 levels; Human Sciences Research Council [South Africa]. *

a) SILENT READING TEST (ELEMENTARY). Standards 1–3; 4 tests.

1) *Paragraphs.* 1951 and 1963 tests essentially the same as tests copyrighted 1947.

2) *Sentences.* 1951 tests essentially the same as tests copyrighted 1947.

3) *Vocabulary.* 1961 tests essentially the same as tests copyrighted 1947–51.

4) *Speed.*

b) SILENT READING TESTS (REVISED EDITION). Standards 3–8, 6–10; 3 or 4 scores: vocabulary, paragraphs, sentences (standards 3–8 only), language usage.

For additional information, see 6:811.

[1601]

Southgate Group Reading Tests. Ages 6–7.5, 7–8; 1960–62, c1959–62; 2 tests; Vera Southgate; University of London Press Ltd. [England]. *

a) TEST 1—WORD SELECTION. Ages 6–7.5; 1960–61, c1959.

b) TEST 2—SENTENCE COMPLETION TEST. Ages 7–8; 1962.

For additional information, reviews by M. L. Kellmer Pringle and Magdalen D. Vernon, and an excerpted review by P. E. Vernon of Test 1, see 6:812.

[1602]

Stanford Achievement Test: High School Reading Test. Grades 9–12; 1965–66; catalog uses the title *Stanford High School Reading Test;* subtest of *Stanford Achievement Test: High School Basic Battery;* Eric F. Gardner, Jack C. Merwin, Robert Callis, and Richard Madden; Harcourt Brace Jovanovich, Inc. * For the complete battery entry, see 37.

For additional information and reviews by Robert

H. Bauernfeind and H. Alan Robinson, see 7:707. For reviews of the complete battery, see 7:27 (2 reviews).

REFERENCES THROUGH 1971

1. KAY, PATRICIA M.; TITTLE, CAROL J.; AND WEINER, MAX. "Selecting Tests to Predict the Need for Remediation in a University Open Admissions Population." *Meas & Eval Guid* 4(3):154–9 O '71. * (*PA* 49:11964)

CUMULATIVE NAME INDEX

Kay, P. M.: 1	Weiner, M.: 1
Tittle, C. J.: 1	

[1603]

*****Stanford Achievement Test: Reading Tests.** Grades 1.5–9; 1922–74; 2 editions; Richard Madden, Eric F. Gardner, Herbert C. Rudman, Truman L. Kelley (*a*), Bjorn Karlsen (*b*), and Jack C. Merwin (*b*); Harcourt Brace Jovanovich, Inc. * For the complete battery entry, see 36.

a) 1964 EDITION. Grades 1.5–2.4, 2.5–3.9, 4.0–5.4, 5.5–6.9, 7.0–9.9; 1922–68; catalog uses the title *Stanford Reading Tests;* 5 levels; Braille and large type editions available from American Printing House for the Blind, Inc.

1) *Primary 1 Reading Tests.* Grades 1.5–2.4; 4 scores: word reading, paragraph meaning, vocabulary, word study skills.

2) *Primary 2 Reading Tests.* Grades 2.5–3.9; 3 scores: word meaning, paragraph meaning, word study skills.

3) *Intermediate 1 Reading Tests.* Grades 4.0–5.4; 2 scores: word meaning, paragraph meaning.

4) *Intermediate 2 Reading Tests.* Grades 5.5–6.9; 2 scores: word meaning, paragraph meaning.

5) *Advanced Paragraph Meaning Test.* Grades 7.0–9.9.

b) 1973 EDITION. Grades 1.5–2.4, 2.5–3.4, 3.5–4.4, 4.5–5.4, 5.5–6.9, 7.0–9.5; 1923–74; 6 levels.

1) *Primary Level 1.* Grades 1.5–2.4; 6 scores: reading (word, comprehension, word plus comprehension), word study skills, total, vocabulary.

2) *Primary Level 2.* Grades 2.5–3.4; 6 scores: same as for primary level 1.

3) *Primary Level 3.* Grades 3.5–4.4; 4 scores: comprehension, word study skills, total, vocabulary.

4) *Intermediate Level 1.* Grades 4.5–5.4; 4 scores: same as for primary level 3.

5) *Intermediate Level 2.* Grades 5.5–6.9; 4 scores: same as for primary level 3.

6) *Advanced.* Grades 7.0–9.5; 3 scores: vocabulary, comprehension, total.

For additional information and a review by Arthur E. Traxler of the 1964 edition, see 7:708 (16 references); see also 6:813 (1 reference); for reviews by Helen M. Robinson and Agatha Townsend of an earlier edition, see 5:656; for a review by James R. Hobson, see 4:555 (4 references); for a review by Margaret G. McKim, see 3:503. For reviews of the complete battery, see 7:25 (1 excerpt), 6:26 (1 review, 1 excerpt), 5:25 (1 review), 4:25 (2 reviews), and 3:18 (2 reviews).

REFERENCES THROUGH 1971

1–4. See 4:555.
5. See 6:813.
6–21. See 7:708.

22. GOODENOUGH, F. L. "The Reading Tests of the Stanford Achievement Scale and Other Variables." *J Ed Psychol* 16:523–31 N '25. *

23. FORAN, T. G. "The Present Status of Silent Reading Tests: Part 2, The Measurement of Comprehension." *Cath Univ Am Ed Res B* 2(3):1–51 Mr '27. * (*PA* 2:2610)

24. MOSHER, RAYMOND M. "A Further Note on the Reliability of Reading Tests." *J Ed Psychol* 19:272–4 Ap '28. * (*PA* 2:2623)

25. GIFFORD, CELIA ALLEN. *An Evaluation of Six Primary Reading Tests.* Master's thesis, University of California (Berkeley, Calif.), 1929.

Sequential Tests of Educational Progress: Reading

26. MANUEL, H. T., AND WRIGHT, CARRIE E. "The Language Difficulty of Mexican Children." *J Genetic Psychol* 36:458–68 S '29. * (*PA* 4:304)

27. BOUSFIELD, MAUDELLE B. "The Intelligence and School Achievement of Negro Children." *J Negro Ed* 1:338–95 O '32. * (*PA* 8:3671)

28. ENGELHART, MAX D. "The Relative Contribution of Certain Factors to Individual Differences in Arithmetical Problem Solving Ability." *J Exp Ed* 1:19–27 S 15 '32. * (*PA* 7:1126)

29. CALDWELL, FLOYD F. "Speed as a Factor With Children of Superior and Inferior Intelligence." *J Ed Res* 26:522–4 Mr '33. * (*PA* 7:3046)

30. KNIPE, CHESTER S. *Correlation Between Reading Ages of Three Standard Reading Tests.* Master's thesis, Temple University (Philadelphia, Pa.), 1933.

31. LONG, HOWARD HALE. "Test Results of Third-Grade Negro Children Selected on the Basis of Socio-Economic Status." *J Negro Ed* 4:192–212, 523–52 Ap, O '35. * (*PA* 10:1089)

32. MANUEL, H. T. "A Comparison of Spanish-Speaking and English-Speaking Children in Reading and Arithmetic." *J Appl Psychol* 19:189–202 Ap '35. * (*PA* 9:5346)

33. WILSON, FRANK Y.; BURKE, AGNES; AND FLEMMING, CECILE WHITE. "Sex Differences in Beginning Reading in a Progressive School." *J Ed Res* 32:570–82 Ap '39. * (*PA* 13:4386)

34. ASHFORD, ZELODIOUS WILLIAMS. *Personality: Reading and Spelling Achievement of Mentally Retarded Pupils.* Master's thesis, Illinois State University (Normal, Ill.), 1966.

35. GADZELLA, BERNADETTE M., AND BENTALL, GRACE. "Differences in Mental Ability and Academic Achievement of Two Groups of High School Graduates." *J Ed Res* 60:104–6 N '66. *

36. MCCRACKEN, ROBERT A. "A Two-Year Study of the Reading Achievement of Children Who Were Reading When They Entered First Grade." *J Ed Res* 59:207–10 Ja '66. * (*PA* 40:6506)

37. TRIEGLAFF, ANNETTE LOUISE. *The Relationship Between the Wechsler Intelligence Scale for Children and Reading Scores for the Stanford Achievement Test.* Master's thesis, Sacramento State College (Sacramento, Calif.), 1967.

38. LOWERY, DONELLA W. *An Analysis of the Relationship Between Personality Traits and Reading Comprehension Achievement of Students in Grades Four Through Seven.* Master's thesis, East Tennessee State University (Johnson City, Tenn.), 1968.

39. HAMMERMEISTER, FRIEDA K. "The Stability of Reading Achievement in Deaf Adults." *CEC Selected Conv Papers* 1969:467–76 '69. *

40. PAGE, BEN H. *Predicting Performance in Seventh Grade Advanced Mathematics at Kearns Junior High School.* Master's thesis, University of Utah (Salt Lake City, Utah), 1969.

41. KIDD, LOR RHEBA R. *A Comparison of the Wide Range Achievement Test With the Stanford Achievement Test and Comprehensive Tests of Basic Skills as a Measurement of Reading Achievement.* Master's thesis, California State College (Hayward, Calif.), 1970.

42. PLUMLEIGH, GEORGE ELWOOD, JR. *The Relationship of Selected Variables to the Ability of First-Grade Children to Read and Interpret Maps.* Doctor's thesis, University of Southern California (Los Angeles, Calif.), 1970. (*DAI* 31:5946A)

43. BORNSTEIN, HARRY, AND KANNAPELL, BARBARA. "More on the Effects of Verbal Load on Achievement Tests." *Am Ann Deaf* 116(6):575–9 D '71. * (*PA* 48:7769)

44. CALLENBACH, CARL ANTON. *The Effects of Instruction and Practice in Non-Substantive Test-Taking Techniques Upon the Standardized Reading Test Scores of Selected Second Grade Students.* Doctor's thesis, Pennsylvania State University (University Park, Pa.), 1971. (*DAI* 32:6183A)

45. DAVIS, BOBBIE, AND MCNINCH, GEORGE. "A Comparison of Three Standardized Reading Tests in a Fifth Grade Sample." *South J Ed Res* 5(2):101–12 Ap '71. *

46. DAVIS, BOBBIE SUE. *A Comparative Analysis of Three Widely Used Standardized Reading Achievement Tests for a Selected Group of Elementary School Children.* Doctor's thesis, University of Southern Mississippi (Hattiesburg, Miss.), 1971. (*DAI* 32:4831A)

47. FLEISCHMAN, HOWARD L.; ORR, DAVID B.; AND STRASEL, H. C. "Relationships Between the Subtests of Six Achievement Test Batteries." Abstract. *Proc 79th Ann Conv Am Psychol Assn* 6(1): 109–10 '71. * (*PA* 46:3727)

48. GREEN, RICHARD B., AND ROHWER, WILLIAM D., JR. "SES Differences on Learning and Ability Tests in Black Children." *Am Ed Res J* 8(4):601–9 N '71. * (*PA* 47:11611)

49. HAMMERMEISTER, FRIEDA K. "Reading Achievement in Deaf Adults." *Am Ann Deaf* 116(1):25–8 F '71. *

50. JOHNSON, GARY L., AND HUMMEL, THOMAS J. "Effects of Three Modes of Test Administration on the Reading Achievement Scores of Fifth Graders." *El Sch Guid & Counsel* 6(1):21–6 O '71. * (*PA* 49:7853)

51. LIEDTKE, WERNER. "Mathematics Learning and Pupil Characteristics." *Alberta J Ed Res* (Canada) 17(3):143–53 S '71. * (*PA* 48:1864)

52. NEWMAN, ANABEL POWELL. *Longitudinal Study of Pupils Who Were Underachieving in Reading in First Grade.* Doctor's

thesis, State University of New York (Buffalo, N.Y.), 1971. (*DAI* 32:2313A)

53. TRIDER, MARY S. "The Right to Read and Standardized Testing: A Necessary Dimension." *Read Teach* 24(4):320–30 Ja '71. * (*PA* 46:11521)

CUMULATIVE NAME INDEX

[1604]

★**Sucher-Allred Reading Placement Inventory.** Reading level grades 1–9; 1968–71; SARPI; subtests referred to as *Sucher-Allred Word-Recognition Test* and *Sucher-Allred Oral Reading Paragraph Test;* 3 major scores: independent, instructional, and frustrational grade reading levels; Floyd Sucher and Ruel A. Allred; Brigham Young University Press. *

REFERENCES THROUGH 1971

1. KUEHN, JOHN ARTHUR. *A Word Recognition Test as a Placement Tool for Reading Instruction and the Relationship Between Reading Scores Received by Elementary Students on a Battery of Standardized and Informal Reading Tests.* Master's thesis, Brigham Young University (Provo, Utah), 1969.

CUMULATIVE NAME INDEX

[1605]

Survey of Primary Reading Development. Grades 1–2, 2–4; 1957–64; SPRD; J. Richard Harsh and Dorothy Soeberg; Educational Testing Service (Berkeley Office). *

For additional information and a review by Allen Berger, see 7:709; for reviews by Thomas C. Barrett and Russell G. Stauffer of the test for grades 1–2, see 6:814.

[1606]

Survey of Reading Achievement: California Survey Series. Grades 7–9, 9–12; 1959; all items from *California Reading Test;* Ernest W. Tiegs and Willis W. Clark; CTB/McGraw-Hill. *

For additional information and reviews by Clarence Derrick and J. Raymond Gerberich, see 6:815.

[1607]

Survey Tests of Reading. Grades 3–6, 7–13; 1931–32; 2 tests; L. J. O'Rourke; O'Rourke Publications. *
a) CENTRAL THOUGHT TEST. Grades 3–6, 7–13; 1931–32.
b) POWER TEST. Grades 3–13; 1931.

[1608]

Tests of Academic Progress: Reading. Grades 9–12; 1964–66; Dale P. Scannell and Henry P. Smith; Houghton Mifflin Co. * For the complete battery entry, see 44.

For additional information and a review by Marvin D. Glock, see 7:710 (2 references). For a review of the complete battery, see 7:31.

REFERENCES THROUGH 1971
1–2. See 7:710.

CUMULATIVE NAME INDEX

Caldwell, J. R.: 1	Meyers, C. E.: 1
Glock, M. D.: rev, 7:710	Michael, W. B.: 1
Goolsby, T. M.: 2	Schrader, D. R.: 1

[1609]

Tests of Reading: Inter-American Series. Grades 1, 2–3, 4–6, 7–9, 10–13; 1950–73; revision of *Tests of Reading: Cooperative Inter-American Tests;* parallel editions in English and Spanish; 5 levels; Herschel T. Manuel; Guidance Testing Associates. *
a) LEVEL 1, PRIMARY. Grade 1; 1966–73; 3 scores: vocabulary, comprehension, total.
b) LEVEL 2, PRIMARY. Grades 2–3; 1962–73; 5 scores: vocabulary, comprehension (level, speed, total), total.
c) LEVEL 3, ELEMENTARY. Grades 4–6; 1962–73; 5 scores: same as for Level 2.
d) LEVEL 4, INTERMEDIATE. Grades 7–9; 1962–73; 5 scores: same as for Level 2.
e) LEVEL 5, ADVANCED. Grades 10–13; 1962–67; 5 scores: same as for Level 2.

For additional information and a review by Georgia S. Adams, see 7:711 (4 references); see also 6:818 (4 references); for reviews by Jacob S. Orleans and Frederick L. Westover of the earlier edition, see 4:557 (4 references).

REFERENCES THROUGH 1971
1–4. See 4:557.
5–8. See 6:818.
9–12. See 7:711.

CUMULATIVE NAME INDEX

Adams, G. S.: rev, 7:711	McCranie, J.: 2
Arnold, R. D.: 12	Manuel, H. T.: 4, 6, 10–1
Bou, I. R.: 1	Martin, R. P.: 9
Chenault, V. M.: 5	Orleans, J. S.: rev, 4:557
Einspahr, M. H.: 7	Westover, F. L.: rev, 4:557
Fife, R. H.: 4	Zimmerer, A. M.: 8
Kelley, F.: 3	

[1610]

Traxler High School Reading Test, Revised. Grades 10–12; 1938–67; 5 scores: rate, story comprehension, main ideas, total comprehension, total; 1966 tests identical with tests copyrighted 1938–39 except for minor changes in 12 items; Arthur E. Traxler; Bobbs-Merrill Co., Inc. *
For additional information and a review by Robert A. Forsyth, see 7:712; for a review by Harold D. Carter, see 4:559 (4 references); for reviews by Alvin C. Eurich, Constance M. McCullough, and C. Gilbert Wrenn, and excerpted reviews by E. L. Abell and J. Wayne Wrightstone, see 2:1578.

REFERENCES THROUGH 1971
1–4. See 4:559.
5. AUKERMAN, ROBERT C., JR. "Differences in the Reading Status of Good and Poor Eleventh Grade Students." *J Ed Res* 41:498–515 Mr '48. * (*PA* 22:4599)
6. SMITH, DONALD E. P. "A Note on 'Equivalent Forms.'" *J Develop Read* 1:62–3 su '58. *
7. THALBERG, STANTON P. "Reading Rate and Immediate Versus Delayed Retention." *J Ed Psychol* 58:373–8 D '67. * (*PA* 42:3379)

CUMULATIVE NAME INDEX

Abell, E. L.: exc, 2:1578	Blommers, P.: 3
Aukerman, R. C.: 5	Carter, H. D.: rev, 4:559

Eurich, A. C.: rev, 2:1578	Thalberg, S. P.: 7
Forsyth, R. A.: rev, 7:712	Traxler, A. E.: 1–2
Lindquist, E. F.: 3	Tuft, E. N.: 4
McCullough, C. M.: rev, 2: 1578	Wrenn, C. G.: rev, 2:1578
Preston, R. C.: 4	Wrightstone, J. W.: exc, 2: 1578
Smith, D. E. P.: 6	

[1611]

Traxler Silent Reading Test. Grades 7–10; 1934–69; 6 scores: reading rate, story comprehension, word meaning, paragraph meaning, total comprehension, total; 1969 tests identical with tests copyrighted 1934 except for conversion of all items to multiple choice form; Arthur E. Traxler; Bobbs-Merrill Co., Inc. *
For additional information and a review by William E. Coffman, see 7:713; for a review by J. Thomas Hastings, see 4:560 (2 references); for reviews by Robert L. McCaul and Miles A. Tinker and an excerpted review by J. Wayne Wrightstone, see 2:1579 (3 references); for reviews by Frederick B. Davis and Spencer Shank, see 1:1114.

REFERENCES THROUGH 1971
1–3. See 2:1579.
4–5. See 4:560.
6. TRAXLER, ARTHUR. "Sex Differences in Comprehension Among Junior High School Students." *Ed* 89(4):312–4 Ap–My '69. *

CUMULATIVE NAME INDEX

Blanchard, H. L.: 4	Stoddard, G. D.: 1
Coffman, W. E.: rev, 7:713	Tinker, M. A.: rev, 2:1579
Davis, F. B.: rev, 1:1114	Traxler, A.: 6
Hastings, J. T.: rev, 4:560	Traxler, A. E.: 2–3, 5
McCaul, R. L.: rev, 2:1579	Wrightstone, J. W.: exc, 2: 1579
Ruch, G. M.: 1	
Shank, S.: rev, 1:1114	

[1612]

Van Wagenen Analytical Reading Scales. Grades 4–6, 7–9, 10–12; 1953–54; 6 or 7 scores: central thought, simple details, complex ideas, inferences, interpretation, total, word meaning (Form M only); Part 3 of *Diagnostic Examination of Silent Reading Abilities;* 3 levels; M. J. Van Wagenen; Van Wagenen Psycho-Educational Laboratories. *
a) INTERMEDIATE DIVISION. Grades 4–6; 1953.
b) JUNIOR DIVISON. Grades 7–9; 1953.
c) SENIOR DIVISION. Grades 10–12; 1953–54.
For reference to reviews of the *Diagnostic Examination of Silent Reading Abilities,* see 1622.

[1613]

W.A.L. English Comprehension Test. High school; 1962–65; 4 scores: recognition vocabulary, recall vocabulary, reading comprehension, total; Australian Council for Educational Research [Australia]. *
For additional information, see 6:819.

[1614]

★Wide-span Reading Test. Ages 7–15; 1972; Alan Brimer (incorporating material by Herbert Gross); Thomas Nelson & Sons Ltd. [England]. *

[1615]

Williams Primary Reading Test. Grades 1, 2–3; 1926–55; Allan J. Williams; Bobbs-Merrill Co., Inc. *
For additional information, see 5:658; for a review by Alice N. Jameson of the original edition, see 3:508.

REFERENCES THROUGH 1971
1. GIFFORD, CELIA ALLEN. *An Evaluation of Six Primary Reading Tests.* Master's thesis, University of California (Berkeley, Calif.), 1929.
2. BAKER, FLORENCE, AND BROOM, M. E. "Concerning One Criterion for the Choice of Primary Reading Tests." *J Appl Psychol* 16:419–20 Ag '32. * (*PA* 7:4098)

[1616]

Williams Reading Test for Grades 4–9. 1929; Allan J. Williams; Bobbs-Merrill Co., Inc. *

REFERENCES THROUGH 1971

1. FORAN, T. G., AND ROCK, ROBERT J., JR. "The Reliability of Some Silent Reading Tests." *Cath Univ Am Ed Res B* 5(6): 1–23 Je '30. * (*PA* 5:2921)

[Out of Print Since TIP I]

A.C.E.R. Silent Reading Tests, Forms A and B, R:2, 5:616 (1 review) ; Forms C and D, R:3, 6:782 (2 reviews, 1 reference)

Achievement Test in Silent Reading: Dominion Tests, R:5, 5:619 (4 reviews)

Ballard's Reading Tests, R:88

Burt's Reading Tests, R:9

Chapman Reading Comprehension Test, R:91, 5:623 (1 review)

Detroit Reading Test, T:1399

Detroit Word Recognition Test, R:20

Diagnostic Paragraph Comprehension: Group Achievement Tests: Niagara Edition, R:31, 5:13b

Elementary Reading: Every Pupil Scholarship Test, 6:788

Elementary Reading: Every Pupil Test, R:94, 6:789

Emporia Silent Reading Test, R:28, 2:1534 (2 reviews)

Gates Advanced Primary Reading Tests, 6:790 (3 reviews, 4 references) ; for a revision, see the Primary B level of the *Gates-MacGinitie Reading Tests,* 1552

Gates Basic Reading Tests, R:98, 6:791 (8 reviews, 1 excerpt, 9 references)

Gates Primary Reading Tests, 6:792 (4 reviews, 10 references) ; for a revision, see the Primary A level of the *Gates-MacGinitie Reading Tests,* 1552

Gates Reading Survey, 6:793 (4 reviews, 7 references) ; for a revision, see the grades 3–9 levels of the *Gates-MacGinitie Reading Tests,* 1552

General Reading Test: Ohio Senior Survey Tests, R:99, 4:534

Kansas Primary Reading Test, R:102, 4:539 (2 reviews)

Kelley-Greene Reading Comprehension Test, R:35, 5:636 (2 reviews, 1 reference)

Los Angeles Elementary Reading Test, R:39, 4:541 (1 review)

Manchester Reading Comprehension Test (Sen.) 1, 7:695 (2 reviews, 1 reference), R:42

Nelson-Lohmann Reading Test, R:104, 6:801 (1 review)

Primary Reading: Every Pupil Scholarship Test, 6:803

Primary Reading: Every Pupil Test, R:105, 6:804 (2 reviews)

Primary Reading Test, R:106, 3:494 (1 review, 1 reference)

Purdue Reading Test, R:55, 5:643 (1 review)

Reading: Seven Plus Assessment, R:63, 4:548

Sangren-Woody Reading Test, R:107, 4:551 (2 reviews, 7 references)

Silent Reading Comprehension: Iowa Every-Pupil Tests of Basic Skills, R:71, 4:554 (2 reviews)

Stone-Webster Test in Beginning Reading, R:109, 3:504 (1 review, 1 reference)

Techniques in Reading Comprehension: Every Pupil Test, R:110, 6:816 (2 reviews)

DIAGNOSTIC

[1617]

California Phonics Survey. Grades 7–12 and college; 1956–63; CPS; shortened version of *Stanford Diagnostic Phonics Survey, Research Edition;* 9 error analysis scores for Form 1 (Form 2 yields total score only) : long-short vowel confusion, other vowel confusion, consonants-confusion with blends and digraphs, consonant-vowel reversals, configuration, endings, negatives-opposites-sight words, rigidity, total; Grace M. Brown and Alice B. Cottrell; CTB/McGraw-Hill. *

For additional information and a review by Constance M. McCullough, see 7:714 (1 reference) ; for a review by Thomas E. Culliton, Jr., see 6:820 (1 reference).

REFERENCES THROUGH 1971

1. See 6:820.
2. See 7:714.
3. ILIKA, JOSEPH. "The Third Annual Report of the Phonetic Skills of Teachers." *Yearb Nat Read Conf* 19(2):95–105 '71. *

[1618]

*****Classroom Reading Inventory, Second Edition.** Grades 2–10; 1965–73; CRI; 6 scores: word recognition, independent reading level, instructional reading level, frustration level, hearing capacity level, spelling; Nicholas J. Silvaroli; Wm. C. Brown Co. Publishers. *

For additional information and an excerpted review by Donald L. Cleland of an earlier edition, see 7:715.

REFERENCES THROUGH 1971

1. POWELL, WILLIAM R., AND DUNKELD, COLIN G. "Validity of the IRI Reading Levels." *El Engl* 48(6):637–42 O '71. *

[1619]

★The Cooper-McGuire Diagnostic Word-Analysis Test. Grades 1–5 and over; 1970–72; 32 overlapping tests (spirit masters for local duplicating) with 1 to 13 tests administered at a given reader level; J. Louis Cooper and Marion L. McGuire; Croft Educational Services, Inc. *

[1620]

Cooperative Primary Tests: Word Analysis. Grades 1.5–3; 1965–67; Cooperative Tests and Services. * For the complete battery entry, see 12.

For reviews of the complete battery, see 7:10 (2 excerpts).

[1621]

The Denver Public Schools Reading Inventory. Grades 1–8; 1965–68; 3 scores (instructional level, independent level, capacity level) and ratings of areas of both strength and weakness; based upon the Sheldon Basic Reading Series; Department of Instructional Services, Denver Public Schools. *

For additional information, see 7:716.

[1622]

Diagnostic Examination of Silent Reading Abilities. Grades 4–6, 7–9, 10–12; 1939–54; 4 parts, parts 2 and 3 are in 1 booklet; 1952–54 edition entitled *Dvorak-Van Wagenen Diagnostic Examination of Silent Reading Abilities;* August Dvorak and M. J. Van Wagenen; Van Wagenen Psycho-Educational Laboratories. *

a) PART I, VAN WAGENEN RATE OF COMPREHENSION SCALE. 1939–53; 1953 test identical with test copyrighted 1939.

b) PART 2. 1939–52; 4 scores: perception of relations, vocabulary (context, isolation), information.

c) PART 3. 1939–54; also published separately under the title *Van Wagenen Analytical Reading Scales* (see 1612); 6 scores: central thought, single details, related ideas, inferences, interpretation, total; 1954 test identical with test copyrighted 1939.

d) PART 4, READING FOR IDEAS. 1952–53; rate of reading.

For additional information and reviews by Frederick B. Davis, W. E. Hall, and J. B. Stroud, see 3:480 (2 references); for an excerpted review by Worth J. Osburn, see 2:1532.

REFERENCES THROUGH 1971

1–2. See 3:480.
3. TREACY, JOHN P. "The Relationship of Reading Skills to the Ability to Solve Arithmetic Problems." *J Ed Res* 38:86–96 O '44. * (*PA* 19:809)
4. BROMLEY, ANN, AND CARTER, GERALD C. "Predictability of Success in Mathematics." *J Ed Res* 44:148–50 O '50. * (*PA* 25:5630)
5. BUSWELL, G. T. "The Relationship Between Rate of Thinking and Rate of Reading." *Sch R* 59:339–46 S '51. *
6. HOLMES, JACK A. "Factors Underlying Major Reading Disabilities at the College Level." *Genetic Psychol Monogr* 49: 3–95 F '54. * (*PA* 28:8982)
7. MUNRO, JAMES JACKSON RUTHERFORD. *The Predictive Value of Entrance Reading Test Scores at the University of Washington.* Doctor's thesis, University of Washington (Seattle, Wash.), 1954. (*DA* 14:1179)
8. FLETCHER, JUNIOR EUGENE. *A Study of the Relationships Between Ability to Use Context as an Aid in Reading and Other Verbal Abilities.* Doctor's thesis, University of Washington (Seattle, Wash.), 1959. (*DA* 20:2675)
9. HOLMES, JACK A., AND SINGER, HARRY. *Speed and Power of Reading in High School.* Cooperative Research Monograph No. 14. Washington, D.C.: United States Government Printing Office, 1966. Pp. xii, 183. *

CUMULATIVE NAME INDEX

Bromley, A.: 4
Buswell, G. T.: 5
Carter, G. C.: 4
Davis, F. B.: *rev*, 3:480
Fletcher, J. E.: 8
Hall, W. E.: *rev*, 3:480
Hayter, W. H.: 1
Holmes, J. A.: 6, 9
Munro, J. J. R.: 7
Osburn, W. J.: *exc*, 2:1532
Singer, H.: 9
Stroud, J. B.: *rev*, 3:480
Traxler, A. E.: 2
Treacy, J. P.: 3

[1623]

Diagnostic Reading Examination for Diagnosis of Special Difficulty in Reading. Grades 1–4; [1928–29]; a combination of assessment procedures consisting of the *Revised Stanford-Binet Scales*, Gray's *Standardized Oral Reading Paragraphs*, Monroe's *Standardized Silent Reading Tests*, an adaptation of *Ayres Spelling Scale*, the arithmetic computation subtest of *Stanford Achievement Test: Arithmetic*, and 9 additional tests: alphabet repeating and reading, *Iota Word Test*, letter naming, recognition of orientation, mirror reading, mirror writing, number reversals, word discrimination, sounding; Marion Monroe; Stoelting Co. *

REFERENCES THROUGH 1971

1. DELLA-PIANA, GABRIEL. "Analysis of Oral Reading Errors: Standardization, Norms and Validity." *Reading Teach* 15:254–7 Ja '62. *
2. HERLIN, WAYNE RICHARD. *A Comparison of Oral Reading Errors on the Monroe Diagnostic Reading Examination and the Durrell Analysis of Reading Difficulty.* Doctor's thesis, University of Utah (Salt Lake City, Utah), 1963. (*DA* 24:4084)
3. FLYNN, PAULINE T., AND BYRNE, MARGARET C. "Relationship Between Reading and Selected Auditory Abilities of Third-Grade Children." *J Speech & Hearing Res* 13(4):731–40 D '70. *
4. LARSEN, STEPHEN. "Performance of Achieving and Underachieving Second, Third, and Fourth Grade Children on Tests of Auditory Ability and Oral Form Discrimination." *Kan Studies Ed* 21(1–2): 53–9 sp–su '71. *

CUMULATIVE NAME INDEX

Byrne, M. C.: 3
Della-Piana, G.: 1
Flynn, P. T.: 3
Herlin, W. R.: 2
Larsen, S.: 4

[1624]

Diagnostic Reading Scales, Revised Edition. Grades 1–6 and retarded readers in grades 7–12; 1963–72; DRS; 12 or 13 scores: word recognition, instructional level (oral reading), independent level (silent reading), rate of silent reading (optional), potential level (auditory comprehension), and 8 phonics scores (consonant sounds, vowel sounds, consonant blends, common syllables, blends, letter sounds, initial consonants, auditory discrimination); George D. Spache; CTB/McGraw-Hill. *

For additional information and a review by Rebecca C. Barr, see 7:717 (7 references); for a review by N. Dale Bryant, see 6:821.

REFERENCES THROUGH 1971

1–7. See 7:717.
8. DAHLKE, ANITA B. "Predicting True Reading Gains After Remedial Tutoring," pp. 81–102. In *Diagnostic Viewpoints in Reading.* Edited by Robert E. Leibert. Newark, Del.: International Reading Association, 1971. Pp. viii, 133. *
9. MERLIN, SHIRLEY B. *The Psycholinguistic and Reading Abilities of Educable Mentally Retarded Readers.* Doctor's thesis. West Virginia University (Morgantown, W.Va.), 1971. (*DAI* 32:1921A)
10. POWELL, WILLIAM R., AND DUNKELD, COLIN G. "Validity of the IRI Reading Levels." *El Engl* 48(6):637–42 O '71. *
11. RIGGLE, RICHARD RAY. *Correlations of Articulatory Disability With Various Aspects of Reading for Selected Modalities.* Doctor's thesis, University of Oregon (Eugene, Ore.), 1971. (*DAI* 32:2922A)

CUMULATIVE NAME INDEX

Attea, M.: 2
Barr, R. C.: *rev*, 7:717
Botel, M.: 7
Bradley, J.: 7
Bryant, N. D.: *rev*, 6:821
Dahlke, A. B.: 4, 8
Dunkeld, C. G.: 10
Glaser, N. A.: 1
Kashuba, M.: 7
Mann, G. T.: 6
Merlin, S. B.: 9
Powell, W. R.: 10
Rainwater, H. G.: 5
Riggle, R. R.: 11
Trela, T. M.: 3

[1625]

Diagnostic Reading Test: Pupil Progress Series. Grades 1.9–2.1, 2.2–3, 4–6, 7–8; 1956–70; DRT; various titles used by publisher; catalog uses the title *Pupil Progress Series Reading;* 4 levels; Oliver F. Anderhalter, R. Stephen Gawkoski, and Ruth Colestock; Scholastic Testing Service, Inc. *

a) PRIMARY LEVEL 1. Grades 1.9–2.1; 1956–68; 9 scores: vocabulary (word recognition, word to content relation, words in use, total), rate of reading for meaning, comprehension (recalling information, locating information, reading for descriptions, total).

b) PRIMARY LEVEL 2. Grades 2.2–3; 1956–68; 10 scores: vocabulary (words in use, word meaning, total), rate of reading for meaning, comprehension (recalling information, locating information, reading for meaning, following directions, reading for descriptions, total).

c) ELEMENTARY LEVEL. Grades 4–6; 1956–70; 13 scores: knowledge and use of sources (functions, best sources, use of index, use of table of contents, total), rate of reading for meaning, comprehension (word meaning, reading for recall of information, reading for meaning, reading to locate information, reading for directions or procedures, reading for descriptions, total).

d) ADVANCED LEVEL. Grades 7–8; 1956–70; 13 scores: same as for *c*.

For additional information and reviews by Lawrence M. Kasdon and Gus P. Plessas, see 7:718; for a review by Agatha Townsend, see 6:822.

REFERENCES THROUGH 1971

1. GOSNELL, EMMA SUE. *An Analysis of Questions Contained in Selected Intermediate Standardized Reading Tests.* Master's thesis, Eastern Illinois University (Charleston, Ill.), 1969.

CUMULATIVE NAME INDEX

Gosnell, E. S.: 1
Kasdon, L. M.: *rev*, 7:718
Plessas, G. P.: *rev*, 7:718
Townsend, A.: *rev*, 6:822

Diagnostic Examination of Silent Reading Abilities

[1626]

Diagnostic Reading Tests. Grades kgn–13; 1947–72; DRT; 3 levels; Committee on Diagnostic Reading Tests, Inc.

a) DIAGNOSTIC READING TESTS: KINDERGARTEN THROUGH FOURTH GRADES. Grades kgn–4; 1957–66; 2 sections.

1) *Survey Section.* Grades kgn–1, 1, 2, 3–4; 1957–66; 4 levels.

(a) Reading Readiness Booklet. Grades kgn–1; 5 scores: relationships, eye-hand coordination, visual discrimination, auditory discrimination, vocabulary.

(b) Booklet 1. Grade 1; 12 scores: visual discrimination, auditory discrimination (3 subscores plus total), vocabulary (3 subscores plus total), story reading (2 subscores plus total).

(c) Booklet 2. Grade 2; 3 scores: word recognition, comprehension, total.

(d) Booklet 3. Grades 3–4; 3 scores: same as for (c) above.

2) *Section 4: Word Attack, Part 1: Oral.* Grades 1–8; 1958.

b) DIAGNOSTIC READING TESTS: LOWER LEVEL. Grades 4–8; 1947–72; 2 sections.

1) *Survey Section.* Grades 4–8; 1952–72; 3 parts in 2 booklets; Forms A and B also distributed by Science Research Associates, Inc.; Braille edition available from American Printing House for the Blind, Inc.

(a) Booklet 1: Part 1, Word Recognition and Comprehension. 2 scores: word recognition, comprehension.

(b) Booklet 2: Parts 2 and 3, Vocabulary-Story Reading. 3 scores: vocabulary, rate of reading, story comprehension.

2) *Section 4: Word Attack.* Grades 1–8, 4–13; 1947–69; 2 parts.

(a) Part 1, Oral. Grades 1–8; see a2 above.

(b) Part 2, Silent. Grades 4–13; 1947–69; 3 scores: identification of sounds, syllabication, total.

c) DIAGNOSTIC READING TESTS: [UPPER LEVEL]. Grades 7–13; 1947–71; 5 sections.

1) *Survey Section.* 1947–71; 5 scores: rate of reading, comprehension check, vocabulary, total comprehension, total; Forms A and B also distributed by Science Research Associates, Inc.; Braille edition available from American Printing House for the Blind, Inc.

2) *Section 1: Vocabulary (Revised).* 1947–66; 5 scores: English, mathematics, science, social studies, total.

3) *Section 2: Comprehension: Silent and Auditory.* 1947–66; may be administered as a listening comprehension test.

4) *Section 3: Rates of Reading: Part 1, General.* 1947–63; 4 scores: normal rate of reading, comprehension at normal rate, maximum rate of reading, comprehension at maximum rate.

5) *Section 4: Word Attack.* 1947–63; 2 parts.

(a) Part 1, Oral. 1948–58.

(b) Part 2, Silent. Grades 4–13; see b2(b) above.

For additional information and reviews by Albert J. Kingston and B. H. Van Roekel, see 6:823 (21 references); for reviews by Frederick B. Davis, William W. Turnbull, and Henry Weitz, see 4:531 (19 references).

REFERENCES THROUGH 1971

1–19. See 4:531.
20–40. See 6:823.

41. WRIGHT, JAMES CLYDE. *An Investigation of the Nature of Comprehension Gained Through Reading and Its Relationship to Other Aspects of Reading and to Academic Achievement.* Doctor's thesis, Ohio State University (Columbus, Ohio), 1954. (DA 20:2686)

42. PETERSON, MARGARET JEAN. "Comparison of Flesch Readability Scores With a Test of Reading Comprehension." *J Appl Psychol* 40:35–6 F '56. * (PA 31:3654)

43. STONER, WILLIAM GERALD. *Factors Related to the Underachievement of High School Students.* Doctor's thesis, Stanford University (Stanford, Calif.), 1956. (DA 17:96)

44. AINSWORTH, LABAN LINTON, JR. *An Exploratory Study of the Academic Achievement of Arab Students.* Doctor's thesis, University of Texas (Austin, Tex.), 1957. (DA 17:1702)

45. REED, JAMES C., AND PEPPER, ROGER S. "The Interrelationship of Vocabulary, Comprehension and Rate Among Disabled Readers." *J Exp Ed* 25:331–7 Je '57. * (PA 33:6840)

46. EPPLEY, MARY VINEITA (BOOTS). *The Relationship of Personal Factors and Reading Performance to Academic Achievement of Selected Oregon State College Students.* Doctor's thesis, Oregon State University (Corvallis, Ore.), 1958. (DA 19:730)

47. ROBERTSON, MALCOLM H. "Test Scores and Self-Estimates of Two Curricula Groups." *Personnel & Guid J* 38:746–50 My '60. * (PA 35:2767)

48. ALLMAN, REVA WHITE. "A Study of the Vocabulary Needs of a Class of Juniors and Seniors at the Alabama State College." *J Ed Res* 55:228–31 F '62. *

49. HAYDEN, LILLIAN A. "The Effect of Physical Fatigue on Reading Rate and Comprehension of College Athletes." *Yearb Nat Read Conf* 12:202–5 '63. *

50. DREW, ALFRED S. "The Relationship of General Reading Ability and Other Factors to School and Job Performance of Machine Apprentices." *J Indus Teach Ed* 2:47–60 f '64. *

51. LONG, JOHN M. "Sex Differences in Academic Prediction Based on Scholastic, Personality and Interest Factors." *J Exp Ed* 32:239–48 sp '64. * (PA 39:6058)

52. GERSTEIN, ALVIN I. "Development of a Selection Program for Nursing Candidates." *Nursing Res* 14:254–7 su '65. *

53. LEUTENEGGER, RALPH R.; MUELLER, THEODORE H.; AND WERSHOW, IRVING R. "Auditory Factors in Foreign Language Acquisition." *Mod Lang J* 49:22–31 Ja '65. *

54. EMANS, ROBERT; URBAS, RAYMOND; AND DUMMETT, MARJORIE. "The Meaning of Reading Tests." *J Read* 9:406–9 My '66. * (PA 40:10459)

55. CLAWAR, HARRY J. "A Comparison of the Davis Reading Test and the Survey Section of the Diagnostic Reading Test When Used With Independent-School Pupils." *Ed Rec B* 92:39–42 Jl '67. * (PA 42:1126)

56. COATES, LESLIE F. "The Enigma of the Survey Section of the Diagnostic Reading Tests." *Yearb Nat Read Conf* 17:70–8 '68. *

57. LITTRELL, J. HARVEY. "Teacher Estimates Versus Reading Test Results." *J Read* 12:18–23 O '68. *

58. ERNEST, DAVID J. "The Predication of Academic Success of College Music Majors." *J Res Music Ed* 18(3):273–6 f '70. * (PA 45:8994)

59. LLEWELLYN, HOWARD CHARLES. *The Relationship Between Selected Silent Word Perception Skills and Achievement in First-Year High School Typewriting.* Doctor's thesis, University of North Dakota (Grand Forks, N.D.), 1970. (DAI 31:6454A)

60. MAXON, LLOYD MELVIN. *The Relationship of Certain Mental Factors, Reading Factors, Aptitudes, and Situational Factors to Achievement in Selected Air Force Technical Courses.* Doctor's thesis, North Texas State University (Denton, Tex.), 1970. (DAI 31:3437A)

61. PEPPER, ROGER S. "The Study Skills and Academic Achievement of Marginal Admission Students." *Yearb Nat Read Conf* 19(1):248–53 '71. *

CUMULATIVE NAME INDEX

Wall, C. F.: 28   Wershow, I. R.: 53
Ward, L. R.: 26   Wright, J. C.: 41
Weitz, H.: *rev,* 4:531

[1627]

*Doren Diagnostic Reading Test of Word Recognition Skills, 1973 Edition. Grades 1–4; 1956–73; 13 scores: letter recognition, beginning sounds, whole word recognition, words within words, speech consonants, ending sounds, blending, rhyming, vowels, discriminate guessing, spelling, sight words, total; Margaret Doren; American Guidance Service, Inc. *

For additional information and reviews by B. H. Van Roekel and Verna L. Vickery of an earlier edition, see 5:659.

REFERENCES THROUGH 1971

1. HACKNEY, BEN H., JR. "Reading Achievement and Word Recognition Skills." *Read Teach* 21:515–8 Mr '68. * (*PA* 42:17789)
2. McCALL, ROZANNE A., AND McCALL, ROBERT B. "Comparative Validity of Five Reading Diagnostic Tests." *J Ed Res* 62(7):329–33 Mr '69. *

CUMULATIVE NAME INDEX

Hackney, B. H.: 1   Van Roekel, B. H.: *rev,* 5:659
McCall, R. A.: 2   Vickery, V. L.: *rev,* 5:659
McCall, R. B.: 2

[1628]

Durrell Analysis of Reading Difficulty, New Edition. Grades 1–6; 1937–55, c1933–55; 7 scores: reading (oral, silent), listening, flash words, word analysis, spelling, handwriting; Donald D. Durrell; Harcourt Brace Jovanovich, Inc. *

For additional information and reviews by James Maxwell and George D. Spache, see 5:660; for a review by Helen M. Robinson of the original edition, see 4:561 (2 references); for reviews by Guy L. Bond and Miles A. Tinker, see 2:1533; for a review by Marion Monroe, see 1:1098.

REFERENCES THROUGH 1971

1–2. See 4:561.
3. DUFFY, GERTRUDE BERCHMANS. *A Diagnostic Study of Reading Difficulties in a Third Grade.* Master's thesis, Boston University (Boston, Mass.), 1934.
4. BURNS, BARBARA. *A Diagnostic Study of Reading Difficulties in Fourth Grade.* Master's thesis, Boston University (Boston, Mass.), 1938.
5. SHELDON, WILLIAM D., AND HATCH, SHIRLEY. "Strengths and Weaknesses in Reading of a Group of Third-Grade Children." *El Sch J* 50:445–52 Ap '50. * (*PA* 24:6514)
6. LONG, DONNA JANET. *An Analysis of the Reading Difficulties of Retarded Readers in Second, Fourth, and Sixth Grades.* Doctor's thesis, State University of Iowa (Iowa City, Iowa), 1959. (*DA* 20:924)
7. MITCHELL, MARY K. *The Development of Proficiency in Marking the Oral Reading Section of the Durrell Analysis of Reading Difficulty by the Use of Tape Recordings.* Master's thesis, University of Kansas (Lawrence, Kan.), 1959.
8. DELLA-PIANA, GABRIEL. "Analysis of Oral Reading Errors: Standardization, Norms and Validity." *Read Teach* 15:254–7 Ja '62. *
9. HERLIN, WAYNE RICHARD. *A Comparison of Oral Reading Errors on the Monroe Diagnostic Reading Examination and the Durrell Analysis of Reading Difficulty.* Doctor's thesis, University of Utah (Salt Lake City, Utah), 1963. (*DA* 24:4084)
10. KRIPPNER, STANLEY. "Sociopathic Tendencies and Reading Retardation in Children." *Excep Children* 29:258–66 F '63. *
11. ATTEA, MARY. *A Comparison of Three Diagnostic Reading Tests.* Doctor's thesis, State University of New York (Buffalo, N.Y.), 1966. (*DA* 27:1530A)
12. FLOWER, RICHARD M.; VIEHWEG, RICHARD; AND RUZICKA, WILLIAM R. "The Communicative Disorders of Children With Kernicteric Athetosis: 2, Problems in Language Comprehension and Use." *J Speech & Hearing Disorders* 31:60–8 F '66. * (*PA* 40:9108)
13. OLSON, ARTHUR V. "Relation of Achievement Test Scores and Specific Reading Abilities to the Frostig Test of Visual Perception." *Optom Weekly* 57:31–4 Jl 14 '66. *
14. OLSON, ARTHUR V. "Relation of Achievement Test Scores and Specific Reading Abilities to the Frostig Developmental Test of Visual Perception." *Percept & Motor Skills* 22:179–84 F '66. * (*PA* 40:4750)
15. TRELA, THADDEUS M. "What Do Diagnostic Reading Tests Diagnose?" *El Engl* 43:370–2 Ap '66. *

16. MAXEY, EARL JAMES. *An Investigation of the Rasch Probability Model for Speed in an Oral Reading Test.* Doctor's thesis, University of Iowa (Iowa City, Iowa), 1967. (*DA* 28:3075A)
17. EARLY, GEORGE H., AND SHARPE, THEODORE M. "Developing Perceptual-Motor Skills: Perceptual-Motor Training and Basic Abilities." *Acad Ther* 5(3):235–40+ sp '70. * (*PA* 44:19036)
18. EUBANKS, JOHN LLOYD. *The Relationship of Mental Age to Visual Memory and Word Analysis in Eight, Nine, and Ten Year Old Children of Selected Intellectual Levels.* Doctor's thesis, University of Alabama (University, Ala.), 1970. (*DAI* 31:5196A)
19. LEWIS, FRANKLIN D.; BELL, D. BRUCE; AND ANDERSON, ROBERT P. "Reading Retardation: A Bi-Racial Comparison." *J Read* 13(6):433–6, 474–8 Mr '70. *
20. POWELL, WILLIAM R., AND DUNKELD, COLIN G. "Validity of the IRI Reading Levels." *El Engl* 48(6):637–42 O '71. *

CUMULATIVE NAME INDEX

Anderson, R. P.: 19   Long, D. J.: 6
Attea, M.: 11   Maxey, E. J.: 16
Bell, D. B.: 19   Maxwell, J.: *rev,* 5:660
Bond, G. L.: *rev,* 2:1533   Mitchell, M. K.: 7
Burns, B.: 4   Monroe, M.: *rev,* 1:1098
Della-Piana, G.: 8   Olson, A. V.: 13–4
Duffy, G. B.: 3   Powell, W. R.: 20
Dunkeld, C. G.: 20   Robinson, H. M.: *rev,* 4:561
Durrell, D. D.: 1   Ruzicka, W. R.: 12
Early, G. H.: 17   Sharpe, T. M.: 17
Eubanks, J. L.: 18   Sheldon, W. D.: 5
Flower, R. M.: 12   Spache, G. D.: 2; *rev,* 5:660
Hatch, S.: 5   Tinker, M. A.: *rev,* 2:1533
Herlin, W. R.: 9   Trela, T. M.: 15
Krippner, S.: 10   Viehweg, R.: 12
Lewis, F. D.: 19

[1629]

Gates-McKillop Reading Diagnostic Tests. Grades 2–0 to 6–0; 1926–62; revision of *Gates Reading Diagnostic Tests;* 28 scores: omissions, additions, repetitions, mispronunciation (reversals, partial reversals, total reversals, wrong beginnings, wrong middle, wrong ending, wrong in several parts, total), oral reading total, words–flash presentation, words–untimed presentation, phrases–flash presentation, recognizing and blending common word parts, giving letter sounds, naming capital letters, naming lower-case letters, recognizing the visual form of sounds (nonsense words, initial letters, final letters, vowels), auditory blending, spelling, oral vocabulary, syllabication, auditory discrimination; Arthur I. Gates and Anne S. McKillop; Teachers College Press. *

For additional information and reviews by N. Dale Bryant and Gabriel M. Della-Piana, see 6:824 (2 references); for a review by George D. Spache of the earlier edition, see 5:662; for a review by Worth J. Osburn, see 4:563 (2 references); for a review by T. L. Torgerson, see 3:510 (3 references). For excerpts from related book reviews, see 4:564 (2 excerpts).

REFERENCES THROUGH 1971

1–3. See 3:510.
4–5. See 4:563.
6–7. See 6:824.
8. WILSON, FRANK Y.; BURKE, AGNES; AND FLEMMING, CECILE WHITE. "Sex Differences in Beginning Reading in a Progressive School." *J Ed Res* 32:570–82 Ap '39. * (*PA* 13:4386)
9. RUSSELL, DAVID H. "A Diagnostic Study of Spelling Readiness." *J Ed Res* 37:276–83 D '43. * (*PA* 18:1534)
10. MURRAY, CAROL-FAITH. *A Concurrent Validity Study of the Silent Reading Diagnostic Tests and the Gates Reading Diagnostic Tests.* Master's thesis, San Diego State College (San Diego, Calif.), 1959.
11. ATTEA, MARY. *A Comparison of Three Diagnostic Reading Tests.* Doctor's thesis, State University of New York (Buffalo, N.Y.), 1966. (*DA* 27:1530A)
12. TRELA, THADDEUS M. "What Do Diagnostic Reading Tests Diagnose?" *El Engl* 43:370–2 Ap '66. *
13. BOND, GUY L., AND DYKSTRA, ROBERT. "The Cooperative Research Program in First-Grade Reading Instruction." *Read Res Q* 2:5–142 su '67. * (*PA* 42:4557)
14. BOEHNLEIN, MARY MAHER. *A Structure-of-Intellect Analysis of Two Diagnostic Reading Tests.* Doctor's thesis, Kent State University (Kent, Ohio), 1969. (*DAI* 31:212A)

Diagnostic Reading Tests

15. NURSS, JOANNE R. "A Diagnostic Comparison of Two Third Grade Reading Classes," pp. 42–54. In *Reading Difficulties: Diagnosis, Correction, and Remediation*. Edited by William K. Durr. Newark, Del.: International Reading Association, 1970. Pp. vii, 276. *

16. HORN, WILLIAM ANTHONY. *An Investigation of Language and Reading Abilities of Educable Mentally Retarded and Normal Students in Rural and Urban Areas*. Doctor's thesis, West Virginia University (Morgantown, W.Va.), 1971. *(DAI* 32:6249A)

17. MYKLEBUST, HELMER R.; BANNOCHIE, MARGARET N.; AND KILLEN, JAMES R. Chap. 9, "Learning Disabilities and Cognitive Processes," pp. 213–51. In *Progress in Learning Disabilities*, Vol. 2. Edited by Helmer R. Myklebust. New York: Grune & Stratton, Inc., 1971. Pp. ix, 404. *

18. POWELL, WILLIAM R., AND DUNKELD, COLIN G. "Validity of the IRI Reading Levels." *El Engl* 48(6):637–42 O '71. *

CUMULATIVE NAME INDEX

Attea, M.: 11
Bannochie, M. N.: 17
Boehnlein, M. M.: 14
Bond, E.: 2
Bond, G. L.: 13
Bryant, N. D.: *rev, 6:824*
Burke, A.: 8
Collins, E. M.: 4
Della-Piana, G. M.: *rev, 6: 824*
Dunkeld, C. G.: 18
Dykstra, R.: 13
Flemming, C. W.: 8
Gates, A. I.: 1–3, 5
Halpin, A.: 2
Horan, K.: 2

Horn, W. A.: 16
Karlsen, B.: 7
Killen, J. R.: 17
Murray, C. F.: 7, 10
Myklebust, H. R.: 17
Nurss, J. R.: 15
Osburn, W. J.: *rev, 4:563*
Powell, W. R.: 18
Russell, D. H.: 2, 6, 9
Shaffer, L. F.: *exc, 4:564*
Spache, G. D.: *rev, 5:662*
Tinker, M. A.: *exc, 4:564*
Torgerson, T. L.: *rev, 3:510*
Trela, T. M.: 12
Wilson, F. Y.: 8

[1630]

★**Gillingham-Childs Phonics Proficiency Scales.** Grades 1–12; 1966–73; GCPPS; for use in a phonics training program, especially programs using the book entitled *Remedial Training for Children With Specific Disability in Reading, Spelling, and Penmanship;* 2 series; Educators Publishing Service, Inc. *

a) SERIES I: BASIC READING AND SPELLING. 1966–70; 17 subtest scores in each of 2 areas: reading, spelling; Anna Gillingham, Bessie W. Stillman, and Sally B. Childs.

b) SERIES II: ADVANCED READING. 1970–73; 20 subtest scores; Sally B. Childs and Ralph de S. Childs.

[1631]

Group Diagnostic Reading Aptitude and Achievement Tests. Grades 3–9; 1939; 15 scores: reading (paragraph understanding, speed), word discrimination (vowels, consonants, reversals, additions and omissions), arithmetic, spelling, visual ability (letter memory, form memory), auditory ability (letter memory, discrimination and orientation), motor ability (copying text, crossing out letters), vocabulary; Marion Monroe and Eva Edith Sherman; C. H. Nevins Printing Co. *

For additional information, see 6:825.

REFERENCES THROUGH 1971

1. WITHERSPOON, Y. T. "The Measurement of Indian Children's Achievement in the Academic Tool Subjects."*J Am Indian Ed* 1:5–9 My '62. *

2. GOLDEN, NANCY E., AND STEINER, SHARON R. "Auditory and Visual Functions in Good and Poor Readers." *J Learn Dis* 2(9):476–81 S '69. * *(PA* 45:6666)

3. KLINE, CARL L., AND LEE, NORMA. "A Transcultural Study of Dyslexia: Analysis of Reading Disabilities in 425 Chinese Children Simultaneously Learning to Read and Write in English and in Chinese: A Preliminary Report." *B Orton Soc* 19:67–81 '69. * *(PA* 47:1622)

CUMULATIVE NAME INDEX

Golden, N. E.: 2
Kline, C. L.: 3
Lee, N.: 3

Steiner, S. R.: 2
Witherspoon, Y. T.: 1

[1632]

★**Group Phonics Analysis.** Reading level grades 1–3; 1971; GPA; no scores, 11 areas: numbers, letters, consonants, alphabetization, vowels, short sounds, long vowel sounds in words, vowel digraph rule, final e rule, open and closed syllables, syllabification; Edward Fry; Dreier Educational Systems, Inc. *

[1633]

★**LRA Standard Mastery Tasks in Language.** Grades 1, 2; 1970; 2 levels; Donald E. P. Smith, Judith M. Smith, and Raymond Cabot (*a*); Learning Research Associates, Inc. *

a) PRIMARY 1. Grade 1; 2 scores: letter matching, sound matching.

b) PRIMARY 2. Grade 2; 5 scores: letter naming, letter writing, word naming, word writing, word attack.

[1634]

McCullough Word-Analysis Tests. Grades 4–6; 1962–63, c1960–63; MWAT; 10 scores: phonetic (initial blends and digraphs, phonetic discrimination, matching letters to vowel sounds, sounding whole words, interpreting phonetic symbols, total), structural (dividing words into syllables, root words in affixed forms, total), total; Constance M. McCullough; Personnel Press. *

For additional information and a review by Larry A. Harris, see 7:719 (2 references); for reviews by Emery P. Bliesmer and Albert J. Harris, see 6:826.

REFERENCES THROUGH 1971

1–2. See 7:719.

3. FARR, ROGER, AND ROELKE, PATRICIA. "Measuring Subskills of Reading: Intercorrelations Between Standardized Reading Tests, Teachers' Ratings, and Reading Specialists' Ratings." *J Ed Meas* 8(1):27–32 sp '71. * *(PA* 46:5464)

CUMULATIVE NAME INDEX

Benson, J. P.: 1
Bliesmer, E. P.: *rev, 6:826*
Farr, R.: 3
Harris, A. J.: *rev, 6:826*

Harris, L. A.: *rev, 7:719*
McCall, R. A.: 2
McCall, R. B.: 2
Roelke, P.: 3

[1635]

★**The McGuire-Bumpus Diagnostic Comprehension Test.** Reading levels grades 2.5–3, 4–6; 1971–72; MBDCT; although designed as part of the Croft Inservice Program: Reading Comprehension Skills, the test may be used independently; 4 tests (spirit masters for local duplicating), 12 scores listed below; "mastery" (defined as 2 or fewer errors on each 12-item test) on previous test required before administering Tests B, C, and D; Marion L. McGuire and Marguerite J. Bumpus; Croft Educational Services, Inc. *

a) TEST A, LITERAL READING. 4 scores: recognizing stated details, translation of details, recognizing pattern words, recognizing the main idea.

b) TEST B, INTERPRETIVE READING. 3 scores: getting implied details, finding pattern clues, inferring the main idea.

c) TEST C, ANALYTIC READING. 3 scores: determining the main question, selecting a suitable hypothesis, distinguishing relevant and irrelevant details.

d) TEST D, CRITICAL READING. 2 scores: selecting a criterion as a basis for evaluation, making a judgment based on the criterion.

[1636]

★**Phonics Criterion Test.** Reading level grades 1–3; 1971; PCT; no scores, 99 phoneme grapheme correspondences in 14 areas: easy consonants, short vowels, long and silent vowels, difficult consonants, consonant digraphs, consonant second sounds, schwa sounds, long vowel digraphs, vowel plus r, broad o, diphthongs, difficult vowels, consonant blends, consonant exceptions; Edward Fry; Dreier Educational Systems, Inc. *

[1637]

Phonics Knowledge Survey. Grades 1–6; 1964; PKS; no scores other than item scores in 15 areas: names of letters, consonant sounds, vowels, vowel generalizations, sounds of c and g, sounds of y, consonant blends, digraphs, vowel combinations, vowels followed by r, sounds of qu, sounds of oo, sounds of x, beginning consonant combinations, syllabication; Dolores Durkin and Leonard Meshover; Teachers College Press. *

For additional information and reviews by Ira E. Aaron and Edward B. Fry, see 7:720.

[1638]

Phonovisual Diagnostic Test. Grades 3–12; 1949–58; formerly called *Phonovisual Diagnostic Spelling Test;* a spelling test "designed to discover phonetic weaknesses"; 13 scores: words incorrect, consonant errors (initial, final, 9 blends), vowel errors; Lucille D. Schoolfield and Josephine B. Timberlake; Phonovisual Products, Inc. *

For additional information and reviews by Charles M. Brown and George D. Spache, see 6:829.

[1639]

★Prescriptive Reading Inventory. Grades 1.5–2.5, 2.0–3.5, 3.0–4.5, 4.0–6.5; 1972; PRI; 34 to 42 scores (mastery, needs review, non-mastery) covering 90 reading objectives; 84 percent of the scores based on 3 and 4 item tests; mastery interpreted as 66⅔ and 75 percent correct on 3 and 4 item tests, respectively; also identifies "students who have failed to show mastery of 60 per cent of the objectives" in any of the following categories: recognition of sounds and symbols (grades 1.5–3.5 only), phonic analysis, structural analysis, translation, literal comprehension, interpretive comprehension (2 categories), critical comprehension; 4 levels; CTB/McGraw-Hill. *
a) RED BOOK, LEVEL A. Grades 1.5–2.5; 34 scores (each score based on 3–5 items): recognition of sounds and symbols (2 scores), phonic analysis (4 scores), structural analysis (9 scores), translation (7 scores), literal comprehension (3 scores), interpretive comprehension (7 scores), critical comprehension (2 scores).
b) GREEN BOOK, LEVEL B. Grades 2.0–3.5; 41 scores (each score based on 3–6 items): recognition of sounds and symbols (2 scores), phonic analysis (8 scores), structural analysis (8 scores), translation (7 scores), literal comprehension (3 scores), interpretive comprehension (12 scores), critical comprehension (1 score).
c) BLUE BOOK, LEVEL 3. Grades 3.0–4.5; 42 scores (each score based on 3–8 items): phonic analysis (4 scores), structural analysis (8 scores), translation (8 scores), literal comprehension (5 scores), interpretive comprehension (13 scores), critical comprehension (4 scores).
d) ORANGE BOOK, LEVEL 4. Grades 4.0–6.5; 38 scores (each score based on 3–6 items): phonic analysis (3 scores), structural analysis (5 scores), translation (6 scores), literal comprehension (3 scores), interpretive comprehension (12 scores), critical comprehension (9 scores).

[1640]

★Prescriptive Reading Inventory Interim Tests. Grades 1.5–2.5, 2.0–3.5, 3.0–4.5, 4.0–6.5; 1973; experimental edition; primarily for use after study of a behavior prescribed by the *Prescriptive Reading Inventory;* 163 scores (mastery, needs review, non-mastery) covering 90 reading objectives; mastery interpreted as 80 percent correct; also identifies "students who failed to show mastery of at least 60% of the objec-

tives" in any of the following categories: recognition of sounds and symbols (grades 1.5–3.5 only), phonic analysis, structural analysis, translation, literal comprehension, interpretive comprehension, critical comprehension; 4 levels; CTB/McGraw-Hill. *
a) A (RED) LEVEL. Grades 1.5–2.5; 25 skills tests, 10 comprehension tests in 3 booklets; no manual.
b) B (GREEN) LEVEL. Grades 2.0–3.5; 25 skills tests, 19 comprehension tests in 6 booklets.
c) C (BLUE) LEVEL. Grades 3.0–4.5; 20 skills tests, 27 comprehension tests in 8 booklets.
d) D (ORANGE) LEVEL. Grades 4.0–6.5; 14 skills tests, 28 comprehension tests in 8 booklets.

[1641]

Primary Reading Profiles. Grades 1–2, 2–3; 1953–68; PRP; 6 scores: reading aptitude, auditory association, word recognition, word attack, reading comprehension, total; James B. Stroud, Albert N. Hieronymus, and Paul McKee; Houghton Mifflin Co. *

For additional information and reviews by James R. Hobson and Verna L. Vickery, see 5:665.

REFERENCES THROUGH 1971

1. BREEN, JOSEPH MICHAEL. *Differential Prediction of Intermediate Grade Skills Achievement From Primary Grade Aptitude and Achievement Measures.* Doctor's thesis, University of Connecticut (Storrs, Conn.), 1965. (*DA* 26:5260)
2. BARZ, ANITA I. *Prediction of Secondary School Achievement From Primary Grade Aptitude and Achievement Measures.* Doctor's thesis, St. John's University (Jamaica, N.Y.), 1969. (*DAI* 30:3271A)

CUMULATIVE NAME INDEX

Barz, A. I.: 2　　　　　　Hobson, J. R.: *rev*, 5:665
Breen, J. M.: 1　　　　　Vickery, V. L.: *rev*, 5:665

[1642]

★Reading Diagnostic Probes. Grades 2–5, 3–9; 1970; also called SARA (Systems Approach to Reading Analysis); 2 tests; manuals by Stella B. Warner and William R. Myers; American Testing Co. *
a) READING DIAGNOSTIC PROBE I: PROBES INTO AUDITORY DISCRIMINATION, PHONETIC ANALYSIS. Grades 2–5; SARA I; 9 scores: consonants (initial, final), rhyming elements, blends (initial, digraphs, final), vowels (long, short, digraph); test by the Diagnostic Reading Committee, revision by Stella B. Warner.
b) READING DIAGNOSTIC PROBE II: PROBE INTO STRUCTURAL ANALYSIS. Grades 3–9; SARA II; 12 scores: inflectional endings (3 scores), compound words, contractions, inflectional changes (3 scores), alphabetical order, prefixes, suffixes, syllabication; test by Ronald A. Herbert and William R. Myers, revision by Stella B. Warner.

[1643]

Roswell-Chall Diagnostic Reading Test of Word Analysis Skills. Grades 2–6; 1956–59; no scores, 6 areas: single consonant sounds, consonant combinations, short vowels, rule of silent e, vowel combinations, syllabication; 1959 tests identical with tests copyrighted 1956; 1959 manual essentially the same as 1956 manual; Florence G. Roswell and Jeanne S. Chall; Essay Press, Inc. *

For additional information and reviews by Ira E. Aaron and Emmett Albert Betts, see 6:831 (1 reference); for a review by Byron H. Van Roekel, see 5:667.

REFERENCES THROUGH 1971

1. See 6:831.
2. MCCALL, ROZANNE A., AND MCCALL, ROBERT B. "Comparative Validity of Five Reading Diagnostic Tests." *J Ed Res* 62(7):329–33 Mr '69. *
3. CLAYMAN, DEBORAH P. GOLDWEBER. *The Relationship of Error and Correction of Error in Oral Reading to Visual-Form*

Perception and Word Attack Skills. Doctor's thesis, Columbia University (New York, N.Y.), 1971. (*DAI* 32:5033A)

CUMULATIVE NAME INDEX

Aaron, I. E.: *rev*, 6:831
Betts, E. A.: *rev*, 6:831
Chall, J. S.: 1
Clayman, D. P. G.: 3
McCall, R. A.: 2
McCall, R. B.: 2
Van Roekel, B. H.: *rev*, 5:667

[1644]

Reading Skills Diagnostic Test. Grades 2–8; 1967; 9 scores: letter identification, letter-sound identification, phonetic sounds, phonetic words, inconsistent words, consistent phrases, inconsistent phrases, letters in context, words in context; Richard H. Bloomer; Brador Publications, Inc. *

REFERENCES THROUGH 1971

1. BLOOMER, RICHARD H. "Reading Patterns of the Rejected Child." *Read Teach* 22(4):320–4+ Ja '69. *

CUMULATIVE NAME INDEX

Bloomer, R. H.: 1

[1645]

★**SPIRE Individual Reading Evaluation.** Grades 1–6, 4–10; 1969–71; SPIRE (Student Problem Individual Reading Evaluation); 2 tests: diagnostic reading evaluation, quick placement test; 8 scores: 3 diagnostic scores (individual word recognition, oral reading, silent reading), 2 quick placement scores (individual word recognition, reading) and 3 derived scores (instructional level, frustration level, independent level); 2 levels; Harvey Alpert and Alvin Kravitz; New Dimensions in Education, Inc. *
a) [SPIRE 1.] Grades 1–6; 1969–70.
b) SPIRE 2. Grades 4–10; 1971.

[1646]

The Schonell Reading Tests. Ages 5–15, 6–9, 7–11, 9–13; 1942–55; 7 tests; Fred J. Schonell; Oliver & Boyd [Scotland]. *
a) TEST R1, GRADED WORD READING TEST. Ages 5–15; also called *Graded Reading Vocabulary Test.*
b) TEST R2, SIMPLE PROSE READING TEST. Ages 6–9; also called *My Dog Test.*
c) TEST R3, SILENT READING TEST A. Ages 7–11.
d) TEST R4, SILENT READING TEST B. Ages 9–13.
e) TEST R5, TEST OF ANALYSIS AND SYNTHESIS OF WORDS CONTAINING COMMON PHONIC UNITS. *Out of print.*
f) TEST R6, TEST OF DIRECTIONAL ATTACK ON WORDS. *Out of print.*
g) TEST R7, VISUAL WORD DISCRIMINATION TEST. *Out of print.*
For additional information and a review by R. W. McCulloch, see 5:651 (4 references); for a review by M. L. Kellmer Pringle, see 4:552 (3 references); for a review by Edith I. M. Thomson, see 3:499.

REFERENCES THROUGH 1971

1–3. See 4:552.
4–7. See 5:651.
8. JONES, W. R. "The Influence of Reading Ability in English on the Intelligence Test Scores of Welsh-Speaking Children." *Brit J Ed Psychol* 23:114–20 F '53. * (*PA* 28:4835)
9. PITTS, R., AND SIMON, A. "A Psychological and Educational Study of a Group of Male Prisoners." *Brit J Ed Psychol* 24:106–21 Je '54. * (*PA* 29:2748)
10. SCHMIDT, W. H. O., AND MILLER, W. B. "A Standardisation of Three Reading Tests and a Survey of Reading Abilities in Primary Schools in Durban and Pietermaritzburg." *J Social Res* (South Africa) 6:99–111 D '55. *
11. KEATS, J. A. "The Difficulty of Available Word Recognition Tests for Queensland Children." *Austral J Ed* 2:168–70 N '58. *
12. MEDDLETON, G. "Overlap in Test Scores and Its Relation to Remedial Reading." *Slow Learning Child* (Australia) 6:68–76 N '59. *
13. CURR, W., AND GOURLAY, N. "The Effect of Practice on Performance in Scholastic Tests." *Brit J Ed Psychol* 30:155–67 Je '60. *

14. LEWIS, D. G. "Differences in Attainment Between Primary-Schools in Mixed-Language Areas: Their Dependence on Intelligence and Linguistic Background." *Brit J Ed Psychol* 30:63–70 F '63. *
15. POTTS, ERIC. "A Factorial Study of the Relationship Between the Child's Vocabulary and His Reading Progress at the Infants' Stage." Abstract. *Brit J Ed Psychol* 30:84–6 F '60. *
16. LOVELL, K.; JOHNSON, E.; AND PLATTS, D. "A Summary of a Study of the Reading Ages of Children Who Had Been Given Remedial Teaching." *Brit J Ed Psychol* 32:66–71 F '62. * (*PA* 37:1955)
17. ANDREWS, R. J. "Some Comments on the Use of Standardised Word Reading Tests." *Slow Learning Child* (Australia) 11:176–84 Mr '65. * (*PA* 39:15207)
18. FRANSELLA, FAY, AND GERVER, DAVID. "Multiple Regression Equations for Predicting Reading Age From Chronological Age and WISC Verbal I.Q." *Brit J Ed Psychol* 35:86–9 F '65. * (*PA* 39:10818)
19. LINFOOT, K. W. "An Investigation of the Word Order and Difficulty Level in Schonell's Graded Word Recognition Test (R.1)." *Slow Learning Child* (Australia) 13:158–63 Mr '67. * (*PA* 42:14500)
20. COCHRANE, R. G.; ELKINS, J.; AND RICHMOND, DAWN M. "Analysis of Fourth Grade Testing." *Slow Learning Child* (Australia) 16(3):131–42 N '69. * (*PA* 44:18351)
21. LOCKYER, LINDA, AND RUTTER, MICHAEL. "A Five- to Fifteen-Year Follow-up Study of Infantile Psychosis: 3, Psychological Aspects." *Brit J Psychiatry* 115(525):865–82 Ag '69. * (*PA* 44:10847)
22. BOOKBINDER, G. E. "Variations in Reading Test Norms." *Ed Res* (England) 12(2):99–105 F '70. *
23. O'KELLY, E. "A Method for Detecting Slow Learning Juniors." *Ed Res* (England) 12(2):135–9 F '70. *
24. ELKINS, J. "Some Recent Queensland Norms for Widely Used Standardized Tests." *Slow Learning Child* (Australia) 18(3):142–7 N '71. *
25. YOUNG, DENNIS, AND STIRTON, MARGARET E. "G.W.R. Test Equivalences and Reading Ages." *Remedial Ed* (England) 6(3):7–8 N '71. *

CUMULATIVE NAME INDEX

Andrews, R. J.: 17
Bookbinder, G. E.: 22
Cochrane, R. G.: 20
Curr, W.: 13
Elkins, J.: 20, 24
Fransella, F.: 18
Gerver, D.: 18
Gourlay, N.: 13
Johnson, E.: 16
Jones, W. R.: 8
Keats, J. A.: 11
Lewis, D. G.: 14
Linfoot, K. W.: 19
Lockyer, L.: 21
Lovell, K.: 16
McCulloch, R. W.: *rev*, 5:651
Meddleton, G.: 12
Miller, W. B.: 10
Neale, M. D.: 7
O'Kelly, E.: 23
Pitts, R.: 9
Platts, D.: 16
Potts, E.: 15
Pringle, M. L. K.: 7; *rev*, 4:552
Richmond, D. M.: 20
Rutter, M.: 21
Schmidt, W. H. O.: 10
Schonell, F. E.: 3, 6
Schonell, F. J.: 1–6
Simon, A.: 9
Stirton, M. E.: 25
Thomson, E. I. M.: *rev*, 3:499
Young, D.: 25

[1647]

Silent Reading Diagnostic Tests. Grades 2–6; 1955–70; SRDT; 17 scores based upon 8 tests: words in isolation (test 1), words in context (2), total right (1, 2), initial errors (1, 2), middle errors (1, 2), ending errors (1, 2), orientation errors (1, 2), total errors (1, 2), total omitted (1, 2), visual-structural (3), syllabication (4), word synthesis (5), total right (3, 4, 5), beginning sounds (6), ending sounds (7), vowel and consonant sounds (8), total right (6, 7, 8); Guy L. Bond, Bruce Balow, and Cyril J. Hoyt; Lyons & Carnahan. *

For additional information and reviews by N. Dale Bryant and Roy A. Kress, see 7:722 (7 references); for reviews by Emery P. Bliesmer and Albert J. Kingston of the original edition, see 6:832 (1 reference).

REFERENCES THROUGH 1971

1. See 6:832.
2–8. See 7:722.
9. REYNOLDS, MAYNARD CLINTON. "A Study of the Relationships Between Auditory Characteristics and Specific Silent Reading Abilities." *J Ed Res* 46:439–49 F '53. * (*PA* 28:1492)
10. GLORFELD, PATRICIA. *The Relationship of Word Recognition Deficiencies as Measured by the Silent Reading Diagnostic Tests to the Reading Achievement of Seventh Graders.* Master's thesis, Northern Illinois University (DeKalb, Ill.), 1966.
11. SAMPLE, MELVIN LEON. *A Study of the Relationship of*

Visual Discrimination to the Recall of Words Taught by Visual Method Among Thirty Elementary School Children. Master's thesis, East Tennessee State University (Johnson City, Tenn.), 1966.

CUMULATIVE NAME INDEX

Benz, D. A.: 3, 5	Murray, C. F.: 1–2
Bliesmer, E. P.: *rev*, 6:832	Plattor, E. E.: 8
Bryant, N. D.: *rev*, 7:722	Reynolds, M. C.: 9
Glorfeld, P.: 10	Rosemier, R. A.: 3, 5
Karlsen, B.: 1	Sample, M. L.: 11
Kingston, A. J.: *rev*, 6:832	Todd, E. A.: 6
Kress, R. A.: *rev*, 7:722	Trela, T. M.: 4
McCall, R. A.: 7	Woestehoff, E. S.: 8
McCall, R. B.: 7	

[1648]

★**Sipay Word Analysis Tests.** Grades 2–12; 1974, c1973–74; SWAT; designed to measure oral reading decoding skills in 1 or more of 3 areas: visual analysis, phonic analysis, visual blending; 2 types of scores based on following criteria: "specific strengths and weaknesses" scores (can or probably can perform the skill [68–100% correct], may be able to [51–67% correct], cannot or probably cannot [0–50% correct]), "performance objective" scores (based on at least 95% correct [some examiners may choose to use a lower standard]); 17 tests; Edward R. Sipay; Educators Publishing Service, Inc. *
a) SURVEY TEST. May be administered to help decide which of following tests to administer.
b) TEST 1: LETTER NAMES.
c) TEST 2: SYMBOL-SOUND ASSOCIATION: SINGLE LETTERS.
d) TEST 3: SUBSTITUTION: SINGLE LETTERS.
e) TEST 4: CONSONANT-VOWEL-CONSONANT TRIGRAMS.
f) TEST 5: INITIAL CONSONANT BLENDS AND DIGRAPHS.
g) TEST 6: FINAL CONSONANT BLENDS AND DIGRAPHS.
h) TEST 7: VOWEL COMBINATIONS.
i) TEST 8: OPEN-SYLLABLE GENERALIZATION.
j) TEST 9: FINAL SILENT E GENERALIZATION.
k) TEST 10: VOWEL VERSATILITY.
l) TEST 11: VOWELS PLUS R.
m) TEST 12: SILENT CONSONANTS.
n) TEST 13: VOWEL SOUNDS OF Y.
o) TEST 14: VISUAL ANALYSIS.
p) TEST 15: VISUAL BLENDING.
q) TEST 16: CONTRACTIONS.

[1649]

Standard Reading Inventory. Grades 1–7; 1966, c1963–66; SRI; 4 scores (independent reading level, minimum instructional level, maximum instructional level, frustration level), 6–9 subtest scores (vocabulary in isolation, vocabulary in context, oral word recognition errors, total oral errors, recall after oral reading, recall after silent reading, total comprehension, oral speed, silent speed) at each of 11 reading levels (pre-primer, 1¹, 1², 2¹, 2², 3¹, 3², 4, 5, 6, 7), and various ratings and checklists; Robert A. McCracken; Klamath Printing Co. *
For additional information and a review by H. Alan Robinson, see 7:723 (8 references).

REFERENCES THROUGH 1971
1–8. See 7:723.
9. FROESE, VICTOR. "Word Recognition Tests: Are They Useful Beyond Grade Three." *Read Teach* 24(5):432–8 F '71. * (*PA* 47:11610)
10. POWELL, WILLIAM R., AND DUNKELD, COLIN G. "Validity of the IRI Reading Levels." *El Engl* 48(6):637–42 O '71. *

CUMULATIVE NAME INDEX

Blynn, C. P.: 5	Kasdon, L. M.: 4
Botel, M.: 6	Kashuba, M.: 6
Braddock, B. J.: 7	Kelly, D.: 4
Bradley, J.: 6	McCracken, R. A.: 1, 8
Caccavo, E.: 3	Mullen, N. D.: 8
Childs, F. V.: 2	Powell, W. R.: 10
Dunkeld, C. G.: 10	Robinson, H. A.: *rev*, 7:723
Froese, V.: 9	Robinson, R. V.: 7

Silent Reading Diagnostic Tests

[1650]

The Standard Reading Tests. Reading ages up to 9–0; 1958; SRT; 12 tests; J. C. Daniels and Hunter Diack; Hart-Davis Educational Ltd. [England]. *
a) TEST 1, THE STANDARD TEST OF READING SKILL.
b) TEST 2, COPYING ABSTRACT FIGURES.
c) TEST 3, COPYING A SENTENCE.
d) TEST 4, VISUAL DISCRIMINATION AND ORIENTATION TEST.
e) TEST 5, LETTER-RECOGNITION TEST.
f) TEST 6, AURAL DISCRIMINATION TEST.
g) TEST 7, DIAGNOSTIC WORD-RECOGNITION TESTS.
h) TEST 8, ORAL WORD-RECOGNITION TEST.
i) TEST 9, PICTURE WORD-RECOGNITION TEST.
j) TEST 10, SILENT PROSE-READING AND COMPREHENSION TEST.
k) TEST 11, GRADED SPELLING TEST.
l) TEST 12, GRADED TEST OF READING EXPERIENCE.
For additional information and a review by M. L. Kellmer Pringle, see 7:724; for a review by L. B. Birch, see 6:833 (1 reference).

REFERENCES THROUGH 1971
1. See 6:833.
2. McCRACKEN, ROBERT A. "A Two-Year Study of the Reading Achievement of Children Who Were Reading When They Entered First Grade." *J Ed Res* 59:207–10 Ja '66. * (*PA* 40: 6506)

CUMULATIVE NAME INDEX

Birch, L. B.: *rev*, 6:833	McCracken, R. A.: 2
Daniels, J. C.: 1	Pringle, M. L. K.: *rev*, 7:724
Diack, H.: 1	

[1651]

*Stanford Diagnostic Reading Test.** Grades 2.5–4.5, 4.5–8.5; 1966–71; SDRT; 2 levels; Bjorn Karlsen, Richard Madden, and Eric F. Gardner; Harcourt Brace Jovanovich, Inc. *
a) LEVEL 1. Grades 2.5–4.5; 1966–71; 7 scores: comprehension, vocabulary, auditory discrimination, syllabication, beginning and ending sounds, blending, sound discrimination.
b) LEVEL 2. Grades 4.5–8.5; 1966–68; 8 scores: comprehension (literal, inferential, total), vocabulary, syllabication, sound discrimination, blending, rate.
For additional information and a review by Lawrence M. Kasdon, see 7:725 (3 references).

REFERENCES THROUGH 1971
1–3. See 7:725.
4. HANNI, DONALD. *The Efficacy of a Classroom Reading Program Predicted Upon the Stanford Diagnostic Reading Test.* Master's thesis, Sonoma State College (Rohnert Park, Calif.), 1971.
5. MAHR, ILA RUTH. *An Investigation of the Empirical Validity of the Group Categories of the Stanford Diagnostic Reading Test Instructional Placement Report.* Doctor's thesis, University of Georgia (Athens, Ga.), 1971. (*DAI* 32:3792A)

CUMULATIVE NAME INDEX

Boehnlein, M. M.: 1	Kasdon, L. M.: *rev*, 7:725
Giovino, R.: 3	Mahr, I. R.: 5
Hanni, D.: 4	Shealor, D. A.: 2

[1652]

★**Swansea Test of Phonic Skills, Experimental Version.** Reading ages below 7.5; 1970–71; 6 scores: short vowels, long vowels, initial letter blends, final letter blends, miscellaneous, total; Phillip Williams assisted by Peter Congdon, Margaret Holder, and Norman Sims; published for the Schools Council Research and Development Project in Compensatory Education; Basil Blackwell, Publisher [England]. *

[1653]

*Test of Individual Needs in Reading, Seventh Edition.** Grades 1–6; 1961–71; TINR; test booklet title is *John Bidwell and the Trail to California;* 20

scores: oral reading, comprehension, rate, word analysis (use of context, words beginning alike, beginning consonants, ending consonants, consonant substitutions, speech consonants, consonant blends, reversals, long and short vowels, vowel blends, blending letter sounds, prefixes, suffixes, compound words, recognizing syllables, syllabication, total); the 1970 test involves changes in 5 items but no change in norms; Hap Gilliland; Montana Reading Publications. *

For additional information and reviews by Larry A. Harris and George D. Spache, see 7:726.

[1654]

★Test of Phonic Skills. Reading level grades kgn–3; 1971; TPS; no scores, 19 areas: phone discrimination, print discrimination, initial consonants, final consonants, initial clusters, final clusters, consonant digraphs, selected spelling patterns, long vowels, short vowels, silent -e, vowel digraphs, vocalic/ʒ/ and -r as a vowel, -r controllers, -l and -w controllers, soft or hard -c, soft or hard -g, diphthongs, syllabication principles; taped *Phone Discrimination Test* to be administered if child makes 3 or more errors on phone discrimination subtest; Kenneth J. Smith and Henry M. Truby; Harper & Row, Publishers, Inc. *

[1655]

★Wisconsin Tests of Reading Skill Development: Word Attack. Grades kgn–2, 1, 1–3, 2–4, 3–6; 1970–72; WTRSD:WA; part of the Wisconsin Design for Reading Skill Development; 6–16 "single-skill" scores at each of 5 levels; 80% mastery criterion suggested for each subtest with retesting at next higher level if a child fails not more than one subtest and retesting at next lower level if a child passes not more than one subtest; handbook and planning guide by Wayne Otto (principal investigator) and Eunice Askov; tests and manuals by Karlyn Kamm, Pamela J. Miles, Deborah M. Stewart, Virginia L. Van Blaricom (tests), and Margaret L. Harris (tests); NCS Interpretive Scoring Systems. *
a) LEVEL A. Grades kgn–2; "early readiness" level; 6 scores: rhyming words, rhyming phrases, shapes, letters and numbers, words and phrases, initial consonants.
b) TRANSITION LEVEL A-B. Grade 1; "advanced readiness or preprimer" level; selected items from Levels A and B; 7 scores: rhyming words, rhyming phrases, words and phrases, initial consonants, beginning consonants, ending consonants, consonant blends.
c) LEVEL B. Grades 1–3; "primer or first reader" level; 11 scores: beginning consonants, ending consonants, consonant blends, rhyming elements, short vowels, consonant digraphs, compound words, contractions, base words and endings, plurals, possessives.
d) LEVEL C. Grades 2–4; "second reader" level; 16 scores: consonant variants, consonant blends, long vowels, vowel plus r–a plus l–a plus w, diphthongs, long and short oo, middle vowel, 2 vowels separated, 2 vowels together, final vowel, consonant digraphs, base words, plurals, homonyms, synonyms and antonyms, multiple meanings.
e) LEVEL D. Grades 3–6; "third reader" level; 6 scores: 3-letter consonant blends, silent letters, syllabication, accent, unaccented schwa, possessives.

REFERENCES THROUGH 1971
1. MOE, ALDEN JOHN. *An Investigation of the Uniqueness of Selected Auditory Discrimination Skills Among Kindergarten Children Enrolled in Two Types of Reading Readiness Programs.* Doctor's thesis, University of Minnesota (Minneapolis, Minn.), 1971. (*DAI* 32:6295A)

CUMULATIVE NAME INDEX
Moe, A. J.: 1

[1656]

★Woodcock Reading Mastery Tests. Grades kgn–12; 1972–73; WRMT; 6 scores (letter identification, word identification, word attack, word comprehension, passage comprehension, total) plus derived scores in these same 6 areas at each of 4 levels (easy reading level [96% mastery], reading grade score [90% mastery], failure reading level [75% mastery], relative mastery of grade level); Richard W. Woodcock; American Guidance Service, Inc. *

[Out of Print Since TIP I]

MISCELLANEOUS

[1657]

Basic Sight Word Test. Grades 1–2; 1942; Edward W. Dolch; Garrard Publishing Co. *

REFERENCES THROUGH 1971
1. DOLCH, E. W. "A Basic Sight Vocabulary." *El Sch J* 36:456–60 F '36. * (*PA* 10:3164)
2. HAMMILL, BETH A. *A Comparison of Reader Levels of a First Grade Group of Children With Reading Grade Equivalents on a Standardized Reading Test.* Master's thesis, State University of Iowa (Iowa City, Iowa), 1941.
3. ECKSTEIN, CATHERINE. *Use of the Dolch Basic Sight Word List as a Measure to Determine Reader Level.* Master's thesis, State University of Iowa (Iowa City, Iowa), 1944.
4. SPARROW, JULIA. *Accomplishment on the Dolch Basic Sight Word Test as a Measure of Reader-Level.* Master's thesis, State University of Iowa (Iowa City, Iowa), 1944.
5. McBROOM, MAUDE; SPARROW, JULIA L.; AND ECKSTEIN, CATHERINE G. *A Scale for Determining the Child's Reader Level.* University of Iowa Extension Bulletin, College of Education Series, No. 35. Iowa City, Iowa: State University of Iowa, 1947. Pp. 14. *

CUMULATIVE NAME INDEX
Dolch, E. W.: 1   McBroom, M.: 5
Eckstein, C.: 3   Sparrow, J.: 4
Eckstein, C. G.: 5   Sparrow, J. L.: 5
Hammill, B. A.: 2

[1658]

Botel Reading Inventory. Grades 1–4, 1–6, 1–12; 1961–70; BRI; 4 tests; 9 scores: frustrational, instructional (placement), and free reading grade score for each of tests a, b, and d; Morton Botel; Follett Publishing Co. *
a) WORD RECOGNITION TEST. Grades 1–4; 1961–70; oral reading fluency; 8 "graded" 20-word lists described as samples of reading materials at 8 levels (PP, P, 1^2, 2^1, 2^2, 3^1, 3^2, 4+); 3 grade scores: frustration level (0–65%), instructional level (70–90%), free reading level (95–100%).
b) WORD OPPOSITES TEST. Grades 1–12; 1961–70; a vocabulary test described as "an estimate of reading comprehension"; 10 "graded" 10-word lists described as samples of reading materials at 10 levels (1, 2^1, 2^2, 3^1, 3^2, 4, 5, 6, 7–8, 9–12); 3 grade scores: frustration level (0–60%), instructional level (70–80%), free reading level (90–100%).
c) PHONICS MASTERY TEST. Grades 1–4; 1961–70; "knowledge of key word perception skills"; 3 levels of phonic skills, each level to be mastered 100% before going on to the next.
d) SPELLING PLACEMENT TEST. Grades 1–6; 1970; 5 "graded" 20-word lists described as samples from the

author's *Spelling and Writing Patterns* at 5 levels (1–2, 3, 4, 5, 6) ; 3 grade scores: frustration level (0–80%), instructional level (85–90%), independent level (95–100%).

For additional information, see 7:727 (5 references) ; for reviews by Ira E. Aaron and Charles M. Brown, see 6:834.

REFERENCES THROUGH 1971

1–5. See 7:727.
6. SCHNEIDERHAN, ROSEMARY MALMGREN. *A Correlation of Individual and Group Reading Tests.* Master's thesis, St. Cloud State College (St. Cloud, Minn.), 1963.
7. FINNEGAN, SHIRLEY BOOHER. *Relationships Between Certain Auditory Tasks and the Ability to Recode Nonsense Words.* Doctor's thesis, University of California (Berkeley, Calif.), 1971. (*DAI* 32:2400A)

CUMULATIVE NAME INDEX

Aaron, I. E.: *rev*, 6:834	Kashuba, M.: 4
Botel, M.: 3–4	McCracken, R. A.: 5
Bradley, J.: 4	Mullen, N. D.: 5
Brown, C. M.: *rev*, 6:834	Schneiderhan, R. M.: 6
Davis, M. C. E.: 1	Trela, T. M.: 2
Finnegan, S. B.: 7	

[1659]

Cumulative Reading Record, 1956 Revision. Grades 9–12 ; 1933–56 ; revision of a record by Margaret M. Skinner ; National Council of Teachers of English. *

[1660]

Durrell Listening-Reading Series. Grades 1–2, 3–6, 7–9 ; 1969–70 ; 9 scores: listening (vocabulary, sentences or paragraphs, total—these scores are referred to as "potential reading grade equivalents"), reading (vocabulary, sentences or paragraphs, total—these scores are referred to as "actual reading grade equivalents"), potential minus actual reading grade equivalents (vocabulary, sentences or paragraphs, total—these scores are referred to as "differential" scores) ; 3 levels; Donald D. Durrell, Mary T. Hayes (*a*), and Mary B. Brassard (*b*) ; Harcourt Brace Jovanovich, Inc. *

a) PRIMARY LEVEL. Grades 1–2.
b) INTERMEDIATE LEVEL. Grades 3–6.
c) ADVANCED LEVEL. Grades 7–9.

For additional information and reviews by John R. Bormuth and George D. Spache, see 7:728 (3 references).

REFERENCES THROUGH 1971

1–3. See 7:728.
4. SMITH, CHARLES LEROY. *A Comparison of Selected Standardized Reading Test Scores and Informal Reading Inventory Results at Intermediate Grade Levels.* Doctor's thesis, University of Northern Colorado (Greeley, Colo.), 1970. (*DAI* 31:4046A)
5. BROUSSEAU, PAULA JOAN. *A Study of the Interrelationships of Reading Ability, Listening Ability and Intelligence of Ninth and Tenth Grade Students.* Doctor's thesis, Southern Illinois University (Carbondale, Ill.), 1971. (*DAI* 32:4828A)
6. WADE, VERN JOSEPH. *A Comparison of Selected Standardized Reading Test Scores and Informal Reading Inventory Results at Eighth Grade Level.* Doctor's thesis, University of Northern Colorado (Greeley, Colo.), 1971. (*DAI* 32:3853A)

CUMULATIVE NAME INDEX

Bormuth, J. R.: *rev*, 7:728	Hayes, M. T.: 1
Brassard, M. B.: 2	Smith, C. L.: 4
Brousseau, P. J.: 5	Spache, G. D.: *rev*, 7:728
Durrell, D. D.: 3	Wade, V. J.: 6

[1661]

Durrell-Sullivan Reading Capacity and Achievement Tests. Grades 2.5–4.5, 3–6 ; 1937–45 ; 3–5 scores: word meaning, paragraph meaning, total, spelling (optional), written recall (optional) ; 2 tests; Donald D. Durrell and Helen Blair Sullivan ; Harcourt Brace Jovanovich, Inc. *

a) READING CAPACITY TEST.
b) READING ACHIEVEMENT TEST.

For additional information and a review by James Maxwell, see 5:661 (5 references) ; for a review by Helen M. Robinson, see 4:562 (4 references) ; for reviews by William S. Gray and Marion Monroe and an excerpted review of the original edition, see 1:1099.

REFERENCES THROUGH 1971

1–4. See 4:562.
5–9. See 5:661.
10. WELSH, GEORGE BYRON. *An Investigation of Some Predictive Factors in Auding Ability.* Doctor's thesis, University of Pittsburgh (Pittsburgh, Pa.), 1954. (*DA* 14:2407)
11. CARROW, MARY ARTHUR. "Linguistic Functioning of Bilingual and Monolingual Children." *J Speech & Hearing Disorders* 22:371–80 S '57. * (*PA* 33:4258)
12. RUSSELL, DAVID H. "Auditory Abilities and Achievement in Spelling in the Primary Grades." *J Ed Psychol* 49:315–9 D '58. * (*PA* 36:2KL15R)
13. HARVEY, JOHN C. *Study of the Durrell-Sullivan Reading Capacity Test as a Measure of Intelligence.* Master's thesis, Sacramento State College (Sacramento, Calif.), 1961.
14. TOUSSAINT, ISABELLA HASTIE. *Interrelationships of Reading, Listening, Arithmetic, and Intelligence and Their Implications.* Doctor's thesis, University of Pittsburgh (Pittsburgh, Pa.), 1961. (*DA* 22:819)
15. CLELAND, DONALD L., AND TOUSSAINT, ISABELLA H. "The Interrelationships of Reading, Listening, Arithmetic Computation and Intelligence." *Read Teach* 15:228–31 Ja '62. *
16. YOUNG, FRANCIS A. "Reading, Measures of Intelligence and Refractive Errors." *Am J Optom* 40:257–64 My '63. *
17. SINGER, HARRY. "Validity of the Durrell-Sullivan Reading Capacity Test." *Ed & Psychol Meas* 25:479–91 su '65. * (*PA* 39:15268)
18. WENGER, THELMA WOOD. *A Study of the Effect on Listening Test Scores of Change in Methods of Presentation.* Doctor's thesis, University of Virginia (Charlottesville, Va.), 1967. (*DA* 28:2466A)
19. WILLIAMS, FERN C. *A Comparison of Scores on the Durrell-Sullivan Reading Capacity Test and Auditory Comprehension Paragraphs of the Diagnostic Reading Scales.* Master's thesis, University of Texas (Austin, Tex.), 1967.
20. BRAGG, JANE K. *Six Predictive Reading Capacity Formulas With Actual Reading Achievement for Children in Grades 3–6.* Master's thesis, Rutgers—The State University (New Brunswick, N.J.), 1971.
21. GRUEN, RONALD STEVEN. *Prediction of End-of-Year Reading Achievement for First and Third Grade Pupils.* Doctor's thesis, Pennsylvania State University (University Park, Pa.), 1971. (*DAI* 32:6198A)

CUMULATIVE NAME INDEX

Alden, C. L.: 3	Owen, J. C.: 9
Bliesmer, E. P.: 6, 8	Pugh, G. S.: 4
Bond, G. L.: 7	Robinson, H. M.: *rev*, 4:562
Bragg, J. K.: 20	Russell, D. H.: 12
Carrow, M. A.: 11	Singer, H.: 17
Cleland, D. L.: 15	Sullivan, H. B.: 1, 3
Clymer, T. W.: 7	Tireman, L. S.: 2
Durrell, D. D.: 3	Toussaint, I. H.: 14–5
Gray, W. S.: *rev*, 1:1099	Welsh, G. B.: 10
Gruen, R. S.: 21	Wenger, T. W.: 18
Harvey, J. C.: 13	Williams, F. C.: 19
Maxwell, J.: *rev*, 5:661	Woods, V. E.: 2
Miller, V. J.: 5	Young, F. A.: 16
Monroe, M.: *rev*, 1:1099	

[1662]

Dyslexia Schedule. Children having reading difficulties and first grade entrants ; 1968–69 ; an 89-item questionnaire to be completed by parents ; score based on 23 discriminating items, 21 of which are published separately under the title *School Entrance Check List* (SECL) for screening use ; John McLeod ; Educators Publishing Service, Inc. *

For additional information and a review by Martin Kling, see 7:729 (3 references).

REFERENCES THROUGH 1971

1–3. See 7:729.

CUMULATIVE NAME INDEX

Kling, M.: *rev*, 7:729	McLeod, J.: 1–3

[1663]

Individual Reading Placement Inventory, Field Research Edition. Youths and adults with reading levels up to grade 7 ; 1969 ; IRPI ; 7 grade level scores: independent reading (words, paragraphs), instructional reading (words, paragraphs), frustration (words, paragraphs), present language potential; Edwin H. Smith and Weldon G. Bradtmueller; Follett Publishing Co. *

For additional information and reviews by Edward B. Fry and Albert J. Kingston, see 7:730.

REFERENCES THROUGH 1971
1. WUNDERLICH, ELAINE, AND BRADTMUELLER, MARY. "Teacher Estimates of Reading Levels Compared With IRPI Instructional Level Scores." *J Read* 14(5):303–8 F '71. *

CUMULATIVE NAME INDEX
Bradtmueller, M.: 1   Kingston, A. J.: *rev*, 7:730
Fry, E. B.: *rev*, 7:730   Wunderlich, E.: 1

[1664]
★The Instant Word Recognition Test. Reading level grades 1–4; 1971; IWRT; Edward Fry; Dreier Educational Systems, Inc. *

[1665]
★Inventory of Teacher Knowledge of Reading. Elementary school teachers and college students in methods courses; 1972, c1971; A. Sterl Artley and Veralee B. Hardin; Lucas Brothers Publishers. *

[1666]
Learning Methods Test. Grades kgn, 1, 2, 3; 1954–55; LMT; comparative effectiveness of four methods of teaching new words: visual, phonic, kinesthetic, combination; Robert E. Mills; Mills School. *

For additional information and reviews by Thomas E. Culliton, Jr. and William Eller, see 6:836 (1 reference).

REFERENCES THROUGH 1971
1. See 6:836.
2. MILLS, ESTHER BROWNELL. *Relationships Between Psycholinguistic Abilities of Educable Mentally Retarded Pupils and the Effectiveness of Four Instructional Approaches in the Language Arts.* Doctor's thesis, University of Maryland (College Park, Md.), 1965. (*DA* 27:145A)
3. SAMPLE, MELVIN LEON. *A Study of the Relationship of Visual Discrimination to the Recall of Words Taught by Visual Method Among Thirty Elementary School Children.* Master's thesis, East Tennessee State University (Johnson City, Tenn.), 1966.
4. LONG, RUBY DAVIDSON. *Learning Mode Preference of Educable Mentally Retarded Children.* Doctor's thesis, University of Missouri (Columbia, Mo.), 1967. (*DA* 29:151A)

CUMULATIVE NAME INDEX
Coleman, J. C.: 1   Long, R. D.: 4
Culliton, T. E.: *rev*, 6:836   Mills, E. B.: 2
Eller, W.: *rev*, 6:836   Sample, M. L.: 3

[1667]
★National Test of Basic Words. Grades 1–5; 1970; NTBW; "service words" from preprimer to first reader difficulty arranged in 9 levels; next higher level administered when child has 4 or less errors in a 20-item set; 80% mastery suggested for entire test before instruction in second grade reader; manual by Sue Harrison Halpern; American Testing Co. *

[1668]
OC Diagnostic Syllabizing Test. Grades 4–6; 1960–62; formerly called *OC Diagnostic Syllable Test;* Katherine O'Connor; O'Connor Reading Clinic Publishing Co. *

For additional information, see 6:827.

[1669]
Phonics Test for Teachers. Reading methods courses; 1964; PTT; no scores other than item scores in 10 areas: syllabication, vowels, vowel generalizations, sounds of c and g, sounds of y, digraphs, diphthongs, sounds of oo, sounds of qu, sounds of x; Dolores Durkin; Teachers College Press. *

For additional information and reviews by Ira E. Aaron and Gerald G. Duffy, see 7:721 (2 references).

REFERENCES THROUGH 1971
1–2. See 7:721.

CUMULATIVE NAME INDEX
Aaron, I. E.: *rev*, 7:721   Gibson, G. C.: 1
Duffy, G. G.: *rev*, 7:721   Tyre, B. B.: 2

[1670]
The Reader Rater With Self-Scoring Profile. Ages 15 and over; 1959–65; self-administered survey of reading skills; designed for use either with the Rapid Reading Kit or separately; 12 scores: speed, comprehension, reading habits, reading for details, reading for inferences, reading for main ideas and adjusting speed, summarizing, skimming, recall of information read, unspeeded vocabulary, speeded vocabulary, total; Better Reading Program, Inc. *

For additional information, see 6:837.

[1671]
The Reader's Inventory. Entrants to a reading improvement course for secondary and college students and adults; 1963; information concerning a student's reading interests, attitudes, habits, visual conditions, educational and vocational background, and what he expects to gain from a reading course; George D. Spache and Stanford E. Taylor; Educational Developmental Laboratories, Inc. *

For additional information and reviews by John J. Geyer and David M. Wark, see 7:733.

[1672]
Reading Eye II. Grades 1, 2, 3, 4, 5, 6, 7–8, 9–16 and adults; 1959–69; a portable electronic eye-movement recorder with test materials; 5 reading component scores (fixations, regressions, average span of recognition, average duration of fixation, rate with comprehension), 3 ratings (grade level of reading, relative efficiency, directional attack), and 2 diagnostic categories (visual adjustment, general adjustment to reading); Stanford E. Taylor, Helen Frackenpohl, and James L. Pettee; Educational Developmental Laboratories, Inc. *

For additional information and a review by John J. Geyer, see 7:734 (9 references); for reviews by Arthur S. McDonald and George D. Spache of an earlier model, see 6:838 (3 references). For an excerpt from a related book review, see 6:B478.

REFERENCES THROUGH 1971
1–3. See 6:838.
4–12. See 7:734.
13. SMITH, PETER B. "Eye Movements and Rapid Reading Reconsidered." *Yearb Nat Read Conf* 14:203–9 '65. *
14. TAYLOR, STANFORD E. "Rebuttal to 'Eye Movements and Reading Reconsidered.'" *Yearb Nat Read Conf* 14:210–7 '65. *
15. MANN, GLORIA T. "Eye Movements of Children in Reading English and Hebrew." *J Exp Ed* 36:60–8 su '68. *
16. DIZNEY, HENRY; RANKIN, RICHARD; AND JOHNSTON, JAMES. "Eye-Movement Fixations in Reading as Related to Anxiety in College Females." *Percept & Motor Skills* 28:851–4 Je '69. * (*PA* 43:17454)
17. HANNAH, BETTY RUPARD. *Visual Behavior of Children With Nystagmus While Reading Orally.* Doctor's thesis, University of Arizona (Tucson, Ariz.), 1971. (*DAI* 32:3821A)

CUMULATIVE NAME INDEX
Beyer, D. A.: 9   Mann, G. T.: 15
Brickner, C. A.: 10   Mickish, V. L.: 11
Bryant, N. D.: *exc*, 6:B478   Rankin, R.: 16
Dizney, H.: 16   Ryan, H. J. L.: 8
Erdley, R. R.: 5   Seifert, J. G.: 6
Evans, R. M.: 7   Singer, C. R.: 12
Geyer, J. J.: *rev*, 7:734   Smith, P. B.: 13
Hannah, B. R.: 17   Spache, G. D.: 2; *rev*, 6:838
Johnston, J.: 16   Taylor, S. E.: 1, 3–4, 14
McDonald, A. S.: *rev*, 6:838

[1673]
Reading Versatility Test. Grades 5–8, 8–12, 12–16; 1961–68; RVT; 7 scores: rate and comprehension (fiction, nonfiction, skimming, scanning) and 3 reading rate ratios (fiction/nonfiction, skimming/fiction, scanning/fiction); Arthur S. McDonald, M. Alodia, Harold M. Nason, George Zimny, and James A. Byrne; Educational Developmental Laboratories, Inc. *
For additional information and a review by John J. Geyer, see 7:735

REFERENCES THROUGH 1971
1. See 6:839.
2. McDONALD, ARTHUR S. "Reading Versatility Twelve Years Later." *Yearb Nat Read Conf* 20:168–73 '71. *

CUMULATIVE NAME INDEX
Geyer, J. J.: *rev*, 7:735   Theophemia, M.: 1
McDonald, A. S.: 2

[1674]
Roswell-Chall Auditory Blending Test. Grades 1–4; 1963; Florence G. Roswell and Jeanne S. Chall; Essay Press, Inc. *
For additional information and reviews by Ira E. Aaron and B. H. Van Roekel, see 6:830 (2 references).

REFERENCES THROUGH 1971
1–2. See 6:830.
3. BROWN, LILY. *Auditory Blending Ability as a Perceptual Process and Its Relationship to Reading Success*. Master's thesis, Bank Street College of Education (New York, N.Y.), 1964.
4. ALSHAN, LEONARD M. "Reading Readiness and Reading Achievement." *Proc Ann Conv Int Read Assn* 10:312–3 '65. *
5. HANESIAN, HELEN. *The Relationship of Auditory Abilities to First Grade Reading Achievement*. Doctor's thesis, Columbia University (New York, N.Y.), 1966. (*DA* 27:2883A)
6. BRUININKS, ROBERT H. "Auditory and Visual Perceptual Skills Related to the Reading Performance of Disadvantaged Boys." *Percept & Motor Skills* 29(1):179–86 Ag '69. * (*PA* 44:2835)
7. McNINCH, GEORGE HAAS WILEY. *The Relationships Between Selected Perceptual Factors and Measured First Grade Reading Achievement*. Doctor's thesis, University of Georgia (Athens, Ga.), 1970. (*DAI* 31:3965A)
8. GOLDMAN, RONALD, AND DIXON, SARAH D. "The Relationship of Vocal-Phonic and Articulatory Abilities." *J Learn Dis* 4(5):251–6 My '71. * (*PA* 47:9457)
9. McNINCH, GEORGE. "Auditory Perceptual Factors and Measured First-Grade Reading Achievement." *Read Res Q* 6(4):472–92 su '71. * (*PA* 47:11769)

CUMULATIVE NAME INDEX
Aaron, I. E.: *rev*, 6:830   Goldman, R.: 8
Alshan, L. M.: 4   Hanesian, H.: 5
Blumenthal, S. H.: 2   Huset, M. K.: 1
Brown, L.: 3   McNinch, G.: 9
Bruininks, R. H.: 6   McNinch, G. H. W.: 7
Chall, J.: 2   Roswell, F. G.: 2
Dixon, S. D.: 8   Van Roekel, B. H.: *rev*, 6:830

[1675]
Word Discrimination Test. Grades 1–8; 1958; WDT; no manual; Chas. B. Huelsman, Jr.; Miami University Alumni Association. *
For additional information, see 7:736 (2 references).

REFERENCES THROUGH 1971
1–2. See 7:736.

CUMULATIVE NAME INDEX
Huelsman, C. B.: 1   Robinson, H. A.: 2

[1676]
★**Word Recognition Test.** Preschool to age 8.5; 1970; WRT; Clifford Carver; University of London Press Ltd. [England]. *

[Out of Print Since TIP I]
Eye Movement Camera, T:1686
Functional Readiness Questionnaire for School and College Students (status unknown), R:151, 6:835
SRA Reading Checklist, R:158

ORAL

[1677]
★**Concise Word Reading Tests.** Ages 7–12; 1969; R. J. Andrews; Teaching and Testing Resources [Australia]. *

[1678]
Flash-X Sight Vocabulary Test. Grades 1–2; 1961; 2 scores: sight vocabulary, experience vocabulary; George D. Spache and Stanford E. Taylor; Educational Developmental Laboratories, Inc. *
For additional information, see 6:841.

[1679]
Gilmore Oral Reading Test. Grades 1–8; 1951–68; 3 scores: accuracy, comprehension, rate; John V. Gilmore and Eunice C. Gilmore; Harcourt Brace Jovanovich, Inc. *
For additional information and reviews by Albert J. Harris and Kenneth J. Smith, see 7:737 (17 references); for reviews by Lydia A. Duggins and Maynard C. Reynolds of the original edition, see 5:671.

REFERENCES THROUGH 1971
1–17. See 7:737.
18. CARROW, MARY ARTHUR. "Linguistic Functioning of Bilingual and Monolingual Children." *J Speech & Hearing Disorders* 22:371–80 S '57. * (*PA* 33:4258)
19. CORAH, NORMAN L.; ANTHONY, E. JAMES; PAINTER, PAUL; STERN, JOHN A.; AND THURSTON, DONALD. "Effects of Perinatal Anoxia After Seven Years." *Psychol Monogr* 79(3):1–34 '65. * (*PA* 39:9776)
20. MUMPOWER, D. L., AND RIGGS, SHARON. "Overachievement in Word Accuracy as a Result of Parental Pressure." *Read Teach* 23(8):741–7 My '70. * (*PA* 45:3073)
21. FLEISCHMANN, LILLIAN S. *A Comparison of the Gilmore Oral Reading Test and the Metropolitan Achievement Test in Reading for Grade Placement*. Master's thesis, Sacramento State College (Sacramento, Calif.), 1971.
22. POWELL, WILLIAM R., AND DUNKELD, COLIN G. "Validity of the IRI Reading Levels." *El Engl* 48(6):637–42 O '71. *

CUMULATIVE NAME INDEX
Anthony, E. J.: 19   Kirby, C. L.: 13
Bond, G. L.: 9   Kirby, C. L. L.: 10
Brown, J. L.: 11   Ladd, E. M.: 2
Carrow, M. A.: 18   Means, C. E.: 12
Clark, H. C.: 4   Mumpower, D. L.: 20
Corah, N. L.: 19   Painter, P.: 19
Dollarhide, R. S.: 6   Patty, D. L.: 7
Duggins, L. A.: *rev*, 5:671   Powell, W. R.: 22
Dunkeld, C. G.: 22   Reynolds, M. C.: *rev*, 5:671
Dykstra, R.: 9   Riddle, W. T.: 3
Fleischmann, L. S.: 21   Riggs, S.: 20
Garlock, J.: 6   Sabatino, D. A.: 14–6
Gilmore, J. V.: 1   Simpson, R. L.: 17
Harris, A. J.: *rev*, 7:737   Smith, K. J.: *rev*, 7:737
Hayden, D. L.: 14–6   Stern, J. A.: 19
Higgins, C.: 5   Thurston, D.: 19
Hopkins, K. D.: 6   Trela, T. M.: 8

[1680]
Graded Word Reading Test. Ages 5 and over; 1921–67; GWRT; pronunciation; 2 tests; 1967 manual identical with manual copyrighted 1938 except for addition of revised norms ['54] for *a*; P. E. Vernon; University of London Press Ltd. [England]. *
a) THE BURT (REARRANGED) WORD READING TEST. 1921–67; adaptation for Scottish schools of *Burt's Graded Word Reading Test* ('21).
b) GRADED WORD READING TEST. 1938; for use in Scottish schools.
For additional information, see 7:738 (3 references).

REFERENCES THROUGH 1971
1–3. See 7:738.
4. VERNON, P. E. "A Study of the Norms and the Validity of Certain Mental Tests at a Child Guidance Clinic: Part II." *Brit J Ed Psychol* 7:115–37 Je '37. * (*PA* 11:4827)
5. VERNON, PHILIP E. *The Standardization of a Graded Word Reading Test*. Publications of the Scottish Council for Research in Education, No. 12. London: University of London Press Ltd., 1938. Pp. 43. * (*PA* 18:2282)

6. SCHMIDT, W. H. O., AND MILLER, W. B. "A Standardisation of Three Reading Tests and a Survey of Reading Abilities in Primary Schools in Durban and Pietermaritzburg." *J Social Res* (South Africa) 6:99–111 D '55 *

7. KEATS, J. A. "The Difficulty of Available Word Recognition Tests for Queensland Children." *Austral J Ed* 2:168–70 N '58. *

8. POTTS, ERIC. "A Factorial Study of the Relationship Between the Child's Vocabulary and His Reading Progress at the Infants' Stage." Abstract. *Brit J Ed Psychol* 30:84–6 F '60. *

9. LOVELL, K.; JOHNSON, E.; AND PLATTS, D. "A Summary of a Study of the Reading Ages of Children Who Had Been Given Remedial Teaching." *Brit J Ed Psychol* 32:66–71 F '62. * (*PA* 37:1955)

10. YOUNG, DENNIS, AND STIRTON, MARGARET E. "G.W.R. Test Equivalences and Reading Ages." *Remedial Ed* (England) 6(3):7–8 N '71. *

CUMULATIVE NAME INDEX

Bannon, W. J.: 2
Johnson, E.: 9
Keats, J. A.: 7
Lovell, K.: 9
Miller, W. B.: 6
Payne, J. F.: 3
Phillips, C. J.: 2

Platts, D.: 9
Potts, E.: 8
Schmidt, W. H. O.: 6
Stirton, M. E.: 10
Vernon, P. E.: 1, 4–5
Young, D.: 10

[1681]

Gray Oral Reading Test. Grades 1–16 and adults; 1963–67; GORT; William S. Gray; edited by Helen M. Robinson; Bobbs-Merrill Co., Inc.*

For additional information and reviews by Emery P. Bliesmer, Albert J. Harris, and Paul R. Lohnes, see 6:842.

REFERENCES THROUGH 1971

1. PATTY, DELBERT LEE. *A Comparison of Standardized Oral Reading Test Scores and Informal Reading Inventory Scores.* Doctor's thesis, Ball State University (Muncie, Ind.), 1965. (*DA* 26:5302)

2. KIRBY, CLARA LOU LAUGHLIN. *A Comparison of Scores Obtained on Standardized Oral and Silent Reading Tests and a Cloze Test.* Doctor's thesis, Ball State University (Muncie, Ind.), 1967. (*DA* 28:4512A)

3. STAFFORD, CLARICE M. SALLI. *An Analysis of the Types of Oral Reading Errors in a Sample of Fourth Grade Pupils.* Doctor's thesis, Wayne State University (Detroit, Mich.), 1967. (*DA* 29:1375A)

4. KASDON, LAWRENCE M. "Oral Versus Silent-Oral Diagnosis." *Proc Ann Conv Int Read Assn* 13(4):86–92 '68. *

5. COTLER, SHELDON. "The Effects of Positive and Negative Reinforcement and Test Anxiety on the Reading Performance of Male Elementary School Children." *Genetic Psychol Monogr* 80(1):29–50 Ag '69. * (*PA* 44:5700)

6. HARDIN, VERALEE B., AND AMES, WILBUR S. "A Comparison of the Results of Two Oral Tests." *Read Teach* 22(4):329–34 Ja '69. *

7. KASDON, LAWRENCE M. "Oral Versus Silent-Oral Diagnosis," pp. 86–92. In *Reading Diagnosis and Evaluation.* Edited by Dorothy L. De Boer. Newark, Del.: International Reading Association, 1970. Pp. vi, 138. *

8. KIRBY, CLARA L. "Using the Cloze Procedure as a Testing Technique," pp. 68–77. In *Reading Diagnosis and Evaluation.* Edited by Dorothy L. De Boer. Newark, Del.: International Reading Association, 1970. Pp. vi, 138. *

9. CLAYMAN, DEBORAH P. GOLDWEBER. *The Relationship of Error and Correction of Error in Oral Reading to Visual-Form Perception and Word Attack Skills.* Doctor's thesis, Columbia University (New York, N.Y.), 1971. (*DAI* 32:5033A)

10. HARDY, MIRIAM P.; MELLITS, DAVID; AND WILLIG, SHARON N. "Reading: A Function of Language Usage." *Johns Hopkins Med J* 129(1):43–53 Jl '71. *

11. POWELL, WILLIAM R., AND DUNKELD, COLIN G. "Validity of the IRI Reading Levels." *El Engl* 48(6):637–42 O '71. *

CUMULATIVE NAME INDEX

Ames, W. S.: 6
Bliesmer, E. P.: *rev*, 6:842
Clayman, D. P. G.: 9
Cotler, S.: 5
Dunkeld, C. G.: 11
Hardin, V. B.: 6
Hardy, M. P.: 10
Harris, A. J.: *rev*, 6:842
Kasdon, L. M.: 4, 7

Kirby, C. L.: 8
Kirby, C. L. L.: 2
Lohnes, P. R.: *rev*, 6:842
Mellits, D.: 10
Patty, D. L.: 1
Powell, W. R.: 11
Stafford, C. M. S.: 3
Willig, S. N.: 10

[1682]

Holborn Reading Scale. Ages 5.5–11.0; 1948; 2 scores: word recognition, comprehension; A. F. Watts; George G. Harrap & Co. Ltd. [England]. *

For additional information and a review by Stanley

Nisbet, see 5:635 (1 reference); for a review by C. M. Fleming, see 4:537.

REFERENCES THROUGH 1971

1. See 5:635.

2. SAMPSON, OLIVE C. "Written Composition at 10 Years as an Aspect of Linguistic Development." *Brit J Ed Psychol* 34: 143–50 Je '64. * (*PA* 39:4958)

3. PARKER, D. H. H. "Musical Perception and Backwardness in Reading." *Ed Res* (England) 12(3):244–6 Je '70. * (*PA* 47: 1754)

CUMULATIVE NAME INDEX

Fleming, C. M.: *rev*, 4:537
Nisbet, S.: *rev*, 5:635
Parker, D. H. H.: 3

Sampson, O. C.: 2
Watts, A. F.: 1

[1683]

***Neale Analysis of Reading Ability, Second Edition.** Ages 6–13; 1957–66; NARA; 3 scores (accuracy, comprehension, rate of reading) plus 3 optional supplementary tests (names and sounds of letters, auditory discrimination through simple spelling, blending and recognition of syllables); Marie D. Neale; Macmillan Education Ltd. [England]. *

For additional information, reviews by M. Alan Brimer and Magdalen D. Vernon, and an excerpted review, see 6:843.

REFERENCES THROUGH 1971

1. SAMPSON, OLIVE C. "Reading Skill at Eight Years in Relation to Speech and Other Factors." *Brit J Ed Psychol* 32:12–7 F '62. *

2. NETLEY, C.; RACHMAN, S.; AND TURNER, R. K. "The Effect of Practice on Performance in a Reading Attainment Test." *Brit J Ed Psychol* 35:1–8 F '65. * (*PA* 39:10837)

3. LEVY, PHILIP. "The Reliability of a Difference Between Two Scores: A Re-Examination of Assumptions." *J Clin Psychol* 22:357–9 Jl '66. * (*PA* 40:10632)

4. GOOCH, STAN; LEVY, PHILIP; AND PRINGLE, M. L. KELLMER. "The Interaction of Four Status Variables and Measured Intelligence and Their Effect on Attainment in Two Junior Schools." *Ed Sci* (England) 2:37–46 O '67. *

5. YULE, WILLIAM. "Predicting Reading Ages on Neale's Analysis of Reading Ability." *Brit J Ed Psychol* 37:252–5 Je '67. * (*PA* 41:15822)

6. BOOKBINDER, G. E. "Variations in Reading Test Norms." *Ed Res* (England) 12(2):99–105 F '70. *

7. ANDREWS, R. J., AND ELKINS, J. "The Use of the Neale Analysis of Reading Ability With Lower Grade Primary School Children." *Slow Learning Child* (Australia) 18(1):3–7 Mr '71. * (*PA* 47:1571)

CUMULATIVE NAME INDEX

Andrews, R. J.: 7
Bookbinder, G. E.: 6
Brimer, M. A.: *rev*, 6:843
Elkins, J.: 7
Gooch, S.: 4
Levy, P.: 3–4
Netley, C.: 2

Pringle, M. L. K.: 4
Rachman, S.: 2
Sampson, O. C.: 1
Turner, R. K.: 2
Vernon, M. D.: *rev*, 6:843
Yule, W.: 5

[1684]

★**Oral Reading Criterion Test.** Reading level grades 1–7; 1971; ORCT; 3 reading level scores: independent, instructional, frustration; Edward Fry; Dreier Educational Systems, Inc. *

[1685]

Oral Word Reading Test. Ages 7–11; 1952; A. E. Fieldhouse; New Zealand Council for Educational Research [New Zealand]. *

For additional information and reviews by S. A. Rayner and D. K. Wheeler, see 5:674.

REFERENCES THROUGH 1971

1. KEATS, J. A. "The Difficulty of Available Word Recognition Tests for Queensland Children." *Austral J Ed* 2:168–70 N '58. *

2. MCCREARY, J. R. "Reading Tests With Maori Children." *N Zeal J Ed Studies* 1(1–2):40–50 '66. *

CUMULATIVE NAME INDEX

Keats, J. A.: 1
McCreary, J. R.: 2

Rayner, S. A.: *rev*, 5:674
Wheeler, D. K.: *rev*, 5:674

[1686]

★**Reading Miscue Inventory.** Grades 1–7; 1972; RMI; "deviations" (errors) are called *"miscues* to suggest that they are not random errors but, in fact, are cued by the thought and language of the reader"; tape recorder must be used to record the examinee's reading of a 15–20 minute selection (difficult enough to produce at least 25 errors) and the immediate retelling of what he read; 6 **s**cores: retelling score, percentage breakdown of oral reading errors with comprehension loss (none, partial, total), percentage breakdown of oral reading errors (excluding omissions) with sound similarity (high, some, none) to text, percentage breakdown of oral reading errors (excluding omissions) with graphic similarity (high, some, none) to text, percentage breakdown of oral reading errors (excluding omissions) with grammatical function similarity (identical, indeterminate, different) to text, percentage breakdown of 18 possible oral reading error patterns—corrected, grammatically acceptable, semantically acceptable—characterizing the examinee's ability (strength, partial strength, weakness, overcorrection) in "using the grammatical and meaning cueing systems"; Yetta M. Goodman and Carolyn L. Burke; Macmillan Publishing Co., Inc. *

REFERENCES THROUGH 1971

1. HITTLEMAN, DANIEL RICHARD. *The Readability of Subject Matter Material Re-Written on the Basis of Students' Oral Reading Mis-Cues.* Doctor's thesis, Hofstra University (Hempstead, N.Y.), 1971. (*DAI* 32:5534A)

CUMULATIVE NAME INDEX

Hittleman, D. R.: 1

[1687]

★**St. Lucia Graded Word Reading Test.** Grades 2–7; 1969; R. J. Andrews; Teaching and Testing Resources [Australia]. *

[1688]

Slosson Oral Reading Test. Grades 1–8 and high school; 1963; SORT; no manual; Richard L. Slosson; Slosson Educational Publications, Inc. *

For additional information, see 6:844.

REFERENCES THROUGH 1971

1. DUGGAN, MARY DIONYSIA. *A Study of the Relation Between the Slosson Reading and Intelligence Tests and Other Standardized Tests at the Second Grade Level.* Master's thesis, Cardinal Stritch College (Milwaukee, Wis.), 1968.
2. KEANY, MARY. *A Study of the Relation Between the Slosson Reading and Intelligence Tests and Other Standardized Tests at the Sixth Grade Level.* Master's thesis, Cardinal Stritch College (Milwaukee, Wis.), 1968.
3. KILDUFF, CAROL T. *A Study of the Relation Between the Slosson Reading and Intelligence Tests and Other Standardized Tests at the Fourth Grade Level.* Master's thesis, Cardinal Stritch College (Milwaukee, Wis.), 1969.
4. BRADDOCK, BETTY J., AND ROBINSON, RUTH V. *A Correlation of Slosson Oral Reading Test With the McCracken Word Recognition Subtest.* Master's thesis, Glassboro State College (Glassboro, N.J.), 1970.
5. STUHLER, AGNES M. *An Experimental Study of the Relation Between the Slosson Reading and Intelligence Tests and Other Standardized Tests at the First Grade Level.* Master's thesis, Cardinal Stritch College (Milwaukee, Wis.), 1970.

CUMULATIVE NAME INDEX

Braddock, B. J.: 4   Kilduff, C. T.: 3
Duggan, M. D.: 1   Robinson, R. V.: 4
Keany, M.: 2   Stuhler, A. M.: 5

[1689]

Standardized Oral Reading Check Tests. Grades 1–2, 2–4, 4–6, 6–8; 1923–55; 2 scores: rate, accuracy; William S. Gray; Bobbs-Merrill Co., Inc. *

For additional information and reviews by David H. Russell and Clarence R. Stone, see 2:1570 (1 reference).

REFERENCES THROUGH 1971

1. See 2:1570.
2. STONE, CLARENCE R. "Validity of Tests in Beginning Reading." *El Sch J* 43:361–5 F '43. * (*PA* 18:2605)
3. MACLATCHY, JOSEPHINE H. "An Oral-Reading Test as an Appraisal of Progress." *Ed Res B* 28:230–9 D 7 '49. *
4. ROBINSON, HELEN M. Chap. 5, "Visual Efficiency and Reading," pp. 90–112. In *Clinical Studies in Reading, I.* University of Chicago, Supplementary Educational Monographs, No. 68. Chicago, Ill.: University of Chicago Press, June 1949. Pp. xiv, 173. *
5. SPACHE, GEORGE. "A Comparison of Certain Oral Reading Tests." *J Ed Res* 43:441–52 F '50. * (*PA* 25:562)
6. ROBINSON, HELEN M. "Factors Related to Monocular and Binocular Reading Efficiency." *Am J Optom* 28:337–46 Jl '51. * (*PA* 26:2977)
7. SHEPHERD, EDWIN M. "Reading Efficiency of 809 Average School Children: The Effect of Reversal on Their Performance." *Am J Ophthal* 41:1029–39 Je '56. * (*PA* 31:5081)
8. HARTE, MARY LABOURE. *Anxiety and Defensiveness as Related to Measurable Intelligence and Scholastic Achievement of Selected Institutionalized Children.* Doctor's thesis, Fordham University (New York, N.Y.), 1966. (*DA* 27:2884A)

CUMULATIVE NAME INDEX

Allen, C. H.: 1   Russell, D. H.: *rev,* 2:1570
Camp, C.: 1   Shepherd, E. M.: 7
Harte, M. L.: 8   Spache, G.: 5
Maclatchy, J. H.: 3   Stone, C. R.: 2; *rev,* 2:1570
Robinson, H. M.: 4, 6

[1690]

Standardized Oral Reading Paragraphs. Grades 1–8; 1915; SORP; William S. Gray; Bobbs-Merrill Co., Inc. *

For additional information and reviews by David Kopel and Clarence R. Stone, see 2:1571 (7 references).

REFERENCES THROUGH 1971

1–7. See 2:1571.
8. GRAY, WILLIAM S. "A Co-operative Study in Reading in Eleven Cities of Northern Illinois." *El Sch J* 17:250–65 D '16. *
9. GRAY, WILLIAM S. "A Study of the Emphasis on Various Phases of Reading Instruction in Two Cities." *El Sch J* 17: 178–86 N '16. *
10. GRAY, WILLIAM SCOTT. "Methods of Testing Reading, II." *El Sch J* 16:281–98 F '16. *
11. JUDD, CHARLES HUBBARD. *Measuring the Work of the Public Schools,* pp. 124–61, 255–74. Cleveland, Ohio: The Survey Committee of the Cleveland Foundation, 1916. Pp. 290. *
12. UHL, W. L. "The Use of the Results of Reading Tests as Bases for Planning Remedial Work." *El Sch J* 17:266–75 D '16. *
13. GRAY, CLARENCE TRUMAN. *Types of Reading Ability as Exhibited Through Tests and Laboratory Experiments,* pp. 17–32. Supplementary Educational Monographs, Vol. 1, No. 5. Chicago, Ill.: University of Chicago Press, 1917. Pp. xiv, 196. *
14. WHITE, CECILE W. "A Study in Reading (Gray Oral and Silent Reading Tests) in Indiana Cities." *Ann Conf Ed Meas* 4:102–13 '17. *
15. GRAY, W. S. "A Cooperative Study of Reading in Sixteen Cities in Indiana." *Indiana Univ Studies* 5(37):1–43 Je '18. *
16. McLEOD, L. S. "The Influence of Increasing Difficulty of Reading Material Upon Rate, Errors, and Comprehension in Oral Reading." *El Sch J* 18:523–32 Mr '18. *
17. MONROE, WALTER SCOTT. *Measuring the Results of Teaching,* pp. 39–41, *passim.* Boston, Mass.: Houghton Mifflin Co., 1918. Pp. xviii, 297. *
18. WILSON, G. M., AND HOKE, KREMER J. *How to Measure,* pp. 133–43. New York: Macmillan Co., 1920. Pp. vii, 285. *
19. GATES, ARTHUR I. "An Experimental and Statistical Study of Reading and Reading Tests." *J Ed Psychol* 12:303–14, 378–91, 445–64 S, O, N '21. *
20. WALLIN, J. E. WALLACE. *The Achievement of Subnormal Children in Standardized Educational Tests.* Miami University Bulletin Series 20, No. 7. Miami, Ohio: the University, 1922. Pp. 97. *
21. MONROE, WALTER SCOTT; DeVOSS, JAMES CLARENCE; AND KELLY, FREDERICK JAMES. *Educational Tests and Measurements, Revised Edition,* pp. 135–43. Boston, Mass.: Houghton Mifflin Co., 1924. Pp. xxvii, 521. *
22. HUDSON, ALVA. "Reading Achievement, Interests and Habits of Negro Women." *J Negro Ed* 1:367–73 O '32. * (*PA* 8:3690)
23. WEISENBURG, THEODORE; ROE, ANNE; AND McBRIDE, KATHARINE E. *Adult Intelligence: A Psychological Study of Test Performances.* New York: Commonwealth Fund, 1936. Pp. xiii, 155. * (*PA* 10:3771)
24. LAWSON, JOHN R., AND AVILA, DONALD. "Comparison of Wide Range Achievement Test and Gray Oral Reading Para-

graphs Reading Scores of Mentally Retarded Adults." *Percept & Motor Skills* 14:474 Je '62. * (*PA* 37:3581)

25. DENNEHY, JOHN N. *An Experimental Study of the Influence of the Time Factor Upon the Magnitude of Score on Diagnostic Oral Reading Inventories*. Master's thesis, Central Connecticut State College (New Britain, Conn.), 1966.

26. ELDER, RICHARD D. "Oral Reading Achievement of Scottish and American Children." *El Sch J* 71(4):216–30 Ja '71. *

CUMULATIVE NAME INDEX

Avila, D.: 24	Kopel, D.: *rev*, 2:1571
Buckingham, B. R.: 6	Lawson, J. R.: 24
Dennehy, J. N.: 25	McBride, K. E.: 23
DeVoss, J. C.: 21	McLeod, L. S.: 16
Dolch, E. W.: 6	Monroe, W. S.: 3, 17, 21
Elder, R. D.: 26	Payne, C. S.: 4
Gates, A. I.: 5, 19	Roe, A.: 23
Gray, C. T.: 13	Stone, C. R.: 7; *rev*, 2:1571
Gray, W. S.: 1–2, 8–10, 15	Uhl, W. L.: 12
Hoke, K. J.: 18	Wallin, J. E. W.: 20
Hudson, A.: 22	Weisenburg, T.: 23
Judd, C. H.: 11	White, C. W.: 14
Kelly, F. J.: 21	Wilson, G. M.: 18

[Out of Print Since TIP I]

Graded Word Reading Test, Test 1, R:176
Leavell Analytical Oral Reading Test, R:179, 5:672 (2 reviews)
Oral Diagnostic Test of Word-Analysis Skills, R:170, 5:673 (2 reviews)

READINESS

[1691]

The ABC Inventory to Determine Kindergarten and School Readiness. Entrants to kgn and grade 1; 1965; Normand Adair and George Blesch; Research Concepts. *

For additional information and a review by David P. Weikart, see 7:739 (2 references).

REFERENCES THROUGH 1971

1–2. See 7:739.
3. MANSON, PAUL DIRK. *Pre-Kindergarten Readiness Testing Program Characteristics in Southern Michigan School Districts Using the ABC Inventory*. Doctor's thesis, Michigan State University (East Lansing, Mich.), 1971. (*DAI* 32:5507A)
4. SCRANTON, GARY B. *A Comparison Study of the Hess School Readiness Scale With the ABC Inventory*. Master's thesis, Millersville State College (Millersville, Pa.), 1971.

CUMULATIVE NAME INDEX

Knoll, D. B.: 1	Scranton, G. B.: 4
Lee, R. E.: 2	Weikart, D. P.: *rev*, 7:739
Manson, P. D.: 3	

[1692]

The APELL Test: Assessment Program of Early Learning Levels. Ages 4.5–7; 1969; program for identifying educational deficiencies, suggesting remedial instruction, and retesting; 16 scores: 4 pre-reading (visual discrimination, auditory discrimination, letter names, total), 4 pre-math (attributes, number concepts, number facts, total), 7 language (nouns, pronouns, verbs, adjectives, plurals, prepositions, total), total; Eleanor V. Cochran and James L. Shannon; Edcodyne Corporation. *

For additional information, see 7:740.

REFERENCES THROUGH 1971

1. PROGER, BARTON B. "The APELL Test: A Review: Assessment Program of Early Learning Levels: A Review." *J Spec Ed* 5(2):195–8 su '71. *

CUMULATIVE NAME INDEX

Proger, B. B.: 1

[1693]

Academic Readiness and End of First Grade Progress Scales. Beginning of first grade, end of first grade; 1968–69; ratings by teachers in 14–15 areas:

motor, perceptual-motor (2 scores), persistence, memory, attention, number recognition (*a*) or computational arithmetic (*b*), counting, word recognition, comprehension (*b*), vocabulary, interest in curriculum, social, humor, emotional; 2 levels; Harold F. Burks; Arden Press. *

a) ACADEMIC READINESS SCALE: END OF KINDERGARTEN OR BEGINNING FIRST GRADE. 1968; ARS.

b) END OF FIRST GRADE PROGRESS SCALE. 1969; EFGPS; no manual.

For additional information, see 7:741.

REFERENCES THROUGH 1971

1. MONAHAN, MICHAEL TIMOTHY. *Prediction of First Grade Reading Scores Utilizing Burks' Academic Readiness Scale*. Master's thesis, California State University (Long Beach, Calif.), 1971.

CUMULATIVE NAME INDEX

Monahan, M. T.: 1

[1694]

American School Reading Readiness Test, Revised. First grade entrants; 1941–64; 1964 test identical with tests copyrighted 1941 and 1955 except for changes in titles and sequence of subtests and slight changes in format and drawings; Willis E. Pratt, George W. Stouffer (1964 form), Robert V. Young (1941 and 1955 forms), and Carroll A. Whitmer (1941 and 1955 forms); Bobbs-Merrill Co., Inc. *

For additional information and reviews by Joan Bollenbacher and Helen M. Robinson, see 5:675 (3 references); for reviews by David H. Russell and Paul A. Witty, see 3:513.

REFERENCES THROUGH 1971

1–3. See 5:675.

CUMULATIVE NAME INDEX

Bollenbacher, J.: *rev*, 5:675	Robinson, H. M.: *rev*, 5:675
Delancy, E. O.: 3	Russell, D. H.: *rev*, 3:513
Pratt, W. E.: 1–2	Witty, P. A.: *rev*, 3:513

[1695]

★**Analysis of Readiness Skills: Reading and Mathematics.** Grades kgn–1; 1972, c1969–72; 6 scores: visual perception of letters, letter identification, mathematics (identification, counting, total), total; directions in English and Spanish; Mary C. Rodrigues, William H. Vogler, and James F. Wilson; Houghton Mifflin Co. *

[1696]

The Anton Brenner Developmental Gestalt Test of School Readiness. Ages 5–6; 1964; BGT; also called *Brenner Gestalt Test;* an optional rating scale provides 2 scores: achievement-ability, social-emotional; Anton Brenner; Western Psychological Services. *

For additional information and a review by Dennis J. Deloria, see 7:742 (8 references); see also 6:844a (8 references).

REFERENCES THROUGH 1971

1–8. See 6:844a.
9–16. See 7:742.

CUMULATIVE NAME INDEX

Brenner, A.: 1, 4, 9	Luttgen, G.: 6
Bushey, J. T.: 13	Ralph, J.: 7
Chasey, W. C.: 15	Ralph, J. S.: 5
Deloria, D. J.: *rev*, 7:742	Sandhu, S. S.: 8
Donnelly, F.: 11	Scandary, E. J.: 12
Falik, L. H.: 14	Svagr, V. B.: 10
Hepburn, A. W.: 11	Viewag, W. E.: 3
Hofmann, H.: 2	Worthington, J. D.: 16

[1697]

The Basic Concept Inventory, Field Research Edition. Preschool and kgn; 1967; BCI; school readiness; 4 scores: basic concepts, statement repetition

and comprehension, pattern awareness, total; Siegfried E. Engelmann; Follett Publishing Co. *

For additional information and reviews by Boyd R.
McCandless and James J. McCarthy, see 7:743 (2
references).

REFERENCES THROUGH 1971
1–2. See 7:743.

CUMULATIVE NAME INDEX

Espeseth, V. K.: 2   McCarthy, J. J.: *rev, 7:743*
Hofmeister, A.: 2 | Sears, C. R.: 1
McCandless, B. R.: *rev, 7:743*

[1698]

**Binion-Beck Reading Readiness Test for Kinder-
garten and First Grade.** Grades kgn–1; 1945; Harriet Seay Binion and Roland L. Beck; Psychometric
Affiliates. *

For additional information and reviews by Irving H.
Anderson and Paul A. Witty, see 3:514 (1 reference).

REFERENCES THROUGH 1971
1. See 3:514.

CUMULATIVE NAME INDEX

Anderson, I. H.: *rev, 3:514*   Witty, P. A.: *rev, 3:514*
Binion, H. S.: 1

[1699]

Clymer-Barrett Prereading Battery. First grade
entrants; 1966–69; CBPB; 4 scores: visual discrimination, auditory discrimination, visual-motor, total; short
screening form consisting of 2 of the 6 subtests yields
a single score; 1967 tests identical with tests copyrighted 1966; Theodore Clymer and Thomas C. Barrett; Personnel Press. *

For additional information and reviews by Roger
Farr and Kenneth J. Smith, see 7:744 (2 references).

REFERENCES THROUGH 1971
1–2. See 7:744.
3. HALL, FRANCES POULSON. *A Re-Evaluation of the Predictive
Validity of the Clymer-Barrett Pre-Reading Battery.* Master's
thesis, University of Texas (Austin, Tex.), 1971.
4. MOE, ALDEN JOHN. *An Investigation of the Uniqueness of
Selected Auditory Discrimination Skills Among Kindergarten
Children Enrolled in Two Types of Reading Readiness Programs.*
Doctor's thesis, University of Minnesota (Minneapolis, Minn.),
1971. (*DAI* 32:6295A)

CUMULATIVE NAME INDEX

Farr, R.: *rev, 7:744*   Moe, A. J.: 4
Hall, F. P.: 3   Smith, K. J.: *rev, 7:744*
Johnson, R. E.: 1–2

[1700]

The Contemporary School Readiness Test. First
grade entrants; 1970; CSRT; Clara Elbert Sauer;
Montana Reading Publications. *

For additional information and a review by Gerald G.
Duffy, see 7:745.

[1701]

★Delco Readiness Test. First grade entrants; 1970;
DRT; 3 scores: visual-motor, visual discrimination,
total; Walter M. Rhoades; Delco Readiness Test. *

[1702]

**Gates-MacGinitie Reading Tests: Readiness
Skills.** Grades kgn–1; 1939–69; revision of *Gates
Reading Readiness Tests;* catalog uses the title *Gates-
MacGinitie Readiness Skills Test;* 9 scores: listening
comprehension, auditory discrimination, visual discrimination, following directions, letter recognition, visual-
motor coordination, auditory blending, total, word
recognition; Arthur I. Gates and Walter H. Mac-
Ginitie; Teachers College Press. *

For additional information and reviews by Paul
Conrad Berg and Robert Dykstra, see 7:749 (17

references); see also 6:845 (1 reference); for a
review by F. J. Schonell of the original edition, see
4:566; for reviews by Marion Monroe Cox and Paul A.
Witty, see 3:516 (3 references); for excerpted reviews
by Austin G. Schmidt and one other, see 2:1537 (6
references).

REFERENCES THROUGH 1971
1–5. See 2:1537.
6–8. See 3:516.
9. See 6:845.
10–26. See 7:749.
27. MILLER, FLORENCE BRESSON. *Reading Readiness Tests:
Predictors of Reading Achievement.* Master's thesis, Illinois State
University (Normal, Ill.), 1964.
28. MOE, ALDEN JOHN. *An Investigation of the Uniqueness of
Selected Auditory Discrimination Skills Among Kindergarten
Children Enrolled in Two Types of Reading Readiness Programs.*
Doctor's thesis, University of Minnesota (Minneapolis, Minn.),
1971. (*DAI* 32:6295A)

CUMULATIVE NAME INDEX

Althouse, R. E.: 21   Jansky, J. J.: 16
Anastasiow, N.: 25   Johnson, C. I.: 26
Balow, I. H.: 9–10   Kerfoot, J. F.: 14
Barrett, T. C.: 12   Langford, W. S.: 16
Berg, P. C.: *rev, 7:749*   Loper, D. J.: 15
Bond, E.: 5   Miller, F. B.: 27
Bond, G. L.: 1, 5   Miller, W. D.: 19
Burke, A.: 2   Moe, A. J.: 28
Cox, M. M.: *rev, 3:516*   Norris, R. C.: 19
de Hirsch, K.: 16   Ohnmacht, F. W.: 22–3
Dykstra, R.: 13, 17; *rev, 7:*   Olson, A. V.: 22–3
  749   Russell, D. H.: 5
Everhart, R. W.: 11   Schmidt, A. G.: *exc, 2:1537*
Farr, R.: 25   Schonell, F. J.: *rev, 4:566*
Flemming, C. W.: 2   Silberberg, M.: 20, 24
Furbee, C.: 11   Silberberg, M. C.: 18
Garrison, C. G.: 2   Silberberg, N.: 20, 24
Gates, A. I.: 1, 3–6, 8   Weaver, C. H.: 11
Halpin, A.: 5   Wilson, F. T.: 2, 7
Horan, K.: 5   Witty, P. A.: *rev, 3:516*
Iversen, I.: 20, 24

[1703]

***The Gesell Developmental Tests.** Ages 5–10;
1964–71; GDT; readiness to start school; Frances L.
Ilg, Louise Bates Ames, and Jacqueline Haines (Copy
Form cards); Programs for Education. *

For additional information and excerpted reviews
by L. J. Borstelmann and Edith Meyer Taylor, see
7:750 (5 references).

REFERENCES THROUGH 1971
1–5. See 7:750.
6. KIMBELL, VALERIE W., AND KNIGHT, DAVID W. "The Performance of Two Populations on Selected Readiness Tests."
South J Ed Res 4(3):186–92 Jl '70. *
7. ANDREWS, ANN M. *The Gesell Developmental Test as a
Predictor of School Readiness.* Doctor's thesis, University of
Pennsylvania (Philadelphia, Pa.), 1971. (*DAI* 32:3082A)
8. JENSEN, ARTHUR R. "Do Schools Cheat Minority Children?" *Ed Res* (England) 14(1):3–28 N '71. * (*PA* 49:11953)
9. KAUFMAN, ALAN S. "Piaget and Gesell: A Psychometric
Analysis of Tests Built From Their Tasks." *Child Develop*
42(5):1341–60 N '71. * (*PA* 48:4592)

CUMULATIVE NAME INDEX

Ames, L. B.: 1–3   Jensen, A. R.: 8
Andrews, A. M.: 7   Kaufman, A. S.: 5, 9
Apell, R. J.: 1   Kimbell, V. W.: 6
Borstelmann, L. J.: *exc, 7:750*   Knight, D. W.: 6
Hirst, W. E.: 4   Taylor, E. M.: *exc, 7:750*
Ilg, F. L.: 1–2

[1704]

**Group Test of Reading Readiness: The Dominion
Tests.** Grades kgn, kgn–1; 1949–59; 2 editions;
Ontario Institute for Studies in Education; distributed
by Guidance Centre [Canada]. *
a) [LONG FORM.] Grades kgn–1; 1949–59; 6 scores:
discrimination of objects-symbols-words, listening-
remembering-observing, familiarity with word forms,
memory for word forms, motor coordination, total.
b) [SHORT FORM.] Kgn; 1954–55. *Out of print.*

For additional information and a review by N. Dale
Bryant, see 5:676.

Basic Concept Inventory

REFERENCES THROUGH 1971
1. SAVAGE, H. W. "Validity of the Dominion Group Test of Reading Readiness—Short Form, and Differences Among Groups of Pupils Tested." *Ont J Ed Res* 2:63–70 O '59. *

CUMULATIVE NAME INDEX
Bryant, N. D.: *rev*, 5:676   Savage, H. W.: 1

[1705]
The Harrison-Stroud Reading Readiness Profiles.
Grades kgn–1; 1949–56; 7 scores: using symbols, making visual discriminations (2 scores), using the context, making auditory discriminations, using context and auditory clues, giving the names of letters; M. Lucile Harrison and James B. Stroud; Houghton Mifflin Co. *

For additional information and a review by S. S. Dunn, see 5:677 (2 references); for a review by William S. Gray, see 4:568.

REFERENCES THROUGH 1971
1–2. See 5:677.
3. DURKIN, DOLORES. "A Case-Study Approach Toward an Identification of Factors Associated With Success and Failure in Learning to Read." *Calif J Ed Res* 11:26–33 Ja '60. * (*PA* 34:8336)
4. RALPH, JEAN. "The Brenner-Gestalt Test as a Measure of Readiness for School," pp. 87–101. In *The Inter-Institutional Seminar in Child Development: Collected Papers, 1960.* Greenfield Village, Mich.: Education Department, Henry Ford Museum, [1961]. Pp. vi, 272. *
5. DYKSTRA, ROBERT. *The Relationship Between Selected Reading Readiness Measures of Auditory Discrimination and Reading Achievement at the End of First Grade.* Doctor's thesis, University of Minnesota (Minneapolis, Minn.), 1962. (*DA* 24:195)
6. RANDECKER, HELEN. *A Study to Determine if Chronological Age, Mental Age Scores, and Reading Readiness Tests Predict the Probable Achievement in Reading of First Grade Pupils.* Master's thesis, Wisconsin State University (Whitewater, Wis.), 1963.
7. KERFOOT, JAMES FLETCHER. *The Relationship of Selected Auditory and Visual Reading Readiness Measures to First Grade Reading Achievement and Second Grade Reading and Spelling Achievement.* Doctor's thesis, University of Minnesota (Minneapolis, Minn.), 1964. (*DA* 25:1747)
8. MILLER, FLORENCE BRESSON. *Reading Readiness Tests: Predictors of Reading Achievement.* Master's thesis, Illinois State University (Normal, Ill.), 1964.
9. THACKRAY, D. V. *The Relationship Between Reading Readiness and Reading Progress.* Master's thesis, University of London (London, England), 1964. (Abstract: *Brit J Ed Psychol* 35:252–4)
10. DYKSTRA, ROBERT. "Auditory Discrimination Abilities and Beginning Reading Achievement." *Read Res Q* 1:5–34 sp '66. * (*PA* 40:11011)
11. ASHWORTH, MARY G. *An Empirical Study of the Predictive Validity of the Harrison-Stroud Reading Readiness Profiles With First Grade Pupils in the Warwick Public Schools.* Master's thesis, University of Rhode Island (Kingston, R.I.), 1967.
12. BAGFORD, JACK. "Reading Readiness Scores and Success in Reading." *Read Teach* 21:324–8 Ja '68. * (*PA* 42:17640)
13. MIEZITIS, SOLVEIGA AUSMA. *An Exploratory Study of Divergent Production in Preschoolers.* Doctor's thesis, University of Toronto (Toronto, Ont., Canada), 1968. (*DAI* 30:589A)
14. REHMSTEDT, HELEN. *The Characteristics of Underachievers in Reading According to Potentials as Indicated by Reading Readiness Scores.* Master's thesis, Wisconsin State University (Platteville, Wis.), 1968.
15. SLOBODZIAN, EVELYN BIRDSALL. *The Relationship Between Certain Readiness Measures and Reading Achievement at Level One.* Doctor's thesis, Temple University (Philadelphia, Pa.), 1968. (*DA* 29:1053A)
16. FARR, ROGER, AND ANASTASIOW, NICHOLAS. *Tests of Reading Readiness and Achievement: A Review and Evaluation,* pp. 13–5. Newark, Del.: International Reading Association, 1969. Pp. iv, 51. *
17. EGELAND, BYRON; DI NELLO, MARIO; AND CARR, DONALD. "The Relationship of Intelligence, Visual-Motor, Psycholinguistic and Reading-Readiness Skills With Achievement." *Ed & Psychol Meas* 30(2):451–8 su '70. * (*PA* 45:3056)
18. McNINCH, GEORGE. "Auditory Perceptual Factors and Measured First-Grade Reading Achievement." *Read Res Q* 6(4):472–92 su '71. * (*PA* 47:11769)
19. MOE, ALDEN JOHN. *An Investigation of the Uniqueness of Selected Auditory Discrimination Skills Among Kindergarten Children Enrolled in Two Types of Reading Readiness Programs.* Doctor's thesis, University of Minnesota (Minneapolis, Minn.), 1971. (*DAI* 32:6295A)

CUMULATIVE NAME INDEX
Anastasiow, N.: 16	McNinch, G.: 18
Ashworth, M. G.: 11	Miezitis, S. A.: 13
Bagford, J.: 12	Miller, F. B.: 8
Carr, D.: 17	Moe, A. J.: 19
Di Nello, M.: 17	Mosbo, A. O.: 1
Dunn, S. S.: *rev*, 5:667	Ralph, J.: 4
Durkin, D.: 3	Randecker, H.: 6
Dykstra, R.: 5, 10	Rehmstedt, H.: 14
Egeland, B.: 17	Slobodzian, E. B.: 15
Farr, R.: 16	Spaulding, G.: 2
Gray, W. S.: *rev*, 4:568	Thackray, D. V.: 9
Kerfoot, J. F.: 7	

[1706]
★Initial Survey Test. First grade entrants; 1970–72; IST; skills for "success in beginning primary learning"; 7 scores: language meanings, auditory ability, visual ability, letter recognition, sound-letter relationships, mathematics, total; first five subtests originally published under the title *Initial Reading Survey Test;* Marion Monroe, John C. Manning, Joseph M. Wepman, and E. Glenadine Gibb; Scott, Foresman & Co. *

[1707]
★An Inventory of Primary Skills. Grades kgn–1; 1970; IPS; administered by parent; 20 scores: self information, body identification, body spatial relations, copying designs, alphabet printing, writing numbers, symbol matching, sentence copying, counting, basic arithmetic, copying house, draw-a-man, sight vocabulary, paragraph reading, alphabet knowledge, number knowledge, class concepts, position in space concepts, descriptive concepts, total; no manual; Robert E. Valett; Lear Seigler Inc./Fearon Publishers. *

[1708]
★Kindergarten Behavioural Index: A Screening Technique for Reading Readiness. Grades kgn–1; 1972; KBI; behavior checklist; 38 scores: self identity, handedness, directionality (3 scores), visual-motor coordination (7 scores), rhythm, speech, language structure (2 scores), language sequencing (5 scores), sequential memory (4 scores), language association, behaviour (8 scores), attention (3 scores), total; Enid M. Banks; Australian Council for Educational Research [Australia]. *

[1709]
Kindergarten Evaluation of Learning Potential. Kgn; 1963–69; KELP; prediction of school success based upon the learning performance on KELP items presented as regular instructional activities throughout the kindergarten year; 4 scores: association learning, conceptualization, creative self-expression, total; John A. R. Wilson and Mildred C. Robeck; Webster Division, McGraw-Hill Book Co., Inc. *

For additional information and an excerpted review by Walter R. Borg, see 7:751 (5 references).

REFERENCES THROUGH 1971
1–5. See 7:751.

CUMULATIVE NAME INDEX
Blackman, C. T.: 4	Meredith, W. V.: 5
Borg, W. R.: *exc*, 7:751	Robeck, M. C.: 1–3
Coffey, L. W.: 5	Wilson, J. A. R.: 1–3

[1710]
★LRS Seriation Test. Ages 4–6; 1968; may be used alone or with instructional materials in The Learning Readiness System: Classification and Seriation Kit; 6 scores: 5 factor scores, total; Ralph Scott, Jerald Nelson, and Ann Mary Dunbar; Harper & Row, Publishers, Inc. *

REFERENCES THROUGH 1971
1. SCOTT, RALPH. "Perceptual Readiness as a Predictor of Success in Reading." *Read Teach* 22:36–9 O '68. *

2. SCOTT, RALPH. "Ceiling Level as a Factor in Assessing Disadvantaged Children's Abilities." *Psychol Sch* 6(3):279–82 Jl '69. * (*PA* 44:4172)
3. SCOTT, RALPH. "Perceptual Skills, General Intellectual Ability, Race, and Later Reading Achievement." *Read Teach* 23(7):660–8 Ap '70. * (*PA* 45:3069)

CUMULATIVE NAME INDEX

Scott, R.: 1–3

[1711]

Lee-Clark Reading Readiness Test. Grades kgn–1; 1931–62; LCRRT; 4 scores: letter symbols, concepts, word symbols, total; 1962 test identical with tests copyrighted 1943 and 1951 except for format and, in concepts subtest, revision of all art work and one-half of items; J. Murray Lee and Willis W. Clark; CTB/McGraw-Hill. *

For additional information and a review by Paul Conrad Berg, see 7:752 (15 references); see also 6:846 (9 references); for a review by James R. Hobson of an earlier edition, see 5:678; for reviews by Marion Monroe Cox and David H. Russell, see 3:517.

REFERENCES THROUGH 1971

1–9. See 6:846.
10–24. See 7:752.
25. PETTY, MARY CLARE. "An Experimental Study of Certain Factors Influencing Reading Readiness." *J Ed Psychol* 30:215–30 Mr '39. * (*PA* 13:4885)
26. PECK, L., AND McGLOTHLIN, L. E. "Children's Information and Success in First-Grade Reading." *J Ed Psychol* 31:653–64 D '40. * (*PA* 15:2804)
27. POTTER, MURIEL CATHERINE. "Perception of Symbol Orientation and Early Reading Success." *Teach Col Contrib Ed* 939:1–69 '49. * (*PA* 24:6511)
28. MILLER, FLORENCE BRESSON. *Reading Readiness Tests: Predictors of Reading Achievement.* Master's thesis, Illinois State University (Normal, Ill.), 1964.
29. FIFE, JANICE. *A Longitudinal Study of Relationships Among Reading Readiness Test Scores, Reading and Over-All Achievement Test Scores, and Intelligence Quotients.* Master's thesis, Brigham Young University (Provo, Utah), 1965.
30. AVRIL, DOROTHY VERNON. *An Investigation of the Relationship Between Reading Readiness Test Scores and Reading Achievement in First Grade.* Master's thesis, Glassboro State College (Glassboro, N.J.), 1966.
31. REHMSTEDT, HELEN. *The Characteristics of Underachievers in Reading According to Potentials as Indicated by Reading Readiness Scores.* Master's thesis, Wisconsin State University (Platteville, Wis.), 1968.
32. GUENTHER, GEORGIA S. *A Comparative Analysis of the Predictive Validity of Two Reading Readiness Tests and Their Subtests.* Master's thesis, Indiana University of Pennsylvania (Indiana, Pa.), 1969.
33. BLANTON, WILLIAM ELGIT. *The Interactive Effects of Perceptual Centration and Decentration on Reading Readiness and Reading Achievement at the First Grade Level.* Doctor's thesis, University of Georgia (Athens, Ga.), 1970. (*DAI* 31:5837A)
34. DICK, ROBERT MARCUS, II. *Screening Identification of First Grade Problems in an American Indian Population.* Doctor's thesis, University of North Carolina (Chapel Hill, N.C.), 1971. (*DAI* 32:1209B)
35. FRIEDRICHS, THOMAS DONNELLY. *Prediction of First Grade Teachers' Ratings and Objective Achievement From Ability and Biographical Data.* Doctor's thesis, University of North Carolina (Chapel Hill, N.C.), 1971. (*DAI* 32:1211B)
36. LOWELL, ROBERT E. "Reading Readiness Factors as Predictors of Success in First Grade Reading." *J Learn Dis* 4(10):563–7 D '71. * (*PA* 47:11782)
37. SCRUGGS, ALLIE W. *The Effect of the Fall River and Lowell Head Start Programs on Behavioral Characteristics Associated With Lower Socio-Economic Class Preschool Children.* Doctor's thesis, Boston University (Boston, Mass.), 1971. (*DAI* 32:1949A)

CUMULATIVE NAME INDEX

Anastasiow, N.: 21	Fife, J.: 29
Avril, D. V.: 30	Fitzgibbon, N. H.: 18
Barkley, M. J.: 16	Friedrichs, T. D.: 35
Berg, P. C.: *rev,* 7:752	Gale, D. F.: 12
Blanton, W. E.: 33	Guenther, G. S.: 32
Bridges, J. S.: 23	Henig, M. S.: 3
Clark, W. W.: 1	Hernandez, P. E.: 10
Cox, M. M.: *rev,* 3:517	Hobson, J. R.: *rev,* 5:678
Cunningham, W.: 11	Hopkins, K. D.: 9, 22
Dick, R. M.: 34	Koppitz, E. M.: 5
Dobson, J. C.: 8–9	Lee, D. M.: 1
Farr, R.: 21	Lee, J. M.: 1

Lessler, K.: 23	Petty, M. C.: 25
Lindy, J.: 24	Potter, M. C.: 27
Lloyd, B. A.: 13	Powell, M.: 6–7
Lloyd, R.: 13	Rehmstedt, H.: 31
Lowell, R. E.: 36	Russell, D. H.: *rev,* 3:517
McGlothlin, L. E.: 26	Schoeninger, D. W.: 23
Mardis, V.: 5	Schrager, J.: 24
Merrill, J. D.: 17	Scruggs, A. W.: 37
Miller, F. B.: 28	Seidel, H. E.: 16
Moreau, M.: 4	Sitkei, E. G.: 22
Olson, A. V.: 18	Slobodzian, E. B.: 20
Olson, N. H.: 14, 19	Stephens, T.: 5
Panther, E. E.: 15	Stith, D.: 16
Parsley, K. M.: 6–7	Wilmore, W. W.: 2
Peck, L.: 26	

[1712]

Lippincott Reading Readiness Test (Including Readiness Check List). Grades kgn–1; 1965–73; 1973 test identical with test copyrighted 1965 except for typeface and cover page; Pierce H. McLeod; J. B. Lippincott Co. *

For additional information and a review by Edward R. Sipay, see 7:753 (1 reference).

REFERENCES THROUGH 1971

1. See 7:753.

CUMULATIVE NAME INDEX

Norfleet, M. A.: 1   Sipay, E. S.: *rev,* 7:753

[1713]

McHugh-McParland Reading Readiness Test. Grades kgn–1; 1966–68; 5 scores: rhyming words, beginning sounds, visual discrimination, identifying letters, total; 1968 test identical with test copyrighted 1966; Walter J. McHugh and Myrtle McParland; Cal-State Bookstore. *

For additional information and reviews by Rebecca C. Barr and Edward R. Sipay, see 7:754.

[1714]

The Macmillan Reading Readiness Test, Revised Edition. First grade entrants; 1965–70; 6 or 7 scores: rating scale, visual discrimination, auditory discrimination, vocabulary and concepts, letter names, total for tests 1–5, visual-motor (optional), total for tests 1–6; Albert J. Harris and Edward R. Sipay; Macmillan Publishing Co., Inc. *

For additional information, see 7:755.

[1715]

Maturity Level for School Entrance and Reading Readiness. Grades kgn–1; 1950–59; revision of *School Readiness Inventory;* behavior checklist completed by teachers; 1959 test is essentially a combination of items from the two forms of the original 1950 edition; 2 scores: maturity level, reading readiness; Katharine M. Banham; American Guidance Service, Inc. *

For additional information, see 6:847; for a review by David H. Russell of the original edition, see 4:572.

REFERENCES THROUGH 1971

1. BANHAM, KATHARINE M. "Maturity Level for Reading Readiness: A Check List for the Use of Teachers and Parents as a Supplement to Reading Readiness Tests." *Ed & Psychol Meas* 18:371–5 su '58. * (*PA* 33:11013)
2. TENHOFF, MARVIN LE ROY. *Conditions Associated With Readiness for School Entrance at Selected Ages.* Doctor's thesis, University of Minnesota (Minneapolis, Minn.), 1962. (*DA* 24:150)
3. BILKA, LOISANNE PFEIFER. *An Evaluation of the Predictive Value of Certain Reading Readiness Measures as Related to Method of Instruction, Sex, and Mental Age.* Doctor's thesis, University of Pittsburgh (Pittsburgh, Pa.), 1970 (*DAI* 31:5922A)

CUMULATIVE NAME INDEX

Banham, K. M.: 1   Russell, D. H.: *rev,* 4:572
Bilka, L. P.: 3   Tenhoff, M. L.: 2

LRS Seriation Test

[1716]
Metropolitan Readiness Tests. Grades kgn-1; 1933–69; MRT; 7 or 8 scores: word meaning, listening, matching, alphabet, numbers, copying, total, draw-a-man (optional); Gertrude H. Hildreth, Nellie L. Griffiths, and Mary E. McGauvran; Harcourt Brace Jovanovich, Inc. *

For additional information and reviews by Robert Dykstra and Harry Singer, see 7:757 (124 references); for a review by Eric F. Gardner and an excerpted review by Fay Griffith, see 4:570 (3 references); for a review by Irving H. Anderson of the original edition, see 3:518 (5 references); for a review by W. J. Osburn, see 2:1552 (10 references).

REFERENCES THROUGH 1971

1–10. See 2:1552.
11–15. See 3:518.
16–18. See 4:570.
19–142. See 7:757.
143. WILSON, FRANK T. "Correlation of Information With Other Abilities and Traits in Grade I." *El Sch J* 37:295–301 D '36. * (*PA* 11:2478)
144. GRANT, ALBERT. "An Analysis of the Number Knowledge of First-Grade Pupils According to Levels of Intelligence." *J Exp Ed* 7:63–6 S '38. * (*PA* 13:1672)
145. WILMORE, WALDO W. *Relative Validity of Three Group Readiness Tests in Predicting Reading Achievement.* Master's thesis, University of Kansas (Lawrence, Kan.), 1939. (Abstract: *Univ Kan B Ed* 4:68)
146. HAMMOND, SARAH LOU, AND SKIPPER, DORA S. "Factors Involved in the Adjustment of Children Entering First Grade." *J Ed Res* 56:89–95 O '62. *
147. LOCKHART, HAZEL SHIERRY. *The Relationship of Personality With Reading Readiness.* Master's thesis, Illinois State University (Normal, Ill.), 1964.
148. MILLER, FLORENCE BRESSON. *Reading Readiness Tests: Predictors of Reading Achievement.* Master's thesis, Illinois State University (Normal, Ill.), 1964.
149. DICKERSON, MARJORIE KRAFT. *Readiness Test: Predictor of Reading Achievement in the Primary Grades.* Master's thesis, Illinois State University (Normal, Ill.), 1965.
150. DITTMAR, NANCY SIZEMORE. *Auditory Discrimination: Its Relation to Reading Achievement and Intelligence.* Master's thesis, Illinois State University (Normal, Ill.), 1965.
151. OSBORNE, AARON. *Predicting the Success of First Grade Children.* Master's thesis, East Tennessee State University (Johnson City, Tenn.), 1965.
152. ADAMS, MAMIE JOSEPHINE CUSTER. *Reading Readiness Factors and Reading Achievement of First-Grade Children.* Master's thesis, Illinois State University (Normal, Ill.), 1966.
153. FOSTER, JERRY D. *Academic Readiness and Physical Fitness of Kindergarten Boys and Girls.* Master's thesis, Northern Illinois University (DeKalb, Ill.), 1966.
154. GARRISON, THERESA MAE. *Reading Readiness Factors: Relationship to Reading Achievement.* Master's thesis, Illinois State University (Normal, Ill.), 1966.
155. HADLEY, BONNIE D. *Prediction of Third Grade Arithmetic Achievement Based on First Grade Readiness Tests.* Master's thesis, University of Louisville (Louisville, Ky.), 1966.
156. HAMMOND, FRANCES VIRGINIA. *Reading Readiness: Relationship in Kindergarten With Beginning First-Grade.* Master's thesis, Illinois State University (Normal, Ill.), 1966.
157. COHEN, ISABELLA. "Reading Readiness and Head Start Graduate." *Grad Res Ed & Related Discip* 4:66–80 w '68. *
158. GOOLSBY, THOMAS M. "Culturally Deprived Head Start Subjects' Reading Readiness After Training in Listening." *J Learn Dis* 1:561–4 O '68. * (*PA* 45:3079)
159. GORALSKI, PATRICIA J., AND KERL, JOYCE M. "Kindergarten Teacher Aides and Reading Readiness Minneapolis Public Schools." *J Exp Ed* 37:34–8 w '68. *
160. SPOMER, ESTHER E. *The Comparative Ability of a Test of Visual Perception and Measures of a Readiness Test of Kindergarten Children.* Master's thesis, Fort Hays Kansas State College (Hays, Kan.), 1968.
161. BUTLER, EVELYN AHLEEN (WINETEER). *The Prediction of Success in Reading by Sixth Grade With the Use of the Reading Readiness Test.* Master's thesis, University of Idaho (Moscow, Idaho), 1969.
162. GUENTHER, GEORGIA S. *A Comparative Analysis of the Predictive Validity of Two Reading Readiness Tests and Their Subtests.* Master's thesis, Indiana University of Pennsylvania (Indiana, Pa.), 1969.
163. KELLY, DENNIS E. *Predicting Reading Readiness Using Questionnaires.* Master's thesis, Glassboro State College (Glassboro, N.J.), 1969.
164. BENTZ, DARRELL DEAN. *A Study of the Effect of Perceptual and Language Training Upon Kindergarten Children Reading Readiness Performance.* Doctor's thesis, Oklahoma State University (Stillwater, Okla.), 1970. (*DAI* 31:5922A)

165. BILKA, LOISANNE PFEIFER. *An Evaluation of the Predictive Value of Certain Reading Readiness Measures as Related to Method of Instruction, Sex, and Mental Age.* Doctor's thesis, University of Pittsburgh (Pittsburgh, Pa.), 1970. (*DAI* 31:5922A)
166. BORDEAUX, ELIZABETH ANN. *Auditory and Visual Readiness Factors Related to Reading Achievement in First Grade Based on Three Methods of Instruction.* Doctor's thesis, University of North Carolina (Chapel Hill, N.C.), 1970. (*DAI* 31:5924A)
167. BUDDE, ELAINE HELEN. *The Relationship Between Performance of Kindergarten Children on Selected Motor Tests and the Metropolitan Readiness Tests—Otis-Lennon Mental Ability Test.* Doctor's thesis, University of Wisconsin (Madison, Wis.), 1970. (*DAI* 31:5820A)
168. COULTHARD, DOROTHY BLAKE. *Metropolitan Readiness Tests as Predictor for Success in Reading Achievement.* Master's thesis, Drake University (Des Moines, Iowa), 1970.
169. FRESHOUR, FRANK W. *The Effects of a Patent Education Program on Reading Readiness and Achievement of Disadvantaged First Grade Negro Children.* Doctor's thesis, University of Florida (Gainesville, Fla.), 1970. (*DAI* 32:91A)
170. HIERS, MARGARET HANES. *A Comparison of the Readiness Test Performance of a Group of Primary-Level Educable Mentally Retarded Children Instructed on Visual-Motor Perceptual Tasks and a Comparable Group Receiving No Prescribed Instruction.* Doctor's thesis, University of Georgia (Athens, Ga.), 1970. (*DAI* 31:6440A)
171. MITCHELL, KATHARINE E. *An Early Predictive Test and Its Relationship to Junior High School Achievement.* Doctor's thesis, Syracuse University (Syracuse, N.Y.), 1970. (*DAI* 32:97A)
172. RAGSDALE, NANCY L. *Relationship of Reading Readiness and the Frostig Visual Perception Test.* Master's thesis, Illinois State University (Normal, Ill.), 1970.
173. SLAUGHTER, DIANA T. "Parental Potency and the Achievements of Inner-City Black Children." *Am J Orthopsychiatry* 40(3):433–40 Ap '70. * (*PA* 45:8989)
174. WALKER, PAUL RANDOLPH. *The Validity of Syntax as a Predictor of Reading Success.* Doctor's thesis, University of Maine (Orono, Me.), 1970. (*DAI* 32:682A)
175. WOOD, MILDRED HOPE. *A Longitudinal Study of the Effectiveness of Certain Kindergarten Tests in Predicting Reading Achievement, School Failure, and the Need for Special Services.* Doctor's thesis, Indiana University (Bloomington, Ind.), 1970. (*DAI* 31:5683A)
176. ANDREWS, ANN M. *The Gesell Developmental Test as a Predictor of School Readiness.* Doctor's thesis, University of Pennsylvania (Philadelphia, Pa.), 1971. (*DAI* 32:3082A)
177. ASPRIDY, CHRISOULA. *Kindergarten Block Building Ratings Compared to Self-Concept and Readiness Scores as Predictors of First Grade Reading Achievement.* Doctor's thesis, University of Rochester (Rochester, N.Y.), 1971. (*DAI* 32:2997A)
178. BICKLEY, A. C.; DINNAN, JAMES A.; AND JONES, J. P. "Oral Associates and Reading Readiness." *Yearb Nat Read Conf* 20:14–6 '71. *
179. BLACK, BOB GENE. *Determining the Predictive Value of Selected Measures for First Grade Reading Success.* Doctor's thesis, North Texas State University (Denton, Tex.), 1971. (*DAI* 32:3548A)
180. BURTON, JANICE H. *The Predictive Value of the Metropolitan Readiness Tests for First Grade Achievement for Selected Groups of Children in the Johnson City, Tenn., Public Schools.* Master's thesis, East Tennessee State University (Johnson City, Tenn.), 1971.
181. CLAPP, BEECHER E. *A Study of the Relationships Between a Measure of School Readiness and Subsequent Performance on Reading Tests.* Master's thesis, University of Tennessee (Knoxville, Tenn.), 1971.
182. EVANS, MILDRED MAY BAILEY. *The Effects of a Physical Education Program on Auditory Discrimination Ability, Verbal and Non-Verbal, of Kindergarten Children.* Doctor's thesis, Michigan State University (East Lansing, Mich.), 1971. (*DAI* 32:3073A)
183. FRIEDRICHS, THOMAS DONNELLY. *Prediction of First Grade Teachers' Ratings and Objective Achievement From Ability and Biographical Data.* Doctor's thesis, University of North Carolina (Chapel Hill, N.C.), 1971. (*DAI* 32:1211B)
184. FULK, BARBARA F. *Correlations Between Scores of the Metropolitan Readiness Tests of Matching and Copying and the Stanford Achievement Tests Primary I Battery of Word Reading, Paragraph Meaning, Vocabulary, and Word Study Skills.* Master's thesis, Texas Woman's University (Denton, Tex.), 1971.
185. GAMSKY, NEAL R., AND LLOYD, FAYE WILLIAMS. "A Longitudinal Study of Visual Perceptual Training and Reading Achievement." *J Ed Res* 64(10):451–4 Jl–Ag '71. * (*PA* 47:9831)
186. GEIS, ROBLEY. *The Prediction and Prevention of Reading Failure.* Doctor's thesis, University of Southern California (Los Angeles, Calif.), 1971. (*DAI* 32:5611A)
187. HAMMILL, DONALD, AND WIEDERHOLT, J. LEE. "Appropriateness of the Metropolitan Tests in an Economically De-

prived, Urban Neighborhood." *Psychol Sch* 8(1):49–50 Ja '71. * (*PA* 46:7446)

188. LOWELL, ROBERT E. "Reading Readiness Factors as Predictors of Success in First Grade Reading." *J Learn Dis* 4(10): 563–7 D '71. * (*PA* 47:11782)

189. MCKINNEY, JAMES D. "Factor Analytic Study of the Developmental Test of Visual Perception and the Metropolitan Readiness Test." *Percept & Motor Skills* 33(3):1331–4 D '71. * (*PA* 48:1653)

190. MASON, GEORGE E., AND BLANTON, WILLIAM E. "Semantic Constructs and Beginning Reading." *Yearb Nat Read Conf* 19(1):39–45 '71. *

191. PROGER, BARTON B.; McGOWAN, JOHN R.; BAYUK, ROBERT J., JR.; MANN, LESTER; TREVORROW, RUTH L.; AND MASSA, EDWARD. "The Relative Predictive and Construct Validities of the Otis-Lennon Mental Ability Test, the Lorge-Thorndike Intelligence Test, and the Metropolitan Readiness Test in Grades Two and Four: A Series of Multivariate Analyses." *Ed & Psychol Meas* 31(2):529–38 su '71. *

192. SEDA, MARIA S. A., AND MICHAEL, JOAN J. "The Concurrent Validity of the Sprigle School Screening Readiness Test for a Sample of Preschool and Kindergarten Children." *Ed & Psychol Meas* 31(4):995–7 w '71. * (*PA* 48:1660)

193. SHELDON, HARRY JAY. *An Investigation of Syntactical Ability and Vocabulary Knowledge of First Graders as Related to Reading and Vocabulary Achievement as Measured by the Stanford Achievement Test*. Doctor's thesis, University of Iowa (Iowa City, Iowa), 1971. (*DAI* 32:1201A)

194. SPENCE, ALLYN G.; MISHRA, SHITALA P.; AND GHOZEIL, SUSAN. "Home Language and Performance on Standardized Tests." *El Sch J* 71(6): 309–13 Mr '71. * (*PA* 47:2655)

195. STEVENS, FRANCES ANN BENNETT. *Predicting Third Grade Reading Achievement for Mexican-American Students From Lower Socioeconomic Levels*. Doctor's thesis, New Mexico State University (University Park, N.M.), 1971. (*DAI* 32: 5480A)

196. WHITCRAFT, CAROL JONES. *Levels of Generative Syntax and Linguistic Performance of Young Children From Standard and Non-Standard English Language Environments*. Doctor's thesis, University of Texas (Austin, Tex.), 1971. (*DAI* 32: 5644A)

197. WILLIAMS, ROBERT. "Testing for Number Readiness: Application of the Piagetian Theory of the Child's Development of the Concept of Number." *J Ed Res* 64(9):394–6 My–Je '71. * (*PA* 47:6489)

[1717]

Murphy-Durrell Reading Readiness Analysis. First grade entrants; 1949–65, c1947–65; revision of *Murphy-Durrell Diagnostic Reading Readiness Test;* 6 scores: phonemes, letter names (capitals, lower case, total), learning rate, total; Helen A. Murphy and Donald D. Durrell; Harcourt Brace Jovanovich, Inc. *

For additional information and reviews by Rebecca C. Barr and Harry Singer, see 7:758 (10 references); for reviews by Joan Bollenbacher and S. S. Dunn of the earlier edition, see 5:679 (2 references); see also 4:571 (2 references).

REFERENCES THROUGH 1971

1–2. See 4:571.
3–4. See 5:679.
5–14. See 7:758.
15. BILKA, LOISANNE PFEIFER. *An Evaluation of the Predictive Value of Certain Reading Readiness Measures as Related to Method of Instruction, Sex, and Mental Age*. Doctor's thesis,

University of Pittsburgh (Pittsburgh, Pa.), 1970. (*DAI* 31: 5922A)

16. BORDEAUX, ELIZABETH ANN. *Auditory and Visual Readiness Factors Related to Reading Achievement in First Grade Based on Three Methods of Instruction.* Doctor's thesis, University of North Carolina (Chapel Hill, N.C.), 1970. (*DAI* 31: 5924A)

17. MOTTOLA, RICHARD ALBERT. *The Development of Auditory Discrimination Skills in Kindergarten Children.* Doctor's thesis, University of Connecticut (Storrs, Conn.), 1970. (*DAI* 31: 6284A)

18. GRUEN, RONALD STEVEN. *Prediction of End-of-Year Reading Achievement for First and Third Grade Pupils.* Doctor's thesis, Pennsylvania State University (University Park, Pa.), 1971. (*DAI* 32:6198A)

19. LOWELL, ROBERT E. "Reading Readiness Factors as Predictors of Success in First Grade Reading." *J Learn Dis* 4(10): 563–7 D '71. * (*PA* 47:11782)

20. NEWMAN, ANABEL POWELL. *Longitudinal Study of Pupils Who Were Underachieving in Reading in First Grade.* Doctor's thesis, State University of New York (Buffalo, N.Y.), 1971. (*DAI* 32:2313A)

21. O'PIELA, JOAN MARIE. *Identification of Predictor Variables of Success in First Grade Reading in Culturally Disadvantaged Inner-City Children Who Have Had a Preschool Experience.* Doctor's thesis, Wayne State University (Detroit, Mich.), 1971. (*DAI* 32:6109A)

CUMULATIVE NAME INDEX

Anastasiow, N.: 13
Barr, R. C.: *rev,* 7:758
Beauchamp, J. M.: 10
Biggy, M. V.: 2
Bilka, L. P.: 15
Bollenbacher, J.: *rev,* 5:679
Bond, G. L.: 11
Bordeaux, E. A.: 16
Dunn, S. S.: *rev,* 5:679
Dykstra, R.: 6, 9, 11
Farr, R.: 13
Gruen, R. S.: 18

Kerfoot, J. F.: 7
Lowell, R. E.: 19
Mitchell, B. C.: 12
Mottola, R. A.: 17
Murphy, H. A.: 1
Newman, A. P.: 20
Nicholson, A.: 3–4
Noonan, J. D.: 5
O'Piela, J. M.: 21
Singer, H.: *rev,* 7:758
Ward, B. J.: 14
Weeks, E. E.: 8

[1718]

Parent Readiness Evaluation of Preschoolers. Ages 3–9 to 5–8; 1968–69; PREP; administered by parent; 17 scores: verbal (general information, comprehension, opposites, identification, verbal association, verbal description, listening, language, total), performance (concepts, motor co-ordination, visual-motor association, visual interpretation, auditory memory, visual memory, total), total; A. Edward Ahr and Benita Simons (handbook); Priority Innovations, Inc. *

For additional information and reviews by S. Alan Cohen, Robert E. Valett, and David P. Weikart, see 7:759.

[1719]

★**Pre-Reading Assessment Kit.** Grades kgn–1; 1971–72; PRAK; 18 tests in 4 areas; Ontario Institute for Studies in Education; CTB/McGraw-Hill Ryerson Ltd. [Canada]. *

a) LISTENING UNIT. 6 tests: Rhyming (2 tests), Beginning Sounds (2 tests), Ending Sounds (2 tests).

b) SYMBOL PERCEPTION UNIT. 4 tests: Visual Discrimination (2 tests), Recognition of Letters, Recognition of Words.

c) EXPERIENCE VOCABULARY UNIT. 2 tests.

d) COMPREHENSION UNIT. 6 tests: Classification (2 tests), Emotional Response (2 tests), Cause-Effect and Prediction (2 tests).

[1720]

★**Prereading Expectancy Screening Scales.** First grade entrants; 1973; PRESS; predicting reading problems in beginning readers; 4 scores: visual sequencing, visual/auditory spatial, auditory sequencing, letter identification; Lawrence C. Hartlage and David G. Lucas; Psychologists and Educators, Inc. *

[1721]

Pre-Reading Screening Procedures. First grade entrants of average or superior intelligence; 1968–69;

PSP; identification of children "who make errors in perception and recall of language symbols which often indicate a Specific Language Disability, or dyslexia"; 7 or 8 scores: visual (discrimination of letter forms, discrimination of word forms, visual perception memory), visual-motor (copying, visual perception memory), auditory discrimination, letter knowledge, individual auditory tests (optional); Beth H. Slingerland; Educators Publishing Service, Inc. *

For additional information and reviews by Colleen B. Jamison and Roy A. Kress, see 7:732 (1 reference).

REFERENCES THROUGH 1971

1. See 7:732.
2. OLIPHANT, GENEVIEVE G. *A Study of Factors Involved in Early Identification of Specific Language Disability (Dyslexia).* Doctor's thesis, United States International University (San Diego, Calif.), 1969. (*DAI* 31:305A)

CUMULATIVE NAME INDEX

Jamison, C. B.: *rev,* 7:732   Oliphant, G. G.: 2
Kress, R. A.: *rev,* 7:732   Slingerland, B. H.: 1

[1722]

★**Preschool and Kindergarten Performance Profile.** Preschool and kgn; 1970; PKPP; ratings by teachers; 11 scores: social (interpersonal relations, emotional behavior, safety), intellectual (communication, basic concepts, perceptual development, imagination and creative expression), physical (self-help, gross motor skills, fine visual motor skills), total; Alfred J. DiNola, Bernard P. Kaminsky, and Allan E. Sternfeld; Educational Performance Associates. *

[1723]

Primary Academic Sentiment Scale. Ages 4–4 to 7–3; 1968; PASS; motivation for learning and level of maturity and parental independence; 2 scores: sentiment, dependency; Glen Robbins Thompson; Priority Innovations, Inc. *

For additional information and a review by Jerome Rosner, see 7:760.

[1724]

Reading Aptitude Tests. Grades kgn–1; 1935; also called *Monroe Reading Aptitude Tests;* 5 scores: visual, auditory, motor, articulation, language; Marion Monroe; Houghton Mifflin Co. *

For additional information and a review by Irving H. Anderson, see 3:519 (5 references).

REFERENCES THROUGH 1971

1–5. See 3:519.
6. CURRENT, W. F., AND RUCH, G. M. "Further Studies on the Reliability of Reading Tests." *J Ed Psychol* 17:476–81 O '26. * (*PA* 1:196)
7. CARROLL, MARJORIE WIGHT. "Sex Differences in Reading Readiness at the First Grade Level." *El Engl* 25:370–5 O '48. *
8. WELSH, GEORGE BYRON. *An Investigation of Some Predictive Factors in Auding Ability.* Doctor's thesis, University of Pittsburgh (Pittsburgh, Pa.), 1954. (*DA* 14:2407)
9. BRENNER, ANTON, AND MORSE, NANCY C. "The Measurement of Children's Readiness for School." *Papers Mich Acad Sci Arts & Letters* 41:333–40 '56. * (*PA* 37:6453)
10. DYKSTRA, ROBERT. *The Relationship Between Selected Reading Readiness Measures of Auditory Discrimination and Reading Achievement at the End of First Grade.* Doctor's thesis, University of Minnesota (Minneapolis, Minn.), 1962. (*DA* 24: 195)
11. MEYERS, E.; ORPET, R. E.; ATTWELL, A. A.; AND DINGMAN, H. F. *Primary Abilities at Mental Age Six.* Monographs of the Society for Research in Child Development, Vol. 27, No. 1, Serial No. 82. Lafayette, Ind.: Child Development Publications, 1962. Pp. 40. * (*PA* 38:8462)
12. NASTRI, LETITIA S. *An Experimental Study Investigating the Relationship Between the Articulation Subtest of the Monroe Reading Aptitude Tests and the Mendelson and Robinson Standard Speech Diagnostic Test.* Master's thesis, Southern Connecticut State College (New Haven, Conn.), 1962.
13. PELZ, KURT; PIKE, FRANCES; AND AMES, LOUISE B. "A Proposed Battery of Childhood Tests for Discriminating Between Different Levels of Intactness of Function in Elderly Subjects." *J Genetic Psychol* 100:23–40 Mr '62. * (*PA* 37:975)

14. AMES, LOUISE B., AND ILG, FRANCES L. "Sex Differences in Test Performance of Matched Girl-Boy Pairs in the Five-to-Nine-Year-Old Age Range." *J Genetic Psychol* 104:25–34 Mr '64. * (*PA* 39:4582)

15. KERFOOT, JAMES FLETCHER. *The Relationship of Selected Auditory and Visual Reading Readiness Measures to First Grade Reading Achievement and Second Grade Reading and Spelling Achievement.* Doctor's thesis, University of Minnesota (Minneapolis, Minn.), 1964. (*DA* 25:1747)

16. DYKSTRA, ROBERT. "Auditory Discrimination Abilities and Beginning Reading Achievement." *Reading Res Q* 1:5–34 sp '66. * (*PA* 40:11011)

17. NERLOVE, MARY ELLEN. *Some Factors Affecting Monroe Reading Aptitude Test Scores of Culturally Disadvantaged Kindergarteners.* Master's thesis, Southern Connecticut State College (New Haven, Conn.), 1968.

18. BUSHEY, JAMES THOMAS. *The Relationships Between a Preschool Measure of Readiness and Subsequent Test Performances Among a Group of Private Elementary School Children.* Doctor's thesis, Wayne State University (Detroit, Mich.), 1969. (*DAI* 30:3816A)

19. KIMBELL, VALERIE W., AND KNIGHT, DAVID W. "The Performance of Two Populations on Selected Readiness Tests." *South J Ed Res* 4(3):186–92 Jl '70. *

20. GOLDMAN, RONALD, AND DIXON, SARAH D. "The Relationship of Vocal-Phonic and Articulatory Abilities." *J Learn Dis* 4(5):251–6 My '71. * (*PA* 47:9457)

21. STRAINGE, RENEE EVELYN. *An Analysis of the Results Obtained on the Monroe Reading Aptitude Test for the Kindergarten Classes of the Bridgeport Public School System.* Master's thesis, Southern Connecticut State College (New Haven, Conn.), 1971.

CUMULATIVE NAME INDEX

Ames, L. B.: 13–4	Kirk, S. A.: 3
Anderson, I. H.: *rev,* 3:519	Knight, D. W.: 19
Attwell, A. A.: 11	Meyers, E.: 11
Brenner, A.: 9	Morse, N. C.: 9
Bushey, J. T.: 18	Nastri, L. S.: 12
Carroll, M. W.: 7	Nerlove, M. E.: 17
Current, W. F.: 6	Orpet, R. E.: 11
Dean, C. D.: 2	Pelz, K.: 13
Dingman, H. F.: 11	Pike, F.: 13
Dixon, S. D: 20	Roslow, S.: 4
Dykstra, R.: 10, 16	Ruch, G. M.: 6
Goldman, R.: 20	Spache, G.: 5
Ilg, F. L.: 14	Strainge, R. E.: 21
Kerfoot, J. F.: 15	Welsh, G. B.: 8
Kimbell, V. W.: 19	Wylie, A. E.: 1

[1725]

★Reading Inventory Probe 1. Grades 1–2; 1970–73; also called READI (Reading Evaluation and Diagnostic Inventory); 17 scores: auditory discrimination (3 scores), visual discrimination (9 scores), vocabulary (2 scores), comprehension skills (3 scores); test by the Diagnostic Reading Committee, revision and manual by Stella Warner and Williams Myers; American Testing Co. *

[1726]

Reversal Test. Grade 1 entrants; 1954; Åke W. Edfeldt; Skandinaviska Testförlaget AB [Sweden]. *

[1727]

Riley Preschool Developmental Screening Inventory. Ages 3–5; 1969; RPDSI; school readiness; 2 scores: design, make-a-boy (girl); Clara M. D. Riley; Western Psychological Services. *

For additional information, see 7:761.

[1728]

The School Readiness Checklist. Ages 5–6; 1963–68; booklet title is *Ready or Not;* checklist to be used by parents; John J. Austin, J. Clayton Lafferty, Frederick Leaske (manual), and Fred Cousino (manual); Research Concepts. *

For additional information and a review by Dennis J. Deloria, see 7:762.

[1729]

School Readiness Survey. Ages 4–6; 1967–69; to be administered and scored by parents with school supervision; 8 scores: number concepts, discrimination

of form, color naming, symbol matching, speaking vocabulary, listening vocabulary, general information, total; F. L. Jordan and James Massey; Consulting Psychologists Press, Inc. *

For additional information and excerpted reviews by Dale E. Bennett and Byron Egeland, see 7:763.

[1730]

Screening Test of Academic Readiness. Ages 4-0 to 6-5; 1966; STAR; 9 scores: picture vocabulary, letters, picture completion, copying, picture description, human figure drawing, relationships, numbers, total (IQ); A. Edward Ahr; Priority Innovations, Inc. *

For additional information, a review by Mildred H. Huebner, and an excerpted review by Jon Magoon (with Richard C. Cox), see 7:765 (5 references).

REFERENCES THROUGH 1971
1–5. See 7:765.

CUMULATIVE NAME INDEX

Ahr, A. E.: 1–3	Hutton, J. B.: 5
Cox, R. C.: 4; *exc,* 7:765	Magoon, J.: 4; *exc,* 7:765
Huebner, M. H.: *rev,* 7:765	

[1731]

Sprigle School Readiness Screening Test. Ages 4-6 to 6-9; 1965; SSRST; distribution restricted to physicians and psychologists; Herbert A. Sprigle; Learning to Learn School, Inc. *

For additional information and reviews by Nicholas Anastasiow and Alice Moriarty, see 7:766 (4 references).

REFERENCES THROUGH 1971
1–4. See 7:766.

5. SEDA, MARIA S. *A Validation Study of the Sprigle School Screening Readiness Test.* Master's thesis, California State College (Long Beach, Calif.), 1971.

6. SEDA, MARIA S. A., AND MICHAEL, JOAN J. "The Concurrent Validity of the Sprigle School Screening Readiness Test for a Sample of Preschool and Kindergarten Children." *Ed & Psychol Meas* 31(4):995–7 w '71. * (*PA* 48:1660)

CUMULATIVE NAME INDEX

Anastasiow, N.: *rev,* 7:766	Moriarty, A. E.: *rev,* 7:766
Bottrill, J. H.: 1	Seda, M. S.: 5
Hutton, J. B.: 3–4	Seda, M. S. A.: 6
Lanier, J.: 2	Sprigle, H. A.: 2
Michael, J. J.: 6	

[1732]

The Steinbach Test of Reading Readiness. Grades kgn–1; 1965–66; STRR; 5 scores: letter identification, word memory, auditory discrimination, language comprehension, total; M. Nila Steinbach; Scholastic Testing Service, Inc. *

REFERENCES THROUGH 1971
1. STEINBACH, MARY NILA. *An Experimental Study of Progress in First-Grade Reading.* Doctor's thesis, Catholic University of America (Washington, D.C.), 1940.

CUMULATIVE NAME INDEX
Steinbach, M. N.: 1

[1733]

Van Wagenen Reading Readiness Scales. First grade entrants; 1933–58; 2 parts; Van Wagenen Psycho-Educational Research Laboratories. *

a) PART 1, LISTENING VOCABULARY. 1954–58; Maximilian L. G. Klaeger and M. J. Van Wagenen.

b) PART 2. 1933–58; 1954 test items same as in earlier edition published 1938 under the title *Reading Readiness Test;* 7 scores: range of information, perception of information, opposites, memory span for ideas, word discrimination, word learning, verbal IQ; M. J. Van Wagenen.

For additional information and a review by David H. Russell of an earlier edition of Part 2, see 3:520 (4 references).

Reading Aptitude Tests

REFERENCES THROUGH 1971

1–4. See 3:520.
5. WILSON, FRANK T. "Correlation of Information With Other Abilities and Traits in Grade I." *El Sch J* 37:295–301 D '36. * (*PA* 11:2478)
6. LOPER, DORIS JEAN. *Auditory Discrimination, Intelligence, Achievement, and Background of Experience and Information in a Culturally Disadvantaged First-Grade Population.* Doctor's thesis, Temple University (Philadelphia, Pa.), 1965. (*DA* 26:5873)
7. CHARRY, LAWRENCE BERNARD. *The Relationship Between Prereading and First Grade Reading Performances and Subsequent Achievement in Reading and Other Specified Areas.* Doctor's thesis, Temple University (Philadelphia, Pa.), 1967. (*DA* 28:960A)

CUMULATIVE NAME INDEX

Bond, E.: 3	Horan, K.: 3
Bond, G. L.: 3	Huggett, A. J.: 2
Burke, A.: 1	Johnson, N. E.: 4
Charry, L. B.: 7	Loper, D. J.: 6
Gates, A. I.: 3	Russell, D. H.: 3; *rev,* 3:520
Halpin, A.: 3	Wilson, F. T.: 1, 5

[1734]

Watson Reading-Readiness Test. Grades kgn–1; 1960; 3 scores: subjective test (teacher's ratings of physical, social, emotional, and psychological readiness), objective test, total; G. Milton Watson; Book Society of Canada Ltd. [Canada]. *
For additional information, see 6:851.

[Out of Print Since TIP I]

Classification Test for Beginners in Reading, R:202, 3:515 (2 reviews, 2 references)
Early Detection Inventory, 7:746 (2 reviews), R:183
Evanston Early Identification Scale, 7:747 (1 review, 1 reference), P:426
Reading Readiness Test, R:203, 6:849 (1 review, 1 reference)
Scholastic Reading Readiness Test, R:204, 6:850 (1 review)
Webster Reading-Readiness Test, R:206, 5:682

SPECIAL FIELDS

[1735]

*ANPA Foundation Newspaper Test, 1972 Edition. Grades 7–9, 10–12; 1969–72; newspaper reading ability; 1972 tests identical with experimental tests published 1969; sponsored by National Council for the Social Studies and developed in cooperation with American Newspaper Publishers Association Foundation; Cooperative Tests and Services. *
For additional information, see 7:768.

[1736]

The Adult Basic Reading Inventory. Functionally illiterate adolescents and adults; 1966; ABRI; test booklets with the title *Basic Reading Inventory* (BRI) are available for school use; scores in 5 areas: sight words, sound and letter discrimination, word meaning (reading), word meaning (listening), context reading; Richard W. Burnett; Scholastic Testing Service, Inc. *
For additional information and a review by Albert J. Kingston, see 7:769.

[1737]

*The Iowa Tests of Educational Development: Test 6, Ability to Interpret Reading Materials the Social Studies. Grades 9–12; 1942–67; Forms X–4 and Y–4; more recent Forms X5 and Y5 are not available as separates; prepared under the direction of E. F. Lindquist and Leonard S. Feldt; Science

Research Associates, Inc. * For the complete battery entry, see 20.
For additional information concerning earlier forms, see 6:852. For reviews of the complete battery, see 6:14 (2 reviews), 5:17 (2 reviews), 4:17 (1 review), and 3:12 (3 reviews).

REFERENCES THROUGH 1971

1. LEBSACK, JACOB ROBERT. *Specific Reading Ability as Associated With Subject Matter Achievement.* Doctor's thesis, University of Nebraska (Lincoln, Neb.), 1954. (*DA* 14:1995)
2. COVELL, HAROLD MANFRED. *A Study of the Characteristics of Good and Poor Readers of Social Studies Materials at the Eleventh Grade Level.* Doctor's thesis, Florida State University (Tallahassee, Fla.), 1955. (*DA* 15:1570)

CUMULATIVE NAME INDEX

Covell, H. M.: 2	Lebsack, J. R.: 1

[1738]

*The Iowa Tests of Educational Development: Test 6, Ability to Interpret Reading Materials in the Natural Sciences. Grades 9–12; 1942–67; Forms X–4 and Y–4; more recent Forms X5 and Y5 are not available as separates; prepared under the direction of E. F. Lindquist and Leonard S. Feldt; Science Research Associates, Inc. * For the complete battery entry, see 20.
For additional information concerning earlier forms, see 6:853. For reviews of the complete battery, see 6:14 (2 reviews), 5:17 (2 reviews), 4:17 (1 review), and 3:12 (3 reviews).

REFERENCES THROUGH 1971

1. LEBSACK, JACOB ROBERT. *Specific Reading Ability as Associated With Subject Matter Achievement.* Doctor's thesis, University of Nebraska (Lincoln, Neb.), 1954. (*DA* 14:1995)
2. JOHNSON, JENNINGS O. "The Relationship Between Science Achievement and Selected Student Characteristics." *Sci Ed* 53(4):307–18 O '69. *

CUMULATIVE NAME INDEX

Johnson, J. O.: 2	Lebsack, J. R.: 1

[1739]

Purdue Reading Test for Industrial Supervisors. Supervisors; 1955; Joseph Tiffin and Roy Dunlap; University Book Store. *
For additional information and reviews by Jerome E. Doppelt and Louis C. Nanassy, see 5:644 (1 reference).

REFERENCES THROUGH 1971

1. See 5:644.
2. SCHUCKER, RAYMOND E. *Validity and Reliability of the Purdue Reading Test for Industrial Supervisors.* Master's thesis, Purdue University (Lafayette, Ind.), 1957.
3. KIRCHNER, WAYNE; HANSON, RICHARD; AND BENSON, DALE. "Selecting Foremen With Psychological Tests." *Personnel Adm* 23:27–30 N–D '60. *
4. GRUENFELD, LEOPOLD W. "Selection of Executives for a Training Program." *Personnel Psychol* 14:421–31 w '61. * (*PA* 37:3922)

CUMULATIVE NAME INDEX

Benson, D.: 3	Hanson, R.: 3
Doppelt, J. E.: *rev,* 5:644	Kirchner, W.: 3
Dunlap, R. D.: 1	Nanassy, L. C.: *rev,* 5:644
Gruenfeld, L. W.: 4	Schucker, R. E.: 2

[1740]

RBH Scientific Reading Test. Employees in technical companies; 1950–69; Richardson, Bellows, Henry & Co., Inc. *
For additional information and a review by Samuel T. Mayo, see 7:772.

[1741]

Reading Adequacy "READ" Test: Individual Placement Series. Adults in industry; 1961–66; 3 scores: reading rate, per cent of comprehension, corrected reading rate; J. H. Norman; Personnel Research Associates, Inc. *

Reading Adequacy "READ" Test

For additional information and a review by Samuel T. Mayo, see 7:773.

[1742]

[Reading: Adult Basic Education Student Survey, Parts 1 and 2.] Poorly educated adults; 1966–67; 2 scores: comprehension, vocabulary; Elvin Rasof and Monroe C. Neff; Follett Publishing Co. *

[1743]

Reading Comprehension Test for Personnel Selection. Applicants for technical training programs with high verbal content; 1965–66; L. R. C. Haward; University of London Press Ltd. [England]. *
For additional information and reviews by M. A. Brimer and Douglas A. Pidgeon, see 7:774 (3 references).

REFERENCES THROUGH 1971
1–3. See 7:774.

CUMULATIVE NAME INDEX
Brimer, M. A.: rev, 7:774   Pidgeon, D. A.: rev, 7:774
Haward, L. R. C.: 1–3

[1744]

★Reading/Everyday Activities in Life. High school and "adults at basic education levels"; 1972; R/EAL; functional literacy; Marilyn Lichtman; CAL Press, Inc. *

[1745]

[Robinson-Hall Reading Tests.] College; 1940–49; 4 tests; Francis P. Robinson and Prudence Hall; University Publications Sales, Ohio State University. *
a) A TEST OF READING ABILITY FOR ART.
b) A TEST OF READING ABILITY FOR GEOLOGY.
c) A TEST OF READING ABILITY FOR HISTORY.
d) A TEST OF READING ABILITY FOR FICTION.
For additional information and a review by Robert Murray Bear, see 4:575 (2 references); see also 3:533 (3 references).

REFERENCES THROUGH 1971
1–3. See 3:533.
4–5. See 4:575.
6. TAYLOR, JEANNE K. Establishment of Norms for University of Wyoming Freshmen for the Robinson Reading Tests and the Development of a Comparable Reading Test. Master's thesis, University of Wyoming (Laramie, Wyo.), 1954.
7. MAXWELL, MARTHA J. "An Experimental Investigation of the Effect of Instructional Set and Information on Reading Rate." Yearb Nat Read Conf 14:181–7 '65. *

CUMULATIVE NAME INDEX
Bear, R. M.: rev, 4:575   Maxwell, M. J.: 7
Edgerton, H. A.: 4   Robinson, F. P.: 1–3, 5
Hall, P.: 2   Taylor, J. K.: 6
Hall, W. E.: 5   Thomson, K. F.: 4

[1746]

SRA Reading Index. Job applicants with poor educational backgrounds; 1968; Science Research Associates, Inc. *
For additional information and a review by Dorothy C. Adkins of this test and the SRA Arithmetic Index, see 7:20.

[1747]

Understanding Communication (Verbal Comprehension). Industrial employees at the skilled level or below; 1959, c1956–59; Thelma G. Thurstone and Measurement Research Division, Industrial Relations Center, University of Chicago; the Center. * [The publisher has not replied to our four requests to check the accuracy of this entry.]
For additional information and reviews by C. E. Jurgensen and Donald E. P. Smith, see 6:840.

Reading Adequacy "READ" Test

REFERENCES THROUGH 1971
1. BAEHR, MELANY E.; FURCON, JOHN E.; AND FROEMEL, ERNEST C. Psychological Assessment of Patrolman Qualifications in Relation to Field Performance. Washington, D.C.: United States Government Printing Office, 1969. Pp. vii, 246. *

CUMULATIVE NAME INDEX
Baehr, M. E.: 1   Jurgensen, C. E.: rev, 6:840
Froemel, E. C.: 1   Smith, D. E. P.: rev, 6:840
Furcon, J. E.: 1

[Out of Print Since TIP I]

Interpretation of Reading Materials in the Natural Sciences, 7:770, R:210; now available only as a subtest of Tests of General Educational Development, 48
Interpretation of Reading Materials in the Social Studies, 7:771 (2 reviews, 1 reference), R:211; now available only as a subtest of Tests of General Educational Development, 48
SRA Reading Progress Test, 7:775 (1 review), R:220
Tests of Natural Sciences: Vocabulary and Interpretation of Reading Materials: Cooperative Inter-American Tests, R:221, 4:576 (1 review, 4 references)
Tests of Social Studies: Vocabulary and Interpretation of Reading Materials: Cooperative Inter-American Tests, R:222, 4:577 (4 references)

SPEED

[1748]

*Basic Reading Rate Scale. Grades 3–12; 1971, c1947–71; BRRS; the two forms consist of the first 97 or 98 items in the corresponding 450-item forms of Tinker Speed of Reading Test ('55); Ronald P. Carver (manual) and Miles A. Tinker (test); Revrac Publications. *
For additional information and a review by Leonard S. Feldt of the full length test, see 5:687.

[1749]

Minnesota Speed of Reading Test for College Students. Grades 12–16; 1936; Alvin C. Eurich; University of Minnesota Press. *
For additional information and a review by J. R. Gerberich, see 2:1555 (2 references); for reviews by Frederick B. Davis and Ruth Strang, see 1:1107.

REFERENCES THROUGH 1971
1–2. See 2:1555.
3. EURICH, ALVIN C. "The Relation of Speed of Reading to Comprehension." Sch & Soc 32:404–6 S 20 '30. * (PA 5:764)
4. LITTERER, OSCAR F. "An Experimental Analysis of Reading Performance." J Exp Ed 1:28–33 S 15 '32. * (PA 7:1137)
5. LITTERER, OSCAR F. "An Experimental Study of Visual Apprehension in Reading." J Appl Psychol 17:266–76 Je '33. * (PA 8:496)
6. PACE, C. ROBERT. "Handedness and Reading Ability in High School and College Students." J Ed Res 31:205–10 N '37. * (PA 12:952)
7. SEASHORE, R. H.; STOCKFORD, L. B. O.; AND SWARTZ, B. K. "A Correlational Analysis of Factors in Speed of Reading Tests." Sch & Soc 46:187–92 Ag 7 '37. * (PA 11:5346)
8. GREENE, PAUL C. "Some Relationships Between Placement Scores and Scholastic Rating." Proc Iowa Acad Sci 48:361–6 '41. * (PA 16:2867)
9. BLOMMERS, PAUL, AND LINDQUIST, E. F. "Rate of Comprehension of Reading: Its Measurement and Its Relation to Comprehension." J Ed Psychol 35:449–73 N '44. * (PA 19:1035)
10. SUTHERLAND, JEAN. "The Relationship Between Perceptual Span and Rate of Reading." J Ed Psychol 37:373–80 S '46. * (PA 21:1665)
11. LANIGAN, MARY A. "The Effectiveness of the Otis, the A.C.E. and the Minnesota Speed of Reading Tests for Predicting Success in College." J Ed Res 41:289–96 D '47. * (PA 22:2748)
12. PRESTON, RALPH C., AND TUFT, EDWIN N. "The Reading Habits of Superior College Students." J Exp Ed 16:196–202 Mr '48. * (PA 20:5126)
13. HOLMES, JACK A. "Factors Underlying Major Reading Disabilities at the College Level." Genetic Psychol Monogr 49:3–95 F '54. * (PA 28:8982)

14. KERSH, BERT Y. "An Investigation of the Interpretation of Written Problems Among College Students." *Calif J Ed Res* 5:13-9 Ja '54. * (*PA* 28:7198)
15. SWEENEY, FRANCIS J. "Intelligence, Vocational Interests and Reading Speed of Senior Boys in Catholic High Schools of Los Angeles." *Calif J Ed Res* 5:159-65 S '54. * (*PA* 29:4656)

CUMULATIVE NAME INDEX

Blommers, P.: 9	Paterson, D. G.: 2
Davis, F. B.: *rev*, 1:1107	Preston, R. C.: 12
Eurich, A. C.: 1, 3	Schneidler, G. G.: 2
Gerberich, J. R.: *rev*, 2:1555	Seashore, R. H.: 7
Greene, P. C.: 8	Stockford, L. B. O.: 7
Holmes, J. A.: 13	Strang, R.: *rev*, 1:1107
Kersh, B. Y.: 14	Sutherland, J.: 10
Lanigan, M. A.: 11	Swartz, B. K.: 7
Lindquist, E. F.: 9	Sweeney, F. J.: 15
Litterer, O. F.: 4-5	Tuft, E. N.: 12
Pace, C. R.: 6	Williamson, E. G.: 2

[Out of Print Since TIP I]

Chapman-Cook Speed of Reading Test, R:232, 3:522 (1 review, 1 reference)
Reading Speed and Comprehension: Ohio Senior Survey Tests, R:234, 3:524 (2 reviews)
Tinker Speed of Reading Test, R:231, 5:687 (1 review)

STUDY SKILLS

[1750]

Bristol Achievement Tests: Study Skills. Ages 8-9, 9-10, 10-11, 11-12, 12-13; 1969; 6 scores: properties, structures, processes, explanations, interpretations, total; Alan Brimer, Margaret Fidler, Wynne Harlen, and John Taylor; Thomas Nelson & Sons Ltd. [England]. * For the complete battery entry, see 5.
For additional information and a review by Elizabeth J. Goodacre, see 7:776. For reviews of the complete battery, see 7:4 (2 reviews).

[1751]

College Adjustment and Study Skills Inventory. College; 1968; CASSI; 6 scores: time distribution, attitude and personal adjustment, reading and class participation, taking notes, taking examinations, total; Frank A. Christensen; Personal Growth Press, Inc. *
For additional information and reviews by William A. Mehrens and Walter Pauk, see 7:777.

[1752]

*Comprehensive Tests of Basic Skills: Study Skills.** Grades 2.5-4, 4-6, 6-8, 8-12; 1968-71; CTB/McGraw-Hill. * For the complete battery entry, see 11.
For additional information and a review by Walter Pauk, see 7:778. For reviews of the complete battery, see 7:9 (2 reviews, 3 excerpts).

[1753]

★**The Cornell Class-Reasoning Test.** Grades 4-12; 1964; deductive logic; no manual; Robert H. Ennis, William L. Gardiner, Richard Morrow, Dieter Paulus, and Lucille Ringel; Critical Thinking Project, University of Illinois. *

REFERENCES THROUGH 1971

1. ENNIS, ROBERT H., AND PAULUS, DIETER H. *Critical Thinking Readiness in Grades 1-12 (Phase 1, Deductive Logic in Adolescence).* An unpublished report to the U.S. Office of Education, Cooperative Research Project No. 1680, Cornell University, 1965. Pp. 348. * (ERIC ED003818)

CUMULATIVE NAME INDEX

Ennis, R. H.: 1	Paulus, D. H.: 1

[1754]

★**The Cornell Conditional-Reasoning Test.** Grades 4-12; 1964; deductive logic; no manual; Robert H. Ennis, William L. Gardiner, John Guzzetta, Richard Morrow, Dieter Paulus, and Lucille Ringel; Critical Thinking Project, University of Illinois. *

REFERENCES THROUGH 1971

1. ENNIS, ROBERT H., AND PAULUS, DIETER H. *Critical Thinking Readiness in Grades 1-12 (Phase 1, Deductive Logic in Adolescence).* An unpublished report to the U.S. Office of Education, Cooperative Research Project No. 1680, Cornell University, 1965. Pp. 348. * (ERIC ED003818)

CUMULATIVE NAME INDEX

Ennis, R. H.: 1	Paulus, D. H.: 1

[1755]

The Cornell Critical Thinking Test. Grades 7-12, 13-16; 1961-71; CCTT; 1971 tests identical with tests copyrighted 1961 except for format; Robert H. Ennis and Jason Millman; Critical Thinking Project, University of Illinois. *
For additional information, see 7:779 (10 references).

REFERENCES THROUGH 1971

1-10. See 7:779.
11. FOLLMAN, JOHN; MILLER, WILLIAM; AND BURG, ELDON. "Statistical Analysis of Three Critical Thinking Tests." *Ed & Psychol Meas* 31(2):519-20 su '71. *
12. TOLMAN, RICHARD. "Student Performance in Lower Division Collegiate General Biology Programs in Selected Community Colleges and Four-Year Institutions in Oregon." *J Res Sci Teach* 8(2):105-12 '71. *

CUMULATIVE NAME INDEX

Brown, L.: 9	Follman, J.: 4-6, 8-11
Brown, T. R.: 3	Follman, J. C.: 7
Burg, E.: 9, 11	Hernandez, D.: 5-6, 10
Craven, G. F.: 2	Miller, W.: 5-6, 10-1
Ennis, R. H.: 1	Tolman, R.: 12

[1756]

★**The Cornell Learning and Study Skills Inventory.** Grades 7-12, 13-16; 1970; CLSSI; 9 scores: goal orientation, activity structure, scholarly skills, lecture mastery, textbook mastery, examination mastery, self mastery, total, reading validity index; Walter Pauk and Russell Cassel; Psychologists and Educators, Inc. *

REFERENCES THROUGH 1971

1. CASSEL, RUSSELL, AND PAUK, WALTER. "Validation of Self-Concept of Typical Student as Substitute for Student's Own Self-Concept." *J Psychol* 73(1):111-4 S '69. * (*PA* 44:5142)
2. CASSEL, RUSSELL N., AND PAUK, WALTER. "Comparing Scores on the Cornell Learning and Study Skills Inventory With GPA and Age." *Cont Ed* 43(1):44-7 O '71. *

CUMULATIVE NAME INDEX

Cassel, R.: 1	Pauk, W.: 1-2
Cassel, R. N.: 2	

[1757]

Evaluation Aptitude Test. Candidates for college and graduate school entrance; 1951-52; 5 scores: neutral syllogisms, emotionally toned syllogisms, total, emotional bias, indecision; DeWitt E. Sell; Psychometric Affiliates. *
For additional information and reviews by J. Thomas Hastings and Walker H. Hill, see 5:691.

[1758]

*The Iowa Tests of Educational Development: Test 9, Use of Sources of Information.** Grades 9-12; 1942-67; Forms X-4 and Y-4; more recent Forms X5 and Y5 are not available as separates; prepared under the direction of E. F. Lindquist and Leonard S. Feldt; Science Research Associates, Inc. *
For the complete battery entry, see 20.
For additional information concerning earlier forms,

see 6:858. For reviews of the complete battery, see 6:14 (2 reviews), 5:17 (2 reviews), 4:17 (1 review), and 3:12 (3 reviews).

REFERENCES THROUGH 1971

1. MOELLER, VERNON E. *A Study of Relationships Between Measures of Academic Achievement, Study Habits and Attitudes, the Ability to Use Reference Materials, and Academic Aptitude in a Large Suburban Illinois High School.* Master's thesis, Northern Illinois University (DeKalb, Ill.), 1963.

CUMULATIVE NAME INDEX

Moeller, V. E.: 1

[1759]

A Library Orientation Test for College Freshmen. Grade 13; 1950–61; Ethel M. Feagley, Dorothy W. Curtiss, Mary V. Gaver, and Esther Greene; Teachers College Press. *

For additional information and a review by Morey J. Wantman, see 6:859 (1 reference); for reviews by Janet G. Afflerbach (with Lois Grimes Afflerbach) and J. Wayne Wrightstone, see 5:693.

REFERENCES THROUGH 1971

1. See 6:859.
2. LEE, CHI HO. *The Library Skills of Prospective Teachers at the University of Georgia.* Doctor's thesis, University of Georgia (Athens, Ga.), 1971. (*DAI* 32:5089A)

CUMULATIVE NAME INDEX

Afflerbach, J. G.: *rev*, 5:693　　Wantman, M. J.: *rev*, 6:859
Afflerbach, L. G.: *rev*, 5:693　　Wrightstone, J. W.: *rev*, 5:
Joyce, W. D.: 1　　　　　　　　693
Lee, C. H.: 2

[1760]

★**Library Tests.** College; 1967–72; 3 tests; no manual; Perfection Form Co. *

a) TEST 1: LIBRARY SURVEY TEST. General knowledge of library.
b) TEST 2: LIBRARY SOURCES AND SKILLS TEST. More detailed knowledge of library.
c) TEST 3: LIBRARY SOURCES AND USES OF INFORMATION. Thorough knowledge of library and research techniques.

[1761]

Logical Reasoning. Grades 9–16 and adults; 1955; Alfred F. Hertzka and J. P. Guilford; Sheridan Psychological Services, Inc. *

For additional information and reviews by Duncan Howie and Charles R. Langmuir, see 5:694 (1 reference).

REFERENCES THROUGH 1971

1. See 5:694.
2. GUILFORD, J. P. *Personality.* New York: McGraw-Hill Book Co., Inc., 1959. Pp. xiii, 562. *
3. MERRIFIELD, P. R.; GUILFORD, J. P.; CHRISTENSEN, P. R.; AND FRICK, J. W. "The Role of Intellectual Factors in Problem Solving." *Psychol Monogr* 76 (10):1–21 '62. *
4. LEMKE, ELMER A.; KLAUSMEIER, HERBERT J.; AND HARRIS, CHESTER W. "Relationship of Selected Cognitive Abilities to Concept Attainment and Information Processing." *J Ed Psychol* 58:27–35 F '67. * (*PA* 41:3959)
5. VERY, PHILIP S. "Differential Factor Structures in Mathematical Ability." *Genetic Psychol Monogr* 75:169–207 My '67. * (*PA* 41:10451)
6. BERGER, RAYMOND M. "Selection of Systems Analysts and Programmer Trainees." *Proc Ann Computer Personnel Res Conf* 6:44–63 '68. *
7. FOLLMAN, JOHN. "Factor Analysis of Three Critical Thinking Tests, One Logical Reasoning Test, and One English Test." *Yearb Nat Read Conf* 18:154–60 '69. *
8. FOLLMAN, JOHN COSGROVE. *A Factor Analytic Study of Three Critical Thinking Tests, One English Test, and One Logical Reasoning Test.* Doctor's thesis, Indiana University (Bloomington, Ind.), 1969. (*DAI* 30:1015A)
9. VANDENBERG, STEVEN G. "A Twin Study of Spatial Ability." *Multiv Behav Res* 4(3):273–94 Jl '69. * (*PA* 44:356)
10. FOLLMAN, JOHN. "Correlational and Factor Analysis of Critical Thinking, Logical Reasoning, and English Total Test Scores." *Fla J Ed Res* 12(1):91–4 Ja '70. *
11. FOLLMAN, JOHN; BROWN, LAURENCE; AND BURG, ELDON. "Factor Analysis of Critical Thinking, Logical Reasoning, and English Subtests." *J Exp Ed* 38(4):11–6 su '70. *

CUMULATIVE NAME INDEX

Berger, R. M.: 6　　　　　Hills, J. R.: 1
Brown, L.: 11　　　　　　Howie, D.: *rev*, 5:694
Burg, E.: 11　　　　　　　Klausmeier, H. J.: 4
Christensen, P. R.: 3　　　Langmuir, C. R.: *rev*, 5:694
Follman, J.: 7, 10–1　　　Lemke, E. A.: 4
Follman, J. C.: 8　　　　　Merrifield, P. R.: 3
Frick, J. W.: 3　　　　　　Vandenberg, S. G.: 9
Guilford, J. P.: 2–3　　　Very, P. S.: 5
Harris, C. W.: 4

[1762]

★**National Test of Library Skills.** Grades 2–4, 4–12; 1967–71; NTLS; 2 levels; Frances Hatfield, Irene Gullette, and William Myers; American Testing Co. *

a) LEVELS 2 TO 4. Grades 2–4; 1971; 4 scores: arrangement of books, parts of a book, card catalog, reference books.
b) LEVELS 4 TO 12. Grades 4–12; 1967–71; 5 scores: same as for level 2–4 plus indexes.

[1763]

Nationwide Library Skills Examination. Grades 4–12; 1962–63; no manual; [Donald R. Honz]; Educational Stimuli. *

For additional information, see 6:860.

[1764]

OC Diagnostic Dictionary Test. Grades 5–8; 1960; Katherine O'Connor; O'Connor Reading Clinic Publishing Co. *

For additional information, see 6:861.

[1765]

SRA Achievement Series: Work-Study Skills. Grades 4–9; 1955–69; an optional supplement to Forms C and D of the series; 3 scores: references, charts, total; Louis P. Thorpe, D. Welty Lefever, and Robert A. Naslund; Science Research Associates, Inc. * For the complete battery entry, see 29.

For additional information, see 7:780; for reviews by Robert L. Ebel and Ruth M. Strang of earlier forms, see 5:696. For reviews of the complete battery, see 7:18 (2 reviews), 6:21 (1 review), and 5:21 (2 reviews).

[1766]

★**Study Attitudes and Methods Survey.** High school and college; 1972; SAMS; 6 scores: academic interest, academic drive, study methods, study anxiety, manipulation, alienation toward authority; William B. Michael, Joan J. Michael, and Wayne S. Zimmerman; Educational and Industrial Testing Service. *

REFERENCES THROUGH 1971

1. MICHAEL, WILLIAM B., AND REEDER, DOUGLAS E. "The Development and Validation of a Preliminary Form of a Study-Habits Inventory." *Ed & Psychol Meas* 12:236–47 su '52. * (*PA* 27:6156)
2. MICHAEL, WILLIAM B.; JONES, ROBERT A.; AND TREMBLY, W. A. "The Factored Dimensions of a Measure of Motivation for College Students." *Ed & Psychol Meas* 19:667–71 w '59. * (*PA* 34:6550)
3. ZIMMERMAN, WAYNE S.; MICHAEL, JOAN J.; AND MICHAEL, WILLIAM B. "The Factored Dimensions of the Study Attitudes and Methods Survey Test—Experimental Form." *Ed & Psychol Meas* 30(2):433–6 su '70. * (*PA* 45:2960)
4. MICHAEL, WILLIAM B.; LEE, YOUNG B.; MICHAEL, JOAN J.; HOOKE, ORA; AND ZIMMERMAN, WAYNE S. "A Partial Redefinition of the Factorial Structure of the Study Attitudes and Methods Survey (SAMS) Test." *Ed & Psychol Meas* 31(2): 545–7 su '71. *

CUMULATIVE NAME INDEX

Hooke, O.: 4　　　　　　Michael, W. B.: 1–4
Jones, R. A.: 2　　　　　Reeder, D. E.: 1
Lee, Y. B.: 4　　　　　　Trembly, W. A.: 2
Michael, J. J.: 3–4　　　Zimmerman, W. S.: 3–4

Iowa Tests of Educational Development: Test 9

[1767]

Study Habits Checklist. Grades 9–14; 1957–67; also published as a pretest and posttest in the authors' booklet entitled *How to Study;* Ralph C. Preston and Morton Botel; Science Research Associates, Inc. *

REFERENCES THROUGH 1971

1. PRESTON, RALPH C. "Improving the Item Validity of Study Habits Inventories." *Ed & Psychol Meas* 21:129–31 sp '61. * (*PA* 36:1KI29P)
2. BROWN, SARA MAE. *Variables Associated With Overachievement and Underachievement.* Doctor's thesis, University of Pennsylvania (Philadelphia, Pa.), 1964.
3. BUTCOFSKY, DON. "Any Learning Skills Taught in High School?" *J Read* 15(3):195–8 D '71. *

CUMULATIVE NAME INDEX

Brown, S. M.: 2   Preston, R. C.: 1
Butcofsky, D.: 3

[1768]

Study Habits Inventory, Revised Edition. Grades 12–16; 1934–41; C. Gilbert Wrenn; Consulting Psychologists Press, Inc. *

For additional information and a review by Douglas E. Scates, see 3:540 (8 references); for reviews by Edward S. Jones and William A. McCall, see 2:1574.

REFERENCES THROUGH 1971

1–8. See 3:540.
9. DOUGLASS, LOWELL N. "A Study of Certain Factors Influencing Academic Achievement With Special Reference to the Health Factor." *J Exp Ed* 7:235–44 Mr '39. * (*PA* 13:5911)
10. SHEFFIELD, EDWARD F. "Achievement of Evening College Students." *J Am Assn Col Reg* 17:319–24 Ap '42. *
11. WAGGONER, R. W., AND ZEIGLER, THORNTON WOODWARD. "Psychiatric Factors in Medical School Students Who Fail." *Am J Psychiatry* 103:369–76 N '46. * (*PA* 21:1671)
12. PORTENIER, LILLIAN G. "Predicting Success in Introductory Psychology." *Ed & Psychol Meas* 8:117–26 sp '48. * (*PA* 22:3730)
13. PRESTON, RALPH C., AND TUFT, EDWIN N. "The Reading Habits of Superior College Students." *J Exp Ed* 16:196–202 Mr '48. * (*PA* 20:5126)
14. GARBER, W. F. "Evaluation of Psychometric Tests for Optometry." *Optom Weekly* 41:7–9 Ja '50. * (*PA* 24:5533)
15. ESHLEMAN, DAWN FORRESTER. *The Relationship of the Wrenn Study Habits Inventory to Personality Adjustment and Achievement of High School Seniors.* Master's thesis, Pennsylvania State College (State College, Pa.), 1951.
16. GEHMAN, WINFIELD SCOTT, JR. *Analysis of a Program Involving Required Psychological Counseling and Other Services for a College Population Having Serious Scholastic Difficulties.* Doctor's thesis, Pennsylvania State College (State College, Pa.), 1951.
17. MUNGER, PAUL F. "Factors Related to Persistence in College of Students Who Ranked in the Lower Third of Their High School Class." *J Counsel Psychol* 1:132–6 f '54. * (*PA* 29:6258)
18. GEHMAN, W. SCOTT. "Problems of College Sophomores With Serious Scholastic Difficulties." *J Counsel Psychol* 2:137–41 su '55. * (*PA* 30:3406)
19. RASMUS, CAROLYN A. *Predictive Value of the Wrenn Study-Habits Inventory in Predicting the Success of Miami University Freshmen.* Master's thesis, Miami University (Oxford, Ohio), 1955.
20. SLAYTON, WILFRED GEORGE. *A Comparison of Successful and Unsuccessful Bible College Students With Respect to Selected Personality Factors.* Doctor's thesis, University of Arizona (Tucson, Ariz.), 1965. (*DA* 26:1487)
21. LIGHT, LOUISE L., AND ALEXAKOS, C. E. "Effect of Individual and Group Counseling on Study Habits." *J Ed Res* 63(10):450–4 Jl–Ag '70. * (*PA* 46:7571)
22. ZEDECK, SHELDON; CRANNY, C. J.; VALE, CAROL A.; AND SMITH, PATRICIA CAIN. "Comparison of 'Joint Moderators' in Three Prediction Techniques." *J Appl Psychol* 55(3):234–40 Je '71. * (*PA* 46:9774)

CUMULATIVE NAME INDEX

Alexakos, C. E.: 21   McCall, W. A.: *rev*, 2:1574
Cranny, C. J.: 22   Munger, P. F.: 17
Douglass, L. N.: 9   Musselman, J. W.: 7
Eshleman, D. F.: 15   Portenier, L. G.: 12
Garber, W. F.: 14   Preston, R. C.: 13
Gehman, W. S.: 16, 18   Rasmus, C. A.: 19
Gordon, H. P.: 3   Reeder, C. W.: 1
Greene, J. E.: 2   Scates, D. E.: *rev*, 3:540
Humber, W. J.: 4   Sheffield, E. F.: 10
Johnson, A. P.: 5–6   Slayton, W. G.: 20
Jones, E. S.: *rev*, 2:1574 Smith, P. C.: 22
Light, L. L.: 21   Staton, T. F.: 2

Traxler, A. E.: 8   Wrenn, C. G.: 4
Tuft, E. N.: 13   Zedeck, S.: 22
Vale, C. A.: 22   Zeigler, T. W.: 11
Waggoner, R. W.: 11

[1769]

Study Performance Test. High school and college; 1934–43; Herbert A. Toops, Grace Shover, and others; Wilbur L. Layton. *

[1770]

The Study Skills Counseling Evaluation. High school and college; 1962; George Demos; Western Psychological Services. *

For additional information and reviews by Stanley E. Davis and W. G. Fleming, see 6:865.

[1771]

Study Skills Test: McGraw-Hill Basic Skills System. Grades 11–14; 1970; also called *MHBSS Study Skills Test;* although designed for use with the MHBSS instructional program, the test may be used independently; 6 scores: problem solving, underlining, library information, study skills information, total, inventory of study habits and attitudes; Alton L. Raygor; McGraw-Hill Book Co., Inc. *

For additional information and a review by Walter Pauk, see 7:781.

[1772]

Survey of Study Habits and Attitudes. Grades 7–12, 12–14; 1953–67; SSHA; original edition called *Brown-Holtzman Survey of Study Habits and Attitudes;* 7 scores: study habits (delay avoidance, work methods, total), study attitudes (teacher approval, education acceptance, total), total; William F. Brown and Wayne H. Holtzman; Psychological Corporation. *

For additional information, a review by Carleton B. Shay, and excerpts by Martin J. Higgins and Albert E. Roark (with Scott A. Harrington), see 7:782 (69 references); see also 6:856 (12 references); for reviews by James Deese and C. Gilbert Wrenn (with Roy D. Lewis) of the original edition, see 5:688 (14 references).

REFERENCES THROUGH 1971

1–14. See 5:688.
15–26. See 6:856.
27–95. See 7:782.
96. PAUK, WALTER J. "Are Present Reading Tests Valid for Both Girls and Boys?" *J Ed Res* 53:279–80 Mr '60. *
97. DAR, RIFAAT JEHAN, AND ZIA-UL-HAQ, M. "A Study of Actual Study Habits Among IX Class Boys and Girls of Lahore Area in West Pakistan." *B Ed & Res* (Pakistan) 2:45–56 w '63. *
98. SCHNEYER, J. WESLEY. "Factors Associated With the Progress of Students Enrolled in a College Reading Program." *J Ed Res* 56:340–5 Mr '63. *
99. GIBBONS, K. C., AND SAVAGE, R. D. "Intelligence Study Habits and Personality Factors in Academic Success—A Preliminary Report." *Durham Res R* (England) 5:8–12 S '65. *
100. KEISTER, RUTH V. *The Relationship of Study Habits and Attitudes to Predicted and Achieved Grade Point Average and Reading Skills.* Master's thesis, West Virginia University (Morgantown, W.Va.), 1965.
101. HAYNES, CAROLYN R. *The Relationships of Performances of Seventh Grade Students on Measures of Creativity, Study Habits and Attitudes, Expressed Need for Counseling and Achievement.* Master's thesis, Texas A & M University (College Station, Tex.), 1966.
102. LAMMI, ELEANOR HEINZ. *An Investigation of the Relationship of Interests in Forestry and Study Habits and Attitudes to Grade-point Average.* Master's thesis, North Carolina State University (Raleigh, N.C.), 1966.
103. GROOM, HARRY DEE. *Predicting Achievement Behavior of Academic Probation Students at Brigham Young University.* Master's thesis, Brigham Young University (Provo, Utah), 1968.
104. HASLAM, WARREN L., AND BROWN, WILLIAM F. "Effectiveness of Study-Skills Instruction for High School Sophomores." *J Ed Psychol* 59:223–6 Ag '68. * (*PA* 42:16153)
105. COOPER, B., AND FOY, J. M. "Students' Study Habits,

Attitudes and Academic Attainment." *Univ Q* (England) 23(2): 203–12 sp '69. *

106. BRAUN, PETER H. *Subjective and Psychometric Non-Cognitive Scales in Relation to Over- and Under-Achievement.* Master's thesis, University of Alberta (Edmonton, Alta., Canada), 1970.

107. CAZZELLE, JACKIE GENE. *A Study of Non-Intellective Variables Related to the Academic Success and Adjustment of College Freshmen From Low Socioeconomic Backgrounds.* Doctor's thesis, Oklahoma State University (Stillwater, Okla.), 1970. (*DAI* 31:5118A)

108. CURL, GERALD ALLEN. *A Comparison of Freshman Achievers and Non-Achievers From Economically Deprived Families.* Doctor's thesis, University of Illinois (Urbana, Ill.), 1970. (*DAI* 31:4455A)

109. JOHNS, DANIEL JAY. *Correlates of Academic Success in a Predominantly Black, Open-Door, Public, Urban Community College.* Doctor's thesis, University of Virginia (Charlottesville, Va.), 1970. (*DAI* 31:4464A)

110. MOTE, THOMAS ALLAN, JR. *Student Grade Perception and the Prediction of Academic Achievement.* Doctor's thesis, University of Texas (Austin, Tex.), 1970. (*DAI* 32:3794A)

111. STARKS, WALTER LIVINGSTON. *The Relationship of Residence and Economic Factors to the First Semester Academic Achievement of College of Business Administration and College of Agriculture 1969 Freshmen, Male Students.* Doctor's thesis, Oklahoma State University (Stillwater, Okla.), 1970. (*DAI* 31: 5805A)

112. BENGEL, JAMES ELWOOD. *The Relationship Between Self-Attitudes, Academic Performance and Student-Centered Teaching for First Semester Agricultural Institute Students at North Carolina State University.* Doctor's thesis, University of North Carolina (Chapel Hill, N.C.), 1971. (*DAI* 32:2412A)

113. BEYER, DARRELL ERICK. *An Analysis of Selected Intellectual and Nonintellectual Characteristics of Dropouts and Survivors in a Private College.* Doctor's thesis, Baylor University (Waco, Tex.), 1971. (*DAI* 32:3773A)

114. CARDWELL, JESSE FRANKLIN. *A Comparative Study of Intellectually Able Students Who Completed and Who Did Not Complete an Honors and Advanced Placement Program.* Doctor's thesis, George Peabody College for Teachers (Nashville, Tenn.), 1971. (*DAI* 32:1939A)

115. COWELL, M. D., AND ENTWISTLE, N. J. "The Relationships Between Personality, Study Attitudes and Academic Performance in a Technical College." *Brit J Ed Psychol* 41(1):85–90 F '71. * (*PA* 46:9542)

116. DISPENZIERI, ANGELO; GINIGER, SEYMOUR; REICHMAN, WALTER; AND LEVY, MARGUERITE. "College Performance of Disadvantaged Students as a Function of Ability and Personality." *J Counsel Psychol* 18(4):298–305 Jl '71. * (*PA* 46:11687)

117. ENTWISTLE, N. J., AND BRENNAN, T. "The Academic Performance of Students: 2, Types of Successful Students." *Brit J Ed Psychol* 41(3):268–76 N '71. * (*PA* 47:11759)

118. ENTWISTLE, N. J.; NISBET, JENNIFER; ENTWISTLE, DOROTHY; AND COWELL, M. D. "The Academic Performance of Students: 1, Prediction From Scales of Motivation and Study Methods." *Brit J Ed Psychol* 41(3):258–67 N '71. * (*PA* 47: 11781)

119. GARRISON, CLIFFORD BEVERLY. *A Comparative Investigation of Behavorial Counseling Group Techniques Used to Modify Study Skills, Attitudes and Achievement of Selected High School Pupils.* Doctor's thesis, State University of New York (Buffalo, N.Y.), 1971. (*DAI* 32:1271A)

120. HARVEY, RAYMOND CHESTERFIELD, JR. *The Relationship of Study Habits and Attitudes to College Subcultures and to Personality Types.* Doctor's thesis, East Texas State University (Commerce, Tex.), 1971. (*DAI* 32:6030B)

121. JOHNSON, LEONARD ROSS. *A Comparative Investigation of Achievement Motivation in Vocational-Technical and Transfer Students in Selected Texas Junior Colleges.* Doctor's thesis, Baylor University (Waco, Tex.), 1971. (*DAI* 32:3790A)

122. LEWIS, ROBERT WILLIAM, JR. *The Effects of a Planned Group Guidance Program for College-Bound High School Seniors on Selected Guidance Program Variables.* Doctor's thesis, University of Maine (Orono, Me.), 1971. (*DAI* 32:2421A)

123. MOTE, THOMAS A., JR. "Uncontrolled vs. Controlled Administration of the SSHA." *Interam J Psychol* (Mexico) 5(3–4):159–61 '71. * (*PA* 48:12167)

124. PEPPER, ROGER S. "The Study Skills and Academic Achievement of Marginal Admission Students." *Yearb Nat Read Conf* 19(1):248–53 '71. *

125. PHILLIPS, GEORGE O., SR. "Study Habits and Attitudes of Disadvantaged Students in a College Reading and Study Skills Program." *Yearb Nat Read Conf* 19(2):152–7 '71. *

126. SHEPPS, FLORENCE P., AND SHEPPS, R. RONALD. "Relationship of Study Habits and School Attitudes to Achievement in Mathematics and Reading." *J Ed Res* 65(2):71–3 O '71. * (*PA* 48:1841, title only)

127. WEIGEL, RICHARD G.; WEIGEL, VIRGINIA M.; AND HEBERT, JOHN A. "Non-Volunteer Subjects: Temporal Effects." *Psychol Rep* 28(1):191–2 F '71. * (*PA* 46:5449)

128. ZEDECK, SHELDON. "Identification of Moderator Variables by Discriminant Analysis in a Multipredictable Group Validation Model." *J Appl Psychol* 55(4):364–71 Ag '71. * (*PA* 47:1947)

Survey of Study Habits and Attitudes

CUMULATIVE NAME INDEX

[1773]

A Test on Use of the Dictionary. High school and college; 1955–63; 6 scores: pronunciation, meaning, spelling, derivation, usage, total; George D. Spache; Reading Laboratory and Clinic. *

For additional information, see 6:866.

[1774]

★**The Uncritical Inference Test.** College; 1955–67; UIT; no manual; William V. Haney; International Society for General Semantics. *

REFERENCES THROUGH 1971

1. HANEY, WILLIAM VALENTINE. *Measurement of the Ability to Discriminate Between Inferential and Descriptive Statements.*

Doctor's thesis, Northwestern University (Evanston, Ill.), 1953. (*DA* 14:405)

2. HANEY, WILLIAM V. "Are Accident-Prone Drivers Unconscious-Inference Prone?" *Gen Semantics B* 20–21:79–80 '57. *

3. HANEY, WILLIAM V. "Police Experience and Uncritical Inference Behavior." *Gen Semantics B* 22–23:51–4 '58. *

4. HANEY, WILLIAM V. "The Uncritical Inference Test: Applications." *Gen Semantics B* 28–29:26 '61–62. *

5. KOTTMAN, E. JOHN. "Intension and Uncritical Inference Behavior." *ETC* 26(1):53–7 Mr '69. *

CUMULATIVE NAME INDEX

Haney, W. V.: 1–4   Kottman, E. J.: 5

[1775]
Watson-Glaser Critical Thinking Appraisal.

Grades 9–16 and adults; 1942–64; formerly called *Watson-Glaser Tests of Critical Thinking;* Goodwin Watson and Edward M. Glaser; Harcourt Brace Jovanovich, Inc. *

For additional information and excerpted reviews by John O. Crites and G. C. Helmstadter, see 7:783 (74 references); see also 6:867 (24 references); for reviews by Walker H. Hill and Carl I. Hovland of an earlier edition, see 5:700 (8 references); for a review by Robert H. Thouless and an excerpted review by Harold P. Fawcett, see 3:544 (3 references).

REFERENCES THROUGH 1971

1–3. See 3:544.
4–11. See 5:700.
12–35. See 6:867.
36–109. See 7:783.

110. SHNEIDMAN, EDWIN S. "The Case of El: Psychological Test Data." *J Proj Tech* 25:131–54 Je '61. * (*PA* 36:21K31S)

111. D'AOUST, THÉRÈSE. *Predictive Validity of Four Psychometric Tests in a Selected School of Nursing.* Master's thesis, Catholic University of America (Washington, D.C.), 1963.

112. OBST, FRANCES. "A Study of Abilities of Women Students Entering the Colleges of Letters and Science and Applied Arts at the University of California, Los Angeles." *J Ed Res* 57:84–6 O '63. *

113. LYSAUGHT, JEROME P. "Further Analysis of Success Among Auto-Instructional Programmers." *Teaching Aid News* 4:6–11 O 15 '64. *

114. LYSAUGHT, JEROME P. "Selecting Instructional Programmers: New Research Into Characteristics of Successful Programmers." *Training Directors J* 18:8–14 Je '64. *

115. COYLE, F. A., JR., AND BERNARD, J. L. "Logical Thinking and Paranoid Schizophrenia." *J Psychol* 60:283–9 Jl '65. *

116. KROCKOVER, GERALD H. "The Development of Critical Thinking Through Science Instruction." *Proc Iowa Acad Sci* 72:402–4 '65. *

117. LIVINGSTON, HOWARD. "An Investigation of the Effect of Instruction in General Semantics on Critical Reading Ability." *Calif J Ed Res* 16:93–6 Mr '65. * (*PA* 39:10787)

118. QUINN, PATRICK V. "Critical Thinking and Openmindedness in Pupils From Public and Catholic Secondary Schools." *J Social Psychol* 66:23–30 Je '65. * (*PA* 39:14915)

119. STALNAKER, ASHFORD W. "The Watson-Glaser Critical Thinking Appraisal as a Predictor of Programming Performance." *Proc Ann Computer Personnel Res Conf* 3:75–7 '65. *

120. WENBERG, BURNESS G., AND INGERSOLL, RALPH W. "Medical Dietetics: Part 2, The Development of Evaluative Techniques." *J Am Dietetic Assn* 47:298–300 O '65. *

121. ALEXAKOS, C. E. "Predictive Efficiency of Two Multivariate Statistical Techniques in Comparison With Clinical Predictions." *J Ed Psychol* 57:297–306 O '66. * (*PA* 40:12756)

122. STEPHENS, JAMES ALBERT. *A Study of the Correlation Between Critical Thinking Abilities and Achievement in Algebra Involving Advanced Placement.* Master's thesis, North Carolina State University (Raleigh, N.C.), 1966.

123. CROSSON, ROBERT F. "An Investigation Into Certain Personality Variables Among Capital Trial Jurors." Abstract. *Proc 76th Ann Conv Am Psychol Assn* 3:371–2 '68. * (*PA* 43:887, title only)

124. GRACE, JAMES L., JR. "Critical Thinking Ability of Students in Catholic and Public High Schools." *Nat Cath Ed Assn B* 65:49–57 N '68. *

125. PILLAI, N. P., AND NAYAR, P. P. "The Role of Critical Thinking in Science Achievement." *J Ed Res & Exten* (India) 5:1–8 Jl '68. *

126. BROADHURST, NORMAN A. "A Measure of Some Learning Outcomes in Matriculation Chemistry in South Australia." *Austral Sci Teach J* 15(3):67–70 N '69. *

127. WENBERG, BURNESS G.; INGERSOLL, RALPH W.; AND DOHNER, CHARLES W. "Evaluation of Dietetic Interns." *J Am Dietetic Assn* 54(4):297–301 Ap '69. *

128. LA FOREST, JAMES RENE. *Relation of Critical Thinking to Program Planning.* Doctor's thesis, North Carolina State University (Raleigh, N.C.), 1970. (*DAI* 32:1253A)

129. PARSLEY, JAMES FRANCIS, JR. *A Comparison of the Ability of Ninth Grade Students to Apply Several Critical Thinking Skills to Problematic Content Presented Through Two Different Media.* Doctor's thesis, Ohio University (Athens, Ohio), 1970. (*DAI* 31:4629A)

130. POEL, ROBERT HERMAN. *Critical Thinking as Related to PSSC and Non-PSSC Physics Programs.* Doctor's thesis, Western Michigan University (Kalamazoo, Mich.), 1970. (*DAI* 31:3983A)

131. SKINNER, SAMUEL BALLOU. *A Study of the Effect of the St. Andrews Presbyterian College Natural Science Course Upon Critical Thinking Ability.* Doctor's thesis, University of North Carolina (Chapel Hill, N.C.), 1970. (*DAI* 31:3984A)

132. BETRES, JAMES JOHN. *A Study in the Development of the Critical Thinking Skills of Preservice Elementary Teachers.* Doctor's thesis, Ohio University (Athens, Ohio), 1971. (*DAI* 32:2520A)

133. DAVIS, WALTER NEWTON. *Authoritarianism and Selected Trait Patterns of School Administrators: Seventeen Case Studies.* Doctor's thesis, North Texas State University (Denton, Tex.), 1971. (*DAI* 32:1777A)

134. DISPENZIERI, ANGELO; GINIGER, SEYMOUR; REICHMAN, WALTER; AND LEVY, MARGUERITE. "College Performance of Disadvantaged Students as a Function of Ability and Personality." *J Counsel Psychol* 18(4):298–305 Jl '71. * (*PA* 46:11687)

135. FOLLMAN, JOHN; MILLER, WILLIAM; AND BURG, ELDON. "Statistical Analysis of Three Critical Thinking Tests." *Ed & Psychol Meas* 31(2):519–20 su '71. *

136. HJELMHAUG, NOEL NELS. *Context Instruction and the Ability of College Students to Transfer Learning.* Doctor's thesis, Indiana University (Bloomington, Ind.), 1971. (*DAI* 32:1356A)

137. JAMES, REUBEN J. *Traits Associated With the Initial and Persistent Interest in the Study of College Science.* Doctor's thesis, State University of New York (Buffalo, N.Y.), 1971. (*DAI* 32:1296A)

138. KOOKER, EARL W. "The Relationship Between Performance in a Graduate Course in Statistics and the Miller Analogies Test and the Watson-Glaser Critical Thinking Appraisal." *J Psychol* 77(2):165–9 Mr '71. * (*PA* 46:1772)

139. LEWIS, DARRELL R., AND DAHL, TOR. "The Test of Understanding in College Economics and Its Construct Validity." *J Econ Ed* 2(2):155–66 sp '71. *

140. LOWE, A. J.; FOLLMAN, JOHN; BURLEY, WADE; AND FOLLMAN, JOHNNY. "Psychometric Analysis of Critical Reading and Critical Thinking Test Scores—Twelfth Grade." *Yearb Nat Read Conf* 20:142–7 '71. *

141. O'TOOLE, DENNIS MARTIN. *An Accountability Evaluation of an In-Service Economic Education Experience.* Doctor's thesis, Ohio University (Athens, Ohio), 1971. (*DAI* 32:2315A)

142. RADEBAUGH, BYRON F., AND JOHNSON, JAMES A. "Excellent Teachers: What Makes Them Outstanding? Phase 2." *Ill Sch Res* 7(3):12–20 sp '71. *

143. SMITH, RICHARD LEE. *A Factor-Analytic Study of Critical Reading/Thinking, Influenceability, and Related Factors.* Doctor's thesis, University of Maine (Orono, Me.), 1971. (*DAI* 32:6229A)

144. WILLIAMS, BILLY RICHARD. *Critical Thinking Ability as Affected by a Unit on Symbolic Logic.* Doctor's thesis, Arizona State University (Tempe, Ariz.), 1971. (*DAI* 31:6434A)

CUMULATIVE NAME INDEX

Alexakos, C. E.: 121
Alspaugh, C. A.: 95
Alston, D. N.: 78
Armstrong, N. A.: 96
Barker, L. L.: 72
Bass, J. C.: 18
Beckman, V. E.: 36
Bergman, L. M. E.: 23
Bernard, J. L.: 115
Bessent, E. W.: 26
Betres, J. J.: 132
Bledsoe, J. C.: 8
Bostrom, E. A.: 79
Bradberry, R. D.: 65
Brakken, E.: 47
Braun, J. R.: 80
Brembeck, W. L.: 4–5
Broadhurst, N. A.: 81, 97, 126
Brouillette, O. J.: 66
Brown, L.: 101
Brownell, J. A.: 7
Burg, E.: 101, 135
Burley, W.: 140
Burton, A.: 3
Canter, R. R.: 6
Carleton, F. O.: 98
Carnes, D. D.: 82
Chang, E. C. F.: 83
Combs, C. M.: 67
Cook, J.: 9
Corell, J. H.: 68

Cousins, J. E.: 39
Coyle, F. A.: 115
Crane, W. J.: 29
Crawford, C. D.: 14
Crites, J. O.: *exc,* 7:783
Crosson, R. F.: 123
Dahl, T.: 139
D'Aoust, T.: 111
Davis, W. N.: 133
De Graaf, C.: 10
De Martino, H. A.: 99
Denney, L. L.: 69
Dirr, P. M.: 51
Dispenzieri, A.: 134
Dohner, C. W.: 127
Duckworth, J. B.: 70
Ennis, R. H.: 11
Fawcett, H. P.: *exc,* 3:544
Flora, L. D.: 52
Follman, J.: 84–6, 100–1, 105, 135, 140
Follman, J. C.: 87
Frank, A. D.: 55, 88
Friend, C. M.: 15
Geckler, J. W.: 48
George, K. D.: 71
Gibson, J. W.: 72
Giniger, S.: 134
Glaser, E. M.: 1
Glidden, G. W.: 43
Goss, R. G.: 93

Grace, J. L.: 124
Gruner, C. R.: 103
Haas, M. G.: 40
Hardesty, D. L.: 73
Harkless, R.: 102
Helm, C. R.: 56
Helmstadter, G. C.: *exc*, 7:783
Henkel, E. T.: 74
Herber, H. L.: 19
Hernandez, D.: 85–6
Hernandez, D. E.: 105
Hill, W. H.: *rev*, 5:700
Hjelmhaug, N. N.: 136
Hollenbach, J. W.: 10
Hovland, C. I.: *rev*, 5:700
Howell, W. S.: 2
Hunt, E. J.: 57
Hunter, N. W.: 75
Ingersoll, R. W.: 120, 127
Jabs, M. L.: 89
Jackson, T. R.: 27
James, R. J.: 137
Jenkins, A. C.: 53
Joël, W.: 3
Johnson, J. A.: 142
Jones, R. S.: 30
Jones, W. S.: 73
Juergenson, E. M.: 16
Kaiser, H. F.: 30
Kenoyer, M. F.: 37
Kibler, R. J.: 72
Kirtley, D.: 102
Kooker, E. W.: 138
Krockover, G. H.: 116
La Forest, J. R.: 128
Land, M.: 41
Larter, S. J.: 90
Levy, M.: 134
Lewis, D. R.: 139
Livingston, H.: 117
Lowe, A. J.: 140
Luck, J. I.: 103
Luton, J. N.: 13
Lysaught, J. P.: 42, 44–5, 104, 107, 113–4
Miller, W.: 85–6, 105, 135
Milton, O.: 24
Moffett, C. R.: 12
Moskovis, L. M.: 58, 106

Nayar, P. P.: 125
Ness, J. H.: 59
Nunnery, M. Y.: 17, 20
Obst, F.: 112
Opdyke, D.: 60
O'Toole, D. M.: 141
Owens, T. R.: 54
Parsley, J. F.: 129
Pierleoni, R. G.: 44, 104, 107
Pillai, N. P.: 125
Poel, R. H.: 130
Quinn, P. V.: 34, 118
Radebaugh, B. F.: 142
Reichman, W.: 134
Renner, J. W.: 94
Roaden, A. L.: 54
Roby, T. B.: 61
Rodd, W. G.: 21
Rust, V. I.: 22, 25, 28, 30
Sellers, J. R.: 64
Seymour, P. J.: 49
Shatin, L.: 60
Shneidman, E. S.: 110
Shockley, J. T.: 31
Singer, E.: 61
Skelly, C. G.: 38
Skinner, S. B.: 131
Smith, J. R.: 91
Smith, P. M.: 35
Smith, R. G.: 50
Smith, R. L.: 143
Snider, C. F. B.: 108
Snider, J. G.: 46
Stalnaker, A. W.: 119
Stephens, J. A.: 122
Taylor, P. A.: 90
Thouless, R. H.: *rev*, 3:544
Titus, H. E.: 92–3
Trela, T. M.: 32, 62
Troxel, V. A.: 108
Walton, F. X.: 76
Welsch, L. A.: 63
Wenberg, B. G.: 120, 127
Westbrook, B. W.: 64
Wevrick, L.: 109
Williams, B. R.: 144
Yager, R. E.: 77
Yoesting, C.: 94
Zubek, J. P.: 15

[1776]

★**Wisconsin Tests of Reading Skill Development: Study Skills.** Grades kgn–1, 1–2, 2–3, 3–4, 4–5, 5–6, 6–7; 1970–73; WTRSD:SS; part of the Wisconsin Design for Reading Skill Development; 2–14 "single-skill" scores at each of 7 levels; 80% mastery criterion suggested for each subtest, with retesting at next higher level if a child fails not more than one subtest and retesting at next lower level if a child passes not more than one subtest; handbook and planning guide by Wayne Otto (principal investigator), Eunice Askov, and Robert D. Chester; manuals by Deborah M. Stewart, Karlyn Kamm, James Allen, and Diane K. Sals (*c–e*); NCS Interpretive Scoring Systems. *

a) LEVEL A. Grades kgn–1; 2 scores: position of objects, measurement (size); test by Karlyn Kamm, Deborah M. Stewart, and Virginia L. Van Blaricom.
b) LEVEL B. Grades 1–2; 4 scores: picture symbols, picture grids, measurement (distance), graphs (relative amounts); test by Karlyn Kamm, Deborah M. Stewart, and Virginia L. Van Blaricom.

c) LEVEL C. Grades 2–3; 10 scores: nonpictorial symbols, color keys, number-letter grids, measurement (size, distance), graphs (exact amounts, differences), tables (relative amounts, one cell), alphabetizing; test by Karlyn Kamm, Deborah M. Stewart, Virginia L. Van Blaricom, James Allen, and Mary L. Ramberg.
d) LEVEL D. Grades 3–4; 12 scores: point and line symbols, scale (whole units), graphs (differences, approximate amounts), tables (differences), indexes, tables of contents, alphabetizing, guide words, headings and subheadings, selecting sources, facts or opinions; test by Karlyn Kamm, Deborah M. Stewart, Virginia L. Van Blaricom, Evelyn Weible, James Allen, J. Laird Marshall, Mary L. Ramberg, and Diane K. Sals.
e) LEVEL E. Grades 4–5; 14 scores: point-line-area symbols, intermediate directions, scale (multiple whole units), graphs (differences, purpose and summary), tables (multiplicative differences, purpose and summary), indexes, dictionary meanings, cross references, guide words, guide cards, specialized references, fact checking.
f) LEVEL F. Grades 5–6; 12 scores: maps (analysis), map projections, inset maps, different scales, graphs (differences), schedules (relationship), *Subject Index*, dictionary pronunciation, card filing rules, Dewey Decimal System, outlining, catalog cards.
g) LEVEL G. Grades 6–7; 10 scores: maps (synthesis), latitude and longitude, meridians and parallels, scale (fractional units), graphs (multiplicative differences, projecting and relating), schedules (problem solving), *Reader's Guide*, card catalogs, outlining.

[Out of Print Since TIP I]

Ability to Learn (Exploratory and Corrective Inventory), T:1519
Application of Certain Principles of Logical Reasoning, R:256, 2:1528 (4 references)
Bennett Use of Library Test, R:258, 4:578 (1 review)
California Study Methods Survey, R:236, 6:857 (2 reviews, 2 excerpts, 9 references)
Cooperative Dictionary Test, R:259, 5:690 (1 review)
Edmiston How to Study Test, R:262, 4:580
Library Usage Test, R:268, 3:537 (1 review)
Peabody Library Information Test, R:241, 3:538 (1 review, 2 excerpts, 2 references)
Senior High School Library and Reference Skills Test, R:274, 6:863
Special Reading Test: Ohio Senior Survey Tests, R:275, 3:539 (1 review)
Spitzer Study Skills Test, R:244, 6:864 (2 reviews, 1 reference)
Stanford Achievement Test: Study Skills, R:276, 5:698 (2 reviews)
Survey of Study Habits, R:249, 4:583 (1 review, 1 reference)
Test of Critical Thinking, R:279, 4:584
Test of Study Skills, R:280, 5:699 (2 reviews)
Tyler-Kimber Study Skills Test, R:251, 2:1580 (4 reviews, 1 reference)
Work-Study Skills: Iowa Every-Pupil Tests of Basic Skills, R:254, 4:588 (1 review)

READING – SEVENTH MMY

REVIEWS BY *Ira E. Aaron, Georgia S. Adams, Nicholas Anastasiow, Rebecca C. Barr, Robert H. Bauernfeind, Paul Conrad Berg, Allen Berger, Donald B. Black, John R. Bormuth, M. A. Brimer, N. Dale Bryant, Carolyn L. Burke, Thorsten R. Carlson, William E. Coffman, S. Alan Cohen, Frederick B. Davis, Dennis J. Deloria, Evelyn Deno, Gerald G. Duffy, Robert Dykstra, Roger Farr, Robert A. Forsyth, Edward B. Fry, John J. Geyer, Marvin D. Glock, Elizabeth J. Goodacre, Arlen R. Gullickson, John T. Guthrie, Albert J. Harris, Larry A. Harris, Mildred H. Huebner, Colleen B. Jamison, Lawrence M. Kasdon, Willard A. Kerr, Albert J. Kingston, Martin Kling, Roy A. Kress, Boyd R. McCandless, James J. McCarthy, Constance M. McCullough, Lester Mann, Samuel T. Mayo, William A. Mehrens, Jason Millman, Ronald W. Mitchell, Alice E. Moriarty, John Nisbet, Walter Pauk, Douglas A. Pidgeon, Gus P. Plessas, M. L. Kellmer Pringle, Earl F. Rankin, H. Alan Robinson, Jerome Rosner, Roger A. Ruth, Richard Rystrom, Carleton B. Shay, Harry Singer, Edward R. Sipay, Kenneth J. Smith, George D. Spache, Arthur E. Traxler, Robert E. Valett, Byron H. Van Roekel, David M. Wark, and David P. Weikart.*

[682]

★**Burnett Reading Series: Survey Test.** Grades 1.5–2.4, 2.5–3.9, 4.0–6.9, 7.0–9.9, 10.0–12.9; 1966–70; 5 levels; 1–2 forms; preliminary technical report ('67, 11 pages, for *a–d*); $5.60 per 35 tests, postage extra; 50¢ per specimen set of any one level, cash orders only; technical report free; (50) minutes; Richard W. Burnett; Scholastic Testing Service, Inc. *

a) PRIMARY 1. Grades 1.5–2.4; 1966–69; 4 scores: word identification, word meaning, comprehension, total; Forms A ('67, 16 pages), B ('68, 16 pages); manual ('69, 21 pages).

b) PRIMARY 2. Grades 2.5–3.9; 1966–69; scores same as for Primary 1; Forms A ('67, 16 pages, identical with test published in 1966), B ('68, 16 pages); manual ('69, 21 pages).

c) INTERMEDIATE. Grades 4.0–6.9; 1966–69; scores same as for Primary 1; Forms A ('67, 16 pages, identical with test published in 1966), B ('68, 16 pages); manual ('69, 28 pages); separate answer sheets (NCS) must be used; $5 per 50 answer sheets; $1.50 per set of scoring materials for Intermediate, Advanced, and Senior Levels; scoring service, 20¢ per test.

d) ADVANCED. Grades 7.0–9.9; 1967; 4 scores: vocabulary, comprehension, total, rate and accuracy; Form A (16 pages); manual (21 pages); remaining details same as for Intermediate.

e) SENIOR. Grades 10.0–12.9; 1968–70; scores same as for Advanced; Form A ('68, 16 pages); manual ('70, 11 pages); no norms; no data on reliability; remaining details as for Intermediate.

ROGER FARR, *Associate Professor of Education and Director, Reading Clinic, Indiana University, Bloomington, Indiana.*

This test has been developed primarily to serve as a general survey of students' reading ability. It is commendable that the author has developed his test in five levels so that each level covers only a limited achievement range. Regretfully, many survey tests available today attempt to cover a wide span of achievement levels and thereby decrease their validity.

The makeup of the subtests is the major weakness of the Burnett tests. The first three levels of the test include a test of word identification. The task in each item on this subtest is to select from four alternatives a word read by the teacher. At the Intermediate level, many of these items include three non-words and one actual word. For example, in Form B, on one item the word the examiner reads is *character* and the four choices are: "character, charcter, caracker, and cahicter." Obviously, some children will not have to hear the teacher read anything to select the correct response. In addition, the author's definition of "word identification" as used in this test is an extremely narrow one. The author has emphasized a very careful and precise listening to sounds and the matching of the sounds to a configuration of letters.

Other items on the word identification test seem to be measuring a visual recognition of correctly spelled words. An example of this from the Intermediate level, Form B, is an item including these four choices: "inaxaustable, inexhaustible, inexhaustibel, and enexhastable." From a descriptive linguist's point of view each of the first three of these letter configurations is a possible orthographic representation of the spoken word *inexhaustible*.

The comprehension subtest on all five levels of the series utilizes a modified cloze procedure. The task for the examinee is to select from three alternatives the correct choice for a blank in a passage. The major weakness of this section as a measure of reading comprehension is that some of the items are measuring dialect patterns rather than reading comprehension. For example, in Primary 2, Form A, the examinee must select the word *were* rather than *was* for the blank in a sentence. Certainly the dialect patterns of some children would lead them to select *was*.

Other correct choices on the comprehension test seem to be rather arbitrary. For example, in Primary 1, Form A, the correct choice for a sentence is "my grandmother had *promised* she would send a surprise." However, it certainly seems quite feasible for a child to select *agreed,* one of the alternatives given, for this blank. Finally, the use of the cloze technique to measure higher level comprehension skills such as critical reading and making inferences is questionable. It seems quite logical to assume that the comprehension subtests in this series may be measuring at best only literal comprehension.

The vocabulary subtest for the first two levels follows the common practice of asking examinees to match a picture with one of four words. This type of item is subject to cultural bias which affects picture interpretation and thus reduces the test's validity. For example, in Primary 1, Form A, a horse, a cow, a squirrel, and a split rail fence, all pictured, may not be common to the backgrounds of many inner city first grade children.

The interpretation of test scores at all levels of the series is extremely difficult because of the lack of description of the norming population. Test users are told in the technical manual that the 141 schools were selected from the total population of schools that have been using other Scholastic Testing Service tests; the 44,025 students in these schools were administered the Burnett tests. That this population is not described in any other way negates the use of the norm tables provided in the manuals. Neither the manual for the fifth level of the test nor the technical manual describes how the norms of this level of the test were developed. Presumably they were developed in the same manner as those for the other levels of the test, but this is not stated in any of the publisher's materials.

Test validity for the total test scores of the first three levels of the test were developed by correlating the Burnett scores with reading scores on the *Stanford Achievement Test*. Correlations range from a low of .74 for sixth graders to a high of .86 for first graders. These correlations are fairly substantial and indicate that there exists at least over 50 percent commonality in what the two tests are measuring. However, the samples for these studies are extremely small (48 to 70) and also undescribed; therefore, a test user is not able to place much faith in this evidence. Despite suggestions that the subtest scores can be used for diagnostic purposes, no subtest validity evidence is provided anywhere in the manual.

K-R 21 reliabilities are reported for the first four levels for total test and subtest scores. These reliabilities are based at each level on approximately 1,500 students randomly selected from the norming population. The total test reliabilities range from .92 to .94. The subtest reliabilities range from .77 to .93. The higher reliabilities for the subtests are usually achieved on the comprehension subtests. These reliabilities seem to indicate that the total test scores are quite reliable but that the subtest scores, with the possible exception of the comprehension subtests, are not stable enough to be used independently for diagnostic purposes.

In summary, it seems that the Burnett tests

Burnett Reading Series

reflect several major weaknesses. Test norms are incomplete and poorly described; validity evidence for the various subtests is completely missing; and serious questions can be raised concerning the interpretation of a number of items on all levels of the test. There are certainly more carefully and completely developed reading tests available to the test user.

[683]

*California Achievement Tests: Reading, 1970 Edition.** Grades 1.5–2, 2–4, 4–6, 6–9, 9–12; 1933–70; previous edition (see 6:784) still available; 3 scores: vocabulary, comprehension, total; 1 form; 5 levels; for battery manuals and accessories, see 5; separate answer sheets (CompuScan [NCS], Digitek, IBM 1230) may be used in grades 4–12; postage extra; original edition by Ernest W. Tiegs and Willis W. Clark; CTB/McGraw-Hill. *

a) LEVEL 1. Grades 1.5–2; Form A ('70, 12 pages); 2 editions; $2.45 per specimen set of both editions, postpaid; 46(65) minutes.

1) *Hand Scorable Booklet.* $5 per 35 tests.
2) *CompuScan Machine Scorable Booklet.* $7.70 per 35 tests; scoring service, 27¢ and over per test.

b) LEVEL 2. Grades 2–4; Form A ('70, 12 pages); 2 editions; prices same as for level 1; 40(68) minutes.

1) *Hand Scorable Booklet.*
2) *CompuScan Machine Scorable Booklet.*

c) LEVEL 3. Grades 4–6; Form A ('70, 14 pages); $6 per 35 tests; $2.50 per 50 answer sheets; $1 per IBM hand scoring stencil; $2 per specimen set, postpaid; CompuScan scoring service, 22¢ and over per test; 45(70) minutes.

d) LEVEL 4. Grades 6–9; Form A ('70, 15 pages); prices same as for level 3; 50(75) minutes.

e) LEVEL 5. Grades 9–12; Form A ('70, 16 pages); prices same as for level 3; 50(75) minutes.

REFERENCES

1–5. See 5:622.
6–18. See 6:784.
19. MOE, IVER L. *Auding as a Predictive Measure of Reading Performance in Primary Grades.* Doctor's thesis, University of Florida (Gainesville, Fla.), 1957. (*DA* 18:121)
20. TURNER, DANIEL. *A Study of Speech Effectiveness and Personal and Social Adjustment Among Ninth Grade Pupils.* Doctor's thesis, Boston University (Boston, Mass.), 1957. (*DA* 17:2902)
21. McCULLOUGH, RAYMOND OLIVER, JR. *The Reading Growth of Three Hundred Recent High School Graduates.* Doctor's thesis, Pennsylvania State University (University Park, Pa.), 1958. (*DA* 19:1251)
22. SEAY, LESTEN CLARE. *A Study to Determine Some Relations Between Changes in Reading Skills and Self-Concepts Accompanying a Remedial Program for Boys With Low Reading Ability and Reasonably Normal Intelligence.* Doctor's thesis, North Texas State College (Denton, Tex.), 1960. (*DA* 21:2598)
23. SIPAY, EDWARD ROBERT. *A Comparison of Standardized Reading Achievement Test Scores and Functional Reading Levels.* Doctor's thesis, University of Connecticut (Storrs, Conn.), 1961. (*DA* 22:2639)
24. LOPEZ, DANIEL CLARENCE. *Effects of Test Format on the Reading Scores of Fifth Grade Children.* Doctor's thesis, Stanford University (Stanford, Calif.), 1962. (*DA* 23:1972)
25. BROWN, SANDRA ROSE. *A Comparison of Five Widely Used Standardized Reading Tests and an Informal Reading Inventory for a Selected Group of Elementary School Children.* Doctor's thesis, University of Georgia (Athens, Ga.), 1963. (*DA* 25:996)
26. WILLIAMS, JOAN LEE. *A Comparison of Standardized Reading Test Scores and Informal Reading Inventory Scores.* Doctor's thesis, Southern Illinois University (Carbondale, Ill.), 1963. (*DA* 24:5262)
27. BUCK, JAMES R., JR. *Some Identifiable Characteristics of Students Entering Negro Senior Colleges in Mississippi.* Doctor's thesis, George Peabody College for Teachers (Nashville, Tenn.), 1964. (*DA* 25:5039)
28. CAMPBELL, W.; SHEPPARD, C.; BOBBE, CAROL; AND

LAMBERTI, ELAINE. "An Evaluation of the California Achievement Test, Elementary, Form W, Reading Comprehension." *J Ed Res* 58:75–7 O '64. *
29. COOPER, BERNICE. "An Analysis of the Reading Achievement of White and Negro Pupils in Certain Public Schools of Georgia." *Sch R* 72:462–71 w '64. * (*PA* 39:8697)
30. JONES, ROBERT A.; KAPLAN, ROBERT; AND MICHAEL, WILLIAM B. "The Predictive Validity of a Modified Battery of Tests in Language Skills for Foreign Students at an American University." *Ed & Psychol Meas* 24:961–5 w '64. * (*PA* 39:8687)
31. PETTY, EDGAR LAWTON. *The Effect of Four Methods of Recording Answers to Standardized Test Items on Mean Achievement at Four Grade Levels.* Doctor's thesis, University of Oklahoma (Norman, Okla.), 1964. (*DA* 25:3405)
32. SCHECK, ROSE RAYNOR. *An Investigation of Children's Knowledge of Single and of Multiple Meanings of Words and Reading Comprehension.* Doctor's thesis, Temple University (Philadelphia, Pa.), 1964. (*DA* 25:6657)
33. KARLIN, ROBERT, AND JOLLY, HAYDEN. "The Use of Alternate Forms of Standardized Reading Tests." *Read Teach* 19:187–91+ D '65. *
34. MICHAEL, WILLIAM B.; HANEY, RUSSELL; AND BROWN, STEPHEN W. "The Predictive Validity of a Battery of Diversified Measures Relative to Success in Student Nursing." *Ed & Psychol Meas* 25:579–84 su '65. * (*PA* 39:15247)
35. WILSON, JAMES JOHN, III. *The Relationship of Reading Achievement, Patterns of Eye Movements, and Emotional and Personality Adjustment.* Doctor's thesis, Arizona State University (Tempe, Ariz.), 1965. (*DA* 26:1999)
36. SUTHERLAND, SAMUEL PHILIP. *A Factor Analytic Study of Tests Designed to Measure Reading Ability.* Doctor's thesis, University of Southern California (Los Angeles, Calif.), 1966. (*DA* 27:4141A)
37. BURKE, JACK DALE. *The Predictive Validity of English Language Screening Instruments for Foreign Students Entering the University of Southern California.* Doctor's thesis, University of Southern California (Los Angeles, Calif.), 1968. (*DA* 29:3118A)
38. DAVIS, WILLIAM QUINBY. *A Study of Test Score Comparability Among Five Widely Used Reading Survey Tests.* Doctor's thesis, Southern Illinois University (Carbondale, Ill.), 1968. (*DA* 29:4370A)
39. EGGERS, PATRICIA M. *A Study of the Adjacent Test Levels of the California Reading Test for Remedial Reading Placement.* Master's thesis, California State College (Los Angeles, Calif.), 1968.
40. FARR, ROGER. "The Convergent and Discriminant Validity of Several Upper Level Reading Tests." *Yearb Nat Read Conf* 17:181–91 '68. *
41. BOTEL, MORTON. "A Comparative Study of the Validity of the Botel Reading Inventory and Selected Standardized Tests." *Proc Ann Conv Int Read Assn* 13(1):721–7 '69. *
42. FARR, ROGER, AND ANASTASIOW, NICHOLAS. *Tests of Reading Readiness and Achievement: A Review and Evaluation,* pp. 25–30. Newark, Del.: International Reading Association, 1969. Pp. iv, 51. *
43. GOSNELL, EMMA SUE. *An Analysis of Questions Contained in Selected Intermediate Standardized Reading Tests.* Master's thesis, Eastern Illinois University (Charleston, Ill.), 1969.
44. LOVETT, CARL JAMES. *An Analysis of the Relationship of Several Variables to Achievement in First Year Algebra.* Doctor's thesis, University of Texas (Austin, Tex.), 1969. (*DAI* 30:1470A)
45. RAKES, THOMAS. *A Comparison of the Results of the California Reading Test With an Informal Reading Inventory as Revealed by a Sampling of Fifteen Special Needs Students.* Master's thesis, East Tennessee State University (Johnson City, Tenn.), 1969.
46. KRIPPNER, STANLEY. "Reading Improvement and Its Correlates." *Percept & Motor Skills* 31(3):727–31 D '70. * (*PA* 45:10694)
47. MARS, PAUL ARNE. *High School Geometry Achievement as Related to Reading Achievement, Arithmetic Achievement, and General Intelligence in the Public Schools of Lincoln Nebraska.* Doctor's thesis, University of Nebraska (Lincoln, Neb.), 1970. (*DAI* 31:1691A)

For reviews by John C. Flanagan and James R. Hobson of an earlier edition, see 4:530 (1 excerpt); for a review by Frederick B. Davis, see 2:1563; for reviews by Ivan A. Booker and Joseph C. Dewey, see 1:1110. For reviews of earlier editions of the complete battery, see 6:3 (2 reviews), 5:2 (1 review), 4:2 (3 reviews), 3:15 (1 review), 2:1193 (2 reviews), and 1:876 (1 review, 1 excerpt).

[684]

★The Carver-Darby Chunked Reading Test.
Grades 9–16 and adults; 1970; CDCRT; 3 scores:
efficiency, accuracy, rate; Forms A, B, (18 pages);
manual (33 pages); separate answer sheets (IBM
1230) must be used; $10 per 25 tests; $2.50 per 50
answer sheets; $4 per specimen set; postpaid; 25(35–
40) minutes; Ronald P. Carver and Charles A. Darby,
Jr.; American Institutes for Research. *

ARLEN R. GULLICKSON, *Research Assistant,
College of Education, University of Minnesota,
Minneapolis, Minnesota.*

PURPOSE. CDCRT has been designed "to
measure the information stored during reading
and is appropriate for mature language users,
such as high school students, college students,
or adults." It is to be used to assess individual
students in order to diagnose reading difficulties
and prescribe possible treatments; to study information processing by setting up and testing
hypotheses through analyses of individual score
patterns; and to measure individual differences
in reading comprehension.

TEST DEVELOPMENT AND DESIGN. Each of the
two forms consists of six reading passages, the
first of which is used as a sample test. On the
back side of the page following each reading
passage, the passage has been rewritten into 20
segments. Each of these 20 parts consists of the
material written as five "chunks" of meaningfully related words. One chunk in each five-
chunk part has been reworded so that the original meaning of that passage is changed. After
reading the original passage, the examinee must
(without referring back to the original passage)
determine which chunk has been changed in
meaning for each of the 20 parts.

The final test forms, A and B, were the result
of a four-step process. Twelve passages and
their related questions were written, tested with
a sample of 60 college students, and then
revised. The revised passages and questions
were then organized into two "parallel" forms,
A and B. Directions were written and later
revised after the two forms were administered
individually to five students. At that time an
"optimal" test time limit of 25 minutes was set.

Three scores are obtained for each person:
(*a*) efficiency, the total number of questions
answered correctly; (*b*) rate, the number of
the last item attempted; (*c*) accuracy, the
percent of attempted items which were answered
correctly. The rate and accuracy scores are
included to aid in "diagnosing the source of

the reader's difficulty which is producing his
low efficiency score."

ADMINISTRATION. The directions for administering the test are clear and well written. They
state that "the test has been designed so that
no one can finish all the items and still answer
them accurately." However, the manual provides no support for that statement. The
directions also state, "all passages are equally
difficult." This statement is not documented and
it appears that no serious attempt was made to
insure an equal difficulty level for all passages.
Certainly if these two test directions are made
as facts, they should be justified since both are
expected to have a pronounced effect on the
manner in which individuals complete the test.

A potential problem of test administration
may result if the students, while answering
questions, do turn back to reread portions of
the original passage. The authors recognize this
problem and indicate that students should be
monitored during the test, but efficient monitoring could become difficult to accomplish if the
group being tested is large.

The test manual indicates that one function
of the scores is to determine an individual's
absolute change in reading score. To facilitate
that use, the directions instruct students not to
skip questions. Since this is a timed test which
most individuals will not finish, the raw test
scores should be corrected for chance. The
manual does correct for chance in one part of
its validity study, but the reported norms are
not corrected for chance. Also, in the section
on scoring there is no indication that individual
scores should be corrected for chance nor are
any directions given for correcting for chance.

NORMS. "Preliminary norms" (means and
standard deviations) are based on a sample
size of 41. This group is described only as
"41 college student volunteers." No information
regarding age, sex, or educational experience
was given. The only indication of the group's
reading ability is this statement, "a comparison
of the means and standard deviations of the
tested group on two other standardized reading
tests indicates that the group was above average
and restricted in range." For anyone using this
test with college students, that description of
the individuals tested is little, if any, better than
nothing. The norms are wholly unsatisfactory
for any group, especially for high school students and adults, for whom this test was specifically intended. A large or representative sample,

Carver-Darby Chunked Reading Test

perhaps, cannot be reasonably expected for such a new test, but the manual should at least describe the persons tested, not to mention having a sample of all major categories of individuals for whom the test is intended.

RELIABILITY. Since the test is speeded, the alternate forms method of determining reliability has been used. Reliability coefficients, standard deviations, and standard errors of measurement are given for each form. The reliability coefficients for the three scores, efficiency (.81), accuracy (.65), and rate (.76) are not high. The 95 percent confidence interval for accuracy, whose reliability is lowest, ranges from .43 to .81. Even for efficiency, whose reliability is highest, the 95 percent confidence interval ranges from .67 to .89. For the ill-defined population, the assurance that true reliability coefficients fall within these *large* confidence interval ranges leaves one with very little confidence in the precision of these reported reliabilities.

In order to address the situation of measuring individual student changes, the manual introduced a new measure of reliability. An explanation of this method of reliability estimation is given in neither the manual nor any other published source. The lack of an explanation renders this reliability measure useless to potential CDCRT users.

VALIDITY. A study involving 61 paid college students who took both the CDCRT and the *Nelson-Denny Reading Test* supports the claim that the CDCRT does discriminate between persons who have read the passages before responding to the test items and those who did not read the passages before responding. The results for the group tested also indicate that the CDCRT did a better job at this type of discrimination than did the Nelson-Denny test.

A further attempt to provide construct and concurrent validity involved a separate study. That study (apparently the same study from which the reliability data were obtained) attempted to show the validity of the efficiency, accuracy and rate scores. Correlation coefficients were obtained for these variables with comparable variables in the *Nelson-Denny Reading Test,* the *Davis Reading Test,* and the *Tinker Speed of Reading Test.* Unfortunately, the criticisms of unrepresentative sample and large interval estimates of reliability apply equally to the concurrent validity study.

A validity concern of serious nature involves the manual's attempt to "help" the consumer assess and diagnose an individual's reading difficulties. The manual includes six categories of mature readers and gives hypothesized attributes of the readers in each category and the approximate percent of the pupils tested who fell into each category. No information is given to substantiate either the categorization or the hypothesized attributes for diagnosis. Consequently, persons utilizing that aspect of the test must accept on faith alone the developers' insight. The authors place no restrictions on who should use the test. Consequently, many novices may use it and accept as correct the manual's interpretation of the test scores and diagnoses of possible reading problems. The theoretical or empirical support for the categorizations and hypotheses should have been presented along with appropriate cautions for use. In addition, the CDCRT should have been labeled "for research use only" at this time.

This reviewer would expect both the type of material and the difficulty level of the material to greatly affect an individual's reading comprehension and speed. For example, one would not expect an individual to read a novel and a physics text with the same speeds or with the same comprehensions. No information is given to support the position that the CDCRT is of the correct reading level for the individuals it proposes to test nor does the manual indicate for what type of reading material these variables are being measured. Also, it would seem that both the type of material read and the average level of reading difficulty would differ across the groups of individuals to be tested, yet no mention of this issue is made.

SUMMARY. While the test's ideas and format appear to be promising, at the present time the CDCRT is clearly not ready for general use. The test purports to be both a valid measure of information stored during reading, and "an indicator of individual differences in reading comprehension." These claims have not been substantiated by the manual. The reliability and validity studies reported can be best described as pilot studies from which the test appears to have some promise. If the claims made by the manual are to have credibility, they will have to be supported by data from a representative sample of sufficient size to provide accurate estimates of the test's reliability and validity.

Carver-Darby Chunked Reading Test

RICHARD RYSTROM, *Associate Professor of Reading, University of Georgia, Athens, Georgia.*

This test is unique in that it measures an examinee's ability to recall "chunks" of information rather than his ability to answer questions about an essay. The test items consist of five essays divided into 100 phrases/clauses of from one to five words in length. One phrase from each succession of five "has been changed in meaning from the original passage. The examinee's task for a single test item is to identify the changed chunk in each set of five chunks." The authors feel their test has the following advantages: "it indicates comprehension·at the sentence level"; "it employs meaningful units of measurement," i.e., chunks; and it discriminates "between readers and nonreaders of [test] passages" more effectively than most comprehension tests.

The test provides the user with three scores: efficiency, the total number of items answered correctly; rate, the number of the last item attempted; and accuracy, the percentage of attempted items which were answered correctly. While no normative data for the test are presented, the manual does identify six different types of readers; each type and the probable proportion of college students in each category are described. Intercorrelations between subtests and alternate-form reliabilities are presented in the manual. Concurrent validity was measured by correlating this test with three other reading tests. Construct validity was measured by comparing the test results of subjects who read the essays before taking the test with results of subjects who took the test without reading the essays. Since a test question does not consist of a single correct answer and several distracter answers, this test cannot be validated by correlating test sections with the total score or by using factor analysis. The authors do not present content validity data.

Several of the following comments raise questions about the validity of this test: First, a test question rarely corresponds to an individual sentence. For example, in the first test passage (Form A) an examinee answers 20 test items about 17 sentences; each sentence is divided into 2 to 12 chunks but each item contains 5 chunks. Second, commas between main clauses and nonrestrictive modifiers in the reading passages are sometimes deleted in the test section. These deletions appear to be typographical errors. Third, there does not appear to be any meaningful or consistent basis used for dividing sentences into chunks. Sometimes the division occurs between a noun phrase and a verb phrase, or between a noun head and a following prepositional phrase, or between a main clause and its nonrestrictive modifier. At other times a division is made between items which cannot be divided in any meaningful way. Fourth, some of the changes made in the test items leave the examinee with a tangle of ·meaningfully unrelated structures, e.g., "In twelve states, moving across a county line is sufficient, unless you are ineligible for six months." Also, it is impossible to interpret any three adjacent sentences which have been changed in the test section. An examinee must first read a passage which makes sense; he must then read an additional passage which does not make sense and identify those items which were changed.

This test assumes that meaning occurs only within sentences. At no point is an examinee asked to identify an item which is the conjunction of two prior ideas which were stated in different sentences, a technique which does measure one type of comprehension. Nor does the test distinguish between chunk identification and redundancy, the reformulation of an idea at a different level of specificity. Writers do not usually state single, fully developed ideas. Instead they present a matrix of ideas which they then weave together into a complete fabric. That is, a writer might state pieces of an idea, then come back later to some particular idea from a different point of view. He reformulates his ideas until he has woven the fabric he wishes to communicate to a reader; this reformulation of an idea is one type of redundancy. This test may measure comprehension because examinees who do well on the test are capable of employing redundancy to identify disparate chunks; subjects who comprehend well are also better able to pick out nonsensical or contradictory chunks. If the time limit were removed from the testing situation, it might be impossible to discriminate between examinees who had read the passages and taken the test and those who simply took the test. When the time limit is employed, the test measures how well an examinee can recall units of writing from memory and how quickly he can use redundancy to support his memory capabilities.

The idea of isolating and examining chunks of information should be pursued. Its immediate application does not seem to be in testing, but rather in examining relationships between chunking and the transfer of meaning. As a research technique, the idea of chunking could lead to substantial discoveries about the nature of communication; this information might then be applied to writing a test to measure differences in how readers handle chunks of information. Such a test would indicate *how* different readers read differently, not simply that they do.

In summary, examiners will wish to thoroughly familiarize themselves with the construction of this test before attempting to administer it. While the data presented indicate that the test discriminates between subjects who read the essays and those who did not read the essays before answering the test questions, there is some question about what skills the test measures. This test quantifies the amount of information which a reader can identify, but it fails to identify the more important relationships between chunking and meaning. Without a consistent theoretical basis for dividing the sentences into chunks, the test does not provide information about the nature of the reading act.

[685]
★Comprehensive Tests of Basic Skills: Reading. Grades 2.5–4, 4–6, 6–8, 8–12; 1968–70; 3 scores: vocabulary, comprehension, total; 2 forms; 4 levels; for battery manuals and accessories, see 9; separate answer sheets (CompuScan [NCS], Digitek, IBM 1230, Scoreze) must be used for levels 2–4; postage extra; $1.75 per specimen set of any one level, postpaid; CTB/McGraw-Hill. *
a) LEVEL I. Grades 2.5–4; Forms Q ('68, 8 pages), R ('69, 8 pages); $5.35 per 35 tests; 49(70) minutes.
b) LEVEL 2. Grades 4–6; Forms Q ('68, 13 pages), R ('69, 13 pages); $5.75 per 35 tests; $2.50 per 50 Digitek or IBM answer sheets; $3 per 50 CompuScan answer sheets; $2.75 per 25 Scoreze answer sheets; $1 per IBM hand scoring stencil; CompuScan scoring service, 17¢ and over per test; 52(75) minutes.
c) LEVEL 3. Grades 6–8; Forms Q ('68, 13 pages), R ('69, 13 pages); prices same as for level 2; 46(65) minutes.
d) LEVEL 4. Grades 8–12; Forms Q ('68, 13 pages), R ('69, 13 pages); prices same as for level 2; 41(60) minutes.

EARL F. RANKIN, *Professor of Education, University of Kentucky, Lexington, Kentucky.*

The reading test of the *Comprehensive Tests of Basic Skills* is a group survey test yielding conventional scores for vocabulary, comprehension, and total reading, like many similar tests. As such, its greatest value lies in evaluating total groups with respect to general level of reading skill and in selecting cases of reading disability which are in need of more intensive diagnosis. Its value as a selecting device for cases of read-

ing disability is considerably enhanced by its joint use with the *California Short-Form Test of Mental Maturity* to measure the gap between anticipated achievement and actual achievement in reading. The administration of both of these tests to a large number of individuals in the standardization sample made it possible to derive valid anticipated achievement scores for the reading test from the intelligence test scores. In the writer's opinion, this is a highly desirable feature.

As its title implies, the test is designed to measure basic skills as distinct from "higher mental processes." One might wonder about the validity of a reading test which is intentionally constructed to exclude the "higher mental processes." However, this would be an unwarranted criticism. The intellectual processes measured are "recognition and/or application, translation, interpretation, and analysis." This classification system was adapted from Bloom's *Taxonomy of Educational Objectives.* These processes are commonly measured by many reading tests. In fact, a number of higher order cognitive processes (as defined by Bloom) are not usually measured in tests of reading. The very high correlations reported in the Technical Report between this reading test and the reading subtest of the *California Achievement Tests* and also with the CTMM-SF indicate that the CTBS reading test is certainly not measuring merely low level skills. Indeed, the correlation coefficients ranging from .82 to .92 between the total reading scores of the CTBS and the CAT suggest that despite the alleged differences in rationale and emphasis claimed by the publisher of these two tests, they are measuring essentially the same thing.

The classification of each test item in the CTBS reading test in terms of the presumed intellectual process is supposedly one of the distinctive features of the test. In the writer's opinion, this feature is not of much diagnostic value to the teacher. The precision of the classification is subject to question. The Test Coordinator's Handbook indicates that the process by which items were classified was somewhat loose and simplified. More importantly, the number of test items designed as measuring one particular intellectual process may be as few as only three or four in the test as a whole. Hence, little reliability could be expected from such a measurement. The main value, then, of the intellectual process classification is that it aided in constructing a test which measures a variety of educationally significant processes. The test constructors have done a commendable job of avoiding an excess of factual items and making effective use of a hierarchical classification of cognitive operations in constructing tests which provide a developmental sequence from the first grade through secondary school.

The CTBS reading test has a number of distinctive features. The use of overlapping levels at grades 4, 6, and 8 allows a choice of levels for the measurement of reading at these grades for schools where the reading level is below or above average. This feature is particularly desirable for schools in culturally disadvantaged areas. Another good feature is a choice of norms for use in interpreting test results. Separate norms are provided for public and Catholic schools and also for large cities. Minority groups are proportionately represented in these norms. Many users of this test will be attracted by the variety of scoring service reports offered by the publishers to help teachers interpret both individual and group results. The use of confidence bands for reporting percentile ranks and the reporting of only significant differences between anticipated and actual achievement are worthwhile features of the Individual Test Record. A variety of derived scores are provided for interpreting test results—grade equivalents, percentile ranks, stanines, and standard scores. Manuals for the test, including the Technical Report, the Test Coordinator's Handbook, and the Examiner's Manual, are exceedingly comprehensive. The first two manuals, if understood by public school personnel, should be very helpful. This statement should be interpreted as a criticism not of the manuals, but of the sophistication of the intended users. The writer suspects that an in-service program would be necessary to enable the average user of these manuals to comprehend the wealth of technical material and very sound advice found in these publications.

From a technical point of view, the CTBS reading test is a model of good test construction. Norms are based upon an exceedingly large standardization sample of representative students. K-R 20 reliabilities at each grade level for vocabulary, comprehension, and total scores are almost all above .90, with standard errors of the measurement ranging from .25 to 1.01 (in grade equivalent units). Interform reliability coefficients, a more rigorous evaluation, tend

to be in the high .80's for the total reading score. Little evidence exists at present concerning the statistical validity of the CTBS reading test, with the exception of the previously mentioned correlations with the CAT and the CTMM-SF. However, the test constructors were very rigorous in the steps taken to insure content validity. An analysis of these procedures and the results presented in great detail in the Technical Report indicate that the CTBS reading test is probably a highly valid test for its purpose. The final judgment of this reading test's validity will rest upon the results of more scientific studies and upon the assessment of practitioners in the field.

For reviews of the complete battery, see 9 (2 reviews, 3 excerpts).

[686]
★Delaware County Silent Reading Test, Second Edition. Grades 1², 2¹, 2², 3¹, 3², 4, 5, 6, 7, 8; 1965; 5 scores: interpretation, organization, vocabulary, structural analysis, total; 10 levels; 1 form (6 pages); story booklets (4–11 pages); teacher's guide (2 pages) for each level; no manual; no data on reliability; no norms; $1.75 per 25 tests; $3.25 per 25 story booklets; $3 per specimen set; postpaid; [45–90] minutes in 2 sessions; Judson E. Newburg and Nicholas A. Spennato; Delaware County Reading Council. *

ALLEN BERGER, *Associate Professor of Reading Education, The University of Alberta, Edmonton, Alberta, Canada.*

The *Delaware County Silent Reading Test* is a "group informal reading inventory" that claims to sample the following skills: interpretation of ideas, organization of ideas, vocabulary, and structural analysis. The purpose of the test is "to measure pupil achievement in typical....grade reading material." A secondary purpose of the test beyond the first grade level is "to give a general rating of the pupils' ability to express ideas in written form." The test, or inventory, is composed of 10 booklets, each containing a story selected for its interest and readability. Because there is no manual, this reviewer discussed the test with one of the test authors; the essence of the discussion is reflected in this review.

The readability for each of the 10 stories was determined by the Spache Readability Formula and, for the upper level stories, the Dale-Chall Readability Formula. Accompanying each story is a six-page pupil response form, an answer key, and a one-leaf teacher's guide. The stories, pupil response forms, answer keys, and teacher's guide are separate for each level.

The stories designated as appropriate for grades 1² and 2¹ were written by local reading consultants; the remaining stories are from published materials. One story, "The Young Fireman" (for grade 2²) is identified as having appeared in the 1931 *Elson-Gray Basic Reader.*

After reading a story, each pupil responds to the total of 20 items which comprise the four subtests at each level. There are no sample items on which to practice. The first subtest (interpretation of ideas) also serves to indicate the pupil's writing ability. Of the 8 items in this subtest, approximately 6 (on varying levels) are sentence or sentence-completion items. Pupils obtain "good," "average," or "poor" written language ratings depending upon criteria involving their sentences, the number of misspelled words, and the number of "errors in the mechanics of writing."

The developers recommend that the first two parts of the test (interpretation of ideas and organization of ideas) be given in one sitting to children in grades 1 and 2, and the remainder (vocabulary and structural analysis) be given at another time. Pupils beyond grade 2 can complete the level on which they are being tested in approximately 45 minutes, which is about the same amount of time needed by pupils in grades 1 and 2 to complete half of the test. Since the test stresses interpretation rather than recall, the children can look back at the story.

Prior to development of its present form, the instrument was administered to approximately 50,000 elementary and junior high children, about 5,000 per grade level, in selected schools in Delaware County. Norms, however, have not been prepared yet, nor are validity or reliability data available.

The one-leaf teacher's guide for each level contains information about administering the test and rating the pupils within certain ranges on the basis of their total scores. No reference is made to the 50,000 children tested, nor is there any written information to indicate exactly how the readability and interest levels of each story were determined.

This reviewer is surprised that the data obtained from testing approximately 50,000 children have not been processed to make the test more meaningful. While the appropriateness of the passages in the test was determined by readability formulas, the additional data could have been used to determine predictive validity,

norms, etc. It is also surprising that no test manual is available.

Of further concern is the lack of information on the interpretation of pupil scores. For instance, the teacher's guides for grades 4 through 8 state: "This test is difficult; it is designed to challenge good....readers. Few pupils are expected to achieve perfect papers." What this means is that the scores will tend to reflect the frustration level of the children. No evidence is available to indicate that consideration of this point is reflected in the total reading achievement ratings (e.g., excellent, good, average, poor, very poor), which are provided in each teacher's guide.

The developers of this instrument are to be commended for their awareness of the need for a group diagnostic test to tap some of the higher level reading skills. But one wonders whether or not the test actually reflects the stated purpose of measuring reading achievement in typical grade level material, for most of the reading passages are relatively short pieces of fiction. The secondary purpose of providing an indication of skill in written expression is also highly suspect. Furthermore, there is no manual, nor any written information about validity, reliability, norms, interest level and readability levels of passages, or rationale behind the interpretation of test scores. In short, until more complete test characteristics are available, this instrument should be used for research purposes only, and even then with caution.

[687]

*Emporia Reading Tests.** 1, 2 semesters in grades 1, 2–3, 4–6, 7–8; 1962–64; first published in the Every Pupil Scholarship Test series; Forms A, B, ('64, 4 pages); 2 levels (labeled Tests 1, 2) within each of 4 tests; $1.75 per 25 tests, postage extra; 75¢ per specimen set of any one test, postpaid; M. W. Sanders, Marjorie Barnett (*a–b*), Donald E. Carline (*c–d*), Ed. L. Eaton (*d*), Angie Seybold (*c*), and Stafford E. Studer (*d*); Data Processing and Educational Measurement Center. *
a) EMPORIA PRIMARY READING TEST. 1, 2 semesters grade 1; special directions (no date, 3 pages); manual ('64, 3 pages); (40–60) minutes.
b) EMPORIA ELEMENTARY READING TEST. 1, 2 semesters grades 2–3; manual ('64, 4 pages); 15(25) minutes.
c) EMPORIA INTERMEDIATE READING TEST. 1, 2 semesters grades 4–6; manual ('64 4 pages); 25(35) minutes.
d) EMPORIA JUNIOR HIGH SCHOOL READING TEST. 1, 2 semesters grades 7–8; manual ('64, 4 pages); 25(35) minutes.

RONALD W. MITCHELL, *Assistant Executive Secretary, International Reading Association, Newark, Delaware.*

The opening sentence in each of the three test manuals (primary, elementary, and intermediate and junior high school) states that the reading test at each particular level is made up of four equivalent forms. No statistical evidence is presented to support this statement. An examination of the actual tests causes this writer to doubt the validity of the assumption that the forms within each test are equivalent. In the primary test, for example, two of the forms contain a paragraph reading subtest and two subtests requiring the child to read a complete sentence. In the other two forms there is no paragraph reading subtest and only one test involving complete sentences. Subsequently the two latter forms contain more subtests requiring the child to react to words in isolation. In the junior high test all four forms have approximately the same number of paragraph reading questions. Three of the forms, however, have about 2.5 times as many questions in the vocabulary subtest as the fourth form. Under the circumstances it is difficult to believe that the forms within the test are in fact equivalent.

Reliability for the tests was, according to the manual, determined by the split-half method. Since all the tests above the primary level are timed, the appropriateness of the the spilt-half method must be questioned. In the case of speeded tests, this method tends to produce inflated estimates of reliability.

The manuals at each level assure the user of the validity of the the test, since each item was "carefully selected and checked against reputable criteria." The criteria suggested include such things as word lists, textbooks and criticisms of teachers and supervisors. No hard data of any type, however, are presented.

There is also a lack of information on the norm group. While the number of students used to establish the norms is indicated, no mention is made of norm group characteristics, such as socioeconomic background, geographical location, or intelligence.

Interpretation of test results would seem to be difficult. For one thing, there is no indication of what the test is intended to measure other than "reading." One may make inferences on some subtests, such as Part 2 of the junior high school test which appears to be a standard type of vocabulary test. But Part 1 of the same test is a paragraph reading section, and one is left to ascertain for himself whether the test measures general comprehension or specific types of

comprehension, such as the ability to draw inferences or to evaluate. To further confuse matters, the manual suggests that both the junior high and intermediate tests lend themselves to diagnostic interpretation, since each test is divided into "three distinct parts." An inspection of the tests, however, reveals that the intermediate test has only one part, a paragraph reading section, while the junior high test has two parts, paragraph reading and vocabulary. If either test has three distinct parts, this reviewer was unable to find them.

This reviewer also questions the appropriateness of certain remarks made in the test manual in the section, "Translating Scores into School Marks." It is suggested that the percentile scores can be changed to letter school marks with comparative ease simply by assigning an "A" to percentile scores of 90 and above, "B" to 75–89, etc. After reading this section, some teachers might feel justified in determining a child's report card grade or even his grade for the year solely on the basis of the test results. This would indeed be unfortunate.

Because of the limitations stated above, particularly the absence of sound reliability and validity data and the failure to identify specifically what the test is attempting to measure, this reviewer would hesitate to recommend the use of this test.

[688]

★GAP Reading Comprehension Test. Grades 2–7; 1965–70; GAP; cloze technique with approximately every tenth word omitted; Forms B, R, ('65, 4 pages); 15(20) minutes; J. McLeod.
a) AUSTRALIAN EDITION. 1965–67; revised manual ('67, 8 pages); Aus $4 per 100 tests, postpaid within Australia; specimen set free; Heinemann Australia Pty Ltd. *
b) BRITISH EDITION. 1965–70; manual ('70, 14 pages); 40p per 10 sets of both forms; 15p per manual; postage extra; specimen set not available; manual edited by Derick Unwin; Heinemann Educational Books Ltd. *

DONALD B. BLACK, *Professor of Educational Psychology, The University of Calgary, Calgary, Alberta, Canada.*

GAP represents an application of the "cloze" technique, which is based on linguistic redundancy. Its application in this test is in the form of a sentence completion item format, the blanks calling for words indicative of the testee's comprehension of the paragraph of which the sentence is a part. While this is the very strength of the technique, it is also its weakness. The words chosen to close the gap (no pun intended) must have a very high probability of occurrence in this context, i.e., high redundancy, or there will be scoring difficulties. This means that for any age group, the missing words must have a low readability level, which will result in skewed score distributions. From the norms reported in the manual of the Australian edition, this appears to have happened. While this skewing is not necessarily undesirable in itself, it does have implications for the use of the test and the interpretation of those test analysis statistics premised on an assumption of normalcy. This reviewer would suggest that apart from GAP's being an interesting test which children would enjoy taking, it will have its greatest value in being an effective initial screening device for reading comprehension.

Some comment should be made about the manuals pertaining to both the Australian and United Kingdom norming populations, since both manuals must be read to get overall statistical information about the test. First, in both cases the initial norming population does not seem to be consistently defined and certainly is not shown to be representative of the available universe. It is not clear which norms are used in either manual except that comparison of conversion tables in each suggests that these are from different populations. The test statistics, i.e., reliability, etc., are reported for Forms M and J, no longer available. No data are provided as to the relationship between these two particular forms and the two, B and R, for which norms are given. The manuals suggest that users give both forms to improve score reliability. The reported statistics should probably be viewed with some caution because of the apparently skewed score distributions suggested by the norming sample and noted earlier. The norms provide age equivalents in both editions of the manual. Percentile norms would have to be determined locally.

In summary, the theory underlying the test and its item format application seems inherently sound. In the application of theory to practice, the very demands of the language have resulted in an instrument better suited to the initial identification of children with learning difficulties, whether they have reading problems per se or simply show the manifestations of a non-indigenous and neophyte anglophile struggling with a new language. Even a cursory adherence by the author and publishers to the *Standards for Educational and Psychological Tests and Manuals* would greatly assist the discriminating user who is looking for something novel.

EARL F. RANKIN, *Professor of Education, University of Kentucky, Lexington, Kentucky.*

The *GAP Reading Comprehension Test* was constructed through the use of the "cloze procedure." The cloze procedure is a word deletion technique which can be used to construct reading tests. Typically, words are deleted on a random or "every-*n*th" basis from a printed passage and replaced with underlined blank spaces. The person taking such a test is asked to fill in the missing words in the blank spaces interspersed throughout the test. The raw score on this type test is obtained by counting the number of "correct" words filled in. Usually the "correct" answer is the precise word which had been deleted in constructing the test. Cloze tests can be constructed easily by persons who are totally unfamiliar with the intricacies of other forms of test construction. Rankin[1] and Jenkinson[2] first showed that cloze test scores are highly correlated with the scores of standardized reading tests.

GAP, the first published cloze test, is based upon a modified cloze procedure utilizing certain "refinements" which should make it superior to an informal cloze test which can be constructed by any teacher. The alleged refinements consist of a different method of word selection and scoring. Instead of selecting words on a strictly objective basis, the authors of GAP deleted "approximately" one word in ten. The deletion ratio was approximate because deletions were restricted to blanks for which there was a consensus among a group of presumably efficient readers. (The degree of consensus required is not specified in the manual nor is a reason given for labeling undergraduate education students as "efficient readers.") Scoring of the correct responses is determined by agreement with the consensual responses of the efficient readers. Presumably the consensual response would take precedence in determining the correct answer if the consensual response differs from the word deleted.

On theoretical grounds, one might question

1 RANKIN, EARL FREDERICK, JR. *An Evaluation of the Cloze Procedure as a Technique for Measuring Reading Comprehension.* Doctor's thesis, University of Michigan (Ann Arbor, Mich.), 1957. (*DA* 19:733)
2 JENKINSON, MARION DIXON. *Selected Processes and Difficulties in Reading Comprehension.* Doctor's thesis, University of Chicago (Chicago, Ill.), 1957.

the value of the previously described modifications. If the deleted words are only those which are completely redundant to "efficient readers," they cease to be a representative sample of the degree of redundancy in the total passage. It is precisely this measurement of redundancy in a particular passage for a particular reader that forms the rationale for the cloze procedure in the measurement of comprehension. On practical grounds, the use of these modifications of the cloze procedure (which are rather arduous and time consuming) will have to be justified by the pragmatic results of such refinements.

GAP has several attractive features. Unlike most reading tests, it has no test items to influence test performance. The reader is exposed only to the mutilated text. Test performance is little influenced by guessing, since there are no printed alternatives from which to choose. Cheating on the test can be reduced by giving alternate forms to students in adjacent seats. This procedure is facilitated by the fact that the two test forms are printed on paper of different color. It should be noted that since Forms B and R are not of equivalent difficulty, derived scores, not raw scores, must be used when both forms are administered.

Although the manual reveals that the test was standardized on pupils in grades 2 through 7, there is no direct indication of the age group for whom the test is intended. Presumably, this one test can be administered to children in a broad spectrum of age and grade levels. If so, one wonders about the suitability of the material for readers of widely different ages. Imagine the reaction of a seventh grader to this practice passage which appears on both forms of the test: "A big dog sat by his kennel. He had _____ big bone in his mouth. A little _____ sat by his kennel. He had a _____ bone in his mouth." The passages in the test vary from easy to difficult, but every reader must attempt to cope with all passages. Consequently, considerable tolerance for frustration is assumed. For example, on Form B, the average reader with a chronological age of 8-0 gets only 9 out of the 42 items correct. A raw score of only 2 out of 42 items is average for a person with a chronological age of 7-3. Such difficulty must surely influence the validity of the test for young readers. This writer seriously questions the validity of GAP over the large age range indicated in the manual.

The standardization sample for the test appears adequate for the United Kingdom and Australia, but not for the United States. Norms for the test were limited to reading ages. The limitations of such norms are widely known. It is unfortunate that no standard score norms have been produced. In addition, reading quotients obtained by dividing the reading age by the chronological age and multiplying by 100 are given in the manual. Because of the many problems inherent in such quotients, most test makers have long since abandoned them. There is no reason why deviation quotients based upon standard scores within age or grade level could not have been provided for this test.

The administration of GAP takes only 15 minutes. This should be a highly desirable feature. However, the interform reliability of the test is only .83, which is not high enough for use with individuals. When the two forms are combined to represent an 88-item test taking 30 minutes, the estimated reliability is .91. Thus, combining both forms would be suggested for individual usage. Of course, the use of 30 minutes of testing time for a test which yields only one global score for comprehension has certain limitations. Suggestions for diagnostic usage of these results through retrospective reports from individual students along lines suggested by Jenkinson should be included in the manual to make the test more helpful to the teacher.

Concurrent validity coefficients in the manual (British edition) between GAP and reading tests by Schonell and Watts range from .75 to .81. Indeed, GAP correlates about as well with these two tests as they correlate with each other. These validity coefficients are quite high, but they are no higher than several other investigators have obtained with conventional, informally constructed cloze tests. Thus, from the standpoint of validity, one wonders about the superiority of this published cloze test over teacher-constructed cloze tests. Apparently the refinements introduced in the construction of this test have not been particularly productive. It should be noted that Greene [3] also found that a modified cloze procedure did not produce a more valid test than the conventional procedure, which can be used much more easily by untrained persons.

In conclusion, the writer believes that GAP is not superior to a cloze test that any classroom

3 GREENE, FRANK PIERREPONT. *A Modified Cloze Procedure for Assessing Adult Reading Comprehension.* Doctor's thesis, University of Michigan (Ann Arbor, Mich.), 1964. (*DA* 25: 5734)

teacher could devise. In fact, the teacher might do a better job of test construction by selecting passages more suitable to the particular age level of his students. The possible advantage of being able to use norms in interpreting results is limited by the fact that the norms for GAP leave much to be desired. The use of cloze test percentage criteria provided by Bormuth [4] and Rankin and Culhane [5] together with a conventional cloze test would provide an interpretation of cloze test results equal to, if not better than, the use of normative results from the GAP.

[689]

*Gates-MacGinitie Reading Tests. Grades 1, 2, 3, 2.5–3, 4–6, 7–9; 1926–65; Primary A is a revision of the *Gates Primary Reading Tests;* Primary B is a revision of the *Gates Advanced Primary Reading Tests;* the other tests in this series are revisions of the *Gates Reading Survey;* 6 levels; 2 editions in grades 4–9; technical manual ('65, 24 pages); cash orders postpaid; Arthur I. Gates and Walter H. MacGinitie; Teachers College Press. *

a) PRIMARY A. Grade 1; 1926–65; 2 scores: vocabulary, comprehension; Forms 1, 2, ('64, 8 pages); manual ('65, 8 pages); $3.60 per 35 tests; 60¢ per specimen set; 40(50) minutes in 2 sessions.

b) PRIMARY B. Grade 2; 1926–65; remaining details same as for Primary A.

c) PRIMARY C. Grade 3; 1939–65; 2 scores: vocabulary, comprehension; forms and prices same as for Primary A; 50(60) minutes in 2 sessions.

d) PRIMARY CS. Grades 2.5–3; 1926–65; speed and accuracy; Forms 1, 2, 3, ('64, 3 pages); manual ('65, 8 pages); $2.40 per 35 tests; 60¢ per specimen set; 7(15) minutes.

e) SURVEY D. Grades 4–6; 1939–65; 3 scores: speed and accuracy, vocabulary, comprehension; $3.60 per 35 tests of either edition.

1) *Consumable Booklet Edition.* Forms 1, 2, 3, ('64, 8 pages); manual ('65, 12 pages); 60¢ per specimen set; 45(60) minutes in 2 sessions.

2) *Separate Answer Sheet Edition.* Forms 1M, 2M, 3M, ('64, 8 pages); manual ('65, 16 pages); separate answer sheets (Digitek, IBM 805, IBM 1230, MRC, NCS) must be used; $2.20 per 35 Digitek answer sheets; $2 per 35 IBM answer sheets; $2.40 per 35 MRC answer sheets; $18.75 per 250 NCS answer sheets; $1.50 per set of IBM 805 scoring stencils; 50¢ per specimen set; MRC scoring service, 20¢ and over per test; 46(60) minutes in 2 sessions.

f) SURVEY E. Grades 7–9; 1939–65; $3.60 per 35 tests of either edition; 44(60) minutes in 2 sessions.

1) *Consumable Booklet Edition.* Forms 1, 2, 3, ('64, 8 pages); manual ('65, 12 pages); 60¢ per specimen set.

2) *Separate Answer Sheet Edition.* Forms 1M, 2M, 3M, ('64, 8 pages); manual ('65, 16 pages); answer sheets and prices same as for e2.

REFERENCES

1–7. See 3:486.
8–9. See 5:632.
10. See 6:792.
11. FARRANT, ROLAND H. "The Intellective Abilities of Deaf and Hearing Children Compared by Factor Analyses." *Am Ann Deaf* 109:306–25 My '64. * (*PA* 39:2442)
12. DAVIS, WILLIAM QUINBY. *A Study of Test Score Comparability Among Five Widely Used Reading Survey Tests.* Doctor's thesis, Southern Illinois University (Carbondale, Ill.), 1968. (*DA* 29:4370A)
13. FARR, ROGER, AND ANASTASIOW, NICHOLAS. *Tests of Reading Readiness and Achievement: A Review and Evaluation,* pp. 30–4. Newark, Del.: International Reading Association, 1969. Pp. iv, 51. *
14. RODGERS, DENIS CYRIL. *An Investigation of the Auditory Memory Abilities of Grade 2 Retarded-Underachieving Readers and Competent-Achieving Readers Under Conditions of Reinforcement and Non-Reinforcement.* Doctor's thesis, University of Toronto (Toronto, Ont., Canada), 1969. (*DAI* 31:2196A)
15. ROELKE, PATRICIA LYNN. *Reading Comprehension as a Function of Three Dimensions of Word Meaning.* Doctor's thesis, Indiana University (Bloomington, Ind.), 1969. (*DAI* 30:5300A)
16. WALLACE, GERALD. *A Study of the Relationship of Selected Visual Perceptual Capabilities and Intelligence to Achievement in Reading of Educable Mentally Retarded Children.* Doctor's thesis, University of Oregon (Eugene, Ore.), 1969. (*DAI* 30:3336A)
17. ALLEN, JOHN EDWARD. *A Survey of Third Grade Reading in the State of Utah.* Doctor's thesis, University of Utah (Salt Lake City, Utah), 1970. (*DAI* 31:2165A)
18. GAULKE, MARY FLORENCE. *A Longitudinal Two-Generation Study of Parent-Child Relationships on Selected Reading Skills and Aptitudes.* Doctor's thesis, University of Oregon (Eugene, Ore.), 1970. (*DAI* 31:3371A)

CAROLYN L. BURKE, *Assistant Professor of Education, and Associate Director, Reading Miscue Research, Wayne State University, Detroit, Michigan.*[1]

Though there is a teacher's manual for each level and a technical manual for the entire test, the authors do not present their view of the reading process or their rationale for the focus of the test. Such information must be surmised from the material itself.

VOCABULARY. At the primary levels, the authors state that "the Vocabulary Test samples the child's ability to recognize or analyze isolated words." The child is called on to select the word which matches the picture. In so doing he must make very fine graphic and phonemic discriminations between words with minimal contrasts. The distinctions the child must make are much more minute and detailed than the general application of any "sounding out" or word attack strategy in the context of a reading situation.

These minimal contrasts accumulate in their effect as the section continues and result in tricking or confusing the examinee. This effect is heightened with the increased use of less familiar stimulus words near the end of the first grade section and in the second and third grade sections. The compounded effect of these two situations is illustrated by a selection in which the picture is a hanging light fixture and the four words are *chocolate, chimpanzee, chandelier,* and *chiffonier* (Primary B). Even a reader

4 BORMUTH, JOHN ROBERT. "Comparable Cloze and Multiple-Choice Comprehension Test Scores." *J Read* 10:291–9 '67. *
5 RANKIN, EARL F., AND CULHANE, JOSEPH W. "Comparable Cloze and Multiple-Choice Comprehension Test Scores." *J Read* 13(3):193–8 D '69. *

1 Assisted by Kenneth Goodman, Yetta Goodman, and Peter Rousch.

proficient in word attack strategies will have trouble with items not in his oral vocabulary.

At least two items will hinder the child who has adjusted to the word attack strategy of the text. With the pictured item a comb and a choice of *comb* and *come* (Primary A), with the pictured item a medal and choice of *medal* and *meddle* (Primary B), no attack strategy will work; simple recognition is called for.

At the levels for grades 4–9 the authors state that "the Vocabulary Test samples the student's reading vocabulary." The reader indicates which of five words "means most nearly the same" as the key word. Since the key words are in isolation, the student is forced to bring his own background meaning to the reading. If this differs from the authors' intention, confusion and time loss result.

SPEED AND ACCURACY. This subtest for grades 2.5 and higher was designed to test "how rapidly students can read with understanding" material "of relatively uniform difficulty."

A sixth grader, asked by this reviewer to select the correct answer from the four alternatives on the basis of a single word selected from the paragraph to be read, answered correctly 20 out of 36 items. A second student scored 24 out of 36 with no time pressure. With speed as the critical factor, reading the paragraphs may not be the most effective procedure for handling this section. The reader who treats it as an association task might be the most successful.

COMPREHENSION. This section is meant to measure "the student's ability to read complete prose passages with understanding." At Levels A and B, the student selects one of four pictures to match a sentence or paragraph. At Level C, there are two multiple choice questions following each selection. A cloze-like procedure involving multiple choice answers is used at Levels D and E.

At Primary Levels A and B, the answers to many of the questions are built entirely upon one word. For example, one item asks "Which is the boy who is shooting marbles?" Marbles are involved in all four of the pictures, only the action *shooting* discriminates the correct response. Such items measure, in effect, vocabulary and not comprehension.

Twenty-one of the 48 questions at the Primary C level can be answered without reading the paragraph. These questions call for use of commonly accepted information or direct recall of facts; for example, "How many Great Lakes are there?" "What is a dinghy?" and "The jet stream is a _____." At this level too, some items look more like vocabulary than comprehension tasks, since the answers depend upon developing from the paragraph such word definitions as adults are people over twelve; twice a year means every six months; and every morning means daily. The remaining items involve either the implementation of common background knowledge or the simple recognition of a key item from the text.

The use of a cloze-like procedure (choosing from five words a word which has been deleted from a paragraph) in the upper grade levels is more delimiting than the multiple choice format. These cloze-like items actually test the student's control of structural and semantic text restraints, which may contribute to comprehension but is not the same.

SUMMARY. Processes in isolation do not function as they do when part of a more complex structure. The set of skills and strategies that make for success in taking this test may have no direct relationship to those called into use by a successful reader. The component which the authors state is the most significant—comprehension—is the least touched. If comprehension can be understood to involve judging a reader's ability to interrelate information and draw conclusions, while avoiding the use of background and simple recall information, it would seem necessary to use much longer and more fully developed reading selections.

BYRON H. VAN ROEKEL, *Professor of Teacher Education, Michigan State University, East Lansing, Michigan.*

The manuals for the *Gates-MacGinitie Reading Tests* report these to be "a new series of tests designed to cover grades 1 through 12." They are intended to "replace the *Gates Reading Readiness Test,* the *Gates Primary Reading Tests,* and *Gates Advanced Primary Reading Tests,* and the *Gates Reading Survey.*" It is claimed that "the content of the new series is more up to date, more varied, and more typical of current reading material for children."

This reviewer wishes that the previous comment could have been said with as much authority of reason as forwardness of assurance, for it is evident that these tests, in general, are merely a new coat cut from the same old piece of cloth. The major changes reflected in the

Gates-MacGinitie tests are matters of format and structure. Whereas each of the subtests of the Gates Primary and Advanced Primary tests was printed in separate test booklets, the subtests for each level of the Gates-MacGinitie tests are combined in one test booklet and the latter are now available in both hand scored and machine scored editions. These changes apparently stem from criticisms registered by reviewers of the 1958 edition of the *Gates Advanced Primary Reading Tests*.

The vocabulary subtests for the Primary A, B, and C levels are very similar to the word recognition subtests of the earlier Advanced Primary and Primary tests, except, of course, that the pictures and words which make up the stem of each of the items and the words which make up the responses to these items have been changed. Except for the last 40 items of Primary C, each of the items consists of a picture followed by four words, and "the child's task is to circle the word that best corresponds to the picture." The last 40 items of Primary C consist "of a test word followed by four other words, one of which is similar in meaning to the test word. The format is similar to the picture exercises, with the test word replacing the picture in function. The child's task is to circle the word that means most nearly the same as the test word." Eller's criticism (6:792) of the word recognition subtest of the *Gates Primary Reading Tests* is equally apropos in this instance:

The sight vocabulary tested is restricted to words which can be defined easily with pictures, with the result that about 75 percent [substitute "90 per cent" for the current test] of the correct answers are nouns * it is unfortunate that Type PWR [the current vocabulary tests] cannot include any of the short, abstract words (these, from, was, etc.) which account for a large proportion of word recognition errors in grades 1 and 2.

The comprehension subtests for the A, B, and C levels reflect some change in item structure from previous Gates tests in the sense that some of the items now require inference and abstraction rather than strictly testing the ability to follow printed directions.

The development of the Survey D and E levels has eliminated the most severe limitations of the *Gates Reading Survey* by reducing the grade range covered by a single test. Survey D is intended for grades 4–6 and Survey E for grades 7–9, the two tests combined now serving a grade range 1.5 grades less than formerly

served by the *Gates Reading Survey* alone. The new tests do not differ materially in content and structure from their predecessor. There are still three subtests: Speed and Accuracy, Vocabulary, and Comprehension. The speed and accuracy test requires the reading of rather short paragraphs, all of similar difficulty, each followed by a simple multiple choice item measuring comprehension of the inferential type. The comprehension subtest involves very short paragraphs of increasing difficulty in which comprehension is measured by asking the pupil to choose appropriate words to fit two or three omissions in the paragraph. The vocabulary subtest requires the simple matching of a word with the correct synonym among five choices.

The level manuals and the technical manual are quite complete, well organized, and easy to follow. The standardization appears to have been rather carefully done. The tryout sample and the norming group appear to have been quite adequate, although no attempt is made to describe either group, except to say that the communities were carefully selected on the basis of size, geographical location, average educational level, and average family income.

Alternate-form and split-half reliability coefficients are reported. Alternate-form reliabilities range from .78 to .89, except on the speed and accuracy subtests, where the coefficients tend to be somewhat lower. Intertest correlations fall substantially below alternate-form reliabilities. This is a marked improvement over previous Gates tests, for which intertest correlations nearly approached the alternate-form reliabilities.

The Gates-MacGinitie tests reflect a marked improvement over their predecessors. A number of the faults of the Gates tests appear to have been corrected. The intertest correlations are low enough to permit a rough analysis of reading difficulties, especially if these tests are used as a diagnostic supplement to reading tests published as a part of achievement test batteries. Used alone, however, these tests probably function best as survey tests.

J Ed Meas 6(2):114–6 su '69. William R. Powell. * This edition makes no claims for diagnostic features as did the earlier editions. * does not differ materially from earlier editions. * Directions are clear and former weaknesses due to lack of specific statements on the time limits has been remedied. * Sample items and directions appear on the same page as test items and this arrangement could effect the usefulness of norm data for speeded tests as some students might begin working mentally before timing officially begins. * The hand scoring answer keys are cumbersome in that the strips must be cut apart into several pieces with the answers on both sides. The scorer loses time in turning and hunting. A lay-over key would have been better. * The nature and extent of content revision is somewhat vague being referred to as "more up to date, more varied, and more typical of current reading material for children." The item types and basic form of the subtests remain unchanged. * No mention of validity is made in the manual and apparently no attempt has been made to organize data for specific use as evidence of validity. Content validity as such is not discussed. * As compared with other general reading tests, the *Gates-MacGinitie Reading Tests* would provide usable data on achievement in comprehension, vocabulary, and speed. It would be of limited value if information about specific reading subskills were needed. The earlier Gates tests were criticized due to use of one instrument to measure a wide range of grades (3–10). It was challenged as being inappropriate for the highest and lowest levels tested. By breaking down the test into different levels this situation has been remedied. Whether the breakdown has gone too far to be of practical value remains to be seen. Some question also arises as to the speededness of the vocabulary and comprehension tests. Although these tests are considered power tests, 15–25% of the pupils were unable to complete them in the allotted time. The test manual does not indicate the proper interpretation of the obtained score for translation into classroom practice. The implication is given that the grade score obtained by a student is the instructional reading level for him. This implication is not supported by other evidence and the absence of caution and clarification on the matter to the teacher lessens the effectiveness of use of the test results. While not peculiar to just the Gates-MacGinitie Tests, survey or general reading tests tend to produce frustration or prefrustration level scores. An explanation of this interpretation relating the obtained test scores to functional reading levels (independent, instructional, frustration) needs a full discussion in the manual. Then, and only then, will teacher

estimates and test scores become more compatible. Even with limitations, the Gates-MacGinitie Reading Tests will undoubtedly continue to enjoy widespread use which was established by the earlier editions.

For reviews by William Eller and Coleman Morrison of Gates Primary Reading Tests, *see 6:792; for reviews by William S. Gray and George Spache of an earlier edition, see 3:486. For a review by Kenneth D. Hopkins of* Gates Advanced Primary Reading Tests, *see 6:790; for reviews by Virginia Seavey and George Spache of an earlier edition, see 3:484. For reviews by George Spache and Morey J. Wantman of* Gates Reading Survey, *see 6:793; for reviews by Dorothy E. Holberg and Herbert F. Spitzer of an earlier edition, see 3:487.*

[690]
★Gates-MacGinitie Reading Tests: Survey F. Grades 10–12; 1969–70; 3 scores: speed and accuracy, vocabulary, comprehension; 2 forms; 2 editions; technical supplement ('70, 6 pages) ; $3.60 per 35 tests, postage extra; 49(60) minutes; Arthur I. Gates and Walter H. MacGinitie; Teachers College Press. *
a) CONSUMABLE BOOKLET EDITION. Forms 1, 2, ('69, 8 pages) ; manual ('69, 12 pages) ; 60¢ per specimen set.
b) SEPARATE ANSWER SHEET EDITION. Forms 1M, 2M, ('69, 8 pages) ; manual ('69, 16 pages) ; separate answer sheets (Digitek, IBM 805, IBM 1230, MRC, NCS) must be used; $2 per 35 IBM 805 answer sheets; $2 per 35 IBM 1230 answer sheets; $2.20 per 35 Digitek answer sheets; $2.40 per 35 MRC answer sheets; $18.75 per 250 NCS answer sheets; $1.50 per set of scoring stencils; 60¢ per specimen set; MRC scoring service, 20¢ and over per test.

JASON MILLMAN, *Professor of Educational Research Methodology, Cornell University, Ithaca, New York.*

The construction of Survey F for grades 10–12 in the image of the lower grade tests completes the K-12 series of *Gates-MacGinitie Reading Tests.* The usefulness of reading tests for the high school student is open to question. Potential users should compare their informational needs with the nature of the scores available from these tests. These scores will be discussed in detail, together with other information about these tests.

SPEED AND ACCURACY SCORES. The first test in the set of three consists of 36 very short passages, with the last word of the passage to be selected from among four options. The speed score is the number of passages completed; the accuracy score is the number of passages completed correctly.

The questions appear easy to answer after the

passage is read and thus quite appropriate for a test of reading speed and accuracy. I would like to have seen data presented by the publishers to confirm my expectation that given generous time limits and exhortations to read carefully, most students in grades 10–12 would answer most questions correctly.

Although the content of this test is impressive in view of its intended purpose, the directions for administration and the shortness of the test (four minutes) have undoubtedly lessened its reliability. The directions do not make clear what it takes to do well on the test, nor do they give the student a running start. Further, four minutes is just too short a time in which to assess reading speed and accuracy.

The alternate-form reliability ranges from .64 to .81—not very acceptable. If I wished to measure the speed and accuracy with which students could read easy material of the sort found in this test, and if I were willing to use local rather than the national norms, I would (*a*) use one form of the test as a warm-up, (*b*) construct additional practice items, or (*c*) give both forms of the test and average the scores.

VOCABULARY SCORE. Knowledge of word meaning is measured by a 50-item, synonym-type, multiple choice test. One answer is clearly best in all cases. The test has a liberal 15-minute time limit and no penalty for guessing. The test has an adequate .90 alternate-form reliability.

COMPREHENSION SCORE. Twenty-one short passages are used to measure reading comprehension. In each passage, two or three words are omitted (52 in all) and in each case the student is to select from among five options the word he thinks was omitted. Students are told to make the best guess they can. The time limit of 25 minutes is not so generous as for the vocabulary test, but still about 80 percent are said to complete all items.

Potential users of Survey F should study a specimen set to be sure that the authors' conception of reading comprehension agrees with their own. Although the testing format is appealing to this reviewer and appears capable of measuring a large number of comprehension skills, the instrument (like the corresponding test in Survey E for grades 7–9) seems to measure *primarily* vocabulary and determining-meaning-from-context skills. For example, students must know the meaning of such words as "commodious," "centage," "prosaic," and "propagated," and further, that one does not "reach a mes-

sage," "hinder an injury," or "begin to life." I found myself eliminating options because the paragraph didn't make sense when they were included.

Measured only slightly (if at all) are such skills as drawing from context inferences about the meaning of a specific word; recognizing a writer's purpose, attitude, tone, and mood; identifying a writer's techniques; and drawing inferences from content. Although these skills may be more important for a senior high student than for a student in a lower grade, a test user might prefer not to measure them and thus be attracted to the more limited concept of comprehension embodied in Survey F.

The comprehension test has high alternate-form reliability (about .88). (The corrected odd-even reliability reported is spurious because of the dependence among items based on the same passage.) The correlation between the comprehension score and the vocabulary score is extremely high (about .85). This correlation, when corrections are made for the unreliability of both tests, rises to .95! *Word meaning skills are evidently inherent in the comprehension test.* The comprehension test also correlates highly (.79) with Lorge-Thorndike verbal IQ scores.

OTHER INFORMATION. The teacher's manual and technical supplement are written with clarity and competence. No exaggerated claims are made and the user is alerted to possible dangers in interpretation.

For each raw score, the corresponding normalized standard scores and percentile ranks at three points during the school year are provided for each of grades 10 to 12. The teacher's manual leads the user to believe (incorrectly) that Table 5 (Percentile Equivalents of Standard Scores) is appropriate to assess the relative standing of the *mean* score of a class. The technical supplement, however, does point out that Table 5 was not constructed from a distribution of class averages.

Survey F and the verbal battery of the *Lorge-Thorndike Intelligence Tests* were administered to the same standardization sample; Survey F scores were "adjusted by the same proportion as was required to adjust the mean and standard deviation of....[the pupils'] intelligence test scores to conform to the national average." The procedure used in obtaining the standardization sample for the Lorge-Thorndike test is first rate.

The technical supplement provides several

Gates-MacGinitie Reading Tests: Survey F

tables useful in judging the statistical significance of differences between pairs of the four available scores. The explanations regarding interpretation of such differences are especially well done.

Both machine and hand scoring forms are available. Financial saving and speed of scoring would suggest that these older students use the separate answer sheet rather than write directly in the test booklet.

SUMMARY. Survey F provides reading test scores for students in grades 10 to 12. The speed and accuracy test has an appealing format but only marginal reliability. For test users who are prepared to substitute local for national norms, several suggestions are made for increasing the reliability of this test. The vocabulary test has good psychometric properties.

Reading comprehension is also measured in an appealing way. Knowledge of word meanings and ability to determine meaning from context are judged to be the skills needed to do well on this test. Potential users are cautioned to consider whether or not they want a reading comprehension test for senior high school students that does not reflect the other skills thought by many to be part of reading comprehension.

Norming procedures are good and interpretive tables ample. The teacher's manual and technical supplement were prepared in excellent psychometric fashion.

[691]
★Group Reading Test. Ages 6–10; 1968–69; GRT; Forms A, B, ('69, 2 pages) ; manual ('68, 35 pages) ; 50p per 20 tests; 30p per scoring stencil; 25p per manual; 90p per specimen set; postage extra; 13(20) minutes; D. Young; University of London Press, Ltd. *

[692]
★McGrath Test of Reading Skills, Second Edition. Grades 1–13; 1965–67; 4 scores: oral word recognition, oral paragraph reading, silent reading vocabulary, oral reading rate; individual; 1 form ('67, 24 pages—7 pages of which is the manual) ; normative population not described; $15 per 20 tests; $1.25 per sample copy; postage extra; (5–10) minutes; Joseph E. McGrath; McGrath Reading Clinic. *

BYRON H. VAN ROEKEL, *Professor of Teacher Education, Michigan State University, East Lansing, Michigan.*

This test apparently proceeds on several assumptions, none of which will find much support in the literature dealing with either measurement or the assessment of individual reading performance. The manual, which is the

first seven pages of the test booklet, makes the following claims :

Most reading tests are too time-consuming and difficult to be administered or interpreted by anyone who has not been specially trained as a reading consultant or clinician. Consequently, many children and adults are not identified as poor readers and are allowed to continue through life with a serious reading disability. * The pattern of errors and the general performance in oral reading can give the examiner important clues regarding any weakness in word recognition, besides pointing to reasons for low comprehension. Poor habits in oral reading are usually carried over to silent reading. The result is low comprehension. * The greatest reason for low comprehension is a lack of knowledge in word meanings. Therefore, the results of this third test can be used to estimate the comprehension level in silent reading.

Even a meager acquaintance with reading tests now in print should make one aware that most reading tests are group tests which do not assume special training in reading instruction as a prerequisite for test administration and rarely have a time limit exceeding 40 or 50 minutes. It takes but simple arithmetic to reveal the economy effected through the administration of a 40-minute group test to a class of 25 pupils versus the administration of a 10-minute individual test to these same pupils.

Although most writers concede some value to oral reading as a diagnostic tool, some basic differences between oral and silent reading have been identified. This at least opens to question the degree to which one can assume that oral and silent reading are overt and implicit expressions of the same basic mental processes.

It has long been recognized that knowing the meaning of words is a great asset to children in their schoolwork and that it has its values in out-of-school activities. However, there is some evidence to suggest that knowledge of word meanings may not be so closely related to reading success as are some other factors and that the prediction of general level of reading achievement from measures of vocabulary is questionable.

The technical characteristics of this test are even less defensible than the assumptions on which its content is based. The manual is completely devoid of information which a prospective test user needs to make judgments about the merits of this test. It carries not even a hint regarding the selection of content, and data on the construction of the test are conspicuous by their complete absence. The manual carries one reference to validity, if a vaguely worded statement about comparisons with results from other tests may be construed to signify validity.

This test reflects practically none of the characteristics of good test construction, there is no evidence of a tryout, and the manual of instructions falls far below technical standards.

[693]

★McMenemy Measure of Reading Ability. Grades 3, 5–6, 7–8; 1964–68; 1 form; 3 levels; separate answer sheets (Digitek-IBM 805, IBM 1230) must be used; $3.85 per 35 tests; 5¢ per answer sheet; postage extra; $1.50 per specimen set, postpaid; Richard A. McMenemy; the Author. *
a) PRIMARY. Grade 3; 1964–67; 1 form ('64, 8 pages); mimeographed manual ['67, 13 pages]; 45(70) minutes.
b) INTERMEDIATE. Grades 5–6; 1966–68; 3 scores: vocabulary, comprehension, total; 1 form ('66, 13 pages); mimeographed manual ('68, 14 pages); no data on reliability; no norms for grade 6; 50(60) minutes.
c) ADVANCED. Grades 7–8; 1965–68; 1 form ('65, 15 pages); mimeographed manual ('68, 14 pages); no data on reliability; no norms for grade 7; 65(75) minutes.

MARVIN D. GLOCK, *Professor of Educational Psychology, Cornell University, Ithaca, New York.*

This test is designed to measure "functional or assimilative" type reading in grades 3 through 8. The authors state that this involves the following four important abilities: (*a*) "To be able to select and recall important specific facts," (*b*) "To be able to select the main idea or central thought of a paragraph," (*c*) "To follow printed directions," (*d*) "To select relevant from irrelevant facts."

The author claims that these instruments are "different from most commercially made tests and have many strengths and advantages." He makes the following claims for the primary level:

a) There are no picture clues to help the pupil; he must be able to read words—not decipher pictures.
b) The control on the vocabulary is intentionally very slight. This challenges the pupil to get meaning from context when he doesn't know a word.
c) The content of the items involves many subject areas, e.g., science, social studies, simple poetry, and items of general interest to children. Most children look upon the test as entertaining and interesting.
d) The picture on the cover is a useful device that enables the teacher to materially reduce the tension in the testing situation.
e) The test has been judged by experienced teachers and testing personnel to be a pleasant and valuable way to introduce machine-scored answer sheets to primary aged children.
f) The norming population consisted of over 8,000 children in Portland and surrounding areas. This insures meaningful results above and beyond any commercially made measures presently available. Item analysis and all statistical work has been done by highly professional testing experts who had no commercial interest in the results.

Let me comment on the above points. The author makes some sweeping generalizations about "commercial" tests that he may be hardpressed to defend in the light of the evidence he presents. Of course, his test is "commercial" in that he offers it for sale.

a) There are a number of tests that use no pictures at the primary level. But even when they do, such use cannot be seen invariably as "clues to help the pupil." For example, in the *Metropolitan Achievement Tests* a picture is shown along with four words in an attempt to measure word knowledge. The pupil chooses the correct word for the picture. In the same test a measure of the pupil's ability to read and comprehend sentences is developed by showing a picture along with three sentences, one of which describes the picture. The pupil must read and understand the sentence before he can relate it to the picture. The picture does not serve as a cue to understanding the sentence.

b) The author claims that because there has been little control of vocabulary, the pupil gets meaning from context. This conclusion is not substantiated by any data in the manual. There are word-analysis techniques that children can use and stereotyped expressions which are helpful in getting meaning. Furthermore, it is questionable that the author has used no control. Because of his classroom experience, he may have unconsciously controlled the vocabulary of the selections; this appears likely.

c) It is true that the author has included materials on a variety of subjects, but whether these very short, unrelated paragraphs account for children's interest in taking the test is debatable. This interest may well be due to the pupils' being able to follow through on a series of tasks where reinforcement comes continually and immediately.

d) Of course, no picture or aids of any kind will materially reduce tension in children when the climate for testing is poor. Unless the teacher establishes with children the concept that testing is not for punishing but for helping, no extraneous device will satisfactorily reduce anxiety.

e) Other publishers have introduced separate answer sheets to children in a variety of ways. There is nothing novel about the answer sheets for this particular instrument.

f) The author gives no information about the norming population, other than that it included 8,000 children from the Portland area.

There are no data on how the sample was obtained nor any analysis of the sample. It is difficult, therefore, to know what the author means when he indicates that the selection of 8,000 children in Portland and the surrounding area "insures meaningful results above and beyond any commercially made measure presently available." If he is referring to local norms, certainly there is nothing to preclude developing them from any test data. Neither are there any data to support his implication that there may be some dishonesty among test publishers because they have a "commercial" interest in the results.

The author includes such a list of strengths and advantages of his instrument for the other two levels as well. However, rather than react to them, let us point up several other observations. There is no reported validity at any level of the instrument. No item analysis data are included. No reliability coefficients are reported.

In the upper two levels, the tests are divided into two parts, vocabulary and comprehension. Yet in both comprehension sections, study skill items are included and are so classified in the Key to Diagnosis. Reference is made only to the total score. The Key to Diagnosis is only a listing of items which the author believes measure ability to Interpret Factual Data, Inference and Interpretation, Vocabulary, Reading for Detail, and Study Skills. No data are given to support this classification.

The author suggests that the SCAT Verbal is most appropriate in relating a pupil's ability to his achievement on this test. No evidence is given to support this conclusion.

In the intermediate and advanced levels vocabulary is measured by selecting from five choices the meaning of a word as used in a sentence and by presenting a word with two sets of five possible choices, i.e., 10 choices in all. Only one set of choices contains the answer. This has the effect of cutting down the number of items on the test, thus decreasing sampling possibilities.

In measuring comprehension, it is questionable whether the depth of comprehension can be determined by very short paragraphs and questions that probe quite superficially. Furthermore, in a number of instances the astute reader could answer the question without reading the paragraph. Also, some items are probably not measuring what the author intended.

In summary, until the author can present more evidence that his test is superior to a number of other widely used instruments, it would not seem advisable to recommend the use of his instrument. Local norms can be developed for any test and this is advisable. However, local or national norms are of little use when based on such a weak instrument.

RONALD W. MITCHELL, *Assistant Executive Secretary, International Reading Association, Newark, Delaware.*

The primary level consists of 46 questions based on accompanying paragraphs. The reading material increases in length from three short sentences to three paragraphs.

Both the intermediate and advanced levels contain questions designed, according to the author, to measure vocabulary and reading comprehension. Vocabulary is measured by asking the student to select from a list of 5 or 10 words the synonym for the stimulus word which is presented in either a short sentence or in isolation. In the comprehension section, the student answers questions based on accompanying paragraphs. The author puts much more stress on vocabulary in the advanced level, which contains 114 vocabulary items as compared to 54 on the intermediate level.

According to the manuals, "the overriding consideration" of the test is "to arrive as closely as possible to a pupil's *functional* reading level." Thus, the test attempts to cover several skill areas. Questions in the comprehension section of each level are designed to measure the abilities to interpret factual data, draw inferences, note detail, find the main idea, and, on the intermediate and advanced levels, use study skills. While there are no subscores in these categories and the author does in fact state that the final test score is a composite one describing nothing other than "general reading achievement," each item is keyed to one or more of the skill areas listed above. Thus, the test has a certain degree of diagnostic usefulness, since the teacher can locate areas of weakness for a particular student.

The norms were developed on students from the Portland schools. Although the norm group included representation from all socioeconomic levels in the Portland area, the author recommends that the test user construct local norms.

Split-half reliability is reported for the primary level in terms of a standard error of measurement of 2.5. This is the only technical or statistical information related to test reliability or validity contained in the manuals. It should be pointed out that the test is timed; therefore, the split-half method of establishing reliability must be questioned, since it can result in inflated estimates when used with speeded tests.

This reviewer did contact the test author by telephone and found that the standard error has recently been computed for the intermediate (SE = 3.5) and advanced (SE = 3.0) levels of the test by using a split-half method. The reviewer further learned that validation studies on the test as a whole are now underway; however, no technical manual is planned at this time.

The manual accompanying the advanced level contains a section outlining the proper use of the test score. This would appear to be a valuable aid to a classroom teacher whose background in testing may be limited. By following suggested uses, the teacher is more likely to derive full benefit from the testing, as well as to avoid misuse of test data. Unfortunately, validation information is again lacking, so it is questionable how much faith could be placed in such suggested uses as predicting future performance.

It should be pointed out that all three levels contain questions of such common knowledge that many students could respond correctly without reading the related paragraphs. A study by this reviewer [1] on similar questions contained in subtests of the *Gates Basic Reading Tests,* however, failed to demonstrate that such questions have an adverse effect on test validity.

In conclusion, while the test appears to have reasonable face or content validity, one's confidence in this measuring instrument would certainly be strengthened by more substantial supporting information related to validity and reliability.

[694]

★**Maintaining Reading Efficiency Tests.** Grades 7–16 and adults; 1966–70; MRET; 3 scores: rate, comprehension accuracy, reading efficiency; 5 forms; reading booklet ('70, 13 pages) for each test; test booklet ('70, 4 pages); norms ['66, 2 pages] for Test 1 (grade 9) and Test 2 (grades 9 and 13) only; no manual; no data on reliability; $5 per 20 reading booklets; $2 per 20 test booklets; $2 per specimen set; cash orders postpaid; [20] minutes; Lyle L. Miller; Developmental Reading Distributors. *
a) TEST 1, HISTORY OF BRAZIL, 1970 REVISION. 1966–70.
b) TEST 2, HISTORY OF JAPAN, 1970 REVISION. 1966–70.

1 MITCHELL, RONALD W. *A Comparison of Children's Responses to an Original and Experimental Form of Subtests GS and ND of the Gates Basic Reading Tests.* Doctor's thesis, University of Minnesota (Minneapolis, Minn.), 1967.

c) TEST 3, HISTORY OF INDIA. 1970.
d) TEST 4, HISTORY OF NEW ZEALAND. 1970.
e) TEST 5, HISTORY OF SWITZERLAND. 1970.

[695]

Manchester Reading Comprehension Test (Sen.)
1. Ages 13.5–15; 1959; 1 form (8 pages); manual (8 pages); 57½p per 20 tests; 10p per manual; 15p per specimen set; postage extra; 45(50) minutes; Stephen Wiseman and Jack Wrigley (test); University of London Press Ltd. *

REFERENCE

1. See 6:796.

ELIZABETH J. GOODACRE, *Lecturer, Institute of Education, University of London, London, England.*

This test, "designed for use in English secondary schools," is a timed test which asks the pupil to read a short prose passage and answer questions requiring inference from what is read as well as straight recall of factual detail. Forty-nine of the questions are multiple choice and the remaining 11 require answers to be written. No information is presented on the reasons for using two types of questions, on the effect of guessing, or on the extent to which slow-writing children are penalized.

The test was standardized on 6,679 boys and 6,763 girls, the total age group of an English industrial city. This should be remembered if the test is being used with children from rural areas or small towns. A split-half reliability of .95 and a K-R (not further identified) of .94 are reported.

There is no information about the test's validity. Since the test was calibrated against the Watts-Vernon Comprehension Test, one might have expected information on the association between the tests.

Although it is well known that the performance of boys and that of girls tend to differ on tests of reading, this is one of the few tests in this country which provides separate norms for boys and girls. In England at the present time, there are insufficient tests for secondary school children and the choice available to teachers at this age level is decidedly limited. However, since the secondary schools are being reorganized on the basis of the comprehensive principle, it could be argued that the need for a test intended, as this one is, to be of assistance with vocational guidance preparatory to leaving school has lessened and that the Manchester test is therefore of limited use. The test appears to be fairly reliable, but it fails to provide information about the contribution of particular forms of comprehension to the total score and so cannot provide the teacher with information about an individual pupil's weaknesses in particular areas.

JOHN NISBET, *Professor of Education, University of Aberdeen, Aberdeen, Scotland.*

Nothing is said in the manual about the construction of this test. The passages of prose and the questions appear no different from the conventional comprehension exercises widely used in schools. The standardisation is based on the scores of over 13,000 Manchester 14-year-olds, with separate norms for boys and girls.

Layout and instructions follow the established model of the Moray House tests.

The test is neat, clear, and economical of space without crowding, though dull by comparison with more expensive and colourful American achievement tests. Eleven short passages of prose in boldface type stand out from the 60 questions, of which 22 are open-ended and the rest multiple choice.

There is a good range of scores covering performance around average level: one standard deviation above and one below average at age 14.5 spread over 26 points of raw score. Norms are "converted scores" with mean 100 and standard deviation 15; but the tables range down to 50 and up to 150, figures which surely convey a false sense of precision. There is no information on validity or correlations with other measures. Inspection suggests that vocabulary knowledge is a substantial factor, and 11 of the 60 items are straight vocabulary questions answerable without reference to the preceding texts.

On average, boys' scores are slightly higher than girls'. The choice of passages provides an explanation. In addition to the conventional literary prose extracts, there are technical passages on airflow, binocular vision, population census, and a cricket match. The sampling of different kinds of prose is commendable, but the inclusion of questions on cricket unfortunately makes the test unsuitable for export or for use in cross-cultural studies.

The test has been calibrated against the Watts-Vernon Test used in nationwide literacy surveys in England since 1948. Watts-Vernon, though preferable, is a restricted test, and this test offers an acceptable alternative for general use.

[696]

*Metropolitan Achievement Tests: Reading Tests.** Grades 2.5–3.4, 3.5–4.9, 5.0–6.9, 7.0–9.5; 1931–71; 3 scores: word knowledge, reading, total; 2 forms; 4 levels; battery teacher's handbook ('71, 16–17 pages) for each level; $6.50 per 35 tests; 70¢ per set of hand scoring stencils; 50¢ per battery handbook; $2 per battery specimen set of any one level; postage extra; Walter N. Durost, Harold H. Bixler, J. Wayne Wrightstone, George A. Prescott, and Irving H. Balow; Harcourt Brace Jovanovich, Inc. *

a) PRIMARY 2 READING TESTS. Grades 2.5–3.4; Forms F ('70, 8 pages), G ('71, 8 pages); directions ('70, 8 pages); scoring service, $1.25 and over per test; 48(60) minutes.

b) ELEMENTARY READING TESTS. Grades 3.5–4.9; Forms F ('70, 8 pages), G ('71, 8 pages); battery directions ('70, 13 pages); separate answer sheets (MRC) may be used; $7.50 per 100 answer sheets; 80¢ per MRC hand scoring stencil; hand scoring service, $1.25 and over per test; MRC scoring service, 23¢ and over per test; 40(50) minutes.

c) INTERMEDIATE READING TESTS. Grades 5.0–6.9; Forms F ('70, 7 pages), G ('71, 7 pages); battery directions ('70, 19 pages); separate answer sheets (Digitek, IBM 805, IBM 1230, MRC) may be used; $2.80 per 35 Digitek or IBM 1230 answer sheets; $2.50 per 35 MRC answer sheets; $2.30 per 35 IBM 805 answer sheets; 80¢ per scoring stencil; MRC scoring service, 23¢ and over per test; IBM scoring service, 50¢ and over per test; 40(50) minutes.

d) ADVANCED READING TESTS. Grades 7.0–9.5; Forms F ('70, 8 pages), G ('71, 8 pages); battery directions ('70, 19 pages); answer sheets, prices, and time same as for intermediate level.

REFERENCES

1–4. See 6:797.
5. SIPAY, EDWARD ROBERT. *A Comparison of Standardized Reading Achievement Test Scores and Functional Reading Levels.* Doctor's thesis, University of Connecticut (Storrs, Conn.), 1961. (*DA* 22:2639)
6. BROWN, SANDRA ROSE. *A Comparison of Five Widely Used Standardized Reading Tests and an Informal Reading Inventory for a Selected Group of Elementary School Children.* Doctor's thesis, University of Georgia (Athens, Ga.), 1963. (*DA* 25:996)
7. WILLIAMS, JOAN LEE. *A Comparison of Standardized Reading Test Scores and Informal Reading Inventory Scores.* Doctor's thesis, Southern Illinois University (Carbondale, Ill.), 1963. (*DA* 24:5262)
8. KAUFMAN, MAURICE. "A Follow-Up Study on Reading Test Results." *Am Ann Deaf* 110:420–3 My '65. * (*PA* 39:15989)
9. FURTH, HANS G. "A Comparison of Reading Test Norms of Deaf and Hearing Children." *Am Ann Deaf* 111:461–2 Mr '66. * (*PA* 40:10371)
10. SUTHERLAND, SAMUEL PHILIP. *A Factor Analytic Study of Tests Designed to Measure Reading Ability.* Doctor's thesis, University of Southern California (Los Angeles, Calif.), 1966. (*DA* 27:4141A)
11. ARNOLD, RICHARD D. "Reliability Coefficients of Certain Tests Used in the San Antonio Language Research Project." Abstract. *AERA Paper Abstr* 1968:92 '68. *
12. DAVIS, WILLIAM QUINBY. *A Study of Test Score Comparability Among Five Widely Used Reading Survey Tests.* Doctor's thesis, Southern Illinois University (Carbondale, Ill.), 1968. (*DA* 29:4370A)
13. ROBINSON, H. ALAN, AND HANSON, EARL. "Reliability of Measures of Reading Achievement." *Read Teach* 21:307–13+ Ja '68. * (*PA* 42:17652)
14. ARNOLD, RICHARD D. "Reliability of Test Scores for the Young 'Bilingual' Disadvantaged." *Read Teach* 22(4):341–5 Ja '69. *
15. FARR, ROGER, AND ANASTASIOW, NICHOLAS. *Tests of Reading Readiness and Achievement: A Review and Evaluation,* pp. 36–42. Newark, Del.: International Reading Association, 1969. Pp. iv, 51. *
16. GROPPER, ROBERT L. *Comprehension of Narrative Passages by Fourth-Grade Children as a Function of Listening Rate and Eleven Predictor Variables.* Doctor's thesis, George Peabody College for Teachers (Nashville, Tenn.), 1969. (*DAI* 30:4827A)
17. MICELI, FRANK. *The Performance of Culturally Disadvantaged Students on a Cross-Culturally Translated Stand-*

ardized Reading Test. Doctor's thesis, New York University (New York, N.Y.), 1969. (DAI 31:1251A)
18. ROELKE, PATRICIA LYNN. Reading Comprehension as a Function of Three Dimensions of Word Meaning. Doctor's thesis, Indiana University (Bloomington, Ind.), 1969. (DAI 30: 5300A)
19. BRANDINGER, ALICE L. Programmed Instruction, Sign Language, and Formal Directions to a Reading Test for Deaf High School Students. Doctor's thesis, Rutgers—The State University (New Brunswick, N.J.), 1970. (DAI 31:3405A)
20. BRUININKS, ROBERT H., AND LUCKER, WILLIAM G. "Change and Stability in Correlations Between Intelligence and Reading Test Scores Among Disadvantaged Children." J Read Behav 2(4):295–305 f '70. * (PA 46:5700)

For a review by H. Alan Robinson of an earlier edition, see 6:797; for reviews by James R. Hobson and Margaret G. McKim, see 4:543; for a review by D. A. Worcester, see 2:1551; for reviews by Ivan A. Booker and Joseph C. Dewey, see 1:1105. For reviews of an earlier edition of the complete battery, see 6:15 (3 reviews), 4:18 (1 review), 2:1189 (2 reviews), and 1:874 (3 reviews).

[697]

*New Developmental Reading Tests. Grades 1–2.5, 2.5–3, 4–6; 1955–68; revision of Developmental Reading Tests; 2 forms; 3 levels; postage extra; Guy L. Bond, Bruce Balow, and Cyril J. Hoyt; Lyons & Carnahan, Inc. *
a) PRIMARY TESTS. Grades 1–2.5, 2.5–3; 1955–65; 4 scores: word recognition, comprehending significant ideas, comprehending specific instructions, average grade score; 2 levels; manual ('65, 16 pages); $5.80 per 35 tests; $1 per set of scoring stencils; 60¢ per specimen set; 40(60) minutes in 2 or 3 sessions.
  1) Lower Primary Reading. Grades 1–2.5; Forms L-1, L-2, ('65, 16 pages).
  2) Upper Primary Reading. Grades 2.5–3; Forms U-1, U-2, ('65, 16 pages).
b) INTERMEDIATE TESTS. Grades 4–6; 1959–68; 5 basic scores: (1) vocabulary, (2) reading for information, (3) reading for relationships, (4) reading for interpretation, (5) reading for appreciation, plus 3 combination scores—literal comprehension (2 and 3), creative comprehension (4 and 5), and general comprehension (2, 3, 4, and 5); Forms A, B, ('68, 22 pages); manual ('68, 37 pages); no intercorrelations are presented for the 8 scores; $6 per 35 tests; separate answer sheets (Digitek) may be used; $5.60 per 100 answer sheets; $1 per specimen set (must be purchased to obtain manual and keys); scoring service, 15¢ to 50¢ per test; 50(75) minutes.

REFERENCES

1. LAMB, GEORGE STANWOOD. The Effect of Verbal Cues Upon Second and Third Grade Pupils' Responses on a Group Reading Test. Doctor's thesis, University of Minnesota (Minneapolis, Minn.), 1965. (DA 26:5871)
2. LAMB, GEORGE S. "Teacher Verbal Cues and Pupil Performance on a Group Reading Test." J Ed Psychol 58:332–6 D '67. * (PA 42:4486)
3. ROSEN, CARL L., AND OHNMACHT, FRED. "Perception, Readiness, and Reading Achievement in First Grade." Proc Ann Conv Int Read Assn 12(4):33–9 '68. *
4. WASSON, JOHN BRUCE. The Influence of Time Limits on Reading Comprehension Tests Among Fifth Grade Pupils of Differing Abilities. Doctor's thesis, University of Minnesota (Minneapolis, Minn.), 1969. (DAI 30:3807A)

FREDERICK B. DAVIS, Professor of Education, University of Pennsylvania, Philadelphia, Pennsylvania; and Director, Test Research Service, Bronxville, New York.

In Part 1 of both the Lower and Upper Primary tests, basic vocabulary is measured by items that require the examinee to circle the one of four words that "tells about the picture" presented in each item. The extent to which this word "tells about" the picture in some of the items is debatable. For example, items 16 in Form L-1 and 21 in Form L-2 both illustrate music with a picture of a grand piano that has no music visible on it. Item 9 in Form L-1 shows a kitten with one paw on a ball of string. Both pet and catch are included in the item but only the former is keyed as correct. Is this fair?

Quick inspection shows that 17 of the 36 vocabulary items in Form L-1 have the keyed word-picture combination repeated in Form L-2. This lack of independence of the two forms makes their equivalent-forms reliability coefficients spuriously high and reduces the appropriateness of the tests for estimating pupil growth (one of the purposes of measurement mentioned in the manual).

Ten minutes are allowed for first and second graders to complete 36 items in the Lower Primary tests and for second and third graders to complete 42 items in the Upper Primary tests. No data to show the actual numbers of items attempted in the time limit are available in the manual, but allowing only about 15 seconds per item when the pupils have to draw a circle around the word they select as correct seems on the low side for tests that are intended to be "power tests." Fortunately, the vocabulary tests are properly corrected for chance success.

Comprehension of sentences and short paragraphs is measured in Part 2 by 40 four-choice items. Surprisingly, scores on Part 2 are not corrected for chance success. What seem like easily avoidable faults characterize some items scattered throughout the tests. For example, item 35 in Form L-2 reads: "The toy was an _____. animal airplane game frog." Most pupils will avoid the last two choices simply because "an game" and "an frog" neither sound nor look right to them. Item 2 in Form L-2 reads: "This can go on water. It can go _____. not want fast like." Most pupils will rule out the first two choices because these words are not used colloquially after "go."

Part 3 measures comprehension of specific instructions by means of 26 items (at the Lower Primary level) or 32 items (at the Upper Primary level) that require the examinee to mark on the test booklet with letters or lines. Some of the keyed responses to these may be

New Developmental Reading Tests

difficult to defend. For example, item 17 in Form L-1 shows a boy in a cart, a girl, and a school building. The item reads: "The boy was riding a wagon away from the school. Put C on the one not riding." If an examinee marks the school, is he wrong? The key credits the girl only.

The test manual describes the tests, their scoring, and the recording of scores on a graphic profile. The rationale for use of what are called "Lines of Importance" (drawn vertically to represent one "Allowable Variation" above and one below each examinee's grade placement) is not given. In fact, the use of the profile chart is not clearly explained. The illustrative example, using Phil Rand's scores, does not help significantly. For example, scores between the Lines of Importance are said to be considered "satisfactory," yet one of Phil's scores that is between the lines is labeled "good." The basic question about whether or not there are significant differences (at some designated level) among Phil's part scores is not even asked, much less answered. It is difficult to see how the quality of an examinee's performance can be satisfactorily evaluated by scores on a measuring instrument like the *New Developmental Reading Tests* without reference to normative data like percentile ranks for scores obtained at each of several grade placements. Yet such data are not provided for the Lower and Upper Primary tests.

In a discussion under the heading "Diagnostic Use of Test Results" in the manual, Allowable Variations appear to be measured from an examinee's obtained grade score rather than from his actual grade placement, presumably in an effort to identify significant differences between scores. Since data in the manual indicate that differences among part scores of about 2 raw score points (and, as it happens in general, about .2 grade score points) are significantly different from zero differences at the .15 level or better, the Allowable Variations of .3, .4, or .6 grade score points may identify only extremely significant differences. Use of the same Allowable Variations, as suggested, for identifying significant differences between average reading grade scores derived from Forms 1 and 2 would seem to be so overly conservative as to be inappropriate. Data in Table 2 suggest that the standard error of measurement of the difference between two pupils' average scores

would be only about .8 raw score points for either Primary test.

Forms A and B of the Intermediate tests for grades 4–6 provide eight scores each, as listed in the entry above. The 60 items in Part 1 are straightforward four-choice recognition-vocabulary items. The source of the sampling of the 120 words tested is not given. It may be unfortunate that the distracters in each item are not all of the same part of speech as the keyed choice, but no glaringly poor items are apparent. The 30 items in Part 2 test for accuracy in getting details from passages. In spite of its title, Part 3 appears to measure much the same mental functions with its 30 items. Thus, the sum of scores on Parts 2 and 3 yields a good measure of literal comprehension of content.

The 30 items in Part 4 appear to measure a combination of weaving ideas together and making inferences from the content. Part 5 (also 30 items in length) probably measures this same combination of skills plus, to some degree, ability to recognize the mood, intent, or purpose of a passage. The dangers of using items that measure this last ability are illustrated by the second sample, for which some readers may argue that choices *a* and *b* are about equally satisfactory answers, though only choice *b* is keyed as correct. The combined score of Parts 4 and 5 may perhaps be regarded functionally as a measure of reasoning in reading, even though it is labeled "Creative Comprehension."

The short passages on which the reading items are based seem interesting and are so chosen that, by and large, items cannot be answered confidently without reference to the passages. The scoring procedures properly include a correction for chance success.

Information about the standardization sample of the Intermediate test indicates that over 100 schools were included and that geographical location and community type, size, and socioeconomic level were taken into account in constructing the normative samples. Percentile ranks and stanines are provided in the manual for raw scores of examinees at the end of grade 3 and at the middle and end of each of grades 4, 5, and 6. Grade scores ranging from 2.7 to 11.2 are also given, although there is no evidence in the manual that pupils below grade 3.9 or above grade 6.9 were actually tested. If extrapolation was used to estimate grade scores below 3.9 and above 6.9, great caution should be

New Developmental Reading Tests

exercised in reporting such scores, because they will almost always be misinterpreted.

The data pertaining to reliability and accuracy of measurement given in the manual indicate that the tests are satisfactory in these respects. Virtually no information about the practical uses of the standard errors of measurement is provided in the manual. Unfortunately, these data are reported in raw scores instead of in grade scores, stanines, and percentile bands. Hence, teachers and counselors are likely to use such scores improperly when they fail to recognize that they do not know how to employ them with the derived scores that are reported.

SUMMARY. The *New Developmental Reading Tests* measure fairly well a number of important components of comprehension. Inadequate normative data are available for the Lower and Upper Primary tests. Although helpful suggestions are given for using the test scores to improve instruction, the interpretive aids that are needed to make the tests as useful as they could be are not provided. To the reviewer, this seems to be their most serious limitation.

ARTHUR E. TRAXLER, *Adjunct Lecturer in Education, University of Miami, Coral Gables, Florida.*

The *Developmental Reading Tests,* 1955–61 edition, the forerunner of the present edition known as the *New Developmental Reading Tests,* were rather severely criticized, and justifiably so, by Fry and Townsend in *The Sixth MMY.* The *New Developmental Reading Tests,* while not free from limitations, are a distinct improvement over the older edition, particularly in the case of the manuals accompanying the tests. Most of the reading material of the tests is well chosen, the directions for administering and scoring are clear and appropriate, most of the test items are free from ambiguity, the format and printing of the test booklets are above average, and the aspects of reading that the tests undertake to measure are worthwhile and suited to the age levels of the pupils.

Since the preceding edition was not accompanied by a test manual, no useful information was available concerning reliability and validity, intercorrelation of part scores, standardization population, or norms. In the present edition, an effort was made to correct these faults. Even so, there is a noticeable unevenness in the statistical information made available for the different levels.

Nearly all the items in the Primary tests obviously have only one correct response, although in a few instances, such as the picture for item 14 of the L-1 form, there may be some doubt. While the Primary tests themselves appear to be good, the manual is, for several reasons, rather inadequate. First, the directions for scoring Parts 1 and 2, both of which consist of four-choice items, do not agree with one another as to correction for guessing. Second, the basis for establishing norms is stated in terms so vague and general as to have little meaning. Third, the uncommon term "Allowable Variation" used in connection with the graphic profile of individual pupil scores needs more explanation.

Further inadequacies occur in shortcomings in the technical data given in the Primary manual: (*a*) Although the correlation between the two forms at each level is satisfactorily high, a lack of information about the relative difficulty of the forms leads to doubt as to whether they are interchangeable and whether they may be used for test-retest purposes. (*b*) At one point, the test manual refers to the "low intercorrelations" among the part scores, but the reported data do not support characterization of the intercorrelations as "low." (*c*) A more glaring weakness in the technical data given in the manual is that the question of validity of the tests at the Primary levels seems to have been ignored.

The Intermediate level contains five subtests designed for a total working time of 50 minutes, exclusive of directions. Its appearance is that of a well-designed test, with good items and well chosen reading materials, although portions of it may be difficult for the range of pupil ability usually found in the intermediate grades. All items are four-choice, and the number of right answers is corrected for guessing in each part, a scoring procedure that greatly reduces the probability that some pupils will obtain respectable grade scores by chance.

The manual appears to be much better than the one for the Primary levels. It is forthright, well organized, and clearly written, and the standardization and statistical work on the test scores bears the mark of the professional in test construction and use. The standardization population for the Intermediate level, while by no means comparable in scope to that for such instruments as the Stanford reading tests, compares favorably with that for many tests. It consisted of 15,000 pupils representing five major geographical areas and three community types.

Reliabilities are reported both in terms of internal-consistency coefficients and between-forms correlations. The reliability coefficients for vocabulary, for the subtotal comprehension scores, and for the general comprehension score would warrant use of these scores in appraising individual pupils. The reliabilities for the individual parts are well above the level needed for group evaluation but, with the exception of vocabulary, tend to be a bit low for individual appraisal.

The manual contains a good discussion of the content validity of the Intermediate level. As is true of the manual for the Primary tests, the Intermediate manual lacks precise information ·about the relative difficulty of the two forms. This question might readily have been cared for by means of the extensive norms tables for each form had the information given in the manual indicated whether or not the pupils taking Form A and those taking Form B were random samples of the same or equivalent populations.

In summary, the reading material and item structure of the *New Developmental Reading Tests* are good, with a very few exceptions. The information contained in the manual for the Lower and Upper Primary tests is not adequate relative to standardization, consistency of scoring procedures, norms, reliability and validity data, and comparability of forms. The manual for the Intermediate level (1968) is much improved over the one for the Primary level (1965). The 1968 manual clearly sets forth the reading abilities the tests undertake to measure, the administration and scoring procedures to be followed, the well-conceived standardization procedures used, statistical and other information concerning reliability and validity, tables including three types of norms, and valuable suggestions concerning use of test results. Limitations include rather inadequate explanation of the norm tables and vague information concerning the comparability of the norm groups for the alternate forms of the test. Overall, this reviewer would recommend the *New Developmental Reading Tests* for cautious use in analyzing the reading abilities of individual pupils in the primary and intermediate grades.

For reviews by Edward B. Fry and Agatha Townsend of the original edition, see 6:787.

New Developmental Reading Tests

[698]

★OISE Achievement Tests in Silent Reading: Advanced Primary Battery. Grade 2; 1969-71; 5 scores: words in use, multiple word meanings, Part A comprehension, Part B comprehension, total; Forms A, B, ('69, 21 pages); manual ('70, 16 pages); technical handbook ('71, 34 pages); Can $4 per 25 tests; 75¢ per set of scoring stencils; $2 per handbook; $1 per specimen set; postage extra; 90(110) minutes in 3 sessions; Ontario Institute for Studies in Education and Patricia Tracy (handbook); distributed by Guidance Centre. *

[699]

★Progressive Achievement Tests of Reading. Standards 2-4 and Forms I-IV; 1969-70; PATR; raw scores are converted into "levels of achievement" regardless of age or class and into percentile ranks within half-year age groups; 2 forms; 2 tests; 7 overlapping levels called Parts 2 (Standard 2), 3 (3), 4 (4), 5 (Form I), 6 (II), 7 (III), 8 (IV) in a single booklet; manual ('69, 32 pages); separate answer sheets must be used; NZ 15¢ per 20 answer sheets for any one level; 60¢ per specimen set; postpaid within New Zealand; Warwick B. Elley and Neil A. Reid; New Zealand Council for Educational Research. *
a) READING COMPREHENSION. Forms A ('69, 23 pages), B ('70, 23 pages); $1.60 per 20 tests; 40(50) minutes.
b) READING VOCABULARY. Forms A ('69, 12 pages), B ('70, 12 pages); $1.20 per 20 tests; 30(40) minutes.

N Z J Ed Studies 5(1):69-71 My'70. Milton L. Clark. * Successful use of the tests....may be predicted on two very fundamental bases: firstly, the painstaking efforts which appear to have been made to ensure that the objectives and emphases of the tests "reflect the aims and practices of New Zealand teachers"; and secondly, the succinct but informative expositions on interpreting and using the test results which appear in the Teacher's Manual. An impressive amount of planning is reported on the production of these tests. * The two facets of reading comprehension covered by the PAT—literal and implied meaning—are only briefly defined in the manual (page 5), but on each scoring key the classification used for each item is given as a guide to general diagnosis and remedial treatment. However, only a single comprehension score is provided because of the high correlation found between factual and inferential comprehension skills defined by these tests. Nevertheless, the construct of comprehension employed, both in terms of the general skill definitions given, as well as the type of items used to measure each skill, would be generally accepted as valid. It is consistent with research findings on the nature of reading comprehension ability. Furthermore, it would seem that the New Zealand teacher's view of the reading comprehension process, as interpreted by the reading specialists employed in writing the PAT material, is in conformity with the objectives made explicit in some of the better known reading tests published overseas. There is a close similarity between the PAT and the well established Iowa Tests of Basic Skills in Reading evident not only in the type of reading passages and questions employed, but also in general organisation. The PAT material is also not unlike that used in the ETS Sequential Tests of Educational Progress in Reading. Unique characteristics of the PAT reading tests derive from the relative weighting of types of passages and items employed, and the local flavour of a number of the passages—which will no doubt appeal to children tested. A valuable feature of these tests is the provision of "level" scores. These give a basis for determining the pupil's "absolute" level of development rather than a "relative" level of performance such as that obtained by means of normalized scores. Ten levels are identified, ranging from a "very limited grasp of reading to an adult level of competence in the skills tested." Comprehension level scores are related in a very practical table to illustrative reading material of suitable difficulty level, Elley's scaling of the readability of the test passages, and an equivalent age level. The vocabulary level scores have been equated to an approximate vocabulary size as well as an equivalent age level. * The NZCER Test Division is to be congratulated for achieving a balanced perspective between developmental level on the one hand and relative level of performance on the other in their presentation of interpretative data. * highly reliable and valid testing instruments. The tests themselves are clearly presented in an attractive format, and the comprehension test passages make interesting reading. The standard of reporting on relevant research data is good, and information from further statistical studies of test validity has been promised. Standardization data indicates careful sampling, and scaling procedures have resulted in a single scale from which norms for each age group (in half years) have been calculated. The simple tables of norms are commendably clear. To sum up, the PAT Reading, Form A, has all the marks of a most professional job, and the authors are to be complimented. It seems highly probable that test users outside of New Zealand will be interested in this material.

Slow Learning Child 16(3):185–7 N '69. J. Elkins. * An excellent 32 page manual * The authors indicate a wide range of possible uses to which these tests might be put by teachers. Most of these, such as grouping for instruction, identifying gifted and retarded readers, and classifying students entering the New Zealand education system, are realistic. However, for selecting materials and methods, group tests of this type provide only a small portion of necessary information. * The content validity of these tests appears very satisfactory, though the New Zealand setting of some comprehension passages make it more suitable for New Zealand children but less suitable for one of the stated uses "to help classify school entrants from outside the New Zealand public education system." Some evidence supportive of concurrent validity is provided, but as yet little is known of the predictive stability of the tests. * The internal consistency of the tests is very satisfactory. * A useful adjunct is a list of materials of difficulty level suited to each level score. It appears inconvenient that the Level scores are calculated on the marking key but the Percentile Ranks from a table in the Manual. Also teachers are told to ignore the subdivisions a, b, c....for each level, as these are used only for entering the P.R. table. It would be preferable to have these norms in terms of raw scores. Also, an age unit of 6 months is too coarse. * These tests have been very thoroughly constructed. Both comprehension passages and questions have been classified according to stated objectives. The marking keys show clearly which comprehension questions are factual and which inferential. This augments the diagnostic possibilities of the test. This reviewer considers that "Cloze" procedure reading comprehension tests are more efficient and less time-consuming than the traditional approach used here. Also the predictive value of reading vocabulary tests in addition to reading comprehension and general ability measures is not large. However, as tests which could be used widely by teachers, especially in relation to immediate classroom procedures, the PAT Reading Tests should prove most useful.

[700]

★RBH Basic Reading and Word Test. Disadvantaged adults; 1968–69; 1 form ('68, 4 pages); manual ['69, 7 pages]; directions (no date, 2 pages); $4.50 per 25 tests; $1.50 per manual; 50¢ per key; $1.50 per specimen set; postage extra; (25–30) minutes; Richardson, Bellows, Henry & Co., Inc. *

RBH Basic Reading and Word Test

THORSTEN R. CARLSON, *Professor of Education, Sonoma State College, Rohnert Park, California.*

The title of this test might be misleading. An examination of the test indicates that it seeks to measure reading vocabulary. The test manual claims that the test measures "reading-vocabulary" and reading comprehension. It would seem to measure comprehension only incidentally to the degree that comprehension is required for the reading of the directions and of each vocabulary item.

The test contains 80 true-false items arranged in order of difficulty from the easiest to the most difficult. Few data are provided on the validity of the test. The authors state that the test has high face validity. It does seem to measure reading vocabulary, but no information is provided on how the sampling of words was selected. What were the sources of the words? A significant number seem to be "old-fashioned" such as, divan, leghorn, violin cello, fodder, backgammon, and raiment. In other words, the reviewer would seriously question the attestation in the manual of high face validity.

What control was exercised over types of words? Why are 15 of the 80 words concerned with animals? What was done to distribute the vocabulary sampling among various areas of human knowledge and experience? Were the choices of words distributed among the various parts of speech? In what proportions and why? The items seem to contain a disproportionate share of nouns.

The nature of the items makes it difficult to determine which word is most significant or which word is being tested. "A *pump* is a *vegetable.*" "A *hammer* is a *tool.*" Which of the italicized words in each item is the principal word? Also, to what extent are the items a test of syntax or comprehension of meaning units larger than single words?

A reference to Thorndike and Lorge, *The Teacher's Wordbook of 30,000 Words,* indicates that many words, in the judgment of this reviewer, occur too infrequently in reading matter to merit their placement in the first half of the test or in the test at all. If the items are graded in difficulty, it is not apparent from reference to the data on utility in a wordlist such as that of Thorndike and Lorge. Casual examination of difficulty gradation reveals such strange contiguous items as *rabbits* and *contribution,*

square and *vehicle, spaniel* and *dragoon, orange* and *display.*

The most specific treatment of validity in the manual cites correlations of −.20 and .29 between the test and an estimate of learning rate and a composite learning criterion, respectively. Both these validity criteria seem tenuous, but even assuming their relevance, the magnitude of correlation for each is not reassuring.

The only other evidence of validity is a statement that a "substantial correlation" was obtained "between the test's overall score and a widely used test of reading comprehension." The name of the test with which it was correlated is not provided.

An obtained correlation of .77 was used as a base to set up a grade expectancy chart for scores on the test. It is difficult to understand what the validity or usefulness of a grade equivalent can be in evaluating an adult's reading competence.

A split-half reliability of .86 was obtained from a study of 100 applicants for a skills training program. Even this modest coefficient may be an overestimate because of the variability of the group tested on educational factors related to reading comprehension.

Percentile norms and "scaled scores" are provided. The manual should have used the term "standard score" instead of "scale score." The norms seem to be adequate. The "scaled scores" are linear transformations with mean 20 and a standard deviation 5.

The format of the test is practical but unimaginative and unattractive. The test is available only in single form.

In summary, the test lacks convincing reliability and validity data. The vocabulary content seems old-fashioned, poorly graded in difficulty, and, in all, rather unimpressive as a sampling of vocabulary. The single form also limits the usefulness of the test. More adequate tests, in the judgment of the reviewer, are available for the purposes ostensibly served by this instrument.

[701]

RBH Test of Reading Comprehension. Business and industry; 1951–63; 1 form ('51, 8 pages); manual ['63, 10 pages]; directions (no date, 2 pages); $5.50 per 25 tests; 50¢ per key; $1.50 per manual; $1.50 per specimen set; postage extra; 20(25) minutes; Richardson, Bellows, Henry & Co., Inc. *

THORSTEN R. CARLSON, *Professor of Education, Sonoma State College, Rohnert Park, California.*

This test contains six articles on subjects related to business and industry. Three-option multiple choice items are used to evaluate comprehension. Each selection of 200 to 275 words is covered by six or seven test items. The items call for the identification of specific factual information. The items and the reading selection are on the same page, thus permitting referral from the items to the selection for verification of correct answer. The decoys seem to be attractive enough to make such referral a slow process and thus force a rather careful initial reading of each selection.

The test has a copyright date of 1951. The norming data carry a date of 1963. The nature of the articles and the age of the test would give an evaluator pause as to the up-to-dateness and the current accuracy of the material.

The test comes in a single form. The format seems acceptable but drab. The length of line for the reading selections seems excessive from the point of view of readability and reader interest.

The norms seem to indicate that the test is quite easy for the sample on which it was normed. In fact, the mean of 31, with a maximum score of 40 and a standard deviation of 7, would indicate a skewed distribution. Under such circumstances, a percentile or scale score system may be difficult to interpret. There was apparently no statistical normalizing of the data in setting up the scale score system, which is based on a mean of 20 and a standard deviation of 5. The authors should probably have used the term "standard score" instead of "scale score." The question should be raised as to the usefulness of such a system for users of the test, most of whom would have little test sophistication.

The quoted reliability coefficients seem adequate. However, for evaluation, the mean and standard deviation should be available for each coefficient. Though the manual disclaims the time factor, there is a time limit. Since the quoted means are high, one may probably presume a high mean for the samples used in the reliability studies. Considering the time factor and the probability of a high mean, it may be that the quoted reliabilities are spuriously high.

Little information is provided on validity. If the criterion measures are accepted as suitable, the coefficients of .17 to .46 are not reassuring. None of the criterion measures seems to be a measure of reading comprehension. Performance ratings on the job would seem to be of dubious value in determining whether a reading test truly measures reading comprehension. Some other established test of reading comprehension or some informal measure of reading competence would have been a more acceptable criterion.

In summary, the reliability and validity data for this test are not convincing. The norms seem adequate, though users might question the value of a unique scale score system. The content of the test is technical and this feature, combined with the factual nature of the items, will induce a meticulous type of reading behavior. The format does not help to enliven the test or motivate the reader. The single form limits the usefulness of the test. The reviewer does not recommend this instrument. Those seeking a test for use with adults should carefully evaluate other available instruments.

WILLARD A. KERR, *Professor of Psychology and Head of the Department, Middle Tennessee State University, Murfreesboro, Tennessee.*

This test is an 8-page booklet containing six carefully selected articles about business and industry. Each article is followed by questions which test understanding. Basic subject matter was taken from "training manuals, safety manuals, and publicity releases, all [of which] might be given an hourly-paid employee. The questions asked....are clearly answered in the article and are not intended to measure critical thinking. The examinee is alloted 20 minutes for reading the articles and answering the [40] questions."

Casual reading of the articles evokes quick interest. They have been employed primarily on male personnel in the oil industry but also with women in the nursing profession. Content, however, is appropriate to occupations in general. Means and sigmas are provided on 12 groups of operating personnel and 24 classifications of applicants. Also, 63 correlation coefficients are supplied with 30 other ability and motivational test variables. The RBH correlates .38 to .82 with various learning ability tests. Percentile norms are provided for 1,185 operating industrial personnel and 4,716 industrial job applicants.

This instrument appears to possess high reliability and face validity plus satisfactory demonstrated validity.

Nine validity studies (7 in oil industry, 2 in

nursing) were conducted. These yielded correlations (between test scores and performance criteria such as supervisors' ratings and grades) ranging between .18 and .46. Criteria predicted in most of these studies are quite complex. For reading comprehension alone to predict such criteria at a median level of about .23 is more than satisfactory. It is unusual for a single variable to predict a complex phenomenon at so high a level. The explanation here probably lies in the fact that reading comprehension tests (including the RBH one) measure *more* than "one variable." They are also disguised partial tests of intelligence involving unknown loadings of the factors of memory, logical reasoning, and verbal fluency. The manual does not directly explore the problem of how much validity would remain were these factors partialed out. On the other hand, the test has excellent face validity and its practical usefulness is demonstrated.

[702]

★Reading Comprehension Test DE. Ages 10-0 to 12-6; 1963-67; formerly called *Reading Comprehension Test 1;* 1 form ['63, 11 pages]; mimeographed provisional manual ['63, 9 pages]; provisional norms ['67, 1 page] for ages 10-0 to 11-11 only; no data on reliability; 5p per test, postpaid within U.K.; manual and norms free on request from NFER; (40-45) minutes; E. L. Barnard; published for the National Foundation for Educational Research in England and Wales; Ginn & Co. Ltd. *

[703]

*Reading Test AD. Ages 7-6 to 11-1; 1956-70; formerly called *Sentence Reading Test 1;* 1 form ['60, 4 pages, identical with test published in 1956 except for format]; manual ('70, 8 pages, identical with manual published in 1956 except for title); 4p per test; 7p per manual; postpaid within U.K.; 15(20) minutes; A. F. Watts; published for the National Foundation for Educational Research in England and Wales; Ginn & Co. Ltd. *

For reviews by Reginald R. Dale and Stephen Wiseman, see 5:652.

[704]

★Reading Test: McGraw-Hill Basic Skills System. Grades 11-14; 1970; also called *MHBSS Reading Test;* although designed for use with the MHBSS instructional program, the test may be used independently; 7 scores: 2 reading rates (recreational, study), flexibility, retention, skimming and scanning, paragraph comprehension, total; Forms A, B, (34 pages); manual (48 pages); separate answer sheets (Digitek, IBM 1230, Scoreze) must be used; $7.25 per 25 tests; $2.50 per 50 IBM or Digitek answer sheets; $3 per 25 Scoreze answer sheets; $1 per IBM or Digitek scoring stencil; postage extra; $1.25 per specimen set, postpaid; IBM scoring service, 25¢ and over per test ($20 minimum); 66(76) minutes; Alton L. Raygor; McGraw-Hill Book Co., Inc. *

RBH Test of Reading Comprehension

DONALD B. BLACK, *Professor of Educational Psychology, The University of Calgary, Calgary, Alberta, Canada.*

This reading test is a welcome addition at a level where reading skills are of considerable importance and concern. The items appear both timely and interesting to the student, i.e., the test content appears to have a high face validity.

The manual is most complete and a model of desirable format. The norms tables and descriptions of the various scores are well presented. The schools and institutions participating in the norming are listed but no rationale is given for their being chosen or for the number of students from each. In fact, the manual cautions the reader that "no real effort" was made to select representative samples. Subsequent use of the norms tables and test statistics based on these samples must take this into account. It is not surprising, therefore, that the manual encourages the development of local norms.

For the most part, the statistics are based on the combined norming populations, which include samples in ability levels ranging from high school juniors to sophomores in four-year colleges. Item difficulties are given for the combined groups by form. The item difficulties and numbers of items comprising each subscore give some clue as to why the K-R 20 reliabilities are lower than one might normally expect and particularly so with such a heterogeneous sample. Interestingly, K-R 20's are reported for the Skimming and Scanning subscore, which is acknowledged to be speeded. The manual cautions about the spuriously high reliability coefficients which result, and then proceeds to report standard errors of measurement based on these figures.

Intercorrelations of part scores are given for two samples of 84 and 67 cases. These samples are not presented as being representative but the data presented do show gratifyingly low intercorrelations where these might be expected.

Summing up, this test shows promise; it appears to have high face validity. The manual is a model of format. Its deficiencies are directly related to the very newness of the test, e.g., the lack of adequate norming samples expected in tests today. While there is emphasis placed on the necessary relation of the test to local objectives and on the need for local norms, the lack of representative "national" or regional norms reflects a deficiency which will hopefully be corrected in future revisions of the manual.

[705]

★**Reading Tests A and BD.** 1, 2–4 years primary school; 1967–70; 1 form; 2 levels; 5p per test; post-paid within U.K.; published for the National Foundation for Educational Research in England and Wales; Ginn & Co. Ltd. *
a) READING TEST A. 1 year primary school; 1968–70; formerly called *Primary Reading Test 1;* 1 form ['68, 8 pages]; mimeographed instructions ['68, 6 pages]; provisional norms ('70, 2 pages); no data on reliability; instructions and norms free on request from NFER; (20–30) minutes.
b) READING TEST BD. 2–4 years primary school; 1967–69; formerly called *Primary Reading Test 2;* 1 form ['67, 6 pages]; manual ['69, 16 pages]; 13p per manual; 20(30) minutes.

[706]

*****SRA Achievement Series: Reading.** Grades 1–2, 2–4, 4–9; 1954–69; 2 forms; 5 levels in 3 booklets; no specific manuals; for series manuals and accessories, see 18; postage extra; Louis P. Thorpe, D. Welty Lefever, and Robert A. Naslund; Science Research Associates, Inc. *
a) HAND SCORED EDITION. Grades 1–2, 2–4; 1954–68; 2 levels.
  1) *Grades 1–2.* 5 scores: verbal-pictorial association, language perception, comprehension, vocabulary, total; Forms C, D, ('63, 36 pages); $5.85 per 25 tests; 120(185) minutes in 4 sessions.
  2) *Grades 2–4.* 3 scores: comprehension, vocabulary, total; Forms C ('63, 27 pages), D ('57, 27 pages); $3.75 per 25 tests; 90(120) minutes in 2 sessions.
b) MULTILEVEL EDITION. Grades 4–9; 1963–69; 3 scores: comprehension, vocabulary, total; Forms C, D, ('63, 25 pages); 3 levels: blue (grades 4.5–6.5), green (grades 6.5–8.5), and red (grades 8.5–9) in a single booklet; separate series answer sheets (Digitek, Docu-Tran, IBM 805, IBM 1230) must be used; $8.70 per 25 tests; $9.30 per 100 DocuTran answer sheets; 70(77) minutes.

REFERENCES
1. KARLIN, ROBERT, AND JOLLY, HAYDEN. "The Use of Alternate Forms of Standardized Reading Tests." *Read Teach* 19:187–91+ D '65. *
2. SUTHERLAND, SAMUEL PHILIP. *A Factor Analytic Study of Tests Designed to Measure Reading Ability.* Doctor's thesis, University of Southern California (Los Angeles, Calif.), 1966. (DA 27:4141A)
3. ZEMAN, SAMUEL STEVE. *The Relationship Between the Measured Reading Comprehension and the Basic Sentence Types and Sentence Structural Patterns in Compositions Written by Second and Third Grade Children.* Doctor's thesis, Lehigh University (Bethlehem, Pa.), 1966. (DA 27:3243A)
4. DAVIS, WILLIAM QUINBY. *A Study of Test Score Comparability Among Five Widely Used Reading Survey Tests.* Doctor's thesis, Southern Illinois University (Carbondale, Ill.), 1968. (DA 29:4370A)
5. ANASTASIOW, NICHOLAS J. "Fourth Through Sixth Grade Student Performance Differences on STEP and SRA Achievement Tests." *Meas & Eval Guid* 2(3):149–52 f '69. * (PA 44:13276)
6. HAFNER, LAWRENCE E.; WEAVER, WENDELL W.; AND POWELL, KATHRYN. "Psychological and Perceptual Correlates of Reading Achievement Among Fourth Graders." *J Read Behav* 2(4):281–90 f '70. * (PA 46:5663)

JOHN T. GUTHRIE, *Assistant Professor of Education, The Johns Hopkins University, Baltimore, Maryland.*

The purpose of this test is to "measure the pupil's ability to understand the overall theme of the story, identify the main idea in paragraphs, infer logical ideas, retain significant details and understand the meaning of words in context." The validity of this reading test could be assessed by correlating it with other widely used reading tests. However, this reviewer could not locate any studies reporting such data; the authors report no information on predictive or concurrent validity.

The face validity of the test may be described by listing the subtests: paragraph comprehension, vocabulary, and total. The level for grades 1–2 also includes the subtests verbal-pictorial association and language perception. The inclusion of the language perception subtest is peculiar. The function of the whole test as a general reading ability measure rather than a diagnostic device does not require this subtest.

The computation of total reading score at the level for grades 1–2 is also amiss. The language perception subtest contributes almost half of the points making up the total score. Thus, the total reading score is weighted too heavily with the language perception subtest. Reflecting this bias, the language perception subtest correlated .90 with the total reading score in its present form.

The comprehension subtests at all levels are commendable. The passages are interesting and the multiple choice questions require a broad range of skills such as recall, inference, and the identification of central themes. Most admirable is the exclusion of vocabulary items from this subtest.

The vocabulary subtests, however, are questionable. At all levels, they require the recognition of the meaning of words in context. However, the words and contexts are identical to those of the paragraph comprehension section administered immediately before. It is not surprising that the correlation between the vocabulary and comprehension subtests is .73 for Form C and .80 for Form D. This confounding should be eliminated if separate scores for vocabulary and comprehension are to be provided.

The K-R 20 reliabilities are uniformly high for all subtests at all levels: comprehension, .79 to .90, with median .86; vocabulary, .76 to .92, with median .88; and total score, .90 to .98, with median .94. Alternate forms correlated .83 when administered one year apart. Since the correlation is likely to have been deflated because of the long time interval between testings, the reliability over time is comfortably high.

The usability of this test is substantial. Teachers or administrators without special training can easily administer and interpret the test. The instructions are clear and extensive color coding of booklets, answer sheets, and items makes the communication of directions easy.

The standardization of the test and the construction of norms leave room for further refinement. For example, although the various geographic regions are well represented in the standardization sample, the socioeconomic status and intelligence of the sample are not described. Are students with IQ's below 85 or students in remedial reading classes included in the sample? This information is vital to the interpretation of a low score and the placement of a student who scores poorly on the test. Since this test is often used to place students in special classes, either gifted or remedial, information is needed about the characteristics of the children who represent the high and low ends of the norm group. Finally, separate norms for boys and girls are not provided. Since girls are so frequently superior to boys in reading, different norms would facilitate both the interpretation of scores and a variety of administrative decisions.

For a review by Edward B. Fry of earlier forms, see 6:808; for a review by N. Dale Bryant and Clarence Derrick, see 5:649. For reviews of the complete battery, see 18 (2 reviews), 6:21 (1 review), and 5:21 (2 reviews).

[707]

★Stanford Achievement Test: High School Reading Test. Grades 9–12; 1965–66; catalog uses the title *Stanford High School Reading Test;* subtest of *Stanford Achievement Test: High School Basic Battery;* Form W ('65, 6 pages); no specific manual; battery manual ('65, 48 pages); supplementary directions ('66, 4 pages) for each type of answer sheet; separate answer sheets (IBM 805, IBM 1230) must be used; $8.20 per 35 tests; $2.30 per 35 IBM 805 answer sheets; $2.80 per 35 IBM 1230 answer sheets; 70¢ per scoring stencil; $1.20 per battery manual; $2 per specimen set; postage extra; scoring service, 19¢ and over per test; 40(45) minutes; Eric F. Gardner, Jack C. Merwin, Robert Callis, and Richard Madden; Harcourt Brace Jovanovich, Inc. *

ROBERT H. BAUERNFEIND, *Professor of Educational Psychology, Northern Illinois University, DeKalb, Illinois.*

This appears to be a very satisfactory test of reading comprehension for high school students. It is built around two item types—cloze items, in which the student must select words for blanks in a paragraph, and conventional comprehension items in which the student answers questions about a paragraph he has read. In this 65-item test there are 23 cloze items and 42 conventional comprehension items.

There is a stress on historical materials in the paragraphs, but I think one should not criticize that fact. Reading is a single-factor skill, at least in the upper grades. Correlations among reliable power tests of reading comprehension seem consistently to run in the .80's and low .90's. To paraphrase both L. L. Thurstone and Gertrude Stein, "A poor reader is a poor reader is a poor reader." Whether the authors had used more or fewer historical passages, one's students would score at about the same level.

In general, the items are clear and well written. I dislike picking on individual items, but, really, item 14 shouldn't have happened. This is an item in which answer 2 is marked as 5, 3 as 6, 4 as 7, and 5 as 8. Such an item can really stop a poor student, and it is bound to annoy any red-blooded student as further evidence of the insensitivity of the "Establishment."

This test is given with a 40-minute time limit, and the authors imply that the test—including the preliminaries—can be given in 45 minutes. This is true, if one is using the plan wherein the students have previously marked the preliminary information on their answer sheets so that on testing day they are greeted with their pre-coded answer sheets and the actual test booklets. But if one is using the second and third page of the manual—the plan where students code their answer sheets and take a "short break" before they begin the test—the time needed is going to run closer to 55 minutes.

There could also be a problem with the 40-minute time limit. The manual includes a general statement to the effect that all of the Stanford high school tests were designed as power measures, and the authors have repeatedly made this assumption in calculating their reliability coefficients, but the manual includes no data indicating the percentages of various groups who actually finish the test in a 40-minute period. If a high school elects to give this test, this matter of power vs. speed should be checked on its own students. (Incidentally, that is good practice on any test, whether or not the authors report power vs. speed data for various groups.)

This test also looks good technically. It is readable and attractive; the answer sheets are easy to work with; the national norms appear to be soundly developed; the reliability coefficients typically run around .91; and the difficulty level appears to be about right for high school students, with the national median representing about 54 percent of the items/correct.

The test purchaser should also note the excellent national "rights analysis" data given in the manual. These data could be very helpful if the test purchaser has similar data for his own students.

H. ALAN ROBINSON, *Professor of Reading, Hofstra University, Hempstead, New York.*

The *Stanford High School Reading Test* is a very fine survey tool for appraising the results of a student's interaction with certain specific types of reading tasks. The test renders only one score based on the accomplishment of two different approaches to testing reading achievement: (*a*) a type of cloze procedure in which the student selects the best of four choices to fit into the running context of blank spots in a short paragraph (ranging from 4 to 12 lines); (*b*) questions, following longer paragraphs (ranging from 14 to 47 lines), in which the student selects one of four responses regarding details, main ideas, implications, or conclusions.

The single score does not make the test useful as a diagnostic tool but enhances its value as a reliable measure of reading comprehension. For the enterprising, the test can be converted into a semi-diagnostic instrument by developing an answer key which clusters together those responses which appear to be measuring the same subskill. Such an evaluation may give the teacher some rough insights into strengths and weaknesses which need further evaluation. One can see why the test designers did not include such a key for fear of appearing to label the test *diagnostic* when it is not.

In fact, the authors, as well as the publisher, are to be congratulated for their caution against making broad generalities, for their extensive experimentation and standardization procedures, and for their sincere efforts to produce a valid and reliable instrument. The format is clear, and directions for administering and scoring are unambiguous. Norms are based on 22,-699 students from 58 schools in 39 states. Raw scores are converted to standard scores, and the standard scores are converted to both percentile ranks and stanines. As the manual indicates, norms are based on midyear achievement; hence, if the test is administered at another time, appropriate allowance must be made.

Content validity for the selections used appears to be established, and there is a fair sampling from science, social studies, and arts and humanities. Technical subjects incorporating mathematical symbols and appropriate graphics are not represented. Nor is concrete information presented about the content validity of the reading skills chosen for the test. The authors do warn, however, that a school should compare the content of the test with the content of the school curriculum to be sure that the test is an appropriate measuring device for the instructional objectives of the particular school.

The technical adequacy of each test item was evaluated on the basis of tryouts during the development of the test. Items that proved too difficult or too easy were dropped. The majority of students appear to be able to complete the test during the 40-minute working period; hence, the test is called a power test. On the other hand, no information is presented about the students who could not do so. Those who finish early are advised to go back and check their answers. One wonders what the slower workers could have done if they had been allowed to go back, particularly since the score is based on number right, with no penalty for guessing.

Split-half reliability on Form X (Form W has no such reliability data) for all grades combined (9–12) is high—.92. As the manual indicates, these reliability data concern the homogeneity of the content (internal consistency) and do not concern intercorrelation of forms and consistency in time (test-retest).

In spite of a few limitations and with the understanding that this test, like all other standardized reading tests of this nature, measures only a specific type of reading achievement, this test ranks as one of the very best survey tests of secondary school reading achievement available today. It has been carefully designed, broadly and precisely tested, and well produced. It adequately serves its objectives as a rough measure of reading achievement for comparative purposes and as an instrument of identification upon which further evaluation of reading strengths and weaknesses may be based.

For reviews of the complete battery, see 27 (2 reviews).

[708]

Stanford Achievement Test: Reading Tests. Grades 1.5–2.4, 2.5–3.9, 4.0–5.4, 5.5–6.9, 7.0–9.9; 1922–68; catalog uses the title *Stanford Reading Tests;*

3 forms; 5 levels; battery technical supplement ('66, 55 pages); expected grade score tables ('68, 10 pages) based on *Otis-Lennon Mental Ability Test* available on request; supplementary directions ['64–66, 1–2 pages] for each type of answer sheet; separate answer sheets (Digitek, Harbor, IBM 805, IBM 1230) may be used for grades 4–9; $2 per battery technical supplement, postage extra; Braille and large type editions available from American Printing House for the Blind; Truman L. Kelley, Richard Madden, Eric F. Gardner, and Herbert C. Rudman; Harcourt Brace Jovanovich, Inc. *

a) PRIMARY I READING TESTS. Grades 1.5–2.4; 4 scores: word reading, paragraph meaning, vocabulary, word study skills; Forms W, X, Y, ('66, 8 pages); battery directions for administering ('64, 32 pages); $6.20 per 35 tests; $1 per battery scoring key; $1.75 per battery specimen set; 83(95) minutes.

b) PRIMARY 2 READING TESTS. Grades 2.5–3.9; 3 scores: word meaning, paragraph meaning, word study skills; Forms W, X, Y, ('66, 7 pages); battery directions for administering ('64, 32 pages); $6.20 per 35 tests; $1.30 per battery scoring key; $1.75 per battery specimen set; 72(85) minutes.

c) INTERMEDIATE I READING TESTS. Grades 4.0–5.4; 2 scores: word meaning, paragraph meaning; Forms W, X, ('64, 7 pages), Y ('65, 7 pages); directions for administering ('64, 8 pages); $6.20 per 35 tests; 60¢ per scoring key; $2.30 per 35 IBM 805 answer sheets; $2.80 per 35 Digitek or IBM 1230 answer sheets; $3 per 100 Harbor answer cards; 70¢ per Digitek or IBM scoring stencil; $1.75 per specimen set; Harbor or IBM scoring service, 19¢ and over per test; 40(48) minutes.

d) INTERMEDIATE 2 READING TESTS. Grades 5.5–6.9; 2 scores: word meaning, paragraph meaning; Forms W, X, ('64, 7 pages), Y ('65, 7 pages); directions for administering ('64, 10 pages); prices same as for *c;* 42(50) minutes.

e) ADVANCED PARAGRAPH MEANING TEST. Grades 7.0–9.9; Forms W, X, ('64, 5 pages), Y ('65, 5 pages); directions for administering ('64, 10 pages); $5.90 per 35 tests; remaining prices same as for *c;* 30(35) minutes.

REFERENCES

1–4. See 4:555.
5. See 6:813.
6. SMITH, GARY RICHARD. *An Examination of Selected Measures of Achievement and Aptitude for Use in Normative Grade Placement of Science Concepts on Light.* Doctor's thesis, Northwestern University (Evanston, Ill.), 1960. *(DA* 21:2952)
7. LONG, JOHN ADAM, JR. *Some Aspects of an Oral-Visual Presentation of an Achievement Test to Educable, Mentally Retarded Pupils.* Doctor's thesis, Pennsylvania State University (University Park, Pa.), 1962. *(DA* 23:3728)
8. BROWN, SANDRA ROSE. *A Comparison of Five Widely Used Standardized Reading Tests and an Informal Reading Inventory for a Selected Group of Elementary School Children.* Doctor's thesis, University of Georgia (Athens, Ga.), 1963. (*DA* 25:996)
9. DAVIS, M. CATHERINE ELIZABETH. *The Relative Effectiveness of Certain Evaluative Criteria for Determining Reading Levels.* Doctor's thesis, Temple University (Philadelphia, Pa.), 1964. *(DA* 25:3967)
10. ATHEY, IRENE JOWETT. *Reading-Personality Patterns at the Junior High School Level.* Doctor's thesis, University of California (Berkeley, Calif.), 1965. *(DA* 26:861)
11. NAMKIN, SIDNEY. *The Stability of Achievement Test Scores: A Longitudinal Study of the Reading and Arithmetic Subtests of the Stanford Achievement Test.* Doctor's thesis, Rutgers—The State University (New Brunswick, N.J.), 1966. *(DA* 27:398A)
12. BOND, GUY L., AND DYKSTRA, ROBERT. "The Cooperative Research Program in First-Grade Reading Instruction." *Read Res Q* 2:5–142 su '67. * (*PA* 42:4557)
13. ISBITZ, SARAH FAY. *An Analysis of the Stanford Reading Tests in Relation to the Los Angeles City School District's Curriculum.* Master's thesis, University of Southern California (Los Angeles, Calif.), 1967.
14. TRELA, THADDEUS M. "Comparing Achievement on Tests of General and Critical Reading." *J Read Specialist* 6:140–2 My '67. * (*PA* 41:14190)
15. DAVIS, WILLIAM QUINBY. *A Study of Test Score Comparability Among Five Widely Used Reading Survey Tests.* Doctor's thesis, Southern Illinois University (Carbondale, Ill.), 1968. *(DA* 29:4370A)
16. POTTS, MARION. "A Comparison of Vocabulary Introduced in Several First-Grade Readers to That of Two Primary Reading Tests." *J Ed Res* 61:285 F '68. *
17. ATHEY, IRENE J., AND HOLMES, JACK A. *Reading Success and Personality Characteristics in Junior High School Students.* University of California Publications in Education, Vol. 18. Berkeley, Calif.: University of California Press, 1969. Pp. viii, 80. *
18. COHEN, JERRY MARVIN. *A Study of the Validity of the Predictor Variables Used for Determining the Admission of Ninth Grade Students to the College Preparatory and Vocational-Technical Curricula in the Tenth Grade of the Baltimore City Public Schools.* Doctor's thesis, George Washington University (Washington, D.C.), 1969. *(DAI* 30:1328A)
19. FARR, ROGER, AND ANASTASIOW, NICHOLAS. *Tests of Reading Readiness and Achievement: A Review and Evaluation,* pp. 42–5. Newark, Del.: International Reading Association, 1969. Pp. iv, 51. *
20. GASPAR, MARY A. *A Descriptive Study of the Characteristics of Students Who Show a High Discrepancy Between Scores in the S.R.A. Primary Mental Ability Test and the Stanford Achievement Test in Reading.* Master's thesis, Chapman College (Orange, Calif.), 1969.
21. JOHNSON, GARY LANE. *An Experimental Study of the Effects of Three Modes of Test Administration on the Reading Achievement of Fifth Graders Grouped According to Test Anxiety and Sex.* Doctor's thesis, Ohio University (Athens, Ohio), 1969. *(DAI* 30:3789A)

ARTHUR E. TRAXLER, *Adjunct Lecturer in Education, University of Miami, Coral Cables, Florida.*

The *Stanford Reading Tests,* a portion of the well-known *Stanford Achievement Test* battery, are published both in combination with the rest of that extensive battery and in a separate booklet. This review is concerned primarily with the separate-booklet edition, but it takes into account certain supplementary technical materials which are available only for the complete battery.

Starting in 1923, five editions of the Stanford tests have been published. The median time interval between editions has been 11 years, a period long enough to reflect changes in instructional and measurement procedures but not so long as to put the tests far out of adjustment with those changes.

The current edition resembles preceding editions in that it provides for a survey of reading achievement mainly in terms of word meaning and paragraph meaning. It represents an improvement over the 1953 edition and earlier editions in three noteworthy ways:

a) Nearly all the reading material and test items are new, and these take account of modern changes in theory and practice of reading instruction and of improvements in techniques of testing. The task of filling each blank in the paragraph meaning test is objectified by having the pupil indicate his choice from four suggested responses. More attention than formerly is given to including in the overall score such reading skills as getting the central thought, drawing conclusions, and recognizing feelings, a need implied by Robinson and Townsend in their reviews of the 1953 edition in *The Fifth MMY*.

b) The current edition consists of five levels, instead of four as formerly. In line with the contemporary emphasis on early childhood education, the new Primary I level is suitable for most children in the last half of grade 1, as well as in the first half of grade 2, while preceding editions were seldom usable below grade 2.

c) The Primary I level is designed to measure four aspects of reading achievement, and the intercorrelations among these four aspects are not especially high, according to data given in the Technical Supplement for the battery. Thus it would seem that the Primary I level may have some limited diagnostic properties, even though this level, like the other levels, is purported to be a survey test only.

By contrast, two features of the 1964 edition would seem to be a step backward from the 1953 edition:

a) The current edition has just three published forms—W, X, and Y—instead of five, as in the higher levels of the preceding edition. This fact somewhat limits the possibility of repeated measurement without repetition of a form with the same pupils, as, for example, in a longitudinal follow-up study.

b) The Advanced level, for grades 7, 8, and 9, contains no word-meaning test, as did the last edition and as do the other levels of the current edition. Thus, the entire Advanced reading test consists of paragraph meaning only. While the correlation between word meaning and paragraph meaning is high, it is probably no higher in grades 7, 8, and 9 than it is in the elementary grades. Hence, word meaning would seem to be as nearly differentiated from paragraph meaning, and as useful, at the junior high school level as at the lower levels. The omission of word meaning from the advanced level seems regrettable, even though the paragraph-meaning test at this level is unusually well constructed.

Reliabilities of the scores on the *Stanford Reading Tests* are high enough to warrant use of the Stanford tests in appraising the reading ability of individual pupils.

Very little solid evidence concerning the validity of these reading tests is available. The authors recommend that each school evaluate the content validity of the tests in the Stanford battery through comparison of the test content with the content of their own curriculum, but they appropriately call attention to the fact that this procedure is not very meaningful for tests of word meaning and paragraph meaning. It would have been helpful to schools and reviewers in their efforts to infer validity if more precise information had been given in the Technical Supplement concerning the exact source of the test words in the word-meaning test at the different levels and concerning the field classification and reading difficulty of the paragraphs used in the paragraph-meaning test.

The national standardization of the *Stanford Achievement Test,* including the reading tests, compares favorably with that of any other achievement test this reviewer has seen. The 264 participating school systems were drawn to represent all 50 states and provided over 850,-000 pupils. Public and private schools, regions of the country, racial balance, and other characteristics were, as nearly as possible, proportional to the national distribution of population.

The three types of norms developed—grade scores, percentiles, and stanines—are extensively discussed and explained. A limitation not mentioned in the Technical Supplement (this is applicable to various other tests as well) is that, because a raw score on the Stanford is simply the number of right responses, without correction for guessing or chance factors, it is possible for a pupil, under certain conditions, to obtain a grade-equivalent score not more than two grades below his actual grade placement simply by blind guessing and without reading the test at all.

The format and printing are excellent. Color is used to good advantage without reducing legibility. Separate booklets of Directions for Administering each level contain essential information relative to interpretation, reliability, validity, and use of test results. Notwithstanding these valuable aids, users should be informed that for deeper understanding and use the Technical Supplement is indispensable. Since this supplement is an optional accessory, it has been observed that some otherwise knowledgeable users are not aware of its existence.

Everything considered and notwithstanding the few limitations that have been mentioned, this reviewer regards the *Stanford Reading Tests* as the best series of reading tests now published for making annual or semiannual surveys of the reading achievement of pupils

Stanford Achievement Test: Reading Tests

throughout the elementary and junior high school grades. The foregoing statement should be qualified by pointing out that in grade 1 less advanced pupils may be more adequately measured by a somewhat easier test, such as the Primary 1 level of the *Metropolitan Reading Test*.

For reviews by Helen M. Robinson and Agatha Townsend of an earlier edition, see 5:656; for a review by James R. Hobson, see 4:555; for a review by Margaret G. McKim, see 3:503. For reviews of the complete battery, see 25 (1 excerpt), 6:26 (1 review, 1 excerpt), 5:25 (1 review), 4:25 (2 reviews), and 3:18 (2 reviews).

[709]

*Survey of Primary Reading Development. Grades 1–2, 2–4; 1957–64; SPRD; 2 forms; 2 levels; postage extra; J. Richard Harsh and Dorothy Soeberg; Educational Testing Service (Western Office). *
a) FORMS A-1 AND B-1. Grades 1–2; 1957; Forms A-1, B-1, (15 pages); manual (48 pages); $3 per 20 tests; 50¢ per manual; $1 per specimen set; (30–60) minutes.
b) FORMS C AND D. Grades 2–4; 1964; Forms C, D, (15 pages); manual (64 pages); $3 per 20 tests; $1 per manual; $1.50 per specimen set; administration time not reported.

ALLEN BERGER, *Associate Professor of Reading Education, The University of Alberta, Edmonton, Alberta, Canada.*

Two new forms of this test have appeared since Stauffer and Barrett reviewed Forms A-1 and B-1 in *The Sixth Mental Measurements Yearbook*. No changes seem to have been made in Forms A-1 and B-1, or the manual for those forms, and this reviewer would make the same general comments about them as did Stauffer and Barrett.

Forms C and D "proceed from form comparison and sight vocabulary to successively more complex tasks in reading comprehension." The five subtests tap the following: form comparison, word recognition, sentence comprehension, story comprehension, and pictorial-narrative reading.

One of the striking differences between the earlier forms and the latter forms involves the typography. Whereas Forms A-1 and B-1 appear to be printed in medium or boldface 18-point type, Forms C and D are printed in ordinary lower-case type, beginning with 14-point type and changing to 12-point type in the fourth subtest. At that point the line width on Forms C and D is nearly twice that recommended for children in grades 2–4 by Tinker

and others. Since most children are farsighted until 7½ years of age, this reviewer wonders what effect this typography will have not only on the attitude of children toward taking tests but also on the validity of the testing instrument. No reference is made to typography in the manual.

The manual for Forms C and D comes closer than the earlier manual (for Forms A-1 and B-1) to meeting the standards of reporting suggested in the 1955 *Technical Recommendations for Achievement Tests* and the 1966 *Standards for Educational and Psychological Tests and Manuals*. Whereas the manual for Forms A-1 and B-1 contains fewer than 10 lines of information about reliability, four and one-half pages of reliability information are presented in the manual for the newer forms, with data on mean and standard deviation for each grade level of each subtest as well as for the total score. The total score reliability coefficients reported for Forms C and D are, respectively: grade 2, .85 and .87; grade 3, .86 and .84; and grade 4, .82 and .89. The higher reliability coefficients of .91 for both Forms A-1 and B-1 reflect in part the use of the split-half method in contrast to the use of K-R 21 for Forms C and D.

The newer manual contains more than three pages of information on validity in contrast to the four paragraphs appearing in the earlier manual. Empirical validity was obtained "by relating the test scores to teacher ratings of the pupils tested." Total score validity coefficients between teacher rating and reading comprehension score range from .45 to .62. These validity coefficients reflect a drop from the .79 reported earlier for Forms A-1 and B-1.

The newer manual contains more normative information. For example, the earlier manual reports only that "Form A of the test was administered to 10,000 first, second, and third grade children in 60 schools of eight school districts in Los Angeles County." A similar kind of statement is made about Form B. However, the newer manual presents a breakdown of the data by grade levels and both subtests and total score. The manual for Forms C and D indicates that the mean IQ "of the combined samples from the norming reference group was 108.24."

Directions for administering the test are simple and straightforward. An unexplained inconsistency, however, appears in the directions for subtest 4 and subtest 5 of Forms C and D. In the sample exercise for subtest 4, children are given feedback as to the accuracy of their response, whereas in the sample exercise for subtest 5 no such feedback is given to the children.

Nearly one-third of both manuals contains information on instructional activities for the teacher to use with children who fall into certain ranges according to the total test score. While it is commendable that there is a specific kind of instruction as a result of taking the test, one wonders if the test manual is the place to have these instructional activities.

In summary, this reviewer agrees in general with the comments made in earlier reviews of Forms A-1 and B-1. It is encouraging to find more complete reporting of data in the more recently published manual for Forms C and D. The newer manual indicates that the normative population contains children of slightly above average intelligence from southern California; the test user must, of course, determine if the children to be tested are comparable to the population on which the norms were based. Another caution involves the typography in the latter part of Forms C and D as well as the lower validity and reliability coefficients for these two newer forms. In short, while the SPRD is usable, this instrument would be even more useful if the recommendations contained in previous reviews (which perhaps appeared too late to be acted upon) were incorporated and if the better features of Forms A-1 and B-1 were reflected in newer Forms C and D.

For reviews by Thomas C. Barrett and Russell G. Stauffer of a, see 6:814.

[710]

★Tests of Academic Progress: Reading. Grades 9–12; 1964–66; Form 1 ('64, 24 pages); 4 levels (grades 9, 10, 11, 12) in a single booklet; no specific manual; battery teacher's manual ('64, 62 pages); battery manual for administrators, supervisors, and counselors ('65, 45 pages); battery norms booklet for IQ levels ('66, 26 pages); separate answer cards (MRC) must be used; 30¢ per test; $3 per 100 MRC answer cards; MRC keys not available; scoring service, 27¢ per test; $1.20 per battery teacher's manual; 96¢ per battery administrator's manual; 60¢ per battery norms booklet; $3 per specimen set of the complete battery; postage extra; 60(70) minutes; Dale P. Scannell and Henry P. Smith; Houghton Mifflin Co. *

REFERENCES

1. CALDWELL, JAMES R.; MICHAEL, WILLIAM B.; SCHRADER, DONALD R.; AND MEYERS, C. E. "Comparative Validities and Working Times for Composites of Structure-of-Intellect Tests and Algebra Grades and Composites of Traditional Test Measures and Algebra Grades in the Prediction of Success in Tenth-Grade Geometry." *Ed & Psychol Meas* 30(4):955-9 w '70. *
2. GOOLSBY, THOMAS M., JR. "The Appropriateness of the Tests of Academic Progress for an Experimental School." *Ed & Psychol Meas* 30(4):967-70 w '70. *

MARVIN D. GLOCK, *Professor of Educational Psychology, Cornell University, Ithaca, New York.*

The items of this test "can be classified into four broad categories: identification of explicitly stated facts, details and relationships; comprehension of information which has been identified; application of information in drawing conclusions and forming inferences; and, evaluation of the theme or purpose of the writer." Various types of reading selections are included, such as natural history, geography, biography, and history.

Items are of the multiple choice type, each having five choices. Paragraphs on which the questions are based vary in length from about 150 to 400 words, thus providing an opportunity for testing more than superficial comprehension. The test is arranged in a multilevel format, which permits a student in any grade to respond only to those items at his level.

Two types of scores are reported: within-grade percentile ranks and normalized standard scores. A very carefully selected national sample reflects such factors as size of community, socio-economic characteristics, and type of school.

The authors point out that information on content validity is perhaps more important than criterion-related validity. Although they are collecting data on correlation with other achievement tests, they rightly emphasize that low or high relationships with these tests will not necessarily prove the worth of their test. One would have to use a clearly better test as the criterion to draw these conclusions. In examining the test, one finds evidence of considerable care in the enhancement of content validity. Selections from varied subject areas are included. Although the various comprehension skills are not sampled as widely as one might wish, they require reading skill far beyond that of determining the literal meaning. It should be noted that there is no measure of reading rate or rate of comprehension.

Reliability was determined by the split-half procedure. Coefficients ranging from .90 to .93 are reported by grades. The authors warn that alternate-form reliabilities would probably have been lower. The ample time allotment, however, does not seem to place a premium on speed.

In summary, this reading test is among the

better tests for measuring comprehension at the secondary level. Reliability is adequate and considerable attention was given to content validity. Norms are based on a representative national sample.

For a review of the complete battery, see 31.

[711]

*Tests of Reading: Inter-American Series. Grades 1, 2–3, 4–6, 7–9, 10–13; 1950–67; revision of still-in-print *Tests of Reading: Cooperative Inter-American Tests;* a series of parallel tests and manuals in English and Spanish; 5 levels; series manual ('67, 99 pages) ; series technical report ('67, 70 pages) ; tentative norms, publisher recommends use of local norms; $1 per manual; $1 per technical report; postage extra; 50¢ per specimen set of any one level, postpaid; Herschel T. Manuel; Guidance Testing Associates. *

a) LEVEL 1, PRIMARY. Grade 1; 1966–67; 3 scores: vocabulary, comprehension, total; English language Forms CE, DE, ('66, 12 pages) ; Spanish language Forms CEs, DEs, ('66, 12 pages) ; directions ('66, 4 pages) ; $3.50 per 25 tests; 18(28) minutes.

b) LEVEL 2, PRIMARY. Grades 2–3; 1962–67; 5 scores: vocabulary, comprehension (level, speed, total), total; English language Forms CE, DE, ('62, 16 pages) ; Spanish language Forms CEs, DEs, ('62, 16 pages) ; directions ['65, 6 pages] ; $4 per 25 tests; 23(35) minutes.

c) LEVEL 3, ELEMENTARY. Grades 4–6; 1962–67; 5 scores as in *b;* English language Forms CE, DE, ('62, 15 pages) ; Spanish language Forms CEs, ('62, 15 pages), DEs ('62, 16 pages) ; combined directions ['65, 4 pages] for Levels 3–5; separate answer sheets (IBM 805, IBM 1230) must be used; $4 per 25 tests; $4 per 100 answer sheets; 20¢ per IBM 805 scoring stencil; 10¢ per IBM 1230 scoring key; 41(50) minutes.

d) LEVEL 4, INTERMEDIATE. Grades 7–9; 1962–67; 5 scores as in *b;* English language Forms CE, DE, ('62, 16 pages) ; Spanish language Forms CEs, DEs, ('62, 16 pages) ; remaining details same as for Level 3.

e) LEVEL 5, ADVANCED. Grades 10–13; 1962–67; 5 scores as in *b;* English language Forms CE, DE, ('62, 16 pages) ; Spanish language Forms CEs, DEs, ('62, 16 pages) ; remaining details same as for Level 3.

REFERENCES

1–4. See 4:557.
5–8. See 6:818.
9. MARTIN, RICHARD PANTALL. *The Adjustment of Latin-American Male Students in Selected Private Secondary Schools in the United States.* Doctor's thesis, Northwestern University (Evanston, Ill.), 1954. (*DA* 14:1605)
10. MANUEL, HERSCHEL T. *The Preparation and Evaluation of Inter-Language Testing Materials.* Unpublished report to the U.S. Office of Education, Cooperative Research Project No. 681, University of Texas, 1963. Pp. vii, 112. * (ERIC ED 001 702)
11. MANUEL, HERSCHEL T. *Development of Inter-American Test Materials.* Unpublished report to the U.S. Office of Education, Cooperative Research Project No. 2621, University of Texas, December 1966. Pp. vii, 99. * (ERIC ED 010 670)
12. ARNOLD, RICHARD D. "Reliability of Test Scores for the Young 'Bilingual' Disadvantaged." *Read Teach* 22(4): 341–5 Ja '69. *

GEORGIA S. ADAMS, *Professor of Education, California State College, Los Angeles, California.*

This series of parallel reading tests in English and Spanish has been designed in part to provide comparable measures of reading competency in these languages, for use in bilingual communities and in cross-cultural educational research. The authors are frank in reporting the difficulties encountered in attempting to achieve equivalent English and Spanish editions and recommend caution in the use of the test and interpretation of the results; e.g., in pretesting and posttesting, it is recommended that half of the pupils take Form C first and Form D for posttesting, while the other pupils follow the reverse pattern.

Most of the criticisms of the 1950 series (made by Orleans and Westover in the 4th MMY) do not apply to this revision. Since five levels have replaced three (for the same span of grades), measurement can be more efficiently done (i.e., with a smaller percentage of questions at inappropriate difficulty levels for the examinees). The 1950 series was criticized for using exact translation of English into Spanish, with no supporting evidence for the validity of this approach. In preparing this series, the Spanish edition was revised on the basis of considerable research so as to "approach more nearly the ideal of expressing in standard Spanish the same content as in English and in language of similar difficulty." Procedures used in attaining equivalence between the parallel Spanish and English tests are summarized in the technical report. A test of reading speed, recommended by Westover in the 4th MMY, has been included at all levels except grades 1–2. While the earlier series provided no data on reliability and validity, considerable relevant data are provided for the current series. Normative data, although much more extensive than for the 1950 series, still make no claims to representativeness.

RELIABILITY. The median alternate-form reliabilities (within grades) for the English and Spanish editions are .82 and .68, respectively, for subtests, and .90 and .84, respectively, for total scores. Since most of the intercorrelations between subtests exceed .70, only large intraindividual differences between subtest scores are statistically significant.

VALIDITY. In general, test items have been competently written; great care has been exercised to see that the Spanish translation is comparable to the English in both content and difficulty. Results from a preliminary administration were used in item analysis; items were selected in terms of difficulty values and discrimination indices (with total score on each subtest having been used as the criterion). More evidence should be provided concerning the decision-making processes of test construction, e.g., how words were selected for vocabulary tests, what standards were used for item-subtest relationships, what range of difficulty values was considered acceptable, and the like. Studies should be conducted on the extent to which speed of work contributes to score variance.

NORMS. The publishers recommend the development of local and regional norms. The manual provides aids in setting up local tables of percentile or standard score norms. The manual includes 77 pages of normative data in bewildering variety. The reviewer would recommend that most of these data be presented in a supplement. For example, for the Puerto Rican norms, only those for the total population should be presented in the manual, with the breakdown into urban, rural, and private school samples reserved for a supplement. With the exception of the Puerto Rican norms, based on island-wide administration, all other norms are based on samples which are not presented as representative.

There are many instances of carelessness in reporting the norming data, with the number of cases occasionally missing, and the month of administration and data on sample characteristics frequently missing.

USABILITY. The tests are clearly printed on good quality paper; two types of answer sheets (one not requiring use of special pencils) are available for use in grades 4 and above. The directions for administering and time limits are the same for Levels 3, 4, and 5, thus permitting the simultaneous use of different levels in the same classroom. Fortunately, grade level designations are not printed on the tests.

The directions for administering should be printed in large type like that used for the tests. The manual should be reorganized for greater efficiency and convenience.

The art work for the primary tests, though not attractive, is adequate for clarity.

SUMMARY. The reliability of subtest scores on the Spanish edition is inadequate for measuring intraindividual differences. Data on the speededness of the tests and on the extent to which reliability is improved by the use of easier (lower level) tests should be presented.

Care has been taken to make the English and Spanish editions as nearly parallel as possible.

The format is good, and instructions are clear.

Use of these tests should probably be limited to cross-cultural research and to assessment of reading competency in bilingual communities. These tests could be very useful in measuring the vocabulary and reading comprehension of children entering U.S. schools from Mexico, Cuba, Puerto Rico, and other Latin American countries. Different provisions could then be made for children with high reading ability in their own language, as distinguished from those with little reading ability in either English or Spanish. For example, the former group could be provided with Spanish editions of textbooks in mathematics, social studies, science, and other subjects so that they could progress in these areas while they were learning English. Reading test results would help one choose Spanish textbooks at the right level of reading difficulty.

For reviews by Jacob S. Orleans and Frederick L. Westover of the earlier edition, see 4:557.

[712]

*Traxler High School Reading Test, Revised. Grades 10–12; 1938–67; 5 scores: rate, story comprehension, main ideas, total comprehension, total; Forms A, B, ('66, 16 pages, identical with the 1938 edition except for minor changes in 12 items); manual ('67, 17 pages); norms and reliability data are for the 1938 edition; $4.60 per 35 tests; separate answer sheets (IBM 1230) may be used; $2 per 35 answer sheets; 50¢ per scoring stencil; 35¢ per manual; 60¢ per specimen set; postage extra; 50(60) minutes; Arthur E. Traxler; Bobbs-Merrill Co., Inc. *

REFERENCES

1–4. See 4:559.

ROBERT A. FORSYTH, *Assistant Professor of Education, The University of Iowa, Iowa City, Iowa.*

The similarities of this revision with the original 1938 edition are best described by the following statement by the author:

The 1966 revision of this test was not extensive. It was designed to correct and bring up to date the information contained in certain items, particularly items in Part II, and to strengthen a few weak items. * The content of Part I of Form A, as well as the questions in that part, remain unchanged, and the only revisions in that part of Form B were changes in three words in the last paragraph of the story. In Part II, Main Ideas in Paragraphs, revisions were made in eight items of Form A and four items of Form B.

Because the changes were so minor, most of the favorable and unfavorable comments concerning this test in *The Second* and *Fourth Yearbooks* still apply. Therefore, the remainder of this review is concerned only with the appropriateness of the test for current high school students and an evaluation of the new data supplied for the revised form.

With the wealth of new ideas and new problems in the social sciences and natural sciences, it seems inappropriate to have high school students reading essentially the same materials that students of their parents' generation read over 30 years ago. One can't help but feel that student motivation would be much greater with reading passages based on more current topics from high school science and social studies textbooks.

The major reason for using essentially the same test seems obvious. "An effort was made to keep the difficulty of each form unchanged *so that existing norms could be used with the revised tests* [italics added] until new ones could be established, if changes in the reading ability of high school pupils seemed to require revised norms." Evidence regarding the comparability of revised Form A with revised Form B and revised Form A with unrevised Form A was gathered in the fall of 1966 by giving these forms to equivalent groups of 11th graders in three high schools. From these data, the author concludes: "Revised Form A is closely equivalent in difficulty to Unrevised Form A. Thus the norms for the unrevised test are applicable to Revised Form A." Assuming that the forms *are* equivalent in difficulty (and other score distribution characteristics, such as variability), the conclusion about the applicability of norms is open to question. The fact that two random samples of 11th graders in 1966 scored at the "same" level on both editions does not provide evidence of the appropriateness of the old norms for current high school students. In all likelihood, the 1938 norms do not accurately reflect current student performance on *either* edition.

Another conclusion reached on the basis of the 1966 data was: "That part [Story Comprehension] of Form B [revised] appears to be a little more difficult than the corresponding part of Form A [revised], and some allowance should be made for that fact when the norms are used." How this allowance is to be determined is not discussed.

The author indicates that the present norms will be reviewed as new information is obtained. As indicated above, however, he concludes that the existing norms can be utilized with the revised forms. Therefore, it is implied that no new standardization of the new forms will be undertaken in the near future. This limits the usefulness of this test for the high school students of the seventies.

No new validity or reliability evidence is reported; the manual still reports the reliabilities obtained for the 1938 forms. Since these reliability data are not very complete (reliabilities are not reported for subtests by grade levels), it would have been beneficial to include additional reliability data. Also, no additional validity evidence is given. Only item validities for the 1938 form are discussed. This lack of additional evidence of reliability and validity is extremely surprising. Since the test has been in use since 1938, one would expect that much additional data would have accumulated.

As a final comment on the lack of sufficient data, it is interesting to note that no subtest intercorrelation data are given. Thus, it is impossible to estimate the reliability of difference scores.

In summary, the revised version of the *Traxler High School Reading Test* is a very superficial attempt to update a relatively old test. Potential users of a high school reading test which will provide a rate and comprehension score should seek other tests which have more up-to-date norms and better evidence of reliability and validity.

For a review by Harold D. Carter, see 4:559; for reviews by Alvin C. Eurich, Constance M. McCullough, and C. Gilbert Wrenn, see 2:1578 (2 excerpts).

[713]

*Traxler Silent Reading Test. Grades 7-10; 1934-69; TSRT; 6 scores: reading rate, story comprehension, word meaning, paragraph meaning, total comprehension, total; Forms 1, 2, ('69, 15 pages, same as 1934 forms except for conversion of all items to multiple choice form), 3 ('41, c1939, 12 pages), 4 ('42, 12 pages); manual ('69, 27 pages); $4.60 per 35 tests; separate answer sheets (IBM 805, IBM 1230) may be used; $2 per 35 answer sheets; 50¢ per scoring stencil; 35¢ per manual; 60¢ per specimen set; postage extra; (46) minutes, (53) minutes using answer sheets; Arthur E. Traxler; Bobbs-Merrill Co., Inc. *

REFERENCES

1-3. See 2:1579.
4-5. See 4:560.

WILLIAM E. COFFMAN, *E. F. Lindquist Professor of Educational Measurement, The University of Iowa, Iowa City, Iowa.*

The reader who has turned to this review seeking guidance on whether or not to introduce the *Traxler Silent Reading Test* into his school's testing program can save valuable time by stopping at the end of the next sentence. Nobody looking for a new reading test in the 1970's should give it serious consideration; the test was not judged outstanding at the time it was introduced, and nothing of significance has been done in the last 30 years to improve either the test forms themselves or the teacher's handbook that accompanies them.

The reader who comes to the review for an evaluation of a test he is already using or who is simply browsing may wish to see some documentation of this judgment. After all, the test has exhibited unusual longevity. The publishers still offer the 1939 and the 1942 forms (Forms 3 and 4) in their pristine state, untouched by modern hands, and the 1934 forms (Forms 1 and 2) have a 1969 copyright only as a result of a little tinkering. In contrast, tests that were clearly superior in a technical sense even in 1942 have long since given way to revised forms or been quietly retired. The Teacher's Handbook has a 1969 copyright date, but it still contains this passage: "Mean scores on the various parts of Forms 1 and 2 are shown in Table IV. *Forms 3 and 4 were not available when the data for this table were collected*" [italics added].

This is not an isolated instance. Most of the fragmentary data in the Teacher's Handbook are based on studies conducted at the time Forms 1 and 2 were developed in the early 1930's, in spite of the fact that the author reports that more than a million copies of the tests have been used over the last 30 years. The typical report of validity is based on "a class of seventh grade pupils" otherwise not identified, "fifty-four pupils near the end of Grade 6," or "fifty-eight pupils who were about to enter the seventh grade of the University of Chicago High School." Sometimes the coefficients of correlation are accompanied by the mean scores on the tests, but no standard deviations are reported. Even if the data were up-to-date, it would be impossible to make any meaningful comparisons between data reported in the handbook and data collected in one's own school. Nor are the norms likely to prove informative. They are based on "high school freshmen and sophomores participating in the Michigan statewide testing program in 1937 and 1938.... combined with scores from schools in widely distributed parts of the United States which made their data available to the author and the

publisher." Even though the handbook carries a 1969 copyright, it states: "(It is planned to check these norms as soon as new data can be collected from schools using the test and to revise them, if necessary.)" Apparently, it has taken a long time to check the norms.

The norms certainly need checking. First, there has been a significant change in level of performance on reading tests since the 1930's, so that percentile scores based on the tables in the handbook are probably inflated. Second, it is claimed that raw scores on the four forms are equivalent throughout the range of scores. A single table is provided relating raw scores to percentile scores, and it is to be used with all four forms of the test. Other tables give median scores by grades and grade equivalents for raw scores. Furthermore, it is said that the equivalence is not disturbed if pupils mark answers on IBM 805 or 1230 answer sheets. These are exorbitant claims; they should be supported by convincing data. Actually, the few data that are reported cast doubts on the claims, and a detailed examination of data published by the Educational Records Bureau between 1946 and 1966 strongly suggests that Forms 2 and 4 are significantly more difficult than Forms 1 and 3.

In view of the inadequacy of the technical data, how can one account for the apparent popularity of the test? Perhaps it is simply that many users have built up their own reference data over the years at the local level or through the Educational Records Bureau. If so, interpretations may have some validity in spite of the inadequacy of the data provided by the publisher. Thus, it might be legitimate for a long-term user to continue using a test that is no longer adequate for a new user. However, it would be well for such a user to compare his results with those from a test with more adequate technical support, such as the *Davis Reading Test,* which replaced the Traxler in 1967 as the recommended test in the Educational Records Bureau's program.

Another possible explanation of the continuing use of the test is that it provides a separate reading rate score; most competing tests do not provide pure rate scores, and authorities tend to discount their value. However, if one wishes to determine reading rate, one might just as well construct his own reading rate test using a variety of reading material likely to be interest-

Traxler Silent Reading Test

ing to today's junior high school students. At this time the simple animal stories that provide the text for the rate test seem somewhat remote from the adolescent world, and the published norms are of no use as a basis of comparison.

The passage of time has not improved the representativeness of the vocabulary sample, either. Originally, the item pool was based on words from the fourth through the tenth thousand of the Thorndike and Lorge *Teacher's Word Book of 30,000 Words*. However, the final selection was made from pretest data indicating which were "most satisfactory." The sample was judged by a reviewer in *The 1940 Mental Measurements Yearbook*, Robert L. McCaul, to contain "too large a percentage of words peculiar mainly to English literature," and the passing years require only that the statement be modified by adding "as taught in the schools of the 1930's."

In *The Fourth Mental Measurements Yearbook*, Thomas Hastings wrote: "It is quite unfortunate that virtually all the adverse criticisms made at least 11 years ago are still valid." It is necessary only to change *11* to *30* to make the statement valid for 1970.

For a review by J. Thomas Hastings, see 4:560; for reviews by Robert L. McCaul and Miles A. Tinker, see 2:1579 (1 excerpt); for reviews by Frederick B. Davis and Spencer Shank, see 1:1114.

[Other Tests]

For other tests new or revised since *The Sixth Mental Measurements Yearbook*, see the following in *Reading Tests and Reviews:*

1. ★A.C.E.R. Lower Grades Reading Test
8. *Buffalo Reading Test for Speed and Comprehension
11. *Canadian English Achievement Test (CEAT)
14. ★Comprehensive Primary Reading Scales
15. ★Comprehensive Reading Scales
16. *Cooperative Reading Comprehension Test, Form Y
17. *Cooperative Reading Comprehension Test, Forms L and M
23. *Elementary Reading: Every Pupil Achievement Test
32. ★Group Reading Assessment
52. *Primary Reading: Every Pupil Achievement Test
54. ★Primary Reading Test 2
57. ★Reading Comprehension Test
61. ★Reading for Understanding Placement Test
68. ★Secondary Reading Tests 1–3
80. *Tests of Reading: Cooperative Inter-American Tests
84. ★Van Wagenen Analytical Reading Scales
85. *W.A.L. English Comprehension Test

DIAGNOSTIC

[714]

California Phonics Survey. Grades 7–12 and college; 1956–63; CPS; shortened version of *Stanford Diagnostic Phonics Survey, Research Edition;* 9 error analysis scores for Form 1 (Form 2 yields total score only) : long-short vowel confusion, other vowel confusion, consonants-confusion with blends and digraphs, consonant-vowel reversals, configuration, endings, negatives-opposites-sight words, rigidity, total; Forms 1, 2, ('62) in a single booklet (8 pages) ; manual ('63, 44 pages) ; may be administered by examiner but tape recording (3¾ ips) is recommended; no data on reliability of subscores; $3.50 per 35 tests; $5.95 per tape; separate answer sheets (IBM 805, Scoreze) may be used (must be used if administered by tape) ; $2.50 per 50 IBM answer sheets; $2.50 per 25 Scoreze answer sheets for Form 1 only; $6.75 per set of IBM scoring stencils for Form 1; 75¢ per IBM scoring stencil for Form 2; postage extra; $1 per specimen set (without tape), postpaid; (40–45) minutes; Grace M. Brown and Alice B. Cottrell; CTB/McGraw-Hill. *

REFERENCES

1. See 6:820.
2. TYRE, BETTY BRANNEN. *An Investigation of Three Procedures Employed in Teaching Word Recognition Skills to Pre-Service Teachers Within an Introductory Reading Course.* Doctor's thesis, University of Southern Mississippi (Hattiesburg, Miss.), 1968. (DA 29:3029A)

CONSTANCE M. McCULLOUGH, *Professor of Education, San Francisco State College, San Francisco, California.*

The *California Phonics Survey* is the product of extensive study for standardization purposes since work on its development began in 1954. Coefficients of reliability (parallel forms and K-R 20) in grades 4 through 13 range from .89 to .93, showing the high confidence which can be placed in the instrument.

Particularly interesting is the study of the performance of 1,652 college freshmen in three institutions in California, comparing the test score on a prototype of the CPS with the score on a reading test used in all three institutions. A triangular pattern emerged, in which students scoring low on the phonics test tended to score low on the reading test, whereas good readers and poor readers could be found among the high scorers in the phonics test. The conclusion drawn was that phonic adequacy, which the test purports to measure, is a necessary but not a sufficient basis for reading proficiency in English.

The test was originally based upon the errors students made in sounding out words. It includes all of the phonemes which occur in a list of 3,000 words most frequently taught to and used by elementary school children, 91 percent of the spellings occurring on that list (1). The authors have attempted to delete words whose pronunciations vary markedly from region to region and those which have acceptable alternate pronunciations within regions.

The scores of 47 seventh graders on this group test have been compared with scores on various individually administered phonics tests. The rank order correlation between the individual and group testings was .89. The authors thus established the group test as a worthy competitor of the individual test as far as total score is concerned. Obviously the group test cannot yield the information about individual behavior in attempts to attack words that can be observed in individually administered oral tests. It can, however, lead to a decision that such observation is desirable for more precise understanding of the process leading to error.

The test contains five parts, or "exercises," totaling 75 items in all, with a pattern of five possible responses. For example, in Exercise 1, item 2, the examiner presents the spoken word *like,* and the student is to choose the correct written form from among the following: sir, nap, book, lick, None. Some of the items in the same exercise involve nonsense words, such as item 5, in which the examiner says, rog—rog—rog, and the student must choose among: rog, bot, pab, zen, None. In this way the authors avoid having correct choices entirely dependent upon previous visual experience with the words.

Some of the test items are useful for more than one diagnostic purpose. For example, the diagnostic analysis chart in the manual shows that the stimulus word *cheer* brought a wrong answer of *chair* (classified as "Other Vowel Confusion") and of *clear* (classified as "Consonants").

This example brings the reviewer to some of the features of the test which might be altered in future revisions. Probably most phonics tests, whether individually or otherwise administered, need to be reviewed for the inclusion of items which reveal dialect, regional, or foreign language characteristics rather than actual phonetic difficulty injurious to comprehension. That a child in Tennessee reads *Tinnissee* for *Tennessee* does not suggest the need of training in phonics. If a child reads *chair* as *cheer* and gathers from context that it is something sat upon rather than uttered, he is showing his early ear and speech training, not his need for remediation in phonics. A child from a Japanese background may well choose *blandish* for the spelling of the spoken word *brandish.* There is

such a thing also as being so concerned with finding the right word that the pleasure of identifying a part reduces one's wariness in accepting the remainder. Thus the choice of *trep* for *threep* might be natural for a child whose home language has reduced all initial /th/'s to /t/.

A fine addition to the test might be separate diagnostic advice indicating the items and choices which would be characteristic of children of a particular language or dialect background, with the suggestion of the speech training which should precede the visual phonics experience or with the suggestion that for reading purposes the distinction in the case of that student may not be important.

The diagnostic analysis chart confirms the impression which the test itself gives the reader, that many of the wrong answers have little diagnostic value. It would seem that each item could serve more than one or two diagnostic purposes. It is almost inconceivable that some of the wrong responses could ever have been gathered from the actual errors of students in individual oral reading. An interesting experiment might be to give the spoken stimulus words and ask students to write each word in as many plausible ways as they can think of. Many implausible creations can be gathered in this way.

Exercises 1, 2, and 3 require the student to find the word which the examiner has uttered. Exercise 4 requires that he find a word that rhymes with the spoken word. Thus, the first four exercises reverse the natural reading task, which is to conjure up the spoken symbol from the printed without aid. Exercise 5 is the only one in which the student must analyze the printed forms without aid. It contains 15 items.

Since publication of this pioneer work in the assessment of phonic adequacy at levels above the primary grades, other tests have been devised, such as the one by this reviewer. The pioneer work is still unique in that all of its exercises test and retest many of the same elements, whereas its competitors attempt to confine a given part (exercise) to a given skill. The *California Phonics Survey* can be counted on to identify the points of weakness in a number of phoneme-grapheme understandings of students in fourth grade and above. The reasons for misunderstanding require further investigation through the use of other techniques or instruments.

California Phonics Survey

For a review by Thomas E. Culliton, Jr., see 6:820.

[715]
★**Classroom Reading Inventory.** Grades 2–8; 1965–69; CRI; 6 scores: word recognition, independent reading level, instructional reading level, frustration level, hearing capacity level, spelling; individual in part; Forms A, B, ('69, 14 pages); manual ('69, 13 pages plus test materials; perforated pages permit test materials to be removed from the manual); record sheets and teacher's worksheets ('69, 10–12 pages) must be reproduced locally; no data on reliability; no norms; $1.95 per manual, postage extra; (12) minutes for individual parts, administration time for spelling not reported; Nicholas J. Silvaroli; Wm. C. Brown Co. Publishers. *

Read Teach 22(8):757 My '69. Donald L. Cleland. * Silvaroli has provided an answer to the ubiquitous question: "Where can the teacher find a compact volume which includes appropriately graded reading materials, wordlists, and suggested techniques for ascertaining the instructional needs and levels of students in their classrooms?" The Classroom Reading Inventory (CRI) is designed for the elementary classroom teacher who has not had prior experience with either individual or group diagnostic measures. More specifically, this diagnostic tool may be used with children in grades two through eight and will yield, according to the author, information concerning a child's *hearing-capacity, frustration, instructional,* and *independent* reading levels. Part I (the graded wordlists) and Part II (graded oral paragraphs) are designed to be administered individually, while Part III (spelling survey) may be administered to a group. After the teacher has gained some facility in administering the CRI, she should be able to administer the tests, excluding the spelling survey, to a child in approximately fifteen minutes. According to the author, the testing can be done at the teacher's desk while the other children are engaged in quiet seatwork activity. The booklet is economically priced, with the added feature that permission is granted by the publisher to reproduce the *Inventory Record,* Pp. 17 through 26. While some may question the validity of such concepts as *hearing-capacity, frustration, instructional,* and *independent* reading levels and their practicality in a learning situation, yet those who are convinced of their feasibility in a total reading program will find the CRI a most valuable adjunct, when judiciously used, to their repertoire of teaching skills.

California Phonics Survey

[716]
★**The Denver Public Schools Reading Inventory.** Grades 1–8; 1965–68; 3 scores (instructional level, independent level, capacity level) and ratings of areas of both strength and weakness; based upon the *Sheldon Basic Reading Series;* individual; inventory ('68, 31 pages, entitled *Let's Read Together*); manual ('68, 26 pages); scoring booklet ('68, 14 pages, entitled *Reading Inventory*); no data on reliability; no norms; 60¢ per inventory; 15¢ per scoring booklet; 40¢ per manual; $1.15 per specimen set; postpaid; [30–40] minutes; Department of Instructional Services, Denver Public Schools. *

[717]
Diagnostic Reading Scales. Grades 1–8 and retarded readers in grades 9–12; 1963; DRS; 10 or 11 scores: word recognition, instructional level (oral reading), independent level (silent reading), rate of silent reading (optional), potential level (auditory comprehension), and 6 phonics scores (consonant sounds, vowel sounds, consonant blends, common syllables, blends, letter sounds); individual; 1 form (28 pages); record booklet (29 pages); manual (27 pages); no data on reliability of rate of silent reading and phonics scores; $1.10 per test; $9.60 per 35 record booklets and manual; 50¢ per manual; postage extra; $1.90 per specimen set, postpaid; [20–30] minutes; George D. Spache; CTB/McGraw-Hill. *

REFERENCES
1. GLASER, NICHOLAS ADAM. *A Comparison of Specific Reading Skills of Advanced and Retarded Readers of Fifth Grade Reading Achievement.* Doctor's thesis, University of Oregon (Eugene, Ore.), 1964. (*DA* 25:5785)
2. ATTEA, MARY. *A Comparison of Three Diagnostic Reading Tests.* Doctor's thesis, State University of New York (Buffalo, N.Y.), 1966. (*DA* 27:1530A)
3. TRELA, THADDEUS M. "What Do Diagnostic Reading Tests Diagnose?" *El Engl* 43:370–2 Ap '66. *
4. DAHLKE, ANITA B. *The Use of WISC Scores to Predict Reading Improvement After Remedial Tutoring.* Doctor's thesis, University of Florida (Gainesville, Fla.), 1968. (*DAI* 30:165A)
5. RAINWATER, HAROLD G. "Reading Problem Indicators Among Children With Reading Problems." *Psychol* 5:81–3 N '68. *
6. MANN, GLORIA T. "Reversal Reading Errors in Children Trained in Dual Directionality." *Read Teach* 22(7):646–8 Ap '69. *
7. BOTEL, MORTON; BRADLEY, JOHN; AND KASHUBA, MICHAEL. "The Validity of Informal Reading Testing," pp. 85–103. In *Reading Difficulties: Diagnosis, Correction, and Remediation.* Edited by William K. Durr. Newark, Del.: International Reading Association, 1970. Pp. vii, 276. *

REBECCA C. BARR, *Director, The Reading Clinic, The University of Chicago, Chicago, Illinois.*

The scales present a systematic approach to the diagnosis of reading skills at the elementary school level and, for retarded readers, at the secondary level. The tests determine Instructional, Independent, and Potential Reading Levels and specify patterns of reading skill development (word attack and analysis and sight recognition). The instrument is beautifully conceived but standardization leaves much to be desired.

The battery consists of three word recognition lists, two reading passages at each of 11 levels ranging from first to eighth grade in difficulty, and six supplementary phonics tests. The battery is individually administered; the examiner records the child's oral reading responses. The component tests will be discussed in the order in which they are administered.

WORD RECOGNITION LISTS. The main use of the word lists is to provide an estimate of the level of the passage that the child should be able to read in the second part of the test. The lists also give evidence about the child's word analysis and sight recognition of words in isolation.

The three lists, 40–50 words each, compose overlapping samples of words of increasing difficulty. Words were selected on the basis of adequate discrimination and appropriate difficulty. Estimates of reliability (.87 to .96, using K-R 21) and predictive validity (.65 to .78, using the Instructional Level as criterion) are sufficiently high to justify use of the lists for the purpose specified.

READING PASSAGES. Each passage is followed by seven or eight questions. Contrary to the description in the manual, the reviewer found that comprehension questions at all levels tend to test memory of literally stated content. The highest passage level that the child reads with 85 percent comprehension is judged to be his Instructional Level. Oral reading errors include omissions, additions, reversals, substitutions, aided words (aid given after five seconds) and repetitions of more than one word. Accurate recording of oral reading errors requires considerable clinical experience and judgment on the part of the examiner.

Silent reading of the passages follows the oral reading, using a passage at the level just above a pupil's obtained Instructional Level. The highest passage level that the child reads with 60 percent comprehension is judged to be his Independent Reading Level.

Following the silent reading, the examiner reads aloud passages beginning at the level just above the child's Independent Level. The highest passage level that the child listens to with not more than a specified number of errors is judged to be his Potential Level.

The 22 passages used to measure oral and silent reading and auditory comprehension were selected to be representative of the type and range of reading actually employed at each grade level. Most passages through the fourth grade level tend to describe experiences of children. Beyond this level, passages have been selected from several content areas. Because of variation in content and because only two passages are used to assign a grade score, the scores beyond the fourth grade level can be significantly affected by the interests and past experience of the reader.

According to the manual, readability estimates reflecting vocabulary and sentence length were used to select passages. No readability ratings, however, are reported for the passages. Each passage was compared with comparable passages at the same level on other reading tests. Information concerning the difficulty of individual passages selected is not included in the manual. The omission of such data would not be unusual for the ordinary achievement test in which a mean score of several passages is used to determine the grade score. In the present test, estimates of reading are sometimes based on only one passage at a level. For this reason it is important to have such information as mean scores, standard deviations, and standard errors for both oral reading errors and comprehension for each passage. Apparently, as reported by Bryant in a review of this test in *The Sixth MMY* (6:821), the criterion oral reading error scores and criterion comprehension scores for each passage are one standard deviation below obtained mean score for the oral reading presentation.

Reliability and validity of the passages were assessed by using a variety of different samples. Frequently the samples were inadequately described in terms of age or grade composition. For this reason, accurate interpretation of information presented is difficult. It is apparent from a review of studies reported that a more systematic standardization of the scales is necessary before comparisons between observations made from different passages can be justified. For example, reliability of passages at one level should be checked by administering both passages under the same reading or listening condition. Likewise, once passage reliabilities for each condition are determined, systematic differences between conditions should be specified and passages graded accordingly. More than two passages at each level would avoid the problem of a level's being expended—and it might provide the opportunity for a more reliable estimate (if the examiner wished to base the estimate on the average of two passages, rather than on one).

PHONICS TESTS. Skill in recognition and use of letter sounds (Tests 1, 2, and 6), consonant blends (Test 3), common syllables (Test 4), and blending sounds into a coherent whole (Test 5) are tested in the six supplementary phonics tests. Although grade norms are provided, the examiner is advised against using them. No data are included concerning the construction or standardization of the supplementary tests.

SUMMARY. The scales are useful as an informal diagnostic instrument through which a teacher or clinician can acquire in a short time considerable information about a child's language and reading skill development. The use of the passage scores to assign grade norms and to make comparisons among instructional, independent, and potential levels cannot be justified on the basis of standardization information presented in the manual. The scales appear to be most valid for children reading at the first to fourth grade levels.

For a review by N. Dale Bryant, see 6:821.

[718]

Diagnostic Reading Test: Pupil Progress Series. Grades 1.9–2.1, 2.2–3, 4–6, 7–8; 1956–70; DRT; various titles used by publisher; catalog uses the title *Pupil Progress Series Reading;* 2 forms; 4 levels; technical manual ('65, 17 pages) ; $7 per 35 tests, postage extra ; 50¢ per specimen set, cash orders only ; Oliver F. Anderhalter, R. Stephen Gawkoski, and Ruth Colestock ; Scholastic Testing Service, Inc. *
a) PRIMARY LEVEL 1. Grades 1.9–2.1 ; 1956–68 ; 9 scores : vocabulary (word recognition, word to content relation, words in use, total), rate of reading for meaning, comprehension (recalling information, locating information, reading for descriptions, total) ; Forms A ('56, 12 pages), B ('57, 12 pages) ; manual ('68, 12 pages) ; [40–50] minutes.
b) PRIMARY LEVEL 2. Grades 2.2–3 ; 1956–68 ; 10 scores : vocabulary (words in use, word meaning, total), rate of reading for meaning, comprehension (same as for a plus following directions, reading for meaning) ; Forms A ('56, 12 pages), B ('57, 15 pages) ; manual ('68, 16 pages) ; [50–60] minutes.
c) ELEMENTARY LEVEL. Grades 4–6 ; 1956–70 ; 13 scores : knowledge and use of sources (functions, best sources, use of index, use of table of contents, total), rate of reading for meaning, comprehension (same as for a plus word meaning, reading for meaning, reading for directions or procedures) ; Forms A ('56, 16 pages), B ('57, 18 pages) ; NCS directions for administering ('70, 16 pages) ; directions for hand scoring ['70, 15 pages] for this and the Advanced Level ; separate answer sheets (NCS) may be used ; $5 per 50 answer sheets ; $1.50 per school scoring kit ; scoring service, 20¢ and over per test ; [50–60] minutes.
d) ADVANCED LEVEL. Grades 7–8 ; 1956–70 ; 13 scores : same as for c; Forms A ('56, 16 pages), B ('57, 20 pages) ; NCS directions for administering ('70, 16 pages) ; remaining details same as for c.

LAWRENCE M. KASDON, *Associate Professor of Education, Ferkauf Graduate School, Yeshiva University, New York, New York.*

Still pertinent to these tests are the reviews in earlier MMY's (5:650, 6:822) by Stauffer, Traxler, and Townsend. Townsend criticized the DRT not only for not yielding a clinically sound picture of reading problems. She criticized the curricular validity of the tests, particularly for lack of any auditory or word attack tests at the primary and elementary levels. The content of the comprehension subtests, as well as the heavy use of fact questions, caused her concern with the primary and elementary levels. Since Townsend wrote her review in *The Sixth MMY,* the accelerated shift in social values has made the content of some of the comprehension subtests even more inappropriate. Her criticism of the elementary level Use of the Index subtest, in terms of the questions asked, is still pertinent. She agreed with the earlier reviewers of the test that the norms should be based on a wider sampling than 37 schools in 9 states.

In *The Fifth MMY* Traxler criticized some of the norms, particularly those for the Functions of Common Sources subtest of the elementary battery. Since the 15 questions require yes-no answers, a chance score of seven would equal the 75th percentile on Form A and the 70th on Form B. He further points out that since the three levels were normed in the spring, "the percentile norms for the first half of each grade must have been found by interpolation— a somewhat hazardous procedure." In her summary of the previous reviews in *The Sixth MMY,* Townsend stated that Traxler was critical of the reliability of the part scores. Townsend said : "It is unfortunate that the publisher has not profited from these suggestions for the improvement of the public school edition." And now it is necessary to say this again.

At the primary levels, reliability was calculated by use of the K-R 21 ; at the elementary and advanced levels both K-R and split-half reliabilities are offered for Form A while for Form B, only the K-R with a sprinkling of split-halves at the advanced level. The authors point out in the manual that the reliabilities for the three total scores for both forms are high enough for individual and group analysis, ranging from .75 for Comprehension, on Primary 1, Form A to .96 for Comprehension on the advanced level, Form A. Except for the Primary 1, Form A, Comprehension, this advice is satisfactory. In terms of the low reliabilities of some of the part scores, the authors point out :

"The statistical data for the part scores indicate that these scores may be used for class analysis but should not be given much weight in the individual counseling situation."

The formulas used to compute reliability present a problem. The authors point out that, strictly speaking, neither the K-R nor the split-half should have been used with the Rate test. They further state that split-half reliability generally provides an "over-estimate" of reliability and that the Kuder-Richardson provides an "excellent approximation of the reliability of power tests." The authors use a 75 percent cutoff of items attempted to differentiate between a speed test and a power test. In the technical report, Locating Information, primary level 1, is designated as a speed test; at the elementary level, five of the ten subtests are largely speed tests; and at the advanced level, three of the subtests are largely speed tests. Thus, the reliability for those tests which are speeded is overestimated and to the degree that they contribute to the total scores, such as Comprehension, the reliability of the total scores is also overestimated. Because some of the subtests are speeded and there are two forms of the test, alternate-form reliability should be supplied, particularly since the two forms were standardized in different years.

For a test to be useful as a diagnostic instrument it should have sufficient easy material to assess below average performance adequately. The *Diagnostic Reading Test* does not always meet this criterion. On Locating Information, Primary 1, if the pupil answers 4 out of 20 questions, his score falls at the 50th percentile. On Primary 2, Form A (grade placement 2.0–2.49), one question answered correctly places him at the 30th percentile on Reading for Meaning and two questions correct, at the 60th percentile. On the elementary level, Form A, (Grade Placement 4.0–4.49), two correct answers on either Recalling Information or Reading Directions place the pupil at the 50th percentile. On Form B, for the same grade placement, one correct answer for a fourth grader places him at the 50th percentile on Use of the Table of Contents. It is not until a child is in the upper half of the sixth grade that he needs to have more than two correct answers on this subtest to fall at the 50th percentile. On the advanced level, Form A, it takes 3 correct replies, out of 11, to reach the 50th percentile on Reading Directions.

The pictures in the tests are dated and the format needs improvement. However, the format of the new test manuals appears to be satisfactory. The directions for administering the tests are clear. However, the directions for finding the median, on the class analysis chart, are somewhat complicated. In view of the shortcomings discussed above, calculating the median with such precision may not prove to be very useful.

This test has been in use for a long time and has been critiqued sufficiently that if the authors used all available information and revised the test, it should then be able to fulfill its mission as a diagnostic instrument. At present, the best use that can be made of the DRT is as a survey instrument.

GUS P. PLESSAS, *Professor of Education and Chairman of the Department of Teacher Education, Sacramento State College, Sacramento, California.*

The *Diagnostic Reading Test* comes in four levels with two comparable forms at each level. The test is intended for use in grades 1 through 8 to assess strong and weak areas of reading among individuals or groups.

For grade 1 and beginning grade 2, the Primary Level 1 battery consists of seven measures to evaluate reading abilities in three areas. Test 1, on simple identification of words in print; Test 2, on matching words with pictures; and Test 3, on indicating missing words in sentences, are combined to evaluate reading vocabulary. Test 4, on rate of reading, assesses the second area of reading. Test 5, on recall of information; Test 6, on locating information; and Test 7, on identifying pictures from written descriptions, are combined to measure the area of reading comprehension.

For grades 2 and 3, the Primary Level 2 battery covers the same general areas as does the Primary Level 1 battery, with only a few differences. The Primary Level 2 battery does not include a measure of word identification but does include two additional measures of comprehension, reading for meaning and following directions.

For the intermediate (4–6) and upper (7–8) grades, the Elementary and Advanced Levels, respectively, are designed to accomplish the same purposes in the areas of study skills, reading speed, and comprehension. There are 10 subtests in each level. Four subtests are devoted

Diagnostic Reading Test

to knowledge and use of reference materials, two subtests are on reading rate, and six subtests are on word meaning and comprehension, two subtests being counted in both rate and comprehension subscores.

Although the term *Diagnostic* is used in the title of the series, there are some questions concerning the diagnostic value of subscores secured from administering tests of a particular level. Consider, for example, the significance of low scores on Words in Use and Word Meaning in the Primary Level 2 battery. Does an inadequate performance on these measures suggest a weakness in reading vocabulary or in word identification skills? Again, what is the meaning of low scores on all the measures relating to knowledge and use of common reference materials in the Elementary Level test? Are the low scores actually indicative of deficiencies in various reference skills? Perhaps such scores are outcomes of poor comprehension or word recognition abilities? How important is the rate of reading score, especially at the Primary levels? If a pupil's rate is slow, what factors would account for this deficiency? In short, scores indicating weakness could perhaps be attributed to many factors, so that performances on various measures may not be easy to interpret. Unfortunately, the section in the manual on interpreting and applying the results seems incomplete insofar as deriving diagnostic information is concerned. Perhaps the best statement on this matter appears in the introduction of the Diagnostic Reading Technical Report, where the authors suggest that teachers who study each right and wrong answer may derive information of greater value than the value from the profile of subscores. If this is so, the task of the classroom teacher is greatly increased in the process of interpreting reading performances.

A related problem concerning the DRT centers on the validity of the subtests. No research evidence supports a division of subskills in the measurement of reading, especially on aspects of vocabulary and comprehension. Uncertainty still remains, relative to the methods of measuring vocabulary apart from considerations of quality and dimensions of the words used. For instance, time limits imposed on vocabulary tests may confound the results so that neither vocabulary nor speed is measured. Rather, a combination of the two may produce an unknown estimate, particularly for the slow but careful reader. Unfortunately, all measures of reading vocabulary in the DRT are timed. Research shows that even the reliability of a vocabulary measure is affected when the test is timed.

Validity studies have not as yet justified the division of comprehension into discrete subskills. Because a lack of knowledge exists about basic aspects of comprehension, real doubt is cast on the validity of subtests that purportedly measure specific components of comprehension. The *Diagnostic Reading Test* is no exception to this validity problem. Another difficulty affecting validity concerns the time limits as imposed on tests of comprehension. When the measurement of comprehension is timed, the result is not power of comprehension but rather speed of comprehension. Still another problem affecting the validity of the comprehension measures relates to the opportunities for students to refer to the selection while answering the questions. This practice in taking the DRT confounds the outcome so that immediate memory may be tested rather than a valid measure of comprehension.

Again, the time limits on the rate of reading tests appear too short to insure high reliability. On the Elementary and Advanced Level tests, only 90 seconds are allowed on the rate of reading measures. Perhaps two or three times that length would seem appropriate to support any confidence in the results. Some question must also be raised about the increasing difficulty level of the passages used in the measure of reading rate in the Primary 1 and 2 batteries. The effect of this measurement problem indeed influences the validity of the scores when materials to be read are either easy or hard for students in a test situation.

The dates of the standardization program and the representation of the sample in the preparation of national norms raise questions. Original norms for both forms were secured from studies conducted over a decade ago, with the first data collected in May 1956 for Form A and May 1957 for Form B. According to the authors, however, subsequent independent checks in 1960 and 1964 disclosed "no major shifts in the performance of groups." But no information is available on any verification of the published norms since 1964. Confidence in the norms may be further diminished by the fact that the sampling of pupils includes 11,510 students from 37 schools in eight states for the stand-

Diagnostic Reading Test

ardization of Form A and 12,199 students for Form B.

In sum, the *Diagnostic Reading Test* is lacking as a clinical or diagnostic instrument. However, when the vocabulary or comprehension subtests are combined to produce total scores, the value of the test is greatly increased as a gross measure of reading ability.

For a review by Agatha Townsend, see 6:822.

[719]

*McCullough Word-Analysis Tests. Grades 4–6; 1962–63, c1960–63; MWAT; 10 scores: phonetic (initial blends and digraphs, phonetic discrimination, matching letters to vowel sounds, sounding whole words, interpreting phonetic symbols, total), structural (dividing words into syllables, root words in affixed forms, total), total; 1 form ('62, 8 pages); manual ('63, 23 pages); pupil's individual record ('62, 4 pages); $5.40 per 35 tests; 78¢ per specimen set; postpaid; [70] minutes in 7 sessions; Constance M. McCullough; Personnel Press, Inc. *

REFERENCES

1. BENSON, JEAN POWER. *Fifth Grade Students' Knowledge of Certain Word Analysis Skills and Their Ability to Transfer This Knowledge Into Functional Reading Situations.* Doctor's thesis, Colorado State College (Greeley, Colo.), 1968. (*DA* 29:1031A)
2. McCALL, ROZANNE A., AND McCALL, ROBERT B. "Comparative Validity of Five Reading Diagnostic Tests." *J Ed Res* 62(7):329–33 Mr '69. *

LARRY A. HARRIS, *Associate Professor of Education, The University of North Dakota, Grand Forks, North Dakota.*

The *McCullough Word-Analysis Tests* are a highly useful battery of seven subtests designed to measure certain phonetic and structural analysis skills. Generally the tests are well constructed and provide an accurate assessment on one specific component of the reading process: decoding. Properly used, with a clear understanding of the author's purpose for constructing the instrument, results obtained with these tests can be quite helpful to the classroom teacher as well as to the reading specialist.

A brief but valuable teacher's manual accompanies the tests. Clear language is used in the manual to identify the objectives of the tests, to describe the contents of each subtest, and to explain the uniqueness of the instrument. The title of each subtest clearly and accurately identifies the skill it measures (with one exception which is noted later).

Perhaps the major limitation of these tests is that no validity data are provided. While study of the items and subtests offers some assurance that the instrument has face validity, no empirical evidence is given to support this view.

Neither is an effort made to validate the tests by relating the items and subtests to a definitive discussion of word-analysis.

Reliability coefficients reported for the subtests, based on K-R 21, are generally in the .83–.96 range. One subtest, Test 6, Dividing Words Into Syllables, is considerably below this range (.76 for grade 4; .68 for grades 5 and 6). An appropriate cautionary note is given regarding the interpretation of this subtest. No standard error of measurement figures are reported for the tests, thus making it difficult for the teacher to determine with any certainty the probable accuracy of a child's score.

Although the test is described in the manual as a diagnostic instrument useful for identifying specific skill deficiencies, no data regarding the intercorrelations of the subtests are reported. Thus it is impossible to determine the overlap between subtests. The manual states that analysis of the scores of the normative pupils indicates that the seven subtests are measuring different skills and can be used for diagnostic purposes. Without supporting evidence, such claims are of doubtful value.

The McCullough tests are fairly comprehensive in their assessment of word-analysis skills. Unfortunately the word recognition technique typically emphasized in the intermediate grade reading program, using context clues, is not measured by these tests. This omission is evidently due to the fact that context clues are tied closely to meaning. Indeed, one of the strengths of these tests is that they focus specifically on word analysis, thus avoiding results that are contaminated by comprehension considerations. This may explain the absence of a test on using context. Regardless of the reason for omitting an assessment of context clues from this battery, however, the teacher will want to gather some additional information on this skill to have a complete picture of each child's word-analysis skills.

Despite an apparent attempt by the author to limit the content of these tests to the mechanical aspects of word-analysis, one subtest, Test 4, Sounding Whole Words, is, in part, a vocabulary test. In this test, the child is asked to read silently three nonsense words and mark the one that sounds like a word he has heard. For example, the phonetic spelling of shirt is given (*shert*) along with *sterb* and *skerd*. The examinee must choose the nonsense word (*shert*) that sounds like an actual word. It is quite likely that some intermediate grade youngsters may be able to decode certain words such as *drewp*, but be unfamiliar with the word (droop). A similar problem may be created by *knoock* (nook), *swai* (sway), and other items (depending on the individual child's background). Consequently, scores obtained on Test 4 must be viewed with caution, since more than the ability to sound whole words is required to respond correctly.

Test 5, Interpreting Phonetic Symbols, requires the examinee to use a pronunciation key to solve new words. Each word is spelled phonetically and marked for pronunciation in four different ways. The examinee must choose the alternative that is marked correctly. As with any phonics task, regional and subcultural variations in pronunciation should be considered in scoring Test 5. No caution to this effect is found in the manual, however.

An excellent but brief discussion on the proper use of the norms is presented in the manual. Originally the test was developed for diagnostic and instructional purposes. Norms are seldom needed for these purposes since each child's progress toward mastery of a skill is of interest, not his relationship to the performance of other youngsters. Despite this enlightened view and excellent statement in the manual regarding the limited value of norms, considerable time and space are then devoted to norms. This problem is further compounded by the inadequate information presented in the manual regarding development of the norms.

For example, the sample of youngsters selected for norming purposes are described in only a superficial manner. A single class in each of 23 schools was tested at each grade level. No information is given to describe how the classes were selected or whether any attempt was made to include heterogeneous groups. Furthermore, while the manual states that an effort was made to balance the sample on the variables of socio-economic status and mental ability, no information is given to demonstrate the effectiveness of this effort. Indeed, the mean IQ of the sample was considerably above average (108.5), indicating that the "balancing" attempt was not successful. Technical information supposedly available on request from the publisher (according to the manual) was not provided for this reviewer when requested.

In addition, the norms were established only on youngsters who had been taught using the Ginn Basic Readers. This is presented as an important control by the publisher, since the materials and methods used with the sample can influence the development of children's word-analysis skills. The manual suggests that this control in terms of prior instruction makes the norms free from the effects of "extreme" methods. While this logic is sound, it seems prudent to add that because of this control, the norms may be inappropriate to some degree for children who are taught by another method, or with other materials. Since norms are useful only to the extent that examinees resemble the norming population, this factor should be considered in making comparisons.

Also with regard to norms, the manual explains that teachers should take into consideration the skills that have been emphasized in their classes when deciding what score is satisfactory on a test. In a sixth grade classroom, for example, every pupil might be expected to earn a perfect score of 30 correct on Test 5. That score would indicate *mastery* for the purposes of the teacher's instruction. Again, with this discussion, the manual seems to suggest criterion-referenced scoring as opposed to norm-referenced scoring. This approach, particularly on a diagnostically and instructionally oriented instrument, is commendable. It is unfortunate that norms receive so much attention in the manual since the test author and publisher appear to understand the limitations of norms for this instrument.

Several aspects of these tests deserve special commendation. First, the tests are untimed. This is important in obtaining a measure of word-analysis skill based on power and not confounded by speed factors. Second, an excellent record booklet encourages the teacher to use the information from one subtest in conjunction with information obtained from other subtests. By entering the information for each child on the various record sheets, the teacher can systematically determine where a difficulty lies. Patterns of errors are easily identified in this way. The manual also provides a class record sheet and suggests ways for determining which word-analysis skills are relatively low for a group as a whole. Third, the tests carefully avoid isolating sounds, but instead direct the examiner to refer to "the sound heard at the beginning of boy," for example. Fourth, separate norms are reported for boys and girls. With a wealth of research evidence demonstrating the

McCullough Word-Analysis Tests

consistent difference in achievement between these two groups, it is appropriate that separate norms be provided.

Despite the limitations identified here, the *McCullough Word-Analysis Tests* stand as the best single instrument of its type currently available for assessing the mechanical aspects of word-analysis. Used as a diagnostic device, these tests can be quite helpful in identifying intermediate grade youngsters who have specific difficulties that may interfere with the higher order cognitive processes that depend on accurate word recognition.

For reviews by Emery P. Bliesmer and Albert J. Harris, see 6:826.

[720]

Phonics Knowledge Survey. Grades 1–6; 1964; PKS; individual; content card (2 pages); response record (8 pages); manual (4 pages); no data on reliability; no norms; $3.75 per set of content card, 25 response records, and manual; 50¢ per specimen set; postpaid; (10–30) minutes; Dolores Durkin and Leonard Meshover; Teachers College Press. *

IRA E. AARON, *Professor of Education and Head of the Reading Department, The University of Georgia, Athens, Georgia.*

This 15-part individually administered survey is designed to assist teachers in assessing pupil knowledge of phonics. Skills checked are names of letters; consonant sounds; long and short vowel sounds; vowel generalizations; consonant blends; digraphs (consonant); vowel combinations (diphthongs and digraphs); vowels followed by *r*; sounds of *qu*, *c* and *g*, *y*, *oo*, and *x*; beginning consonant combinations (digraphs); and syllabication.

The Content Card used by the child and the Response Record are easy to read and uncluttered. Directions on the Response Record are clear and brief. Results from individual items may be summarized on a detachable summary sheet, the last two pages of the Response Record. The Content Card, made of cardboard, is durable enough to withstand handling by numbers of children.

The child being tested looks at the Content Card, which contains the letters, letter combinations, and nonsense "words" on which he is being questioned. Sections on the Content Card are divided by heavy lines and are numbered in large, heavy type. The examiner records correctness of responses by checking a "right" or "wrong" blank on the right side of each page

opposite the questions or by underlining letters or combinations not known by the child.

The pattern followed in the Response Record is very practical. The statements and questions to be used by the examiner are presented in bold type in each section. In four subsections involving phonics or syllabication principles, the generalizations are presented in boxes just above the questions to be used by the examiner. Such information assists the teacher who is not thoroughly grounded in these generalizations.

No reliability or validity data are presented. Since this instrument is a somewhat formalized informal inventory, the absence of these data is not disturbing. The content, however, covers most of the important phonics skills and understandings.

The content may be challenged at points. The first vowel generalization checked (double vowel principle) is the one with the greatest number of exceptions. The questions asked are stated in such a way that one may infer that letters make sounds rather than represent them. The principle of the sound represented by *y* in the second syllable for a two-syllable word ignores regional differences for places where the short *i* rather than the long *e* sound is heard as these words are pronounced.

Used by an experienced reading teacher, this informal instrument should pinpoint strengths and weaknesses in most phonics skills. However, many existing informal inventories, some taking less time than this one, are being used by teachers. An instrument of this nature should be a part of a larger assessment of word attack skills, as the authors imply. An individual inventory built around the instructional program being used would be more helpful to a teacher. Even so, the reading teacher who does not know the phonics skills well enough to prepare his own inventory may find this one useful.

EDWARD B. FRY, *Professor of Education and Director, Reading Center, Rutgers, The State University, New Brunswick, New Jersey.*

This is a good individual survey that covers most of the basic phonics taught in the elementary grade levels of most basal readers. As the authors point out, it is not intended to be exhaustive and this is to its credit—an exhaustive phonics inventory would probably do more to confuse, than aid, reading teachers.

The test is quite simply constructed and consists of only two basic parts: (*a*) a Content

Card that has letters and letter combinations for the child to look at, and (*b*) a Response Record that contains directions for the teacher to read plus a place to record student responses.

There are no norms, as the test is not standardized; rather, this test is an excellent example of "content validity." This instrument is made for teachers who want to know if Johnny can, for example, sound out all his short vowels and who are not concerned that the ability to sound out four short vowels would place him at the 43rd percentile for 3rd graders.

Time needed to complete the test ranges from 10 to 30 minutes, but there are probably teachers who would want to give only one or two items and then teach that content for a while before giving the balance of the test, as the items are in an approximate order of difficulty which corresponds to the order in which they are introduced in most basal reading series. It is perhaps an oversight that the test directions do not suggest this partial testing procedure. The directions do suggest that the teacher could skip sections that she feels are too difficult.

The scoring is simply the number of correct items in 15 categories such as names of letters, consonant sounds, sounds of *y*, etc. It is a minor but perhaps difficult-to-avoid flaw of the survey that there is great inequality of value of each of the 15 categories. For example, Part 11, Sounds of QU, is hardly of equal weight with Part 3, Vowels: Long and Short. Also, if the goal is to aid the teacher, it might make more sense to separate short vowels and several of the ways long vowel sounds are made. Sounds of QU and Sounds of X could then be lumped together in a section on minor consonant sounds. This would also give a bit more equality of weight in terms of time needed to teach the various phonics sounds.

By making the following comments on the content of the test the reviewer does not wish to imply that the test is loaded with errors or that he does not basically approve of the contents and method of testing:

a) One of the old standard vowel generalizations, "When there are two vowels within a syllable, the first is usually long and the second is silent" is not always found to be true by this reviewer or at least one other reading specialist, Theodore Clymer. In fact, Clymer feels, based on frequency counts, that it is true less than half of the time because of such exceptions as *au, ow, oi, oy, ea* (bread), etc. The solution?

Teach vowel digraphs—*ee* makes the long *e* sound, etc.

b) Linguists or phonics enthusiasts might squirm a bit at seeing *ou* a diphthong and *au* a digraph making the broad *o* sound, plus several other things, all scrambled together in Part 9, Vowel Combinations.

c) There are several glaring omissions. There is no mention of the schwa. Also missing are two additional sounds of *u* which are neither long nor short (for example, the *u* in "put" and the *u* in "rule"). But the problem here is that these sounds would be difficult to test using the method, employed throughout the test, of simply asking a child what sound this letter or this combination of letters makes.

d) A study of any of the phonics frequency studies in the literature would probably dictate the removal of few bits of this test. For example, it is of little import that *x* sometimes makes the *gz* and *z* sound—it usually only makes the *ks* sound as in "box." The initial consonant combinations of *ps* in psalm and *gn* in gnaw are so infrequent that these had probably better be taught as sight words in the elementary school. We see some of the same problem in Part 15, Syllabication: "When *x* is preceded and followed by vowels, the *x* is in the same syllable as the preceding vowel, as in *tax* i."

The authors should be congratulated for taking the modern position that *y* at the end of a multisyllabic word such as "carry" makes the long *e* sound. And they are ahead of many of the older phonics materials by definitely separating initial consonant blends (such as *bl*) from consonant digraphs (such as *sh*).

A few teachers (but not this reviewer) might find fault with having the student pronounce the phonics sounds in isolation. There is a school of thought which holds that a phonics sound should be taught only in the context of a word. Hence, if a child had been instructed under this procedure he might have great difficulty with this survey. But you can't please everybody.

It is possible to read quite well at adult levels with a relatively poor knowledge of phonics. Hence, the knowledge gained from this survey is not necessarily imperative for reading improvement, but it is very helpful to those who wish to incorporate phonics into their reading curriculum and measure the amount the students know.

Phonics Knowledge Survey

In summary, the *Phonics Knowledge Survey* is a good instrument for any elementary teacher and for remedial reading teachers at any level. The directions are clear and the test is simple to administer and score. It is not standardized, but its content is valid and in harmony with most basal reading series and with phonics methods.

[721]

★**Phonics Test for Teachers.** Reading method courses; 1964; PTT; 1 form (8 pages); manual (4 pages); no data on reliability; no norms; $3.75 per set of 25 tests, 25 keys, and manual; 75¢ per specimen set; postage extra; (45) minutes; Dolores Durkin; Teachers College Press. *

REFERENCES

1. GIBSON, G. C. *A Study of Phonics Knowledge of Certain Louisiana Elementary School Teachers.* Doctor's thesis, Louisiana State University (Baton Rouge, La.), 1968. (*DA* 29: 1362A)
2. TYRE, BETTY BRANNEN. *An Investigation of Three Procedures Employed in Teaching Word Recognition Skills to Pre-Service Teachers Within an Introductory Reading Course.* Doctor's thesis, University of Southern Mississippi (Hattiesburg, Miss.), 1968. (*DA* 29:3029A)

IRA E. AARON, *Professor of Education and Head of the Reading Department, The University of Georgia, Athens, Georgia.*

This inventory of teacher knowledge of selected phonics skills is designed to assess strengths and weaknesses in areas such as syllabication; long and short vowels; vowel generalizations; sounds of *c* and *g*, *oo*, *qu*, *x*, and *y*; digraphs; and diphthongs. The author considers the content included to be a bare minimum for reading teachers. Phonics information likely to be known by all teachers or prospective teachers—such as the sound-symbol associations of most consonants—and highly technical information are omitted.

The test booklet is designed for self-administration and self-scoring. Even the slowest student should be able to complete the test, score it, and record the results within the 45-minute period suggested in the manual. On each page, space for summarizing results is provided. The answer key, which repeats important ideas from each item and presents the correct answers, is kept by the student. This unique feature should motivate further study on the part of students who perform poorly on the test.

In addition to the test booklet and answer key, test materials include a combined set of directions and a group summary sheet. Two pages are devoted to directions and two to the summary form. Information in this manual is presented in a clear and concise form.

The information and directions presented in the self-administering test booklet are clear and easy to follow in most instances. However, the abrupt change in type of response requested from section to section is disconcerting. For example, for each item, subtest 1 (Syllabication) instructs the student to draw a line between the syllables in a nonsense word and then write the principle involved, whereas subtest 2 (Vowels: Long and Short) asks that the student underline one of three words in each of ten rows that begin with a long (in the first five rows) or short vowel sound (in the last five rows). In fact, 6 different patterns of responding are called for in the 10 subsections of the test. Nonsense words are used in three subsections whereas real words are used in other subtests. No attempt seems to have been made to tighten up the item format.

Though the directions are usually clear, their grouping in the section on "Sounds of *c* and *g*" may be somewhat confusing. Two sets of directions precede two rows of words. The first task is to underline in the first row the word beginning with the "soft" sound; the second is to underline in the second row the word beginning with the "hard" sound. The hurried teacher could easily fail to note the change from "soft" to "hard" in the second set of directions and mark the wrong word even though he knows the difference in "soft" and "hard" sounds of *c* and *g*.

The section on diphthongs oversimplifies diphthongs in its introductory information and could lead to the teaching of an inaccurate concept. The introduction states that diphthongs are "certain combinations of vowels" and that in these combinations sometimes *y* and *w* function as vowels. If one ignores that the author is making no distinction between vowel sounds and vowel letters, the statements are acceptable to this point. Next, however, the student is asked to underline in an exercise the two letters "that make up the diphthong" in each of six words from among ten possibilities. In the words *they* and *few,* the long vowel sounds—which actually are diphthongs—are represented by *ey* (long *a*) and *ew* (long *u*). The single vowel letters *a* and *u*, as well as others, may also represent diphthong sounds, as in *able* and *music*. Since the inventory items are somewhat instructive as well as evaluative, an incorrect concept could easily be developed by the student—or by the teacher using the test.

No reliability, validity, or normative data are

Phonics Test for Teachers

presented in the brief manual. Since this instrument is intended as a testing-teaching informal inventory, the omission of these data is not disturbing. The items are likely to assess with reasonable adequacy what the author intended them to measure.

Most of the 10 sections contain only one item measuring a particular phonics skill. While it would be desirable to have more items from the standpoint of reliability, it would be impractical in terms of testing time required.

The omission of easier phonics items as well as those that are highly technical can be justified in view of the intended audience. However, the content may be criticized on several counts. One of the syllabication principles included (a vowel followed by *x* forms a syllable) is of little utility since relatively few words contain the letter *x*. The first nonsense word under vowel generalizations (*aif*) tests the "double vowel, long sound of first letter" principle, which is one of the least useful generalizations. Other important phonics generalizations (as the "*r* controller" and "final *e*" principles) are not included. The second item (*adsy*) under "sounds of *y*" (final *y* in words of two syllables usually represents the long *e* sound) does not consider the regional differences noted particularly in such words (short *i* instead of long *e*). The use of terminology that implies that letters have sounds rather than represent sounds may disturb some methodology teachers. The definition of a consonant digraph (as noted in the key) limits consonant digraphs to two consonant letters representing a single sound that is unlike that usually associated with either letter; thus, the sounds represented by *wr* and *mb* (as in *write* and *dumb*) are excluded.

Despite these shortcomings, the test could be of some help to reading methodology teachers and in-service leaders in assessing phonics knowledge of teachers and prospective teachers. It appears to be a testing-teaching device that one teacher found useful in her methodology courses and then decided to publish. It is doubtful, though, that other persons well grounded in phonics knowledge would want to use the inventory. They probably would prepare their own to cover those points they think are important in phonics.

GERALD G. DUFFY, *Associate Professor of Education, Michigan State University, East Lansing, Michigan.*

Phonics Test for Teachers

This test is designed "to help teachers and student teachers identify what they do and do not know about phonics" and is intended to be used in reading methods courses. The implication is that methods instructors, by using this test, will be able to assess the degree to which students understand the relationship between English sounds and English spelling and prescribe appropriate instruction.

The test is self-administering and can be corrected either by the instructor or by the students themselves. The author emphasizes there is no one best way to use the test. She suggests that it may be given before, during, or following instruction in sound-letter association but leaves the final decision regarding its administration to the user.

The test consists of 10 brief subtests: assessing student knowledge in the areas of syllabication, long and short vowels, vowel generalizations, sounds of *c* and *g*, sounds of *y*, digraphs, diphthongs, sounds of *oo*, sounds of *qu*, and sounds of *x*. During the course of the test, the student makes a total of 60 responses, of which 39 consist of underlining or checking the correct answer, while the balance are open-ended. Examples of the latter include: "Define the term *consonant digraph*"; "In the space provided, write any word in which the 'long' sound of *oo* is heard"; "Why would the letter *y* most likely record this particular vowel sound?"

The major strength of the test is that it is the only one known to this reviewer which is designed to assess phonic knowledge of teachers. Further, most items are clearly written and the choice of responses is generally unambiguous. Users should note, however, the author's interpretation of phonic elements such as diphthongs, which includes the *ew* in "few" and the *ey* in "they" in addition to the usual *oi, oy, ou,* and *ow* combinations.

The test's major weakness is that it is not standardized, with apparently no attempt being made to gather either normative data or information regarding validity and reliability. Consequently, the test user has no way of determining the relative value of a given score. Another weakness may be the author's decision to include subtests on rather esoteric elements such as the two sounds of *qu* and the three sounds of *x* while failing to assess more utilitarian elements such as the schwa sound. In addition, some users may prefer a test having no open-ended responses, particularly if they wish to have students correct the test themselves as the author suggests.

In summary, this test may be useful for methods instructors who heretofore have constructed their own informal instruments to assess student knowledge of phoneme-to-grapheme correspondences prior to providing instruction in how phonics should be taught to children. The degree to which this test is successful, however, will depend upon the extent to which the user adapts it to his particular needs. It is clearly an informal diagnostic tool, rather than a standardized instrument, and demands that it be used as such.

[722]

*Silent Reading Diagnostic Tests. Grades 2–6; 1955–70; SRDT; 17 scores based upon 8 tests: words in isolation (test 1), words in context (2), total right (1, 2), initial errors (1, 2), middle errors (1, 2), ending errors (1, 2), orientation errors (1, 2), total errors (1, 2), total omitted (1, 2), visual-structural (3), syllabication (4), word synthesis (5), total right (3, 4, 5), beginning sounds (6), ending sounds (7), vowel and consonant sounds (8), total right (6, 7, 8); 1 form ('70, 16 pages); manual ('70, 31 pages); $5 per 20 tests; $2.80 per specimen set (must be purchased to obtain manual and scoring cards); postage extra; (90) minutes in 2 or 3 sessions; Guy L. Bond, Bruce Balow, and Cyril J. Hoyt; Lyons & Carnahan. *

REFERENCES

1. See 6:832.
2. MURRAY, CAROL-FAITH. A Concurrent Validity Study of the Silent Reading Diagnostic Tests and the Gates Reading Diagnostic Tests. Master's thesis, San Diego State College (San Diego, Calif.), 1959.
3. BENZ, DONALD A., AND ROSEMIER, ROBERT A. "Concurrent Validity of the Gates Level of Comprehension Test and the Bond, Clymer, Hoyt Reading Diagnostic Tests." Ed & Psychol Meas 26:1057–62 w '66. * (PA 41:4989)
4. TRELA, THADDEUS M. "What Do Diagnostic Reading Tests Diagnose?" El Engl 43:370–2 Ap '66. *
5. BENZ, DONALD A., AND ROSEMIER, ROBERT A. "Word Analysis and Comprehension." Read Teach 21:558–63 Mr '68. *
6. TODD, ELEANOR ARDICE. A Clinical Study of the Developmental Test of Visual Perception and Its Relationship to Reading Retardation and Specific Reading Skills. Doctor's thesis, University of Georgia (Athens, Ga.), 1968. (DAI 30:629A)
7. McCALL, ROZANNE A., AND McCALL, ROBERT B. "Comparative Validity of Five Reading Diagnostic Tests." J Ed Res 62(7):329–33 Mr '69. *
8. PLATTOR, EMMA E., AND WOESTEHOFF, ELLSWORTH S. "Specific Reading Disabilities of Disadvantaged Children," pp. 55–60. In Reading Difficulties: Diagnosis, Correction, and Remediation. Edited by William K. Durr. Newark, Del.: International Reading Association, 1970. Pp. vii, 276. *

N. DALE BRYANT, Professor of Psychology and Education, Teachers College, Columbia University, New York, New York.

The Silent Reading Diagnostic Tests provide diagnostic information about word recognition and analysis skills to be used in conjunction with the usual silent reading achievement scores. This instrument consists of eight group-administered subtests requiring about 80 minutes of timed testing plus about 10 to 20 minutes for instructions and other administrative tasks. Testing is accomplished in three, or sometimes two, sessions and booklets are not reusable. The tests are "designed to help the classroom teacher analyze the specific reading needs of his pupils" and are "designed to be used with pupils of any age who read at second through sixth grade levels." It is evident, however, that some subtests are more appropriate for primary level readers, while others are more appropriate for those reading at higher levels. The fact that the tests are timed may limit some examinees, though the manual claims that the time "is sufficient for upper grade level readers to attempt all items and for primary grade level readers to demonstrate their reading power."

Two of the tests, 1 and 2, relate to accurate word recognition. Test 1, Words in Isolation, consists of 54 items in which the examinee looks at a picture and selects one of five printed words to identify the picture. The distractors use reversal, incorrect spelling, and other modifications of the answer or of other words that could logically be the answer. Four types of errors are identified on the scoring key and are used to obtain four separate scores. For example, for a picture of a cart with large wheels, the answer is "wheels" and the distractors are "chart" (initial error), "wagem" (ending error), "wanog" (orientation error), and "whills" (middle error). The Rights score not only reflects accuracy of word recognition but probably has less general intelligence variance than most reading vocabulary achievement tests, a distinct advantage in diagnostic work.

Test 2, Words in Context, is identical to Test 1 except that instead of pictures, sentences with blanks are presented, the context making the correct choice fairly obvious. The same four types of errors are noted. Tests 1 and 2 correlate about .8 to .9 within different grades. Thus, the two scores are very properly combined.

In addition to the Total Right score, a Total Omitted score and a Total Errors score for Tests 1 and 2 are used and converted to grade equivalents. Total Errors and Total Omitted scores have a relationship that does not lend itself to meaningful use of separate norms for each. For example, an examinee giving an erroneous answer for only one item and omitting only one item would have a Rights grade equivalent of 7.0 but an Omits grade equivalent of 4.0 and an Error grade equivalent of 7.4. A nonreader, marking each item at random, would most probably achieve a Rights grade equivalent of 1.8 but would have a grade equivalent above 4.0 on Omits. Reliabilities are not given for omit or error scores. A single score based upon the raw score corrected for guessing would have some distinct advantages in comparison to the currently used scores.

The number of each of the four types of errors is presently converted to a grade equivalent. A difference of one error can make a grade equivalent difference of as much as 1.5 years. The proportion of each type of error could be useful if proportion norms were available for individuals making approximately the same Rights score. The error scores as used currently must be judged with considerable insight and caution.

Test 3, Visual-Structural Analysis, measures the ability to identify root words, usually by recognizing and separating common affixes from them. Each of the 30 items consists of a word and three choices of "the root word; that is, the word from which the first word was made," e.g., "eaten: at eat ten." This kind of item encourages guessing, and a nonreader marking at random for each item would score about fourth grade level. The manual warns that the test functions best at upper grade levels, but the reviewer would question its meaningfulness for primary level scores where there are many errors. A test of ability to use root words in getting the meaning of unfamiliar words would be more useful diagnostically and might correlate only moderately with Test 3.

Test 4, Syllabication, shows three different ways of separating words into syllables and requires the examinee to select the correct one. Of the 30 items, 25 are keyed to six rules of syllabication and 5 require only counting the number of syllables.

Test 5, Word Synthesis, presents a series of paragraphs with lines that end in hyphenated words. Comprehension questions are asked that require the examinee to correctly blend the hyphenated word so as to recognize it. A person guessing at the answers would be likely to do slightly better than chance, since the comprehension questions provide some clues as to the answer. The score probably reflects comprehension skills as well as the blending of hyphenated words.

Test 6, Beginning Sounds, Test 7, Ending Sounds, and Test 8, Vowel and Consonant Sounds all require the examinee to listen to a word the teacher pronounces and select the one

of four choices that has the same beginning or ending. The tests intercorrelate about .5 to .8 within different grades. Test 8 uses single vowels or consonants; Test 6 uses consonant blends and digraphs predominantly, and Test 7 uses common word endings. For most children, the skill demonstrated on these three tests will probably be indicative of decoding skill in reading, but, particularly among children with disability, some who can perform adequately on encoding and matching tasks, such as those in Tests 6, 7, and 8, may be unable to perform the comparable decoding skills in reading.

Reliabilities based upon an unstated number of third or fourth grade children appear adequate for diagnostic use, being predominantly in the .90 to .95 level, with that for Syllabication the only one as low as .80.

The graphic profile used to plot a grade equivalent score for each examinee lists grade in school, chronological age, reading expectancy, measures of silent reading achievement, and each subscore. As discussed earlier, the plotting of Omits and Errors and the plotting of each of the four error types can be misleading. For the other variables, the "lines of importance" established as one-half year above and below the average reading achievement grade equivalent are reasonable for suggesting that variations outside the lines represent strengths or weaknesses. If, however, reading achievement measures vary greatly from one another, these lines are less useful. While the distance between the lines should probably vary at different grade levels, this refinement would add too much complexity to the use of the profile with little gain in meaningfulness.

In addition to the separate tests, Tests 1 and 2 are combined (as noted above) and Tests 6, 7, and 8 are also properly combined. Tests 3, 4, and 5 are combined, even though Test 3 has only low or moderate correlations with Tests 4 and 5 and the latter two tests correlate only .35 to .64 over different grades.

In addition to grade equivalent norms for each test and combination of tests, percentile and stanine norms by grade are given. The normative sample consisted of 2,500 children in grades 2 through 7, stratified so as to be representative of the socioeconomic distributions of 10 cities in three states. It is difficult to judge the appropriateness of the norms for other localities. Even a distribution of socioeconomic levels for the normative group would

add a great deal to the value of the norms. However, the manual states that the vast majority
of children in the schools "were making normal
progress in reading development," so the norms
are presumably intended as an approximation
of national norms.

The manual is clearly written. A substantial
section on interpreting test results is included.
It not only discusses diagnostic meaning of
scores but also makes some general and rather
limited remedial suggestions. Scoring is simple
but lengthy, with the use of 14 scoring stencils,
6 of which must be used for five different
scores.

In computing the reading expectancy level,
the example in the manual should be followed
rather than the formula, which omits dividing
IQ by 100.

There are many dimensions of silent reading
that need to be diagnostically measured, including various aspects of comprehension. Factors
in silent reading beyond the word level are not
measured by the *Silent Reading Diagnostic
Tests*. However, this instrument, with the cautions suggested above, provides certain information about word recognition and analysis
skills in silent reading that can be helpful to
the classroom teacher and that can be useful
to the reading clinician. The clinician is likely
to use oral reading and other individual tests
to supplement the group measures, even in the
areas of silent reading being measured by these
tests. Generally, these tests provide limited but
useful diagnostic information.

Roy A. Kress, *Professor of Psychology and
Educational Psychology, Temple University,
Philadelphia, Pennsylvania.*

The 1970 edition of the *Silent Reading
Diagnostic Tests* is a shortened version of the
1955 edition. The number of subtests has been
reduced from 11 to 8 and the time shortened
to approximately 80 minutes of testing time.
Designed as a group diagnostic measure of
various skills important for success in reading
in grades 2 through 6, it purports to measure
the ability to: (*a*) "recognize words in isolation," (*b*) "recognize words in context," (*c*)
"identify root words," (*d*) "separate words
into syllables," (*e*) "apply the common rules
of syllabication," (*f*) "synthesize, or blend,
words," (*g*) "distinguish beginning sounds,"
(*h*) "distinguish ending sounds," and (*i*) "distinguish vowel and consonant sounds."

Because of the range of reading maturity it
attempts to measure, 10-minute time limits have
been set for each of the first five subtests as an
estimated time for upper grade pupils to finish
each test. Younger pupils may often not finish,
but the authors indicate this is sufficient time
"for primary grade level readers to demonstrate
their reading power." The administration instructions call for three testing periods for the
younger grades and two periods for older pupils.

Test 1: Words in Isolation consists of 54
items, each one a picture with five possible
answers identifying the picture. The distracters
have been planned to permit an analysis of a
child's errors as being due to difficulty with the
initial, medial, or final portion of a word or
an error in directional attack (orientation).
However, most of the distracters are either
scrambled or improper spellings of the word, or
a complete or partial reversal. Often only the
required response is correctly spelled. The distracters are frequently designed to mislead the
child for whom the correct word is not a part
of his sight vocabulary (i.e., item 17 depicts a
teacher at a chalkboard writing subtraction
exercises. The responses are *treacher, teacher,
teachler, aritmethic, lezzon.* In the analysis of
errors, the selection of *treacher* indicates difficulty with the initial portion of the word,
teachler with the final portion, *aritmethic* an
error of orientation, and *lezzon* a medial error.)
The artificiality of the task leads one to question
the validity of the test except as a measure of
pure sight vocabulary.

Test 2: Words in Context consists of 30
incomplete sentences, each with a blank space
followed by a list of five possible responses,
only one of which will complete the sentence.
Again the distracters are incorrectly spelled or
jumbled words (e.g., item 30: "He could drive
the _____. otomobile, machine, automo-
ble, turck, trartor"). The reviewer feels that the
child who decides upon *otomobile* as a response
has *not demonstrated* difficulty with the initial
portion of the stimulus, as the authors suggest
in the manual, but instead has demonstrated
that he does not know the word *machine,* that
he also does not know how to spell *automobile*
but does have, among other things, reasonably
mature word analysis abilities and does use
context clues to good advantage.

Test 3: Visual-Structural Analysis and Test
4: Syllabication consist of 30 items each and

Silent Reading Diagnostic Tests

measure various aspects of structural analysis and syllabication abilities. All distracters are actual words and the items appear to measure, in ascending order of difficulty, the more mature word recognition abilities (exclusive of dictionary skills) expected of upper elementary students.

Test 5: Word Synthesis consists of eight paragraphs with hyphenated words at the end of each line. Each paragraph is followed by a series of sentences and numbered blank spaces (cloze procedure) designed to measure the child's understanding of the paragraph. Four possible responses are provided for each of the numbered blanks—30 in all. The hyphenated words are usually monosyllabic or are hyphenated within, rather than between, the syllables when they are polysyllabic. The authors state that this measures the ability to "blend" words. This reviewer feels the technique is artificial and that the distortion in the separation of the hyphenated words interferes with the reader's comprehension and does not measure skills applicable in the normal process of reading.

Tests 6 (Beginning Sounds), 7 (Ending Sounds), and 8 (Vowel and Consonant Sounds) consist of 30 items each. Here, the test administrator pronounces a word and the child identifies, from a multiple choice group of four letters or letter groups, the graphic response which matches the initial or final sound in the word heard. However, a variety of artificial graphic representations are included throughout, making these very questionable measures of the phonetic abilities supposedly being asessed; e.g., in Test 6, for the beginning sound in *natural* the child is to select *pn* from pn, un, tn, nt; in Test 7, for the ending sound in *decay,* he is to select *quet* from khak, kayn, cove, quet; in Test 8, for the vowel sound at the beginning of the word *urn* he is to select *i* from x, i, v, a.

The manual indicates that the tests were standardized using a sample of 2,500 pupils "representative of approximately 38,000," following "stratified sampling procedures." Split-half reliabilities for each subtest, obtained by using *two* "randomly selected classrooms," range from a high of .95 for Test 1 to a low of .80 for Test 4.

No validity data are presented. Instead, "content validity" is claimed on the basis of the description of the tests: "tasks required of the pupil are the kinds which adequately maturing

Silent Reading Diagnostic Tests

readers are required to do in their everyday use of reading."

The manual provides tables for converting each subtest and certain combinations of subtests to grade equivalents, stanines, and percentile ratings. These are recorded on a profile on the pupil test booklet and provide a scale of strengths and weaknesses in the subtest areas for each student. The authors suggest that this information may be used as a starting point in planning a particular child's instructional program in reading.

This reviewer questions the value of such an artificial measure as a "diagnostic measure" of children's reading abilities. Obviously, whatever is being measured is related to reading ability and may be positively correlated with particular skill processes in reading. It is doubtful, however, that such an instrument will aid the teacher in the analysis of "specific reading needs of his pupils" beyond providing a related grade-equivalent or percentile score similar to that obtained on most standardized group reading achievement measures. Its purpose, as a diagnostic instrument, is defeated by the artificiality inherent in the stimuli employed.

For reviews by Emery P. Bliesmer and Albert J. Kingston of the original edition, see 6:832.

[723]

★**Standard Reading Inventory.** Grades 1–7; 1966, c1963–66; SRI; 4 scores (independent reading level, minimum instructional level, maximum instructional level, frustration level), 6 to 9 subtest scores (vocabulary in isolation, vocabulary in context, oral word recognition errors, total oral errors, recall after oral reading, recall after silent reading, total comprehension, oral speed, silent speed) at each of 11 reading levels (preprimer, 1^1, 1^2, 2^1, 2^2, 3^1, 3^2, 4, 5, 6, 7), and various ratings and checklistings; individual; record booklets: Forms A, B, ('63, 20 pages); manual ('66, 64 pages); $5 per 25 record booklets; $4 per set of manual and word cards; $6 per set of manual, word cards, and 5 copies of each form; cash orders postpaid; (30–120) minutes; Robert A. McCracken; Klamath Printing Co. *

REFERENCES

1. McCRACKEN, ROBERT ALLEN. *The Development and Validation of the Standard Reading Inventory for the Individual Appraisal of Reading Performance in Grades 1 Through 6.* Doctor's thesis, Syracuse University (Syracuse, N.Y.), 1963. (*DA* 24:5200)
2. CHILDS, FRANCES V. *An Independent Study to Check the Validity of the Standard Reading Inventory in Appraising the Reading Achievement of Students in Third and Fourth Grades.* Master's thesis, Western Washington State College (Bellingham, Wash.), 1966.
3. CACCAVO, EMIL. *The Listening Comprehension Level of an Informal Reading Inventory as a Predictor of Intelligence of Elementary School Children.* Doctor's thesis, New York University (New York, N.Y.), 1968. (*DAI* 30:164A)
4. KASDON, LAWRENCE M., AND KELLY, DEAN. "Simulation: In-Service Education for Teachers of Reading." *J Exp Ed* 38(1):79–86 f '69. *

5. BLYNN, CATHERINE PETERS. *A Determination of the Practicality of Making the Use of an Informal Reading Inventory More Applicable to the Needs of the Classroom Teachers.* Doctor's thesis, Lehigh University (Bethlehem, Pa.), 1970. (*DAI* 31:5240A)

6. BOTEL, MORTON; BRADLEY, JOHN; AND KASHUBA, MICHAEL. "The Validity of Informal Reading Testing," pp. 85–103. In *Reading Difficulties: Diagnosis, Correction, and Remediation.* Edited by William K. Durr. Newark, Del.: International Reading Association, 1970. Pp. vii, 276. *

7. BRADDOCK, BETTY J., AND ROBINSON, RUTH V. *A Correlation of Slosson Oral Reading Test With the McCracken Word Recognition Subtest.* Master's thesis, Glassboro State College (Glassboro, N.J.), 1970.

8. McCRACKEN, ROBERT A., AND MULLEN, NEILL D. "The Validity of Certain Measures in an I.R.I.," pp. 104–10. In *Reading Difficulties: Diagnosis, Correction, and Remediation.* Edited by William K. Durr. Newark, Del.: International Reading Association, 1970. Pp. vii, 276. *

H. ALAN ROBINSON, *Professor of Reading, Hofstra University, Hempstead, New York.*

This informal reading inventory for the elementary grades consists of "eleven stories for oral reading, eight stories for silent reading, and eleven word lists for measuring word pronouncing ability in isolation." The stories and word lists are at 11 basal reading book levels from preprimer through grade 7. The test is designed to measure word recognition in isolation and in context, errors in oral reading, comprehension, word meaning, and speed of oral and of silent reading.

The content of the test is based on three basal reading series. Content validity was obtained through (*a*) vocabulary control; (*b*) basing sentence length, content, and general style on the three series; and (*c*) the use of the Spache and Dale-Chall readability formulas as a basis for analyzing the basal readers and as a guide in writing the stories. Content validity was corroborated by testing children in grades 1–6, and through the evaluations of experts in the field.

Alternate-form reliabilities, based on the testing of 60 children in grades 1–6, ranged from .86 to .91 for the level scores and from .68 to .99 (median .93) for the subtest scores.

Although the test is titled the *Standard Reading Inventory,* it is not standardized, for information about specific norming procedures is lacking. On the other hand, the data about validity and reliability assure more comparable and consistent results than are normally obtained on a teacher-constructed informal reading inventory.

The very formalizing of an informal inventory, however, raises important questions about usefulness, particularly if the test is to render diagnostic information: Does this inventory do any better a job of placing a pupil on an appropriate instructional or independent reading level for material other than the small samples of reading represented in this test or on the "typical" standardized reading survey test? Does the test really furnish adequate diagnostic information about oral reading errors when the scoring is quantitative rather than qualitative? Obviously there are no absolute answers to these questions but they must be raised by a reviewer whose own conceptual framework about evaluating reading is in a state of flux. Won't reading levels change in relation to the type of material read? Wouldn't it be more meaningful to analyze oral reading errors or miscues in the light of psycholinguistic principles?

The materials to be used for test administration are attractive and printed clearly, but there are a few problems in regard to organization and administration: (*a*) The manual is bound with the selections to be read by the pupils and it is cumbersome for the examiner to leaf back and forth. (*b*) Some concepts are hazy or introduced with inadequate explanation—e.g., distinctions among questionable, definite, minimum, and maximum instructional levels; distinctions between word recognition errors and total errors; lack of a silent reading selection at the preprimer level; inclusion and exclusion of certain levels of reading selections. (*c*) The scoring of oral errors seems needlessly complex and confusing.

As is true of any evaluative tool, the *Standard Reading Inventory* has weaknesses and limitations. Its major contribution is in providing more information, particularly when utilized by a keen examiner, about the process of reading as opposed to the product normally measured by group standardized silent reading tests. It is useful as a rough, semidiagnostic tool when an examiner wants to learn more about a given learner and how he reads certain kinds of materials.

[724]

The Standard Reading Tests. Reading ages up to 9-0; 1958; SRT; individual; 1 form; 12 tests; manual (128 pages, see *1* below) includes all test materials; no data on reliability; norms for Tests 1, 11, and 12 only; £1.50 per manual, postage extra; administration time not reported for Tests 1–11; J. C. Daniels and Hunter Diack; Chatto & Windus Ltd. *

a) TEST 1, THE STANDARD TEST OF READING SKILL.
b) TEST 2, COPYING ABSTRACT FIGURES.
c) TEST 3, COPYING A SENTENCE.
d) TEST 4, VISUAL DISCRIMINATION AND ORIENTATION TEST.
e) TEST 5, LETTER-RECOGNITION TEST.
f) TEST 6, AURAL DISCRIMINATION TEST.

g) TEST 7, DIAGNOSTIC WORD-RECOGNITION TESTS.
h) TEST 8, ORAL WORD-RECOGNITION TEST.
i) TEST 9, PICTURE WORD-RECOGNITION TEST.
j) TEST 10, SILENT PROSE-READING AND COMPREHENSION TEST.
k) TEST 11, GRADED SPELLING TEST.
l) TEST 12, GRADED TEST OF READING EXPERIENCE. (20) minutes.

REFERENCE

1. See 6:833.

M. L. KELLMER PRINGLE, *Director, National Children's Bureau, London, England.*

Since a fairly detailed description of this test battery has been given in *The Sixth Mental Measurements Yearbook,* it will not be repeated here, except to say that the authors regard Test 1 (which, in essence, is one of word-recognition) as the key test "to be given to every child who....has not fully mastered all the skills involved in reading." A retest at six-month intervals is recommended while one or more of the other tests are to be administered in accordance with a particular pupil's needs.

As has been noted by a previous reviewer, data on reliability and validity remain conspicuous by their absence. Nor is there any indication in the manual that they can be found elsewhere. This is a serious omission, all the more so as the battery was first published some 12 years ago. Yet the authors claim that "the Standard Reading Test estimates of reading ability are on a finer scale of grading and the corresponding Reading Ages are, statistically, more reliable at the earliest levels of reading" because in order to attain a reading age of 7 years, the child has to read 68 different words compared with a considerably smaller number on other tests of this type. This claim is reasonable enough but actual standardisation figures would make it rather more convincing.

In considering the relative merits and limitations of the tests, it is useful to bear in mind that the authors espouse the phonic approach in teaching reading.

The handbook is clearly printed and the tests are well set out. Each of them is preceded by unambiguous instructions which are straightforward and easily mastered. While it is the most comprehensive diagnostic battery designed for British children, the total absence of standardisation data is a serious limitation. A further drawback is the lack of a scoring form or test booklet on which the examiner can record details of the child's performance. If the authors were to rectify these omissions, the value of

the tests would be considerably enhanced. Overall, then, their main value lies in the facts that they cover a wide range of reading skills so that the results supply a detailed profile of weaknesses, gaps, and confusions and that no special training is required to administer or interpret them.

For a review by L. B. Birch, see 6:833.

[725]

★Stanford Diagnostic Reading Test. Grades 2.5-4.5, 4.5-8.5; 1966-68; SDRT; 2 levels; Bjorn Karlsen, Richard Madden, and Eric F. Gardner; Harcourt Brace Jovanovich, Inc. *

a) LEVEL 1. Grades 2.5-4.5; 7 scores: comprehension, vocabulary, auditory discrimination, syllabication, beginning and ending sounds, blending, sound discrimination; Forms W ('66, 8 pages), X ('68, 8 pages); manual ('66, 32 pages); $7.90 per 35 tests; 50¢ per key; $1.75 per specimen set; postage extra; scoring service, $2 per test; 137(162) minutes in 4 sessions.
b) LEVEL 2. Grades 4.5-8.5; 8 scores: comprehension (literal, inferential, total), vocabulary, syllabication, sound discrimination, blending, rate; 2 editions; 91(111) minutes in 3 sessions.
1) *Hand Scorable Edition.* Forms W ('66, 8 pages), X ('68, 8 pages); manual ('66, 32 pages); prices same as for Level 1.
2) *Machine Scorable Edition.* Form W consists of 2 parts: reusable reading comprehension booklet ('66, 4 pages), MRC test-answer booklet ('68, 4 pages); manual ('66, 35 pages); $7 per 35 tests; $7 per 35 answer booklets; postage extra; specimen set not available; scoring service, 45¢ and over per test.

REFERENCES

1. BOEHNLEIN, MARY MAHER. *A Structure-of-Intellect Analysis of Two Diagnostic Reading Tests.* Doctor's thesis, Kent State University (Kent, Ohio), 1969. (*DAI* 31:212A)
2. SHEALOR, DONALD A. *Relationship of Diagnostic Test Scores to Pupils' Participation in a Certain Remedial Program.* Doctor's thesis, United States International University (San Diego, Calif.), 1969. (*DAI* 30:2429A)
3. GIOVINO, ROSEMARIE. *The Perceptual Patterns of Normal and Retarded Readers in Grades Four and Eight.* Doctor's thesis, Boston University (Boston, Mass.), 1970. (*DAI* 31: 2216A)

LAWRENCE M. KASDON, *Associate Professor of Education, Ferkauf Graduate School, Yeshiva University, New York, New York.*

The SDRT is designed to diagnose the individual reading difficulties of pupils and to group pupils according to their instructional needs. The latter objective is an innovation which will be discussed at greater length later in this review.

The authors state that comprehension is the ultimate goal in reading and that other aspects of reading measured in the test are subordinate to it. The subordinate skills areas are vocabulary, word recognition, and rate of reading (Level 2 only). At Level 1, only general comprehension is measured, while Level 2 measures both literal and inferential comprehension on various types of subject matter. Only listening vocabulary is measured, but some teachers and clinicians might want more information on other vocabularies such as sight vocabulary.

The five word-recognition skills at Level 1 and the three at Level 2 should be sufficient to diagnose most pupils' phonic skills—this is the only aspect of word recognition assessed. The Blending subtests are most ingeniously constructed. In Auditory Discrimination (Level 1) the beginning, middle, and ends of words are compared by asking the pupil to determine at which of these three places two words pronounced by the tester are alike. At Level 2, Sound Discrimination requires the pupil to match the phoneme underscored in the stimulus word with the same phoneme, regardless of its spelling, contained in one of three other words. The other aspects of phonics are measured in a conventional manner.

The Rate of Reading is measured on fourth grade material using a multiple choice type of cloze technique. The choices occur about every 15 words. The rate score is based on the number of items attempted, which in turn yields a stanine or percentile score. Unfortunately, an accuracy score was not also developed.

The authors state that the SDRT standardization population came from a set of six communities, fairly normal in terms of median family income and median adult years of schooling. The samples were adjusted slightly so that their performance on Comprehension matched the performance of those in the national standardization of the *Stanford Achievement Test*. Means are given for the standardization population, but not standard deviations. Persons planning to make extensive use of this test would probably want to develop local norms, but should not compare local norms with SDRT norms until the publishers release more information on the standardization population. The tests were normed in October on Form X, so that the norms are most accurate for fall testing.

The test was constructed to give reliable and precise measurement for pupils falling below average in reading. For Level 2, reliability is given for Total Comprehension but not for its subtests. The median split-half reliabilities for Level 1 are .94 and .93 for grades 3 and 4, respectively; for Level 2, .87, .88, .90, and .91 for grades 5–8, respectively. Alternate-form reliability, furnished only for Rate of Reading, should be supplied for other subtests.

For the most part the subtest intercorrelations are substantially below their reliabilities so that fairly reliable difference scores can be obtained when making profile analyses. The authors do not supply standard errors of measurement for difference scores; however, they do recommend that "only differences of two or more stanines for the results of an individual pupil should be considered meaningful."

Individual profiles are plotted on the cover of each pupil's test. A class analysis chart is also supplied to permit a teacher to see at a glance the strengths and weaknesses of his class. A rather detailed section of the manual explains how he can form needs groups based on the above analyses.

The publishers also offer a special scoring and reporting service for Level 2. A unique computer program analyzes each pupil's profile of subtest scores and all pupils having similar problems in reading are grouped. According to the program, 11 groups are possible. Each group's scores come on a separate sheet with the group number, the pupils' names, and their scores on all subtests. The teacher checks the identifying number of the group and by looking on a fold-out of the cover, finds an explanation of the reading characteristics of the pupils falling into the group, as well as instructional suggestions. Lists of sample professional and pupil materials appear on the folder. The inexperienced or overburdened teacher can find a skill area to commence his instruction for the group.

By the use of color and format, directions to the teacher as he administers the test and what he is to say to the pupils are very clearly indicated. Only hand scoring keys are supplied. The publisher claims that 30 tests can be hand scored in 45 minutes! The publisher also says that teachers prefer the keys to scoring grids as they can examine items missed. At another place in the manual, teachers are told not to use individual items for diagnosis. Granted that individual items are unreliable, the teacher must start some place when he is teaching a skill such as auditory discrimination.

This test and its manual have definite possibilities for use in a developmental or corrective reading class as well as in a teachers' workshop. If the teachers came away with nothing but the idea of the primacy of comprehension, and the somewhat hierarchical arrangement under

Stanford Diagnostic Reading Test

comprehension of the other skills measured in this battery, it would have been a good investment of time.

[726]

★Test of Individual Needs in Reading, Sixth Edition. Grades 1–6; 1961–66; TINR; test booklet title is *John Bidwell and the Trail to California;* 20 scores: oral reading, comprehension, rate, word analysis (use of context, words beginning alike, beginning consonants, ending consonants, consonant substitutions, speech consonants, consonant blends, reversals, long and short vowels, vowel blends, blending letter sounds, prefixes, suffixes, compound words, recognizing syllables, syllabication, total); individual; 1 form ('66, 24 pages); manual ('66, 18 pages); no description of normative population; $6.25 per 25 tests; 50¢ per specimen set; postpaid; [25–50] minutes; Hap Gilliland; Montana Reading Clinic Publications. *

LARRY A. HARRIS, *Associate Professor of Education, The University of North Dakota, Grand Forks, North Dakota.*

The *Test of Individual Needs in Reading* attempts to assess so many aspects of reading in a relatively brief period of time (25–50 minutes) that it fails to measure adequately any single skill. In general appearance and content it greatly resembles a teacher-made informal reading inventory. There is considerable doubt in the mind of this reviewer that this test offers any improvement over instruments most teachers can construct themselves.

One part of the test consists of paragraphs roughly graded in terms of reading difficulty. Each reading level (ranging from primer level to grade 7, plus a college level paragraph) is followed by five questions, usually multiple choice. According to the teachers' manual accompanying the test, this part may be used to assess oral reading and silent reading for groups or individuals. The questions are asked following oral or silent reading to assess comprehension.

A second part of the test consists of various word analysis tasks. Lists of real and nonsense words are employed in this section along with a brief (7 sentences) cloze exercise. This part of the test is given only on an individual basis.

According to the manual, the test is designed primarily to determine at what reading level each child can best perform and to "provide additional information for adapting instruction to the individual needs of each student." The comprehension questions are included to verify the grade placement score. The word analysis test is intended to locate specific deficiencies needing corrective or remedial instruction.

Several major factors serve to limit the achievement of these stated purposes. First, the instructions provided for the administration of the test are unclear and especially difficult to follow. Much is left to the discretion of the examiner without adequate attention being given to the consequences of the various alternatives. For example, the manual describes a procedure for testing a small group. Up to five youngsters are started reading the graded paragraphs silently. One at a time, the youngsters are interrupted and taken aside for an oral reading examination. Once this is completed, they return to work on the silent reading test. Since the same paragraphs are used for both silent and oral reading, it seems obvious that some youngsters will profit more than their peers from reading orally late in the testing session when the examiner will doubtless pronounce more difficult words for them. With this procedure each child's silent reading comprehension score is confounded by a listening comprehension factor—some to a greater degree than others, depending on when they are taken aside for the oral reading test. In general, a lack of standardization is evident in the instructions for administration. This becomes a serious problem when, as in the above example, arbitrary decisions can seriously affect the test results.

A second factor closely related to the lack of standardized procedures is the absence of validity and reliability information. Obviously, the validity and reliability of the test are influenced by the conditions under which it is administered. Furthermore, certain characteristics of the test also appear to limit its validity. The reading difficulty of the paragraphs in part one of the test has not been determined scientifically. The only control applied, according to the manual, was the selection of words from various levels of the Thorndike Word List (misspelled "Thorndyke" in the manual). No attention is given to the importance of the sentence structure used, the use of narrative versus expository writing, concept load, or other factors known to affect readability.

Another factor related to the validity of the test concerns the comprehension questions. Some of the questions can be answered without first reading the accompanying paragraphs (e.g., "A farm cost more: a. when John got his, b. now"). Furthermore, some of the questions are not answered in the reading selections and cannot be answered correctly through inference alone. In some cases, several of the alternatives given as answers to the multiple choice questions are correct.

In the word analysis section, as few as five tasks are required of the examinee to assess a given skill. In identifying "vowel blends," for example, the examinee hears five words and must write the vowels he hears in "foil, loud, moon, took, plow." Other subtests are nearly as brief. The limited sample of behavior thus gathered is hardly sufficient to draw conclusions regarding a child's instructional needs. Furthermore, the word analysis test randomly mixes reading tasks with auditory and visual discrimination tasks as well as speech tasks, thus yielding various kinds of information, not all of which bear directly on word analysis.

Another area of concern is the format of the test. Pages in the test booklet are cramped, lacking sufficient margins and clear headings. Sketches are scattered throughout the test booklet in an apparent effort to decorate the pages. These drawings may confuse and will certainly distract some children. Since no task in the test relates to the illustrations, their presence seems unnecessary.

With regard to scoring the test, several problems arise. The scoring system for recording oral reading errors is incomplete; no provision is made for omissions, for example. While the manual suggests that some errors are more significant for instructional purposes than others, no explanation is provided to help the teacher apply and interpret this point of view. In the word analysis section, sounds are isolated by the examiner and the examinee is also required to isolate sounds in responding to certain items. This approach ignores the fact that our language contains no isolated sounds and that distortion occurs when sounds are isolated.

While no norms are provided with the test, two graphs, one for oral reading and one for summarizing all 20 scores obtained from the test, are provided with each test booklet. By completing the graphs, one develops an individual profile supposedly highlighting the child's individual strengths and weaknesses. It is unclear from the instructions provided just how the scores from each subtest are entered on the graphs. Nor does the manual describe how the information revealed by the graphs should be interpreted or translated into an instructional program.

In summary, the *Test of Individual Needs*

in Reading attempts to encompass too much. It lacks clear instructions for administration and is not supported by either validity or reliability data. It is not recommended by this reviewer for general use.

GEORGE D. SPACHE, *Professor Emeritus, University of Florida, Gainesville, Florida.*

The author's intent is to offer an instrument that combines (a) the strengths but not the limitations of an oral reading inventory, (b) a silent reading comprehension test, and (c) a word analysis test. He intends that the test could be used by either the classroom teacher or the reading specialist prior to decisions regarding instructional materials primarily in the first six grades.

The instrument provides for a pupil or a group to read silently as many as possible of a series of passages, answering five questions on each. After silent reading, the pupil's answers are scored, with credit given for all correct answers. Then or at a subsequent session the pupil is asked to read the same selections orally, beginning at a point two steps or grade levels below his first error in silent comprehension. Following this testing or at a later time, the word analysis tests are administered individually to each pupil.

Although his directions are difficult to follow because they are scattered through the manual and the child's test booklet, the author does outline several ingenious ways of using the instrument as an individual or group test. For example, pupils could be tested first as a group in silent comprehension and then in oral reading, as described above. Or, while a small group is reading silently, each may be called to read to the teacher orally. Or, if two teachers are available for the testing, pupils may first read orally to one, and then be sent to the other to finish with silent reading. When only one child is to be tested, he will read the passages orally and answer the questions as the teacher reads them to him, the silent comprehension measure being omitted.

These various testing arrangements raise some questions in this reviewer's mind regarding their equivalence and validity. Is it true, as Gilliland assumes, that comprehension level is the same in silent and oral reading? Or is it not more accurate to say that oral and silent comprehension vary with content, the reader's age and previous training, and his purpose for reading? When the child reads the same passages first silently and then orally, is his oral reading representative of his usual oral reading performance? Or is it not more likely to be better than usual? In this same sequence of silent-oral reading, how does the teacher estimate the pupil's oral reading comprehension?

The group administration of the silent reading test instructs pupils to read "as much as you can." How does the teacher know whether the pupil ceased trying before reaching his maximum level of comprehension; stopped at that point; or continued to answer questions by sheer guess, inference, or by the background information he gained in the earlier paragraphs of this continuous narrative material?

Silent reading speed is also measured, but usually only in the third to fifth grade selections, and then by averaging the pupil's elapsed time on the four selections involved (or on as many of them as he has read). If the child doesn't reach this level, then his silent reading speed is determined by averaging elapsed time on those passages which he read "with less than five errors." Do we then disregard his silent comprehension performance in judging his silent reading rate? How can a rate measure based on reading passages too easy, at grade level, and above grade level be meaningful? How can such a rate measure be compared with other common measures of rate of reading?

The oral reading testing permits a child to read until he fails to recognize five or more words in a selection. Was this standard derived from actual performances of pupils reading passages at their functional levels? Or, as in the common oral reading inventory that the author decries, did he establish an a priori standard, which may be unrelated to the functional level of the child as measured by actual comprehension? In effect, the child is assigned to a basal reader on the basis of his oral performances in easy, average, and difficult passages. Is there any evidence of the validity of such an estimate? Or is it not more true that the type and number of oral errors and their effect upon comprehension vary at different levels of difficulty?

Presumably the child's comprehension has also been evaluated either by prior administration of the group silent test or by asking him the questions as he reads orally. But this comprehension estimate does not influence his assignment to instructional materials, according to the author, since such assignment is determined only by oral reading errors. Does this mean that we choose basal reading levels for children by oral reading errors, as judged by an artificial standard, regardless of the pupil's comprehension level? What do we do when he can read materials silently with adequate comprehension at several grade levels above that indicated by the oral reading errors? Pupils who have really learned to read silently at rates far above their own speech rates are obviously no longer reading verbatim, as expected of them in the oral reading act. If they transfer their rapid reading for ideas from the silent act to their oral reading performance, are they to be penalized by being assigned to a lower level basal? Or, to what reading level do we assign an excellent word caller who reads faultlessly orally at levels far above his ability to comprehend?

By assigning labels to the five questions appended to each reading passage, the author claims to differentiate the reader's skills in recognizing main ideas, verbal memory (a completion item), vocabulary, comprehension (then what are the others measuring?), and inference. Presumably a concentration of errors in one of these types of questions implies a specific comprehension weakness, although the author gives no data on the number of attempts or errors a reader must make before the comparison begins to be meaningful or reliable.

The final section of the *Test of Individual Needs in Reading* attempts to cover word analysis skills. Sixteen phonic and syllabication skills, including reversals and the use of context clues, are included. About 5–10 items comprise each separate test, thus providing a sample of the skill rather than a thorough evaluation. But the norms for many of these indicate that 80–90 percent of the items can be completed by pupils of fourth grade or below. It is true, of course, that some phonic skills should certainly be mastered before this point, such as consonant sounds and blends, vowel sounds, and consonant substitution. But how do we reconcile the fact that 80 percent of the subtest on use of context clues is reached by mid-first grade, while blending letter sounds reaches only a 50 percent level by the fourth grade? There are similar inexplicable variations in the standards for these subtests of word analysis skills. Perhaps part of the explanation is found in the unusual demands or format of some of the tests.

Test of Individual Needs in Reading

Beginning consonant sounds and vowel blends are measured by having the child write the letter or blend in words pronounced to him, while ending consonants are tested by visual matching of final letters in printed words, a much simpler task. Initial consonant substitution is also assayed in the roundabout fashion of having the child read 10 words, each of which varies in initial letter from a word in a preceding list of 10 words. If he can read the second list, it is assumed (not that the words were in his sight vocabulary, as they might well be) that the child was able to generalize from the first list. The subtest of blending letters to form words demands recognition of the phonic principles inherent in a closed syllable, a double vowel, an open syllable, and the final silent e. All in 10 words?

In some ways, the *Test of Individual Needs in Reading* represents an improvement on the naive informal reading inventory, even though it employs some of the same arbitrary and dubious standards. But, as our analysis indicates, it needs considerable refinement in format, content, clarity of directions, and testing sequences. Evidence of construct validity in comparison with other tests, reliability of each portion, and demonstration of the content validity of a continuous narrative of semihistorical material—all these must be clarified.

[Other Tests]

For other tests new or revised since *The Sixth Mental Measurements Yearbook,* see the following in *Reading Tests and Reviews:*

121. *Diagnostic Reading Tests
122. *Doren Diagnostic Reading Test of Word Recognition Skills
128. *OC Diagnostic Syllabizing Test
129. ★Ohio Diagnostic Reading Test
132. *Primary Reading Profiles
133. ★Reading Skills Diagnostic Test

MISCELLANEOUS

[727]

*Botel Reading Inventory. Grades 1–4, 1–6, 1–12; 1961–70; BRI; 4 tests; 9 scores: a frustrational, an instructional (placement), and a free reading grade score for each of tests *a, b,* and *d;* revised manual ('70, 32 pages); no norms; the placement scores for which alternate-form reliabilities are reported are not identified as to whether for tests *a, b,* or *d;* $3 per set of materials needed by the examiner; postage extra; Morton Botel; Follett Educational Corporation. *
a) WORD RECOGNITION TEST. Grades 1–4; 1961–70; oral reading fluency; individual; 8 "graded" 20-word lists described as samples of reading materials at 8 grade levels (PP, P, 1–2, 2–1, 2–2, 3–1, 3–2, 4+); 3 grade

scores: frustration level (0–65%), instructional level (70–90%), free reading level (95–100%); scoring sheets for Forms A ('61, 4 pages), B ('66, 4 pages); $1.50 per 35 scoring sheets; [4–12] minutes.
b) WORD OPPOSITES TEST. Grades 1–12; 1961–70; a vocabulary test described as "an estimate of reading comprehension"; 10 "graded" 10-word lists described as samples of reading materials at 10 grade levels (1, 2–1, 2–2, 3–1, 3–2, 4, 5, 6, 7–8, 9–12); 3 grade scores: frustration level (0–60%), instructional level (70–80%), free reading level (90–100%); the author states that the test may be used in grades 3–12 as a listening test to determine "reading potential"; Forms A ('70, 4 pages), B ('66, 4 pages); $1.50 per 35 tests; administration time not reported.
c) PHONICS MASTERY TEST. Grades 1–4; 1961–70; "knowledge of key word perception skills"; 3 levels of phonic skills, each level to be mastered 100% before going on to the next; Forms A ('61, 4 pages), B ('66, 4 pages); no data on reliability; answer sheet ('61, 4 pages); $1.50 per 35 answer sheets; (15–25) minutes.
d) SPELLING PLACEMENT TEST. Grades 1–6; 1970; 5 "graded" 20-word lists described as samples from the author's *Spelling and Writing Patterns* at 5 grade levels (1–2, 3, 4, 5, 6); 3 grade scores: frustration level (0–80%), instructional level (85–90%), independent level (95–100%); word lists presented in the manual; no data on reliability; [5–10] minutes.

REFERENCES

1. DAVIS, M. CATHERINE ELIZABETH. *The Relative Effectiveness of Certain Evaluative Criteria for Determining Reading Levels.* Doctor's thesis, Temple University (Philadelphia, Pa.), 1964. (*DA* 25:3967)
2. TRELA, THADDEUS M. "What Do Diagnostic Reading Tests Diagnose?" *El Engl* 43:370–2 Ap '66. *
3. BOTEL, MORTON. "A Comparative Study of the Validity of the Botel Reading Inventory and Selected Standardized Tests." *Proc Ann Conv Int Read Assn* 13(1):721–7 '69. *
4. BOTEL, MORTON; BRADLEY, JOHN; AND KASHUBA, MICHAEL. "The Validity of Informal Reading Testing," pp. 85–103. In *Reading Difficulties: Diagnosis, Correction, and Remediation.* Edited by William K. Durr. Newark, Del.: International Reading Association, 1970. Pp. vii, 276. *
5. McCRACKEN, ROBERT A., AND MULLEN, NEILL D. "The Validity of Certain Measures in an I.R.I.," pp. 104–10. In *Reading Difficulties: Diagnosis, Correction, and Remediation.* Edited by William K. Durr. Newark, Del.: International Reading Association, 1970. Pp. vii, 276. *

For reviews by Ira E. Aaron and Charles M. Brown, see 6:834.

[728]

★Durrell Listening-Reading Series. Grades 1–2, 3–6, 7–9; 1969–70; DLRS; 9 scores: listening (vocabulary, sentences or paragraphs, total—these scores are referred to as "potential reading grade equivalents"), reading (vocabulary, sentences or paragraphs, total—these scores are referred to as "actual reading grade equivalents"), potential minus actual reading grade equivalents (vocabulary, sentences or paragraphs, total—these scores are referred to as "differential" scores); 2 forms; 3 levels; no norms for differential scores of individual pupils; no data on validity of differential scores; $1.25 per specimen set of any one level; postage extra; Donald D. Durrell, Mary T. Hayes (*a*), and Mary B. Brassard (*b*); Harcourt Brace Jovanovich, Inc. *
a) PRIMARY LEVEL. Grades 1–2; 2 editions; Forms DE ('69, 16 pages), EF ('70, 16 pages); manual for each form (dates same as for tests, 26 pages); 140(180) minutes in 2 sessions, 2–7 days apart.
  1) *Hand Scorable Edition.* $9 per 35 tests; 30¢ per key.
  2) *MRC Machine Scorable Edition.* $10.50 per 35 tests; scoring service, 55¢ and over per test.

Durrell Listening-Reading Series

b) INTERMEDIATE LEVEL. Grades 3-6; 2 editions; manual for each edition and for each form (dates same as for tests, 29 pages); 170(195) minutes in 2 sessions, 2-7 days apart.

1) *Hand Scorable Edition.* Forms DE ('69, 24 pages), EF ('70, 24 pages); $11.70 per 35 tests; 30¢ per key.

2) *Machine Scorable Edition.* Forms DE ('69, 4 page test-answer folder and 8 page test), EF ('70, 4 page test-answer folder and 8 page test); supplementary directions sheet for each type of test-answer folder; separate answer folders (Digitek, IBM 805, IBM 1230, MRC) must be used; $6.60 per 35 tests; $8.50 per 35 Digitek test-answer folders; $4.40 per 35 IBM 805 test-answer folders; $7 per 35 IBM 1230 test-answer folders; $15 per 100 MRC test-answer folders; $2.10 per set of Digitek scoring stencils; $2.80 per set of IBM scoring stencils; $1 per set of MRC scoring stencils; MRC scoring service, 46¢ and over per test.

c) ADVANCED LEVEL. Grades 7-9; Forms DE ('69, 15 pages), EF ('70, 15 pages); manual for each form (dates same as for tests, 27 pages); supplementary directions sheet for each type of answer folder; $9 per 35 tests; $1 per key; separate answer folders (Digitek, IBM 805, IBM 1230, MRC) may be used; $8.50 per 35 Digitek answer folders; $4.40 per 35 IBM 805 answer folders; $7 per 35 IBM 1230 answer folders; $10 per 100 MRC answer sheets; $2.80 per set of Digitek or IBM scoring stencils; $1 per set of MRC scoring stencils; MRC scoring service, 37¢ and over per test; 160(190) minutes in 2 sessions, 2-7 days apart.

REFERENCES

1. HAYES, MARY THERESE. *Construction and Evaluation of Comparable Measures of English Language Comprehension in Reading and in Listening.* Doctor's thesis, Boston University (Boston, Mass.), 1957. (*DA* 18:1721)
2. BRASSARD, MARY B. *Listening and Reading Comprehension in Intermediate Grades.* Doctor's thesis, Boston University (Boston, Mass.), 1968.
3. DURRELL, DONALD D. "Listening Comprehension Versus Reading Comprehension." *J Read* 12(6):455-60 Mr '69. * (*PA* 43:12784)

JOHN R. BORMUTH, *Associate Professor of Education, The University of Chicago, Chicago, Illinois.*[1]

The tests in the *Durrell Listening-Reading Series* were designed to measure a student's abilities to understand both spoken and written language for the purpose of comparing the two abilities. The publishers claim (albeit with a certain amount of inconsistency, as discussed below) that a measure of a student's language listening ability provides the test user with an estimate of the student's *potential* level of achievement in reading and that by comparing the listening and reading scores the test user can estimate the degree of retardation in reading.

The series contains at each level parallel listening and reading tests that are carefully matched for content, difficulty, and (as far as seemed reasonably possible) type of item and administration procedures. Both the listening

1 The reviewer wishes to acknowledge with thanks the assistance of Mr. Robert M. Bortnick in the preparation of this review.

and the reading tests contain vocabulary and comprehension subtests, each of which is accompanied by separate norms and by a table comparing scores on the listening and reading tests. The norms are expressed in terms of grade placement, stanine, and percentile scores. The publishers have worked out an ingenious way to set up the Primary level for MRC machine scoring in a manner that primary grade children should be able to handle without any special instruction.

The content validity of the *Durrell Listening-Reading Series* is outstanding among standardized vocabulary and comprehension tests. A vocabulary or comprehension test is of little use if it merely ranks students according to their abilities to cope with some nebulous segment of the language. The Durrell tests derive their utility only from the fact that a test user can presumably interpret scores on them as representing an unbiased estimate of the student's ability to cope with a segment of the language that is both explicitly identified and worth being able to deal with. According to the test manual, the designers of the Durrell tests went to unusual lengths in an effort to identify a significant segment of language to be represented in the tests. The words included in the vocabulary subtests, for example, were selected both to be representative of the semantic categories employed in *Roget's Thesaurus,* in an effort to insure that a breadth of semantic content would be tested, and also to be representative of words appearing in frequency counts of words in instructional materials, children's writings, and general adult reading materials. Unfortunately, the test designers did not use a perfectly random procedure for selecting words, and they subsequently discarded words because they were too hard or too easy for many of the students in the grade levels being tested, thereby biasing the sample of words tested in unknown ways and making it less justifiable to interpret the scores as representative of a student's ability to cope with the vocabulary in instructional language. Nevertheless, this interpretation seems more nearly justified with the vocabulary subtests in this series than with most other standardized reading and listening vocabulary tests known to the reviewer.

The test manual describes a similar effort to select for the comprehension subtests sentences and paragraphs representative of the language used in instruction. The test designers attempted to control content for subject matter, discourse patterning, and a number of other variables that seem to determine the comprehension skills a passage requires. However, it is impossible to make strong claims that the language used in the comprehension subtests is actually representative of the language found in instruction, first, because our knowledge of readability remains too limited to permit us to identify all of the variables that must be controlled and, second, because the language sample was again biased in some unknown way by the fact that materials were discarded from the tests when they were considered to be too easy or too hard for many of the students in the grade range being tested. But even so, a test user may interpret a student's score on one of these subtests as representative of his ability to cope with the language in instruction with more justification than he can with the comprehension subtests of most other standardized achievement tests known to the reviewer.

The validity of the vocabulary subtests may also be somewhat impaired by the types of test items used to measure vocabulary skills. The student is given a word orally or in printed form and then is asked to choose from among response alternatives the response bearing a synonymity or association relationship of some sort to the stimulus word. Three, four, and five response alternatives are provided at the Primary, Intermediate, and Advanced levels of the test, respectively. The first validity problem arises from the fact that the items are grouped into sets of from 10 to 32 items, with all stimulus words in a set having to be matched with the same group of alternative responses. Now, in a conventional format, a single vocabulary item tests a student's simultaneous knowledge of two concepts, the stimulus word and the response word, and ordinarily a given pair member is tested no more than once. The practice of using the same alternatives for an entire set of stimulus words reduces the number of concepts tested and thereby reduces the amount of information contained in the student's score. Also, if the student should fail to understand one or more of the response alternatives, this failure will influence his performance on all items in a set and possibly bias the scores unduly.

Another major problem seems to impair the validity of the comparison between a student's listening and reading vocabulary scores, but at the Advanced level only. On the listening vocabulary subtest at the Primary and Intermediate levels the response alternatives are given in the form of a word or phrase printed below a picture illustrating the concept named by that alternative. Undoubtedly, the picture reinforces the concept represented by that alternative and thereby helps the student to remember the alternative even if he cannot read the printed form or memorize it as the teacher reads it while giving instructions for that set of items. Hence, it seems unlikely that an illiterate student would be greatly penalized on these items by his inability to read the response alternatives. However, at the Advanced level the pictures are omitted, thereby forcing a student either to memorize the alternatives as the teacher reads them or to reread the alternatives when he forgets them. These items would seemingly discriminate unjustifiably against the student who has severe reading difficulties but who knows the meanings of the words. They force him to memorize five word-letter associations from a single presentation and to retain them as he is answering 20 or more items, while a person who reads well may refer back to the alternatives as often as he likes. What makes this a serious problem is that the test manual advocates that the listening scores be used as an estimate of a student's learning potential in reading. Thus, the test at the Advanced level is likely to underestimate a poor reader's potential regardless of what his actual potential might be, thereby limiting the usefulness of the tests for what the manual describes as one of their principal purposes.

In the tradition and folklore of reading instruction, a student's ability to comprehend spoken language is regarded as an estimate of the upper limit of his capacity to learn reading comprehension skills. The publishers of these tests provide instruments especially designed to make such comparisons and in the opening statements in the manual specifically advocate this interpretation of the differences between the reading and listening test scores. Curiously, though, the research reported in the manual contradicts the premises on which this practice is based, and the authors deny the validity of the traditional practice in some of their other statements. The manual presents the results of a study in which the tests were administered to students and their reading grade equivalent scores were subtracted from their *potential grade equivalent* scores (the latter scores being

Durrell Listening-Reading Series

obtained by entering the norm table calculated for listening test administered as a reading test) and these difference scores were plotted as a function of the students' grade levels. As the students reached the higher grades and presumably increased in reading ability, their vocabulary reading scores did, in fact, gradually rise toward their vocabulary listening scores, as one would expect from traditional reading theory. However, their sentence and paragraph reading scores rose much more rapidly, equalling their sentence and paragraph listening scores by grade 6 and greatly exceeding them by grade 9, showing rather decisively that listening comprehension does not represent the upper limits of a person's ability to acquire reading comprehension skills. The test manual deals with this contradiction of traditional reading theory and of its own recommendations by suggesting somewhat illogically that a student's reading and listening scores may each be used as an estimate of his capacity to learn the other. This reviewer prefers the alternative interpretation that although reading and listening abilities share some elements in common, they exhibit substantial differences, and that we can no longer use listening abilities to estimate reading aptitude in the simple fashion we heretofore thought possible. In any case, the test user should be cautioned in his attempts to interpret these difference scores. Since the manual does not report the standard error of these difference scores, he has no convenient way to determine if a given difference score is merely a chance phenomenon that would disappear if the student were tested again.

In summary, then, this reviewer believes that these reading and listening tests represent unusually sophisticated work in the selection of test content and that in this respect they present a model for emulation by other test makers. However, the tests lose some of their value because of the designs of the test items. Finally, the test manual itself presents evidence that these tests may not be validly used for the major purpose for which they were designed— "to identify pupils with reading disability, and to measure the degree of retardation in reading as compared to listening." But the reviewer believes that each of the reading and listening tests is useful in its own right and compares very favorably with other available tests of reading and listening abilities.

GEORGE D. SPACHE, *Professor Emeritus, University of Florida, Gainesville, Florida.*

"The *Durrell Listening-Reading Series* is designed to provide a comparison of children's reading and listening abilities." By this comparison, the authors hope "to identify children with reading disability, and to measure the degree of retardation in reading as compared with listening." The series consists of parallel tests of listening and reading comprehension of words, sentences, or paragraphs. The primary level test samples listening vocabulary and sentence listening by having the child assign the word or sentence read to him to one of three given categories. Thus, a word may refer to "part of a house," or "time," or "fanciful people," or the like, while a sentence may refer to something "in space," "imaginary," or "inside the earth." The parallel vocabulary and sentence reading tests at this level require the child to read a word or sentence and then categorize it in the same manner as in the listening tests. At the Intermediate level, the listening vocabulary test becomes one of matching a given word to one of four categories. The paragraph listening test offers selections of contrasting statements which refer to a story the child has just heard. To respond, the child must indicate whether each of eight subsequent statements, emphasizing the contrasts made in the selection, is "True only of" (in reference to each of the subjects of the selection) or "True of both" or that "Answer is not given." The parallel reading tests at this level sample reading vocabulary and paragraph reading in the same format as used in the listening tests. At the Advanced level the format of the listening vocabulary test changes by dropping the pictures representing the categories and by requiring the task of matching a synonym, read to the pupil, to one of a group of five printed words. While these five printed words are read to the child once, there is the assumption that he thus learns them and can reread them to match each in meaning with one of the 20–32 test words pronounced to him. In this reviewer's opinion, this arrangement assumes that testees are quick learners or strong in immediate memory for what may be new vocabulary. At this Advanced level, two systems of responding to the paragraph listening test are required: indicating if a statement related to the selection is true, false, or not given; and, later, matching the relevance of a post-reading statement to one of the story characters by marking the initial of his last name, as D for Dee, J for Jay, or indicating that the statement was true for both characters or not given in the selection.

This series is the third version of parallel listening-reading tests offered by the senior author (*Durrell Analysis of Reading Difficulty*, 1933, and *Durrell-Sullivan Reading Capacity and Achievement Tests*, 1937, precede it) and it is undoubtedly the best, in this reviewer's opinion. Standardization is broader (over 20,-000 pupils); equating of the parallel tests at each level and item analysis to improve discrimination between grade levels were more carefully done; adequate reliability data and standard errors of measurement are now offered; and the reliabilities of the tests are probably now sufficient for the direct comparisons recommended. Content validity was insured by using representative word lists and by varying the types of words. Discrimination between grade levels as measured by number and difficulty of items appears good. All these efforts are distinct improvements upon the earlier versions of these comparative tests.

But construct validity, as measured by the readability levels of the selections or by other measures of the difficulty of the content, and concurrent validity, as determined by correlations with comparable tests, remain weak. We still do not know what is being measured, in terms of cognitive processes, in the listening tests, or whether these tests are a valid way of predicting reading potential. Nor do the authors bother to compare this technique of predicting potential with any of the other existing methods. Correlations with a reading readiness test at first grade and with the reading subtests of an achievement test are cited for the four parts of the Primary battery. Similar correlations are cited for the parts of the Intermediate battery with reading subtests of two achievement batteries. But these purported validity correlations support only the validity of the Durrell reading subtests and prove nothing about the basic rationale of these parallel tests.

The manual justifies the comparison between listening and reading scores as "the most satisfactory measure of 'potential' for reading," a fact not yet demonstrated by any research known to this reviewer. We are asked to accept the authors' assumption that a higher performance on the listening tests than on the reading indicates a potential capacity for functioning on the listening level in reading tasks. Or, conversely, we are to assume that a child functioning lower in reading than listening is a retarded reader and therefore that normal pupils tend to perform at the same levels in reading and listening. However, to cite only a single contradictory study, a large-scale research by Young [1] indicates that the average child can listen to and comprehend materials approximately two years above his own reading level. The authors of the DLRS further state that "a higher score in either of these abilities indicates a 'potential level' for the other." What, then, is the true meaning of the reading-listening comparison? Furthermore, the authors' tables in the various manuals indicate that differences commonly persist between reading and listening grade equivalents, from upper first grade to eighth grade. How, then, does the user interpret the difference between these test results in an individual case?

Other problems in interpretation of the test series are present but unanswered in the manuals, such as the known differences in reading scores according to sex, the role of intelligence in tests of listening, and the freedom of the listening tests from cultural influences or socioeconomic status of the testees. We still do not know whether this series can be used at face value with the culturally disadvantaged, the bilingual, the language-deprived or the intellectually dull, despite the authors' recommendations for such use.

Perhaps the best use of this latest version of parallel listening-reading tests would be as a research instrument to explore those questions for which the authors assume they have the answers. Extended use of the series might eventually serve to clarify the expectation of parallel listening and reading performances in normal and atypical or minority populations. As it is now, we have no real evidence to justify the basic assumptions made by the authors in preparing the series.

[729]
★**Dyslexia Schedule.** Children having reading difficulties and first grade entrants; 1968–69; DS; an 89-item questionnaire to be filled out by the child's parents with score based on 24 discriminating items; 21 of these 24 items are published separately under the title *School Entrance Check List* (SECL) for screening use; schedule ('68, 8 pages); checklist ('68, 4 pages); manual ('69, 32 pages); no norms; 1–24

1 YOUNG, WILLIAM E. "The Relation of Reading Comprehension and Retention to Hearing Comprehension and Retention." *J Exp Ed* 5:30–9 S '36. *

schedules, 20¢ each; 1–99 checklists, 10¢ each; $1 per manual; $1.25 per specimen set; [20–25] minutes for schedule, [10–15] minutes for checklist; John McLeod; Educators Publishing Service, Inc. *

REFERENCES

1. McLeod, John. "Psychological and Psycholinguistic Aspects of Severe Reading Disability in Children: Some Experimental Studies." *Ann Inter Conf Assn Children Learn Dis* 3:186–205 '66. *
2. McLeod, John. *Some Psychological and Psycholinguistic Aspects of Severe Reading Disability in Children.* Doctor's thesis, University of Queensland (Brisbane, Australia), 1966.
3. McLeod, John. "Symposium—Dyslexia: 5, Prediction of Childhood Dyslexia." *Slow Learning Child* 12:143–54 Mr '66. * (PA 40:10461)

Martin Kling, *Associate Professor of Education, Rutgers, The State University, New Brunswick, New Jersey.*

The *Dyslexia Schedule* is an 89-item questionnaire containing 24 items which were based on a literature review of 27 workers in the field who asserted that these kinds of items might be linked with dyslexia.

According to McLeod, "To demand that the correlates of dyslexia be unidimensional and invariant before the concept of childhood dyslexia be regarded as meaningful is unrealistic." Therefore, McLeod attempted to develop a heterogeneous group of items which he believed would reliably predict dyslexia.

By its derivation, the term "dyslexia" simply means disorder of reading. However, according to the Secretary's (HEW) National Advisory Committee on Dyslexia and Related Reading Disorders,[1] presently held views of dyslexia range from a rather stereotyped group of symptoms that are innate to a diversity of symptoms and functional disorders.

In view of such a wide range of opinion, the Committee concluded that the term "dyslexia" serves no useful purpose. In spite of the unsettled definitions of dyslexia, McLeod believes that the following types of items answered by the response "Yes" identify with great accuracy the dyslexic child: the youngster's vision and hearing are normal (items 24 and 27); the youngster was in the hospital before the age of 3 (33); the youngster was separated from one or both parents and seemed different after the separation (36); the youngster bed wets (42a), tells lies or fantasies (43b), fears the dark or nightmares (44c), as well as the making of mistakes (46e); apart from educational problems, the youngster manifests anxiety and/or depression (50); the youngster is now over-

1 *Reading Disorders in the United States: Report of the Secretary's (HEW) National Advisory Committee on Dyslexia and Related Reading Disorders.* Chicago, Ill.: Developmental Learning Materials, 1969. Pp. 63. *

active (66), was overactive in infancy (67), and was overactive before he was born (68); in language, the youngster first began to speak after 2.0 years (7), said two or more words after 2.5 years (71), is immature in speech, saying "fink" for "*think*" (72), mixes up the order of words "hopgrasser" for "grasshopper" (74), omits words by age 3.5 onwards (75), and continually asked the parent to repeat words when he was an infant (76); in addition, youngsters jumble or reverse letters (78), cannot remember short messages or telephone numbers (79), and have difficulty distinguishing right from left (87); finally, if any member of the family has experienced difficulty in reading, this also is an adverse response (88).

However, the items selected to discriminate dyslexics are inadequate on several counts: (*a*) The author's criterion of dyslexia is ill defined. There is no psychological, neurological, or any other objective assessment of dyslexia. (*b*) There is no adequate description of non-dyslexics. (*c*) Samples of dyslexics and non-dyslexics are small in number. It is difficult to see how one can generalize from the 20 youngsters in each group or from the population from which they came. The tryout group consisted of 20 remedial reading students between the ages 6-9 and 12-2, with an average of 9-4 at a Remedial Education Center of the University of Queensland, Australia. The second item revision was based on 23 children whose reading level was one year below the chronological age of grade 2 in the Brisbane Schools, Australia. (*d*) A cutoff score of six adverse responses is inappropriate without supplying frequency distributions as well as contingency tables to ascertain the probability of occurrence of chance answers. (*e*) Most of the adverse responses on the *Dyslexia Schedule* would also apply to disadvantaged youngsters, various ethnic groups, and the emotionally disturbed.

In summary, the reviewer sees no possible reason for the use of the *Dyslexia Schedule*.

[730]

★**Individual Reading Placement Inventory, Field Research Edition.** Youth and adults with reading levels up to grade 7; 1969; IRPI; 7 grade level scores; independent reading (words, paragraphs), instructional reading (words, paragraphs), frustration (words, paragraphs), present language potential; individual; Forms A, B, (8 pages); manual (16 pages); no data on reliability and validity of the 7 grade level scores; $3.60 per 20 tests; $4.50 per set of word recognition wheels, reading cards, and manual; $2.10 per sample set; postage extra; [10–35] minutes; Edwin H. Smith and Weldon G. Bradtmueller; Follett Educational Corporation. *

EDWARD B. FRY, *Professor of Education and Director, Reading Center, Rutgers, The State University, New Brunswick, New Jersey.*

The purpose of the *Individual Reading Placement Inventory* is to assess rapidly the reading ability of illiterate and semiliterate adults and youth. The inventory consists of five parts.

In Part 1, Word Recognition and Analysis, a word is exposed for one second and the student is asked to read it. If he can, he is scored correct under "flash" and if he cannot, he tries to read it a second time when he is allowed more time. If correct, the item is scored correct under "analysis." There are six groups of 20 words; one group for each grade level from 1.5 to 6.5. A pupil progresses through the word groups until he misses two words or more when flashed. This is called his "frustration" level; the group just below that, his instructional level; and the group below that, his independent level.

Part 2, Oral Paragraph Reading, consists of six paragraphs on cards, one each for grades 1 through 6, to be read aloud by the student while the examiner records types of errors (omissions, hesitations, etc.). The examiner then asks the student comprehension questions. The student is presented harder paragraphs until he misses 10 words or two comprehension questions. This is called his frustration level and the test is terminated. The level below his frustration level is his instructional level and the level below that his independent level, as in Part 1.

Part 3, Present Language Potential, is really a listening capacity test. The examiner goes back to the oral paragraph cards used in Part 2 and this time the examiner reads aloud the cards beginning where the student reached his frustration level and continues until the student cannot answer three out of the four questions by listening. The level just below where the student fails to answer three out of four questions is called his "present language potential."

Part 4, Auditory Discrimination, is not really a reading test either. The task is to have the examiner simply read aloud words like "harp, hard, yard, herd" and then ask the student which one begins with a different sound.

Part 5, Letters of the Alphabet, is used only if the student cannot score on Part 1, that is, he can read less than 90 percent of the words in

Group 1. The Letters of the Alphabet consists of the alphabet printed in upper and lower case letters. The student is asked the name of the letter and to give one sound that it makes.

The concept of "independent," "instructional," and "frustration" levels of reading comes from the work of Emmett Betts and represents those reading levels at which the student can read independently with little or no help with good comprehension; the level at which the student needs some help and can read with moderate comprehension; and the frustration level at which no type of reading should be assigned or good comprehension expected. The concept is clear but the evidence that it is valid is lacking. The paragraphs were selected by readability formulas and the words used in the paragraphs were checked against several graded word lists. This is secondhand validity evidence. Firsthand validity would consist of seeing if students reading at the independent level of third grade on this inventory are actually reading third grade material with good comprehension.

The authors state that the initial inventory was revised after it was administered to 410 students located in adult basic education classes in Florida, some southern junior and senior high schools, and a federal prison class. It is laudable that the authors are interested in working with this population, but it tells us nothing about the standardization group for this test. Presumably, there is none, and the user must be satisfied with the validity by way of readability formula and word selection.

The test directions lack exactness; for example, "Many disadvantaged youths and adults consistently drop word endings (s, es, ed, ies, ing) and yet retain meaning. In cases like these, ignore the number of errors of this type and use comprehension as the final criterion for deciding instructional level." However, this inexactness probably contributes to the test's usefulness with special populations.

Hence, if the user wants a test with numerical scores and good validity and standardization, he had best seek elsewhere. But if the user is interested in working individually with disadvantaged adults or youth and in attempting to find out where to begin reading instruction, this inventory could be a definite aid. Oral reading paragraphs and the oral reading of word lists have long been a mainstay diagnostic tool of remedial teachers. The listening sections of this inventory might not find such ready acceptance, but even the authors (judging by the space given them in the manual) probably consider them of minor importance.

ALBERT J. KINGSTON, *Professor of Educational Psychology, The University of Georgia, Athens, Georgia.*

This individually administered test is reminiscent of several older tests developed for appraising the reading skills of elementary school children. Presumably, this inventory, developed for use with older youth and adults, contains materials deemed more suitable than those of previously published instruments. The test consists largely of oral tasks and the examiner records the examinee's answers in a record booklet. The scores attained are said to enable the teacher to determine an individual's independent, instructional and frustration reading levels, as well as his "present language potential" as measured by a listening comprehension check. In addition, the inventory furnishes clues about the student's weaknesses in word recognition. This information is valuable in helping a teacher to match students with methods and materials.

The inventory has five subtests. Part 1 appraises word recognition and analysis. Six lists of 20 words each are arranged according to reading level. These words are printed on specially designed word wheels on which a word is flashed at the student for about one second. The examiner later allows the student to study the word at more leisure to determine whether he can recognize the word by analyzing it. This method of testing sight vocabulary and word analysis has been used successfully for many years. Inexperienced teachers, however, will need practice in order to familiarize themselves with the manipulation of word wheels and the system of notation.

Part 2 is an oral reading test, consisting of six selections. As the examinee reads the chosen selection aloud, the examiner records the performance in the test booklet. The system of notation is a traditional one and experienced reading teachers should have no difficulty with this section of the inventory. Inexperienced teachers, however, will need considerable practice before they can reliably record the student's oral reading ability. The materials utilized in this subtest are durable and well designed. Students read from cards slightly larger than 5 by 8

inches. Print is clear, large, and highly legible. Four comprehension questions are provided for each selection. These tend to elicit knowledge about factual details presented in the passages.

Part 3, Present Language Potential, uses the materials employed in Part 2. The examiner reads the next highest paragraph above the student's frustration level, i.e., the paragraph in which the examinee made 10 or more errors. In this test, however, the examiner reads the passage aloud and asks the examinee to answer the four questions. This test is similar to the widely used listening or auditory comprehension tests. The theory is that listening tests measure a subject's language capabilities and furnish some evidence concerning the degree of improvement which can be expected to result from remedial work.

Part 4, Auditory Discrimination, also represents a conventional approach to assessing an individual's ability to differentiate sounds. Five subtests appraise the student's ability to hear initial consonants, short and long vowel sounds, word endings, and initial blends and digraphs. These tests are read aloud by the examiner and the subject's responses are recorded in the booklet.

Part 5 is designed for use only with those individuals who scored at the lowest level on Part 1. It merely provides a rapid check of the individual's ability to recognize, name and give the sounds for the letters of the alphabet.

The inventory provides a basis for analyzing the reading difficulties of adolescents and adults who read at the sixth grade level or below. The authors have not blazed new and difficult trails in reading assessment. Rather they have relied on more traditional methods of appraisal. They have developed an instrument which appears to have face validity and which should be of value to those who work with nonacademically oriented youth and adults. A major problem of teachers in basic literacy courses has been the tests and instructional materials suitable for these populations. This instrument is likely to offer real help. The format of the test is attractive and easily followed. The equipment provided is sturdy, attractive, and durable.

Additional information concerning the reliability and validity of the subtests should be provided. Intercorrelations among the parts of the inventory would be edifying. The manual does not provide sufficient information to assure that teachers with limited experience can administer, score, and interpret the test results correctly. An example is the helpful checklist of reading difficulties found on the cover of the booklet. The manual suggests that the checklist be used to help summarize the problems found. No suggestions are offered, however, to help the teacher distinguish those which may be symptomatic of serious difficulties from those more susceptible to improvement. Despite these minor shortcomings, however, the inventory should prove to be extremely helpful to teachers of adults and disenchanted youth.

[731]

★National Teacher Examinations: Reading Specialist—Elementary School. College seniors and teachers; 1969-70; Forms RNT1, RNT2, ('69, 20 pages), SNT1 ('70, 20 pages), SNT2 ('70, 19 pages); descriptive booklet ('70, 10 pages); for more complete information, see 582; 120(165) minutes; Educational Testing Service. *

For reviews of the testing program, see 582 (2 reviews), 6:700 (1 review), 5:538 (3 reviews), and 4:802 (1 review).

[732]

★Pre-Reading Screening Procedures. First grade entrants of average or superior intelligence; 1968-69; PSP; 7 scores: visual discrimination (letter forms, word forms), visual perception memory (recognition, recall), copying, auditory discrimination, letter knowledge; 1 form ('68, 10 pages); observation and summary folder ('68, 4 pages); test cards ['69, 18 cards]; manual ('69, 47 pages); no data on reliability and validity; no description of normative population; $2.40 per 12 tests; $2 per set of cards; $1 per manual; $1.25 per specimen set (without cards); postage extra; [40] minutes; Beth H. Slingerland; Educators Publishing Service, Inc. *

REFERENCE

1. SLINGERLAND, BETH H. "Early Identification of Preschool Children Who Might Fail." *Acad Ther* 4(4):245-52 su '69. * (PA 43:17998)

COLLEEN B. JAMISON, *Associate Professor of Education, California State College, Los Angeles, California.*

The PSP was prepared for children at the end of kindergarten or beginning of first grade prior to reading instruction. Its purpose is to find children "who make errors in perception and recall of language symbols" and to "identify [their] academic needs."

The manual recommends the use of the PSP in conjunction with the *Metropolitan Readiness Tests* and the *Pintner-Cunningham Primary Test.* These two tests correlate between .60 and .70; intelligence and readiness tests tend to measure the same abilities at pre-reading levels. No information is given regarding the correlation between the PSP and the other two tests. The reason for administering the three tests is to identify pupils whose PSP scores are much lower than their readiness and intelligence scores. This will likely be a very small number of pupils, since the tasks on the three tests are similar. It would seem more appropriate for the teacher to identify pupils, possibly with the use of a test, for whom he needs additional information. None of the three tests provides enough diagnostic information to assist the teacher; thus, administering all three to every pupil seems wasteful.

Ratings are assigned to each of the seven subtests. The ratings "were worked out from test results of approximately 400 children." No information is given on the procedure used for determining ratings, no information is given on chronological age or grade level, nor are any data on reliability or validity provided.

Specific Language Disability (SLD) is discussed as a special condition to be uncovered. The manual indicates that the search for SLD must be exhaustive because it can be discovered even though teacher reports, parent reports, intelligence, and readiness appear to be normal. The manual contains many statements regarding the consideration of teacher and parent reports and how the child responds, but no direction is given for relating this information, suggesting what to look for, or estimating the magnitude of response necessary for significance. According to the manual, once the condition is identified, the child should be placed into a preventive instruction program; identification must not be delayed until the child has failed. In order to be safe, evidently, all children should follow the instructional procedures recommended by the author.

An example of the impressionistic nature of the diagnosis suggested is the following statement: "Persistant [*sic*] errors of a particular type sometimes tell us a great deal about the child's problem." Some types of errors are listed, but no definition of persistency is given, nor is an indication of what we may be told about which problem.

The instructions require the child to make a diagonal line through the correct answer and to place brackets around a mistake. Some children will have difficulty understanding brackets even after lengthy explanations. The pupil who later decides his first "mistake" is right will really have a problem marking the item.

Tests 1 and 2 assess visual discrimination.

Similar tasks appear on many readiness tests. Tests 3 and 5 assess visual memory. Test 3 is multiple choice, with the child marking the figure or letters identical to the stimulus shown by the examiner. On Test 5 the child reproduces the figure shown. Both tests involve a time lapse between exposure and response; 6 seconds for fewer than 12 children, and 10 seconds for a larger group. Since the time lapse is thus not uniform, results are not comparable. It takes about ten seconds after the time lapse to read the remaining directions, doubling the time between exposure and response. To insure the time lapse, children are to put their pencils on the floor, put hands on head during exposure, then pick up pencils and listen to directions and respond. The confusion of children all getting pencils from the floor and listening to directions would surely affect their memory of the stimulus figure.

Test 4 is a copying task. The use of brackets seems particularly inappropriate for this test since children might not be able to draw a whole figure correctly but could correct mistakes on a figure. The drawings are correct or incorrect, but there are not nearly enough examples given for reliable scoring, and the explanatory criteria are incomplete.

On Test 6 three words are said and the child is to indicate whether they are the same or different: "//" means the same and "XX" means different. If the child uses only one symbol, or confuses the symbols, his answers are wrong, "for he has not followed directions." Marking items wrong for not following directions might place a child in a Specific Language Disability program regardless of his auditory discrimination. To keep his place, the child is to find "the little black boxes," "long black boxes," etc. It would be less confusing if different objects, or even numbers, were used.

Test 7 assesses knowledge of the names of letters, a factor which has been found to correlate highly with reading achievement.

The Echolalia Test and Reproducing a Story are to be given to children who exhibit auditory or conceptual problems. The administration seems unnecessary if the pupils have already been so identified.

Keys are given only for Tests 6 and 7, and they are on different pages. Scoring, therefore, would be difficult until enough tests had been marked for the correct answers to have been memorized.

The Teacher Observation Sheet does not involve rating or ranking, and no comparison is made with norms or with other first graders. Brief comments, rather than checks or one-word answers, are encouraged, yet 27 of the 33 questions can be answered by "yes" or "no." The first question, for example, is, "Does child listen?"

There is no evidence for the validity of the test, yet recommendations for the author's instructional procedures are offered throughout the manual. References to books written by the author may extend the usefulness of the test, but in order to serve as a diagnostic or evaluative tool, the test must be accompanied by information regarding reliability and validity.

Most of the subtests assess more than one characteristic, making judgment regarding the various abilities difficult and subjective. The scoring is highly subjective and not necessarily based on the variable under consideration.

There are many readiness and intelligence tests available for pre-readers, and one with more complete information should be used.

ROY A. KRESS, *Professor of Psychology and Educational Psychology, Temple University, Philadelphia, Pennsylvania.*

This test is designed primarily for the identification of those children at the beginning school age who may show indications of "Specific Language Disabilities." Planned for group administration in groups of 20 or fewer children, it consists of the seven subtests listed in the above entry. Individual auditory testing using two separate subtests, Echolalia Test and Reproducing A Story, is also suggested.

The author recommends that the *Pre-Reading Screening Procedures* should be used in conjunction with the *Pintner-Cunningham Primary Test* and the *Metropolitan Readiness Tests.* Thus, the Summary Sheet also provides ratings in terms of raw score performances for subtests 5, 6, and 7 of the former and subtests 1–6 of the latter. Finally, the child's total performance on each of these three test batteries is evaluated by identifying specific "areas of difficulty" (Visual, Visual-Motor, Auditory, Letter Knowledge, Individual Auditory Tests) and conclusions reached in relation to five stages of readiness or courses of action: (*a*) "Ready for regular classroom beginning," (*b*) "Ready for a slower classroom beginning," (*c*) "Specific Language Disability preventive beginning," (*d*) "Delay conventional beginning to allow time for maturational and language development," and (*e*) "Recommend further individual testing or referral for medical advice."

The materials are well organized, the directions for administration are clear and concise, and the test booklets to be used by the children are planned to accommodate those who are left-handed as well as those who are right-handed. The manual contains a brief discussion of the many aspects of pupil behavior about which teachers should be concerned and which they should be observing and recording. There are suggestions for taking a family history and a very brief analysis of the types of errors a child may make in responding to the various subtests.

As a total testing package, the *Pre-Reading Screening Procedures* with the *Metropolitan Readiness Tests* and the *Pintner-Cunningham Primary Test* would seem to have considerable merit. However, used as a single test battery without supportive information gained from other testing procedures and informal classroom observation, the PSP would require extreme caution in interpreting a child's performance and relating it to specific class placement or to recommended courses of action. The tests are, primarily, only measures of the child's ability to perceive, recall, and reproduce a stimulus. In certain subtests the response is immediate; others ask for delayed recall or reproduction after a few seconds of time. In many instances the stimuli involve letters or words presented in reversed or inverted fashion in an attempt to measure the extent to which the child may be confused about those letters frequently appearing in a "reversal" syndrome or about directional attack in reading. The preponderance of these throughout the test suggests a greater concern with directional attack and orientation than seems justified by the negative results reported in most of the research on laterality and reading. This is especially true when one considers that the tests are designed for use with kindergarten and beginning first grade children.

Information obtained about children through the use of the *Pre-Reading Screening Procedures* merits consideration in making decisions about a child's immediate instructional needs in reading at the beginning school age. However, when used alone, the test certainly does not provide the kind of comprehensive information

needed to reach the definitive conclusions suggested by the "five stages of readiness" reported. Users will need to obtain much additional data about each child through the administration of other tests and the gathering of informal information before decisions can be made about placement and program.

[733]
★**The Reader's Inventory.** Entrants to a reading improvement course for secondary and college students and adults; 1963; information concerning a student's reading interests, attitudes, habits, visual conditions, educational and vocational background, and what he expects to gain from a reading course; 1 form (8 pages); manual (14 pages); no data on reliability; no norms; 25¢ per test; 10¢ per manual (free with 25 tests); 55¢ per specimen set; postage extra; (10–20) minutes; George D. Spache and Stanford E. Taylor; Educational Developmental Laboratories, Inc. *

JOHN J. GEYER, *Associate Professor of Education, Rutgers, The State University, New Brunswick, New Jersey.*

The *Reader's Inventory* is a questionnaire designed to be used at the beginning of a reading improvement course. Its purpose is to provide information the author thought would be useful in course planning and student counseling. Since it is not a test in the usual sense, it has no time limits, requires no monitoring, and could be completed by the student during other than class time.

The RI is concerned with information grouped under four categories: (*a*) reading interests, attitudes, and habits, (*b*) visual survey, (*c*) background of educational and vocational experience, and (*d*) expectations about the course. The accompanying manual discusses possible ramifications of certain answers to the questions included in the first category but barely mentions the other three. The discussions presented tend to be *ex cathedra* in tone and offer little rationale and no evidence for the viewpoints expressed.

Used as a basis for discussion and planning, as suggested, the RI could be a useful instrument for the inexperienced teacher. It does highlight several important areas of concern. Before placing a class order, the experienced teacher should request an examination copy to determine whether this informal instrument is in any way superior to his own.

DAVID M. WARK, *Professor of Psychology, University of Minnesota, Minneapolis, Minnesota.*

To quote the manual, the *Reader's Inventory* "is not a test as such, but rather a vehicle for eliciting a student's personal reactions to reading." There are items designed to draw out the reader's knowledge and feelings about comprehension and study reading habits (15 items), rate and flexibility (22 items), and vocabulary (9 items), and a miscellaneous bag of attitudes and interests not otherwise classifiable (21 items). The response categories—yes, no, not sure, sometimes—are unduly constricting for some items, especially those dealing with attitudes. There is a very reasonable-looking visual survey section, which allows the student to mention any of a broad range of vision problems which may require referral. The final sections ask for a record of prior education, including reading improvement programs, and expectations about improvement. The inventory is devoid of validity, reliability, or normative data. There is not even a single score. These omissions are not oversights by the authors; both are highly reputed and unquestionably competent scholars and scientists. The lack of psychometric basics is due strictly to the fact that the inventory is less a mental measurement tool than a teaching/counseling guide.

The inventory gives a counselor or teacher some insight into a student's reading skills, attitudes, and habits. But those insights are not developed quickly. And no particular patterns appear from the set of responses to the inventory. There are no subscales, no indicators, and only a few checks for internal consistency. To make the counselor's task even harder, the items for each topic are randomized throughout the inventory. There is no convenient way to retrieve and group them. Rather than yielding manageable scores or patterns, the inventory seems designed to stimulate discussion between the teacher and the student—discussion that would allow the teacher to test and clarify his understanding of the student's reading problems. Given time to review each item and response, the instructor could in fact get the necessary insight and at the same time disabuse the student of some foolish ideas while setting the stage for future reading progress. The idea is a good one. The format, at its very best, is cumbersome.

The major advantage of the inventory and manual is that taken together, they teach teachers. The manual contains concise, reasonable, and useful analyses of the meanings of common

responses. Where appropriate, there are suggestions for remedial techniques. These materials give the beginning reading instructor a focused and expert interpretation of research relevant to a particular problem. The manual could be used as a handbook or reference in college and adult reading improvement and as a counseling tool in the clinic.

[734]
*Reading Eye II. Grades 1, 2, 3, 4, 5, 6, 7–8, 9–16 and adults; 1959–69; a portable electronic eye-movement recorder with test materials; 5 reading component scores (fixations, regressions, average span of recognition, average duration of ·fixation, rate with comprehension), 3 ratings (grade level of reading, relative efficiency, directional attack), and 2 diagnostic categories (visual adjustment, general adjustment to reading); individual; 1 model ['69]; 8 test forms ('59, 1 card each) for each of 8 levels; technical manual ('60, 125 pages); operator's manual ('69, 13 pages); graph analyzer ('59, 1 page); reliability data and norms for reading component scores only; $1,800 per recorder; $64 per set of test cards; $2.10 per graph analyzer; $5 per roll recording paper; $2 per operator's manual; $1,890 per complete set of preceding materials plus technical manual and other accessories; scoring service, 31 or more graphs, $2.50 per graph; postage extra; [4] minutes; Stanford E. Taylor, Helen Frackenpohl, and James L. Pettee; Educational Developmental Laboratories, Inc. *

REFERENCES
1–3. See 6:838.
4. TAYLOR, STANFORD E. "Eye Movements in Reading: Facts and Fallacies." *Am Ed Res J* 2:187–202 N '65. * (PA 40: 2225)
5. ERDLEY, RUSSELL RICHARD. *Patterns of Eye Movements in Word Learning.* Doctor's thesis, Florida State University (Tallahassee, Fla.), 1967. (DA 28:2439A)
6. SEIFERT, JOAN G. *The Relationship Between Visual Motor Perception and the Speed of Eye Movements by Selected Boys.* Doctor's thesis, Kent State University (Kent, Ohio), 1967. (DA 28:4493A)
7. EVANS, RICHARD M. "Eye-Movement Photography as a Criterion for Measuring Differences Between Students in i.t.a. and T. O. Reading Instructional Programs." *Ill Sch Res* 4: 52–5 My '68. *
8. RYAN, HARRIET JEANNE LAWRENCE. *Eye-Movement Patterns of More Mature Readers While Decoding New Words.* Doctor's thesis, Florida State University (Tallahassee, Fla.), 1968. (DAI 30:1473A)
9. BEYER, DONALD A. *A Comparative Study of the Reading Performance of Third Grade Children Measured by the Reading Eye Camera and the Gates MacGinitie Reading Tests.* Master's thesis, Cardinal Stritch College (Milwaukee, Wis.), 1969.
10. BRICKNER, C. ANN. "The Analysis of Eye-Movement Recordings From Samples of Underachieving Secondary and Primary Students." *AV Commun R* 18(4):414–24 w '70. *
11. MICKISH, VERLE LEON. *The Relationship of Viewing Skills and Visual Perception.* Doctor's thesis, Arizona State University (Tempe, Ariz.), 1970. (DAI 31:2793A)
12. SINGER, CARROLL ROSENFELD. *Eye Movements, Reading Comprehension, and Vocabulary as Effected by Varying Visual and Auditory Modalities in College Students.* Doctor's thesis, New Mexico State University (University Park, N.M.), 1970. (DAI 31:164A)

JOHN J. GEYER, *Associate Professor of Education, Rutgers, The State University, New Brunswick, New Jersey.*

For reading teachers and clinicians committed to the use of eye-movement measures as a diagnostic tool, the advent of the *Reading Eye II* should be very welcome. It is portable, easily assembled, and simple to operate. The corneal reflection technique of the earlier models has been replaced by a monitoring procedure utilizing photocells, a technique which greatly simplifies the process of measurement. Recording is done directly on a roll of heat-sensitive graph paper, eliminating the difficulties associated with photographic film.

Informal calibration studies conducted by this reviewer showed that the *Reading Eye II* yields measures of number of fixations and regressions and of gross reading time sufficiently accurate for the purposes advertised. It will not yield with any useful accuracy measures of where the eye was pointed or the duration of any single fixation (these measures are not claimed by the manufacturer). Therefore, the usefulness of the *Reading Eye II* is limited to the interpretations validly derived from three gross measures, plus whatever subjective judgments the clinician can justify.

The printed material accompanying the *Reading Eye II* suggests that four areas of interpretation are possible (*3*). Two of these, labeled "Visual Adjustment" and "General Adjustment to Reading," must be determined subjectively "on the basis of the examiner's experience with eye-movement photography." Examples of records purporting to illustrate various conditions are provided.

Most of the conditions illustrated in the manual are either trivial or better determined by other methods. One does not need a *Reading Eye II* to discover that a student has a plastic eye, nor is eye-movement recording the preferred method of diagnosing myopia, hyperopia, or the type of corrective lens being worn. While the examples presented do show that the *Reading Eye II* is capable of reflecting certain extreme conditions, they neither prove nor particularly enhance the diagnostic capabilities of the instrument in the reading clinic.

The two major objective measures, "Relative Reading Efficiency" and "Adequacy of Directional Attack," are both derived from the counts of numbers of fixations and regressions, plus measures of rate and comprehension. Let us examine one of these derived measures for the problems of interpretation inherent in it.

The measure "Relative Reading Efficiency" is defined as the ratio between the rate of reading in words per minute and the sum of the number of fixations and regressions per 100 words (thus the number of regressions receives

double weight in the denominator of the ratio). This ratio, it is asserted, yields a number which is "not only the *expression of efficiency* (rate) but also provides an indication of the *effort or energy* expended to achieve this rate [emphasis in original]." Since the instrument yields relatively poor measures of rate, it would be hoped that the additional element of "energy" is an important one. Unfortunately, it is not clear what "energy" is being measured. The energy necessary to move the eyes, while clearly involved, is trivial. Yet, it is difficult to imagine what other kinds of "energy" might be indicated by these particular measures. The accompanying literature does not discuss this question.

Mathematically, the "Relative Reading Efficiency" ratio would be closely related to the average duration of fixation if the number of regressions were not doubled in the denominator. With the arbitrary doubling of regressions (for which no adequate rationale is presented), it is difficult to understand what this ratio might represent. Psychologically, the ratio assumes that between two readers reading with identical rates and comprehension, the reader using fewer eye movements is the better reader. There is no evidence for this nor any reason to suspect that it is true. Yet it is this measure and the grade level of the selection read in deriving it which are recommended as "the two factors used in planning instruction (grouping, starting point, etc.) and in judging progress when further graphs are taken."

The grade norms furnished with the objective measures do nothing to improve their interpretability and do so much to encourage gross misinterpretations that they should be removed. With or without grade norms, the basic difficulty remains: we know very little about why people differ in their eye-movement patterns or how the differences are related to the central processes of reading. Certain eye-movement characteristics can be related to good and poor reading as measured by tests, but these add little useful information to that provided by the tests against which they were validated.

The *Reading Eye II* is a well-designed and easily-operated instrument which yields little useful information not obtainable from paper-and-pencil tests or mere observations. Its one striking asset is that students are fascinated with the camera and the aura of science that it generates. For those reading specialists who

Reading Eye II

believe that this factor is worth the price, the *Reading Eye II* would be an excellent choice.

For reviews by Arthur S. McDonald and George D. Spache of an earlier model, see 6:838.

[735]

*Reading Versatility Test. Grades 5–8, 8–12, 12–16; 1961–68; RVT; 7 scores: rate and comprehension (fiction, nonfiction, skimming, scanning) and 3 reading rate ratios (fiction/nonfiction, skimming/fiction, scanning/fiction); Forms A and B, C and D, (16 pages, 2 forms per test booklet); 3 levels; manual ('68, 12 pages); no reliability data for comprehension and ratio scores; no norms; 40¢ per test booklet; separate answer sheets may be used; $2.50 per 100 answer sheets; 35¢ per set of scoring stencils for all levels; 85¢ per specimen set of any one level; postage extra; (40–50) minutes; Arthur S. McDonald, M. Alodia, Harold M. Nason, George Zimny, and James A. Byrne; Educational Developmental Laboratories, Inc. *
a) BASIC. Grades 5–8; 1961–68; test booklet ('67).
b) INTERMEDIATE. Grades 8–12; 1968.
c) ADVANCED. Grades 12–16; 1962–68; test booklet ('68).

JOHN J. GEYER, *Associate Professor of Education, Rutgers, The State University, New Brunswick, New Jersey.*

The *Reading Versatility Test* stems from the concern for reading flexibility shown by reading improvement manuals and teachers in recent years. As the test manual points out, the rather general agreement as to the desirability of reading flexibility is seriously weakened by a lack of agreement as to what the term means. Following a brief and shallow discussion of several ways in which "reading flexibility" has been interpreted, the manual defines the flexible reader as "one who is effective in achieving his purpose for reading and efficient in accomplishing this task with a minimum expenditure of psychological and physiological effort." In keeping with this definition, the RVT was designed for the purpose of measuring "the relative effectiveness and efficiency with which the subject reads different kinds of material requiring different approaches."

To accomplish their purpose, the authors of the RVT have gathered four brief prose passages for each form. The reader is instructed to read these passages with varying amounts of attention to detail, ranging from careful reading to scanning for a single answer to a question provided in advance. The passages selected are interesting and seem suited to the kind of reading required. Each is followed by from 1 to 10 multiple choice questions.

The chief difficulty in the use of the RVT is in the interpretations suggested and illustrated in the manual. The major method of interpretation suggested is to compare ratios of the rates of reading achieved on the different sections. Unfortunately, the reliabilities reported for these sections are extremely low. The reliabilities obtained from seven groups for the scanning and skimming sections combined range from .51 to .70. These sections calculated separately, as they are used in interpretation, would have yielded even lower reliabilities. Such scores, included in ratios, can have very little meaning.

Despite the fact that at least seven reliability studies were conducted, no reliability figures are reported for either the rate ratios or the comprehension measures. Since these are the major sources of interpretation suggested in the manual, it can only be assumed that the authors felt that the less said the better. It could hardly be otherwise for the comprehension measures, which are based on 10, 3, or 1 multiple choice items.

Judgments concerning comprehension are based on percentages of items answered and are left to the subjective evaluation of the user. For Parts 1 and 2 the authors suggest a cutoff score of 60 percent, below which a reader is judged "ineffective." Beyond this, however, the examiner is given such advice as:

When an individual reads with adequate (60% or above) comprehension on Parts 1 and 2, and he reads Part 2 at a rate commensurate with his grade level, and Part 1 about 1.5 to 2 times as fast, he can be judged to be partially flexible even if his comprehension on Parts 3 and 4 is inadequate.

The "grade level" judgments are presumably to be based on the norm table included in the manual, although these norms were obtained from subjects reading different material, for different purposes, before an eye-movement camera. Earlier in the manual the user is told that the norms "might represent an average for Parts 1 and 2." Whatever these norms might represent, their use in the context of this test is totally inappropriate, particularly at the grade levels where reading flexibility is typically a concern.

In short, although reading flexibility or versatility may be a skill important enough to be measured, this test will not provide an adequate measure of that skill. The use of ratios of unreliable measures is poor. The calculation of comprehension "percentages" from single item tests is incredible and from tests of 3 to 10 items, too unreliable for any useful purpose. The grade norms included are of dubious applicability and their suggested and implied uses are indefensible. Among many poor reading tests, this reviewer would rank the RVT as being very close to the bottom.

[736]

★**Word Discrimination Test.** Grades 1–8; 1958; WDT; Forms A, B, (4 pages); no manual; no data on reliability; norms based on 1949 testing printed on test booklet; 10¢ per test, postpaid; (15–20) minutes; Chas. B. Huelsman, Jr.; Miami University Alumni Association. *

REFERENCES

1. HUELSMAN, CHARLES BERNARD, JR. *The Visual Perception of Word Form.* Doctor's thesis, University of Chicago (Chicago, Ill.), 1949.
2. ROBINSON, H. ALAN. "Reliability of Measures Related to Reading Success of Average, Disadvantaged, and Advantaged Kindergarten Children." Comments by Samuel Weintraub. *Read Teach* 20:203–9 D '66. * (*PA* 41:3344)

[Other Tests]

For other tests new or revised since *The Sixth Mental Measurements Yearbook,* see the following in *Reading Tests and Reviews:*

ORAL

[737]

*Gilmore Oral Reading Test.** Grades 1–8; 1951–68; GORT; 3 scores: accuracy, comprehension, rate; individual; Forms C, D; record blanks ('68, 12 pages); reading paragraphs ('68, 25 pages) for both forms; manual ('68, 31 pages); $5.50 per 35 record blanks; $3.50 per reading paragraphs; $1 per manual; $1.50 per sample set; postage extra; (15–20) minutes; John V. Gilmore and Eunice C. Gilmore; Harcourt Brace Jovanovich, Inc. *

REFERENCES

1. GILMORE, JOHN V. *The Relationship Between Certain Oral Reading Habits and Oral and Silent Reading Comprehension.* Doctor's thesis, Harvard University (Cambridge, Mass.), 1947.
2. LADD, ELEANOR MARY. *A Comparison of Two Types of Training With Reference to Developing Skill in Diagnostic Oral Reading Testing.* Doctor's thesis, Florida State University (Tallahassee, Fla.), 1961. (*DA* 22:2707)
3. RIDDLE, WILLIAM T. *A Study of the Effects of a Controlled Auditory Distraction Factor Upon the Performance of Selected Students on an Oral Reading Test.* Doctor's thesis, Texas Technological College (Lubbock, Tex.), 1961. (*DA* 22:3096)
4. CLARK, H. CLIFFORD. *An Analysis of Reading Deficiencies and Corrective Treatment Among Freshman Students From the Pacific Area Enrolled at the Church College of Hawaii.* Doctor's thesis, Brigham Young University (Provo, Utah), 1963. (*DA* 24:4050)
5. HIGGINS, CONWELL. "Multiple Predictor Score Cut-Offs Versus Multiple-Regression Cut-Offs in Selection of Academically Talented Children in Grade 3." *Yearb Nat Council Meas Ed* 20:153–64 '63. * (*PA* 38:9247)
6. GARLOCK, JERRY; DOLLARHIDE, ROBERT S.; AND HOPKINS, KENNETH D. "Comparability of Scores on the Wide Range and the Gilmore Oral Reading Tests." *Calif J Ed Res* 16:54–7 Mr '65. * (*PA* 39:10108)
7. PATTY, DELBERT LEE. *A Comparison of Standardized Oral Reading Test Scores and Informal Reading Inventory Scores.* Doctor's thesis, Ball State University (Muncie, Ind.), 1965. (*DA* 26:5302)
8. TRELA, THADDEUS M. "What Do Diagnostic Reading Tests Diagnose?" *El Engl* 43:370–2 Ap '66. *
9. BOND, GUY L., AND DYKSTRA, ROBERT. "The Cooperative Research Program in First-Grade Reading Instruction." *Read Res Q* 2:5–142 su '67. * (*PA* 42:4557)
10. KIRBY, CLARA LOU LAUGHLIN. *A Comparison of Scores Obtained on Standardized Oral and Silent Reading Tests and a Cloze Test.* Doctor's thesis, Ball State University (Muncie, Ind.), 1967. (*DA* 28:4512A)
11. BROWN, JOHN LAWRENCE. *The Frostig Program for the Development of Visual Perception in Relation to Visual Perception Ability and Reading Ability.* Doctor's thesis, University of Southern California (Los Angeles, Calif.), 1969. (*DAI* 30:4822A)
12. MEANS, CHALMERS EDWARD. *A Study of the Relationship Between the Use of Intonation Patterns in Oral Reading and Comprehension in Reading.* Doctor's thesis, Pennsylvania State University (University Park, Pa.), 1969. (*DAI* 30:4689A)
13. KIRBY, CLARA L. "Using the Cloze Procedure as a Testing Technique," pp. 68–77. In *Reading Diagnosis and Evaluation.* Edited by Dorothy L. De Boer. Newark, Del.: International Reading Association, 1970. Pp. vi, 138. *
14. SABATINO, DAVID A., AND HAYDEN, DAVID L. "Information Processing Behaviors Related to Learning Disabilities and Educable Mental Retardation." *Excep Children* 37(1):21–9 S '70. * (*PA* 46:5527)
15. SABATINO, DAVID A., AND HAYDEN, DAVID L. "Psycho-Educational Study of Selected Behavioral Variables With Children Failing the Elementary Grades." *J Exp Ed* 38(4):40–57 su '70. * (*PA* 46:5680–1)
16. SABATINO, DAVID A., AND HAYDEN, DAVID L. "Variation in Information Processing Behaviors: As Related to Chronological Age Differences for Children Failing in the Elementary Grades." *J Learn Dis* 3(8):404–12 Ag '70. *
17. SIMPSON, ROBERT L. "Reading Tests Versus Intelligence Tests as Predictors of High School Graduation." *Psychol Sch* 7(4):363–5 O '70. * (*PA* 46:1870)

ALBERT J. HARRIS, *Emeritus Professor of Education, The City University of New York, New York, New York.*

The new Gilmore Forms C and D replace the original Forms A and B, which are no longer in print. Form D is actually a revision of the material previously in Form A, with new comprehension questions. The content of Form C is new. Each form tells a continuing story about a family, with each paragraph a little longer, more mature, and more difficult than the preceding one. Each of the new forms contains 10 paragraphs, ascending from first grade level at a grade per paragraph.

The paragraphs which the subject reads are printed on strong stock, one paragraph to a page. Each form starts with a picture showing the characters who appear in the first paragraph. These paragraphs are presented in a spiral-bound booklet which contains both forms. There is a separate record blank for each form, on which the examiner records the subject's performance. Each page of the record blank reproduces one paragraph, gives five comprehension questions, and provides a table for tabulating eight types of errors.

Testing must be individual. The examiner is advised to start two paragraphs below the one corresponding to the child's grade placement (e.g., for a fourth grade child, start with paragraph 2). The child should be asked to read orally at sight every paragraph from his "basal" level (the highest at which he makes not more than two errors) to his "ceiling" level (at which he makes ten or more errors). Time is taken with a stopwatch. An error code is provided to assist in quick recording. In scoring for Accuracy and for Comprehension, credit is given for the paragraphs below the basal level, though on the Comprehension score, full credit is not always given.

Norms are given for three aspects of oral reading: Accuracy, Comprehension, and Rate. For Accuracy and Comprehension four types of norms are given: performance ratings (poor, below average, average, above average, superior); stanines; percentile ranks; and grade norms. Norms for Rate provide only three categories: slow, average, and fast. There are separate norms for each form, as Form C is apparently a bit more difficult than Form D.

Evidence of care in constructing the paragraphs is shown in data that indicate fairly regular increases in the paragraphs in length, word difficulty, number of polysyllabic words, mean number of words per sentence, and percentage of complex sentences. The content seems somewhat more appropriate for non-disadvantaged children than for disadvantaged children.

Retest reliability was determined by administering both forms to samples of children in grades 3 and 6. Reliabilities were consistently higher in third grade. The reliability of the Accuracy score is satisfactory (.94) in third grade, a little lower (.84) in sixth grade. Reliabilities for the Comprehension and Rate scores range from .53 to .70 and indicate that these scores fall below accepted standards for the reliability of individual scores.

The Accuracy score is the most important of the three Gilmore scores. It is a measure of fluency as well as of accuracy of word recognition, since hesitations, repetitions, disregard of punctuation, and self-corrected errors are all counted as errors. However, it is less influenced by rate than the composite score on the Gray, which is based on a combination of rate and errors, or the Durrell, which relies entirely on rate.

The Gilmore Comprehension score is based on the answers to five questions per paragraph. This seems to be mainly a measure of short-time recall of directly stated details, with very few questions calling for judgments or inferences. It therefore differs considerably from the kind

of comprehension measured by most silent reading tests. It also has relatively poor reliability. Thus the Comprehension score is disappointing in terms of both content validity and reliability. It might better have been used for a qualitative rating or for a three-step normative scale (good, average, poor).

The Rate score is based on the average rate for the paragraphs read from the basal to, but not including, the ceiling paragraphs. Since the paragraphs increase in difficulty and rate is strongly influenced by such errors as hesitations, repetitions, self-corrections, and words pronounced by examiner (after waiting five seconds), the rate score is not independent of accuracy. Although correlations among the three scores are not given in the manual (a strange omission), a substantial correlation between Rate and Accuracy is to be expected. Eliminating timing in test administration and dropping the Rate score would simplify both administration and scoring, with little loss in useful information.

Despite its shortcomings, the updated Gilmore is among the best standardized tests of accuracy in oral reading of meaningful material now available. The usefulness of the Comprehension and Rate scores is more questionable.

KENNETH J. SMITH, *Professor of Education and Head, Department of Reading, The University of Arizona, Tucson, Arizona.*

A basic assumption of the *Gilmore Oral Reading Test* is open to the question of validity. The test seeks to measure comprehension ability with an oral test. However, one does not normally read orally for his own comprehension, but rather for the benefit of listeners. The act of oral reading requires only the most superficial comprehension; therefore, the skilled oral reader has his concentration elsewhere. If he wished to read for his *own* comprehension, he usually would read silently. The appropriateness of testing a silent reading act (comprehension) with a test of oral skill (fluency, etc.) is extremely doubtful.

Comprehension questions on the Gilmore test consist entirely of factual recall questions on all levels. The test, therefore, is one of memory, not comprehension. The manual makes much of the effort to grade levels of difficulty. Yet it gives as an important characteristic of difficulty the number of words in a paragraph. But

Gilmore Oral Reading Test

an increased number of words per paragraph does not make *comprehension* more difficult; it merely gives the reader more to *remember*. Thus, the increasingly longer passages will cause the reader to "fail" on more items only because he has more facts to remember over a longer period of time, not because of increasing difficulty of comprehension.

The test of accuracy (actually oral word-calling) should be useful in word recognition diagnosis if types of errors are analyzed. However, the scoring practice of weighting different types of "errors" equally seems questionable. One wonders, for instance, if a two-second hesitation is the equivalent of a substitution, or a repetition the equivalent of a "mispronunciation."

The test also is scored for rate, but this would seem to be largely irrelevant to a test of oral reading.

Perhaps much of the difficulty of the *Gilmore Oral Reading Test* can be explained by a brief quotation from the manual: "It is reasonable to assume that if one can read well orally he can read well silently. Oral reading also increases auditory acuity. It enables the pupils to discriminate the sounds of words." Experienced teachers of reading and reading clinicians are well acquainted with the many children who read well orally but not silently (acts requiring different sets of skills). Auditory acuity apparently is confused with discrimination. Oral language acquisition hardly awaits oral reading. These errors perhaps explain the invalid assumptions on which this test is based.

Although administration of the test requires considerable practice, directions seem clear and concise. The scoring blank and tables contribute to the ease of scoring.

The *Gilmore Oral Reading Test* requires individual administration and is rather time consuming, and the results have limited use in view of the invalid assumptions upon which the test is based. It would therefore seem that the time might be much better spent on a well-constructed informal reading inventory which tests oral reading with an oral test and reading comprehension with a silent test, and which samples types of comprehension, not simply recall of details.

For reviews by Lydia A. Duggins and Maynard C. Reynolds of the original edition, see 5:671.

[738]

*Graded Word Reading Test. Ages 5–21; 1921–67; GWRT; pronunciation; individual; 2 tests ['38, 1 card]; manual ('67, 32 pages plus tests, identical with manual copyrighted in 1938 except for addition of revised norms ['54] for *a*); 2½p per test; 20p per manual; postage extra; (5–10) minutes; P. E. Vernon; University of London Press Ltd. *

a) THE BURT (REARRANGED) WORD READING TEST. 1921–67; adaptation for Scottish schools of Cyril Burt's *Graded Word Reading Test* ('21); no data on reliability.

b) GRADED WORD READING TEST. 1938–67; for use in Scottish schools.

REFERENCES

1. VERNON, P. E. *The Standardization of a Graded Word Reading Test, Second Edition.* Publications of the Scottish Council for Research in Education 12. London: University of London Press Ltd., 1967. Pp. 44. *

2. PHILLIPS, C. J., AND BANNON, W. J. "The Stanford-Binet, Form L-M, Third Revision: A Local English Study of Norms, Concurrent Validity and Social Differences." *Brit J Ed Psychol* 38:148–61 Je '68. * (*PA* 42:17000)

3. PAYNE, J. F. "A Comparative Study of the Mental Ability of Seven- and Eight-Year-Old British and West Indian Children in a West Midland Town." *Brit J Ed Psychol* 39(3):326–7 N '69. *

[Other Test]

For another test revised since *The Sixth Mental Measurements Yearbook,* see the following in *Reading Tests and Reviews:*

167. *Gray Oral Reading Test

READINESS

[739]

★The ABC Inventory to Determine Kindergarten and School Readiness. Entrants to kgn and grade 1; 1965; individual; 1 form; record form (2 pages); research edition manual (4 pages); no data on reliability; no data on validity for predicting first grade success; no norms for first grade entrants; $4.90 per 50 record forms; $1 per specimen set; cash orders postpaid; (10–15) minutes; Normand Adair and George Blesch; Research Concepts. *

REFERENCES

1. KNOLL, DONNA B. *A Comparison of the ABC Inventory and Wechsler Preschool and Primary Scale of Intelligence for Predicting Success in Kindergarten.* Master's thesis, Fort Hays Kansas State College (Hays, Kan.), 1968.

2. LEE, RAYMOND E. "Pre-School Grouping of Kindergarten Children." *Ill Sch Res* 7(1):19–21 f '70. *

DAVID P. WEIKART, *President, High/Scope Educational Research Foundation, Ypsilanti, Michigan.*

The *ABC Inventory* was constructed "to identify children who are immature for a standard school program," suggesting a "readiness" concept based on passage of time rather than the acquisition of experience. It can be administered by teachers or other school examiners in an estimated 10 to 15 minutes. Items are divided into four groups in which the child is asked to: first, draw a man; second, answer questions about characteristics of objects; third, answer questions about general topics; and

ABC Inventory

fourth, complete some simple tasks involving numbers and shapes. Correct responses are recorded by the examiner, and a single total score is computed for the test. Scoring instructions and norms for determining readiness age are included on the child's answer sheet, greatly facilitating scoring. The readiness ages range from 3–6 to 6–7 years in one-month intervals. The authors provide tentative indication of a strong relationship with mental age components of intelligence tests (r of .78 with Stanford-Binet MA, N = 14).

The test manual contains only three pages, which include supplementary instructions for administering and scoring the test, followed by some interpretation of scores for children under 5 years and some notes on the construction of the test. The instructions for administering the test are clear and brief, and most examiners will be able to administer the test entirely from the answer sheets after the first few tries. The sections on using the results and notes on construction, however, are merely gestures toward the information that the APA-AERA-NCME Standards describes as essential. For example, the only descriptive characteristics of the standardization group presented are the age, which varied from 4–9 through 4–11, and the enrollment of the schools from which children were drawn. Vital information such as sex, geographical location, socioeconomic status, and ethnic composition are not presented. In addition, the locations and methods of selecting the 15 schools involved in the study are not disclosed.

Evidence for predictive validity was obtained "by comparing 'pass-fail' features between children in the upper and lower half [sic] of the score distribution." Joint percentages and a tetrachoric correlation (.70) are presented. The authors state that a cutoff score of 68 would have identified 37 or 86 percent of the children who failed their first year of school. (The authors do not mention that this same cutoff score failed to identify 46 or 37 percent of the 123 children who passed their first year of school!) That 43 children failed kindergarten out of a total sample of 166 is shocking, a 26 percent failure rate! This figure casts doubt on the appropriateness of these particular kindergartens to many of the children in the sample, and it also casts doubt on the relevance of the test results to other kindergartens. The high failure rate might be a reflection of the age of

the test, as more enlightened procedures have become widespread in early childhood education since 1962, when these results were obtained.

The method used to compute reliability was inappropriate for the purpose: "Scores for children of the same age who enrolled in the same school districts two years apart were compared" using a t test for the equality of means, and the resultant lack of a significant difference was taken by the authors to be evidence of reliability. This is quite different from either stability reliability (test-retest) or internal consistency reliability (split-half), and does not constitute adequate evidence of reliability.

The author's summary remark that "the research edition of the ABC Inventory has been found to be reliable and valid" is directly counter to the APA-AERA-NCME Standards recommendation against such broad, unqualified claims. The statement is likely to be misleading to most users. A truer statement would be that the test shows potential usefulness but is not yet adequately developed and researched. The label "Research Edition" has been on the test since it was published over five years ago, and here, as with many other tests, seems to be taken as a license to release the test permanently without providing adequate development.

In view of the inadequacy of supportive research, I do not recommend the test for the use stated by the authors unless the school system using it develops its own norms and conducts its own validity and reliability studies in order to allow practical interpretation of the scores.

[740]

★The APELL Test: Assessment Program of Early Learning Levels. Ages 4.5-7; 1969; program for identifying educational deficiencies, suggesting remedial instruction, and retesting; 16 scores: 4 pre-reading (visual discrimination, auditory discrimination, letter names, total), 4 pre-math (attributes, number concepts, number facts, total), 7 language (nouns, pronouns, verbs, adjectives, plurals, prepositions, total), total; 1 form (58 pages); manual (110 pages); norms for total score only; no description of normative population; separate answer cards must be used; $8.15 per test; $7.90 per manual; $285 per school set (35 tests plus manual); $17.35 per 35 sets of answer cards (includes scoring service); postpaid; (40) minutes in 2 sessions; Eleanor V. Cochran and James L. Shannon; Edcodyne Corporation. *

[741]

★Academic Readiness and End of First Grade Progress Scales. Beginning of first grade, end of first grade; 1968–69; ratings by teachers in 14–15 areas: motor, perceptual-motor (2 scores), persistence, memory, attention, number recognition (a) or compu-

tational arithmetic (b), counting, word recognition, comprehension (b), vocabulary, interest in curriculum, social, humor, emotional; also includes form for recording opinions of teachers and parents regarding children being considered for retention or special class placement; 1 form; 2 levels; no norms; $2.85 per 25 scales; 10% extra for postage and handing; specimen set not available; [5-10] minutes; Harold F. Burks; Arden Press. *
a) ACADEMIC READINESS SCALE: END OF KINDERGARTEN OR BEGINNING FIRST GRADE. 1968; ARS; 1 form (2 pages); manual ['68, 18 pages]; 50¢ per manual.
b) END OF FIRST GRADE PROGRESS SCALE. 1969; EFGPS; 1 form (2 pages); no manual; no data on reliability.

[742]

The Anton Brenner Developmental Gestalt Test of School Readiness. Ages 5-6; 1964; BGT; also called *Brenner Gestalt Test;* an optional rating scale provides 2 scores: achievement-ability, social-emotional; individual; 1 form; manual (32 pages plus record booklet and number recognition form); record booklet (3 pages); number recognition form (3 pages); $13.50 per set of testing materials, 25 record booklets, and manual; $6.50 per 25 record booklets; $4.50 per set of testing materials; $4 per manual; postpaid; (3-10) minutes; Anton Brenner; Western Psychological Services. *

REFERENCES

1-8. See 6:844a.
9. BRENNER, ANTON. "Nature and Meaning of Readiness for School." *Merrill-Palmer Q* 3:114-35 sp '57. *
10. SVAGR, VIRGINIA BAILEY. *The Value of Perceptual Gestalt Tests in the Prediction of Reading Achievement at Various Grade Levels.* Doctor's thesis, Wayne State University (Detroit, Mich.), 1965. (*DAI* 30:2389A)
11. HEPBURN, ANDREW W., AND DONNELLY, FRANK. "Psychometric Identification of Kindergarten Children With Visual Perceptual Impairment." *Excep Children* 34:708-9 My '68. *
12. SCANDARY, EMMA JANE. *A Study of Early Elementary School Teachers Evaluations of Selected Eye-Hand Coordination Skills of Kindergarten Children.* Doctor's thesis, Michigan State University (East Lansing, Mich.), 1968. (*DAI* 30:177A)
13. BUSHEY, JAMES THOMAS. *The Relationships Between a Preschool Measure of Readiness and Subsequent Test Performances Among a Group of Private Elementary School Children.* Doctor's thesis, Wayne State University (Detroit, Mich.), 1969. (*DAI* 30:3816A)
14. FALIK, LOUIS H. "The Effects of Special Perceptual-Motor Training in Kindergarten on Reading Readiness and on Second Reading Grade Performance." *J Learn Dis* 2(8):395-402 Ag '69. * (*PA* 45:7085)
15. CHASEY, WILLIAM C. "The Effect of Motor Development on School Readiness Skills of Educable Mentally Retarded Children." *Am Correct Ther J* 24(6):180-3 N-D '70. *
16. WORTHINGTON, JAMES D. *Relationships of the Anton Brenner and the Metropolitan Readiness Tests in Yielding Readiness Levels and Predicting Reading Achievement.* Master's thesis, Glassboro State College (Glassboro, N.J.), 1970.

DENNIS J. DELORIA, *Vice President for Research, High/Scope Educational Research Foundation, Ypsilanti, Michigan.*

The *Brenner Gestalt Test* (not to be confused with the *Bender-Gestalt Test*) differs from most readiness tests in the content of the items; where most tests consist of activities similar to those found in typical kindergartens, the BGT primarily contains items of a numeric-perceptual nature.

The test is divided into five subtests: number producing, number recognition, ten dot Gestalt, sentence Gestalt, and draw-a-man. Tasks in each of the subtests include, respectively, placing a specified number of blocks in the examiner's

hand, counting dots arranged in various patterns, copying a ten-dot pattern, copying a simple sentence (without necessarily reading it), and drawing a man. There is an optional set of 16 rating items using a 1 to 5 scale, half of which form an Achievement-Ability rating score and half a Social-Emotional Behavior rating score.

The norms (based on about 750 kindergarten and first grade children in Mt. Clemens, Michigan) are reported for three overlapping age groups: 4-10 to 5-11, 5-1 to 6-2, and 5-5 to 6-6. Scores for the three age groups are divided into quarters and assigned readiness levels of low, average, or high. Test-retest reliabilities ranged from .55 to .74 for intervals of 1 to 7 months; split-half reliabilities of .83 and .92 were also obtained. Validity was assessed using two criteria, the optional teacher ratings from the .Brenner Gestalt Test itself, and the *Metropolitan Readiness Test.* Concurrent social-emotional and achievement-ability teacher ratings correlated .82 (N = 351) and .61 (N = 353), respectively, with the total scores; achievement-ability ratings collected seven months later from first grade teachers correlated about .70 with kindergarten BGT scores. First grade October *Metropolitan Readiness Test* scores correlated .66 (N = 54) and .75 (N = 258), respectively, with the previous January and June kindergarten BGT scores. All in all, the reliability and validity statistics are respectable, but the failure of the manual to provide sufficient description of the Mt. Clemens sample makes it difficult to know to what populations the norms can be generalized.

There are two serious flaws in the manual which, rightly or wrongly, do much to destroy the general credibility of the test. The first problem is the gap between suggested uses of the BGT and validity data supporting those uses, and the second is the careless manner in which many allusions are made to research findings which are not presented in the manual or specifically cited in the references.

Suggested uses for the test, in addition to assessing general school readiness, include identifying early and late maturing children, identifying gifted and retarded children, identifying emotionally disturbed children, testing non-English-speaking children, testing culturally deprived children, assessing socio-emotional behavior, predicting reading and numeric

Anton Brenner Developmental Gestalt Test

readiness, and clinically diagnosing children; yet the only validity data presented in the manual are correlations of the total test score with the *Metropolitan Readiness Test* and with the optional teacher ratings from the *Brenner Gestalt Test* itself. No data are provided to support use of the test to distinguish "maturational" factors from "retardedness" factors, nor to separate "emotional disturbance" from more general socio-emotional behaviors. No data are presented to support use of the test and the current norms with "non-English-speaking children" or "culturally deprived" children.

A number of references are presented at the end of the manual, but they are not specifically cited to support the validity of particular test applications. An examination of the articles revealed generally supportive findings, but the studies either lacked scientific sampling methods, used very small samples, or, for various other reasons, failed to provide findings that could be taken as adequate evidence of validity for the specialized uses. Thus, although many different applications of the test are suggested in the manual, essentially no research findings are presented to support most of them.

The second problem in the manual is the careless manner in which many allusions are made to research findings which are not presented in the manual or specifically cited in the references. For example, "experimental work with the BGT included the testing of children in city and rural schools, private and public schools. It was used on normal and exceptional groups of children within an age range of about 4 years to 24 years. Studies included white, Negro, and Mexican children." None of the findings from these studies is presented in the manual nor are any studies cited as sources for this statement. Another example, much more serious, is the following quotation:

The BGT was correlated with teachers' concurrent and later judgments of children's achievements, abilities, and maturities, and with many standardized tests: Sangren Information Test, Pintner-Cunningham Primary Test, Metropolitan Test, Monroe Reading Aptitude Test, Monroe Basic Reading Test, Gates Reading Test, Harrison-Stroud Test, Stanford-Binet, and the Goodenough Draw-A-Man Test. All tests were correlated with teachers' judgments.

The final conclusion, based on all the research findings, was that the BGT is a valid and reliable measure of school readiness. It can be used in place of any of the above tests for determining school readiness; the BGT adds greatly to the interpretation of the above tests if included in the test batteries with them [italics in the original].

Anton Brenner Developmental Gestalt Test

If research is alluded to in this manner, it should be supported by the presentation of key statistical results, along with enough description of the conditions of the study to allow readers to draw their own conclusions; otherwise, such statements are misleading and should be left out of the manual completely.

The test is not recommended for use by teachers in its present form because of ambiguity of both application and interpretation created by the manual statements cited above, and others similar in nature. The problem is particularly acute with untrained testers, as teachers are likely to be. In essence, the manual suggests that the test may be used to measure a large number of characteristics but then fails to give the concrete information needed by the teacher to interpret the results; moreover, the test development research upon which such information should be based is not presented to allow interpretation by trained psychologists. The basic "readiness" assessment application of the test appears to possess some validity, and to the extent that it does, the test might find use in some situations. However, wherever the test is used, active steps should be taken by experienced psychologists to prevent overinterpretation of results by untrained users.

[743]

★The Basic Concept Inventory, Field Research Edition. Preschool and kgn; 1967; BCI; school readiness; 4 scores: basic concepts, statement repetition and comprehension, pattern awareness, total; individual; 1 form: test and scoring booklet (7 pages) plus 9 picture cards; manual (47 pages); no data on reliability; no norms; $2.97 per 15 tests; $2.58 per set of picture cards; $2.16 per manual; postage extra; specimen set not available; (15–25) minutes; Siegfried E. Engelmann; Follett Educational Corporation. *

REFERENCES

1. SEARS, CHARLES RICHARDS. *A Comparison of the Basic Language Concepts and Psycholinguistic Abilities of Second Grade Boys Who Demonstrate Average and Below Average Levels of Reading Achievement.* Doctor's thesis, Colorado State College (Greeley, Colo.), 1969. (*DAI* 30:1758A)
2. HOFMEISTER, ALAN, AND ESPESETH, V. KNUTE. "Predicting Academic Achievement With TMR Adults and Teen-agers." *Am J Mental Def* 75(1):105–7 Jl '70. *

BOYD R. MCCANDLESS, *Professor of Education and Psychology and Director, Educational Psychology, Emory University, Atlanta, Georgia.*

The *Basic Concept Inventory* items tap a series of concepts, subjectively selected as being basic for performing successfully in new learning situations in the first grade. The Inventory is designed to be a "criterion-referenced" measure—that is, one intended "to evaluate the instruction the child has received on specific, relevant skills." It is recommended that scores be employed to form instructional groups of about five children each. Considerable space (and imaginative, constructive thought) is devoted to guiding the teacher, inductively and deductively, in seeking educational strategies for diagnosing and for instructing the child about concepts he has not mastered.

According to the manual, the inventory "is designed for children who are preparing for beginning academic tasks. It is primarily intended for culturally disadvantaged preschool and kindergarten children, slow learners, emotionally disturbed children, and mentally retarded children."

More than half the manual is taken up with classroom application of the inventory, six case histories, educational strategy, and the basic theory. This material, which includes much of the provocative thinking that characterizes the Bereiter-Engelmann approach to compensatory education and its assessment, should be useful to any teacher interested in diagnostic testing.

The weaknesses of the inventory are typical of those inherent in any research edition. Concepts selected for checking range from simple naming from a picture ("Find the boy") through demonstrating inclusive and exclusive concepts ranging from simple to moderately complex; following directions, simple problem solving, sentence repetition, comprehension, and thought; and demonstration of simple competence in syllabic fusion (e.g., understanding and defining "flow-er," pronounced very slowly). But since the criteria for selection are not given, we must infer that they are subjective—although certainly based on the author's wide and constructive experience.

None of the criteria of formal test construction is satisfied (or, at least, reported). There are no age or grade norms, no reported reliability, and no indicated validity other than the face validity apparent in the items.

The inventory is moderately time consuming; it must be given individually, and an estimated 20 minutes per child is required. Some items have single, others multiple responses. This adds to the clerical load placed on the administrator. Considerable verbalization on the part of the child is required, so that such factors as shyness, dialect, and audibility are bound to affect the performance.

The pupil's test booklet is clearly printed. The nine pictures used for the first 9 items

(which tap a total of 44 concepts and understandings) are attractive, clear, and (appropriately) racially—but not socioeconomically—integrated. The remaining 12 items require no props, but elicit a rather wide range of responses.

The author's goals are worthwhile, the inventory plan is potentially valuable, the test content is promising, the strategy and theory sections of the manual are heuristic, and the reviewer hopes that this Field Research Edition will be employed widely enough so that an eventual sound evaluation of the usefulness of the inventory can be made.

JAMES J. McCARTHY, *Professor of Education, The University of Wisconsin, Madison, Wisconsin.*

The Field Research Edition of *The Basic Concept Inventory,* by Engelmann, is probably an outgrowth of the well-known efforts he and Bereiter undertook with disadvantaged children.[1] The inventory's main strength appears to lie in the concept of structural pedagogy upon which it hinges. Its major weakness lies in the complete lack of data presented, in this edition, on validity, reliability and norms. However, this is not the final edition of the inventory; the author promises further improvements and data, and does seek the suggestions of users concerning administration, scoring, format, and scope.

The BCI is designed for use with "culturally disadvantaged preschool and kindergarten children, slow learners, emotionally disturbed children and mentally retarded children." It is an individually administered instrument which might be administered by a teacher as a basis for gaining insights about the child for remedial instruction. However, when the inventory is used as a basis for special treatment or placement, a trained examiner is recommended. The purpose of the inventory is "to evaluate the instruction in certain beginning, academically-related concepts" given to either a group of children or an individual child. The inventory is billed as a "criterion-referenced" measure as contrasted with the "norm-referenced" measure. The latter essentially contrasts the score of an individual with the average performance of many children like himself. The former is an

1 BEREITER, CARL, AND ENGELMANN, SIEGFRIED. *Teaching Disadvantaged Children in the Preschool.* Englewood Cliffs, N.J.: Prentice-Hall, Inc., 1966. Pp. vii, 312. *

attempt to evaluate instruction without reference to individual aptitudes. In constructing criterion-referenced measures, the attempt is to create items which, when failed by the child, unambiguously imply "a relatively specific educational remedy." While this reviewer feels that Engelmann takes an unnecessarily pessimistic attitude toward the merits of norm-referenced measures, one must subscribe to the virtues of the criterion-referenced measures given that the capabilities of such measures are shown to approximate their promise.

The BCI is a three part "checklist of basic concepts." In the first part, the subject is queried on a series of nine pictures to elicit his degree of understanding of common words and word combinations. In the second part, the child is required to repeat statements and to answer questions implied by the statements, some of which are nonsense sentences. The third part assesses what Engelmann calls "pattern awareness" and includes imitation of movement patterns and digit sequences and a little sound blending. Instructions for administering and scoring the measure are extremely explicit, detailed, and item-specific. These characteristics suggest that the administration of the BCI should be largely left to trained examiners. In general, the child scores zero for a correct task, so the lower the score, the more adequate the child's performance.

Suggestions are given for using the BCI results to assemble children into small instructional groups or to contrast group performance with previous performance, though the real strength of the present edition of the BCI lies in what it can reveal about instructional deficits of the individual child, not a group of children. And to this end nearly five pages of commentary are provided with the aim of attempting to identify specific errors (and occasionally classes of errors) and to suggest instructional implications. Engelmann leads the reader through a series of interpretations, evoking hypotheses and tentative conclusions about BCI performance. He closes this section of the manual by attempting to state guidelines for relating BCI results to a prediction of classroom performance. These interpretations are supplemented with more than a dozen pages of case histories illustrating BCI interpretation and remarks on educational strategy. Ostensibly, while this last mentioned section relates BCI results to remedies and teaching presentations, it appears to

be devoted to what is generally regarded as teaching methods and it uses as a model the strategies evolved by Bereiter and Engelmann.

The test manual contains a short section on the "basic theory" in which the author attempts to demonstrate the consistency of his concepts of "structural pedagogy" with a criterion-referenced measure of achievement. The major contentions appear to be that the teacher changes the child's behavior through manipulating the environment and what the child learns depends on what and how the teacher manipulates. Only certain kinds of environmental manipulations produce desired behavior as indexed by the child's behavior. And we assume the child's behavior can be modified through instruction. Therefore, the BCI is required to provide specific examples of the child's instructional deficits. Engelmann maintains that the teacher, in coping with these deficits, must blame the environment, not the child, for the shortcomings and accept, as his commitment as a teacher, full responsibility for what the child learns.

Engelmann differentiates his orientation from the "cognitive process" orientation, which, he states, "provides only superficial direction for the teacher," assumes to be exhaustive (thus failing to differentiate between important and trivial tasks), and leads the teacher to assume he has remedied a deficit if he has taught the child an application of that skill (e.g., skill, visual association; task, bead stringing). One supporting the "cognitive process" approach might interpret Engelmann's views in this regard as somewhat oversimplified and naive, though not without some justification.

Content and criterion validity, extremely important for a criterion-referenced measure, were considered in constructing the BCI, but items were constructed and selected on an "intuitive and informal" basis. Data on predictive and construct validity, as well as reliability, are promised but not supplied in the 1967 manual. Age norms are neither supplied nor promised for reasons which, to this reviewer, are not convincing.

SUMMARY. Engelmann's BCI is a criterion-referenced test which is associated with an approach to teaching the preschool disadvantaged called "structural pedagogy." This individually administered measure provides indices of specific instructional deficits which, in turn, permit the teacher to form working hypotheses for instruction through environmental manipulation and to assess success in this effort via subsequent performance. More than a modicum of practice and skill is required in the administration and interpretation of this largely clinical instrument. The unified viewpoint which incorporates assessment and instruction as part of the whole educational cloth has great appeal and the BCI, for this reviewer, holds considerable promise. However, the objective observer will remain skeptical of claims for the BCI until data on validity, reliability, and (hopefully) age norms are provided.

[744]

★Clymer-Barrett Prereading Battery. First grade entrants; 1966–69; CBPB; 4 scores: visual discrimination, auditory discrimination, visual-motor, total; short screening form consisting of 2 of the 6 subtests yields a single score; Forms A, B, ('67, 16 pages, identical with tests copyrighted in 1966); manual for Forms A, B, ('69, 32 pages); $5 per 25 tests; $1 per specimen set; postpaid; (90) minutes in 3 sessions, (30) minutes for short form; Theodore Clymer and Thomas C. Barrett; Personnel Press, Inc. *

REFERENCES
1. JOHNSON, ROGER ERLING. A Study of the Validity of the Clymer-Barrett Prereading Battery. Doctor's thesis, University of Minnesota (Minneapolis, Minn.), 1967. (DA 28:3892A)
2. JOHNSON, ROGER E. "The Validity of the Clymer-Barrett Prereading Battery." Read Teach 22(7):609–14 Ap '69. * (PA 45:10670)

ROGER FARR, *Associate Professor of Education and Director, Reading Clinic, Indiana University, Bloomington, Indiana.*

The *Clymer-Barrett Prereading Battery* has two stated purposes: the evaluation of pupils' prereading skills and abilities, and the diagnosis of prereading skills for planning beginning reading instruction. This review will focus on the quality of the test regarding each of these purposes.

If a test has as its purpose the broad evaluation of reading readiness, it should include measures of those skills which are most predictive of success in learning to read. The subtests for the test are listed above. The rationale for the inclusion of the various subtests is based on a number of correlation studies. This research evidence is adequate support for the inclusion of each subtest. However, most of the studies that are cited in the manual do not include any description of the type of initial reading program which occurred between the administration of the readiness measure before reading instruction and the administration of the reading achievement test following instruction. This suggests that the tests are predictive, but under an unknown set of conditions.

Potentially, the most useful aspect of the

battery is the Prereading Rating Scale, which is based on a teacher's classroom observations. This scale includes statements concerning a pupil's ability to follow a story sequence, ability to follow directions, and development in other basic language abilities. However, information concerning the scoring and interpretation of this scale is almost totally lacking. In addition, no validity or reliability evidence for the scale is included in the manual.

While the rationale and support for the inclusion of the various subtests are somewhat adequate, the predictive validity studies reported in the manual are not very impressive. In the first place, the data are impossible to interpret because the populations are not described. A test user would have no way of knowing whether the experimental population is in any way similar to the population he is planning to test. In one table, the correlations between the subtests of the Clymer-Barrett and three different reading achievement tests are shown to range from .29 to .71. The correlations of the Clymer-Barrett total score and the reading achievement tests ranged from .40 to .67. This is almost the same as the level of reading prediction of most group intelligence tests.

The second purpose of the Clymer-Barrett test is its use as a diagnostic instrument for planning beginning reading instruction. Evidence of its diagnostic validity is totally lacking. While the subtests have been shown to be predictive of later reading achievement, there is no evidence in the manual to support the contention that teaching any of the skills included in the battery will increase the probability that a child will learn to read. Indeed, one might argue that the two visual discrimination tests, Recognition of Letters and Matching Words, are not visual discrimination tasks at all but are actually beginning reading tasks. If the pupil can perform these tasks he has probably received formal or informal instruction in performing the tasks. The tests may, therefore, be testing specific reading skills rather than the general area of visual discrimination which the authors have titled these two tasks.

Construct validity evidence also is essential to support any diagnostic use of a test. The authors provide data (again from undescribed populations) to show that the intercorrelations of subtests are low and, therefore, the subtests are measuring different skills. Because of the extremely low reliabilities for the subtests, these data are not valid. A table providing correlations corrected for attenuation would be much more helpful. In order to show the diagnostic validity of the subtests, evidence should be given to indicate how the Clymer-Barrett provides improved instructional decisions and how various combinations of subtests are more predictive than each used alone in making instructional decisions.

Any use of the norms and tables should be cautious. The norming population is not adequately described in terms of percentages representing various socioeconomic groups, geographic distribution, or type of community. The authors state that weighting of larger states and communities was carried out, but they do not explain this procedure further. In addition, the testing in the norming population was accomplished when the students were in the third week of first grade. The authors state that these norms can be used confidently with students tested in kindergarten, but they provide no evidence to support this contention.

Two major strengths of the test include the very clear and concise directions for test administration and the total test reliability. One can administer the test rather easily following the authors' directions and can be fairly sure of its accuracy of measurement for total test performance.

In summary, the *Clymer-Barrett Prereading Battery* is generally no better, but also probably not much worse, than other reading readiness measures. Its predictive validity is about the same as other readiness measures. Its diagnostic validity is also about the same as other reading readiness tests; that is, it is extremely limited.

KENNETH J. SMITH, *Professor of Education and Head, Department of Reading, The University of Arizona, Tucson, Arizona.*

The *Clymer-Barrett Prereading Battery* has at least two strengths which are noteworthy: (*a*) Items within subtests generally have been chosen with care—the Matching Words section seems particularly well done; (*b*) The Prereading Rating Scale for accumulation of teacher observations, although subjective, should be particularly useful.

The test shares with other readiness tests a major problem: no one knows what combination of abilities is requisite to learning to read. Credit is due the authors for making no inordinate claims for this test. The publishers enclose

a letter, however, which claims that the Clymer-Barrett's "content is that which comprises reading itself: Auditory Discrimination; Visual Discrimination; and Visual-Motor Coordination." Whether this combination comprises *the* factors is doubtful. Are other, perhaps more important, factors neglected entirely? How about oral-aural language ability or the ability to associate visual and aural symbols? And if we knew the factors, which would be absolute requisites and which would be only desirable? If a factor is desirable, what is its appropriate weighting?

It is difficult to isolate factors, even when they have been selected. For instance, all subtests on the Clymer-Barrett test ability (and willingness) to follow the directions, in addition to the factor supposedly being tested. "Draw a line through the picture whose name begins like turkey." Many concepts and abilities other than "auditory discrimination" are necessary for the successful completion of this task. If the child is unsuccessful, the reason is unknown and therefore the appropriate instruction is also unknown.

Readiness tests generally serve two purposes: prediction and diagnosis. The Clymer-Barrett claims to be diagnostic, yet the justifications for its subtests are made by showing correlations with success in reading. For example, it is well known that knowledge of letter names is a fairly good *predictor* of success in reading. A variety of reasons could be proposed for this predictive ability. But it is extremely doubtful that knowledge of letter names is in any way a *causal* factor in reading ability. If it is not, then what does the teacher do for the child who does not know letter names? Assume that she has found a factor which will prevent his learning to read? Should she then teach him the letter names on the assumption that this is part of the content "which comprises reading itself?" So it would appear that the test may *predict* future success in reading, but there is no evidence that it will *diagnose* difficulty in factors requisite to reading success and point to an instructional program. Evidence is provided that the Clymer-Barrett is a valid instrument for the *prediction* of success in reading. Evidence is lacking for its validity as a diagnostic instrument. Unfortunately for the teacher who is trying to plan an instructional program, diagnosis is critical, while prediction is of limited value.

In fairness to the *Clymer-Barrett Prereading*

Battery, it should be emphasized that its weaknesses are the weaknesses of all existing readiness tests. The Clymer-Barrett is no worse, and probably better, than most. But the development of a valid diagnostic readiness test awaits much research on those components requisite to the reading process which are susceptible to development through instruction. There is great need for such a test. The Clymer-Barrett is an effort in that direction. It is unfortunate that the publisher's claims are far in excess of the ability of this or any other reading readiness test.

[745]
★The Contemporary School Readiness Test. First grade entrants; 1970; CSRT; reading section individually administered; Form A (11 pages); manual (30 pages); 25¢ per test; 75¢ per specimen set; postpaid; (105) minutes in 2 sessions; Clara Elbert Sauer; Montana Reading Clinic Publications. *

GERALD G. DUFFY, *Associate Professor of Education, Michigan State University, East Lansing, Michigan.*

This is an untimed test intended to be administered at the end of kindergarten or the beginning of first grade. Its purpose, which is not stated until page 28 of the manual, is "to predict the success of children in first grade." The term "success" is not defined.

The test consists of the following nine subtests: Writing My Name; Colors of the Spectrum; Science, Health, and Social Studies; Numbers; Handwriting; Reading; Visual Discrimination; Auditory Discrimination; and Listening Comprehension. No attempt is made to establish content validity or otherwise to explain why these particular subtests were selected. Similarly, the rationale for the approach used in certain subtests is unclear. For instance, Test 3 (Science, Health, and Social Studies) includes some items testing vocabulary and others testing inference, while Test 8 (Auditory Discrimination) is limited to rhyming sounds. No explanation for these emphases is provided.

The various parts of the test, as well as its directions to pupils, seem to be replete with weaknesses. Successful completion of the Colors of the Spectrum test depends as much on understanding the concepts of "bottom," "top," and "next" as on knowledge of the colors. The Numbers test requires students to mark the correct answer in items 1 through 7 and in items 11 through 15, but requires him to fill the blanks in items 8 through 10, a midway switch which may confuse young students. The direc-

tions in several other subtests lack the specificity necessary to insure that a group of young students all will keep their places, a situation compounded by the fact that some students will take longer than others to complete some items but all must wait for the teacher's oral directions before going on to the next item. On the Visual Discrimination subtest, 7 of the 15 items require students to discriminate among pictures and geometric figures (as opposed to letters and numbers), despite the fact that research reveals little relationship between this skill and success in reading. The Reading subtest consists of teaching a five-word, one-sentence "story" to the whole class by using word cards and pictures (provided in the test kit) in repetitive manner, with individual students being retested on both the individual words and the whole "story" one hour later. The reliability of this subtest, based as it is on whole-group, recitation-type learning, is highly questionable.

The scoring varies within the test. On Tests 3, 4, 5, 7, 8, and 9, the student receives one point for each correct response. Points are assigned in other tests on the basis of how well the student does. In the Handwriting test, the child receives one point for each word or letter reproduced, providing that it is "reproduced in a reasonably legible manner." No standard of legibility is provided, however. The total points out of a possible 100 represent the readiness score, with the user referring to norms in the manual to determine percentile score and "level of school readiness." A raw score of between 65 and 82 represents a percentile range of 33 to 67 and a level of school readiness of "AVERAGE—likely to succeed in first grade work."

The statistical data reported in the manual lack precision. For instance, it is stated that the test "was developed through a four year period" by analyzing the test results of "over" 1,000 children; that "more than one-hundred pupils....[in each of the three administrations] were used for establishing norms and obtaining information on validity and reliability"; that "the total sample was about evenly divided between boys and girls"; and that "the children came from a broad range of socio-economic backgrounds." It is difficult to determine just exactly how many subjects were used in collecting the data reported, and the criteria used in selecting subjects are unclear.

The reported reliability data were established by running correlations between Form A and unpublished Form B, while validity data were obtained by correlating the results of this test with the results of the *Metropolitan Achievement Tests: Reading.* While the correlation coefficients reported were encouraging, the small size of the sample and the fact that the geographical representation was limited to Montana, Idaho, and Washington, forces one to conclude that the norming group is not a representative national sample.

In summary, it is felt that the test could be more precise in stating its purpose, in providing information regarding content validity and use of test results, in constructing individual items and directions for subtests, and in reporting normative and validity data. The test is not recommended for use in its present form.

[746]

★**Early Detection Inventory.** Preschool children; 1967; EDI; school readiness; 4 scores: school readiness tasks, social-emotional behavior responses, motor performance, total; medical history and family background supplied by parent; individual; 1 form (15 pages); manual (16 pages); no data on reliability and validity; no norms; $8.25 per 15 tests; $1.20 per manual; postage extra; specimen set not available; testing materials must be assembled locally; [45] minutes; F. E. McGahan and Carolyn McGahan; Follett Educational Corporation. *

MILDRED H. HUEBNER, *Professor of Education and Director, Reading Center, Southern Connecticut State College, New Haven, Connecticut.*

Users of the *Early Detection Inventory,* an individual screening device, will have in convenient booklet form an overall evaluation of each child's readiness for school tasks. The inventory is designed to alert school personnel to the preschool child's readiness in these broad areas: social, emotional, physical, and intellectual development.

The authors suggest that the following personnel be contacted for various parts of the screening: parent, dentist, receptionist, and speech therapist. In addition, they suggest that the readiness section of the inventory be administered by a teacher, school psychologist or counselor, or other professional person.

RECORD FORM. The inventory booklet provides a record form for the various checklists. One page is devoted to the examiner's assessment of the child's social-emotional behavior during the administration of the school readiness tasks. Positive and negative responses are indicated for checking. Examples are "Pleasant, smiling" versus "Disagreeable, frowning," and "Con-

fident, self-assured" versus "Timid, fearful, unsure." Six pages are devoted to assessing the child's school readiness. Examples of tasks are knowing colors, counting pennies, recognizing coins, drawing a person, and copying geometric forms. One page provides a record of eye and dental examination, audiometric evaluation, speech and other physical problems. Four pages include quite detailed questions concerning family and social history, prenatal and birth history, and the child's physical history to date.

MANUAL. The manual gives a rationale for the various items included in the inventory, directions for administration, scoring procedures, and suggestions for uses of results. The authors suggest that the inventory is also "useful with children in transitional classes and ungraded primary classes." In a brief but excellent appendix they give directions for the planning and staffing of a preschool evaluation clinic, with procedures for scheduling and evaluating the numbers of preschool children to be serviced. No information concerning standardization, reliability, or validity has been provided in the manual.

The general guidelines provide a list of additional materials the examiner will need to collect before his session with the child—crayons, pennies, rubber bands, and so on. Detailed instructions for each task are provided, with precisely worded questions for the examiner's use.

SCORING. From the viewpoint of this reviewer, the scoring procedure has been oversimplified, and will prove inadequate in some cases. The examiner is told merely to assign a rating of 1, 2, or 3, based on keys furnished in the booklet. Then an overall readiness evaluation is assigned the child—able to work independently, may need help in specific areas, or will probably need special help. Considering the importance of these judgments, more detailed instructions for scoring and interpreting several of the items will be needed by most of the examiners (except the experienced psychologists) who are suggested by the authors to administer the readiness part of the inventory. Several items are to be rated on a three-point scale: Successful, Partial, Unsuccessful. The child's copying of seven geometric figures would be rated simply as Good, Fair, or Poor. When one considers the variations that can be expected among children's copying of a triangle, to use one example, one should expect a scale of values to be included for ease of scoring. On one page the child is told to draw a whole person. The only scoring direction provided the examiner is to check Successful, Partial, or Unsuccessful. In another section of the manual the examiner will find the statement, "The authors' experience indicates that the child who includes in his picture the major parts of the body in reasonable relationship to each other—head, torso, legs, arms—has enough awareness of body image to be able to operate in a learning situation." Thus the examiner is given the rational for this sub-test, but no clear guidelines as to how to score an individual child's drawing of a person. Psychologists skilled in the *Goodenough-Harris Drawing Test* will be in a better position to make the indicated judgments than would the other personnel suggested by the authors. The authors state, "The inventory is simple and does not require intensive training to administer." They do not indicate any other personnel for scoring and interpreting the results, however. The readiness section, therefore, would be strengthened by the addition of more specific scoring guidelines and by the recommendation that it be administered, scored, and interpreted by trained examiners.

SUMMARY. Many school systems collect much of the data indicated in the EDI, but many do so in a haphazard manner. Sometimes when planning programs, they do not take time to look at the "total picture" of a child even after collecting such data. An organized collection and assessment of information would help school personnel to make an early discovery of differences among school entrants—their strengths and weaknesses. Thus the EDI would be useful in providing not only an overall assessment on which to base the initiation of a successful school program but also a foundation for a continuing study of the individual.

Both the manual and the booklet form need further revision to make this a fully useful tool. It is hoped that the authors will provide information on the groups on which this inventory was built and some data concerning its reliability and validity.

JAMES J. MCCARTHY, *Professor of Education, The University of Wisconsin, Madison, Wisconsin.*

The *Early Detection Inventory* is not a psychometric instrument, but, as the title suggests, an inventory. It is a collection of data gathered from parent questionnaires and from direct assessment of the child. This amalgam is intended to suggest a child's readiness for school and to provide a documentary base for the continuing study of the child. The inventory is designed for use with preschool children as well as children in ungraded primary and transitional classes. Its purpose is to search for behavioral signs that are associated with learning problems, by observation or reports of behavior relating to social and emotional adjustment, gross and fine motor coordination, and language performance. To do this, the inventory provides (a) a series of school readiness tasks, (b) a series of gross and fine motor performance tasks, (c) a checklist of "social-emotional" responses (which are to be characterized as positive or negative based upon the behavior of the child during assessment), (d) a questionnaire on the family-social and medical history, and (e) space for recording outcomes of eye, dental, audiometric, and speech evaluations. The school readiness tasks, social-emotional adjustment, and motor performances of the child are each assigned a rating of one, two, or three and brought forward to a summary page where an overall rating is derived as follows: the overall score is one, if all three ratings are one; three, if all three ratings are three; and two, if the child received any other combinations of performance ratings. An overall rating of one indicates the child has responded adequately in all major tasks and is probably able to work independently. If the overall rating is two, the child may need some specific help and when he gets to school he should be watched carefully. A child with a rating of three was unable to respond adequately in any major task area and will probably need special help. Physical problems and personal data appear on this summary page.

The authors, appreciating the difficulty of assembling these data on many children, suggest the use of a preschool clinic which they estimate would be able to process about 100 children per day. Such a clinic would have 16 stations and require a minimum of about 18 people, including several professionals (teacher, nurse, speech therapist, dentist, psychologist, counselor). This averages out to about one man hour of effort per inventory, exclusive of the time parents spend bringing their children there, completing the family, social and medical history, and bringing the child home.

Early Detection Inventory

The value of such an inventory, whether completed in a clinic or by less economical means, is in having a substantial amount of what is believed to be critical information about a child from the outset. Frank defects will be quickly noted and appropriate referrals can be made. Children with marginal performance can be tagged for special observation and given appropriate educational modifications from their first day in school. And, the inventory will provide a useful data base for retrospective individual and group study.

The inventory is not unique in any of its component parts, for most of its questionnaires, performance tasks and checklists have appeared separately at one time or the other, in one form or the other, in the professional literature. The contribution of the inventory lies in assembling the components and in suggesting a means of data collection and data summary.

In their 16-page manual, the authors describe the intent of each part of the inventory but provide no evidence that such parts, or the collective package, effectively identifies a target group of preschoolers with real or incipient problems. Obviously the physical examination and medical history portions of the inventory are largely immune from this criticism. But the social-emotional behavior checklist, for example, raises many questions. Does it include all pertinent behaviors and exclude irrelevant behaviors? Are examiners capable of making appropriate judgments about behaviors? Will these behaviors vary from one situation to the next and from day to day? Do two observers rate the same subject in the same (or reasonably similar) manner? Is the scoring system such that it really identifies children with social and emotional problems? Do children identified as having social or emotional problems by this scale really have or develop such problems? In short, a good deal of reliability, validity, and experimental data should be brought to bear on this section of the inventory before it is trusted for decision making among large groups of children. The same comments apply to both the school readiness and motor performance sections of the inventory. It may be argued that these sections of the inventory have a certain "face validity" or that since most parts are not novel, the user of the inventory can consult the research literature. Though true, these arguments do not excuse the inventory's authors from the obligation of assembling such data in the manual and pro-

viding research on which extant literature is silent.

In sum, the *Early Detection Inventory* appears to provide a vehicle for a comprehensive screening of preschool and ungraded primary school children in the motor, physical, social-emotional, and school-task readiness areas. As a community project, a preschool clinic could be organized in which the inventory could be administered through the joint cooperation of parents, professionals, and volunteer workers; this is probably the most effective means of gathering the data. The inventory purports to indicate the child's readiness for school although no data are provided to support this claim.

[747]
★Evanston Early Identification Scale, Field Research Edition. Ages 5-0 to 6-3; 1967; EEIS; for identifying children who can be expected to have difficulty in school; 1 form (3 pages); manual (45 pages); no data on reliability; $1.50 per 15 tests; $1.59 per manual; postage extra; specimen set not available; [10-45] minutes; Myril Landsman and Harry Dillard; Follett Educational Corporation. *

REFERENCE
1. FERINDEN, WILLIAM E., JR., AND JACOBSON, SHERMAN. "Early Identification of Learning Disabilities." *J Learn Dis* 3(11):589-93 N '70. *

JAMES J. McCARTHY, *Professor of Education, The University of Wisconsin, Madison, Wisconsin.*

The aim of the EEIS is to provide "a simple, highly efficient screening device for identifying those children who can be expected to have difficulty in school." It is said to be valid for children from ages 5-0 to 6-3 and for "different socioeconomic groups." It can be administered and scored by the teacher, as either an individual or a group test. The child is provided a test booklet and lead pencil and instructed to "Please draw someone; draw anyone that you wish. Draw just one person." Erasures are permitted but children are not allowed to look at each other's drawings. There is no time limit.

In scoring, from 1 to 4 points are given if certain elementary body parts are missing (eyes, nose, mouth, arms, hands, legs, feet, body, and hair or hat). In addition, head, legs and arms must be "connected at approximately correct junctures." Thus, the figure with nothing missing is awarded zero points; the maximum number is 21. The child with a score of 4 or less is regarded as low risk (LR) and "can be expected to have no problems." The child with a score of from 5 through 7 is regarded as middle risk (MR) and "may have some difficulty in school." A child with a score of 8 or greater is regarded as high risk (HR) "and will probably require the attention of special personnel."

The risk classification is said to suggest a course of action to the teacher. The LR child should require no special action, while the status of the MR child is uncertain. Some MR children are simply slow in maturing, while others may require further diagnostic testing or special treatment; the professional judgment of the teacher must supplement the test outcome. The HR children "can be expected to have problems in school" and should be referred to the school psychologist for further testing or special treatment. Children who perform poorly are expected to have "emotional, perceptual, or other problems." It is not a test of artistic ability and, "except in cases of mental retardation, intelligence does not significantly influence the test results."

Tests of this character are clearly needed to call children with potential problems to the attention of school personnel for appropriate action. The aim of the publisher to field a "simple, highly effective screening device" is at least partly achieved in the EEIS. Its obvious advantages include ease and speed of administration. A child or a class can perform the task in a few minutes, and scoring requires evaluation of only 10 aspects of the drawing and does not appear to be difficult or arbitrary. Standards not explicit in the scoring directions can be inferred from 20 pages of sample drawings.

RELIABILITY. No reliability is reported, since the variables tested by the EEIS are said to be influenced by development and are expected to change (hence the narrow age limits for the test). However, some index of stability over short periods of time should be provided to assure users that children's scores do not vary from week to week to any significant degree.

VALIDITY. In a sense, the important test of validity is whether the EEIS predicts the future status of children; it seems to do so rather well. Predictions on the 117 standardization subjects were checked by using EEIS scores of 0–4 as "no referral" and of 8–21 as "referral." Of the 95 children falling into either of these categories, only 8 were incorrectly predicted. No predictions were made on the 22 remaining children, with EEIS scores between 5 and 7; it turned out that about half were referred. Interestingly, group intelligence test scores do not appear to differentiate referred from nonreferred children in the normal range of intelligence. The authors state that "except in cases of mental retardation, intelligence does not significantly influence the test results."

PROBLEMS. Clearly, a larger normative group and further validation work are required, but the authors suggest the promise of such work by billing this version of the EEIS as a "Field Research Edition." The test booklet is constructed so that the scoring page is opposite the page on which the child draws. Unless the scoring page is folded under (this is not explicit in administration instructions), the astute subject could, possibly, relate the two.

SUMMARY. The reviewer was impressed with this little test in terms of its ease and speed of administration, its simplicity of scoring, and its potential for predicting subsequent school problems on the basis of drawings made by children halfway through kindergarten. The need for such an instrument is abundantly clear and it is difficult to imagine an easier test for a teacher to manage. Of course, the present test characteristics are based on too small a sample of children, but the test is appropriately labeled "Field Research Edition" in acknowledgment of this; present data are extremely encouraging. Short term reliability has yet to be demonstrated. The test manual is clearly and honestly written. The promise of this instrument should invite confirming research from school systems and university graduate schools.

JEROME ROSNER, *Research Associate, Learning Research and Development Center, University of Pittsburgh, Pittsburgh, Pennsylvania.*

The EEIS is yet another attempt to assess the young child's ability in drawing the human figure and, in this instance, relate it to subsequent poor performance. The authors propose the EEIS as a "simple, highly efficient screening device for identifying those children who can be expected to have difficulty in school."

The test is easily administered. The scoring criteria are based on the notion that certain body parts are likely to be omitted by the less adequate performer. Hence, specific body features are listed in a 10-item weighted scale (e.g., hair or hat, eyes, nose) and points are charged for their omission. A perfect score is zero; the maximum number of points one can score is 21. As in all tests of this type, certain scoring situations arise that are not specifically described in the stated criteria, but in general less than the usual amount of indecision seems to occur. Interrater reliability (between the two authors) in using the scale is reported at .97. The resultant scores are classified in three (Low, Middle, High) risk categories. The authors contend that a high risk designation (a score of 8 or above) indicates good reason to expect the child to have "problems in school" that will probably require the attention of special school personnel, such as a psychologist; that a low risk designation (a score of 4 or less) indicates that the child can be expected "to have no problems" and the middle risk score (from 5 through 7) "may" indicate difficulty. The manual contains anecdotal case histories of nine children, all of whom were high risk and had been referred for assistance of some sort.

The EEIS was standardized on a population of only 117 children. The authors related, in retrospect, the academic records of fourth, fifth, and sixth grade children with figure drawings (*Metropolitan Readiness Tests*) that had been produced when the children were in kindergarten. By establishing cutoff points, the subjects were placed first in one of two and later one of the three categories. Correlations were computed to determine the validity of the EEIS score in predicting which children would have been referred to a school psychologist because of behavior and/or learning problems. These figures were then compared to actual referral data. Unfortunately, little information is provided regarding the nature of the standardization group, their socioeconomic backgrounds, range of intellectual capacities, or performance records. In addition, no information is given on the specific criteria used for the original determination of the referred population, such as how many of those were false negatives, or the age at which referred.

Test reliability was not investigated. The authors realistically state that developmentally derived abilities do not lend themselves well to test-retest situations. There is reason, however, to explore further in this instance and determine whether test-retest data that take development into consideration could not be obtained during the kindergarten year. If the test is indeed valid for children within the 15-month age range specified, this does not seem to be an impossible consideration.

Admittedly, the test edition is identified as a "Field Research Edition." One assumes that

larger and more detailed studies will be conducted to validate the instrument as well as to support its reliability. The authors present it as "a simple, highly efficient screening device." One must caution that the words "highly efficient" have not, as yet, been adequately supported. Viewed as a manageable, though relatively global, method for scoring figure drawing tests that could provide meaningful information to those concerned with a child's intellectual and emotional development, the test appears to be useful, interesting, and deserving of more elaborate developmental effort. Viewing it, however, as *the* instrument for identifying children who may or may not encounter school problems is not justified from presently available data.

[748]

★First Grade Screening Test. First grade entrants; 1966–69; FGST; intellectual deficiency, central nervous system dysfunction, and emotional disturbance; 1 form ('66, 28 pages); 2 editions: boy's, girl's; manual ('69, 55 pages); $4.75 per 25 tests; $2.25 per manual; postage extra; $2.75 per specimen set, postpaid; (30–45) minutes; John E. Pate and Warren W. Webb; American Guidance Service, Inc. *

J Ed Meas 6(1):36–7 sp '69. Grayce A. Ransom. * The procedures for administering are clear and concise. Separate test booklets are provided for boys and girls to "allow children an opportunity to identify with familiar though different social roles." The difference in the forms is only that the sex of the pictured children is the same as the examinee's. No data supporting the implicit assumption are provided. Although there are no practice exercises, the tasks are suitable and clear to the age group involved. * Delineation of the content universe and the proportions of representative items seems to have been approached superficially. The manual states that the underlying rationale depended on teaching experience, developmental theory, clinical instruments, and research literature. Analysis of the sustaining bibliography of sixteen references dealing with types of behavior which are predictive of school failure does not provide proof of a broad and varied base for the general rationale involved. Moreover, the bibliography includes a number of authors who emphasize perceptual-motor skill development for school readiness, and virtually none who emphasize other types of perceptual skills. The brief description of two small pilot studies using experimental test forms does not specify the process by which the original 40 item test was reduced to the present 27 items.

Analysis of the skills sampled is lacking in the manual. * This test does *not* appear to meet the following specifications as named in the *Standards for Educational and Psychological Tests* (1966) recommended by the joint AERA-APA-NCME committee: C3.1, C3.2, C4.31, C4.32, C4.5, C5.2, C6.3, C7, C7.1, C7.11, C7.12, C7.13, C7.2, C7.21, D1.1, D2, D2.42, D6.1, and D6.31. Although sufficient specific evidence of strong undergirding work for construct validity seems lacking, this test does give empirical evidence of providing a quickly and simply administered screening test for identifying a good percentage of ending kindergarten or beginning first-grade children who are "high risks" for failure in academic work.

[749]
*Gates-MacGinitie Reading Tests: Readiness Skills.** Grades kgn-1; 1939-69; revision of *Gates Reading Readiness Tests;* catalog uses the title *Gates-MacGinitie Readiness Skills Test;* 9 scores: listening comprehension, auditory discrimination, visual discrimination, following directions, letter recognition, visual-motor coordination, auditory blending, total, word recognition; 1 form ('66, 8 pages); manual ('68, 20 pages); technical supplement ('69, 4 pages); $4.25 per 35 tests; 75¢ per specimen set; postage extra; (120) minutes in 4 sessions; Arthur I. Gates and Walter H. MacGinitie; Teachers College Press. *

REFERENCES

1-5. See 2:1537.
6-8. See 3:516.
9. See 6:845.
10. BALOW, IRVING H. *The Relationship of Lateral Dominance Characteristics to Reading Achievement in the First Grade.* Doctor's thesis, University of Minnesota (Minneapolis, Minn.), 1959. (*DA* 20:2138)
11. WEAVER, CARL H.; FURBEE, CATHERINE; AND EVERHART, RODNEY W. "Articulatory Competency and Reading Readiness." *J Speech & Hearing Res* 3:174-80 Je '60. * (*PA* 35:7111)
12. BARRETT, THOMAS CLIFFORD. *The Relationship Between Selected Reading Readiness Measures of Visual Discrimination and First Grade Reading Achievement.* Doctor's thesis, University of Minnesota (Minneapolis, Minn.), 1962. (*DA* 24:193)
13. DYKSTRA, ROBERT. *The Relationship Between Selected Reading Readiness Measures of Auditory Discrimination and Reading Achievement at the End of First Grade.* Doctor's thesis, University of Minnesota (Minneapolis, Minn.), 1962. (*DA* 24:195)
14. KERFOOT, JAMES FLETCHER. *The Relationship of Selected Auditory and Visual Reading Readiness Measures to First Grade Reading Achievement and Second Grade Reading and Spelling Achievement.* Doctor's thesis, University of Minnesota (Minneapolis, Minn.), 1964. (*DA* 25:1747)
15. LOPER, DORIS JEAN. *Auditory Discrimination, Intelligence, Achievement, and Background of Experience and Information in a Culturally Disadvantaged First-Grade Population.* Doctor's thesis, Temple University (Philadelphia, Pa.), 1965. (*DA* 26:5873)
16. DE HIRSCH, KATRINA; JANSKY, JEANNETTE JEFFERSON; AND LANGFORD, WILLIAM S. *Predicting Reading Failure.* New York: Harper & Row, Publishers, Inc., 1966. Pp. xv, 144. *
17. DYKSTRA, ROBERT. "Auditory Discrimination Abilities and Beginning Reading Achievement." *Read Res Q* 1:5-34 sp '66. * (*PA* 40:11011)
18. SILBERBERG, MARGARET CATHERINE. *The Effect of Formal Reading Readiness Training in Kindergarten on Development of Readiness Skills and Growth in Reading.* Doctor's thesis, University of Minnesota (Minneapolis, Minn.), 1966. (*DA* 28:974A)
19. MILLER, W. DUANE, AND NORRIS, RAYMOND C. "Entrance Age and School Success." *J Sch Psychol* 6:47-60 f '67. * (*PA* 42:7867)
20. SILBERBERG, NORMAN; IVERSEN, IVER; AND SILBERBERG, MARGARET. "Predicting End of First Grade Developmental Reading Test Scores From Gates Reading Readiness Test Scores Administered in Kindergarten." Abstract. *Proc 75th Ann Conv Am Psychol Assn* 2:291-2 '67. * (*PA* 41:14224)
21. ALTHOUSE, ROSEMARY ELIZABETH. *Validation of an Individual Reading Readiness Test.* Doctor's thesis, Florida State University (Tallahassee, Fla.), 1968. (*DAI* 30:611A)
22. OHNMACHT, FRED W., AND OLSON, ARTHUR V. "Canonical Analysis of Reading Readiness Measures and the Frostig Developmental Test of Visual Perception." Abstract. *AERA Paper Abstr* 1968:121-2 '68. *
23. OHNMACHT, FRED W., AND OLSON, ARTHUR V. "Canonical Analysis of Reading Readiness Measures and the Frostig Developmental Test of Visual Perception." *Ed & Psychol Meas* 28:479-84 su '68. * (*PA* 42:19278)
24. SILBERBERG, NORMAN; IVERSEN, IVER; AND SILBERBERG, MARGARET. "The Predictive Efficiency of the Gates Reading Readiness Tests." *El Sch J* 68:213-8 Ja '68. *
25. FARR, ROGER, AND ANASTASIOW, NICHOLAS. *Tests of Reading Readiness and Achievement: A Review and Evaluation,* pp. 11-3. Newark, Del.: International Reading Association, 1969. Pp. iv, 51. *
26. JOHNSON, CLIFFORD IVY. *An Analysis of the Predictive Validity of Selective Reading Readiness Factors to Third Grade Reading Achievement.* Doctor's thesis, University of Georgia (Athens, Ga.), 1969. (*DAI* 30:3363A)

PAUL CONRAD BERG, *Professor of Education and Director, Reading Clinic, University of South Carolina, Columbia, South Carolina.*

The stimulus items in the Gates-MacGinitie tests are clearly defined and the pictures are carefully detailed. Words are in primer type or larger and reasonably spaced for ease in discrimination. No clues, however, are given to identify the line which the teacher is describing. In giving directions, the teacher says only, "Move your finger down to the next box," etc. (By contrast, the *Metropolitan Readiness Tests* have an easily identified object at the beginning of each set of stimulus items as a common reference for place of pupil response.) Otherwise, the directions for examiners and the pupils are essentially clear and appropriate.

Compared to many other readiness tests, the 120 minutes of administration time for the Gates-MacGinitie test is excessive. For example, the *Harrison-Stroud Reading Readiness Profiles* normally requires 80-90 minutes to administer (6 subtests), the *Lee-Clark Reading Readiness Test,* only 20 minutes (4 subtests), the *Metropolitan Readiness Tests,* 60 minutes (6 subtests), and the *Murphy-Durrell Reading Readiness Analysis,* 60 minutes (3 subtests). While the Gates-MacGinitie requires the longest administration time, it also has eight subtests, two more than its closest comparison. The relative merits of the longer testing time for the Gates-MacGinitie are not known.

A supplement to the manual presents correlations between the Readiness Skills test taken in October and the *Gates-MacGinitie Reading Test* taken in the following May. The correlations between the total readiness scores and the vocabulary and comprehension scores of the reading test were .60 and .59, respectively, for these first graders.

The data available for this test again indicate the large amount of variance not accounted for between predictive measures and their criteria. Quite correctly, the authors state that "Reading is a complex skill involving many component abilities, but a reading readiness test can measure a child's abilities in only a limited number of areas." Therefore, the authors list some 10 areas of investigation that are necessary but not covered by the test.

Formal as well as informal observations are a necessary part of the continuous task of evaluating and teaching. Normative data seem adequate to give confidence to this test within the limits of the variance it can account for. Whether the administration time, which is longer than that of many tests, recommends it is a matter for the user to decide.

ROBERT DYKSTRA, *Professor of Education, University of Minnesota, Minneapolis, Minnesota.*

This test is intended for use with pupils either finishing kindergarten or beginning first grade, and separate norms are provided. Norm tables for the two groups indicate very little difference in performance, suggesting that little growth takes place in the readiness skills measured by the test during the period between the end of the kindergarten year and the beginning of the first grade. Although it is interesting to find separate norms for kindergarten and first grade youngsters, it is not very helpful in a practical sense. Use of the wrong norm tables for evaluating pupil performance on the test would have no effect on decisions made about that pupil's readiness for reading.

The authors give a brief statement concerning what each of the eight subtests is designed to measure but never discuss the purpose of the test as a whole. It is not clear whether the test is designed to measure general school readiness or the more specific area of reading readiness. Because this test is part of the *Gates-Mac-Ginitie Reading Test* series, the latter possibility is more likely, although no clear statement to that effect can be found. Moreover, the test authors do not indicate whether the test is designed primarily to identify pupils who are ready for formal reading instructions or to diagnose strengths and weaknesses in a pupil's readiness profile. This lack of clarity of purpose

extends to the section of the manual entitled "Interpreting the Scores," where almost no suggestions are offered concerning the instructional implications of a certain level of pupil performance on the test. The teacher is encouraged to obtain a total weighted score for each pupil, to locate the corresponding readiness standard score or readiness percentile score, and to record these scores in the appropriate spaces. Presumably, such information is useful in planning instructional strategies. However, no help is given to teachers in determining what to do instructionally with a pupil whose score falls at the 25th, 50th, 75th, or any other percentile. In fact, the entire discussion focuses on what the teacher might do in working with a pupil who scores very poorly on one or more of the subtests. The impression is given that pupil performance on the various subtests, rather than performance on the test battery as a whole, is the critical factor.

This emphasis on subtest performance is surprising in light of the authors' efforts to maximize the predictive validity of the total test. Multiple regression techniques were utilized to weight the eight subtests in such a way as to provide the best prediction of later reading achievement. (This mention of *reading* achievement, incidentally, comes from the technical supplement, not from the teacher's manual, which fails to clarify whether the test is designed to predict reading readiness, general school readiness, or something else.) The authors report that weighting the subtest scores provides a slight increase in the accuracy of prediction over that which would be obtained by assigning equal weights to the subtests. Because of this interest in maximizing the predictive efficiency of the total test, it is disturbing to find no suggestions to teachers concerning how to interpret any given total score.

The authors' unwillingness to define more explicitly what the test is designed to do and their failure to provide adequate interpretation of test results are unfortunate, because in many ways the test appears to be a good readiness test. Performance on the total test correlates approximately .60 with first grade reading achievement. This relationship is consistent with that obtained for most other readiness batteries. Moreover, most of the subtests appear to measure skills which have been found to be closely related to subsequent reading achievement. Even here, however, some problems can be noted. The

Gates-MacGinitie Reading Tests: Readiness Skills

Auditory Blending test confronts the teacher with the task of pronouncing words such as "R-A-I-N" by dividing them where indicated and pausing one second between the parts. How does one pronounce the consonant /r/ in isolation? How about /n/? Obviously, it is impossible. Some examiners will say, "er-ai-en"; some will say "ra-ai-na"; some will say something else. Because of the artificial nature of the task, because of the difficulties in administering the subtest, and because of low correlations (approximately .30) between performance on this test and first grade reading achievement, inclusion of this subtest in the battery seems questionable.

The technical supplement reports subtest reliabilities, but, surprisingly, no reliability data for the total test. Neither the teachers' manual nor the supplement use the term "validity," which probably relates to the failure of the test authors to state specifically the purpose of the test. The closest the authors come to discussing validity is to include one paragraph and an accompanying table on the subject "Correlations with Reading Achievement" in the technical supplement. Therefore, presumably the test has predictive validity. However, as was pointed out earlier, the test provides no help to teachers in interpreting test performance from a predictive point of view.

The discussion of the norming procedures for the test is very brief, giving no information about the normative sample other than to describe it as being nationwide, consisting of "approximately 4500 children in 35 communities," and being "carefully selected on the basis of size, geographic location, average educational level, and family income." The test user is left with the necessity of trusting the accuracy of those judgments.

One would be remiss in concluding this review without stating a potential strength of the battery. The test is the product of the joint thinking of two highly respected authorities in the field. The test itself, therefore, may well be an excellent one. One cannot make that judgment, however, on the basis of the information provided in the manual and the supplement, which fail badly in (a) informing the user about the purpose for which the test is designed; (b) providing information concerning whether or not the test can adequately do what it is designed to do; and (c) helping the test user to interpret test data once he has collected them.

For a review by F. J. Schonell of the original edition, see 4:566; for reviews by Marion Monroe Cox and Paul A. Witty, see 3:516; see also 2:1537 (2 excerpts).

[750]
★The Gesell Developmental Tests. Ages 5–10; 1964–65; readiness to start school; individual; 1 form; 10 recording sheets ('65, 1 page); manual ('65, 404 pages, see 2 below); $9 per set of test materials (test cards, 1 set of 10 recording sheets, and 2 three-dimensional objects); $25 per 100 sets of the recording sheets; $6.95 per set of instructional cards to assist in evaluating responses to the Incomplete Man subtest; $10.95 per manual; postage extra; (20–30) minutes; Frances L. Ilg and Louise Bates Ames; Programs for Education. *

REFERENCES
1. ILG, FRANCES L.; AMES, LOUISE BATES; AND APELL, RICHARD J. "School Readiness as Evaluated by Gesell Developmental, Visual, and Projective Tests." Genetic Psychol Monogr 71:61–91 F '65. * (PA 39:12943)
2. ILG, FRANCES L., AND AMES, LOUISE BATES. School Readiness: Behavior Tests Used at the Gesell Institute. New York: Harper & Row, Publishers, Inc., 1965. Pp. xiii, 396. *
3. AMES, LOUISE BATES. "Academic Progress in Negro Schools." J Learn Dis 1:570–7 O '68. * (PA 45:3029)
4. HIRST, WILMA E. "Sex as a Predictor Variable for Success in First Grade Reading Achievement." J Learn Dis 2(6): 316–21 Je '69. * (PA 45:7077)
5. KAUFMAN, ALAN STEPHEN. Comparison of Tests Built From Piaget's and Gesell's Tasks: An Analysis of Their Psychometric Properties and Psychological Meaning. Doctor's thesis, Columbia University (New York, N.Y.), 1970. (DAI 31: 5605B)

Child Develop Abstracts 39:164 Je–Ag '65. L. J. Borstelmann. [Review of the manual (2).] This combined text and manual presents the basic educational viewpoint of the Gesell Institute: that children should be entered in school and assigned on the basis of their developmental behavior age, not on the basis of chronological age or IQ. * They have not presented a scoring system for the tests nor have they studied the criterial problems of school readiness assessment. In an initial study of 100 kindergarten children the investigators' global judgments as to readiness were in close agreement with global teacher judgments, and also were highly related to academic section assignments 6 years later. Specifications for examiner and teacher ratings are not given. This volume will be a valuable resource for investigators and school psychologists seeking to develop screening procedures for school entry and initial class assignments. The report deals only with the Gesell Institute data and does not consider or refer to other studies of relevance. The authors' approach assumes the basic issue of school readiness to be placement according to general behavioral maturity within given curricular arrangements. They do not consider either curricular modification in terms of developmental level or curricula as a means of facilitating behavioral growth.

Cont Psychol 10:572–3 D '65. *Edith Meyer Taylor.* [Review of the manual (2).] * The authors do not claim that they intend to present new ideas or procedures. Their principles, their viewpoint and their method of presentation are the ones that have for many years now been the earmark of publications originating in the Gesell group. Here again are the carefully recorded behavior observations, the minute normative tabulations of behavioral items by age; here again the "capsule" portraits of distinct age levels: "five" clearly distinguished from "five and a half" and both much different from "six." Such capsule portraits, highlighting some of the alleged characteristics of the stage, are again here meant to represent norms; necessarily they are again most schematic. As in previous books these portraits are engagingly described: there is the "good Five" or the "Withdrawing Seven." The impression is created that emotional attitudes are part and parcel of the developmental level and the suggestion is given that such attitudes may be modified, mitigated or altogether disappear when the child gets six months older and the next maturity level is reached. There is no mention of dynamic psychological processes and no suggestion that individual experiences, interpersonal relationships or home climate may be possible factors in the creation of emotional attitudes toward school. Nothing is said about children who are not ready for school because they cannot leave their mother or about those who find it too hard not to be the kingpin or about the many others who have their own specific psychological reasons for not adjusting to school. It is understood in this book that any signs of immaturity can be picked up in the developmental examination because they show in the child's performances, in his conversations and in his approach to the situation. There is no doubt that experienced examiners such as our authors and their co-workers have no difficulty recognizing some such manifestations. It is easily evident, to those who have seen them at work, that in the individual case their judgment is guided by many factors besides the less elusive and more objective behavior signs mostly described in the book. The purpose of this book is to help parents and school administrators. It is recommended that examiners must be well trained in the giving of these tests but it is not

Gesell Developmental Tests

specified that they must have psychological insight and sensitivity of their own. Perhaps the omission of emotional and individual factors is justified by the limited purpose of the book; perhaps a more sophisticated approach could lead to misuse and misinterpretation. Yet one cannot help feeling that things are made too simple here and that the reader is not made aware enough of the pitfalls of a "quickie" examination. The labor and skill necessary for a true full appraisal of a child's psychological status and development are not emphasized enough and that seems a serious omission. * Ilg and Ames may here be thanked for lending their warning voice and their prestige to the question of school readiness and the problems of parental educational pressure. May they again help to allay fears and may they succeed in adding weight to efforts of educators and mental health experts who try to delay academic learning for children not ready and to enrich the vistas of those who can learn faster. A special prayer goes for their success in combatting the forces of darkness which try to lure unsuspecting parents into teaching their two-year olds "to read" (instead of helping them first to see things which they might later find worth reading about.)

[751]

★**Kindergarten Evaluation of Learning Potential.** Kgn; 1963–69; KELP; prediction of school success based upon the learning performance on KELP items presented as regular instructional activities throughout the kindergarten year; 4 scores: association learning, conceptualization, creative self-expression, total; 1 form; test booklet ('67, 24 pages), teacher's edition ('67, 8 pages plus test booklet); manual ('66, 259 pages, see 3 below); resources guide ('69, 32 pages); introduction ('67, 8 pages); $129.50 per set of test and instructional materials including 60 test booklets; 54¢ per test booklet; postage extra; John A. R. Wilson and Mildred C. Robeck; Webster Division, McGraw-Hill Book Co., Inc. *

REFERENCES
1. ROBECK, MILDRED C., AND WILSON, JOHN A. R. "Comparison of Binet and the Kindergarten Evaluation of Learning Potential." *Ed & Psychol Meas* 24:393–7 su '64. * (*PA* 39: 5088)
2. WILSON, JOHN A. R., AND ROBECK, MILDRED C. "A Comparison of the Kindergarten Evaluation of Learning Potential (KELP), Readiness, Mental Maturity, Achievement, and Ratings by First Grade Teachers." *Ed & Psychol Meas* 24:409–14 su '64. * (*PA* 39:5108)
3. WILSON, JOHN A. R., AND ROBECK, MILDRED C. *Kindergarten Evaluation of Learning Potential: A Curricular Approach to Evaluation.* St. Louis, Mo.: Webster Division, McGraw-Hill Book Co., 1966. Pp. xvii, 242. *
4. BLACKMAN, CLYDE THOMAS. *A Study Using a Structured Audio-Lingual Approach to the Teaching of English to Spanish-Speaking Kindergarten Pupils in Two Elementary Schools.* Doctor's thesis, University of Houston (Houston, Tex.), 1968. (*DA* 29:2428A)
5. MEREDITH, WILLIAM V., AND COFFEY, LINDA W. "Assessment of KELP as a Treatment Variable in a Headstart Program." *Fla J Ed Res* 12(1):69–78 Ja '70. *

Ed & Psychol Meas 27:757–60 au '67. Walter R. Borg. The KELP technique is an approach to the identification during kindergarten of the learning capacities of children. The first section of the book presents the authors' theoretical rationale, describes the purposes of the instrument, tells something of the development of the items, provides some evidence of validity, and discusses the teacher's role as an observer. * The approach was developed initially as a technique for use in teaching and informal day-to-day evaluation, and it is in this context that it shows the most promise. However, the authors also advocate its use as a formal tool for measuring intellectual development and for this purpose serious questions must be raised. Some of the points that the evaluation specialist might wish to consider include the following: (1) Since the same items are used for both instruction and evaluation, they constitute a biased sample for evaluation and no generalization seems possible to the item universes of which the items are a part. (2) Since specific instruction is given on each item, it would appear that the pupil's behavior on these items would reflect not only his level of development but also the skill of the teacher. The authors present no information that would provide a basis for estimating the magnitude of the teacher skill variable. (3) The instrument relies heavily upon the teacher's ability to function as an unbiased observer. It would seem almost inevitable that halo effect would influence the teacher's judgment, especially for those items where scoring is subjective and calls for a fairly high level of inference. The authors report no studies that would provide a basis for estimating the amount of halo effect. * In the second section of the book, one chapter is devoted to each of the eleven items making up the measure. These chapters follow a standard format, made up of a brief introduction, review of research projects related to the item, a description of the device (if any) used to present the item to the child, guidelines for teaching the behavior measured by the item, and a description of behavior scored "pass" at levels 1, 2, and 3. The research sections are very brief, typically citing three or four studies. This is probably sufficient for most kindergarten teachers but far from adequate for behavioral scientists who might want to use the technique. The book would be improved if the authors follow up a review of a few major studies with a supplemental reference list. The

guidelines for teaching generally appear very useful. * Since the KELP technique is purported to be an evaluation tool, it is difficult to see why the authors suggest departures from a standard approach for some of their items that change the nature of the task without providing any advantages that compensate for the loss of the standard situation. * Most of the scoring instructions would be improved by giving more specific information and a wider range of examples of satisfactory and unsatisfactory behavior. * The KELP appears to have real potential as an aid to the kindergarten teacher in making progress reports and conducting teacher conferences. * The norm tables for the KELP are not provided in the book, but may be obtained from the publishers. Little information is given regarding these norms. * the sampling....chapter is probably the weakest in the book containing only 6 pages of text * The chapter contains almost nothing specific about interpretation of the KELP norms. A sample page from the norm tables would have been helpful. One gets the impression that this chapter was added rather reluctantly in an attempt to give some aspects of a standard measure to an approach that was developed as a day-to-day teaching aid. The authors suggest that "Interpretation by the teacher on a day-to-day basis may continue to be more important than will the year end tabulation" (p 215). At its present stage of development this appears to be the only legitimate use for the KELP technique. The kind of day-to-day appraisal it permits, however, is important and in itself sufficient justification for its own use.

[752]

Lee-Clark Reading Readiness Test. Grades kgn–1; 1931–62; LCRRT; 4 scores: letter symbols, concepts, word symbols, total; 1 form ('62, c1960, 10 pages, identical with tests copyrighted in 1943 and 1951 except for format changes and, in concepts subtest, revision of all art work and half of items); manual ('62, 16 pages); $5 per 35 tests, postage extra; 75¢ per specimen set, postpaid; (20) minutes; J. Murray Lee and Willis W. Clark; CTB/McGraw-Hill. *

REFERENCES

1–9. See 6:846.
10. HERNANDEZ, PATROCINIO ESPIRITUSANTO. *Reading Readiness in Kindergarten.* Doctor's thesis, University of Nebraska (Lincoln, Neb.), 1965. (DA 26:2011)
11. CUNNINGHAM, WILLIAM. *A Thirteen-Year Retrospective Study of Standardized Test Data.* Doctor's thesis, Western Reserve University (Cleveland, Ohio), 1966. (DA 27:3305A)
12. GALE, DARWIN FRED. *A Comparison of Reading Readiness Skills of Mentally Retarded and Normal Children.* Doctor's thesis, Brigham Young University (Provo, Utah), 1967. (DA 28:2090A)
13. LLOYD, BRUCE A., AND LLOYD, ROSALIE. "A Comparison of the Reading Readiness and Mental Maturity Scores of Selected First Grade Pupils in an American School and in a

Belgian School: A Pilot Study." *J Read Specialist* 7:14–7 O
'67. *
  14. OLSON, NORINNE HILCHEY. *An Analysis of the Relationship Between Conventional Reading Readiness Measures
and Intellectual Functioning.* Doctor's thesis, University of
Georgia (Athens, Ga.), 1967. (*DA* 28:4490A)
  15. PANTHER, EDWARD E. "Prediction of First-Grade Reading Achievement." *El Sch J* 68:44–8 O '67. *
  16. SEIDEL, H. E., JR.; BARKLEY, MARY JO; AND STITH,
DORIS. "Evaluation of a Program for Project Head Start."
J Genetic Psychol 110:185–97 Je '67. * (*PA* 41:11718)
  17. MERRILL, JIMMIE DALE. *An Investigation of Teachers'
Informal Estimates of First-Grade Reading Readiness.* Doctor's
thesis, University of Oregon (Eugene, Ore.), 1968. (*DA* 29:
3775A)
  18. OLSON, ARTHUR V., AND FITZGIBBON, NORINNE H. "Factor Analytic Investigation of Two Reading Readiness Tests."
Percept & Motor Skills 27:611–4 O '68. * (*PA* 43:5892)
  19. OLSON, NORINNE H. "An Analysis of the Relationship
Between Conventional Reading Readiness Measures and Intellectual Functioning." Abstract. *AERA Paper Abstr* 1968:
122–3 '68. *
  20. SLOBODZIAN, EVELYN BIRDSALL. *The Relationship Between Certain Readiness Measures and Reading Achievement
at Level One.* Doctor's thesis, Temple University (Philadelphia, Pa.), 1968. (*DA* 29:1053A)
  21. FARR, ROGER, AND ANASTASIOW, NICHOLAS. *Tests of
Reading Readiness and Achievement: A Review and Evaluation,* pp. 15–8. Newark, Del.: International Reading Association, 1969. Pp. iv, 51. *
  22. HOPKINS, KENNETH D., AND SITKEI, E. GEORGE. "Predicting Grade One Reading Performance: Intelligence vs.
Reading Readiness Tests." *J Exp Ed* 37(3):31–3 sp '69. *
  23. LESSLER, KEN; SCHOENINGER, D. W.; AND BRIDGES,
JUDITH S. "Prediction of First Grade Performance." *Percept
& Motor Skills* 31(3):751–6 D '70. * (*PA* 45:10959)
  24. SCHRAGER, JULES, AND LINDY, JANET. "Hyperkinetic
Children: Early Indicators of Potential School Failure." *Commun Mental Health J* 6(6):447–54 D '70. * (*PA* 45:8286)

PAUL CONRAD BERG, *Professor of Education
and Director, Reading Clinic, University of
South Carolina, Columbia, South Carolina.*

This test is designed to help determine which
pupils are ready for reading instruction, as well
as to establish the pattern of maturation of
those not yet ready. The 1962 revision is one of
several since the test first appeared in 1931,
earlier revisions having been reviewed in previous *Mental Measurements Yearbooks.* Changes
in this revision include redrawing and enlarging
stimulus items and replacing several of the
previously used stimulus words with new ones.

The manual reports split-half reliabilities
ranging from .87 to .96. Predictive validity
coefficients range from .13 to .72 (median .54)
when compared with teacher ratings and .14 to
.79 (median .45) when compared with scores
on the *Lee-Clark Reading Test: First Reader.*
With predictive validity coefficients in the .40's
and .50's, only around 16 to 25 percent of the
total variance between the predictive test scores
and the criterion tests has been accounted for.
These data indicate rather clearly what the
authors point out in their manual, that the test
should "by no means be the sole measure or
basis for decision" in evaluating pupil readiness.
To do so would ignore a large area of pupil
behavior untapped by this test. Therefore, the
authors discuss several other factors related to
readiness not measured by this test and suggest

Lee-Clark Reading Readiness Test

ways in which data on these variables can be
obtained.

Hopkins and Sitkei (*22*) administered the
Lee-Clark Reading Readiness Test and the
California Short-Form Test of Mental Maturity
to all pupils entering grade 1 in two elementary
schools in a lower middle class community. The
scores from the two tests were correlated at
the end of the school year with scores on the
Lee-Clark Reading Test: Primer and end-of-
year teacher marks. The predictive validities for
the LCRRT (.57 and .61) exceed those for the
CTMM-SF (.51 and .54) on both criteria,
although the differences are not statistically
significant. The addition of IQ to reading readiness in a multiple regression equation produced
multiple correlations of .62 and .67 for the two
criteria. Since the researchers' summary of their
findings is quite helpful to this present review,
it is quoted in some detail:

In view of the fact that the reading readiness test did
at least as well in predicting first-grade reading performance, it was considered to be preferable to the
intelligence test when other relevant factors are considered: (a) it requires considerably less testing time;
(b) it is more easily and meaningfully interpreted;
(c) the effects of improper interpretation are much
less serious to the pupil; and (d) it is less expensive.

The *Lee-Clark Reading Readiness Test* is
one of the oldest of the better known tests in its
field. Data accumulated over the years indicate
that it has real value as a teacher-aid in evaluating pupils for beginning reading instruction.
However, the readiness factors that it evaluates
are very few in terms of all the variables that
predispose a child to finally learn one way
rather than another. How many, and what
variables should be included in a readiness test
that would give the best possible prediction yet
keep its administration time short and its interpretation simple? For example, Weintraub[1]
suggests from the findings of several studies
that a number subtest is the best single measure
for the prediction of reading ability. Whether
the Lee-Clark would have greater predictive
validity with such an addition is not the question
meant here—rather, the point is that no single
paper and pencil test can possibly cover all of
the significant variables that make up the distance from where a child is in September to
where he will be in May. Thus, because no ideal
instrument that covers significantly more of the
readiness variables is available, the Lee-Clark,

1 WEINTRAUB, SAMUEL. "Readiness Measures for Predicting
Reading Achievement." *Read Teach* 20:551–8 Mr '67. *

with its ease of administration, short testing time, and easily interpreted scores, is a recommended instrument by this reviewer to *help* teachers in their *continuous* task of evaluating and organizing for instruction.

For a review by James R. Hobson of an earlier edition, see 5:678; for reviews by Marion Monroe Cox and David H. Russell, see 3:517.

[753]

★Lippincott Reading Readiness Test (Including Readiness Check List). Grades kgn–1; 1965; 1 form (9 pages); manual (10 pages); no data on reliability and validity; no description of norms population; $6.72 per 25 tests; $1.68 per specimen set; postage extra; administration time not reported; Pierce H. McLeod; J. B. Lippincott Co. *

REFERENCE
1. NORFLEET, MARY ANN. *The Bender Gestalt as a Group Screening Instrument for Reading Readiness.* Doctor's thesis, University of Oregon (Eugene, Ore.), 1969. (*DAI* 31:1083A)

EDWARD R. SIPAY, *Professor of Education and Director of Reading Clinics, State University of New York at Albany, Albany, New York.*

DESCRIPTION. In content this test differs greatly from other reading readiness tests. Only letter knowledge is purportedly measured, while other factors related to reading readiness are "covered" in the Readiness Check List.

The Letter Knowledge Test, also confusingly referred to as a Letter Readiness Test, contains four subtests. In each subtest all 26 letters of the alphabet are tested. Test 1, Identifying Capitals Shown, involves short-term visual memory. A capital letter is shown for five seconds, then the child has to "find it among the letters" and encircle it (five choices are given in each item for Tests 1–3). As with most such tests, if the child can scan the choices very quickly while the stimulus is in view, the task then becomes primarily one of visual discrimination. Although the manual does not give a rationale for the exclusive use of capital letters on this subtest, a letter from the test author indicates that capital letters were used, "because the children usually acquire familiarity with these letter configurations before the lower case letter configurations." Perhaps it is a matter of semantics, but more than "configuration" is involved in this test. Furthermore, children primarily use lower case letters in learning to read. Letter names, not the sounds that letters represent, are used as the oral stimuli of Tests 2–4. On the Identifying Upper Case Letters Named and Identifying Lower Case Letters Named tests, the child

has to match the letter name with its printed counterpart. Test 4, Writing Letters Dictated at Random, requires the child to write the grapheme corresponding to the letter named. The word "random" in the title indicates that the oral stimuli are not given in alphabetical order. No rationale why three different types of letter knowledge need to be tested is presented. Nor is there presented any evidence that the subtests are really measuring different skills.

The Readiness Check List contains 33 statements about the child's physical and psychological development, each of which is to be checked "Yes" or "No" by the teacher.

ADMINISTRATION AND SCORING. No special training is required to administer or to score this group test. However, the directions for doing so leave much to be desired.

Correspondence from the test author states that a recommended group size for testing is 8 to 10. The small size (¾ by ⅞ inches) of most of the letters on the Test 1 stimulus cards, however, would limit the number who could be reliably tested. Some directions are misleading or confusing. For example, at the end of Test 1 the children are directed to "Turn your booklet over." This apparently assumes the booklet has been folded back so that only one page shows, but no such instruction has been given. Again at the beginning of Test 2, they are told to "Turn your booklet over." If both directions are followed, the children will end up back on page 2 rather than on page 3. To add further confusion, after being told to turn over their booklets for a second time, the children are next instructed to "Put your marker under the first line of the next sheet." *[margin note: criticism]*

Three sample items for Test 1 are presented on the cover page of the test booklet. It is of interest to note that the same letter is used as the oral stimulus for the first sample item and the third test item, and that the letters used for the other samples are the correct answers for two other items on the first test page. No sample items are given for the other subtests.

In Test 4, the children are instructed to place their markers under each line. This may cause some problems because the marker may interfere with writing or printing lower case letters which have elements descending below the line.

The tests are scored by comparing the pages in the child's test booklet with the scoring key, which shows the test pages, reduced in size, on which the correct answers are circled. An overlay or mask would greatly simplify the scoring.

Only three brief scoring directions are provided in the manual. It is not clear whether the one regarding multiple responses applies to all the subtests or just to Test 4. The other two refer only to Test 4. One directs the scorer to "accept any recognizable representation of the letter whether upper or lower case"; the other, to "Disregard inversions, reversals and rotations of the letter configuration." For the latter, the rationale, presented in a letter from the test author, is that these are "disregarded since this behavior is a developmental phenomenon common to most children of this age." Regardless of this opinion, the fact remains that these directions leave a great deal open to interpretation and are certain to influence the scores obtained by various testers. For example, if printed responses are acceptable (the manual only mentions *writing* the letter, but printed responses are given in the scoring key), at least five items (b, d, g, p, q) have multiple correct responses. Even if only written letters are acceptable, the same would be true for d, g, p, and q, and perhaps even for b if the scorer were willing to accept a "recognizable representation."

The Readiness Check List statements, which are not categorized in any apparent fashion, are simply checked "Yes" or "No." A number of the statements are ambiguous, stated in very general terms, or are overlapping. For example, does "Appears to have normal vision" refer to near point (reading distance) or far point? (Most five-and-six-year-olds are far sighted.) Or, what criteria does one use to determine the following items, to say nothing of distinguishing between and among them:

Speaks in complete sentences.
Expresses self intelligently in a social situation.
Speaks in a manner appropriate for age level.
Can express ideas in a meaningful manner.
Employs an appropriate vocabulary.

More importantly, simple "Yes" or "No" responses imply that the skill or ability is either present or absent. In reality no such clear-cut distinction can be made, because there are degrees to which such skills or abilities are present. Use of a three or five point scale would help to overcome this misleading impression. Also, there is no apparent recognition that the skills and abilities tested are not all of equal importance in determining reading readiness.

The Readiness Check List is to be used in conjunction with the Letter Knowledge Test. Apparently both are included because: (a) "The use of the Readiness Check List....will enable the teacher to identify the child who may encounter learning difficulties despite an adequate Letter Readiness Test score," and, (b) "The children who rate high on the check list can be expected to succeed in reading even if they have not yet acquired letter knowledge. They lack instruction, not readiness."

Evidently the test author believes that letter knowledge is quite important in learning to read, and/or that letter knowledge is an "effective predictor" of later reading achievement. While it is true that letter knowledge tests often correlate more highly than do other readiness subtest scores with later reading achievement, no cause-effect relationship has been established. Nor has it been shown that any one test allows for accurate prediction of an individual's reading achievement.

SUGGESTED USE OF TEST. The manual states, "Both the Reading Readiness Tests [probably meaning the letter knowledge tests] and the Readiness Check List are screening devices. The use of these screening devices enables the teacher to group children for instruction. In the process of grouping the children, she will identify the children who are in need of referral for further more specific evaluation." According to the manual, most children can be grouped for instructional purposes on the basis of the total test scores obtained on the letter knowledge tests. Cutoff scores are provided for establishing three groups, but little information is available on how these categories were established. Such data would seem important, especially in light of the fact that instructional programs are suggested for each group.

SUMMARY. In its present state, this test has little to recommend it as a test of letter knowledge, let alone as a reading readiness test.

[754]

★McHugh-McParland Reading Readiness Test. Grades kgn–1; 1966–68; 5 scores: rhyming words, beginning sounds, visual discrimination, identifying letters, total; 1 form ('68, 12 pages, identical with test copyrighted in 1966); manual ('68, 10 pages); flash cards ('68); $4.55 per 35 tests; $1 per specimen set; postage extra; (60) minutes in 2 sessions; Walter J. McHugh and Myrtle McParland; Cal-State Bookstore. *

REBECCA C. BARR, *Director, The Reading Clinic, The University of Chicago, Chicago, Illinois.*

Lippincott Reading Readiness Test

The authors have designed this test so that results may be used in grouping children for reading in the first grade. No rationale is given for inclusion of the four subtests: rhyming words, beginning sounds, visual discrimination, and identifying letters.

The test is to be administered at the end of kindergarten or beginning of first grade. Appropriate group size for the two recommended administration sessions is not discussed, even though it may seriously affect the validity of the second and third subtests.

Directions for scoring are clear. Raw scores for each subtest and for total score can be converted to stanines and percentile ranks. A major error in the table for converting raw scores may be extremely confusing to teachers: most of the entries in the total raw score column are in error. For example, a percentile rank of 20 corresponds to a total raw score of 38 rather than to a raw score of 2, as stated in the manual.

Refinement of the test was done using a sample of over 10,000 children from California. Standardization data are reported on a sample of 2,675 children. Test-retest reliability for the total test was reported as .94 on a sample of 646. Predictive validity was evaluated by giving the same sample of children various reading tests as criterion measures. Validity coefficients ranged from .43 to .90 for the total test score. No information concerning concurrent or construct validity is included in the manual.

Test 1, Rhyming Words, consists of 20 items. Children are directed to look at three pictures in the test booklet as the teacher names them and then to mark the picture of the word that does *not* rhyme with the others. Three sample tasks are provided to familiarize children with the directions: the first item is used to develop the concept of rhyming, the second to show the child how to identify with an "x" the word that does not rhyme with the other two, and the third as a practice item in which children are told which words rhyme and are directed to mark the remaining word. For some children, I suspect this subtest may become a measure of following directions rather than rhyming. The test-retest reliability of .82 is not as high as would be desired. The predictive validity using later reading vocabulary and comprehension scores as criterion measures is low, ranging from .10 to .60.

Test 2, Beginning Sounds, contains 18 items. The examiner reads the names of four pictures.

Children are directed to put an "x" on the one which does *not* begin with the same sound as the other three. The reliability of this subtest is adequate (test-retest, .87; odd-even, .90). The predictive validity of this subtest with later reading is comparable to that of most other readiness measures (ranging from .39 to .74).

Test 3, Visual Discrimination, contains 26 items: 8 that involve the perception of letters and 18, the perception of words varying in length from two to four letters. The items (containing letters less than 1¼ inches in height) are presented by the examiner on flash cards. The children are directed as follows: "I will show you a letter or a word on a card. Look at the letter or word all the time that I am showing it, then find the one in your booklet just like the one I showed you and make a circle around it." If the flash card is held up for only three seconds and children are not allowed to record responses until after this time, this subtest actually measures visual memory as well as discrimination. Distance from the teacher could be of considerable importance in clear discrimination of the stimulus and could greatly affect the validity of this test.

The reliability of this subtest is inadequate (.73, .74). The predictive validity of this subtest with later reading vocabulary and comprehension scores is low (ranging from .27 to .48).

The examiner is told that "the directions should be followed precisely, using the exact wording given" and that he should "use the chalkboard for demonstrating with the sample items in Tests 3 and 4." Since no sample items are included with Tests 3 and 4, this may be confusing for the teacher.

Test 4, Identifying Letters, consists of 26 items. Children must choose one capital letter from among seven which corresponds to the letter named by the examiner. This is the most reliable of the four subtests (odd-even, .98; test-retest, .93). Predictive validity is highest for this subtest (ranging from .47 to .88), and it is nearly as high as that for the total test score. The other three subtests make little contribution to the predictive effectiveness of this subtest. Since the first three subtests are not used for diagnostic purposes and contribute little to predictive effectiveness, it is difficult to justify their inclusion in the battery.

As mentioned previously, there are two major difficulties with the directions for administration: The directions for some of the subtests do not appear to be sufficiently clear or complete to assure that most children understand the requirements of the task. The directions for two subtests are incomplete. In the visual discrimination subtest, the distance from the stimulus may affect perception and the validity of this test.

Three of the four subtests cannot be justified in terms of predictive validity and two cannot on the basis of reliability. Because of these major problems, this reviewer cannot recommend this test.

EDWARD R. SIPAY, *Professor of Education and Director of Reading Clinics, State University of New York at Albany, Albany, New York.*

The first of four subtests, Rhyming Words, requires the child to select from three choices the picture whose name does not rhyme with the other two. It therefore samples one aspect of auditory discrimination. Of the 20 items, the correct answer is the last choice in eight, four of which occur in the first seven items. It would be of interest to know what influence this has on test results.

Test 2, Beginning Sounds, has 18 items involving auditory discrimination of the sounds represented mostly by single consonants. The child must select from four choices the picture whose name "does not begin like the others."

On the 26 items in Test 3, Visual Discrimination, the child has to match the letter or word displayed with one of six choices. Although visual discrimination is involved, the subtest would be more appropriately labeled "Visual Memory" because, since the stimulus card is shown for only three seconds, short-term visual memory (as well as attention) would seem to be a key requirement. It would appear that higher levels of ability in visual memory and visual discrimination are required on this subtest than are called for on many reading readiness tests. Apart from the fact that each item has six choices, many of those involving words have distractors which are very similar to the correct response in their configuration and length, some differing in only one element.

Test 4, Identifying Letters, requires the child to select from seven choices the capital letter named by the examiner. The ability to associate all 26 letter names with their graphemes is tested. A rationale for the exclusive use of capital letters is not presented in the manual. Nor is a reason given for the increasingly larger number of choices (from three in Test 1 to seven in Test 4).

ADMINISTERING AND SCORING. The general and specific directions for administering the tests are satisfactory except for the following points: (*a*) Sample items are presented for only the first two subtests. (*b*) Sample B of Test 1 uses "log" and "dog" as the rhyming words. In many parts of the country, however, the pronunciation of the sound represented by the vowel varies, so that the words do not rhyme. (*c*) A few items in Test 2 may cause some problems. For example, the use of "vacuum cleaner" and "Jack-in-the-Box" as oral stimuli may confuse some children as to which beginning sound is meant to be the stimulus. Single words would be more appropriate. (*d*) Item 16 of Test 2 uses "whistle," "wheel," and "wagon" as the words that begin with the same sound. Again this appears to overlook regional dialects because some people pronounce the beginning of "whistle" and "wheel" as /hw/. (*e*) The pace at which the items are to be presented is not indicated for three of the four tests. (*f*) The manual contains more misspelled words than one might expect.

The test is hand scored by comparing the test booklet with a paged scoring key. An overlay or scoring mask would simplify scoring. A table is provided for converting subtest and total test raw scores to stanines and percentile ranks.

VALIDITY AND RELIABILITY. Only information on predictive validity is presented in the manual. Predictive validity coefficients are reported between the McHugh-McParland test and five different reading achievement tests that were administered to first graders nine months after initial testing. Coefficients between the readiness subtests and the achievement subtests range from .10 to .88; and from .43 to .90 between the readiness total score and the achievement test subtests. These coefficients are similar to those reported for other reading readiness tests. Limited information is given concerning the populations employed in deriving the validity and reliability statistics, but it would seem to be a rather restricted sample.

Odd-even reliability coefficients for the subtests are reported to range from .73 to .98. Test-retest coefficients range from .74 to .93 for the subtests, with a reliability of .94 for the total test score. These reliability data compare favorably with those of other standardized readiness tests. However, the manual does not discuss how test users might interpret these data or identify the formulas employed to determine the data. Means, standard deviations, and standard errors of measurement are not reported.

SUGGESTED USE OF TEST RESULTS. On a brief half page, the manual defines five readiness levels and offers teaching suggestions for each. The levels are set up according to standard deviations, apparently with Level C being ±.5 standard deviations from the mean, or taking in approximately the middle 38 percent of the population. Levels B and D each have a range of one standard deviation ($+.5$ to $+1.5$, $-.5$ to -1.5) and Levels A and E beyond. Having thus set up five levels, it is surprising and confusing to find that when teaching suggestions are offered the top two levels are lumped together; and that except for one questionable suggestion, the teaching suggestions are the same for Levels A, B, and C. Apparently the authors either are of the opinion or have evidence, perhaps derived from the data obtained in determining test validity, that, although logical, five levels are not of practical significance. Some of the teaching suggestions are questionable. For example, the manual suggests that children who obtain total raw scores between 52 to 69 should be given a quick review of letter names and beginning sounds. It is quite possible, however, that some children who score within this range will show apparent weaknesses in only one or neither of these areas. Also, the manual should at least indicate that interrelated factors other than those sampled by this test may well influence reading achievement.

SUMMARY. If the reported validity and reliability were shown to hold up with a well-defined representative sample, and if the weaknesses indicated above were corrected, this reviewer would recommend the use of this test. It is not clearly superior to other reading readiness tests, but what test is?

[755]

★The Macmillan Reading Readiness Test, Revised Edition. First grade entrants; 1965–70; 6 or 7 scores: rating scale, visual discrimination, auditory discrimination, vocabulary and concepts, letter names, total for tests 1–5, visual-motor (optional), total for tests 1–6; 1 form ('70, 12 pages); manual ('70, 15 pages); $3 per 10 tests; $1.50 per specimen set; postage extra; (75) or (90) minutes in 3 to 5 sessions; Albert J. Harris and Edward R. Sipay; Macmillan Co. *

[756]

★The Meeting Street School Screening Test. Grades kgn–1; 1969; MSSST; 4 scores: motor patterning, visual-perceptual-motor, language, total; individual; no reading by examinees; manual (130 pages); record form (4 pages); $4.50 per 50 record forms; $10 per manual; cash orders postpaid; (15–20) minutes; Peter K. Hainsworth and Marian L. Siqueland; Crippled Children and Adults of Rhode Island, Inc. *

REFERENCES

1. DENHOFF, ERIC; HAINSWORTH, PETER K.; AND SIQUELAND, MARIAN L. "The Measurement of Psychoneurological Factors Contributing to Learning Efficiency." *J Learn Dis* 1:636–44 N '68. * (PA 45:7080)
2. DENHOFF, ERIC; SIQUELAND, MARIAN L.; KOMICH, M. PATRICIA; AND HAINSWORTH, PETER K. "Developmental and Predictive Characteristics of Items From the Meeting Street School Screening Test." *Develop Med & Child Neurol* 10:220–32 Ap '68. * (PA 42:14055)
3. GAVINO, PURITA GONZALES. *Validation of the Meeting Street School Screening Test.* Master's thesis, Queens University (Kingston, Ont., Canada), 1968.
4. DENHOFF, ERIC. "Detecting Potential Learning Problems at Preschool Medical Examinations." *Tex Med* 65(3):56–9 Mr '69. *

Develop Med & Child Neurol 12(6):814–5 D '70. William Yule. * The diagnostic and therapeutic team at the school have pooled their knowledge and clinical expertise to produce a short screening battery which they hoped would be of value in identifying children who would later have learning difficulties. Would that they had succeeded, but, alas, the resulting instrument is psychometrically inadequate. * The test was standardised on 500 children aged between 5 years 0 months and 7 years 5 months, 50 boys and 50 girls at each half-year level, selected to be representative of the U.S. population. One has to search very thoroughly in the manual to unearth the rest of the relevant test standardisation and construction data. The total test has a re-test reliability of 0.85 over a two to four-week period. However, we are not told how many children were re-tested, nor whether there were any practice effects. The inter-rater reliability is quoted as 0.95, though again the number of children re-examined is not quoted. Validity data are even scarcer, and are presented in ways that are difficult to interpret. In an unpublished study, 20 boys of IQ above 90 were tested on the MSSST, Frostig and ITPA. The total MSSST score correlates 0.77 with ITPA and 0.57 with Frostig. However IQ was not partialled out, and nowhere in the whole manual is a correlation between IQ and MSSST score quoted. Yet, the data were collected. Since both Frostig and ITPA correlate highly in other studies with IQ scores, one is left with the strong impression that Denhoff *et al.* are following in Binet's footsteps and re-discovering items predictive of failure to benefit from ordinary schooling. 163 of the children were followed up over a 2-year period. Looking at their school achievement, of the 44 children in the lowest quartile, 26 scored below an arbitrary cut-off point on the MSSST. However, a further 28 who had scored as low at the time of school entry did not do so badly two years later. Alas, the IQ of the children is not given so we do not know how the MSSST compared in predictive efficiency with more soundly-based instruments. Even so, a 15-minute screening test which achieves even this moderate degree of predictive validity is well worth investigating further. Cross-validation studies are required, and the greatest need is for more constructive validity data. No matter how unfashionable IQ scores may be at present, unless the MSSST can be shown to measure areas other than those measured by the Wechsler scales, it might be simpler to train people other than psychologists in psychometric assessments and interpretation. In the meantime, the MSSST cannot be accepted as a valid predictor of learning difficulties.

[757]

*Metropolitan Readiness Tests. Grades kgn–1; 1933–69; MRT; 7 or 8 scores: word meaning, listening, matching, alphabet, numbers, copying, total, draw-a-man (optional) ; Forms A ('64, 16 pages), B ('66, 16 pages) ; manual ('69, 36 pages) ; no norms for kindergarten; $8.20 per 35 tests; $1.50 per specimen set; postage extra; scoring service, $1.75 per test; (60) minutes in 3 sessions; Gertrude H. Hildreth, Nellie L. Griffiths, and Mary E. McGauvran; Harcourt Brace Jovanovich, Inc. *

REFERENCES

1–10. See 2:1552.
11–15. See 3:518.
16–18. See 4:570.
19. TAYLOR, CHRISTIAN D. "The Effect of Training on Reading Readiness," pp. 63–80. In *Studies in Reading, Vol. 2.* Publications of the Scottish Council for Research in Education 34. London: University of London Press Ltd., 1950. Pp. xv, 113. *
20. PRESCOTT, GEORGE A. "Sex Differences in Metropolitan Readiness Test Results." *J Ed Res* 48:605–10 Ap '55. * (*PA* 30:1629)
21. SUTTON, RACHEL S. "A Study of Certain Factors Associated With Reading Readiness in the Kindergarten." *J Ed Res* 48:531–8 Mr '55. * (*PA* 30:1542)
22. BRENNER, ANTON, AND MORSE, NANCY C. "The Measurement of Children's Readiness for School." *Papers Mich Acad Sci Arts & Letters* 41:333–40 '56. * (*PA* 37:6453)
23. KARLIN, ROBERT. "The Prediction of Reading Success and Reading-Readiness Tests." *El Engl* 34:320–2 My '57. *
24. BREMER, NEVILLE. "Do Readiness Tests Predict Success in Reading?" *El Sch J* 59:222–4 Ja '59. *
25. KOONTZ, EUNICE RABY. *Significant Factors Associated With Reading Achievement in the Primary Grades: A Longitudinal Study.* Doctor's thesis, Ohio State University (Columbus, Ohio), 1960. (*DA* 21:2194)
26. SIMPSON, DOROTHY MARGARET. *Perceptual Readiness and Beginning Reading.* Doctor's thesis, Purdue University (Lafayette, Ind.), 1960. (*DA* 21:1858)
27. AVAKIAN, SONIA ASTRID. "An Investigation of Trait Relationships Among Six-Year-Old Children." *Genetic Psychol Monogr* 63:339–94 My '61. * (*PA* 36:1FF39A)
28. FLAMAND, RUTH K. *The Relationship Between Various Measures of Vocabulary and Performance in Beginning Reading.* Doctor's thesis, Temple University (Philadelphia, Pa.), 1961. (*DA* 22:1463)
29. KOPPITZ, ELIZABETH M.; MARDIS, VERDENA; AND STEPHENS, THOMAS. "A Note on Screening School Beginners With the Bender Gestalt Test." *J Ed Psychol* 52:80–1 Ap '61. * (*PA* 38:3205)
30. KERMOIAN, SAMUEL B. "Teacher Appraisal of First Grade Readiness." *El Engl* 39:196–201 Mr '62. *
31. KINGSTON, ALBERT J., JR. "The Relationship of First-Grade Readiness to Third- and Fourth-Grade Achievement." *J Ed Res* 56:61–7 O '62. *
32. MITCHELL, BLYTHE C. "The Metropolitan Readiness Tests as Predictors of First-Grade Achievement." *Ed & Psychol Meas* 22:765–72 w '62. * (*PA* 37:7195)
33. ROSS, BERNICE B. *Correlation Between Total and Sub-Test Scores on Metropolitan Readiness Tests Scores and Second and Third Grade Metropolitan Reading Tests Scores.* Master's thesis, University of Louisville (Louisville, Ky.), 1962.
34. ABBOTT, ROBERT FRANKLIN. *The Prediction of First Grade Reading and Numbers Achievement by Means of Psychological Tests.* Doctor's thesis, University of Tennessee (Knoxville, Tenn.), 1963. (*DA* 25:1020)
35. DUTTON, WILBUR H. "Growth in Number Readiness in Kindergarten Children." *Arith Teach* 10:251–5 My '63. *
36. IRWIN, JAMES L. *A Study of the Effectiveness of the Metropolitan Readiness Tests as Predictors of Reading Success at the End of the Primary Grades.* Master's thesis, Bowling Green State University (Bowling Green, Ohio), 1963.
37. LETON, DONALD A. "A Factor Analysis of Readiness Tests." *Percept & Motor Skills* 16:915–9 Je '63. * (*PA* 38:6584)
38. MATTICK, WILLIAM E. "Predicting Success in the First Grade." *El Sch J* 63:273–6 F '63. *
39. NASH, PAT NEFF. *The Effectiveness of Composite Predictors of Reading Success in the First Grade.* Doctor's thesis, North Texas State University (Denton, Tex.), 1963. (*DA* 24:1482)
40. BALINKY, JEAN LAHN. *A Configurational Approach to the Prediction of Academic Achievement in First Grade.* Doctor's thesis, Rutgers—The State University (New Brunswick, N.J.), 1964. (*DA* 25:2844)
41. BRYAN, QUENTIN R. "Relative Importance of Intelligence and Visual Perception in Predicting Reading Achievement." *Calif J Ed Res* 15:44–8 Ja '64. * (*PA* 38:9228)
42. MOORE, EARL JAMES. *A Study of the Relationship Between High School and College Scholarship and Selected Test Results for Grades K–12.* Doctor's thesis, University of South Dakota (Vermillion, S.D.), 1964. (*DA* 27:679A)
43. ROMANIUK, ALEXANDER. *An Evaluation of the Effectiveness of the First Grade Readiness Testing Program as Used in West Jasper Place Public Schools.* Master's thesis, University of Alberta (Edmonton, Alta., Canada), 1964.
44. RUTHERFORD, WILLIAM LEWIS. *The Effects of a Perceptual-Motor Training Program on the Performance of Kindergarten Pupils on Metropolitan Readiness Tests.* Doctor's thesis, North Texas State University (Denton, Tex.), 1964. (*DA* 25:4583)
45. SHEA, CAROL ANN. *Visual Discrimination of Words as a Predictor of Reading Readiness.* Doctor's thesis, University of Connecticut (Storrs, Conn.), 1964. (*DA* 25:6321)
46. ZINGLE, HARVEY W., AND HOHOL, A. E. "Predictive Validity of the Metropolitan Readiness Tests." *Alberta J Ed Res* 10:99–104 Je '64. * (*PA* 39:12316)
47. BERGREN, VERA I. *The Relationship Between Scores of the Metropolitan Readiness Test and Scores in Reading Achievement in Grades 1, 2, and 3, 4 and 5.* Master's thesis, Northern Illinois University (DeKalb, Ill.), 1965.
48. BROWN, CLARA HEDGLIN. *The Effectiveness of the Metropolitan Readiness Tests in Predicting Reading Difficulties in the Chico City Elementary Schools as Evidenced by the Reading Records of the 1961, 1962, 1963, 1964 Eighth Grade Classes in the Chico Junior High School.* Master's thesis, Chico State College (Chico, Calif.), 1965.
49. KARZEN, JUDITH MILLER; SUVETOR, HELENE; AND THOMPSON, GLEN. "Predicting First Grade Reading Achievement." *Ill Sch Res* 2:20–2 O '65. *
50. LOCKHART, HAZEL M. "Personality and Reading Readiness." *Ill Sch Res* 2:9–11 O '65. *
51. LOPER, DORIS JEAN. *Auditory Discrimination, Intelligence, Achievement, and Background of Experience and Information in a Culturally Disadvantaged First-Grade Population.* Doctor's thesis, Temple University (Philadelphia, Pa.), 1965. (*DA* 26:5873)
52. McCALL, ROZANNE A., AND McCALL, ROBERT B. "A Comparison of First Grade Reading Tests." *Ill Sch Res* 2:32–7 O '65. *
53. MULLIS, JESSE CARL. *The Prediction of Fifth Grade Achievement as Measured by Teacher Grades and Achievement Test Scores Using First Grade Indices of Prediction.* Doctor's thesis, University of Georgia (Athens, Ga.), 1965. (*DA* 26:6515)
54. ROSEN, CARL LYLE. *A Study of Visual Perception Capabilities of First Grade Pupils and the Relationship Between Visual Perception Training and Reading Achievement.* Doctor's thesis, University of Minnesota (Minneapolis, Minn.), 1965. (*DA* 26:5247)
55. WEISER, MARGARET G. "Three Methods of Appraising Reading Readiness." *Ill Sch Res* 2:23–6 O '65. *

56. WIRT, ROBERT. *Raven-Coloured Progressive Matrices, Metropolitan Readiness, and Detroit First Grade Intelligence Tests as Predictors of Achievement in Primary Grades.* Master's thesis, Central Washington College of Education (Ellensburg, Wash.), 1965.

57. COKER, DONALD ROSS. *The Relationship of Readiness Test Scores to Selected Socio-Economic Factors of Lower Class Families.* Doctor's thesis, University of Arkansas (Fayetteville, Ark.), 1966. (*DA* 27:1196A)

58. KUHN, M. VIRGINICE. *A Comparative Study of Teacher Judgment and Reading Readiness Tests for Predicting Success in Reading in First Grade.* Master's thesis, Cardinal Stritch College (Milwaukee, Wis.), 1966.

59. LANE, SHIRLEY Z. *A Comparative Study Between the Metropolitan Readiness Test and Beginning Reading and the Marianne Frostig Developmental Test of Visual Perception and Beginning Reading.* Master's thesis, Texas Woman's University (Denton, Tex.), 1966.

60. LUNDSTEDT, VERNE. *The Graphic Representation of the Results of a Validity Study on the Metropolitan Readiness Tests.* Master's thesis, San Jose State College (San Jose, Calif.), 1966.

61. MAYANS, ANNA E. *Early Differential Prediction of First Grade Reading Achievement Among Three Culturally Different Kindergarten Groups.* Doctor's thesis, University of Cincinnati (Cincinnati, Ohio), 1966. (*DA* 27:2891A)

62. ROBINSON, H. ALAN. "Reliability of Measures Related to Reading Success of Average, Disadvantaged, and Advantaged Kindergarten Children." Comments by Samuel Weintraub. *Read Teach* 20:203–9 D '66. * (*PA* 41:3344)

63. TAUBER, ROSALYN. "Identification of Potential Learning Disabilities." *Acad Ther Q* 2:116–9+ w '66–67. * (*PA* 41:5004)

64. BOND, GUY L., AND DYKSTRA, ROBERT. "The Cooperative Research Program in First-Grade Reading Instruction." *Read Res Q* 2:5–142 su '67. * (*PA* 42:4557)

65. CHARRY, LAWRENCE BERNARD. *The Relationship Between Prereading and First Grade Reading Performances and Subsequent Achievement in Reading and Other Specified Areas.* Doctor's thesis, Temple University (Philadelphia, Pa.), 1967. (*DA* 28:960A)

66. GALE, DARWIN FRED. *A Comparison of Reading Readiness Skills of Mentally Retarded and Normal Children.* Doctor's thesis, Brigham Young University (Provo, Utah), 1967. (*DA* 28:2090A)

67. GIULIANI, GEORGE ANTHONY. *The Relationship of Self-Concept and Verbal-Mental Ability to Levels of Reading Readiness Amongst Kindergarten Children.* Doctor's thesis, St. John's University (Jamaica, N.Y.), 1967. (*DA* 28:3866B)

68. GLASNAPP, DOUGLAS R. *A Comparative Study of Three Forms of the Metropolitan Readiness Test at Two Socio-Economic Levels.* Master's thesis, George Peabody College (Nashville, Tenn.), 1967.

69. HAGENSON, SARA LOUISE. *The Relation of First Grade Readiness and Achievement Scores Based on Sex, Race, and Age.* Doctor's thesis, University of Southern Mississippi (Hattiesburg, Miss.), 1967. (*DA* 28:3362A)

70. HEMPHILL, AUGUSTA S. *A Comparison of the Bender Visual Motor Gestalt Test and the Metropolitan Readiness Test, Form B, as Measures of First Grade Readiness.* Master's thesis, Southern Methodist University (Dallas, Tex.), 1967.

71. JOHNSON, ROGER ERLING. *A Study of the Validity of the Clymer-Barrett Prereading Battery.* Doctor's thesis, University of Minnesota (Minneapolis, Minn.), 1967. (*DA* 28:3892A)

72. MASON, GEORGE E., AND GEESLIN, DORINE. "The Predictive Validity of the New York State Readiness Test as Measured by the Gates Primary Reading Test and the Stanford Achievement Test, Reading Subsections." *J Ed Res* 61:189 D '67. *

73. MITCHELL, BLYTHE C. "Predictive Validity of the Metropolitan Readiness Tests and the Murphy-Durrell Reading Readiness Analysis for White and for Negro Pupils." *Ed & Psychol Meas* 27:1047–54 w '67. * (*PA* 42:9504)

74. OLSON, NORINNE HILCHEY. *An Analysis of the Relationship Between Conventional Reading Readiness Measures and Intellectual Functioning.* Doctor's thesis, University of Georgia (Athens, Ga.), 1967. (*DA* 28:4490A)

75. STEPHENS, WYATT E.; CUNNINGHAM, ERNEST S.; AND STIGLER, B. J. "Reading Readiness and Eye Hand Preference Patterns in First Grade Children." *Excep Children* 33:481–8 Mr '67. * (*PA* 41:7523)

76. WARTENBERG, HERBERT. *The Relationship Between Success in Beginning Reading and Various Predictive Measures.* Doctor's thesis, Temple University (Philadelphia, Pa.), 1967. (*DA* 28:979A)

77. WEAVER, ANN SULLIVAN. *The Prediction of First Grade Reading Achievement in Culturally Disadvantaged Children.* Doctor's thesis, George Peabody College for Teachers (Nashville, Tenn.), 1967. (*DA* 28:3789A)

78. ALTHOUSE, ROSEMARY ELIZABETH. *Validation of an Individual Reading Readiness Test.* Doctor's thesis, Florida State University (Tallahassee, Fla.), 1968. (*DAI* 30:611A)

79. BAGFORD, JACK. "Reading Readiness Scores and Success in Reading." *Read Teach* 21:324–8 Ja '68. * (*PA* 42:17640)

80. BEAUPRE, ROBERT G., AND KENNARD, ANN. "An Investigation of Pre- and Postmetropolitan Readiness Test Scores for Differing Motor Education Programs." *Ill Sch Res* 5:22–5 N '68. *

81. DAVIS, O. L., JR., AND PERSONKE, CARL R., JR. "Effects of Administering the Metropolitan Readiness Test in English and Spanish to Spanish-Speaking School Entrants." *J Ed Meas* 5:231–4 f '68. * (*PA* 44:11213)

82. DOWD, GERALD JOHN. *Sex and Race Differences in the Effectiveness of Various Composite Predictors of Initial Reading Success and the Relationship of Children's Self-Perceptions to Initial Reading Success.* Doctor's thesis, St. John's University (Jamaica, N.Y.), 1968. (*DA* 29:2999A)

83. HENDERSON, EDMUND H., AND LONG, BARBARA H. "Correlations of Reading Readiness Among Children of Varying Background." *Read Teach* 22:40–4 O '68. *

84. JACOBS, JAMES N.; WIRTHLIN, LENORE D.; AND MILLER, CHARLES B. "A Follow-Up Evaluation of the Frostig Visual-Perceptual Training Program." *Ed Leadership* 26:169–75 N '68. *

85. McCLELLAN, DORINDA ANN. *Factors Which Are Predictive of Reading Success of Low-Socio-Economic Children in Selected First Grades.* Doctor's thesis, Oklahoma State University (Stillwater, Okla.), 1968. (*DAI* 30:933A)

86. MAUSER, AUGUST JOHN. *First Grade Children's Comprehension of Oral Language in Sentences and Success in Beginning Reading Instruction.* Doctor's thesis, Indiana University (Bloomington, Ind.), 1968. (*DAI* 30:70A)

87. MILLER, LUCILLE F. *Comparison of the Marianne Frostig Developmental Test of Visual Perception and the Metropolitan Readiness Tests.* Master's thesis, Central Connecticut State College (New Britain, Conn.), 1968.

88. NESBITT, MARY CATHERINE. *Auding Achievement of First Grade Pupils Related to Selected Pupil Characteristics.* Doctor's thesis, University of Georgia (Athens, Ga.), 1968. (*DA* 29:2445A)

89. OHNMACHT, FRED W., AND OLSON, ARTHUR V. "Canonical Analysis of Reading Readiness Measures and the Frostig Developmental Test of Visual Perception." Abstract. *AERA Paper Abstr* 1968:121–2 '68. *

90. OHNMACHT, FRED W., AND OLSON, ARTHUR V. "Canonical Analysis of Reading Readiness Measures and the Frostig Developmental Test of Visual Perception." *Ed & Psychol Meas* 28:479–84 su '68. * (*PA* 42:19278)

91. OLSON, ARTHUR V., AND FITZGIBBON, NORINNE H. "Factor Analytic Investigation of Two Reading Readiness Tests." *Percept & Motor Skills* 27:611–4 O '68. * (*PA* 43:5892)

92. OLSON, NORINNE H. "An Analysis of the Relationship Between Conventional Reading Readiness Measures and Intellectual Functioning." Abstract. *AERA Paper Abstr* 1968: 122–3 '68. *

93. PAUCK, FREDRICK GLEN. *An Evaluation of the Self-Test as a Predictor of Reading Achievement of Spanish-Speaking First Grade Children.* Doctor's thesis, University of Texas (Austin, Tex.), 1968. (*DAI* 30:72A)

94. ROBINSON, H. ALAN, AND HANSON, EARL. "Reliability of Measures of Reading Achievement." *Read Teach* 21:307–13+ Ja '68. * (*PA* 42:17652)

95. ROSEN, CARL L. "An Investigation of Perceptual Training and Reading Achievement in First Grade." *Am J Optom* 45:322–32 My '68. * (*PA* 42:13476)

96. ROSEN, CARL L., AND OHNMACHT, FRED. "Perception, Readiness, and Reading Achievement in First Grade." *Proc Ann Conv Int Read Assn* 12(4):33–9 '68. *

97. SHEA, CAROL ANN. "Visual Discrimination of Words and Reading Readiness." *Read Teach* 21:361–7 Ja '68. *

98. SMITH, MILTON HOWARD. *Kindergarten Teachers' Judgments of Their Pupils' Readiness for Reading Instruction Compared With Readiness Test Results and First Grade Achievement Measures.* Doctor's thesis, University of Oregon (Eugene, Ore.), 1968. (*DA* 29:2044A)

99. WISE, JAMES H. "Stick Copying of Designs by Preschool and Young School-Age Children." *Percept & Motor Skills* 27:1159–68 D '68. * (*PA* 43:9547)

100. AKERS, JAMES CHESTER. *A Predictive Validity Study of the Metropolitan Readiness Tests.* Doctor's thesis, Oklahoma State University (Stillwater, Okla.), 1969. (*DAI* 31:3765A)

101. ASHBURN, PATRICIA SUE. "Predictive Validity of Beginning Readiness in Relation to Reading Achievement in Primary Grades in Selected Southern Mississippi Schools." *South J Ed Res* 3(1):59–70 Ja '69. *

102. AYERS, JERRY B., AND MASON, GEORGE E. "Differential Effects of Science: A Process Approach Upon Change in Metropolitan Readiness Test Scores Among Kindergarten Children." *Read Teach* 22(5):435–9 F '69. *

103. BAKER, GEORGIA ANN PITCHER. *The Efficiency of Diagnostic, Readiness, and Achievement Instruments as Predictors of Language Arts Achievement: A Longitudinal Study From Kindergarten Through Second Grade.* Doctor's thesis, Purdue University (Lafayette, Ind.), 1969. (*DAI* 30:3624A)

104. BLAND, ROSA BEATRICE. *Relation of Auditory Discrimination to Reading Achievement.* Doctor's thesis, University of Virginia (Charlottesville, Va.), 1969. (*DAI* 31:1655A)

105. BOUGERE, MARGUERITE BONDY. "Selected Factors in Oral Language Related to First-Grade Reading Achievement." *Read Res Q* 5(1):31–58 f '69. *

Metropolitan Readiness Tests

106. BUSHEY, JAMES THOMAS. *The Relationships Between a Preschool Measure of Readiness and Subsequent Test Performances Among a Group of Private Elementary School Children.* Doctor's thesis, Wayne State University (Detroit, Mich.), 1969. (*DAI* 30:3816A)

107. CLUTTS, JOAN BERNIECE RUSSELL. *Predicting Reading Success for the First Grade Child.* Doctor's thesis, University of Missouri (Columbia, Mo.), 1969. (*DAI* 30:3360A)

108. FARR, ROGER, AND ANASTASIOW, NICHOLAS. *Tests of Reading Readiness and Achievement: A Review and Evaluation,* pp. 19–22. Newark, Del.: International Reading Association, 1969. Pp. iv, 51. *

109. GILBERT, VIRGINIA RUTH. *Pre-School Reading Experiences and Related Success in Beginning Reading of a Certain Group of Children.* Doctor's thesis, University of Kansas (Lawrence, Kan.), 1969. (*DAI* 30:2904A)

110. HIRST, WILMA E. "Sex as a Predictor Variable for Success in First Grade Reading Achievement." *J Learn Dis* 2(6):316–21 Je '69. * (*PA* 45:7077)

111. JOHNSON, CLIFFORD IVY. *An Analysis of the Predictive Validity of Selective Reading Readiness Factors to Third Grade Reading Achievement.* Doctor's thesis, University of Georgia (Athens, Ga.), 1969. (*DAI* 30:3363A)

112. JOHNSON, ROGER E. "The Validity of the Clymer-Barrett Prereading Battery." *Read Teach* 22(7):609–14 Ap '69. * (*PA* 45:10670)

113. KAMPSEN, ALICE, AND LYDER, WAURINE. "The Effects of a Visual-Motor Perceptual Training Program on Kindergarten Children." *Kan Studies Ed* 19(3):20–4 Ag '69. *

114. KEIM, RICHARD PAUL. *Visual-Motor Training, Readiness, and Intelligence of Kindergarten Children.* Doctor's thesis, Temple University (Philadelphia, Pa.), 1969. (*DAI* 31:1076A)

115. NIKAS, GEORGE BILL. *Anxiety Levels of Upper-Middle and Upper-Lower Class First Grade Children Prior to and During Formal Reading Instruction.* Doctor's thesis, State University of New York (Buffalo, N.Y.), 1969. (*DAI* 30:2382A)

116. NORFLEET, MARY ANN. *The Bender Gestalt as a Group Screening Instrument for Reading Readiness.* Doctor's thesis, University of Oregon (Eugene, Ore.), 1969. (*DAI* 31:1083A)

117. PERSONKE, CARL R., JR., AND DAVIS, O. L., JR. "Predictive Validity of English and Spanish Versions of a Readiness Test." *El Sch J* 70(2):79–85 N '69. *

118. PLOTNIK, MICHAEL. *An Investigation of the Relationship of the Metropolitan Readiness Test to Reading Achievement.* Master's thesis, California State College (Long Beach, Calif.), 1969.

119. SCOTT, RALPH. "Social Class, Race, Seriating and Reading Readiness: A Study of Their Relationship at the Kindergarten Level." *J Genetic Psychol* 115(1):87–96 S '69. * (*PA* 44:4915)

120. SENK, HELEN M. *The Metropolitan Readiness Test: A Study of Its Validity in Predicting Scholastic Achievement for First Grade Pupils in Warehouse Point School.* Master's thesis, Central Connecticut State College (New Britain, Conn.), 1969.

121. SHINN, BRYON M. "A Study of Teacher Judgment and Readiness Tests as Predictors of Future Achievement." *Ill Sch Res* 6(1):12–5 N '69. *

122. THOMPSON, JUDY K. *A Study of the Relationship Between Reading Skills and Selected Components of Physical Fitness Among First-Grade Children.* Master's thesis, Texas Woman's University (Denton, Tex.), 1969.

123. WALKER, AUDREY JEAN MASSEY. *A Descriptive Study of the Oral Language Progress of Selected Disadvantaged and Advantaged Kindergarten Children.* Doctor's thesis, University of Georgia (Athens, Ga.), 1969. (*DAI* 30:5354A)

124. AUGUST, IRWIN. *A Study of the Effect of a Physical Education Program on Reading Readiness, Visual Perception and Perceptual-Motor Development in Kindergarten Children.* Doctor's thesis, New York University (New York, N.Y.), 1970. (*DAI* 31:2212A)

125. BARTLEY, CHARLES J. *The Metropolitan Readiness Test as a Predictor of Success in Grades One and Two.* Master's thesis, Jersey City State College (Jersey City, N.J.), 1970.

126. COTTEN, JERRY DALE. *A Comparison of the Metropolitan Readiness Tests to the Stanford Achievement Test.* Master's thesis, California State College (Long Beach, Calif.), 1970.

127. FERINDEN, WILLIAM E., JR., AND JACOBSON, SHERMAN. "Early Identification of Learning Disabilities." *J Learn Dis* 3(11):589–93 N '70. *

128. GATES, JOHN ANTHONY. *Selective Factors in Predicting Success in Learning Basic Sight Words and First Grade Reading Achievement.* Doctor's thesis, West Virginia University (Morgantown, W.Va.), 1970. (*DAI* 31:3775A)

129. GOODSTEIN, H. A.; WHITNEY, G.; AND CAWLEY, J. F. "Prediction of Perceptual Reading Disability Among Disadvantaged Children in the Second Grade." *Read Teach* 24(1):23–8 O '70. * (*PA* 45:10955)

130. GOOLSBY, THOMAS M., JR., AND FRARY, ROBERT B. "Validity of the Metropolitan Readiness Test for White and Negro Students in a Southern City." *Ed & Psychol Meas* 30(2):443–50 su '70. * (*PA* 45:2948)

131. HARCKHAM, LAURA D. *Prediction of Reading Achievement in Grades One, Two, Three, and Four Using Kindergarten Measures.* Doctor's thesis, Fordham University (New York, N.Y.), 1970. (*DAI* 31:3266A)

132. HUEBNER, ROBERT. "Sex Difference in the Prediction of First Grade Achievement." *Res J Col Ed Univ Md* 1(1):13–8 Jl '70. *

133. LEE, RAYMOND E. "Pre-School Grouping of Kindergarten Children." *Ill Sch Res* 7(1):19–21 f '70. *

134. MISHRA, SHITALA P., AND HURT, MAURE, JR. "The Use of Metropolitan Readiness Tests With Mexican-American Children." *Calif J Ed Res* 21(4):182–7 S '70. *

135. OZEHOSKY, RICHARD J., AND CLARK, EDWARD T. "Children's Self-Concept and Kindergarten Achievement." *J Psychol* 75(2):185–92 Jl '70. * (*PA* 44:20679)

136. ROBERTS, ARTHUR JAMES. *The Relationship Between Kindergarten Experience and Fine-Muscle Eye-Hand Coordination Abilities of First Grade Children.* Doctor's thesis, Oregon State University (Corvallis, Ore.), 1970. (*DAI* 31:2019A)

137. SCHRAGER, JULES, AND LINDY, JANET. "Hyperkinetic Children: Early Indicators of Potential School Failure." *Commun Mental Health J* 6(6):447–54 D '70. * (*PA* 45:8286)

138. SCOTT, RALPH. "Perceptual Skills, General Intellectual Ability, Race, and Later Reading Achievement." *Read Teach* 23(7):660–8 Ap '70. * (*PA* 45:3069)

139. TROBMAN, PHYLLIS B. *The Metropolitan Readiness Tests Scores vs First Grade Reading Progress.* Master's thesis, Glassboro State College (Glassboro, N.J.), 1970.

140. WORKS, MARIAN NEWMAN. *Some Variables Involved in the Reading Process.* Doctor's thesis, University of Oklahoma (Norman, Okla.), 1970. (*DAI* 31:2765AAA)

141. WORTHINGTON, JAMES D. *Relationships of the Anton Brenner and the Metropolitan Readiness Tests in Yielding Readiness Levels and Predicting Reading Achievement.* Master's thesis, Glassboro State College (Glassboro, N.J.), 1970.

142. ZAESKE, ARNOLD. "The Validity of Predictive Index Tests in · Predicting Reading Failure at the End of Grade One," pp. 28–33. In *Reading Difficulties: Diagnosis, Correction, and Remediation.* Edited by William K. Durr. Newark, Del.: International Reading Association, 1970. Pp. vii, 276. *

ROBERT DYKSTRA, *Professor of Education, University of Minnesota, Minneapolis, Minnesota.*

The MRT is designed to measure readiness for first grade instruction and to provide teachers with information helpful in classifying pupils. The subtests included in the battery are similar to those usually found in reading readiness tests except for the inclusion of the numbers subtest, a general measure of number knowledge, and the exclusion of a measure of auditory discrimination.

The manual provides a wealth of information about administering, scoring, and interpreting the tests. A major strength of this test, as compared with its competitors, is the extensive discussion devoted to interpreting test results. Emphasis is placed on pupil performance on the total battery, and the test authors very clearly caution against undue weight being attributed to subtest scores because of the relatively low reliabilities associated with these shorter tests. Interpretation of total test performance is enhanced by the assignment of letter ratings to raw scores. Five letter ratings are set up in terms of standard deviation distances and are accompanied by specific suggestions concerning the instructional significance of the various levels of performance. For example, pupils scoring an "E" rating on the test, according to the manual, should be assigned to slow sections, should be given further readiness work, or should receive individualized instruction. On the other hand, pupils attaining an "A" rating are judged to be very well prepared for first grade work.

The manual also provides expectancy tables to explain more adequately the relationship between performance on the readiness test and end-of-first-grade achievement. One of these tables records the median Stanford grade equivalents for first grade pupils at each of the five readiness levels. Another set of tables provides data concerning the probability that a pupil at a given readiness level will attain a given level of reading, spelling, or arithmetic achievement by the end of grade 1. These examples illustrate the depth and variety of the kinds of information provided in the manual to help school personnel interpret readiness test data.

The manual does a thorough job of discussing the validity of the test in terms of its content validity, construct validity, and predictive validity. Predictive validity is reported for a number of different samples. In addition, test users are supplied with additional data in mimeographed form from recent validation studies of the instrument. The test authors do a convincing job of describing the validity of the test by discussing the relevance of the content, by demonstrating the test's relationship with other measures of school readiness, and by relating success on the test with success in later achievement.

Reliability data, reported for first grade and kindergarten children, were computed using both split-half and alternate-form techniques. Reliabilities for the total test are generally above .90 for pupils tested at the end of kindergarten or early in grade 1. The reliability of the test appears adequate for the purposes for which it is intended.

The test itself appears to be well constructed and to measure abilities commonly believed to be associated with success in early school learning. The directions for administering the test are concise, and the test is set up in such a way that children can follow the instructions with a minimum of difficulty. Scoring the test presents no problem, except for the copying subtest, for which subjective judgment is involved.

Considerable information is provided about the nature of the standardization group, although it is not clear how representative this group is of first grade pupils as a whole. A

large portion of the standardization group was comprised of pupils who were involved in the Cooperative Research Program of First Grade Reading Instruction, and these pupils were certainly not chosen to participate because of the likelihood of their comprising a representative sample of American first-grade children. Nevertheless, the test manual makes a strong case for underplaying the importance of national norms for predictive measures such as readiness tests, stressing instead that the relationship between an obtained readiness score and later achievement is the crucial factor. The manual also points out that if some external or national guideline of readiness is desired, schools should compare the *median* score of their first grade pupils with national percentile ranks which are provided in the manual.

This test ranks very high among readiness tests. It has undergone careful development, it appears to be valid and reliable, and it provides unusually specific information about the instructional significance of test results. If a school system wishes to administer a readiness test in either kindergarten or first grade, it should find the *Metropolitan Readiness Tests* a useful tool.

HARRY SINGER, *Professor of Education, University of California, Riverside, California.*

In this comprehensive revision of the MRT, the name of the Sentence test has been changed appropriately to Listening. The Information test, although related to vocabulary ability, had a relatively low reliability and has been dropped. An Alphabet test, measuring knowledge of names of 16 lower-case letters, was added and is apparently an excellent addition, competing with other tests in the battery for highest coefficients of reliability and validity (for predicting reading achievement), about .89 and .60, respectively. Unfortunately, the manual does not contain multiple regression equations, which would give the relative weight of the Alphabet and the Numbers tests in predicting achievement. As reported in the manual, the two tests correlate .64 with each other, the highest reported intercorrelation among subtest scores, indicating more overlap with each other than with other tests in the battery.

The scoring key for the Copying test now has verbally stated scoring criteria but omits examples of satisfactory vs. unsatisfactory drawings of the figures. Apparently, this change has not reduced the split-half reliability of the test, which ranges from .79 to .85, or its predictive validity for paragraph meaning, which has remained about the same, .35. However, both criteria and examples would be desirable for a scoring key. If questions on applying the criteria arise, scorers may get some guidance, even though the figures to be copied are different, by referring to the scoring key for the 1949 edition.

Norms are given for the beginning of first grade, but not for kindergarten, despite a footnote in the manual that the tests may be used any time during the kindergarten year. Since some schools are now beginning to initiate reading instruction in kindergarten, norms, recommended groups, and validity data for this school level would be desirable. In the meantime, readiness test results for kindergarten children, particularly precocious kindergarteners, could be interpreted by comparison with the first grade norms.

Despite the apparent care with which items were selected to make up Forms A and B, the low alternate-form reliabilities of the subtests, ranging from .50 for Listening to .86 for Alphabet, support the admonition in the manual that "relatively little significance be attached to the subtest scores of *individual* pupils." However, the alternate-form reliability of .91 for the *total for tests 1-6* is excellent and sufficiently high for use of the total test score with individual pupils.

The assumption underlying all of the *Metropolitan Readiness Tests* is that present level of performance, based upon interaction of maturation and past learning, is the best predictor of future achievement. Unlike the *Murphy-Durrell Reading Readiness Analysis*—which uses a miniature standardized situation for teaching two important components of reading, phoneme-grapheme relations and learning rate, *plus* the past achievement of a reading-related function (knowledge of letters of the alphabet)— the MRT stresses past achievement. Nevertheless, the correlation of .80 between the MRT and the Murphy-Durrell indicates a high degree of overlap in functions assessed by the two tests.

Although past achievement tends to be a good predictor of subsequent achievement, teachers should supplement information derived from the MRT with teaching activities in order to obtain some estimate of *present* ability of pupils to learn, perhaps through the use of experience

charts or the language experience approach. This supplementary information would be important to obtain for all pupils, but particularly for those children whose backgrounds had limited their opportunities to learn those functions assessed by the MRT.

Considerable data are presented in the manual on the predictive validity of the MRT for reading attainment as assessed by the *Stanford Achievement Test: Reading* over the October to May period of first grade. Although these data attest to the predictive validity of the MRT, they also reveal the wide range of variability in May achievement for each category of October readiness. This variability means that in addition to the readiness test scores, other factors should be considered in making predictions or instructional decisions, such as adapting methods and materials to individual differences, criterion for successful achievement, and, probably, teacher effectiveness [1] (*64*).

Teachers should be aware that bilingual children are likely to be handicapped on the MRT, even when given in the other language, because bilingual children tend to be deficient in both languages [2] (*117*). Also, the evidence indicates that the predictive validity coefficients for blacks vs. whites are similar (*69, 73*), but low socioeconomic status is associated with less reliable scores on the MRT (*68*). However, readiness level on the MRT may be improved as a result of reading instruction given in kindergarten (*19*).

Since experienced or inexperienced first grade teachers can closely estimate children's readiness scores on the MRT and can predict their reading achievement about as well as the MRT (*30, 58*), the obvious conclusion is that while the MRT provides reliable and valid data on readiness that may be administratively useful, these data tend only to confirm teacher judgments arrived at during the first few weeks of the school year.

Because teachers do not gain very much educationally useful information from the MRT, they would be best advised to use another test for reading readiness, such as the *Murphy-Durrell Reading Readiness Analysis*.

1 GATES, A. I.; BOND, G. L.; AND RUSSELL, D. H. *Methods of Determining Reading Readiness.* New York: Bureau of Publications, Teachers College, Columbia University, 1939. Pp. iv, 55. *
2 SINGER, HARRY. "Bilingualism and Elementary Education." *Mod Lang J* 40:444–58 D '56. *

For a review by Eric F. Gardner of the previous edition, see 4:570 (1 excerpt); for a review by Irving H. Anderson of the original edition, see 3:518; for a review by W. J. Osburn, see 2:1552.

[758]

Murphy-Durrell Reading Readiness Analysis. First grade entrants; 1949-65, c1947-65; MDRRA; revision of *Murphy-Durrell Diagnostic Reading Readiness Test;* 6 scores: sound recognition, letter names (capitals, lower case, total), learning rate, total; 1 form ('64, 8 pages); flash cards ('65, 1 sheet); manual ('65, 20 pages); $6.20 per 35 tests; $1.50 per specimen set; postage extra; (60) minutes in 2 sessions; Helen A. Murphy and Donald D. Durrell; Harcourt Brace Jovanovich, Inc. *

REFERENCES

1–2. See 4:571.
3–4. See 5:679.
5. NOONAN, JOSEPH D., JR. *An Investigation of the Validity of the Pictures in the Murphy-Durrell Diagnostic Reading Readiness Test.* Master's thesis, Boston University (Boston, Mass.), 1961.
6. DYKSTRA, ROBERT. *The Relationship Between Selected Reading Readiness Measures of Auditory Discrimination and Reading Achievement at the End of First Grade.* Doctor's thesis, University of Minnesota (Minneapolis, Minn.), 1962. (DA 24:195)
7. KERFOOT, JAMES FLETCHER. *The Relationship of Selected Auditory and Visual Reading Readiness Measures to First Grade Reading Achievement and Second Grade Reading and Spelling Achievement.* Doctor's thesis, University of Minnesota (Minneapolis, Minn.), 1964. (DA 25:1747)
8. WEEKS, ERNEST EMMETT. *The Effect of Specific Pre-Reading Materials on Children's Performances on the Murphy-Durrell Diagnostic Reading Readiness Test.* Doctor's thesis, University of Connecticut (Storrs, Conn.), 1964. (DA 25:4586)
9. DYKSTRA, ROBERT. "Auditory Discrimination Abilities and Beginning Reading Achievement." *Read Res Q* 1:5–34 sp '66. * (PA 40:11011)
10. BEAUCHAMP, JOAN M. *The Relationship Between Selected Factors Associated With Reading Readiness and the First Grade Reading Achievement of Students Instructed in the Initial Teaching Alphabet.* Doctor's thesis, Syracuse University (Syracuse, N.Y.), 1967. (DA 28:1200A)
11. BOND, GUY L., AND DYKSTRA, ROBERT. "The Cooperative Research Program in First-Grade Reading Instruction." *Read Res Q* 2:5–142 su '67. * (PA 42:4557)
12. MITCHELL, BLYTHE C. "Predictive Validity of the Metropolitan Readiness Tests and the Murphy-Durrell Reading Readiness Analysis for White and for Negro Pupils." *Ed & Psychol Meas* 27:1047–54 w '67. * (PA 42:9504)
13. FARR, ROGER, AND ANASTASIOW, NICHOLAS. *Tests of Reading Readiness and Achievement: A Review and Evaluation,* pp. 22–4. Newark, Del.: International Reading Association, 1969. Pp. iv, 51. *
14. WARD, BYRON J. "Two Measures of Reading Readiness and First Grade Reading Achievement." *Read Teach* 23(7): 637–9 Ap '70. * (PA 45:3070)

REBECCA C. BARR, *Director, The Reading Clinic, The University of Chicago, Chicago, Illinois.*

Similar to its predecessor, this test consists of three subtests that provide information for grouping children for beginning reading instruction. The new test represents an improvement in construction and standardization.

The Phonemes test measures skill in discriminating beginning and final consonant phonemes. The child is first "taught" the sounds by listening to them in three key words and in isolation. He then selects from four pictures the two that begin or end with the same sound.

The Letter Names test has been substituted for the visual test of the 1949 edition. This subtest measures the child's ability to select from five similar letters the one named by the examiner. All letters, and both capitals and lower case, are tested. This task has been found to be the single best predictor of later reading (11). Directions and scoring for this subtest are clear.

The Learning Rate test is similar in purpose to the comparable subtest in the 1949 test. In contrast, however, the new subtest is well conceived, with clear directions and test procedures. It is to be used with a group of children, the size determined by the examiner. Nine words are taught during a 20-minute period. Each word is presented in print on the chalkboard, on flashcards, and in the test booklet. The examiner names the word, stresses the meaning, and informally checks learning. No measure of learning is obtained at the end of the teaching session. One hour after teaching, children are asked to identify each word in a multiple choice task, first from among three of the words taught and then from among three words similar in form.

The answer booklet is well organized so that scoring may be done efficiently. Raw scores for the three subtests (including upper and lower case letters separately and a total) and the total score can be converted into percentiles, stanines, and quartiles. The standardization is based on a sample of 12,231 first grade students from 65 school systems in twelve states.

Split-half reliabilities, standard deviations, and individual item difficulties are based upon the scores of 200 children randomly selected from the standardization sample.

The total test is highly reliable (.98); Phonemes and Letter Names show adequate reliability (.94 and .97, respectively); reliability of Learning Rate is somewhat low (.88). The two subtests most closely related to the total score are Phonemes and Letter Names (.84 and .88, respectively), with Learning Rate showing a considerably lower degree of relationship (.48).

The total score on the Murphy-Durrell was compared with the *Metropolitan Readiness Tests* (.80) and with the *Pintner-Cunningham Primary Test* (.64) As would be expected on the basis of content similarity, the Murphy-Durrell and the Metropolitan seem to be measuring similar abilities.

No estimates of the relationship of the subtests with concurrent measures of the ability are reported. For example, an independent measure of the child's auditory discrimination would be useful to test whether or not the Phonemes test was validly measuring this ability. A sampling of words learned during the first several months of instruction could be used to check the validity of the Learning Rate test. Given the fact that the predictive validity of most readiness tests tends to be low, other evidence that such tests measure what they purport to measure is needed.

The predictive validity, using the *Stanford Achievement Test: Reading* administered at the end of first grade as the criterion, was based upon 200 students from one state—Kansas. The use of this limited sample, instead of the more representative national sample, in assessing predictive validity is not explained. The predictive validity of the total score ranges from .65 to .66. Although these coefficients are not high, they are comparable to those obtained by most presently available readiness instruments. Coefficients for Phonemes and Letter Names tend to be low (.59 to .62 and .54 to .57, respectively). The predictive effectiveness of Learning Rate is inadequate (.38 to .48).

The three subtests do not appear to be measuring the same ability. The correlation is highest between the Phonemes and Letter Names (.59) and somewhat lower between these tests and Learning Rate (.53 and .37, respectively).

Because of the low correlations of Learning Rate with the other subtests, the authors see it as serving "the unique purpose of measuring a different component of pupil's readiness to read." If all subtests are in fact measuring different aptitudes necessary for reading, then a low degree of relationships among subtests is desirable. The validity of the Learning Rate test is not adequately supported by data reported. The contribution of this subtest to the predictive effectiveness of the total score was not assessed, but it appears to be negligible.

The authors discuss in the manual the use of test results. Instructional suggestions are made for children in the highest quarter, two middle quarters, and lowest quarter on total test scores. It is stated that children in a particular quarter will know a certain number of letter names and phonemes and remember a specified number of words. Such generalizations are inappropriate in view of the low subtest intercorrelations.

For teachers who analyze subtest score patterns and errors of their pupils, the individual item difficulties reported in the manual reveal which items are most often correct or incorrect. Instructional suggestions that help the teacher to make diagnostic use of such information would be more appropriate in terms of the standardization findings and more useful for instructional planning which considers the needs of the children than are the instructional suggestions made.

In the discussion of instruction, the authors state that "any missing phoneme or unfamiliar letter will handicap the learning of words containing it." At the present time, little is known about how children actually learn to read, the strategies involved, and the possible sequences of skill development. Children appear to develop different strategies, some using cues primarily from sentence syntax, some using word cues, and some using letter or letter combination cues. I am not aware of research which conclusively supports the statement that lack of letter knowledge will impede word learning.

In summary, this is a well constructed and well standardized test. The Phonemes and Letter Names tests possess adequate reliability. Their predictive validities are similar to other commonly used readiness measures. Standardization norms are based on an adequate sample. Such information recommends the first two subtests. These subtests may also be useful as a source of items to be learned. The Learning Rate test is well designed, but reliability and validity coefficients do not recommend its use for other than diagnostic purposes.

HARRY SINGER, *Professor of Education, University of California, Riverside, California.*

This substantially revised test is based upon a laudatory concept of assessing reading readiness. Of the three subtests, two—Phonemes and Learning Rate—are based upon standardized teaching-learning situations. These two subtests tend to overcome differences in pupil performance due to past experience. Moreover, they articulate well with two major approaches to teaching word recognition, phonics and sight words. The best test of readiness is learning in the actual teaching situation; these first two subtests of the *Murphy-Durrell Reading Readiness Analysis* approach this ideal.

However, the third subtest, Letter Names, merely tests previous achievement and indicates which children had the ability and the opportunity to acquire knowledge of letter names prior to first grade. It also overlaps with the Phonemes subtest, since some letter names are identical to their phonemes.

Although knowledge of letter names per se is not intrinsically related to the reading process, such knowledge is nevertheless important in learning to read because it enables teachers to communicate with children about letters during the teaching-learning process. Moreover, the earlier pupils learn letter names, the sooner they can organize and conceptualize information about the attributes of letters and letter sounds and how to use them in reading. In general, letter names are learned early. According to the authors, the average child can identify 20 capital letters and 14 lower-case letters at the beginning of first grade.

The revised test contains adequate technical data on sample characteristics, reliability, and validity to overcome almost all of the criticisms (see 5:679) leveled at the first edition of the test. But parallel-form reliability and use of the test for pretesting and posttesting are precluded because there is only one form.

Although the Murphy-Durrell is one of the best reading readiness tests, it has some weaknesses. Though directions for taking the test are generally clear, the directions for the Phonemes test may mislead some pupils. The directions merely imply but do not explicitly state that two choices out of four in each row are to be selected. Consequently, some capable but not test-wise pupils might mark only one response and hence obtain, at best, half credit for the item.

The split-half reliabilities of the subtests are quite high: .94 for Phonemes, .97 for Letter Names, and .88 for Learning Rate. The Murphy-Durrell has a very high concurrent validity coefficient of .80 with the *Metropolitan Readiness Tests*. In general, the correlations of the Murphy-Durrell subtests given in September with the *Stanford Achievement Test: Reading* administered in May are substantial, ranging from .38 between Learning Rate and Word Study Skills to .62 between Phonemes and Word Study Skills. However, the magnitude of these correlations does not preclude that some pupils will be high on one test and low on another or that they will have low reading readiness and high reading achievement. Consequently, as with all reading readiness tests, teachers must supplement the test results with judgments based on continuous assessment of pupil performance and, of course, must update their judgments throughout the year.

The basic assumption of the Learning Rate test may be only partially valid. Scores on this subtest are assumed to represent sight words learned in the test's teaching-learning situation. Only by pretesting the list of sight words may the tester validly conclude that pupils had, in fact, learned the sight words during the test. Moreover, logical analysis of this subtest suggests that the pupils may be only learning to discriminate the initial letter or first two letters of the words. The discrimination task in the first part of the test (nine items) can be accomplished through mere recognition of initial consonants of the words, but in the second part of the test (also nine items), where each key word and one of the decoy items have the same initial consonant, the pupil has to discriminate on more than the initial consonant to identify the key word.

No correction is made for guessing on any of the subtests. Consequently, the expected chance score on Phonemes is 24 which places the pupil at the 16th percentile. On Letter Names the expected chance score of 5.2 for each part is at the 8th percentile for Capital Letters and the 12th percentile for Lower Case Letters. On Learning Rate, the expected chance score is 6, which is the 24th percentile.

The norms, based on 12,231 entering first graders in 65 school systems, appear to be representative but do not include schools from the deep South and Southwest. However, there is some evidence (*12*) that the Murphy-Durrell predictive validity is about the same for white and black samples. Since normative data are not provided for kindergarten children, schools that assess reading readiness and initiate reading instruction at this level would need to construct local norms.

Despite these criticisms, the Murphy-Durrell is still one of the best reading readiness tests. It provides information useful to the teacher for adapting reading instruction to individual differences in pupil mode and rate of learning.

For reviews by Joan Bollenbacher and S. S. Dunn of the earlier edition, see 5:679.

[759]
★**Parent Readiness Evaluation of Preschoolers.** Ages 3-9 to 5-8; 1968–69; PREP; test administered by parent; 17 scores: verbal (general information,

comprehension, opposites, identification, verbal association, verbal description, listening, language, total), performance (concepts, motor co-ordination, visual-motor association, visual interpretation, auditory memory, visual memory, total), total; individual; 1 form; manual ('68, 28 pages) ; descriptive sheet ['69, 2 pages] ; child's test booklet ('68, 68 pages) ; parent handbook ('68, 41 pages) ; no data on reliability; norms consist of "average raw score ranges" for 4-month age groups; $1.25 per test; $1 per parent handbook; cash orders postpaid; (60–90) minutes in 2 sessions; A. Edward Ahr and Benita Simons (handbook) ; Priority Innovations, Inc. *

S. ALAN COHEN, *Associate Professor of Education and Director, Reading and Language Arts Center, Yeshiva University, New York, New York.*

PREP should have been printed in *Woman's Day* or *Good Housekeeping.* Reviewing it for this *Mental Measurements Yearbook* grants PREP a dignity it certainly does not deserve. A reported .91 test-retest reliability notwithstanding, PREP is an unprofessional test booklet, designed unprofessionally for use by non-professionals in assessing whether or not their offspring are average in some ambiguous category called "readiness." Is PREP "readiness" reading readiness? Is it readiness for succeeding in preschool? Kindergarten? First grade? Is average PREP like average intelligence on a Stanford-Binet or Wechsler? Who knows? The test publisher offers us no validity data.

Except for a claim that PREP has a sort of face validity ("PREP will highlight the strengths and weaknesses of the child in various skills and ability areas," says the test order form), the test booklet offers no case for its validity. Even in professional hands, poorly validated tests are dangerous. But unvalidated tests in laymen's hands could be a disaster for the poor child whose score is below or above his parents' expectations. In this case, lack of validity is, in laymen's terms, lack of a specific statement of purpose. Without such a statement, the uninitiated parent can interpret the results in the most unpredictable manner.

Even if we were to accept that simple statement of face validity, the "preliminary" reliability coefficients reported for 11 of the 14 subtests are too low to justify diagnostic use of the subtests with individual children. Other technicalities also militate against accepting this instrument as a serious contribution to the professional testing field. Reliability testing, otherwise not described, is said to have been based on "eleven kindergartners." PREP's author sug-

gests that the battery can be divided in half to be administered in two separate sittings. But he offers no correlation between this mode of administration and the one-sitting mode.

PREP is divided into two categories of subtests: verbal and performance. Performance subtests include Concepts, a task similar to picture vocabulary in the *SRA Primary Mental Abilities.* Why Concepts is more performance than verbal is, ordinarily, a semantic irrelevance. But with the absence of validity data, the question becomes crucial to test interpretation, for Thurstone demonstrated that this type of task is included in a *verbal* factor loading not unlike vocabulary. PREP simply lists it as Performance, apparently arbitrarily.

Perhaps the best that can be said is that PREP offers a trained clinician a collection of familiar educational and psychological-type test items he may want to use as an unstandardized clinical tool. Perhaps, too, PREP warns psychometricians that their professional secrecy and their tendency to withhold details of test results from parents who have both the legal and moral right to know, has led to the creation of dangerous, inaccurate, or misleading instruments for parent use. That a market for PREP exists suggests to this reviewer that early childhood psychometricians must reexamine their own practices.

ROBERT E. VALETT, *Professor of Education, Fresno State College, Fresno, California.*

In a prefacing letter to parents, the author of PREP mistakenly states that "never before have parents been given the opportunity to evaluate their own child with a test." Parents have, however, been provided with such opportunities before (e.g., see 763).

The manual presents general directions for parents, explaining that the test is to be presented as a game, although "the precise wording of the specific directions must be used." The test is divided into a verbal and a performance section, each requiring 30 to 45 minutes to administer. Testing items are to be picked up from around the home or obtained from local stores. A total of 150 major tasks are presented in the subtests indicated above. Many items have been taken directly from the Stanford-Binet, WISC, and ITPA, and other tasks are similar to those found in these commonly used standardized tests.

The PREP offers little evidence of its validity. However, its face and content validity with first grade curricular expectations appear to be high. The normative data are limited and misleading in their present form and would only tend to further confuse parents. If used in conjunction with a psychoeducational consultant, however, the test could be a most useful means of involving parents in the early evaluation and subsequent remediation of specific learning disabilities; to this end, the instrument and accompanying handbook for parents appear to be a worthwhile contribution for professional consideration in teacher training as well as in parent education.

DAVID P. WEIKART, *President, High/Scope Educational Research Foundation, Ypsilanti, Michigan.*

Parent Readiness Evaluation of Preschoolers is unusual because it is intended to be administered by parents to their own children about the time of preregistration for kindergarten. The manual states, "It gives parents the opportunity to become more involved with their child, to obtain objective information and to use the data to further their child's development."

For a test intended to be administered by parents, it is quite elaborate and time consuming. There are 14 subtests, each requiring prior familiarization by the parent. In addition, some 15 objects must be secured for use in administering the test; while they are all commonplace, in a particular home on a particular day there are likely to be several unavailable (e.g., bananas, bubble gum). Reading the PREP manual to familiarize oneself with the items could easily take a bright parent a full hour. Collecting the objects could easily consume a half hour if two or three were not immediately available. The two test sessions themselves require 30 to 45 minutes each. Scoring the test and looking up scores in the test norms might easily involve another half hour. Thus, in order to obtain a valid test score, the parent must be motivated enough to spend about three hours or more in the process. Obviously, such a test is not for all parents.

The major drawback of the test becomes apparent at the end of the whole process. For all his trouble, the parent only learns if his child is below average, average, or above average for each of the 17 scores—the manual provides no further interpretations or recommendations to guide the parent.

In an apparent attempt to deal with the problem of putting the test results to practical use, the publisher has provided a companion Parent Handbook intended to suggest activities that the parent and child can perform in order to help develop the child's skills and abilities at home. The attempt is laudable to the extent that it avoids suggesting the dubious practice of delaying the child's entry into kindergarten as some authorities do, and also to the extent that the activities are basically sound and likely to be helpful. However, the handbook bears only the most tenuous relationship to the test, and the lack of correspondence between subtest names and handbook chapter titles is very confusing. If a child performs poorly on a particular subtest, say Opposites, the parent may have difficulty locating those activities in the handbook bearing on the necessary skills and concepts to improve his ability in that area.

The subtests are grouped into verbal and performance categories, and the two subtotals are included in the norm table. Most of the subtests seem to consist of items which should be reasonably familiar to middleclass American children and include typical school activities similar in nature to those of any number of other tests for children of this age. The formats of seven of the subtests (Comprehension, Opposites, Verbal Description, Listening, Language, Visual-Motor Association, and Visual Interpretation) closely resemble the formats of subtests on the *Illinois Test of Psycholinguistic Abilities,* although the wording is different.

Within subtests many of the items seem needlessly repetitious, such as the Listening subtest, where it seems that 5 instead of 15 items would probably suffice, and the Identification subtest, which might do with 3 or so instead of 10. The narrow range indicated for these two subtests on the norm table across all ages would seem to support shortened versions. In general, it appears that many other subtests could be shortened without compromising the test, following adequate test development research, thus considerably reducing the load on the parents who administer it.

Except for the instructions about administering and scoring the test, which are clear but involved, the test manual essentially follows none of the major recommendations presented in the APA-AERA-NCME *Standards for Educational and Psychological Tests and Manuals.* For example, no information was provided

Parent Readiness Evaluation of Preschoolers

about how many children were used in the standardization sample or about the population from which the standardization sample was drawn. Without such information it is impossible to determine what an average score on the test signifies. Also, no evidence of validity is included in the manual, such as empirical verification that children obtaining "average" scores can indeed function adequately in school, or that those scoring "below average" do poorly in school. No information about reliability was included in the manual, but an advertising flyer for the tests presents one-month test-retest reliabilities of .91, .82, and .89 for the total, verbal, and performance totals, respectively. These figures are based on a sample of only 11 children, selection and ages unspecified.

In summary, because of the lack of information necessary to properly interpret and use the results, coupled with the excessive time required for proper administration, the test is not recommended for use by parents. The *School Readiness Survey* would seem to be a much more appropriate alternative test for use by parents. Moreover, if trained examiners are considering giving the test, they could give both the Stanford-Binet and the ITPA in about the same amount of time and arrive at much more interpretable scores supported by careful and extensive research.

[760]

★**Primary Academic Sentiment Scale.** Ages 4-4 to 7-3; 1968; PASS; motivation for learning and level of maturity and parental independence; 2 scores: sentiment, dependency; 1 form (40 pages); manual (19 pages); scoring sheet (1 page); $20 per set of 35 tests, 35 scoring sheets, and manual; $2.50 per specimen set; cash orders postpaid; (50) minutes; Glen Robbins Thompson; Priority Innovations, Inc. *

JEROME ROSNER, *Research Associate, Learning Research and Development Center, University of Pittsburgh, Pittsburgh, Pennsylvania.*

This test is designed to "obtain objective information about a child's motivation for learning and his relative level of maturity and parental independence." The former is expressed quantitatively as a Sentiment Quotient (SQ); the latter in a Dependency Stanine (DS).

The test, designed for group administration, consists of 38 items which, in the main, ask the child to indicate an attitude or preference in response to a given situation. The items are presented orally by the examiner. The children respond by marking pictures. The response choices are designed so that one is presumably more closely related to traditional academic tasks than are the others; another is intended to be an interesting, competing, academically nonessential activity; and the third apparently attempts to present a situation that should appeal strongly to a dependent, immature child. Choice of the one considered most closely related to academic success factors is given credit in determination of the SQ. Choice of the one most weighted with dependency factors is credited in the scaling for the DS. Choice of the "academically irrelevant" behavior results in no credit toward either of the two scales.

The premise that a child cannot display high dependency *and* high motivation on the same item should be questioned seriously. Highly dependent children frequently are motivated toward academic success if only for the resultant social approval. Eight items are included that do not provide for a choice of activity but, instead, question the child on whether his parents take him to the zoo, museum, or on trips, and about mother's and father's favorite activity (read, talk on the phone, watch television?). The validity of these items is tentative at best.

The manual is clearly written. Instructions are specifically stated. Each item is presented in a standardized manner; a script has been written for each. Following the script may cause trouble, however, because the examiner is told to offer such reinforcing comments as "good" and "you are doing it right" after the children respond to many of the items. It is conceivable that these comments might well reinforce responses in a way that would distort the test's validity. The response drawings are simple line sketches that do not appear to confuse most four- and five-year-olds. All representations of human faces and figures are drawn as black solid forms. This hopefully provides a culturally unbiased presentation.

PASS was standardized on a population of 480 preschool, kindergarten, and first grade children living in suburban Chicago. No information is provided concerning the socioeconomic, racial, sex, or age distribution of this population. The author reports a K-R 20 reliability of .58 for the 480 children in this study. In addition, correlations between PASS scores and certain other measures are reported. Other data showed a significant difference between "high" and "low" groups on both the SQ and DS when compared to teachers' ranking of their students along an "academic interest dimension." Unfortunately, only mean scores for the groups are reported, unaccompanied by standard deviations or other relevant data.

The author of PASS does not contend that the instrument is a predictor of academic success. Rather, he proposes that it is a reliable method to assess quantitatively a child's motivation and emotional maturity and that it would facilitate experimental programs designed to probe and alter attitudes toward school and learning. This may well be the case but more studies are required to support the proposition.

[761]

★Riley Preschool Developmental Screening Inventory. Ages 3–5; 1969; RPDSI; school readiness; 2 scores: design, make-a-boy (girl); individual; 1 form (4 pages); manual (12 pages plus test); no data on reliability; $7.50 per 25 tests and manual; $6.50 per 25 tests; $2.50 per manual; postpaid; [3–10] minutes; Clara M. D. Riley; Western Psychological Services. *

[762]

★The School Readiness Checklist. Ages 5–6; 1963–68; booklet title is Ready or Not; checklist to be used by parents; 1 form ('63, 8 pages); manual ('68, 94 pages plus test); no data on reliability and validity; $1.50 per 10 copies; $3.95 per manual; cash orders postpaid; black child illustrated edition available; Spanish edition available; [10–20] minutes; John J. Austin, J. Clayton Lafferty, Frederick Leaske (manual), and Fred Cousino (manual); Research Concepts. *

DENNIS J. DELORIA, Vice President for Research, High/Scope Educational Research Foundation, Ypsilanti, Michigan.

The School Readiness Checklist is a short questionnaire for parents, containing 43 items requiring Yes or No answers. The checklist should take less than 10 minutes to complete and does not require the presence of the child. Although no subtest scores are computed, items are presented in seven groups: growth and age, general activity related to growth, practical skills, remembering, understanding, general knowledge, and attitudes and interests. At the end of the form is a score classification table with five categories, ordered according to the number of Yes responses on the test. For each category the "approximate state of readiness for school" and "possible action" are presented. The former ranges from "readiness reasonably assured" through "readiness unlikely," and the latter from "school entrance" through "consultation with school personnel, physician, psychologist." The manual makes no further attempt to interpret the scores, which seems appropriate, considering the casual nature of the

checklist. Parents with additional questions are urged by the form to consult with local school personnel.

The handbook which accompanies the test does not present the "essential" test development data recommended in Standards for Educational and Psychological Tests and Manuals, omitting such important information as norm sample characteristics, test validity data, and test reliability data. The first half of the handbook consists of a general discussion of readiness, not specifically related to the checklist at all, and the second half consists of two research studies using the checklist. The two studies seem most related to validity, the first comparing checklist scores to kindergarten teachers' judgments of readiness, and the second comparing checklist scores with teachers' judgments, psychologists' judgments, and four standardized instruments. The results of both studies are clearly supportive, but neither does much to inspire confidence in the checklist as a screening device on which to base practical decisions. Part of the reason for this lies within the actual results of the studies as discussed below, but part of the reason rests with insufficient analysis. For example, the second study obtained measurements on the Stanford-Binet and other tests, but no correlation coefficients are presented to summarize their relationships with the checklist.

The studies highlight one problem in particular: there was such a low incidence of scores below the "readiness doubtful" score of 30 (5 out of 278 in the first study and 7 out of 116 in the second) that the practical importance of data gathered through use of the checklist is questionable. In addition, teachers' judgments conflicted with some of the low scores (1 and 2) and also with some of the high scores (18 and 16), casting more doubt on the usefulness of the scores. When the cutoff score was increased to 36 in the first study, a disproportionately large number of children (72) failed to evidence readiness on the test in comparison to the actual number that teachers judged not ready (22). Considering, on the other hand, that about 75 percent of the children fall in the top two categories of the test, having a large group of mothers complete the form may have the effect of reassuring most of them about their children's readiness. For the 25 percent or so that fall at or below the "readiness questionable" category, early consultation would probably be beneficial, even though most of them would in fact be judged "ready" by teachers.

As a side comment, one nagging implication of the word "readiness" is that if a child is not "ready," his entry into school should be delayed until he is "ready." This is a deplorable conclusion, since it amounts to depriving help to the child who is most in need of help, on the basis of the false assumption that "readiness" depends merely on the passage of time and not on the experiences of the child during that time. If available evidence suggests a child is not ready for a normal kindergarten, the most direct solution would be to provide special compensatory experiences to help him become ready. Recent data from preschool research have convincingly demonstrated that high quality preschool programs can have a profound effect in helping young children overcome readiness problems.

In conclusion, the test would seem to be useful as an icebreaker for mothers of entering children at a registration meeting or as a device to help parents make up their minds whether or not to consult with school personnel about their child, but not as a formal screening device used to delay school entry or to assign children to special educational classes.

[763]

★**School Readiness Survey.** Ages 4–6; 1967–69; to be administered and scored by parents with school supervision; 8 scores: number concepts, discrimination of form, color naming, symbol matching, speaking vocabulary, listening vocabulary, general information, total; 1 form ('69, 30 pages); manual ('67, 14 pages); $9.50 per 25 tests; 50¢ per manual; 75¢ per specimen set; postage extra; [15–30] minutes; F. L. Jordan and James Massey; Consulting Psychologists Press, Inc. *

J Ed Meas 7(1):58–9 sp '70. Byron Egeland. * The seven sections and general readiness checklist were derived by asking "several" kindergarten teachers what characteristics they found in their most successful students. In addition, the authors studied "many" kindergarten evaluation forms with regard to what skills and qualities kindergarten children were graded on during their initial school experience. The authors selected items from existing readiness surveys which appeared to be measuring the readiness skills specified by the kindergarten teachers and found on the kindergarten evaluation forms. Only those items were included that could be administered and scored by parents. * It is difficult to judge what skills certain sections of the survey are measuring and how

appropriate the items are for measuring the specified skills. For example, the Professional Manual states that section seven, General Information, is a measure of how mature the child is in observing his environment. In the test booklet used by the parents, section seven is described as a memory test. This section actually contains information and comprehension items similar to those found on the WISC, in addition to analogies, digit span and other short-term memory items. A factor analysis would lend some credibility to the selection of items and help clarify the meaning of the various parts of the test. The test booklet contains directions for administration and scoring as well as suggested remedial exercises which parents can use to help their child get ready for school. The idea of including remedial exercises is appealing even though no data are offered to support the assumption that such exercises enhance a child's school readiness. The instructions for scoring the test are concise although some scorer subjectivity is involved in the General Information and Speaking Vocabulary sections. * The Professional Manual does not contain adequate information regarding reliability, validity, item selection, norming procedures and how to interpret scores. It would be helpful to school personnel to know how to set up local norms and expectancy tables. * The cumulative percentage norms which are given by sex but not by age have been adjusted to compensate for the bias in sampling. Unfortunately, the authors fail to report what kind of correction was applied and whether or not the corrected norms now represent the performance of a cross section of entering kindergarten children. Unaccounted for discrepancies are noted in the cumulative percentages of items passed for certain sections of the survey. The Discrimination of Form section contains 11 items but the cumulative percentages are figured on seven items. The mean raw scores for this section are 6.06 for boys and 6.64 for girls, with s.d.'s of 1.50 and .94 respectively. A raw score of six places the child in the "needs to develop category" and a raw score of seven indicates "borderline readiness." None of the normative sample got more than seven items correct indicating that they are not ready for school according to the Discrimination of Form test. * In a study of 20 children in which parents administered the SRS initially and teachers gave the retest, a correlation of .64 was obtained. Parents tended to score their children two to five points higher than did the teachers. Estimates of reliability based on a test-retest interval of five months provides little useful information since the skills being measured change over short periods of time. Reliability estimates of internal consistency, interscorer agreement, and information concerning the reliability of the part scores are lacking. The standard error of measurement for the whole or part scores is not reported. To determine whether cr not the SRS is useful in predicting school readiness the authors correlated SRS scores with kindergarten teacher's ratings of the progress of 842 children after three and one-half months of school. The resulting correlation was .39. Additional validity data are necessary before the SRS can be considered for use by parents or school personnel in making crucial decisions regarding a child's readiness for school. Noticeably absent is any report of the relationship between SRS scores and other criteria, both concurrently with other readiness tests and predictively with relevant variables such as grade retention, special class placement, school adjustment, and general academic success. *Summary.* Certainly the notion of a parent-administered school readiness screening test which points out a child's strengths and weaknesses and suggests remedial exercises to foster development merits serious attention, but the authors of this particular test have not thoroughly refined the instrument or justified its use on an empirical basis. Based on the information (or lack of) presented in the Professional Manual, the SRS is considered by this reviewer to be in the early stages of experimental development and of little value in making individual decisions regarding a child's readiness for school.

J Read 11:148 N '67. Dale E. Bennett. * The technical data presented in the manual to establish the reliability and validity of the instrument are not particularly rigorous. Certainly one could question whether the correlation between performance on the survey and the rankings of kindergarten teachers as to rate of progress on a five-point scale after three and one-half months in school is sufficient evidence to support the assumption of validity.

[764]

★Screening Test for the Assignment of Remedial Treatments. Ages 4-6 to 6-5; 1968; START; 5 scores: visual memory, auditory memory, visual copying, visual discrimination, total; 1 form (56 pages and 13 cards); manual (31 pages); scoring sheet (1 page); $20 per set of 35 tests and scoring sheets, cards, and manual; $2.50 per specimen set; cash orders postpaid; (60) minutes; A. Edward Ahr; Priority Innovations, Inc. *

EVELYN DENO, *Director, Psycho-Educational Center, University of Minnesota, Minneapolis, Minnesota.*

START is one of many tests now coming on the market that claim to identify children likely to have difficulty in acquisition of school skills before failure to achieve makes unquestionable their vulnerability to failure. Though the instrument is described as a screening test for the assignment of remedial treatments, the manual does not indicate how individual child performance on the test contributes to decisions regarding choice of instructional methods. The discussions regarding use of test data imply that the tests yield evidence as to developmental skills which are known to be "essential for learning." Empirical evidence on the point is not presented.

Similar analytic tests such as the Slingerland and Frostig tests are more clearly related to the instructional theories espoused by their authors. In the case of START, no particular theory of remediation is advanced. The information yielded by the test is presumed to provide information as to status on developmental skills which can be used in a variety of ways described in the manual, such as grouping for instructional purposes, but does not explain what the basis of the grouping would be. If grouping would be for the purpose of improving children's performance in the kinds of behaviors tapped by the test, the relevance or generalizability of improvement in these functions to success in acquisition of specific school skills such as reading remains to be demonstrated. One must assume that test performance in behaviors labeled visual-auditory-motor discrimination functioning is sufficiently pertinent to instructional decisions to warrant the time, energy, and possible effects of mislabeling involved in classification of children on such dimensions.

The manual is well written in its directions and recommendations for administration and in its presentation of technical information. The author has taken into account the activity needs, attentional capabilities, etc. of very young children. The test booklet limits attention to one item at a time and the use of different-colored pages to help identify place in the test seems a valuable measure.

The basis for reliability and validity claims is clearly outlined. Validity claims are based on the criteria of teacher judgments. Data acquired from extensive studies indicate that teachers' judgments are as good a basis for discriminating children prone to learning problems as a variety of professional judgments and psychometric data. However, it is necessary to remember that the teacher makes this judgment from a baseline of "conventional wisdom" about what are likely to be the most effective instructional procedures for most children. Authors of tests which purport to give the teacher more "objective" or readily obtained evidence on the behavior characteristics on which he commonly rests his judgments of a child's capabilities should present evidence that such norm-referenced classification schemes help to move the teacher beyond perpetuation of conventional wisdom toward an empirical, data-based approach to the control of the factors of which learning is a function.

[765]

★Screening Test of Academic Readiness. Ages 4-0 to 6-5; 1966; STAR; 9 scores: picture vocabulary, letters, picture completion, copying, picture description, human figure drawing, relationships, numbers, total (IQ); 1 form (56 pages); manual (42 pages); record form (1 page); no reliability data for subtests; $20 per 35 sets of test and record form, and manual; $2.50 per specimen set; cash orders postpaid; (60) minutes; A. Edward Ahr; Priority Innovations, Inc. *

REFERENCES

1. AHR, AUGUST EDWARD. The Development of a Group Preschool Screening Test of Early School Entrance Potentiality. Doctor's thesis, Loyola University (Chicago, Ill.), 1966. (DA 27:1642A)
2. AHR, A. EDWARD. "The Development of a Group Preschool Screening Test of Early School Entrance Potentiality." Psychol Sch 4:59-63 Ja '67. * (PA 41:4987)
3. AHR, A. EDWARD. "Early School Admission: One District's Experience." El Sch J 67:231-6 F '67. *
4. MAGOON, JON, AND COX, RICHARD C. "An Evaluation of the Screening Test of Academic Readiness." Ed & Psychol Meas 29(4):941-50 w '69. * (PA 44:21527)
5. HUTTON, JERRY BOB. Relationships Between Preschool Screening Test Data and First Grade Academic Performance for Head Start Children. Doctor's thesis, University of Houston (Houston, Tex.), 1970. (DAI 31:395B)

MILDRED H. HUEBNER, Professor of Education and Director, Reading Center, Southern Connecticut State College, New Haven, Connecticut.

The author, a school psychologist, suggests that school systems use this test (a) to help locate the preschool children who are ready early, as well as those who may have learning problems, (b) to screen kindergarten children for individualized help by uncovering their strengths and weaknesses, and (c) to conduct

research by collecting data regarding children's performance patterns on STAR subtests.

The test booklet to be handled by the child is 8½ by 5½ inches, unfortunately small for the age for which it is intended. The child is expected to turn back each page, which presents the examiner with the task of offering special assistance to those children who will find this difficult. Groups of 18 to 72 youngsters have been tested at one time. A second or third person has been recommended to assist with the administration when the group exceeds 20. Considering the nature and purposes of the test, this reviewer would question the advisability of testing such large numbers. The manual suggests limiting a group of disadvantaged preschoolers to 10 or 15. Possibly all teachers should receive similar instructions for limiting the size of any group tested.

All but one page of the test is colored different from the preceding page, affording the examiner and his assistants an opportunity to note readily that everyone is looking at the same page when directions are given. There are several sample pages to insure the children's understanding of the manner of making a response. A possible advantage to be noted for such a small booklet is that distractions for the children can be kept at a minimum when only a few items are met on one page.

To those who have dealt with readiness tests and preprimary tests of mental maturity, the areas measured and many of the items in STAR will look familiar. The author has incorporated language and performance activities in a simple, short test that can be administered to groups of children. There are eight subtests, with about 50 items in which children are told to mark pictures, letters, and numbers named by the examiner; copy a circle, square, and triangle; draw a man; note relationships; follow mazes; count items on several pages; and connect numbers to make a drawing of an Indian head. While the size of the capital letters and of some objects to be counted seems adequate, this reviewer considers several items to be obscure due to the limitations of hand-drawing—such as the "puddle" and the "gown." Young children might be confused, again because of the size and hand-drawing, in selecting pictures of the "rescue," the "mansion," and the person's features. On some pages the items on the following page show through the thin paper.

The manual has been especially well worked-out. The examiner will find detailed instructions for each item, with the time limit of each, which varies from 10 seconds for some to 120 seconds for two items. Actual activities such as finger-play, nursery songs, and games are included, so that the examiner can provide a rest and activity period between the main parts of the test.

Scoring directions are clear-cut and raw scores can be readily compiled on the record form. The total raw score can be converted to a deviation IQ by entering the table supplied in the manual. The norms for this table were obtained from a sample of 1,500 preschool and kindergarten children, ages 4 years to 6 years, five months, in a suburban white population of middle to upper class families.

In summary, this test will be welcomed by school systems that deal with large numbers of preschool and kindergarten children as well as those considered to be educationally disadvantaged. It is a direct answer, in such cases, for those who subscribe to the concept of diagnostic learning situations—know the child before planning his instruction. The test may be considered economical to the extent that it will help large school systems obtain objective test data with group-test procedures, using nonspecialists for scoring purposes. Its chief usefulness, however, will be as an initial screening device—but only if supplemented by several other detecting and predictive measures.

Ed & Psychol Meas 29(4):941–50 w '69. *Jon Magoon and Richard C. Cox.* "An Evaluation of the Screening Test of Academic Readiness." * a group test designed to discriminate between those preschoolers who would be acceptable for early admission to formal schooling, and those who would not. The instrument is intended to aid the school psychologist in identifying a preschooler's learning characteristics, social and emotional difficulties, and developmental and remedial needs. The purpose of this note is to report a wide variety of test and item characteristics for the STAR, gathered from a large heterogeneous national sample, and to evaluate the utility of this instrument in light of these data. The STAR instrument is composed of fifty items, divided into subparts denoted as picture-vocabulary (11 items), letters (5 items), copying (3 items), picture description (7 items), human figure drawing (1 item), relationships (7 items), and numbers (11 items). Subscores are derived for each of these

areas, as well as a total score. * The STAR was administered to a nationwide sample of approximately 4,000 first graders and kindergarteners. * The sample subjects were dispersed geographically across the United States, derived from both urban and exurban environments, and represented widely differing cultural and racial backgrounds. * It must be concluded from these analyses that the STAR provided but a very tenuous measure of lettering, numeration and drawing skills, object and concept identification skills, and picture completion and copying skills. These data seemed to indicate that this "readiness" test measures best those simple skills that are taught through formal systematic instruction. With the exception of numeration and lettering, it is questionable whether there is sufficient construct of factorial validity to scores derived from STAR subtests, for the factor analysis has revealed what is judged to be a structure dimensionality unrelated to scholastic achievement. Consideration of the STAR, as a preschool screening instrument, reveals that its factorial does not fulfill many of the criteria for a school readiness measure as defined by developmental experts. Ilg and Ames (1965) found that readiness tests that are highly related to IQ, as is the case with the STAR, are inadequate measures of a child's developmental level. From these analyses it does not appear that the STAR would be very useful in, as Ahr (1966) suggested, identifying "learning problems or social and emotional difficulties" that are indicators of developmental level. The STAR appeared to be measuring only lettering and numeration skills with any great degree of factorial validity, and this circumstance would probably not qualify the instrument as a readiness measure in developmental terms. Finally, since the STAR scores were found to be highly related to IQ scores, it is likely that there would be little difference between the screening potential of the STAR and an IQ measure.

[766]

★**Sprigle School Readiness Screening Test.** Ages 4-6 to 6-9; 1965; SSRST; individual; for use by pediatricians and school psychologists; 1 form (15 cards and 12 blocks); record form (3 pages); manual (30 pages); distribution restricted to physicians and psychologists; $18 per set of testing materials and 10 record forms; $3.50 per 50 record forms; postage extra; [12] minutes; Herbert A. Sprigle; Learning to Learn School, Inc. *

REFERENCES

1. BOTTRILL, JOHN H. "Effects of Preschool Experience on the School Readiness Level of Privileged and Underprivileged Children." *Excep Children* 34:275 D '67. * (PA 42:6035)

2. SPRIGLE, HERBERT A., AND LANIER, JAMES. "Validation and Standardization of a School Readiness Screening Test." *J Pediatrics* 70:602–7 Ap '67. *

3. HUTTON, JERRY B. "Practice Effects on Intelligence and School Readiness Tests for Preschool Children." *Training Sch B* 65(4):130–4 F '69. * (*PA* 44:4229)

4. HUTTON, JERRY BOB. *Relationships Between Preschool Screening Test Data and First Grade Academic Performance for Head Start Children.* Doctor's thesis, University of Houston (Houston, Tex.), 1970. (*DAI* 31:395B)

NICHOLAS ANASTASIOW, *Director, Institute for Child Study, Indiana University, Bloomington, Indiana.*

The *Sprigle School Readiness Screening Test* is specifically designed as a tool to help the physician in making a quick assessment of young children's mental abilities in answer to queries from parents about their children's readiness to enter school. The manual, as a guide for the physician or nurse in the administration, scoring, and interpretation of scores, is extremely well prepared. A note on the limitations of the test and on general principles of good test administration is included. Interpretation of scores is clearly spelled out in an effort to prevent broader interpretation than the test warrants.

The manual, written for the non-measurement specialist, omits the usual information of interest to those with some background in measurement. Additional information is necessary for an adequate assessment of the SSRST as a measure of mental abilities. It is suggested that such information be supplied in an appendix where it would not detract from the clarity and relevance of the directions for administration and interpretation. Information on test construction is totally lacking. There is a great similarity between many of the items and those on the Stanford-Binet; yet the criteria that were applied in their selection are not discussed. More information is needed on the item sampling procedures used. No means or standard deviations are presented.

The standardization sample was composed of 575 children randomly selected from kindergartens and day nurseries in various areas of the country. Lower-, lower middle-, and middle-class children were included. The norms classify scores into three broad categories: "below average, average to above average, and superior." Considering the length and purpose of the test, this lack of specificity is justified.

The author presents only one type of reliability: test-retest based on 30 randomly selected cases retested after one week by different ex-

aminers. The coefficient of .96 suggests high reliability.

Concurrent validity data, with the *Stanford-Binet Intelligence Scale,* the *Metropolitan Readiness Tests* and *Gates Primary Reading Tests* as criteria, are presented. The correlations with the S-B at all age levels are either .95 or .96. Those for the MRT and the GPRT range from .78 to .92. These coefficients are remarkably high, especially considering the small number of test items and the fact that the age range of each sample is limited to six months.

Since the S-B has a reliability in the range .83 to .91 at the age 5 level, one looks for replication of the correlations between the S-B and the SSRST with a new sample.

If the reliability and validity data in the manual are supported by further research studies, it would appear that this test is a very effective tool for a quick assessment of mental abilities of young preschoolers.

ALICE E. MORIARTY, *Senior Psychologist, The Menninger Foundation, Topeka, Kansas.*

At a time of renewed concerns about what schools teach and how children learn, and with increasing urgency for quick, easy, reliable assessment by persons frequently lacking extensive training in test administration or sophistication about standardization procedures, it is particularly important to examine critically new techniques for these purposes. The *Sprigle School Readiness Screening Test* is one such technique which apparently is based on sound understanding of the cognitive skills required for academic learning in the primary grades and is constructed with appropriate attention to professional standards of scientific reliability and validity.

The SSRST is designed as a screening test to be administered and scored by nurses for the use of pediatricians in counseling parents about school readiness of their preschoolers. For this purpose, the test proposes to measure verbal comprehension, awareness of size relationships, visual discrimination, reasoning ability, understanding of numbers, comprehension of analogies, information background, and ability in spatial relationships. Though we should like more technical information than is available in the manual about item selection and normative procedures, the measured tasks are not unlike those assessed in similar tests by Gates and Hildreth. Randomly selecting 575 children from four geographically dispersed cities and from three socioeconomic levels, the author reported correlations of .95 and .96 between SSRST scores and the Stanford-Binet. From these correlations and the additional fact that there were no negative relationships in individual scores, the author concludes that the SSRST provides an accurate estimate of mental development. Furthermore, correlations with the *Metropolitan Readiness Tests* and the *Gates Primary Reading Tests,* ranging from .78 to .92, suggest that the SSRST is a measure of reading readiness. A test-retest correlation of .96 was reported between scores by two examiners on tests given to 30 randomly selected cases one week apart. Hopefully, the author will repeat reliability studies with a longer time interval between tests. For the more sophisticated examiner, follow-up studies have been promised by the author.

Test materials are colorful and pictured items neat and easily recognizable. Record forms provide space for observations of qualitative aspects of behavior. Directions for test administration are clear and scoring so nearly self-explanatory as to promote objectivity in scoring. It is likely that subject cooperation is enhanced by the initial demand for motor, rather than verbal, response. That is, the subject is required to place a block on the appropriate picture rather than to discriminate verbally. Instructions are given in very simple language which should also minimize differences in subjects' experience with verbal concepts. Appropriate recommendations for providing encouragement, support, and the adherence to standard testing conditions are also clearly stated. Computation of chronological age differs somewhat from standard procedures insofar as days are dropped from the calculation; however, this lack of precision is no doubt a minor objection in a screening device.

For the screening purpose for which it was specifically devised, the SSRST is clearly useful and appropriate to assess cognitive readiness for school, particularly readiness to learn to read. Adequacy of performance is expressed in terms of below average, average, or accelerated performance. Space is also provided for judgments about level of readiness for school; that is, not ready, above average, or readiness skills highly developed. Though IQ ranges of SSRST scores are given for each six-month interval of chronological age between 4-6 and 5-11 and

for a nine-month interval between 6-0 and 6-9, use of IQ is not recommended. In the lowest classification, IQ's in the range between 59 and 91 are useful only in gross assessment of slow development; one would need more refined differentiation in order to make specific recommendations on scores falling within this range.

In choosing between the SSRST and other school readiness tests, the examiner needs to weigh the higher initial cost of the SSRST against decreased time for administration. Furthermore, in making recommendations for individual children, the assessment of cognitive readiness for school needs to be integrated with knowledge of the child's physical, social, and emotional readiness for school. Banham's *Maturity Level for School Entrance and Reading Readiness* might well be examined as an extension of the SSRST, but it is the reviewer's personal opinion that there is no real substitute for careful clinical observations based on experience and knowledge of child behavior. Standardization of behavioral observations—including activity level, sensory accuracy· and openness to new experience, curiosity, coping flexibility and resourcefulness, autonomy and dependency— would clearly add much to school readiness batteries. To my knowledge, this has not yet been done.

[767]

★**Valett Developmental Survey of Basic Learning Abilities.** Ages 2–7; 1966; largely a selection and adaptation of items from many scales, particularly the *Gesell Developmental Schedules;* 7 areas of development: motor integration and physical development, tactile discrimination, auditory discrimination, visual-motor coordination, visual discrimination, language development and verbal fluency, conceptual development; individual; scoring booklet (7 pages); manual (7 pages); workbook (11 pages, paper test items); no data on reliability and validity; no scores or norms for the 7 areas; $10 per 25 sets of scoring booklet and workbook; $3 per set of demonstration materials (some test materials must be assembled locally); 75¢ per manual; $1 per specimen set; postage extra; (60–70) minutes; Robert E. Valett; Consulting Psychologists Press, Inc. *

REFERENCES
1. VALETT, ROBERT. "A Psychoeducational Profile of Basic Learning Abilities." *J Sch Psychol* 4:9–24 w '66. *
2. VALETT, ROBERT. "A Developmental Task Approach to Early Childhood Education." *J Sch Psychol* 5:136–47 w '67. * (*PA* 41:9460)

LESTER MANN, *Director, Special Education, Montgomery County Intermediate Unit, Blue Bell, Pennsylvania.*

The *Valett Developmental Survey of Basic Learning Abilities* is an ambitious attempt to provide a comprehensive evaluation-training *anschauung* and program, relevant and applicable to both early childhood and preschool education and the learning disabilities movements which are dominant forces on the educational scene as this review goes to press; it was presaged by the author's even more ambitious "psychoeducational profile" (*1*) and a "clinical profile" for the Binet. It is a manifestation of that particular movement [1] in psychoeducational assessment which identifies test items with presumptive learning skills; these skills, in turn, are associated with, if not committed to, ability training programs (e.g., Valett's own [2]). A basic tenet of the movement is that various tests, scales, and inventories appropriately assess "basic" learning abilities which, if not properly developed, or if deficited, may constitute "learning disabilities" deleterious to later formal curriculum learning. These skills are to be trained prior to formal academic training or the latter is to be constituted along ability-disability lines [3]; the conceptual and pragmatic validity of these approaches has been questioned.[4]

The results of the survey are to be used, variously: as a "growth record"; to provide a guide to teachers for "individual evaluation and in concrete curriculum planning"; to assist "educational therapists, remedial tutors, and psychologists" as part of "their more intensive diagnostic examination"; and to help them "in planning the subsequent treatment of the child." It can also be used "directly in consulting with parents as to the child's educational needs and how the family environment and stimulation may contribute to the child's growth and development," etc.

More specifically, the survey is "concerned with those all-important developmental tasks prerequisite to more formal learning" and to assist the tester "to guide the young child onward through a program of sequential developmental experiences." It classifies and arranges 233 "basic developmental tasks" in the seven major ability areas listed above. The author has borrowed from a variety of developmental scales and tests, as well as developing his own tasks. Kephart, Hauserman, Binet, Frostig, Wechsler, Doll, and Gesell are among his distinguished resource persons.

The tasks in the various ability areas are arranged "developmentally" in ascending order of difficulty between the ages of 2 and 7. "Only a few items have been selected at any age level —just enough to give the teacher an estimate of the child's task proficiency and to stimulate further investigation if needed." It is assumed that an appropriately mature 7-year-old will have "accomplished" all of the tasks surveyed.

The total of 233 tasks constituting the survey range in number from a low of 11 for Tactile Discrimination to a high of 67 tasks for Conceptual Development. While one might readily concede that conceptual development is more important than tactile discrimination for general learning, it would seem that the author has confused the importance of test items for reliable measurement with the hypothesized or factual importance of the putative "abilities" he seeks to survey.

Within the various ability areas, there is a range of 1 to 4 items for any particular age level. Within the various ability areas, too, some items appear to assess development over a range of two years, others cover six months, one year, or one and one-half years, though the author's scaling practices and definitions make it difficult to determine precisely the age level intended; there is no consistency from one ability area to another in these respects nor explanations of the inconsistencies.

The survey comes to the user in the form of a manual, workbook, a scoring booklet, and testing cards. Additional materials to be used in the survey "may be easily obtained from school supplies or toy stores." The 7-page test manual discusses the purpose, rationale, construction, and materials of the survey and gives some brief indications for administration and scoring. Guides for administration are inadequate, particularly for the novice psychometrist to whom the survey is directed. Less than 2 pages are devoted to assistance in the scoring of 233 items —modest help, indeed.

No examples are given of the correct, partially correct, or incorrect responses that the teacher is expected to score. While many of a child's responses will be simple and should pre-

[1] KIRK, SAMUEL A. "Illinois Test of Psycholinguistic Abilities: Its Origin and Implications." *Learning Disorders* 3:83–91 '68. *
BATEMAN, BARBARA. "Three Approaches to Diagnosis and Educational Planning for Children With Learning Disabilities." *Acad Ther Q* 2:215–22 su '67. *
[2] VALETT, ROBERT E. *The Remediation of Learning Disabilities: A Handbook of Psychoeducational Resource Programs.* Palo Alto, Calif.: Consulting Psychologists Press, 1967. Pp. 228.
[3] BATEMAN, BARBARA. "Implications of a Learning Disability Approach for Teaching Educable Retardates." *Mental Retard* 5:23–5 Je '67. *
[4] MANN, LESTER. "Fractional Practices in Special Education: A Critique." *J Excep Children* 33:311–7 Ja '67. *
MANN, LESTER. "Are We Fractionating Too Much?" *Acad Ther* 5(2):85–91 w '69–70. *

sent no scoring problem, others will most certainly be problematic, such as those in Motor Integration and Physical Development where the examiner is admonished to look for "cross-pattern creeping" and "smooth running" as "behavioral goals," without instruction from the manual. The scoring of motor items on the basis of a child's verbal report (presumably often a verbally impaired one) is another questionable practice. Thus a testee who cannot tell the examiner he rides a scooter (a developmental task at the 6-year level), or a bicycle (a task at the 7-year level), earns 2 negative scores for Motor Integration and Physical Development.

The Workbook employed to assist in the paper and pencil testing aspects of the survey is attractive; it should be appealing to children and present no problems in deployment. In format, it is indeed superior to many traditional work and test books. The demonstration materials, i.e., testing cards provided by the publisher, are also attractive but poorly packaged and of uncertain durability.

The survey's scoring booklet has its developmental tasks numbered seriatim from item 1 for Motor Integration and Physical Development through item 233 for Conceptual Development. This is a poor format for a survey which is purportedly developmental. The booklet is excessively crowded and cluttered. The various tasks or demands and questions which the examiner poses are presented herein rather than in the manual. The child's responses are scored according to the seriatim numbers on the left side of the page of the scoring booklet, while the presumed age level for which the response is intended is confusingly and inconveniently located on the right, and mated with initials denoting the source of the item, e.g., 2B for an item at the 2nd year developmental level adopted from the Binet scale.

Neither the test manual nor the author's article discussing the survey provides any clear justification for his choice of items to assess various basic ability areas. (It is difficult to see why an answer to "tell me in what way cookies and cake are alike" is a task of Language Development and Verbal Fluency while the response to "stomp your feet softly" is one of Conceptual Development.) Generally, Valett's justifications are weak for the relevance or reality of his basic skill areas; his classifications were selected, apparently, on the basis that

"they appear to be logical constructs with a sound rationale and with distinct educational implications" (1). This is an insufficient answer when a user is advised that "lack of successful accomplishment in one or more Survey areas may indicate distinct limitations to further learning and that educational programs should then be developed accordingly" and when the user (typically a teacher) is not conversant with the whys, wherefores, and pitfalls of testing. The Developmental Survey is innocent of reliability statistics, or validity reports to support its claims or justify its applications.

ROGER A. RUTH, *Assistant Professor of Education, University of Victoria, Victoria, British Columbia, Canada.*

The Valett survey consists, in the main, of a cafeteria sampling of items from a number of well-established measures of intellectual ability and perceptual and motor development. Like other cafeteria offerings that promise quick service at minimum price, the resultant fare, while appetizing in appearance, proves to be poorly prepared and difficult to digest.

Its 233 graded items draw largely upon the work of Terman, Gesell, Wechsler, Frostig, and Kephart; some of the items were devised by the author on the basis of his clinical experience, the nature and breadth of which are unspecified.

The manual offers no information on reliability or validity and no normative sampling of the appropriateness of item placement. To the sophisticated test user, these omissions alone would raise a red flag signifying, "Let the buyer beware." Unfortunately, the survey addresses itself nominally to "teachers of nursery school classes, special preschool programs, kindergartens, and primary classes for the retarded and educationally handicapped," many of whom might be expected not to be alert to these tell-tale signs of insufficient research and development.

In the absence of reliability and validity data for the survey, such measures might be assumed by the naive user to inhere in the selection of items from reputable test batteries. This assumption is, of course, unwarranted when the items are withdrawn from their original presentation context. Terman, for example, noted that when the authorized abbreviation of his Binet scale (from 122 subtests to 80) was utilized, the error of measurement increased by 20 percent. One can only conjecture at the magnitude of error resulting when two items, from among five, of one subtest, from among six, are taken to constitute Valett's measure of "Language Development and Verbal Fluency" at the "4½ year" level.

Terman explicitly repudiated the legitimacy of making normative assumptions when items from his scale were administered otherwise than in the standardized *order*. It seems reasonable to expect that the test authors from whom Valett borrows would similarly repudiate using their normative data to support developmental assumptions based on discrete items removed from context.

Quite aside from context considerations, it is at times difficult to divine Valett's rationale for age-level assignment of items. The manual states that, "The norms given in many instances are those for accomplishment by the overwhelming majority of children and may seem somewhat late; however, this provides some safeguards against overconcern." On the contrary, it might be expected that the test user, told items are so conservatively placed in the survey, should feel real reason for concern if a child fails a task at his age level.

How accurate, then, is the statement about conservative placement? One item that permits ready evaluation is the building of a three-block bridge, a Binet task used as Valett's single measure of "Visual-Motor Coordination" at the year 3 level. Terman placed this item at the year 3 level as one of six subtests passed, on the average, by 73 percent of three-year-olds. But in the Binet standardization, the child builds his bridge after having watched the examiner demonstrate the building; while in Valett's administration, the examiner is directed to demonstrate only with a picture of the completed task. The latter procedure appears the more difficult perceptual problem. Whether it is in fact simpler, and therefore conservatively placed in the Valett scale as it is claimed, can only be determined by a normative sampling under the revised directions.

The manual recommends estimating developmental level only within a one-year approximation. Since it also suggests that "the Survey can be used directly in consulting with parents," even this range of approximation may involve some hazard to both teacher and child, given the absence of reliability data and validity studies with which to justify this reference to a reasonably critical parent.

The directions for administration are generally adequate, though falling far short of the specificity usually employed in the instruments from which the items are borrowed. Entry level in each of the seven subtest areas is specified as two years below the chronological age of the child. No further directions are given as to procedures to be followed if a child misses items at this level or the number of successive failures that should be permitted before proceeding to the next subtest. No time limits are specified for any of the tasks, even though such restrictions are imposed on various items in their original standardization.

Most users will find the scoring directions inadequate. For one example, among many, the "Year 5" item, "Draw a picture for me—any picture will do like a house or a person or anything you want," is given no scoring criteria whatever. Users who have struggled with Goodenough's book-length scoring standards for a child's drawing of a man would be very curious about the criteria by which Valett would determine that a child's drawing of, say, a space rocket indicates Year 5 Motor Integration and Physical Development. Items on the survey calling for the drawing of a line, a circle, a cross, a square, and a triangle are similarly innocent of scoring criteria, even though these items are taken from tests where such criteria are specified in great detail.

To further compound the scoring problem, most "developmental levels" are surveyed with from two to four items, but no indication is given as to the proportion of items that must be failed to indicate inadequacy at a given level. Individual items may be assigned full credit, no credit, or half credit and "the total points may be entered on the summary sheet." Such totals, however, have no meaning, expressed or implied. The manual makes no attempt to relate numerical total to developmental level; as of course it should not do without a normalizing study.

The manual suggests that the survey will be useful to educational therapists, remedial tutors, and psychologists as part of a more intensive diagnostic examination. It is, however, these more sophisticated test users who should have the greatest concern for the degree to which pre-exposure in the survey to items drawn in exact form from better standardized, more fully developed instruments may invalidate later use of these instruments. "Educational therapists" should require more evidence than is presented that the items selected for the survey sample adequately the constructs they are purported to measure, and of the relevance of the remedial measures recommended in the manual to developmental inadequacy in these areas.

Given the current high level of interest in assessment and remediation of learning disabilities, an instrument that could accomplish the stated purposes of the Valett survey would meet an enthusiastic reception. The survey has not been demonstrated to accomplish these purposes. At its present stage of development, it is so often in violation of the *Standards for Educational and Psychological Tests and Manuals* as to militate against its circulation to its intended clientele.

[Other Tests]

For other tests new or revised since *The Sixth Mental Measurements Yearbook,* see the following in *Reading Tests and Reviews:*

180. *American School Reading Readiness Test
186.1. ★Keystone Ready to Read Tests
198. ★Steinbach Test of Reading Readiness
200. *Van Wagenen Reading Readiness Scales

SPECIAL FIELDS

[768]

★**ANPA Foundation Newspaper Test, 1969 Experimental Edition.** Grades 7–9, 10–12; 1969; newspaper reading ability; Forms 1, 2, (4 pages) ; 2 levels; manual (19 pages) ; simulated newspapers (4 pages) for each form; descriptive leaflet (4 pages) ; reliability and norms data based on prepublication forms; $1 per 10 tests; $2.50 per 10 newspapers; $1.50 per manual; $2 per specimen set; cash orders postpaid; (40–50) minutes; sponsored by National Council for the Social Studies and developed in cooperation with American Newspaper Publishers Association Foundation; Cooperative Tests and Services. *

[769]

★**The Adult Basic Reading Inventory.** Functionally illiterate adolescents and adults; 1966; ABRI; test booklets with the title *Basic Reading Inventory* (BRI) are available for school use; scores in 5 areas: sight words, sound and letter discrimination, word meaning (reading), word meaning (listening), context reading; Form A (16 pages) ; manual (23 pages) ; technical report (4 pages) ; no data on reliability for scores on Parts 1, 2, 4, and 5; no norms; $6.50 per 20 tests, 20 line markers, and manual, postage extra; 50¢ per specimen set, cash orders only; (60) minutes; Richard W. Burnett; Scholastic Testing Service, Inc. *

ALBERT J. KINGSTON, *Professor of Educational Psychology, The University of Georgia, Athens, Georgia.*

The ABRI is designed to identify functional illiterates, defined as those able to function between the fourth and fifth grade levels of reading achievement. It also is claimed that the inventory will identify the strengths and weaknesses of those whose reading skills are comparable to those of children enrolled in the second, third, and fourth grades.

The inventory consists of five subtests. Part 1 is designed to test sight vocabulary and represents a traditional format. The section contains 20 pictures of common objects. Each picture is followed by four words and the testee is asked to underline the word which tells what is pictured. It should be noted that this type of test procedure is suitable only for measuring a knowledge of nouns. Generally, poor readers have considerable difficulty with verbs, adjectives, adverbs, prepositions, and conjunctions. Although Part 1 may be helpful in identifying illiterates, the failure to provide measures of structural words raises some question about the diagnostic value of the test.

Part 2 is designed to measure the ability to hear and to associate beginning consonants (10 items) and beginning blends and digraphs (10 items). The examiner reads a stimulus word while the examinee underlines the word which begins like the one he hears. Part 3 consists of a silent reading task designed to appraise the individual's knowledge of word meanings. The words are presented out of context, and the examinee underlines the one of three words which means the same or nearly the same as the stimulus word. The author fails to explain the rationale for choosing the 40 words in this part but states that the examinee's performance is indicative of his proper instructional level.

Part 4 is parallel to Part 3. The identical format and words are employed in both sections. The sole difference between the two parts is that in this section the examiner reads the stimulus word while the examinee uses a marker to find and underline the word which means the "same." The author believes that the discrepancy between scores on Part 4 and other parts has significance for identifying individuals who are most likely to profit from literacy training. No mention is made of possible practice effects or motivational effects resulting from the use of identical materials, first in silent reading and next in oral presentation.

Part 5 consists of three reading selections, labeled Context Reading. The three selections are graded according to difficulty. Each reading selection is followed by five multiple choice items designed to check comprehension. Each comprehension check contains one or more negative items in which the examinee is asked to select the response which is *not* in the story. Generally, adults suspected of being illiterate are naive about short-answer tests. In this reviewer's opinion, the use of negative questions may unduly confuse some of those for whom the test is designed.

The format of the ABRI is rather ordinary, but adequate. Print is large and so spaced that few individuals are likely to encounter difficulty in taking the test. Examinees respond in the test booklet, a procedure often recommended when testing illiterate adults. Although the use of line markers may help some individuals, it may bother others. At any rate, some reading specialists are likely to question their value. The scoring system is somewhat unusual. Right scores are tallied for each subtest and converted to percentages. Each subtest then yields a number correct and a percent score. The purpose or meaning of the percentage conversions is not explained, although the author states that a criterion of no more than three errors (about 70 percent) should be expected at the examinee's proper instructional level. Presumably this level is comparable to that proposed by Betts and commonly used by reading teachers. Those who are familiar with Betts' concept of independent, instructional, and frustration levels recognize that they are at best rough estimates of an individual's reading performance. Important factors such as motivation and personality must also be considered in instructing an individual or selecting materials for the purpose.

Although the manual provides adequate information concerning administration and scoring, it fails to provide sufficient information concerning the rationale, reliability, and validity. Some additional information, however, is provided in a four-page technical report. This supplement indicates adequate reliability with a group of 38 adults. It also reports correlations between the ABRI and the *Gates Advanced Primary Reading Tests*. It is interesting to note that these data report coefficients for ABRI vocabulary, ABRI comprehension, and ABRI total scores. Which subtests were combined to achieve vocabulary and comprehension scores is not explained.

A number of questions concerning the inventory remain. No reliability for part scores (except Part 3) is given, although the instrument was published in 1965. As the inventory is designed for use with adults, one might expect that more information concerning its usefulness with adults would be provided. Norms based upon various adult groups would be helpful. The practice of comparing adult reading performance with that of primary grade children is at least a dubious one. It is likely that most skilled reading specialists will have greater faith in informal methods of diagnosis.

[770]
*Interpretation of Reading Materials in the Natural Sciences: Tests of General Educational Development, Test 3. Candidates for high school equivalency certificates; 1944–70; subtest of the battery *Tests of General Educational Development;* tests administered only at Official GED Centers; state departments of education in all states now authorize the use of the GED battery for high school certification; Forms H ('61), J ('62), K ('65), L ('65), CC ('68), EE ('70), FF ('70); revised manual ('64, 15 pages); Handbook of Policies and Procedures for Operation, third edition ('68, 41 pages); State Department of Education Policies ('69, 85 pages); tests rented only; annual rental fee: $6 per battery, $2 per set of scoring stencils; postage extra; special editions available for the blind and partially sighted; (120) minutes; General Educational Development Testing Service of the American Council on Education.

For reviews of earlier editions of the complete battery, see 5:27 (1 review), 4:26 (1 review), and 3:20 (2 reviews).

[771]
*Interpretation of Reading Materials in the Social Studies: Tests of General Educational Development, Test 2. Candidates for high school equivalency certificates; 1944–70; subtest of the battery *Tests of General Educational Development;* tests administered only at Official GED Centers; state departments of education in all states now authorize the use of the GED battery for high school certification; Forms H ('61), J ('62), K ('65), L ('65), CC ('68), EE ('70), FF ('70); revised manual ('64, 15 pages); Handbook of Policies and Procedures for Operation, third edition ('68, 41 pages); State Department of Education Policies ('69, 85 pages); tests rented only; annual rental fee: $6 per battery, $2 per set of scoring stencils; postage extra; special editions available for the blind and partially sighted; (120) minutes; General Educational Development Testing Service of the American Council on Education.

REFERENCE

1. See 3:528.

For reviews by W. E. Hall and C. Robert Pace, see 3:528. For reviews of earlier editions of the complete battery, see 5:27 (1 review), 4:26 (1 review), and 3:20 (2 reviews).

[772]
★RBH Scientific Reading Test. Employees in technical companies; 1950–69; 1 form ('50, 11 pages);

manual ('69, 5 pages); directions ['50, 1 page]; $5.50 per 25 tests; 50¢ per key; $1.50 per manual; $1.50 per specimen set; postage extra; 60(65) minutes; Richardson, Bellows, Henry & Co., Inc. *

SAMUEL T. MAYO, *Professor of Educational Psychology, Loyola University of Chicago, Chicago, Illinois.*

This test consists of 11 paragraphs of text from various scientific disciplines and 52 multiple choice items based upon the passages. No description of the development of the test or the selection of the norm samples (which are presumed to be convenient cluster samples from customers) is given.

The typography is poor and amateurish. The test appears to have been typed single-spaced on an ordinary typewriter and then printed by photo-offset. Only one figure is used, a much-too-small graph. The lines of text extend to a full page in width, making them unnecessarily difficult to read. Furthermore, the quality of the typing is poor. Mercifully, however, the items are set in two columns.

Since separate answer sheets are not used, it is necessary to turn pages five times to score the test.

The so-called "manual" furnished with the specimen set consists of four unnumbered pages with a title sheet, reproduced from typed copy. The manual states that "no specific prior knowledge is required to read the material and all information necessary to answering the multiple choice questions which follow is included in the paragraphs. To minimize the effect of special study the 11 paragraphs were selected from widely diverse scientific disciplines." The prior knowledge promise is violated in several places, e.g., in Paragraph K, in which one finds the word "adiabatic," which is undefined in the test and which must remain obscure to those without appropriate background.

The manual's statement about the diversity of the 11 paragraphs seems a bit too strong, according to the reviewer's classification of the disciplines. Two are in chemistry and from three to five are in physics, depending upon whether the one paragraph each on meteorology and astronomy is classified as physics. Two are in philosophy of science, one is in biology, and one is in psychology (although this is in psychophysics, thereby overlapping physics). Several disciplines come to mind which are not included but which very well could be, such as geology (a natural, since some of the norms

were taken from workers in the petroleum industry); one or more subdisciplines under biology, such as anatomy or physiology; statistics (especially in conjunction with simple graphs such as pie charts or bar graphs); anthropology; and economics.

Very sparse evidence of reliability and validity is given. The manual says, "The test has face validity for industrial and retail salesmen who are expected to know technical information about products but experience for this use is currently lacking." The manual also reports two validity coefficients of .24 and .37 for samples of 160 and 43 persons, respectively. These validity coefficients seem to be about par for the course. Odd-even reliabilities of .93 and .88 are reported for the same samples. These seem satisfactory for this type of reliability coefficient, but how satisfactory is the odd-even coefficient by itself?

We should suspend judgment on this test until we have more hard-nosed evidence of its validity. There may be serious problems in developing a criterion variable on the job. The reviewer is unconvinced that the test represents a good work sample of the literature which a technical worker is required to read on the job. Surely there must be more realistic paragraph samples than the ones used here! The "reading ease" may need to be improved. The reading passages seem to be unnecessarily abstruse. The test needs better face validity as a public-relations gesture. There was a general feeling of disappointment in or anger toward the test among some subjects tested by this reviewer. It is recommended that the publisher improve the content and typography and provide a decent manual with adequate technical information.

[773]

Reading Adequacy "READ" Test: Individual Placement Series. Adults in industry; 1961–66; 3 scores: reading rate, per cent of comprehension, corrected reading rate; Form C ('61, 4 pages); no specific manual; series manual ('66, 107 pages); $3.70 per 20 tests; 50¢ per key; $2.50 per series manual; $3.20 per specimen set; cash orders postpaid; [13–20] minutes; J. H. Norman; Personnel Research Associates, Inc. *

SAMUEL T. MAYO, *Professor of Educational Psychology, Loyola University of Chicago, Chicago, Illinois.*

A quick estimate of reading rate is provided by this relatively short test. The examinee is allowed to read for three minutes as far as he

Reading Adequacy "READ" Test

can in a reading passage of approximately 1,600 words. He then circles the number at the right hand side of the line in which he finished. This number indicates directly the rate in number of words per minute. One limitation is the lack of ceiling. This reviewer tested some subjects who had taken speed-reading courses and were able to finish in half the alloted time. For such people, the rate score is a serious underestimate. After the three-minute period the examinee answers 20 multiple choice items based upon the first four paragraphs, which nearly everyone is assumed to be able to complete. This would seem to be a reasonable assumption.

The manual states that the "results obtained from the 'READ' test are particularly helpful in the interpretation of scores from other tests" in the series and "in counseling employees or determining the general reading level of specific groups." However, the "counseling" aspect is suspect, since evidence of reliability is not satisfactory. Only one coefficient is reported, a test-retest coefficient of .69 for an N of 37. Not given are characteristics of individuals in the sample, the variability of the sample, and the time interval between administrations. The reported estimate of .69 suggests that the test may fairly be applied to groups of workers but that individual diagnosis is not warranted. Furthermore, the value .69 does not compare favorably with alternate-form coefficients reported for other cognitive tests. In addition, it is not specified which rate score (corrected or uncorrected) this coefficient was based upon.

Validity coefficients are reported for eight occupational groups, although only group labels and sizes of samples are given. Neither are the kinds of criterion measures, standard deviations, nor characteristics of persons given. The coefficients range from 0 to .86, with median .26. Some evidence of concurrent validity is furnished by this reviewer's own data, in which the rate score on this test correlated .74 and .51, respectively, with the rate scores on the *Nelson-Denny Reading Test* and the *SRA Reading Progress Test*.

The test produces three scores: raw (uncorrected) reading rate, reading comprehension score, and corrected reading rate (the product of the uncorrected and the comprehension score expressed as a proportion). It is not made clear in the norms in every case which score was used, although where specified, the corrected score was used. The percentile norms appear adequate as to sample size. Four occupational groups (clerical, shop, engineering, and supervisory, along with the total industry norm group) are reported separately. Sample sizes in the four groups range from 376 to 537, the total industry sample having 6,971 cases. Median scores are reported on 15 job classifications, among which sample sizes range from 16 to 407. These may be helpful pending availability of, but not in lieu of, preferable local norms.

In summary, this is a short test which can yield a quick estimate of reading speed. Little evidence is reported on its reliability and validity. Much more evidence is needed before firm recommendations can be made. In view of the very few available reading tests for industrial workers, this one should be considered along with the others. However, application should be restricted to groups rather than individual diagnosis.

[774]
★Reading Comprehension Test for Personnel Selection. Applicants for technical training programs with high verbal content; 1965–66; 1 form ['66, 4 pages]; manual ('65, 35 pages); 37½p per 20 tests; 20p per manual; 22½p per specimen set; postage extra; 15(20) minutes; L. R. C. Haward; University of London Press Ltd. *

REFERENCES
1. HAWARD, L. R. C. "A Simple Selection Test for Nurses." Letter. *Lancet* 271:1269–70 D 15 '56. *
2. HAWARD, L. R. C. "Reading Assessment." *Nursing Times* 53:1414–6 D 13 '58. *
3. HAWARD, L. R. C. "A Reading Comprehension Test for Nurse Training." *Nursing Res* 10:38–42 w '61. *

M. A. BRIMER, *Head of Research Unit, School of Education, University of Bristol, Bristol, England.*

This test consists of 25 free-response questions on a single 316-word passage, describing the cerebellum, slightly adapted from a physiology textbook. The test items were drawn, after analysis for difficulty only, from an original set of 100 trial questions administered to an unspecified sample of 100 subjects. Five of the retained questions are, in practice, true-false items without any correction for chance scoring. All questions seek to elicit specific information contained in the passage and do not involve inference or comprehension of the gist of the passage. The questions can be answered by scanning the passage and without reading it in its entirety; moreover, many of the questions can be answered from prior knowledge and without reference to the passage. Whenever they cannot, it is because the questions rely upon textual reference and sometimes upon confusion, as for example in the question, "Does the cortex differ from the cerebellum?"

A list of correct answers is given in the manual, but apart from a statement that scoring is easy, no guidance is given on the mode of scoring or the extent to which the free response given may validly differ from the model answer. The manual recommends the use of raw scores and percentages of the possible score. Sten scores and percentiles are also given, based upon a "standardising sample," unspecified except that it is said to contain 360 males and 359 females varying in age from 15 to 65. The mean score is 17.6, which is high for a test of 25 items, and the standard deviation of 4.9 implies that discrimination above the mean is inadequate (range of 1.5 standard deviations).

Mixed reliability data, some derived from such small samples as to be valueless, are given. A split-half reliability of .87 was obtained by testing 200 nurses. Test-retest coefficients derived from 100 adults and 151 adolescents are .95 and .91, respectively. A confused summary table attributes an N of 582 to both a split-half coefficient of .88 and a test-retest coefficient of .94, yet the incompleteness of the table suggests that the appropriate N's are 264 and 382, respectively.

Evidence of predictive validity is the correlation of scores with end-of-year examination results and with instructors' ratings. The most substantial evidence was derived from three separate samples of student nurses, for whom the validity coefficients range from .24 to .57. The low predictive validity is attributed to previous knowledge of physiology among the students. A much higher set of coefficients, ranging from .69 to .91, was obtained in correlating test performance with instructors' ratings, though, by the author's admission, test scores were available to the instructors at the time of making their ratings.

The author asserts for his test: "The criterion of its success must lie with the ability of the test to diagnose complex reading disabilities which are likely to be relevant in any course of technical training." Yet, no specific evidence of diagnostic effectiveness is presented anywhere in the manual and indeed it is difficult to see how such a test could pretend to diagnostic validity, when nothing in its construction has been designed to achieve it. The evidence which the author appears to consider relevant to diagnostic function is the finding that among 85

students in one follow-up study, all students who scored 12 or less (equivalent to a percentile rank of 18) failed their examination and all who scored 22 or more (percentile 83) passed their examination. No further information on the follow-up study is given. A reported cross-validation study on 47 entrants to a nurses' training school is no more convincing, and the reference to work carried out in 22 hospitals is vague.

The interpretation section of the manual speaks broadly about "potential failures," "cerebral dysfunction," the function of the cortex in language formulation, without directly implying that the test involves such concepts. General advice on dealing with reading disabilities is offered and reference is made to other publications.

A final table reports correlation coefficients of scores with three different intelligence scales. None of these reaches the 5 percent level of significance.

The author's claim that the test is diagnostic is completely unsupported by published evidence. The reported method of construction is inadequate, if not incompetent. The norms are based on an inadequately identified sample and the raw score distribution suggests poor discrimination. Those wishing to make use of a reading comprehension test for selection would do well to choose another established test. Publishers might seek to be more discriminating before publishing such a test.

Douglas A. Pidgeon, *Deputy Director, National Foundation for Educational Research, Slough, Bucks, England.*

The purpose of this test, according to the author, "is to measure the ability of the examinee to benefit from a course of technical instruction with a high verbal content." More specifically, "it evaluates his potential for independent study and assesses his ability to read, to deal with technical terminology, to concentrate upon a specific item whilst scanning through a condensed but wide range of information, and to determine the relevance of each unit of information as it is encountered." All this is achieved in a 15-minute test, by reading a 316-word passage describing the cerebellum and answering 25 open-ended questions.

As supportive evidence of its validity, scores obtained from nine student groups (N between 19 and 151) were correlated with their marks on a written examination held at the end of a course of training. The coefficients varied between .24 and .74 (mean .41), but as no further details of either the course or the examination are supplied it is difficult to evaluate them. A further set of correlations is also given, between scores on the test and an instructor's ratings on the student's ability to deal with text matter. These range between .69 and .94 (mean .83), and seem remarkably high until one reads in the manual that the instructor made his ratings *after* seeing the test scores.

The test was constructed by taking a difficult passage from a standard textbook on physiology and revising it by reducing the proportion of monosyllabic words to make it more difficult. One hundred questions were then written presumably with no preconceived plan. Following a pretest, the questions were put in order of difficulty and every fourth question selected to form the final test.

This reviewer arranged for the test to be given to 109 sixth form (grade 12) pupils in two secondary schools in England. It turned out to be on the easy side with a definite negative skew (mean score 17.2) although the manual states that it has a slight positive skew, which is odd because the norms provided indicate a median score between 18 and 19. Its K-R reliability was .81 and split-half, .85.

It is doubtful whether the test is measuring any useful form of reading *comprehension* as none of the questions requires the students to make any deductions of any kind. A testee could score very well on this test and yet not have understood the reading matter and, more important, not be able to use or remember the information given. Five of the 25 items require a "yes" or "no" response, and a number of confusing trick questions are included. The last question, for example, wants the name of the organ described in the passage. In the sample tests, only 17 managed to find the correct answer—cerebellum; 47, yielding a positive point biserial with total score, gave "brain" and it is difficult to see why they should be scored wrong; a further 36, probably including some who had opted out of this kind of exercise by this time, omitted the question. The questions also dodge about the passage and, with the emphasis on speed, appear to be measuring searching behaviour more than the ability to understanding meaning.

In this reviewer's opinion this is a bad test.

Its content is so appalling that even if it did provide useful information to a teacher (and on the evidence provided, this is extremely doubtful), its backwash effects on students' study habits would surely be so great as to prohibit its use.

[775]
*SRA Reading Progress Test. Employees; 1962–63; test booklet title is *Reading Progress Test;* 4 scores: vocabulary, logical thinking, reading for information, rate; 1 form ('62, 22 pages); manual ('63, 4 pages); interpretive booklet ('62, 8 pages); separate answer sheets (IBM 805) must be used; $17.75 per 25 tests; $2.35 per 25 answer sheets; 75¢ per set of scoring stencils; $4 per 25 interpretive booklets; 25¢ per manual; $1.95 per specimen set; postage extra; (45–60) minutes; Science Research Associates, Inc. *

SAMUEL T. MAYO, *Professor of Educational Psychology, Loyola University of Chicago, Chicago, Illinois.*

Of the three tests reviewed by this reviewer in this volume, the present test has the most attractive typography but the least amount of dependable technical data. Typography is important but is not one of the most crucial aspects of a test. It cannot compensate for the lack of normative data or lack of description of the rationale for the rules used in interpretation as furnished in a booklet for examinees.

Consisting of 163 multiple choice items divided into four sections, the test yields the four scores shown above, each section yielding one of the four scores. Scoring is number right.

Most of the items appear to be satisfactory, although a few are ambiguous. For example, item 116 is based upon a reading passage whose relevant sections read:

a new theory of oil formation....states that oil is primarily formed after catastrophic landslides have buried large quantities of plants and animals on the ocean floor. These landslides, or "turbidity currents," are dislodged by earthquakes from the rim of the continental shelf or occur at river mouths when silt builds up to a critical level. Once buried and cut off from oxygen, according to this hypothesis, plant and animal life decays and produces petroleum.

The item stem is, "According to theory, petroleum can be formed by" and the choices are easily narrowed down to "A. material deposited on the ocean floor following earthquakes" and "C. decay of plants and animals." Option C is keyed, but the reviewer fails to see why option A would not be equally acceptable.

No bona fide manual was furnished with the review set, but rather a 4-page Administrator's Manual and an 8-page Interpretive Booklet (4 by 9 inches) which purports to interpret scores for the examinee. There is no description of the development of the items or of the test. No normative data are given.

The diminutive interpretive booklet has so many things wrong with it that space does not permit a complete listing. It has a table for quick conversion of raw scores to so-called "Scale Scores." There is no explanation of the process by which raw scores were transformed into scale scores in making up the table. Also, there is one glaring numerical error in the total number of items on the Reading for Information row of the table, i.e., "49" instead of "50." The scale scores may be easy for an examinee or naive person to accept, but the specialist will be disturbed, as was this reviewer, if he studies the table a while and tries to fathom the rationale. The scale scores range from 50 to 100. The first two raw scores, Vocabulary Knowledge and Logical Thinking, have their maximum possible scores (i.e., total number of items, 60 and 50, respectively) transformed to scale scores of 100. In the case of the third score, Reading for Information, the erroneous total of 49 was transformed into a scale score of 100. Furthermore, one might logically expect the raw scores corresponding to a scale score of 50 (the minimum) to be the same percentage of total possible raw score. This is not the case, since the percentages are 38, 36, and 35, respectively. Again, there is no explanation. As a further empirical investigation of the characteristics of the transformation relationships, the reviewer plotted scale scores against the three raw score scales on ordinary graph paper. The first two scores plotted as straight lines, barring slight rounding errors. The third (Reading for Information) plotted linearly except for the range 90 to 100 on the scale scores, where it makes a mysterious bend toward the middle curve. Even when the erroneous maximum of 49 is considered, the curve should have plotted as a straight line, as did the other two.

The so-called "scale scores" are divided into four unequal ranges, 92 to 100, 79 to 91, 61 to 78, and below 61. Thus, it may be seen that the ranges are 9, 13, 18, and 11, respectively. No explanation is given as to how and why these ranges were set up as they were. For each range the booklet gives a brief paragraph which purports to interpret characteristics of members within the range. As an example, for the range 92 to 100, the interpretive booklet reads:

Results of the test indicate that persons whose scores fall into the 92-to-100 range are most likely to be those whose jobs depend upon a high degree of language skill and word proficiency. Persons scoring in this range are rated *excellent* readers and are frequently editors, writers, professors, top-level executives, or professional people. In Vocabulary, this group got no more than six words wrong; in Logical Thinking, no more than five wrong; and in Reading for Information, no more than seven wrong.

It is confusing to try to interpret what "seven wrong" means in this table. The lowest raw score shown in this range is 43, and the highest score shown in the next lower range is 41, 42 not appearing at all. If one attempts to interpret seven wrong in terms of the total of 49, he lands on a raw score of 42, which is on the border between the top two ranges but *in* neither. If one uses the true total of 50, seven wrong lands him on a raw score of 43. The latter relationship checks out correctly for the other two scales. However, the confusion remains.

In some of the other ranges, there are additional erroneous statements of fact regarding the Reading for Information scores. For example, for the range 79 to 91 the statement is made that such persons had "8 to 15 wrong." The raw scores corresponding to these numbers wrong are 41 and 35, respectively. Simple arithmetic will show that a raw score of 41 for the erroneous total of 49 does, indeed, yield 8 wrong; however subtracting 15 from 49 yields a raw score of 14 rather than 15. It was noted that 15 wrong in 50 items would, of course, yield a raw score of 35, but that would mean a change in the rules.

As was pointed out previously, there are no true norms furnished. What aids for interpretation are here, are presented without the rationale for their development, so that the user cannot determine whether they were developed from empirical tryout or rationally "from the armchair." Psychometrists who either learn from this review about the pitfalls of interpretation in the sheer use of the numbers or who figure out the pitfalls for themselves will undoubtedly, as in the case of the reviewer, have their confidence shaken in all other aspects as well. For example, how can an enlightened person accept at face value any statement in the interpretive booklet that such-and-such a range is characteristic of any kind of occupational group? To put it another way, what evidence, if any, is there of the practical validity of the instrument? Nowhere in the specimen set was

SRA Reading Progress Test

there any statement of the purpose of the test. In the publisher's 1970 catalog appears the statement, "This test is primarily a training tool, but the first three sections can be used in selection programs." Furthermore, nowhere are intercorrelations among the scores reported.

The only technical data reported are K-R (not further identified) coefficients for the first three sections. All three are in the middle .90's. However, no information on sample size or characteristics of examinees is reported.

This reviewer's own intercorrelational data on 50 students and faculty in a university showed a lack of independence among the first three scores of this test (correlations ranging from .56 to .79). Rate was relatively independent of other scores ($-.15$ to $-.33$). The rate score correlated moderately with the uncorrected rate score of the *Reading Adequacy "READ" Test* and the rate score of the *Nelson-Denny Reading Test* (.51 and .45, respectively). Correlations of the first three scores of the *SRA Reading Progress Test* with Nelson-Denny vocabulary and comprehension scores were moderate. Only one, Logical Thinking and Nelson-Denny comprehension (.26) failed to reach significance at the .05 level. The vocabulary scores of the two tests correlated .61. The remaining four intercorrelations ranged from .42 to .46.

In summary, it is unfortunate that much money was spent on a test with beautiful typography, while a little more was not spent on technical aspects which should have been reported to the user. The test appears to have some face validity. The interpretive booklet is suspect for reasons given above. Finally, the test may turn out to be valid, reliable, and useful, but for the present the issues remain in doubt, pending more work by publisher or users.

[Other Test]

For another test new since *The Sixth Mental Measurements Yearbook,* see the following in *Reading Tests and Reviews:*

217. ★Reading : Adult Basic Education Student Survey

STUDY SKILLS

[776]

★**Bristol Achievement Tests: Study Skills.** Ages 8-0 to 9-11, 9-0 to 10-11, 10-0 to 11-11, 11-0 to 12-11, 12-0 to 13-11; 1969; BAT; 6 scores: properties, structures, processes, explanations, interpretations, total; Forms A, B, ['69, 8 pages]; 5 levels; administrative

SRA Reading Progress Test

manual ['69, 8 pages] for each level; battery interpretive manual ('69, 78 pages) ; battery profile ['69, 2 pages] for each form; £1.90 per 25 tests; £1 per 25 profiles; 60p per teacher's set (without interpretive manual) of any one level (must be purchased to obtain administrative manual and keys) ; 75p per interpretive manual; postage extra; 50(55) minutes; Alan Brimer, Margaret Fidler, Wynne Harlen, and John Taylor; Thomas Nelson & Sons Ltd. *

ELIZABETH J. GOODACRE, *Lecturer, Institute of Education, University of London, London, England.*

The designers of this battery suggest that these study skills tests represent the most ambitious of the three areas of achievement measurement attempted by the *Bristol Achievement Tests.* The authors define study skills as the degree of application which children are able to bring to bear on the study of the world around them—skills important in the study of environmental and natural science subjects.

The subtests involving structures and processes seem to be attempts to test concepts within the area of "centration" and reversibility and serialisation. The subtest on properties of materials and situations appears to involve a considerable element of verbal ability as well as ideas based on categorisation. The development of some of these abilities is known to be related to the degree of stimulation in the home, and the fact that there were losses from the standardisation sample through absence might be important in consideration of a child's performance on these tests. Also, the test makers had to secure schools that were prepared to test each child with the six tests of the battery. So although the schools were originally selected in terms of their type, urban-rural character, and size to represent a national sample of children throughout England and Wales, the standardisation may in effect have been carried out on the basis of "good attenders" in cooperative schools, and this should be remembered if use of the test with a typical group is being considered.

Using correlations between subtest scores on parallel forms of the tests (two-week intervals), the reliabilities quoted are lower than those usually considered acceptable. Subtest reliabilities range from .57 to .97, with the median .73. Total score reliabilities range from .83 to .93. The lower figures are more often found for some subtests at the higher levels.

Statistical data on the validity of the test were not available at the time of publication and the user is asked to consider the rational validity of the tests on the basis of curriculum sampling and test construction. The manual suggests that only a small sample of the possible content can be represented, and it is not claimed that the test items deal with "the essential content of environmental study and natural science elements in the curriculum for each level of the tests." The number of items in each test part differs and there were differences in the size of the "pool" of items which qualified as statistically satisfactory for each part at the different levels; e.g., in Level 4, subtest on processes (15 items), only 15 items satisfied the discrimination criteria, in contrast to Level 1, test of properties (15 items), for which 103 items satisfied statistical criteria. With these facts in mind, it is difficult to see how a progression of difficulty in some of the subtests at particular levels was satisfactorily achieved.

The manual suggests that the *Bristol Achievement Tests* are to be used as diagnostic measures revealing individual difficulties, although it is also stated that the purpose of the subtest scores is not to suggest what kind of attention should be given but rather that a case for further study has been made out and that an "appropriate diagnostic test" might reveal where teaching could be more profitably placed. In regard to the Study Skills, it is difficult to see how this approach could be carried out in practice. The standard errors of many of the subtests are such that the usefulness of the scores for diagnostic purposes is limited. These tests would appear to be of little assistance to a busy teacher if she has developed her own powers of observation in a rich classroom environment where children are actively encouraged to show these skills in operation. In certain circumstances, some of the subtests might have value as measures of concept attainment.

For a review of the complete battery, see 4.

[777]
★College Adjustment and Study Skills Inventory. College; 1968; CASSI; 6 scores: time distribution, attitude and personal adjustment, reading and class participation, taking notes, taking examinations, total; 1 form (3 pages) ; manual (9 pages plus inventory) ; no data on reliability; separate answer sheets must be used; $8 per set of 10 inventories, 50 answer sheets, and manual; $7.50 per 25 inventories; $10 per 100 answer sheets; $1 per manual; cash orders only; (15–20) minutes; Frank A. Christensen; Personal Growth Press, Inc. *

WILLIAM A. MEHRENS, *Professor of Education, Michigan State University, East Lansing, Michigan.*

The CASSI contains 57 questions for which the subject is to respond on a four-point scale from Very Often to Very Seldom. It yields the six scores listed above, with the five subtests containing 10, 24, 10, 8, and 5 questions respectively.

The primary purpose of the CASSI is to "serve as a counseling tool to assist the Counselor in evaluating characteristics that are important to a student's success in college." The test was devised by reviewing several how to study texts and compiling 150 questions "felt to be indicative of success in college." These were submitted to "three professional counselors" (not described further) who placed each question in one of the five categories. After eliminating an unspecified number of "duplicates and questions outside the scope of the inventory" the remainder were given to 66 college students who were divided into two groups: a group of B or better students and a group of C or below students. The final 57 questions were selected "on their discriminatory power and usefulness in a counseling situation." No data concerning the discrimination indexes are reported in the manual. Nor are we told anything about the college students. We don't know, for example, their grade levels, whether or not they were equated on scholastic aptitude, or the ratio of boys to girls.

The 57-question inventory was apparently normed on 250 students from nine very unrepresentative Midwestern colleges. However, the table giving the means and standard deviations is based on an N of 146. We are not told whether these 146 students are a part of the 250 in the norm group or if they are from another sample.

There are no reliability data on the inventory. There is a matrix of intercorrelations of the 5 subtests and total. The subtests correlate from between .25 and .53 with each other and from .51 to .83 with the total test. One's are entered in the main diagonal and could be mistaken by a novice for reliability measures. There is no way to discern whether the relatively low intercorrelations obtained are because the subtests are actually measuring different traits or whether they reflect unreliability in the inventory. Certainly one would not expect subtests of 5, 8, and 10 items each to be very reliable.

College Adjustment and Study Skills Inventory

On the same page of the manual as the table of means and standard deviations and the table of intercorrelations is a paragraph which apparently is meant to portray some validity evidence. A rank order correlation coefficient of .19 between CASSI and grade point averages for 98 unspecified students is reported.

Although the data included in the manual are less extensive and more poorly explained than what one would expect in a good term paper, the inventory may not be completely useless. Most of the questions seem to measure what they are supposed to measure. There are, however, some notable exceptions. Three of the 10 questions which are purported to measure the trait of "Time Distribution" seem to be somewhat lacking in face validity. They are as follows:

  3. Do you have a study time schedule that you follow *very* closely?
  5. Do you usually do your studying in the same places?
  19. Do you study where there are many things to distract you?

Item 3 must be answered "Very Often" for maximum credit. Following a time schedule very closely seems unduly rigid and probably a poor habit. Assignments occasionally come in bunches, students do feel ill some days, and going to that occasional spontaneous party which conflicts with a study time schedule may well contribute to mental health. Items 5 and 19 just do not seem related to "Time Distribution."

There are other questions in the inventory with which one could find minor faults, but basically they are straightforward in wording. Therefore this inventory, like most others, could easily be faked if the subject was so inclined.

In summary, this inventory contains 57 questions, for the most part appearing to have some face validity. There are no reliability data and only very marginal validity data. The norms are based on a small, atypical sample and probably present misleading information. The minimal technical data available are presented poorly in the manual. This inventory should be used only for research purposes until it is further developed. At the present time it compares very unfavorably with similar inventories such as the Brown-Holtzman *Survey of Study Habits and Attitudes.*

WALTER PAUK, *Professor of Education and Director, Cornell Reading-Study Center, Cornell University, Ithaca, New York.*

College Adjustment and Study Skills Inventory

The author states that the CASSI was developed "to provide a new type of inventory which is easy to administer and score, that can be used as a counseling tool."

The inventory of 57 items is, indeed, easy to administer for the following three reasons: (*a*) no special pencils nor separate machine scored sheets are needed; (*b*) no timing is necessary, and the relatively short inventory can be completed in about 15 to 20 minutes; and (*c*) the directions consist of only seven short sentences.

The special answer sheet bears a 4-point scale consisting of these descriptive terms: Very Often, Often, Seldom, Very Seldom. From the student's point of view, it is a bit cumbersome to encircle such relatively large areas of words over and over again. Another negative aspect is that two of the terms on the scale begin with the word "very." Since the positions of the rating terms are often reversed from item to item, there is a very real danger of a student's encircling the unintended answer by picking up his cue from seeing only the word "very"; that is, encircling "very seldom" instead of "very often" or vice versa.

From the counselor's point of view, the hand scoring of the items is rather tedious. It takes about 10 minutes to count, multiply, and add the various weights to obtain the five different part scores and the one total score. Then there is the task of converting the raw scores into percentiles.

This inventory, like other similar inventories, may be used as an opening wedge for counseling, but the big assumption is that the counselors will be well versed in study skills, learning theory, and academic attitudes. Without being supplemented by such expert knowledge, this inventory, as well as others, will fall far short of its intended use.

One of the major shortcomings of this inventory, as well as of almost all others, is the manual's lack of information about study skills to fortify a counselor. Authors of almost all study skills inventories attempt to get around this problem by including a bibliography of books. But, again, the assumption is that counselors will procure, read, and digest such recommended books.

With 24 of the items already devoted to the category of Attitude and Personal Adjustment, it is difficult to see how the remaining 33 items can be stretched adequately to cover the other four major categories. Actually, the category of Taking Examinations is drastically slighted, being composed of only five items. Only two of the five items deal with *taking* examinations; the other three items deal with *preparing* for examinations.

The category of Taking [lecture] Notes consists of eight items, only five of which pertain to the actual task of taking notes. No mention is made, for instance, of the following activities which are important to note taking: using shorthand or notehand; using abbreviations; redoing notes by rewriting or typing; listening instead of writing; engaging in doodling; and so forth.

In addition to the omission of many key items, there is also the omission of three vastly important categories: educational and career goals, general skills of studying and learning, and studying for examinations.

This reviewer believes that the 57 items which compose this inventory are insufficient to cover adequately the five categories which the author claims to cover. It is understandable that there is a constant tug to keep a test short so that it can be completed within a reasonably short time span; but it would be far better to sacrifice time to gain excellence. Other inventories are much longer; for example, the number of items on the SSHA has been increased from 75 to 100; the *Survey of Reading/Study Efficiency* consists of 144 items; and the *California Study Methods Survey* is made up of 150 items. One should not conclude, however, that the greater the number of items, the better the test. There are also the exceedingly important considerations of pertinence and precision.

In this inventory, there are more than several items which work against themselves internally. For example, "Do you space your study over several periods of time rather than cramming at the last minute?" The two ideas embedded in this item are: Do you distribute your assignment load over several periods of time; and Do you resort to cramming at the last minute? This is an incongruous pair, because they do not complement each other. The item should revolve around either of the following pairs. One complementary pair is: Do you start to study well in advance of the due date; or Do you wait until the last minute? The other pair is: Do you study an extra-long assignment continuously until you finish it; or Do you study an extra-long assignment by breaking it up into several shorter periods of time? In other words, this last pair

deals with the concept of "massed practice" versus "distributed practice." The first pair deals with "getting started early" versus "leaving-it-to-the-last-minute" so that cramming is the only alternative.

Another ambiguous item is: "Do you usually get along with your parents?" In a rating scale which is already based on degrees (Very Often, Often, Seldom, Very Seldom), how does one deal with the word "usually" which is already part of the item? Does the student then say, "I *usually* very seldom get along with my parents." Including such qualifiers in the items themselves, when a rating scale other than Yes-No is used, is a mistake frequently made by authors of study skills inventories. In addition to the ambiguous items already pointed out, 15 other items are equally ambiguous or open to question as to correctness. According to this reviewer, there are some items which refer to practices that are *not* good study skills but yet are listed by the author as desirable.

SUMMARY. The inventory is of doubtful value for the following four reasons: first, it includes many ambiguous items; second, some of the items do not tap important study skills; third, several major categories of study skills and attitudes are completely left out; and fourth, the manual offers virtually no help to the counselor or instructor. The best college-level inventory so far available is the *Survey of Study Habits and Attitudes* by Brown and Holtzman. This 100-item inventory, which covers almost all of the essential study skills and attitudes, is admirably suited for use as an instrument for group assessment, as well as for individual counseling.

[778]
★**Comprehensive Tests of Basic Skills: Study Skills.** Grades 2.5–4, 4–6, 6–8, 8–12; 1968–70; 2 forms; 4 levels; for battery manuals and accessories, see 9; separate answer sheets (CompuScan [NCS], IBM 1230, Scoreze) must be used for levels 2–4; postage extra; $1.75 per specimen set of any one level, postpaid; CTB/McGraw-Hill. *
a) LEVEL 1. Grades 2.5–4; Forms Q ('68, 6 pages), R ('69, 6 pages); $5 per 35 tests; 21(40) minutes.
b) LEVEL 2. Grades 4–6; Forms Q ('68, 9 pages), R ('69, 9 pages); $5.35 per 35 tests; $2.50 per 50 Digitek or IBM answer sheets; $3 per 50 CompuScan answer sheets; $2.75 per 25 Scoreze answer sheets; $1 per IBM hand scoring stencil; CompuScan scoring service, 17¢ and over per test; 32(50) minutes.
c) LEVEL 3. Grades 6–8; Forms Q ('68, 10 pages), R ('69, 10 pages); prices same as for level 2; 30(50) minutes.
d) LEVEL 4. Grades 8–12; Forms Q ('68, 10 pages), R ('69, 10 pages); prices same as for level 2; 29(50) minutes.

WALTER PAUK, *Professor of Education and Director, Cornell Reading-Study Center, Cornell University, Ithaca, New York.*

These tests were developed to measure the ability of students to use library catalog cards, atlases, almanacs, indexes, books, encyclopedias, maps, graphs, diagrams, and charts. The tests do not, however, deal with the more basic psychological factors of effective study, such as attitudes toward school, and study skills actually used.

A close inspection reveals that each test item was carefully constructed to deal specifically with each of the categories of study skills enumerated above. The technical report attests to the meticulous care given toward constructing a valid test. But since "performance is dependent on possession of relevant knowledge" in these categories, it would have been of value to have data on whether or not there are real differences between equated groups of students, if one group was previously taught the type of material on the test and the other group was not.

The K-R 20 reliabilities within grades range from .77 to .92 with median .89. Alternate-form reliabilities range from .72 to .88 with median .83. In almost all cases, the reliabilities for the study skills test are decidedly lower than those for the other tests in the parent battery.

At the first level, the test consists of 30 items; 20 items measuring the ability to use reference materials (dictionary, library catalog cards, and books); and 10 items measuring the ability to use graphic materials (picture map and topographic map). All of the test items are ingenious in that they not only establish the categories for the succeeding tests, but also begin with items that are basic, natural, and logical. All higher levels include two subtests: Using Reference Materials (20 items) and Using Graphic Materials (30 items).

At grades 2.5–4, the readability level of a test is especially important. It is understandable that if the vocabulary is too difficult for the intended user of a test, then the test is probably measuring the reading ability rather than the study skills achievement of the pupil. The grade placements, according to the Spache Readability Formula, for the two forms at this level are: Form Q, 3.6; Form R, 3.7. The difficulty that students would encounter in dealing with an item containing unfamiliar words is illustrated by the following option: "a musical group." Both words, *musical* and *group* are unfamiliar

words. To complicate matters even more, the question itself contains four unfamiliar words; hence, it is improbable that an answer by a student with a reading level below 3.7 would be valid.

All of the items on graphic material in Level 2 are exceptionally well constructed and deal with the major skills of translation, interpretation, and analysis. Some items call for the skill of converting symbols into units of measure or for identification of objects; others call for establishing relationships between objects and between various data; others call for drawing conclusions based on data; and still others call for making inferences that extend beyond the given data, yet based on such data.

At Level 2, the Dale-Chall Readability Formula shows the grade placement for Test 9, Forms Q and R, to be at the 7–8th grade level; for Test 10, Forms Q and R, at the 5–6th grade level. The relatively high readability levels for both forms of Test 9 are due to unfamiliar words such as: almanac, atlas, bibliography, contents, dictionary, encyclopedia, glossary, handbook, and index. Some suggestions for overcoming the readability problem are: (a) use synonyms such as *part* for *syllable;* (b) substitute library catalog cards which contain fewer unfamiliar words; and (c) choose examples of dictionary entries containing fewer unfamiliar words which would still test the student's ability without any sacrifice of level or precision.

At Level 3, the Dale-Chall Formula shows the grade placement for Test 9, Forms Q and R, to be at the 7–8th grade level; for Test 10, Forms Q and R, at the 5–6th grade level.

An ambiguous item presents a dilemma at this level: "Which country gained most in aluminum production between 1964 and 1966?" The question which might most naturally enter the student's mind is whether the item means the largest increase in percentage or in bulk. The correct answer is bulk increase. This bulk increase was a mere 20 percent; whereas, another country's increase, though small in bulk, was close to 80 percent. Such a quandary would never have occurred if the word "tonnage" had been inserted directly after the word "most."

At Level 4, the Dale-Chall Formula shows the grade placement for Tests 9 and 10, Forms Q and R, to be at the 7–8th grade level.

At this level, all 30 test items in Using Graphic Materials are designed to test the students' abilities to convert symbols, make relationships, draw conclusions, and make inferences. The graphic materials in this test are on a high level of the type that one would find in textbooks.

Here again, at Level 4, ambiguity appears. "The two areas that will grow the least in population between 1965 and 2000 are." The question which might most naturally enter the student's mind is: Does the question mean the smallest increase in percentage or in bulk? The correct answer deals with sheer numbers, not percentages! The paradox is that the country which had the smallest increase in the number of people, had the largest percentage increase in the number of people. The increase was 88 percent; yet this is the country called for in the answer as having the *smallest* increase. To make the question clear, the words "in population" should be replaced by "in number of people." Actually, the counterpart question on Form R actually does include the words "in number of people"; consequently is not ambiguous.

Despite the problems mentioned, these tests are the finest yet devised. The rationale is clear and logical; the design a masterpiece of sequential and interlocking categories; the test items polished almost to perfection; the format inviting; the content challenging; the supporting research plentiful; and the overall coordination almost flawless. A great team must have put the pieces together to create the complete picture.

For reviews of the complete battery, see 9 (2 reviews, 3 excerpts).

[779]
★The Cornell Critical Thinking Test. Grades 7–12, 13 and over; 1961–71; CCTT; 1 form; 2 levels; manual ('71, 19 pages); separate answer sheets (Digitek) may be used; 30¢ per test; 2¢ per answer sheet; $1 per specimen set; postpaid; (50) minutes; Robert H. Ennis and Jason Millman; Critical Thinking Project, University of Illinois. *
a) LEVEL X. Grades 7–12; 1 form ('71, 15 pages, identical with test copyrighted in 1961 except for format).
b) LEVEL Z. Grades 13 and over; 1 form ('71, 13 pages, identical with test copyrighted in 1961 except for format).

REFERENCES
1. ENNIS, ROBERT H. "A Concept of Critical Thinking: A Proposed Basis for Research in the Teaching and Evaluation of Critical Thinking Ability." *Harvard Ed R* 32:81–111 w '62. * (*PA* 37:458)
2. CRAVEN, GENE FRANCIS. *Critical Thinking Abilities and Understanding of Science by Science Teacher-Candidates at Oregon State University.* Doctor's thesis, Oregon State University (Corvallis, Ore.), 1966. (*DA* 27:125A)
3. BROWN, TERRANCE RALPH. *Attitudes Toward Science and Critical Thinking Abilities of Chemistry and Non-Chemistry Students in the Tacoma Public Schools.* Doctor's thesis, Oregon State University (Corvallis, Ore.), 1967. (*DA* 28:1611A)
4. FOLLMAN, JOHN. "Factor Analysis of Three Critical Think-

ing Tests, One Logical Reasoning Test, and One English Test." *Yearb Nat Read Conf* 18:154–60 '69. *
5. FOLLMAN, JOHN; HERNANDEZ, DAVID; AND MILLER, WILLIAM. "Canonical Correlation of Scholastic Aptitude and Critical Thinking." *Psychol* 6(3):3–6 Ag '69. * (*PA* 44:2853)
6. FOLLMAN, JOHN; MILLER, WILLIAM; AND HERNANDEZ, DAVID. "Factor Analysis of Achievement, Scholastic Aptitude, and Critical Thinking Subtests." *J Exp Ed* 38(1):48–53 f '69. * (*PA* 45:10901)
7. FOLLMAN, JOHN COSGROVE. *A Factor Analytic Study of Three Critical Thinking Tests, One English Test, and One Logical Reasoning Test.* Doctor's thesis, Indiana University (Bloomington, Ind.), 1969. (*DAI* 30:1015A)
8. FOLLMAN, JOHN. "Correlational and Factor Analysis of Critical Thinking, Logical Reasoning, and English Total Test Scores." *Fla J Ed Res* 12(1):91–4 Ja '70. *
9. FOLLMAN, JOHN; BROWN, LAURENCE; AND BURG, ELDON. "Factor Analysis of Critical Thinking, Logical Reasoning, and English Subtests." *J Exp Ed* 38(4):11–6 su '70. *
10. MILLER, WILLIAM; FOLLMAN, JOHN; AND HERNANDEZ, DAVID E. "Discriminant Analysis of School Children in Integrated and Non-Integrated Schools Using Tests of Critical Thinking." *Fla J Ed Res* 12(1):63–8 Ja '70. *

[780]
*SRA Achievement Series: Work-Study Skills. Grades 4–9; 1955–69; an optional supplement to the Multilevel Edition of the series; 3 scores: references, charts, total; Forms C, D, ('63, 32 pages); 3 levels: blue (grades 4.5–6.5), green (grades 6.5–8.5), and red (grades 8.5–9) in a single booklet; no specific manual; for series manuals and accessories, see 18; separate series answer sheets (Digitek, DocuTran, IBM 805, IBM 1230) must be used; $10.35 per 25 tests; $9.30 per 100 DocuTran answer sheets; postage extra; 70(80) minutes; Louis P. Thorpe, D. Welty Lefever, and Robert A. Naslund; Science Research Associates, Inc. *

For reviews by Robert L. Ebel and Ruth M. Strang of earlier forms, see 5:696. For reviews of the complete battery, see 18 (2 reviews), 6:21 (1 review), and 5:21 (2 reviews).

[781]
★Study Skills Test: McGraw-Hill Basic Skills System. Grades 11–14; 1970; also called *MHBSS Study Skills Test;* although designed for use with the MHBSS instructional program, the test may be used independently; 6 scores: problem solving, underlining, library information, study skills information, test total, inventory of study habits and attitudes; Forms A, B, (27 pages); manual (39 pages); separate answer sheets (Digitek, IBM 1230, Scoreze) must be used; $9 per 25 tests; $2.50 per 50 IBM or Digitek answer sheets; $3 per 25 Scoreze answer sheets; $1 per IBM or Digitek scoring stencil; postage extra; $1.25 per specimen set, postpaid; IBM scoring service, 25¢ and over per test ($20 minimum); 46(56) minutes for test, 10(20) minutes for inventory; Alton L. Raygor; McGraw-Hill Book Co., Inc. *

WALTER PAUK, *Professor of Education and Director, Cornell Reading-Study Center, Cornell University, Ithaca, New York.*

Each form of this test is divided into four parts: Problem Solving, Underlining, Library Information, and Study Skills Information.

The 15 items in Part 1, Problem Solving, fall into three categories: verbal analogies, number series, and configuration series. The verbal analogy items are stated in sentence form; the number series and the configuration series items are stated in conventional form. All three categories are similar in that they measure the student's ability to perceive relationships. It is, therefore, difficult to see how the 15 items can justifiably be classified as study skills, since they do not deal with the *attitudes* that students have toward school, nor with academic work *habits,* nor with such *tools* of study as library catalogue cards, atlases, almanacs, indexes, books, and encyclopedias. Rather, the items in Part 1 deal with reasoning ability—a component of intelligence.

Part 2, Underlining, contains 10 questions based on 18 separate passages that have already been underlined. The student's task is to read each passage to determine whether the underlining is too much, incomplete, a misrepresentation of the text, or correct. The score is a measure of a skill which is dependent on the student's "ability to analyze the structure of the material being read."

Most of the passages are short; many consist merely of two or three sentences. Such brief passages preclude a reader's seeing the specific passage in fuller context. Usually a reader needs the preceding and succeeding paragraphs to see the thrust or sequence of the author's ideas. Without context, it is often almost guesswork to differentiate between an important supporting point and the main point.

There is still a more crucial deficiency. The author of the test recognizes that there will be "an immense range of individual differences among entering students....because of inadequate preparation or achievement in high school." Yet the 36 passages included in Part 2 of both Form A and Form B are at an unusually high level of readability.[1] For example, for the average tenth grader, there are but 5 passages at his level, while 31 passages are above this level. For the average eleventh and twelfth graders, there are 16 passages at or below their levels, while 20 passages are above. There are seven passages that are even beyond the reading level of the average college graduate (grade 16+).

The high readability levels of so many passages introduce a serious confounding factor; that is, it is difficult to know what is being measured: the student's ability to underline or his ability to read.

Part 3, Library Information, is composed of 20 multiple choice test items designed to meas-

ure a student's proficiency in using the library. These items test his knowledge about reference books, library catalogue cards, and parts of a book.

The four questions dealing with a library catalogue card call for identifying the author, the publisher, the subject, and the library card as an author card, a subject card, or a title card. As far as parts of a book are concerned, there are two questions that deal with the purpose of the glossary and the appendix. There is also one question that deals with the skill of alphabetizing.

It would seem that college students might feel that such questions are elementary, and that an undue amount of effort is put forth to transmit a tiny bit of information that could be gotten easily and almost instantly by pulling out a drawer in almost any library.

The 20 multiple choice test items in Part 4, Study Skills Information, do not lend themselves toward finding out the student's present personal study skills, habits, or attitudes; rather, the test items try to find out what he has learned *about* study skills, habits, and attitudes. Such information, presumably, was to have been gotten from the "Study Skills Section" of the McGraw-Hill Basic Skills System. Several examples of the questions are: "What is meant by the SQ3R technique of studying?" "What does 'rote learning' mean?" "What does 'skimming' mean?" All of these questions presuppose prior instruction.

Almost all of the test items in this part are not in consonance with the objectives of an independent study skills inventory.

SUMMARY. The *Study Skills Test* probably fulfills the purpose for which it was designed: to measure what students have learned and retained after using the "Study Skills Section" of the Basic Skills System. As an independent instrument to assess the academic attitudes, study skills, and work habits of students, however, it falls woefully short; but this is understandable: it was not designed to fulfill that purpose.

INVENTORY OF STUDY HABITS AND ATTITUDES. The 49 items of this inventory are clustered to make seven subscales of 7 items each: Listening and Note Taking, General Study Habits, Relationships with Teachers and Courses, Motivation, Organization of Effort, Concentration, and Emotional Problems. The inventory, however,

[1] DALE, EDGAR, AND CHALL, JEANNE S. "A Formula for Predicting Readability: Instructions." *Ed Res B* 27:37-54 F 17 '48.

Study Skills Test: McGraw-Hill Basic Skills System

fails to include items to cover the following categories: academic goals, career goals, textbook studying, studying for examinations, and taking examinations.

The manual does not provide counselors with either direct information about study skills or with suggested references. The assumption seems to be that counselors are well versed in study skills. This reviewer has not found this to be the case.

It is reported in the manual that "separate scores for each of these seven-item subscales are not sufficiently reliable and, therefore, are not reported." This unreliability may be due, in part, to the following four conditions: first, the "yes-no" scale makes it very difficult for some students to answer consistently test items that contain words of *degree;* for example, "I always put studying first." Some students may interpret "always" to mean strictly 100 percent of the time; whereas, other students may feel that "most of the time" (perhaps 75 to 85 percent) earns a "yes."

Second, statements that are too general, such as, "I tend to daydream when I study," are most difficult to answer consistently and honestly on a "yes-no" scale. There is hardly a student who does not, at one time or another, fall into daydreaming. The crucial question here is whether or not the student can put daydreams aside and get on with the job of studying. A five-point scale would probably be an advantage.

Third, including two conditions or actions in one statement can elicit inconsistent answers from students in similar situations: for example, the test item, "I often get moody and can't study at all." Some students get moody and can't study, while other students get moody and study hard but perhaps inefficiently.

Fourth, ambiguity of statements could also lead to inconsistent answers. For example, the test item, "My class notes are sometimes difficult to understand later," could be "yes" for two entirely different reasons: first, not being able to decipher the notes because of poor handwriting; and second, not getting sufficient information into the notes so that the idea can be recreated later.

It is difficult to find a niche for this inventory. It does not really complement the *Study Skills Test* because the data are so unrelated; yet, it cannot stand alone because it is so unreliable and incomplete. It may, however, be used by a knowledgeable counselor as an "opening wedge."

[782]

Survey of Study Habits and Attitudes. Grades 7–12, 12–14; 1953–67; SSHA; original edition called *Brown-Holtzman Survey of Study Habits and Attitudes;* 7 scores: study habits (delay avoidance, work methods, total), study attitudes (teacher approval, education acceptance, total), total; 1 form; 2 levels; manual ('67, 30 pages); separate answer sheets (IBM 805, IBM 1230) must be used; $3.50 per 25 tests; $1 per manual and IBM 805 scoring keys; 90¢ per manual and IBM 1230 scoring keys; $1.25 per specimen set of either level; postage extra; (20–25) minutes; William F. Brown and Wayne H. Holtzman; Psychological Corporation. *
a) FORM H. Grades 7–12; 1967; 1 form (6 pages).
b) FORM C. Grades 12–14; 1965–67; 1 form ('65, 6 pages).

REFERENCES
1–14. See 5:688.
15–26. See 6:856.
27. AINSWORTH, LABAN LINTON, JR. *An Exploratory Study of the Academic Achievement of Arab Students.* Doctor's thesis, University of Texas (Austin, Tex.), 1957. (*DA* 17:1702)
28. CURRIE, CAROLINE. *The Relationship of Certain Selected Factors to Achievement in Freshman Composition.* Doctor's thesis, Northwestern University (Evanston, Ill.), 1957. (*DA* 18:884)
29. DIENER, CHARLES L. *A Comparison of Over-Achieving and Under-Achieving Students at the University of Arkansas.* Doctor's thesis, University of Arkansas (Fayetteville, Ark.), 1957. (*DA* 17:1692)
30. KRUMBOLTZ, JOHN D., AND FARQUHAR, WILLIAM W. "Reliability and Validity of the n-Achievement Test." *J Consult Psychol* 21:226–8 Je '57. * (*PA* 32:5966)
31. CASEY, DONALD DEAN. *A Study of Relationships Between Measures of Academic Aptitude, Academic Achievement, and Study Habits and Attitudes in an Ohio High School.* Master's thesis, Ohio State University (Columbus, Ohio), 1960.
32. DARTER, CLARENCE LESLIE, JR. *A Comparative Study of Over-Achieving and Under-Achieving Ninth-Grade Students.* Doctor's thesis, Texas Technological College (Lubbock, Tex.), 1961. (*DA* 22:1462)
33. MCGUIRE, CARSON; HINDSMAN, EDWIN; KING, F. J.; AND JENNINGS, EARL. "Dimensions of Talented Behavior." *Ed & Psychol Meas* 21:3–38 sp '61. * (*PA* 36:1KH03M)
34. BROWN, WILLIAM F. "Academic Adjustment Counseling Through Peer-Group Interaction," pp. 131–5. (*PA* 37:5632) In *Personality Factors on the College Campus: Review of a Symposium.* Edited by Robert L. Sutherland and others. Austin, Tex.: Hogg Foundation for Mental Health, 1962. Pp. xxii, 242. * (*PA* 37:5621)
35. COVINGTON, JAMES DONALD. *A Study of Selected Personal Characteristics of Entering College Students.* Doctor's thesis, Auburn University (Auburn, Ala.), 1962. (*DA* 23:3197)
36. DOLLAR, ROBERT JOSEPH. *A Study of Certain Psychosocial Differences Among Dormitory, Fraternity, and Off-Campus Freshman Men at Oklahoma State University.* Doctor's thesis, Oklahoma State University (Stillwater, Okla.), 1963. (*DA* 25:961)
37. GAWRONSKI, DANIEL ANTHONY. *A Comparative Study of Differences Existing Among Overachieving, Normal Achieving and Underachieving High School Seniors.* Doctor's thesis, Northwestern University (Evanston, Ill.), 1963. (*DA* 25:292)
38. BROWN, FREDRICK G. "Study Habits and Attitudes, College Experience, and College Success." *Personnel & Guid J* 43:287–92 N '64. * (*PA* 39:10767)
39. BROWN, FREDRICK G., AND DUBOIS, THOMAS E. "Correlates of Academic Success for High-Ability Freshman Men." *Personnel & Guid J* 42:603–7 F '64. * (*PA* 39:5820)
40. CAMPBELL, ARTHUR GLENN. *Student Evaluation of a College Preparation Seminar Before and After College Attendance.* Master's thesis, Southwest Texas State College (San Marcos, Tex.), 1964.
41. CORDES, CAROLYN. *A Normative, Validity, and Subscale Intercorrelation Analysis of the Revised Brown-Holtzman Survey of Study Habits and Attitudes for Grades 7–12.* Master's thesis, Southwest Texas State College (San Marcos, Tex.), 1964.
42. DE SENA, PAUL A. "The Effectiveness of Two Study Habits Inventories in Predicting Consistent Over-, Under- and Normal Achievement in College." Comment by Henry Borow. *J Counsel Psychol* 11:388–94 w '64. * (*PA* 39:8570)

43. DE SENA, PAUL A. "The Role of Consistency in Identifying Characteristics of Three Levels of Achievement." *Personnel & Guid J* 43:145–9 O '64. * (*PA* 39:10713)

44. GLIDDEN, GEORGE WAYNE. *Factors That Influence Achievement in Senior High School American History.* Doctor's thesis, University of Nebraska (Lincoln, Neb.), 1964. (*DA* 25: 3429)

45. KARAS, SHAWKY FALTAOUS. *A Study of Personality and Socioeconomic Factors and Mathematics Achievement.* Doctor's thesis, Columbia University (New York, N.Y.), 1964. (*DA* 28:5191B)

46. KNIGHT, JAMES, AND CHANSKY, NORMAN M. "Anxiety, Study Problems, and Achievement." *Personnel & Guid J* 43: 45–6 S '64. *

47. MARTENS, BRUNO. "The Relationship of Intelligence, Attitudes and Study Habits to Academic Achievement." *Can Ed & Res Dig* 4:268–72 D '64. *

48. MURPHY, VINCENT M. "Manifest Anxiety and Self-Description With Respect to Study Habits and Attitudes." *J Col Stud Personnel* 6:79–81 D '64. *

49. RIGHTHAND, HERBERT. *A Comparison of Technical Institute Freshman Dropouts and Persisting Students With Respect to Sociological and Psychological Characteristics.* Doctor's thesis, University of Connecticut (Storrs, Conn.), 1964. (*DA* 25:4550)

50. STARR, FAY HAVEN. *Antecedents and Concomitants of Change in Teacher Evaluation of Pupil Performance.* Doctor's thesis, University of Texas (Austin, Tex.), 1964. (*DA* 25:-2862)

51. GAWRONSKI, DANIEL A., AND MATHIS, CLAUDE. "Differences Between Over-Achieving, Normal Achieving, and Under-Achieving High School Students." *Psychol Sch* 2:152–5 Ap '65. *

52. PANDEY, JAGDISH. "Hindi Adaptation of Brown-Holtzman's Survey of Study Habits and Attitudes (SSHA)." *Indian Psychol R* 2:53–8 Jl '65. * (*PA* 40:2141)

53. RIGHTHAND, HERBERT. "Identifying Technical Institute Dropouts." *Personnel & Guid J* 44:68–72 S '65. *

54. WEAVER, HAZEL STEWART. *Characteristics of High School Girls Which May Lead to Early Marriage.* Doctor's thesis, North Texas State University (Denton, Tex.), 1965. (*DA* 25: 7094)

55. BROWN, FREDERICK G., AND SCOTT, DAVID A. "The Unpredictability of Predictability." *J Ed Meas* 3:297–301 w '66. *

56. FALCK, FRANCES ELIZABETH. *An Analysis of Achievement and Attitudes of Freshman Participants in the Federal Work-Study Program at the University of Colorado.* Doctor's thesis, University of Colorado (Boulder, Colo.), 1966. (*DA* 28:1263A)

57. HOOVER, BASIL. *College Students Who Did Not Seek Counseling During a Period of Academic Difficulty.* Doctor's thesis, University of Florida (Gainesville, Fla.), 1966. (*DA* 28:1298A)

58. KEARNEY, DOROTHY LUCILLE. *Selected Non-Intellectual Factors as Predictors of Academic Success in Junior College Intellectually Capable Students.* Doctor's thesis, University of Southern California (Los Angeles, Calif.), 1966. (*DA* 27:395A)

59. MALCOLM, RICHARD WARD. *An Analysis of Selected Conditional Admissions at the University of Southern California.* Doctor's thesis, University of Southern California (Los Angeles, Calif.), 1966. (*DA* 27:115A)

60. MEANS, HESTER RICE. *An Analysis of the First Freshman Class of the DeKalb Junior College.* Doctor's thesis, University of Georgia (Athens, Ga.), 1966. (*DA* 27:1552A)

61. PANDEY, JAGDISH. "Response Set on Survey of Study Habits and Attitudes (Hindi Adaptation)." *Psychol Studies* 11:9–14 Ja '66. * (*PA* 40:-041)

62. GARDNER, JAMES M. "Validity of a Study Attitude Questionnaire for Predicting Academic Success." *Psychol Rep* 21: 935–6 D '67. * (*PA* 42:7849)

63. GERRY, ROBERT. *Computer-Learner Interaction in Problem Solving Tasks.* Doctor's thesis, University of Texas (Austin, Tex.), 1967. (*DA* 28:3997A)

64. MEHDI, BAQER. "Differential Factors in Pupil Success in Science, Arts and Commerce Courses at the Higher Secondary Stage." *Indian Ed R* 2:92–104 Jl '67. * (*PA* 41:14220)

65. MOSKOVIS, LEFTERIE MICHAEL. *An Identification of Certain Similarities and Differences Between Successful and Unsuccessful College Level Beginning Shorthand Students and Transcription Students.* Doctor's thesis, Michigan State University (East Lansing, Mich.), 1967. (*DA* 28:4826A)

66. PETERSON, RONALD SKEEN. *A Longitudinal Study of Nonintellective Characteristics of College Dropouts.* Doctor's thesis, University of Oregon (Eugene, Ore.), 1967. (*DA* 28: 2076A)

67. RILEY, RUSSELL HOWARD. *Cheating Propensity of High School Students as a Function of Certain Key Perceptions.* Doctor's thesis, Colorado State College (Greeley, Colo.), 1967. (*DA* 28:2455A)

68. WEIGEL, RICHARD G., AND WEIGEL, VIRGINIA M. "The Relationship of Knowledge and Usage of Study Skill Techniques to Academic Performance." *J Ed Res* 61:78–80 O '67. *

69. DWIVEDI, CHANDRA BHAL, AND SHARMA, MAHESH DUTT. "Validity of Survey of Study Habits and Attitudes (SSHA)." *Indian Psychol R* 4:120–2 Ja '68. * (*PA* 43:11821)

70. GORDON, JAMES ROSCOE. *Listening, Attitude, and Intelligence Tests to Predict Academic Achievement.* Doctor's thesis, Colorado State College (Greeley, Colo.), 1968. (*DA* 29:2522A)

71. HOLTZMAN, WAYNE H., AND BROWN, WILLIAM F. "Evaluating the Study Habits and Attitudes of High School Students." *J Ed Psychol* 59:404–9 D '68. * (*PA* 43:1756)

72. MARSHALL, JOSEPH JEMERSON. *Non-Cognitive Variables as a Predictor of Academic Achievement Among Freshmen, Sophomores, and Juniors at Abilene Christian College.* Doctor's thesis, Baylor University (Waco, Tex.), 1968. (*DA* 29:3833A)

73. MITCHELL, JAMES V. "The Identification of Student Personality Characteristics Related to Perceptions of the School Environment." *Sch R* 76:50–9 Mr '68. * (*PA* 43:3006)

74. MUNDAY, LEO. "Correlations Between ACT and Other Predictors of Academic Success in College." *Col & Univ* 44: 67–76 f '68. *

75. O'DONNELL, PATRICK IAN. *Predictors of Freshman Academic Success and Their Relationship to Attrition.* Doctor's thesis, University of Southern California (Los Angeles, Calif.), 1968. (*DA* 29:798A)

76. PLANISEK, R. J., AND MERRIFIELD, P. R. "Ability, Study Habits, and Academic Performance Correlates of the Theoretical-Practical Value Characteristics Inventory (TPCI)." Abstract. *Proc 76th Ann Conv Am Psychol Assn* 3:159–60 '68. *

77. BANGS, ARTHUR J. *The Parental Perception of Certain Inventoried Traits of a Selected Group of Male Adolescent Offspring.* Doctor's thesis, Catholic University of America (Washington, D.C.), 1969. (*DAI* 30:1810A)

78. CORRENTI, RICHARD J. *Predictors of Success in the Study of Computer Programming at Two-Year Institutions of Higher Education.* Doctor's thesis, Ohio University (Athens, Ohio), 1969. (*DAI* 30:3718A)

79. DESIDERATO, OTELLO, AND KOSKINEN, PATRICIA. "Anxiety, Study Habits, and Academic Achievement." *J Counsel Psychol* 16(2):162–5 Mr '69. * (*PA* 43:10360)

80. FITZPATRICK, JOHN CHARLES. *The Relationships Between the Relative Effectiveness of Two Teaching Methods and Selected Non-Cognitive Variables of College Students.* Doctor's thesis, Fordham University (New York, N.Y.), 1969. (*DAI* 30:5284A)

81. GEHLHAUSEN, PAUL EDWARD. *An Exploration of Selected Factors Associated With Success of Beginning Engineering Students at Tri-State College.* Doctor's thesis, Purdue University (Lafayette, Ind.), 1969. (*DAI* 30:3724A)

82. HO, MAN KEUNG. *The Effect of Group Counseling on the Academic Performance, Study Habits and Attitudes, and the Interpersonal Adjustment of Foreign Students.* Doctor's thesis, Florida State University (Tallahassee, Fla.), 1969. (*DAI* 30:5237A)

83. HUCKABEE, MALCOM W. "Personality and Academic Aptitude Correlates of Cognitive Control Principles." *South J Ed Res* 3(1):1–9 Ja '69. *

84. JOSHI, MOHAN C., AND PANDEY, JAGDISH. "Study Habits and Attitudes of Rural Urban Adolescents." *Indian Psychol R* 5(2):150–5 Ja '69. *

85. KHAN, S. B., AND ROBERTS, DENNIS M. "Relationships Among Study Habits and Attitudes, Aptitude and Grade 8 Achievement." *Ed & Psychol Meas* 29(4):951–5 w '69. * (*PA* 44:21525)

86. KOOKER, EARL W., AND BELLAMY, ROY Q. "Some Psychometric Differences Between Graduates and Dropouts." *Psychol* 6(2):65–70 My '69. * (*PA* 43:14868)

87. MONTGOMERY, MARY ANN. *An Investigation of Students Who Succeed Academically and Those Who Do Not Succeed Academically in a Community College.* Doctor's thesis, University of Pittsburgh (Pittsburgh, Pa.), 1969. (*DAI* 31:1578A)

88. RUSSELL, JACK. *An Investigation of the Relationship Between College Freshman Withdrawal and Certain Critical Personality and Study Orientation Factors.* Doctor's thesis, University of Southern California (Los Angeles, Calif.), 1969. (*DAI* 30:1437A)

89. GALLESSICH, JUNE. "An Investigation of Correlates of Academic Success of Freshmen Engineering Students." *J Counsel Psychol* 17(2):173–6 Mr '-o. * (*PA* 44:9340)

90. GREEN, JOE L. *An Analysis of Factors Related to Academic Achievement in Introductory Geography at the University of Arkansas.* Doctor's thesis, University of Arkansas (Fayetteville, Ark.), 1970. (*DAI* 31:1510A)

91. KHAN, S. B. "Affective Correlates of Academic Achievement: A Longitudinal Study." *Meas & Eval Guid* 3(2):76–80 su '70. * (*PA* 45:1360)

92. LIN, YI-GUANG, AND MCKEACHIE, WILBERT J. "Aptitude, Anxiety, Study Habits, and Academic Achievement." *J Counsel Psychol* 17(4):306–9 Jl '70. * (*PA* 44:21601)

93. MOSKOVIS, L. MICHAEL. "Similarities and Differences of College-Level Successful and Unsuccessful Shorthand Students." *Delta Pi Epsilon J* 12(2):12–6 F '70. *

94. RUBIN, DOROTHY. "Halo Effect in Self-Rated Attitudes of Certain Black College Freshmen." *Psychol Rep* 26(3):940 Je '70. * (*PA* 45:1281)

95. THOMAS, RUSSELL EARLE. *Discriminant Function Analysis of Probationary and Non-Probationary Students' Measured Values, Personality Needs, and Socio-Economic Background Factors.* Doctor's thesis, Purdue University (Lafayette, Ind.), 1970. (*DAI* 31:1589A)

Survey of Study Habits and Attitudes

Carleton B. Shay, *Professor of Education and Associate Dean, School of Education, California State College, Los Angeles, California.*

The revised SSHA, the result of eight years of research, differs in several significant ways from the original edition. Most of the original items were retained, but the inventory was lengthened from 75 to 100 items. Separate scoring keys for men and women were eliminated, a high school level form was introduced, and the inventory was subdivided into four subscales. The developmental program leading to these changes is carefully explained and supported by data. The data are impressive, though incomplete, for an inventory of this type.

The SSHA consists of numbered statements, arranged in two columns per page, to which the student is directed to respond in one of five ways: Rarely (0–15% of the time), Sometimes (16–35%), Frequently (36–65%), Generally (66–85%), or Almost Always (86–100%). Statements for college and high school forms are almost the same, differing only in vocabulary level, age referents, and the like. The basic content and arrangement of both levels are identical, and the same answer sheets and scoring keys are used for both. Four 25-item subscales are delineated: Work Methods, Delay Avoidance, Teacher Approval, and Education Acceptance. Scores on the first two subscales may be combined to yield a score for Study Habits; similarly, the last two subscales combine to form Study Attitudes. The total score is labeled Study Orientation.

The lowest Form C subscale reliability coefficient (K-R 8) is .87; the lowest 4-week test-retest coefficient is .88, and the lowest 14-week test-retest coefficient is .83. These are high for 25-item scales. Unfortunately, small samples were used (though this should deflate the coefficients), and only data for a 4-week interval are available for Form H, all correlations being at least .93.

Evidence for validity is presented in terms of low correlation coefficients (mean .21 for C, .27 for H) between SSHA and aptitude tests and higher correlations (mean .36 for C, .49 for H) between SSHA and grades, which suggest that the test is related to grades but is not just a measure of ability. Partial correlation coefficients (average .43) between SSHA Form H and grades, with aptitude level held constant, also support this notion. In addition, multiple correlation coefficients combining SSHA with aptitude test scores show that the correlation with grades is increased from .07 to .16 over the correlation of grades with aptitude scores alone. Although these are modest increases, they are in a promising direction; however, no evidence is given for crossvalidation of these results.

Intercorrelation coefficients of SSHA subscale scores range from .51 to .75, minimally supportive of the success of the attempt to create unique subscales of use to counselors. Counselors requested these subscales; it is hoped these high correlations will deter them from considering the subscales measures of unique traits.

As pointed out by previous reviewers, the most troublesome aspect of SSHA validity deals with the inventory's use as a predictor. The basic assumption underlying the inventory is that some students earn poor grades because of poor study habits and attitudes, and that if these habits and attitudes can be identified and changed, their grades will improve. The prediction which follows is that students with poor habits and attitudes will earn low grades, and those with good habits and attitudes will earn high grades; thus, the inventory can select those students who will earn good grades. The trouble with this assumption is that a student may know proper study habits and attitudes but fail to employ them, and besides, there are many other reasons for good and poor grades. Validation studies cited in the manual did not use the SSHA as a selection instrument, and in view of its complete dependence upon frankness of responding, the inventory might never be used in this way. Studies of its usefulness in counseling, particularly those which show that a change of study habits and attitudes results in a change of grades, have yet to be conducted. Until then, its ultimate justification for use must rest on unverified assumptions.

Percentile norms for college freshmen, based upon 3,054 cases from nine different colleges, are presented for Form C. Form H norms are given for two levels, grades 7–9 and 10–12, based upon 5,425 and 5,793 cases, respectively. Colleges and school systems included in the norm sample are listed and seem to have a regional bias, but representative norms in the traditional geographical sense may not be important. Recent studies suggest that type of institution and college academic field may be related to study habits and attitudes; thus these factors should be explored further as normable variables.

The SSHA is easy to use and to score; directions are clear and complete. Each answer sheet includes a diagnostic profile, which can be filled in by the student. Instructions for completing this profile call for blackening subtest percentile bars as deviations from the median. A student can readily gain the impression that scores below the median are "low" and scores above are "high." No discussion is given about how large differences need to be, either between subscales or in comparison with the norm group, in order to be important.

In summary, the *Survey of Study Habits and Attitudes* has been carefully devised and has satisfactory reliability; there is statistical evidence for some of the least important aspects of validity. Its use as a predictor is unwarranted, and subscale scores should be interpreted with caution. Additional research is needed to justify its use as a screening or diagnostic instrument. Nonetheless, it is a good teaching aid for teachers and counselors—and useful to those students who are frank in responding and motivated to improve.

J Counsel Psychol 14:392–3 Jl '67. Martin J. Higgins. * All of the items scored for men and women in the original SSHA have been retained in the current revision, and the basic format of the inventory remains unchanged. It is therefore possible to obtain from the revised form scores which are comparable to the scores derived from the original form. Some of the original unscored items have been changed, and new items have been added which extend the length of the inventory from 75 to 100 items and, consequently, lengthen the time of administration. The 1965 revision also makes it possible to score four basic subscales that may prove especially useful in counseling. Another advantage of the new revision is that separate scoring procedures for men and women are no longer necessary and data from both sexes can be subjected to the same analytic procedures. The purposes of the SSHA are (*a*) to identify students whose study habits and attitudes are different from those of students who earn high grades, (*b*) to aid in understanding students with academic difficulties, and (*c*) to provide a basis for helping such students improve their study habits and attitudes and, thus, more fully realize their potentials. * Subscale intercorrela-

tions and weighted averages of correlations were obtained for nine college samples. The weighted averages of obtained intercorrelations range from .49 to .71. The highest correlations are found between the two study habits scales (DA versus WM = .70) and the two study attitude scales (TA versus EA = .69). It would appear that there is considerable overlap between subscales of the SSHA which will reduce the unique variance accounted for by the various scales. * the SSHA appears to have adequate validity and reliability and is feasible to administer and score. It may have considerable use as a counseling aid in high schools, junior colleges, and 4-year institutions. It provides a counseling key which identifies those areas where the performance of the client is most different from the performance of those students who typically obtain high scholastic averages. In trying to diagnose the nature of a student's academic difficulties the counselor may find it worthwhile to discuss the student's response to the items identified with the counseling key. In addition to its use as a counseling aid, it would appear that the SSHA would also be useful as a research tool and as a screening instrument. Although the SSHA has not really been validated as a screening instrument, its low correlation with typical measures of scholastic ability and moderate correlation with grade-point average may make it useful in screening applicants who are especially homogeneous in terms of their academic ability.

J Ed Meas 6(2):120–2 su '69. Albert E. Roark and Scott A. Harrington. * The SSHA is recommended for use as (*a*) screening instrument, (*b*) diagnostic instrument, (*c*) teaching aid, and (*d*) research tool. The reviewers feel that its utility in these areas is severely limited because the SSHA is not a test in the usual sense, but a self-report instrument and has all the inherent weaknesses of this type of measure. A major weakness of the SSHA is that scores can be manipulated by the student at will. This point is mentioned in the manual as a limitation regarding its use as a selection tool, but is not stressed sufficiently with respect to the other suggested areas of use. Its use as a screening instrument is limited to the detection of students who may need counseling on study habits and attitudes. As a diagnostic instrument, giving proper consideration to its self-report limitations, the various scores and the counseling key may provide useful data. The manual

Survey of Study Habits and Attitudes

does not show how to use the SSHA as a teaching aid or provide empirical support of its usefulness. The usefulness of the SSHA as a research tool is severely limited by its susceptibility to faked scores. Nevertheless, the SSHA has demonstrated a suitable level of reliability, and predictive relationship with G.P.A., to warrant its inclusion in research studies where the above mentioned limitations are recognized and minimized. * A counseling key is provided which identifies responses different from the characteristic responses of high scholastic achievers. It is recommended that the counselor discuss all these responses with the student. It does not seem that the mechanistic approach recommended would be acceptable to most professional counselors. Also, it is difficult to assess how much the counseling key would add to the effectiveness of a "skillful" counselor, aside from serving as a possible point of departure. No studies are cited which demonstrate academic improvement as a result of using the counseling key in counseling. The diagnostic profile helps present a clear, meaningful picture of the scores to the student, although the suggestion that the profile should not be given to the student is not explained. * Test-retest reliabilities calculated after 4- and 14-week intervals vary from .83 to .94 which appear satisfactory, although complete data (mean and standard deviation) are not reported on the 14-week study. A period longer than fourteen weeks is desirable in deriving a test-retest reliability coefficient for the uses advocated. It would have been beneficial to also have the standard error of measurement presented, particularly in light of the predictive claims made for the instrument and suggested applications in assessing change in study habits and attitudes after counseling. * In general, Form C of the SSHA is a considerable improvement over the earlier edition. The main improvement results from making one set of norms applicable to both sexes. Also, the division of the survey into subscales should prove helpful in diagnosis of study problems. The manual is still too ambitious in the uses recommended for the SSHA and does not stress sufficiently that the instrument's validity depends on frank and accurate responses. The comments in reviews of the earlier edition, except those on norms and diagnosis, are still applicable to Form C. The SSHA is a well constructed instrument and within the limitations mentioned in the review may be of considerable

value in working with college bound high school seniors and college freshmen.

For reviews by James Deese and C. Gilbert Wrenn (with Roy D. Lewis) of the original edition, see 5:688.

[783]
Watson-Glaser Critical Thinking Appraisal. Grades 9–16 and adults; 1942–64; WGCTA; formerly called *Watson-Glaser Tests of Critical Thinking;* Forms YM, ZM, ('64, c1951–61, 8 pages); manual ('64, 16 pages); separate answer sheets (Digitek, IBM 805, IBM 1230) must be used; $10 per 35 tests; $2.30 per 35 IBM 805 answer sheets; $2.80 per 35 Digitek or IBM 1230 answer sheets; 70¢ per IBM scoring stencil; Digitek scoring stencils not available; $2 per specimen set; postage extra; IBM scoring service, 19¢ and over per test; (50–60) minutes; Goodwin Watson and Edward M. Glaser; Harcourt Brace Jovanovich, Inc. *

REFERENCES

1–3. See 3:544.
4–11. See 5:700.
12–35. See 6:867.
36. BECKMAN, VERNON EARL. *An Investigation and Analysis of the Contributions to Critical Thinking Made by Courses in Argumentation and Discussion in Selected Colleges.* Doctor's thesis, University of Minnesota (Minneapolis, Minn.), 1956. (*DA* 16:2551)
37. KENOYER, MARIE FRANCIS. *The Influence of Religious Life on Three Levels of Perceptual Processes.* Doctor's thesis, Fordham University (New York, N.Y.), 1961. (*DA* 22:909)
38. SKELLY, CLYDE G. *Some Variables Which Differentiate the Highly Intelligent and Highly Divergent Thinking Adolescent.* Doctor's thesis, University of Connecticut (Storrs, Conn.), 1961. (*DA* 22:2699)
39. COUSINS, JACK EUGENE. *The Development of Reflective Thinking in an Eighth Grade Social Studies Class.* Doctor's thesis, Indiana University (Bloomington, Ind.), 1962. (*DA* 24:195)
40. HAAS, MARY GERALDINE. *A Comparative Study of Critical Thinking, Flexibility of Thinking, and Reading Ability Involving Religious and Lay College Seniors.* Doctor's thesis, Fordham University (New York, N.Y.), 1963. (*DA* 24:622)
41. LAND, MELVIN. "Psychological Tests as Predictors for Scholastic Achievement of Dental Students." *J Dental Ed* 27: 25–30 Mr '63. *
42. LYSAUGHT, JEROME P. "An Analysis of Factors Related to Success in Constructing Programed Learning Sequences." *J Programed Instr* 2:35–42 f '63. * (*PA* 38:10415)
43. GLIDDEN, GEORGE WAYNE. *Factors That Influence Achievement in Senior High School American History.* Doctor's thesis, University of Nebraska (Lincoln, Neb.), 1964. (*DA* 25:3429)
44. LYSAUGHT, JEROME P., AND PIERLEONI, ROBERT G. "A Comparison of Predicted and Actual Success in Auto-Instructional Programing." *J Programed Instr* 3(4):14–23 '64. *
45. LYSAUGHT, JEROME PAUL. *An Analysis of Factors Related to Success in Constructing Programmed Learning Sequences.* Doctor's thesis, University of Rochester (Rochester, N.Y.), 1964. (*DA* 25:1749)
46. SNIDER, JAMES GRANT. *Some Correlates of All-Inclusive Conceptualization in High School Pupils.* Doctor's thesis, Stanford University (Stanford, Calif.), 1964. (*DA* 25:4005)
47. BRAKKEN, EARL. "Intellectual Factors in PSSC and Conventional High School Physics." *J Res Sci Teach* 3(1):19–25 '65. *
48. GECKLER, JACK WILLIAM. *Critical Thinking, Dogmatism, Social Status, and Religious Affiliation of Tenth-Grade Students.* Doctor's thesis, University of Tennessee (Knoxville, Tenn.), 1965. (*DA* 26:886)
49. SEYMOUR, PAUL JOHN. *A Study of the Relationships Between the Communication Skills and a Selected Set of Predictors and of the Relationships Among the Communication Skills.* Doctor's thesis, University of Minnesota (Minneapolis, Minn.), 1965. (*DA* 26:549)
50. SMITH, ROBERT GOUGH. *An Evaluation of Selected Aspects of a Teacher Education Admissions Program.* Doctor's thesis, North Texas State University (Denton, Tex.), 1965. (*DA* 26:3771)
51. DIRR, PIERRE MARIE. *Intellectual Variables in Achievement in Modern Algebra.* Doctor's thesis, Catholic University of America (Washington, D.C.), 1966. (*DA* 27:2873A)
52. FLORA, LARRY DALE. *Predicting Academic Success at Lynchburg College From Multiple Correlational Analysis of Four Selected Predictor Variables.* Doctor's thesis, University

of Virginia (Charlottesville, Va.), 1966. (*DA* 27:2276A) (Abstract: *Ed R* 4:53–5)

53. JENKINS, ALICE CRAWFORD. *The Relationship of Certain Measurable Factors to Academic Success in Freshman Biology.* Doctor's thesis, New York University (New York, N.Y.), 1966. (*DA* 27:2279A)

54. OWENS, THOMAS R., AND ROADEN, ARLISS L. "Predicting Academic Success in Master's Degree Programs in Education." *J Ed Res* 60:124–6 N '66. *

55. FRANK, ALLAN DANIEL. *An Experimental Study in Improving the Critical Thinking Ability of High School Students Enrolled in a Beginning Speech Course.* Doctor's thesis, University of Wisconsin (Madison, Wisc.), 1967. (*DA* 28:5168A)

56. HELM, CHRISTOPHER R. *Watson-Glaser–DAT Graduate Norms.* Master's thesis, University of Toledo (Toledo, Ohio), 1967.

57. HUNT, EDITH JOAN. *The Critical Thinking Ability of Teachers and Its Relationship to the Teachers' Classroom Verbal Behavior and Perceptions of Teaching Purposes.* Doctor's thesis, University of Maryland (College Park, Md.), 1967. (*DA* 28:4511A)

58. MOSKOVIS, LEFTERIE MICHAEL. *An Identification of Certain Similarities and Differences Between Successful and Unsuccessful College Level Beginning Shorthand Students and Transcription Students.* Doctor's thesis, Michigan State University (East Lansing, Mich.), 1967. (*DA* 28:4826A)

59. NESS, JOHN HJORT. *The Effects of a Beginning Speech Course on Critical Thinking Ability.* Doctor's thesis, University of Minnesota (Minneapolis, Minn.), 1967. (*DA* 28:5171A)

60. SHATIN, LEO, AND OPDYKE, DAVID. "A Critical Thinking Appraisal and Its Correlates." *J Med Ed* 42:789–92 Ag '67. *

61. SINGER, ESTELLE, AND ROBY, THORNTON B. "Dimensions of Decision-Making Behavior." *Percept & Motor Skills* 24:571–95 Ap '67. * (*PA* 41:9933)

62. TRELA, THADDEUS M. "Comparing Achievement on Tests of General and Critical Reading." *J Read Specialist* 6:140–2 My '67. * (*PA* 41:14190)

63. WELSCH, LAWRENCE A. *The Supervisor's Employee Appraisal Heuristic: The Contribution of Selected Measures of Enployee Aptitude, Intelligence and Personality.* Doctor's thesis, University of Pittsburgh (Pittsburgh, Pa.), 1967. (*DA* 28:4321A)

64. WESTBROOK, BERT W., AND SELLERS, JAMES R. "Critical Thinking, Intelligence, and Vocabulary." *Ed & Psychol Meas* 27:443–6 su '67. * (*PA* 41:13634)

65. BRADBERRY, RONALD DAVID. *Relationships Among Critical Thinking Ability, Personality Attributes, and Attitudes of Students in a Teacher Education Program.* Doctor's thesis, North Texas State University (Denton, Tex.), 1968. (*DA* 29:163A)

66. BROUILLETTE, OSCAR JASON. *An Interdisciplinary Comparison of the Critical Thinking Objective Among Science and Non-Science Majors in Higher Education.* Doctor's thesis, University of Southern Mississippi (Hattiesburg, Miss.), 1968. (*DA* 29:2877A)

67. COMBS, CLYDE MAURICE, JR. *An Experiment With Independent Study in Science Education.* Doctor's thesis, University of Mississippi (University, Miss.), 1968. (*DA* 29:3489A)

68. CORELL, JOAN HELENE. *Comparison of Two Methods of Counseling With Academically Deteriorated University Upperclassmen.* Doctor's thesis, Indiana University (Bloomington, Ind.), 1968. (*DA* 29:1419A)

69. DENNEY, LOREN L. *The Relationships Between Teaching Method, Critical Thinking and Other Selected Teacher Traits.* Doctor's thesis, University of Missouri (Columbia, Mo.), 1968. (*DA* 29:2586A)

70. DUCKWORTH, JOSEPH BATTERSBY. *The Effect of Instruction in General Semantics on the Critical Thinking of Tenth and Eleventh Grade Students.* Doctor's thesis, Wayne State University (Detroit, Mich.), 1968. (*DA* 29:4180A)

71. GEORGE, KENNETH D. "The Effect of Critical-Thinking Ability Upon Course Grades in Biology." *Sci Ed* 52:421–6 D '68. *

72. GIBSON, JAMES W.; KIBLER, ROBERT J.; AND BARKER, LARRY L. "Some Relationships Between Selected Creativity and Critical Thinking Measures." *Psychol Rep* 23:707–14 D '68. * (*PA* 43:9748)

73. HARDESTY, D. L., AND JONES, W. S. "Characteristics of Judged High Potential Management Personnel—The Operations of an Industrial Assessment Center." *Personnel Psychol* 21:85–98 sp '68. * (*PA* 42:16197)

74. HENKEL, E. THOMAS. "Undergraduate Physics Instruction and Critical Thinking Ability." *J Res Sci Teach* 5(1):89–94 '68. *

75. HUNTER, NORMAN W. *A Study of Factors Which May Affect a Student's Success in Quantitative Analysis.* Doctor's thesis, University of Toledo (Toledo, Ohio), 1968. (*DA* 29:2437A)

76. WALTON, FRANCIS XAVIER. *An Investigation of Differences Between More Effective and Less Effective Counselors With Regard to Selected Variables.* Doctor's thesis, University of South Carolina (Columbia, S.C.), 1968. (*DA* 29:3844A)

77. YAGER, ROBERT E. "Critical Thinking and Reference Materials in the Physical Science Classroom." *Sch Sci & Math* 68:743–6 N '68. *

78. ALSTON, DORIS NEWSOME. *An Investigation of the Criti-*

cal Reading Ability of Classroom Teachers in Relation to Selected Background Factors. Doctor's thesis, Florida State University (Tallahassee, Fla.), 1969. (*DAI* 31:1106A)

79. BOSTROM, EDWIN ALBERT. *The Effect of Class Size on Critical Thinking Skills.* Doctor's thesis, Arizona State University (Tempe, Ariz.), 1969. (*DA* 29:2032A)

80. BRAUN, JOHN R. "Search for Correlates of Self-Actualization." *Percept & Motor Skills* 28(2):557–8 Ap '69. * (*PA* 43:15764)

81. BROADHURST, NORMAN ARTHUR. *A Study of Selected Teacher Factors and Learning Outcomes in Chemistry in Secondary Schools in South Australia.* Doctor's thesis, Oregon State University (Corvallis, Ore.), 1969. (*DAI* 30:485A)

82. CARNES, DuWAYNE DOUGLAS. *A Study of the Critical Thinking Ability of Secondary Summer School Mathematics Students.* Doctor's thesis, University of Mississippi (University, Miss.), 1969. (*DAI* 30:2242A)

83. CHANG, EDWARD C. F. *Norms and Correlates of the Watson-Glaser Critical Thinking Appraisal and Selected Variables for Negro College Students.* Doctor's thesis, University of Oklahoma (Norman, Okla.), 1969. (*DAI* 30:1860A)

84. FOLLMAN, JOHN. "Factor Analysis of Three Critical Thinking Tests, One Logical Reasoning Test, and One English Test." *Yearb Nat Read Conf* 18:154–60 '69. *

85. FOLLMAN, JOHN; HERNANDEZ, DAVID; AND MILLER, WILLIAM. "Canonical Correlation of Scholastic Aptitude and Critical Thinking." *Psychol* 6(3):3–6 Ag '69. * (*PA* 44:2853)

86. FOLLMAN, JOHN; MILLER, WILLIAM; AND HERNANDEZ, DAVID. "Factor Analysis of Achievement, Scholastic Aptitude, and Critical Thinking Subtests." *J Exp Ed* 38(1):48–53 f '69. * (*PA* 45:10901)

87. FOLLMAN, JOHN COSGROVE. *A Factor Analytic Study of Three Critical Thinking Tests, One English Test, and One Logical Reasoning Test.* Doctor's thesis, Indiana University (Bloomington, Ind.), 1969. (*DAI* 30:1015A)

88. FRANK, ALLAN D. "Teaching High School Speech to Improve Critical-Thinking Ability." *Speech Teach* 18(4):296–302 N '69. *

89. JABS, MAX LEWIS. *An Experimental Study of the Comparative Effects of Initiating Structure and Consideration Leadership on the Educational Growth of College Students.* Doctor's thesis, University of Connecticut (Storrs, Conn.), 1969. (*DAI* 30:2762A)

90. LARTER, S. J., AND TAYLOR, P. A. "A Study of Aspects of Critical Thinking." *Manitoba J Ed* 5(1):35–53 N '69. *

91. SMITH, JOHN RAYMOND. *A Comparison of Two Methods of Conducting Introductory College Physics Laboratories.* Doctor's thesis, Colorado State College (Greeley, Colo.), 1969. (*DAI* 30:4159A)

92. TITUS, H. EDWIN. "Prediction of Supervisory Success by Use of Standard Psychological Tests." *J Psychol* 72(1):35–40 My '69. * (*PA* 43:16503)

93. TITUS, H. EDWIN, AND GOSS, RICHARD G. "Psychometric Comparison of Old and Young Supervisors." *Psychol Rep* 24(3):727–33 Je '69. * (*PA* 44:1447)

94. YOESTING, CLARENCE, AND RENNER, JOHN W. "Is Critical Thinking an Outcome of a College General Physical Science Course?" *Sch Sci & Math* 69(3):199–206 Mr '69. *

95. ALSPAUGH, CAROL ANN. *A Study of the Relationships Between Student Characteristics and Proficiency in Symbolic and Algebraic Computer Programming.* Doctor's thesis, University of Missouri (Columbia, Mo.), 1970. (*DAI* 31:4627B)

96. ARMSTRONG, NOLAN ANCEL. *The Effect of Two Instructional Inquiry Strategies on Critical Thinking and Achievement in Eighth Grade Social Studies.* Doctor's thesis, Indiana University (Bloomington, Ind.), 1970. (*DAI* 31:1611A)

97. BROADHURST, NORMAN A. "An Item Analysis of the Watson-Glaser Critical Thinking Appraisal (Form YM)." *Sci Ed* 54(2):127–32 Ap–Je '70. *

98. CARLETON, FREDERICK O. "Relationships Between Follow-Up Evaluations and Information Developed in a Management Assessment Center." Abstract. *Proc 78th Ann Conv Am Psychol Assn* 5(2):565–6 '70. * (*PA* 44:19655)

99. DE MARTINO, HUGO A. *The Relations Between Certain Motivational Variables and Attitudes About Mental Illness in Student Psychiatric Nurses.* Doctor's thesis, St. John's University (Jamaica, N.Y.), 1970. (*DAI* 31:3036A)

100. FOLLMAN, JOHN. "Correlational and Factor Analysis of Critical Thinking, Logical Reasoning, and English Total Test Scores." *Fla J Ed Res* 12(1):91–4 Ja '70. *

101. FOLLMAN, JOHN; BROWN, LAURENCE; AND BURG, ELDON. "Factor Analysis of Critical Thinking, Logical Reasoning, and English Subtests." *J Exp Ed* 38(4):11–6 su '70. *

102. KIRTLEY, DONALD, AND HARKLESS, RICHARD. "Student Political Activity in Relation to Personal and Social Adjustment." *J Psychol* 75(2):253–6 Jl '70. * (*PA* 44:20780)

103. LUCK, JAMES I., AND GRUNER, CHARLES R. "Note on Authoritarianism and Critical Thinking Ability." *Psychol Rep* 27(2):380 O '70. * (*PA* 45:6954)

104. LYSAUGHT, JEROME P., AND PIERLEONI, ROBERT G. "Predicting Individual Success in Programing Self-Instructional Materials." *AV Commun R* 18(1):5–24 sp '70. * (*PA* 44:13334)

105. MILLER, WILLIAM; FOLLMAN, JOHN; AND HERNANDEZ, DAVID E. "Discriminant Analysis of School Children in Inte-

grated and Non-Integrated Schools Using Tests of Critical Thinking." *Fla J Ed Res* 12(1):63–8 Ja '70. *
106. MOSKOVIS, L. MICHAEL. "Similarities and Differences of College-Level Successful and Unsuccessful Shorthand Students." *Delta Pi Epsilon J* 12(2):12–6 F '70. *
107. PIERLEONI, ROBERT G., AND LYSAUGHT, JEROME P. "A Decision Ladder for Predicting Programmer Success." *NSPI J* 9(5):6–7+ Je '70. *
108. TROXEL, VERNE A., AND SNIDER, C. F. BILL. "Correlations Among Student Outcomes on the Test of Understanding Science, Watson-Glaser Critical Thinking Appraisal, and the American Chemical Society Cooperative Examination—General Chemistry." *Sch Sci & Math* 70(1):73–6 Ja '70. *
109. WEVRICK, L. "Evaluation of the Personnel Test Battery," pp. 1–5. In *Applied Research in Public Personnel Administration.* By L. Wevrick and others. Personnel Report No. 702. Chicago, Ill.: Public Personnel Association, 1970. Pp. 29. *

J Counsel Psychol 12:328–30 f '65. John O. Crites. * The authors....do not endorse the use of part-scores because of their low reliability, but they do state that they can be utilized "to analyze the critical thinking abilities of a class or larger group and to determine in the light of such analysis the types of critical thinking most needed by the group" (Manual, p. 9). How such an analysis might be carried out was not indicated; consequently, conservative practice in both counseling and research would suggest using only the total score, at least until more is known about the psychometric characteristics of the part-scores. * Percentiles are given for each grade (9–12) and for the combined grades, but *not* separately for sex. Since males and females typically differ on ability measures, this lack of sex data for the test is definitely a shortcoming of the norms. It should also be noted that caution should be exercised in using the combined grades percentiles, since an inspection of the raw scores across grades reveals that they tend to be higher at the upper levels. The norms for the college and employed groups are less extensive and complete than those for the grades, and probably should be supplemented with local norms, as the test authors suggest. * The two new forms of the Watson-Glaser, YM and ZM, are supposedly equivalent, but they differ as much as six raw score points at the same percentile, particularly in the middle of the distribution. * There appears to be insufficient range on the test, however, for college students, particularly those in their last year. For a group of 200 female college seniors the lowest raw score was 37 and the highest was 97, with a mean = 74.4 and a S.D. = 9.6. These data raise a question about whether the Watson-Glaser is appropriate for use at the higher educational levels, as the Manual implies. For the lower grades it seems to be sufficiently internally consistent to use with individuals, but it would be highly desirable to know what the

test-retest coefficients for the test are, especially since scores appear to change as individuals grow older. * The only statement made in the Manual (p. 15) about the test's *predictive* validity is that: "The *Critical Thinking Appraisal* is a potentially useful instrument for predicting performance in situations involving critical thinking." In other words, there are no data on the usefulness of the Watson-Glaser in predicting future behavior. CONCLUSIONS. The Watson-Glaser represents an approach to the measurement of ability which is novel, as far as item content and format are concerned, and it is a laudable approach. It is also one which data on the test justify as empirically useful. The test appears to measure not only general intelligence but also certain logical reasoning abilities. Some questions can be raised about the scoring key and the applicability of the test at the higher educational levels, but in general it seems to be quite adequate for the appraisal of critical thinking at the secondary school level and possibly the freshman year of college. Little is known about its stability over time and its usefulness in prediction, but its internal consistency is high and its concurrent validity is acceptable. If a more difficult form could be devised for the selection of graduate students, it might be very valuable as a measure of those critical and logical abilities which are so important in counseling and research activities.

J Ed Meas 2:254–6 D '65. G. C. Helmstadter. * this instrument could provide an excellent criterion measure for those who claim their instruction results in the "ability to think" rather than simply the acquisition of subject matter * The directions in the manual for administering the test and for scoring and obtaining derived scores are given clearly enough for any conscientious person to use. And, in general, the test seems to be an excellent one when judged with respect to the practical criteria of the importance of the trait measured and the feasibility of using the instrument. Similarly, when judged against the technical criteria of standardization, reliability and validity, this critical thinking appraisal seems to be an instrument well worth attempting to use in a wide variety of educational assessment, selection and research situations. * the test has been carefully standardized * While some users might welcome a wider variety of normative groups, especially among the college and adult populations, all should be thankful that the groups used for

obtaining norms have been clearly enough described (both verbally and in terms of scores
on the Otis Gamma Test) to prevent misun-
derstandings of score interpretation. * it does
seem strange that when two forms of a test are
available and an equivalent raw score table is
presented, no correlation between the two forms
is given. Interestingly, an examination of both
the median item discrimination indexes and the
reliabilities for the various subtests suggests that
form YM is likely to be slightly superior to
form ZM. * To a far greater extent than is
true of any other published test of which this
reviewer is aware, the behaviors measured are
spelled out clearly and specifically, thus eliminating many of the ambiguities that usually
exist when attempting to determine whether a
measure is appropriate for a particular use. Unfortunately, no predictive validity coefficients
are reported. While it is true, as the manual
points out, that "the predictive validity of this
test, as of any other test or selective device,
tends to be unique and must be established
empirically in each situation where the test is to
be used," it is always helpful to the prospective
buyer to know whether a test has been useful as
a predictor in situations similar to his. * In summary, the Watson-Glaser Critical Thinking Appraisal represents a highly professional attempt
to measure an important characteristic. And,
while there may be some flaws in the test, it is
doubtful whether a significantly better measure
will be found until there is a major breakthrough
either in test technology or in our understanding of the "thinking" process. Similarly, while
some additional information about a test is always helpful, if all publishers were as cautious
in their verbal claims, as precise in their test
description, and as inclusive with respect to
crucial data, there would be no ethical problem
in the publishing of tests.

*For reviews by Walker H. Hill and Carl I.
Hovland of an earlier edition, see 5:700; for a
review by Robert H. Thouless, see 3:544 (1
excerpt).*

[Other Test]
For another test new since *The Sixth Mental Measurements Yearbook,* see the following in *Reading Tests
and Reviews:*

244.1. ★Study Habits Checklist

TIP II SCANNING INDEX

This classified index of all tests in *Tests in Print II* can be used to determine what tests are available in areas besides reading. Citations are to test entry numbers in TIP II. The population for which a test is intended is included. Stars indicate tests not previously listed in an MMY; asterisks indicate tests revised or supplemented since last listed. The reading portion of this index, the only part relevant to this monograph, is repeated at the end of this volume.

ACHIEVEMENT BATTERIES

Academic Proficiency Battery [South Africa], college entrants, see 1

Adult Basic Education Student Survey, poorly educated adults in basic education classes, see 2

Adult Basic Learning Examination, adults with achievement levels grades 1–12, see 3

American School Achievement Tests, grades 1–9, see 4

Bristol Achievement Tests [England], ages 8–13, see 5

*CLEP General Examinations: Humanities, 1–2 years of college or equivalent, see 6

*California Achievement Tests, grades 1–14, see 7

Canadian Tests of Basic Skills [Canada], grades 3–8, see 8

Classification and Placement Examination, grade 8 and high school entrants, see 9

*College-Level Examination Program General Examinations, 1–2 years of college or equivalent, see 10

*Comprehensive Tests of Basic Skills, grades kgn–12, see 11

Cooperative Primary Tests, grades 1.5–3, see 12

★*Educational Skills Tests: College Edition*, open-door college entrants, see 13

General Tests of Language and Arithmetic [South Africa], standards 5–7, see 14

Gray-Votaw-Rogers General Achievement Tests, grades 1–9, see 15

★*Guidance Test for Junior Secondary Bantu Pupils in Form 3* [South Africa], see 16

High School Fundamentals Evaluation Test, grades 9–12, see 17

Iowa High School Content Examination, grades 11–13, see 18

*Iowa Tests of Basic Skills, grades 1.7–9, see 19

*Iowa Tests of Educational Development, grades 9–12, see 20

Ligondé Equivalence Test [Canada], adults who left elementary or secondary school 15–20 years ago, see 21

*Metropolitan Achievement Tests, grades kgn–9, see 22

National Achievement Tests, grades 4–9, see 23

*National Educational Development Tests, grades 7–10, see 24

*National Teacher Examinations: Common Examinations, college seniors and teachers, see 25

Peabody Individual Achievement Test, grades kgn–12, see 26

★*Primary Survey Tests*, grades 2–3, see 27

Public School Achievement Tests, grades 3–8, see 28

*SRA Achievement Series, grades 1–9, see 29

*SRA Assessment Survey, grades 1–12, see 30

*SRA High School Placement Test, grade 9 entrants, see 31

*STS Closed High School Placement Test, grade 9 entrants, see 32

*STS Educational Development Series, grades 2–12, see 33

*Scholastic Proficiency Battery [South Africa], standards 8–10, see 34

*Sequential Tests of Educational Progress, grades 4–14, see 35

*Stanford Achievement Test, grades 1.5–9, see 36

Stanford Achievement Test: High School Basic Battery, grades 9–12, see 37

*Stanford Early School Achievement Test, grades kgn–1.5, see 38

★*Stanford Test of Academic Skills*, grades 8–12 and first year junior/community college, see 39

Survey of College Achievement, grades 13–14, see 40

*Teacher Education Examination Program: General Professional Examinations, college seniors preparing to teach, see 41

*Test for High School Entrants, high school entrants, see 42

Test of Reading and Number: Inter-American Series, grade 4 entrants, see 43

*Tests of Academic Progress, grades 9–12, see 44

ENGLISH

LITERATURE

SPELLING

VOCABULARY

FINE ARTS

ART

MUSIC

FOREIGN LANGUAGES

ARABIC

CHINESE

ENGLISH

FRENCH

SPANISH

INTELLIGENCE

GROUP

INDIVIDUAL

SPECIFIC

MATHEMATICS

ALGEBRA

ARITHMETIC

CALCULUS

GEOMETRY

SPECIAL FIELDS

TRIGONOMETRY

MISCELLANEOUS

AGRICULTURE

BLIND

BUSINESS EDUCATION

COMPUTATIONAL & TESTING DEVICES

★*Bowman Chronological Age Calculator*, see 802
Bowman M.A. and I.Q. Kalculator, see 803
**Chronological Age Computer*, ages 3–7 to 19–5, see 804
Dominion Table for Converting Mental Age to I.Q. [Canada], see 805
Grade Averaging Charts, see 806
I.Q. Calculator, see 807
★*Mental Age Calculator*, see 808
**Multiple Purpose Self Trainer*, high school and adults, see 809
Psychometric Research and Service Chart Showing the Davis Difficulty and Discrimination Indices for Item Analysis [India], see 810
Rapid-Rater, see 811
★*Ratio I.Q. Computer*, see 812

COURTSHIP & MARRIAGE

★*Albert Mate Selection Check List*, premarital counselees, see 813
California Marriage Readiness Evaluation, premarital counselees, see 814
Caring Relationship Inventory, marital counselees, see 815
Courtship Analysis, adults, see 816
Dating Problems Checklist, high school and college, see 817
El Senoussi Multiphasic Marital Inventory, premarital and marital counselees, see 818
★*I-Am Sentence Completion Test*, marital counselees, see 819
Individual and Family Developmental Review, counselees and therapy patients, see 820
★*Love Attitudes Inventory*, grades 12–16, see 821
Male Impotence Test, adult males, see 822
Marital Communication Inventory, adults, see 823
★*Marital Diagnostic Inventory*, marital counselees, see 824
Marital Roles Inventory, marital counselees, see 825
Marriage Adjustment Form, adults, see 826
Marriage Adjustment Inventory, marital counselees, see 827
Marriage Adjustment Sentence Completion Survey, marital counselees, see 828
Marriage Analysis, married couples in counseling, see 829
★*Marriage Expectation Inventories*, engaged and married couples, see 830
Marriage-Personality Inventory, individuals and couples, see 831
Marriage Prediction Schedule, adults, see 832
Marriage Role Expectation Inventory, adolescents and adults, see 833
**Marriage Scale (For Measuring Compatibility of Interests)*, premarital or married counselees, see 834
★*Marriage Skills Analysis*, marital counselees, see 835
Otto Pre-Marital Counseling Schedules, adult couples, see 836
★*Pair Attraction Inventory*, college and adults, see 837
Sex Knowledge Inventory, sex education classes in high school and college and adults, see 838
Sexual Development Scale for Females, adult females, see 839
**Taylor-Johnson Temperament Analysis*, grades 7–16 and adults, see 840
Thorman Family Relations Conference Situation Questionnaire, families receiving therapy, see 841

DRIVING & SAFETY EDUCATION

**American Automobile Association Driver Testing Apparatus*, drivers, see 842
**Bicycle Safety—Performance and Skill Tests*, ages 10–16, see 843
Driver Attitude Survey, drivers, see 844
★*Driving Skill Exercises*, automobile drivers, see 845
General Test on Traffic and Driving Knowledge, drivers, see 846
Hannaford Industrial Safety Attitude Scales, industry, see 847
McGlade Road Test for Use in Driver Licensing, Education and Employment, prospective drivers, see 848
Road Test Check List for Passenger Car Drivers, passenger car drivers, see 849
Siebrecht Attitude Scale, grades 9–16 and adults, see 850
★*Simplified Road Test*, drivers, see 851

EDUCATION

Academic Freedom Survey, college students and faculty, see 852
**CLEP Subject Examination in History of American Education*, 1 semester or equivalent, see 853
**CLEP Subject Examination in Tests and Measurements*, 1 semester or equivalent, see 854
★*Classroom Atmosphere Questionnaire*, grades 4–9, see 855
★*Comprehensive Teaching and Training Evaluation*, college and training programs, see 856
★*Counseling Services Assessment Blank*, college and adult counseling clients, see 857
**Course Evaluation Questionnaire*, high school and college, see 858
Diagnostic Teacher-Rating Scale, grades 4–12, see 859
★*Educational Values Assessment Questionnaire*, adults, see 860
Faculty Morale Scale for Institutional Improvement, college faculty, see 861
★*General Tests of Language and Arithmetic for Students* [South Africa], first and second year Bantu candidates for primary teacher's certificate, see 862
**Graduate Record Examinations Advanced Education Test*, graduate school candidates, see 863
**Illinois Course Evaluation Questionnaire*, college, see 864
Illinois Ratings of Teacher Effectiveness, grades 9–12, see 865
Illinois Teacher Evaluation Questionnaire, grades 7–12, see 866
**Junior Index of Motivation*, grades 7–12, see 867
Minnesota Teacher Attitude Inventory, elementary and secondary school teachers and students in grades 12–17, see 868
**National Teacher Examinations*, college seniors and teachers, see 869
**National Teacher Examinations: Early Childhood Education*, college seniors and teachers, see 870
**National Teacher Examinations: Education in an Urban Setting*, college seniors and teachers, see 871
**National Teacher Examinations: Education in the Elementary School*, college seniors and teachers, see 872
**National Teacher Examinations: Education of Mentally Retarded*, college seniors and teachers, see 873
★*National Teacher Examinations: Educational Administration and Supervision*, prospective principals, see 874
★*National Teacher Examinations: Guidance Counselor*, prospective guidance counselors, see 875

HANDWRITING

HEALTH & PHYSICAL EDUCATION

HOME ECONOMICS

RELIGIOUS EDUCATION

Achievement Test in Jewish History, junior high school, see 1020

★*Achievement Test—Jewish Life and Observances,* grades 5–7, see 1021

★*Achievement Test—The State of Israel,* "pupils who have completed an organized course of study on the State of Israel," see 1022

★*Bible and You,* ages 13 and over, see 1023

★*Biblical Survey Test,* college, see 1024

Concordia Bible Information Inventory, grades 4–8, see 1025

Inventory of Religious Activities and Interests, high school and college students considering church-related occupations and theological school students, see 1025A

Religious Attitudes Inventory, religious counselees, see 1026

Standardized Bible Content Tests, Bible college, see 1027

Theological School Inventory, incoming seminary students, see 1028

Youth Research Survey, ages 13–19, see 1029

SCORING MACHINES & SERVICES

Automata EDT 1200 Educational Data Terminal, see 1030

Hankes Scoring Service, see 1031

IBM 1230 Optical Mark Scoring Reader, see 1032

★*IBM 3881 Optical Mark Reader,* see 1033

MRC Scoring and Reporting Services, see 1034

NCS Scoring and Reporting Services, see 1035

NCS Sentry 70, see 1036

OpScan Test Scoring and Document Scanning System, see 1037

Psychological Resources, see 1038

SOCIOECONOMIC STATUS

American Home Scale, grades 8–16, see 1039

Environmental Participation Index, culturally disadvantaged ages 12 and over, see 1040

Home Index, grades 4–12, see 1040A

Socio-Economic Status Scales [India], urban students, adults, and rural families, see 1041

STATISTICS

CLEP Subject Examination in Statistics, 1 semester or equivalent, see 1042

★*Objective Tests in Mathematics: Statistics* [England], ages 15 and over, see 1043

TEST PROGRAMS

ACT Assessment, candidates for college entrance, see 1044

Advanced Placement Examinations, high school students desiring credit for college level courses or admission to advanced courses, see 1045

Canadian Test Battery, Grade 10 [Canada], see 1046

Canadian Test Battery, Grades 8–9 [Canada], grades 8.5–9.0, see 1047

College Board Admissions Testing Program, candidates for college entrance, see 1048

★*College Guidance Program,* grade 11, see 1049

College-Level Examination Program, 1–2 years of college or equivalent, see 1050

College Placement Tests, entering college freshmen, see 1051

Comparative Guidance and Placement Program, entrants to two-year colleges and vocational-technical institutes, see 1052

Graduate Record Examinations: National Program for Graduate School Selection, graduate school candidates, see 1053

Junior College Placement Program, junior college entrants, see 1054

National Guidance Testing Program, grades 1.5–14, see 1055

National Science Foundation Graduate Fellowship Testing Program, applicants for N.S.F. fellowships for graduate study in the sciences, see 1056

★*Ohio Survey Tests,* grades 4, 6, 8, and 10, see 1057

Project Talent Test Battery, grades 9–12, see 1058

Secondary School Admission Test, grades 5–10, see 1059

★*Service for Admission to College and University Testing Program* [Canada], candidates for college entrance, see 1060

★*Testing Academic Achievement,* high school students desiring credit for college level courses or advanced placement, entering college freshmen, and 1–2 years of college or equivalent, see 1061

Undergraduate Program for Counseling and Evaluation, college, see 1062

MULTI-APTITUDE BATTERIES

Academic Promise Tests, grades 6–9, see 1063

★*Academic-Technical Aptitude Tests* [South Africa], "coloured pupils" in standards 6–8, see 1064

★*Aptitude Test for Junior Secondary Pupils* [South Africa], Bantus in Form I, see 1065

Aptitude Tests for Occupations, grades 9–13 and adults, see 1066

★*Armed Services Vocational Aptitude Battery,* high school, see 1067

Detroit General Aptitudes Examination, grades 6–12, see 1068

Differential Aptitude Tests, grades 8–12 and adults, see 1069

Differential Test Battery [England], ages 7 to "top university level," see 1070

Employee Aptitude Survey, ages 16 and over, see 1071

Flanagan Aptitude Classification Tests, grades 9–12 and adults, see 1072

General Aptitude Test Battery, grades 9–12 and adults, see 1073

Guilford-Zimmerman Aptitude Survey, grades 9–16 and adults, see 1074

High Level Battery: Test A/75 [South Africa], adults with at least 12 years of education, see 1075

★*International Primary Factors Test Battery,* grades 5 and over, see 1076

Jastak Test of Potential Ability and Behavior Stability, ages 11.5–14.5, see 1077

Job-Tests Program, adults, see 1078

★*Junior Aptitude Tests for Indian South Africans* [South Africa], standards 6–8, see 1079

Measurement of Skill, adults, see 1080

PERSONALITY

NONPROJECTIVE

PROJECTIVE

Social Relations Test [South Africa], adult males, see 1509

Sound-Apperception Test, ages 16 and over, see 1510

South African Picture Analysis Test [The Netherlands], ages 5–13, see 1511

Structured Doll Play Test, ages 2–6, see 1512

Structured-Objective Rorschach Test, adults, see 1513

Symbol Elaboration Test, ages 6 and over, see 1514

Symonds Picture-Story Test, grades 7–12, see 1515

Szondi Test [Switzerland], ages 5 and over, see 1516

*Tasks of Emotional Development Test, ages 6–11 and adolescents, see 1517

Test of Family Attitudes [Belgium], ages 6–12, see 1518

Thematic Apperception Test, ages 4 and over, see 1519

Thematic Apperception Test for African Subjects [South Africa], ages 10 and over, see 1520

★This I Believe Test, grades 9 and over, see 1521

Tomkins-Horn Picture Arrangement Test, ages 10 and over, see 1522

Toy World Test [France], ages 2 and over, see 1523

Tree Test [Switzerland], ages 9 and over, see 1524

Twitchell-Allen Three-Dimensional Personality Test, ages 3 and over (sighted and sightless), see 1525

Visual Apperception Test '60, ages 6 and over, see 1526

Washington University Sentence Completion Test, ages 12 and over, see 1527

Zulliger Individual and Group Test [Switzerland], ages 3 and over, see 1528

READING

A.C.E.R. Lower Grades Reading Test: Level 1 [Australia], grade 1, see 1529

★ACER Primary Reading Survey Tests [Australia], grades 3–6, see 1530

A.C.E.R. Silent Reading Tests: Standardized for Use in New Zealand [New Zealand], ages 9–12, see 1531

American School Achievement Tests: Reading, grades 2–9, see 1532

American School Reading Tests, grades 10–13, see 1533

Buffalo Reading Test for Speed and Comprehension, grades 9–16, see 1534

Burnett Reading Series: Survey Test, grades 1.5–12, see 1535

*California Achievement Tests: Reading, grades 1–14, see 1536

*Carver-Darby Chunked Reading Test, grades 9–16 and adults, see 1537

Commerce Reading Comprehension Test, grades 12–16 and adults, see 1538

Comprehension Test for Training College Students [England], training college students and applicants for admission, see 1539

Comprehensive Primary Reading Scales, grade 1, see 1540

Comprehensive Reading Scales, grades 4–12, see 1541

*Comprehensive Tests of Basic Skills: Reading, grades kgn–12, see 1542

Cooperative Primary Tests: Reading, grades 1.5–3, see 1543

Cooperative Reading Comprehension Test, Form Y [Australia], secondary forms 5–6 and university, see 1544

Cooperative Reading Comprehension Test, Forms L and M [Australia], secondary forms 2–4, see 1545

Davis Reading Test, grades 8–13, see 1546

Delaware County Silent Reading Test, grades 1.5–8, see 1547

★Edinburgh Reading Tests [England], ages 8.5–12.5, see 1548

Emporia Reading Tests, grades 1–8, see 1549

GAP Reading Comprehension Test [Australia], grades 2–7, see 1550

★GAPADOL [Australia], ages 10 and over, see 1551

*Gates-MacGinitie Reading Tests, grades 1–9, see 1552

Gates-MacGinitie Reading Tests: Survey F, grades 10–12, see 1553

Group Reading Assessment [England], end of first year junior school, see 1554

Group Reading Test [England], ages 6–10, see 1555

High School Reading Test: National Achievement Tests, grades 7–12, see 1556

Individual Reading Test [Australia], ages 6-0 to 9-9, see 1557

★Informal Reading Assessment Tests [Canada], grades 1–3, see 1558

★Inventory-Survey Tests, grades 4–8, see 1559

*Iowa Silent Reading Tests, grades 4–16, see 1560

Kelvin Measurement of Reading Ability [Scotland], ages 8–12, see 1561

Kingston Test of Silent Reading [England], ages 7–11, see 1562

Lee-Clark Reading Test, grades 1–2, see 1563

McGrath Test of Reading Skills, grades 1–13, see 1564

McMenemy Measure of Reading Ability, grades 3 and 5–8, see 1565

Maintaining Reading Efficiency Tests, grades 7–16 and adults, see 1566

*Metropolitan Achievement Tests: Reading Tests, grades 2–9, see 1567

Minnesota Reading Examination for College Students, grades 9–16, see 1568

Monroe's Standardized Silent Reading Test, grades 3–12, see 1569

N.B. Silent Reading Tests (Beginners): Reading Comprehension Test [South Africa], substandard B, see 1570

*National Teacher Examinations: Reading Specialist, college seniors and teachers, see 1571

Nelson-Denny Reading Test, grades 9–16 and adults, see 1572

Nelson Reading Test, grades 3–9, see 1573

New Developmental Reading Tests, grades 1–6, see 1574

OISE Achievement Tests in Silent Reading: Advanced Primary Battery [Canada], grade 2, see 1575

Pressey Diagnostic Reading Tests, grades 3–9, see 1576

★Primary Reading Survey Tests, grades 2–3, see 1577

Primary Reading Test: Acorn Achievement Tests, grades 2–3, see 1578

Progressive Achievement Tests of Reading [New Zealand], standards 2–4 and Forms I–IV (ages 8–14), see 1579

RBH Basic Reading and Word Test, disadvantaged adults, see 1580

RBH Test of Reading Comprehension, business and industry, see 1581

*Reading Comprehension: Canadian English Achievement Test [Canada], grades 8.5–9.0, see 1582

Reading Comprehension: Cooperative English Tests, grades 9–14, see 1583

Reading Comprehension Test, college entrants, see 1584

*Reading Comprehension Test DE [England], ages 10–12.5, see 1585

Reading Comprehension Test: National Achievemen*

DIAGNOSTIC

MISCELLANEOUS

ORAL

READINESS

SPECIAL FIELDS

★*Reading/Everyday Activities in Life,* high school and "adults at basic education levels," see 1744
Robinson-Hall Reading Tests, college, see 1745
SRA Reading Index, job applicants with poor educational backgrounds, see 1746
Understanding Communication (Verbal Comprehension), industrial employees at the skilled level or below, see 1747

SPEED

*Basic Reading Rate Scale, grades 3–12, see 1748
Minnesota Speed of Reading Test for College Students, grades 12–16, see 1749

STUDY SKILLS

Bristol Achievement Tests: Study Skills [England], ages 8–13, see 1750
College Adjustment and Study Skills Inventory, college, see 1751
*Comprehensive Tests of Basic Skills: Study Skills, grades 2.5–12, see 1752
★*Cornell Class-Reasoning Test,* grades 4–12, see 1753
★*Cornell Conditional-Reasoning Test,* grades 4–12, see 1754
Cornell Critical Thinking Test, grades 7–16, see 1755
★*Cornell Learning and Study Skills Inventory,* grades 7–16, see 1756
Evaluation Aptitude Test, candidates for college and graduate school entrance, see 1757

*Iowa Tests of Educational Development: Use of Sources of Information, grades 9–12, see 1758
Library Orientation Test for College Freshmen, grade 13, see 1759
★*Library Tests,* college, see 1760
Logical Reasoning, grades 9–16 and adults, see 1761
★*National Test of Library Skills,* grades 2–12, see 1762
Nationwide Library Skills Examination, grades 4–12, see 1763
OC Diagnostic Dictionary Test, grades 5–8, see 1764
SRA Achievement Series: Work-Study Skills, grades 4–9, see 1765
★*Study Attitudes and Methods Survey,* high school and college, see 1766
Study Habits Checklist, grades 9–14, see 1767
Study Habits Inventory, grades 12–16, see 1768
Study Performance Test, high school and college, see 1769
Study Skills Counseling Evaluation, high school and college, see 1770
Study Skills Test: McGraw-Hill Basic Skills System, grades 11–14, see 1771
Survey of Study Habits and Attitudes, grades 7–14, see 1772
Test on Use of the Dictionary, high school and college, see 1773
★*Uncritical Inference Test,* college, see 1774
Watson-Glaser Critical Thinking Appraisal, grades 9–16 and adults, see 1775
★*Wisconsin Tests of Reading Skill Development: Study Skills,* grades kgn–7, see 1776

SCIENCE

Adkins-McBride General Science Test, high school, see 1777
Borman-Sanders Elementary Science Test, grades 5–8, see 1778
*CLEP General Examinations: Natural Sciences, 1–2 years of college or equivalent, see 1779
Cooperative Science Tests: Advanced General Science, grades 8–9, see 1780
Cooperative Science Tests: General Science, grades 7–9, see 1781
Elementary Science Test: National Achievement Tests, grades 4–6, see 1782
Emporia General Science Test, 1–2 semesters high school, see 1783
★*General Science Test* [South Africa], matriculants and higher, see 1784
General Science Test: National Achievement Tests, grades 7–9, see 1785
General Science III: Achievement Examinations for Secondary Schools, high school, see 1786
*Iowa Tests of Educational Development: General Background in the Natural Sciences, grades 9–12, see 1787
*National Teacher Examinations: Biology and General Science, college seniors and teachers, see 1788
*National Teacher Examinations: Chemistry, Physics and General Science, college seniors and teachers, see 1789
SRA Achievement Series: Science, grades 4–9, see 1790
*Science: Minnesota High School Achievement Examinations, grades 7–9, see 1791
Science Tests: Content Evaluation Series, grades 8–9, see 1792

Scientific Knowledge and Aptitude Test [India], high school, see 1793
*Sequential Tests of Educational Progress: Science, grades 4–14, see 1794
Stanford Achievement Test: High School Science Test, grades 9–12, see 1795
Stanford Achievement Test: Science, grades 5.5–9.9, see 1796
*Teacher Education Examination Program: Biology and General Science, college seniors preparing to teach secondary school, see 1797
*Teacher Education Examination Program: Chemistry, Physics and General Science, college seniors preparing to teach secondary school, see 1798
Tests of Academic Progress: Science, grades 9–12, see 1799

BIOLOGY

*Advanced Placement Examination in Biology, high school students desiring credit for college level courses or admission to advanced courses, see 1800
*BSCS Achievement Tests, grade 10, see 1801
*Biological Science: Interaction of Experiments and Ideas, grades 10–12, see 1802
*Biology: Minnesota High School Achievement Examinations, high school, see 1803
*CLEP Subject Examination in Biology, 1 year or equivalent, see 1804
*College Board Achievement Test in Biology, candidates for college entrance, see 1805
*College Placement Test in Biology, entering college freshmen, see 1806

CHEMISTRY

GEOLOGY

MISCELLANEOUS

PHYSICS

SENSORY-MOTOR

D-K Scale of Lateral Dominance, grades 2–6, see 1874
Developmental Test of Visual-Motor Integration, ages 2–15, see 1875
★Frostig Movement Skills Test Battery, ages 6–12, see 1876
Harris Tests of Lateral Dominance, ages 7 and over, see 1877
*Leavell Hand-Eye Coordinator Tests, ages 8–14, see 1878
MKM Picture Arrangement Test, grades kgn–6, see 1879
*Moore Eye-Hand Coordination and Color-Matching Test, ages 2 and over, see 1880
Perceptual Forms Test, ages 5–8, see 1881
Primary Visual Motor Test, ages 4–8, see 1882
Purdue Perceptual-Motor Survey, ages 6–10, see 1883
★Rosner Perceptual Survey, ages 5–12, see 1884
Southern California Kinesthesia and Tactile Perception Tests, ages 4–8, see 1885
Southern California Perceptual-Motor Tests, ages 4–8, see 1886
*Southern California Sensory Integration Tests, ages 4–10 with learning problems, see 1887
★Spatial Orientation Memory Test, ages 5–8, see 1888
★Symbol Digit Modalities Test, ages 8 and over, see 1889
Trankell's Laterality Tests [Sweden], left-handed children in grades 1–2, see 1890
★Wold Digit-Symbol Test, ages 6–16, see 1891
★Wold Sentence Copying Test, grades 2–8, see 1892
★Wold Visuo-Motor Test, ages 6–16, see 1893

MOTOR

★Devereux Test of Extremity Coordination, emotionally handicapped and neurologically impaired ages 4–10, see 1894
Lincoln-Oseretsky Motor Development Scale, ages 6–14, see 1895
★Manual Accuracy and Speed Test, ages 4 and over, see 1896
★Motor Problems Inventory, preschool–grade 5, see 1897
Oseretsky Tests of Motor Proficiency: A Translation From the Portuguese Adaptation, ages 4–16, see 1898
Perrin Motor Coordination Test, adults, see 1899
Rail-Walking Test, ages 5 and over, see 1900
Smedley Hand Dynamometer, ages 6–18, see 1901
Southern California Motor Accuracy Test, ages 4–7 with nervous system dysfunction, see 1902
★Teaching Research Motor-Development Scale, moderately and severely retarded (preschool–grade 12), see 1903
★Test of Motor Impairment [Canada], ages 5–14, see 1904

VISION

A-B-C Vision Test for Ocular Dominance, ages 5 and over, see 1905
AO Sight Screener, adults, see 1906
Atlantic City Eye Test, grades 1 and over, see 1907
Basic Screen Test—Vision: Measurement of Skill Test 12, job applicants, see 1908
Burnham-Clark-Munsell Color Memory Test, adults, see 1909
Dennis Visual Perception Scale, grades 1–6, see 1910
Dvorine Pseudo-Isochromatic Plates, ages 3 and over, see 1911
Farnsworth Dichotomous Test for Color Blindness: Panel D–15, ages 12 and over, see 1912
Farnsworth-Munsell 100-Hue Test for the Examination of Color Discrimination, mental ages 12 and over, see 1913
★Guy's Colour Vision Test for Young Children [England], ages 3–5 and handicapped, see 1914
*Inter-Society Color Council Color Aptitude Test, adults, see 1915
Keystone Ready-to-Read Tests, school entrants, see 1916
Keystone Tests of Binocular Skill, grades 1 and over, see 1917
*Keystone Visual Screening Tests, preschool and over, see 1918
MKM Binocular Preschool Test, preschool, see 1919
MKM Monocular and Binocular Reading Test, grades 1 and over, see 1920
Marianne Frostig Developmental Test of Visual Perception, ages 3–8, see 1921
★Motor-Free Visual Perception Test, ages 4–8, see 1922
Ortho-Rater, adults, see 1923
*Pseudo-Isochromatic Plates for Testing Color Perception, ages 7 and over, see 1924
School Vision Tester, grades kgn and over, see 1925
★Sheridan Gardiner Test of Visual Acuity [England], ages 5 and over, see 1926
★Sloan Achromatopsia Test, individuals suspected of total color blindness, see 1927
Southern California Figure-Ground Visual Perception Test, ages 4–10, see 1928
Spache Binocular Reading Test, nonreaders and grades 1 and over, see 1929
★Speed of Color Discrimination Test, college, see 1930
Stycar Vision Tests [England], ages 6 months to 7 years, see 1931
Test for Colour-Blindness [Japan], ages 4 and over, see 1932
★3-D Test of Visualization Skill, ages 3–8, see 1933
Titmus Vision Tester, ages 3 and over, see 1934
★Visualization Test of Three Dimensional Orthographic Shape, high school and college, see 1935

SOCIAL STUDIES

American History—Government—Problems of Democracy: Acorn Achievement Tests, grades 9–16, see 1936
American School Achievement Tests: Social Studies and Science, grades 4–9, see 1937
*CLEP General Examinations: Social Sciences and History, 1–2 years of college or equivalent, see 1938
*College Board Achievement Test in American History and Social Studies, candidates for college entrance, see 1939
*College Board Achievement Test in European History

CONTEMPORARY AFFAIRS

ECONOMICS

GEOGRAPHY

HISTORY

POLITICAL SCIENCE

*CLEP Subject Examination in American Government, 1 semester or equivalent, see 2004
Cooperative Social Studies Tests: American Government, grades 10–12, see 2005
Cooperative Social Studies Tests: Civics, grades 8–9, see 2006
Cooperative Social Studies Tests: Problems of Democracy, grades 10–12, see 2007
★Government/Objective Tests, 1 semester grades 11–12, see 2008
*Graduate Record Examinations Advanced Political Science Test, graduate school candidates, see 2009
★National Teacher Examinations: Texas Government, college seniors and teachers, see 2010
Patterson Test or Study Exercises on the Constitution of the United States, grades 9–16 and adults, see 2011
Principles of Democracy Test, grades 9–12, see 2012

Sare-Sanders American Government Test, high school and college, see 2013
Sare-Sanders Constitution Test, high school and college, see 2014
*Social Studies Grade 12 (American Problems): Minnesota High School Achievement Examinations, grade 12, see 2015
*Undergraduate Program Field Tests: Political Science Test, college, see 2016

SOCIOLOGY

*CLEP Subject Examination in Introductory Sociology, 1 year or equivalent, see 2017
*Graduate Record Examinations Advanced Sociology Test, graduate school candidates, see 2018
Sare-Sanders Sociology Test, high school and college, see 2019
*Undergraduate Program Field Tests: Sociology Test, college, see 2020

SPEECH AND HEARING

★Diagnostic Test of Speechreading, deaf children ages 4–9, see 2021
★Multiple-Choice Intelligibility Test, college, see 2022
★Ohio Tests of Articulation and Perception of Sounds, ages 5–8, see 2023
Preschool Language Scale, ages 2–6, see 2024
Reynell Developmental Language Scales [England], children ages 1–5 with delayed or deviant language development, see 2025
*Undergraduate Program Field Tests: Speech Pathology and Audiology Test, college, see 2026

HEARING

*Ambco Audiometers, ages 10 and over, see 2027
Ambco Speech Test Record, ages 3 and over, see 2027A
*Auditory Discrimination Test, ages 5–8, see 2028
★Auditory Memory Span Test, ages 5–8, see 2029
★Auditory Sequential Memory Test, grades 5–8, see 2030
Auditory Tests, grades 2 and over, see 2031
*Beltone Audiometers, grades kgn and over, see 2032
Comprehension of Oral Language: Inter-American Series, grade 1, see 2033
*Eckstein Audiometers, grades kgn and over, see 2034
★Flowers-Costello Tests of Central Auditory Abilities, grades kgn–6, see 2035
★Four Tone Screening for Older Children and Adults, ages 8 and over, see 2036
Goldman-Fristoe-Woodcock Test of Auditory Discrimination, ages 4 and over, see 2037
*Grason-Stadler Audiometers, ages 6 and over, see 2038
Hearing of Speech Tests, ages 3–12, see 2039
Hollien-Thompson Group Hearing Test, grades 1 and over, see 2040
★Kindergarten Auditory Screening Test, grades kgn–1, see 2041
★Lindamood Auditory Conceptualization Test, grades kgn–12, see 2042
*Maico Audiometers, grades kgn and over, see 2043
*Maico Hearing Impairment Calculator, see 2044
Massachusetts Hearing Test, grades 1–16 and adults, see 2045
Modified Rhyme Hearing Test, grades 4 and over, see 2046

*National Teacher Examinations: Audiology, college seniors and teachers, see 2047
New Group Pure Tone Hearing Test, grades 1 and over, see 2048
★Oliphant Auditory Discrimination Memory Test, grades 2–6, see 2049
★Oliphant Auditory Synthesizing Test, grade 1, see 2050
Pritchard-Fox Phoneme Auditory Discrimination Tests: Test Four, kgn and over, see 2051
Robbins Speech Sound Discrimination and Verbal Imagery Type Tests, ages 4 and over, see 2052
Rush Hughes (PB 50): Phonetically Balanced Lists 5–12, grades 2 and over, see 2053
Screening Test for Auditory Perception, grades 2–6, see 2054
Stycar Hearing Tests [England], ages 6 months to 7 years, see 2055
Test of Listening Accuracy in Children, ages 5–9, see 2056
★Test of Non-Verbal Auditory Discrimination, ages 6–8, see 2057
★Tracor Audiometers, infants and older, see 2058
Verbal Auditory Screening for Children, ages 3–8, see 2059
★Washington Speech Sound Discrimination Test, ages 3–5, see 2060
★Word Intelligibility by Picture Identification, hearing impaired children ages 5–13, see 2061
★ZECO Pure Tone Screening for Children, ages 3–8, see 2062
*Zenith Audiometers, preschool and over, see 2063–4

SPEECH

Arizona Articulation Proficiency Scale, mental ages 2–14 and over, see 2065
★Boston Diagnostic Aphasia Examination, aphasic patients, see 2066
★Bzoch-League Receptive-Expressive Emergent Language Scale: For the Measurement of Language Skills in Infancy, birth to age 3, see 2067
Communicative Evaluation Chart From Infancy to Five Years, see 2068
Deep Test of Articulation, all reading levels, see 2069

★*Edinburgh Articulation Test* [Scotland], ages 3–5, see 2070

Examining for Aphasia, adolescents and adults, see 2071

★*Fairview Language Evaluation Scale,* mentally retarded, see 2072

★*Fisher-Logemann Test of Articulation Competence,* preschool and over, see 2073

Forms From Diagnostic Methods in Speech Pathology, children and adults with speech problems, see 2074

Goldman-Fristoe Test of Articulation, ages 2 and over, see 2075

Halstead Aphasia Test, adults, see 2076

Houston Test for Language Development, ages 6 months to 6 years, see 2077

Language Facility Test, ages 3 and over, see 2078

Language Modalities Test for Aphasia, adults, see 2079

Minnesota Test for Differential Diagnosis of Aphasia, adults, see 2080

National Teacher Examinations: Speech-Communication and Theatre, college seniors and teachers, see 2081

National Teacher Examinations: Speech Pathology, college seniors and teachers, see 2082

Nationwide Speech Examination, grades 4–12, see 2083

★*Northwestern Syntax Screening Test,* ages 3–7, see 2084

Orzeck Aphasia Evaluation, mental and brain damaged patients, see 2085

Photo Articulation Test, ages 3–12, see 2086

Porch Index of Communicative Ability, adults, see 2087

Predictive Screening Test of Articulation, grade 1, see 2088

Riley Articulation and Language Test, grades kgn–2, see 2089

Screening Deep Test of Articulation, grades kgn and over, see 2090

Screening Speech Articulation Test, ages 3.5–8.5, see 2091

Sklar Aphasia Scale, brain damaged adults, see 2092

Speech Defect Questionnaire, ages 6 and over, see 2093

Speech Diagnostic Chart, grades 1–8, see 2094

Templin-Darley Tests of Articulation, ages 3 and over, see 2095

★*Undergraduate Program Field Tests: Drama and Theatre Test,* college, see 2096

Utah Test of Language Development, ages 1.5 to 14.5, see 2097

Verbal Language Development Scale, birth to age 15, see 2098

Weidner-Fensch Speech Screening Test, grades 1–3, see 2099

VOCATIONS

★*ACT Assessment of Career Development,* grades 8–11, see 2100

★*ACT Career Planning Program,* entrants to postsecondary educational institutions, see 2101

Aptitude Inventory, employee applicants, see 2102

★*Career Maturity Inventory,* grades 6–12, see 2103

★*Classification Test Battery* [South Africa], illiterate and semiliterate applicants for unskilled and semi-skilled mining jobs, see 2104

Dailey Vocational Tests, grades 8–12 and adults, see 2105

ETSA Tests, job applicants, see 2106

Flanagan Industrial Tests, business and industry, see 2107

Individual Placement Series, high school and adults, see 2108

★*New Mexico Career Education Test Series,* grades 9–12, see 2109

Personal History Index, job applicants, see 2110

Steward Basic Factors Inventory, applicants for sales and office positions, see 2111

Steward Personnel Tests, applicants for sales and office positions, see 2112

TAV Selection System, adults, see 2113

Vocational Planning Inventory, vocational students in grades 8–12 and grade 13 entrants, see 2114

WLW Employment Inventory, adults, see 2115

★*Wide Range Employment Sample Test,* ages 16–35 (normal and handicapped), see 2116

CLERICAL

ACER Short Clerical Test—Form C [Australia], ages 13 and over, see 2117

A.C.E.R. Speed and Accuracy Tests [Australia], ages 13.5 and over, see 2118

APT Dictation Test, stenographers, see 2119

★*Appraisal of Occupational Aptitudes,* high school and adults, see 2120

Clerical Skills Series, clerical workers and applicants, see 2121

Clerical Tests, applicants for clerical positions, see 2122

Clerical Tests, Series N, applicants for clerical positions not involving frequent use of typewriter or verbal skill, see 2123

Clerical Tests, Series V, applicants for typing and stenographic positions, see 2124

Clerical Worker Examination, clerical workers, see 2125

Cross Reference Test, clerical job applicants, see 2126

Curtis Verbal-Clerical Skills Tests, applicants for clerical positions, see 2127

General Clerical Ability Test, job applicants, see 2128

General Clerical Test, grades 9–16 and clerical job applicants, see 2129

Group Test 20 [England], ages 15 and over, see 2130

Group Tests 61A, 64, and 66A [England], clerical applicants, see 2131

Hay Clerical Test Battery, applicants for clerical positions, see 2132

L & L Clerical Tests, applicants for office positions, see 2133

McCann Typing Tests, applicants for typing positions, see 2134

Minnesota Clerical Test, grades 8–12 and adults, see 2135

Office Skills Achievement Test, employees, see 2136

Office Worker Test, office workers, see 2137

O'Rourke Clerical Aptitude Test, Junior Grade, applicants for clerical positions, see 2138

Personnel Institute Clerical Tests, clerical personnel and typists-stenographers-secretaries, see 2139

Personnel Research Institute Clerical Battery, applicants for clerical positions, see 2140

Personnel Research Institute Test of Shorthand Skills, stenographers, see 2141

Purdue Clerical Adaptability Test, applicants for clerical positions, see 2142

RBH Checking Test, applicants for clerical and stenographic positions, see 2143

RBH Classifying Test, business and industry, see 2144

RBH Number Checking Test, business and industry, see 2145

INTERESTS

MANUAL DEXTERITY

APT Manual Dexterity Test, automobile and truck mechanics and mechanics' helpers, see 2222

Crawford Small Parts Dexterity Test, high school and adults, see 2223

Crissey Dexterity Test, job applicants, see 2224

Hand-Tool Dexterity Test, adolescents and adults, see 2225

Manipulative Aptitude Test, grades 9–16 and adults, see 2226

Minnesota Rate of Manipulation Test, grade 7 to adults, see 2227

O'Connor Finger Dexterity Test, ages 14 and over, see 2228

O'Connor Tweezer Dexterity Test, ages 14 and over, see 2229

★*One Hole Test,* job applicants, see 2230

Pennsylvania Bi-Manual Worksample, ages 16 and over, see 2231

Practical Dexterity Board, ages 8 and over, see 2232

Purdue Hand Precision Test, ages 17 and over, see 2233

Purdue Pegboard, grades 9–16 and adults, see 2234

Stromberg Dexterity Test, trade school and adults, see 2235

Yarn Dexterity Test, textile workers and applicants, see 2236

MECHANICAL ABILITY

A.C.E.R. Mechanical Comprehension Test [Australia], ages 13.5 and over, see 2237

A.C.E.R. Mechanical Reasoning Test [Australia], ages 13–9 and over, see 2238

Bennett Mechanical Comprehension Test, grades 9–12 and adults, see 2239

Chriswell Structural Dexterity Test, grades 7–9, see 2240

College Placement Test in Spatial Relations, entering college freshmen, see 2241

Cox Mechanical and Manual Tests [England], boys ages 10 and over, see 2242

Curtis Object Completion and Space Form Tests, applicants for mechanical and technical jobs, see 2243

Detroit Mechanical Aptitudes Examination, grades 7–16, see 2244

Flags: A Test of Space Thinking, industrial employees, see 2245

Form Perception Test [South Africa], illiterate and semiliterate adults, see 2246

Form Relations Group Test [England], ages 14 and over, see 2247

Group Test 80A [England], ages 15 and over, see 2248

Group Test 81 [England], ages 14 and over, see 2249

Group Test 82 [England], ages 14.5 and over, see 2250

MacQuarrie Test for Mechanical Ability, grades 7 and over, see 2251

Mechanical Aptitude Test: Acorn National Aptitude Tests, grades 7–16 and adults, see 2252

Mechanical Comprehension Test [South Africa], male technical apprentices and trainee engineer applicants, see 2253

Mechanical Information Test [England], ages 15 and over, see 2254

Mechanical Movements: A Test of Mechanical Comprehension, industrial employees, see 2255

Mechanical Reasoning: Differential Aptitude Tests, grades 8–12 and adults, see 2256

Mellenbruch Mechanical Motivation Test, grades 6–16 and adults, see 2257

Minnesota Spatial Relations Test, ages 11 and over, see 2258

O'Connor Wiggly Block, ages 16 and over, see 2259

O'Rourke Mechanical Aptitude Test, grades 7–12 and adults, see 2260

Perceptual Battery [South Africa], job applicants with at least 10 years of education, see 2261

Primary Mechanical Ability Tests, applicants for positions requiring mechanical ability, see 2262

Purdue Mechanical Adaptability Test, males ages 15 and over, see 2263

RBH Three-Dimensional Space Test, industrial workers in mechanical fields, see 2264

RBH Two-Dimensional Space Test, business and industry, see 2265

Revised Minnesota Paper Form Board Test, grades 9–16 and adults, see 2266

SRA Mechanical Aptitudes, grades 9–12 and adults, see 2267

Space Relations: Differential Aptitude Tests, grades 8–12 and adults, see 2268

Spatial Tests EG, 2, and 3 [England], ages 10–13 and 15–17, see 2269

Spatial Visualization Test: Dailey Vocational Tests, grades 8–12 and adults, see 2270

Vincent Mechanical Diagrams Test [England], ages 15 and over, see 2271

Weights and Pulleys: A Test of Intuitive Mechanics, engineering students and industrial employees, see 2272

MISCELLANEOUS

Alpha Biographical Inventory, grades 9–12, see 2273

Biographical Index, college and industry, see 2274

Business Judgment Test, adults, see 2275

Conference Evaluation, conference participants, see 2276

Conference Meeting Rating Scale, conference leaders and participants, see 2277

★*Continuous Letter Checking and Continuous Symbol Checking* [South Africa], ages 12 and over, see 2278–9

Gullo Workshop and Seminar Evaluation, workshop and seminar participants, see 2280

Job Attitude Analysis, production and clerical workers, see 2281

Mathematical and Technical Test [England], ages 11 and over, see 2282

Minnesota Importance Questionnaire, vocational counselees, see 2283

★*Minnesota Job Description Questionnaire,* employees and supervisors, see 2284

Minnesota Satisfaction Questionnaire, business and industry, see 2285

Per-Flu-Dex Tests, college and industry, see 2286

RBH Breadth of Information, business and industry, see 2287

Self-Rating Scale for Leadership Qualifications, adults, see 2288

Tear Ballot for Industry, employees in industry, see 2289

Test Orientation Procedure, job applicants and trainees, see 2290

Tests A/9 and A/10 [South Africa], applicants for technical and apprentice jobs, see 2291

Whisler Strategy Test, business and industry, see 2292

Work Information Inventory, employee groups in industry, see 2293

Colleges of Podiatry Admission Test, grades 14 and over, see 2354
Medical College Admission Test, applicants for admission to member colleges of the Association of American Medical Colleges, see 2355
Medical School Instructor Attitude Inventory, medical school faculty members, see 2356
✝*Optometry College Admission Test,* optometry college applicants, see 2357
Veterinary Aptitude Test, veterinary school applicants, see 2358

MISCELLANEOUS

Architectural School Aptitude Test, architectural school applicants, see 2359
Chemical Operators Selection Test, chemical operators and applicants, see 2360
Fire Promotion Tests, prospective firemen promotees, see 2361
Firefighter Test, prospective firemen, see 2362
Fireman Examination, prospective firemen, see 2363
General Municipal Employees Performance (Efficiency) Rating System, municipal employees, see 2364
Journalism Test, high school, see 2365
★*Law Enforcement Perception Questionnaire,* law enforcement personnel, see 2366
Memory and Observation Tests for Policeman, prospective policemen, see 2367
Police Performance Rating System, policemen, see 2368
Police Promotion Tests, prospective policemen promotees, see 2369
Policeman Examination, prospective policemen, see 2370
Policeman Test, policemen and prospective policemen, see 2371
Potter-Nash Aptitude Test for Lumber Inspectors and Other General Personnel Who Handle Lumber, employees in woodworking industries, see 2372
★*Test for Firefighter B-1,* firemen and prospective firemen, see 2373
★*Test for Police Officer A-1,* policemen and prospective policemen, see 2374
Visual Comprehension Test for Detective, prospective police detectives, see 2375

NURSING

Achievement Tests in Nursing, students in schools of registered nursing, see 2376
Achievement Tests in Practical Nursing, practical nursing students, see 2377
Empathy Inventory, nursing instructors, see 2378
Entrance Examination for Schools of Nursing, nursing school applicants, see 2379
Entrance Examination for Schools of Practical Nursing, practical nursing school applicants, see 2380
George Washington University Series Nursing Tests, prospective nurses, see 2381
Luther Hospital Sentence Completions, prospective nursing students, see 2382
NLN Achievement Tests for Schools Preparing Registered Nurses, students in state-approved schools preparing registered nurses, see 2383
NLN Aide Selection Test, applicants for aide positions in hospitals and home health agencies, see 2384
NLN Practical Nursing Achievement Tests, students in state-approved schools of practical nursing, see 2385
NLN Pre-Admission and Classification Examination, practical nursing school entrants, see 2386
NLN Pre-Nursing and Guidance Examination, applicants for admission to state-approved schools preparing registered nurses, see 2387
Netherne Study Difficulties Battery for Student Nurses [England], student nurses, see 2388
Nurse Attitudes Inventory, prospective nursing students, see 2389
PSB-Aptitude for Practical Nursing Examination, applicants for admission to practical nursing schools, see 2390

RESEARCH

Research Personnel Review Form, research and engineering and scientific firms, see 2391
Supervisor's Evaluation of Research Personnel, research personnel, see 2392
Surveys of Research Administration and Environment, research and engineering and scientific firms, see 2393
Technical Personnel Recruiting Inventory, research and engineering and scientific firms, see 2394

SELLING

Aptitudes Associates Test of Sales Aptitude, applicants for sales positions, see 2395
Combination Inventory, Form 2, prospective debit life insurance salesmen, see 2396
Detroit Retail Selling Inventory, candidates for training in retail selling, see 2397
Evaluation Record, prospective life insurance agency managers, see 2398
Hall Salespower Inventory, salesmen, see 2399
Hanes Sales Selection Inventory, insurance and printing salesmen, see 2400
Information Index, life and health insurance agents, see 2401
LIAMA Inventory of Job Attitudes, life insurance field personnel, see 2402
Personnel Institute Hiring Kit, applicants for sales positions, see 2403
SRA Sales Attitudes Check List, applicants for sales positions, see 2404
Sales Aptitude Test, job applicants, see 2405
Sales Comprehension Test, applicants for sales positions, see 2406
Sales Method Index, life insurance agents, see 2407
Sales Motivation Inventory, applicants for sales positions, see 2408
Sales Sentence Completion Blank, applicants for sales positions, see 2409
Steward Life Insurance Knowledge Test, applicants for life insurance agent or supervisory positions, see 2410
Steward Occupational Objectives Inventory, applicants for supervisory positions in life insurance companies or agencies, see 2411
Steward Personal Background Inventory, applicants for sales positions, see 2412
Test for Ability to Sell: George Washington University Series, grades 7–16 and adults, see 2413
★*Test of Retail Sales Insight,* retail clerks and students, see 2414

SKILLED TRADES

Electrical Sophistication Test, job applicants, see 2415
Fiesenheiser Test of Ability to Read Drawings, trade school and adults, see 2416
Mechanical Familiarity Test, job applicants, see 2417
Mechanical Handyman Test, maintenance workers, see 2418
Mechanical Knowledge Test, job applicants, see 2419

SUPERVISION

TRANSPORTATION

PUBLISHERS DIRECTORY
AND INDEX

This directory and index gives the addresses and tests of all publishers represented in this volume. References are to entry numbers, not to page numbers. Stars indicate test publishers with test catalogs listing 10 or more tests. Tests not originating in the country of publication are identified by listing in brackets the country in which the test was originally prepared and published. All foreign tests distributed by United States publishers are listed; however, United States tests distributed by foreign publishers are listed only if the tests have been revised or supplemented for foreign use.

★American Guidance Service, Inc., Publishers' Bldg., Circle Pines, Minn. 55014:
Doren Diagnostic Reading Test of Word Recognition Skills, 1627
Maturity Level for School Entrance and Reading Readiness, 1715
Woodcock Reading Mastery Tests, 1656

American Printing House for the Blind, Inc., 1839 Frankfort Ave., Louisville, Ky. 40206:
Diagnostic Reading Tests, 1626
Sequential Tests of Educational Progress: Reading, 1599
Stanford Achievement Test: Reading Tests, 1603

American Testing Co., 6301 S.W. Fifth St., Fort Lauderdale, Fla. 33317:
National Test of Basic Words, 1667
National Test of Library Skills, 1762
Reading Diagnostic Probes, 1642
Reading Inventory Probe 1, 1725

Arden Press, 8331 Alvarado Drive, Huntington Beach, Calif. 92646:
Academic Readiness and End of First Grade Progress Scales, 1693

★Australian Council for Educational Research, P.O. Box 210, Hawthorn, Vic. 3122, Australia:
A.C.E.R. Lower Grades Reading Test, 1529
ACER Primary Reading Survey Tests, 1530
Cooperative Reading Comprehension Test, Forms L and M [United States], 1545
Cooperative Reading Comprehension Test, Form Y [United States], 1544
Individual Reading Test, 1557
Kindergarten Behavioural Index, 1708
Progressive Achievement Tests of Reading [New Zealand], 1579
W.A.L. English Comprehension Test, 1613

Better Reading Program, Inc., 8 South Michigan Ave., Chicago, Ill. 60603:
Reader Rater With Self-Scoring Profile, 1670

Blackwell (Basil), Publisher, 5 Alfred St., Oxford, England:
Swansea Test of Phonic Skills, 1652

★Bobbs-Merrill Co., Inc. (The), 4300 West 62nd St., Indianapolis, Ind. 46268:
American School Achievement Tests: Reading, 1532
American School Reading Readiness Test, 1694
American School Reading Tests, 1533

Gray Oral Reading Test, 1681
Monroe's Standardized Silent Reading Test, 1569
Pressey Diagnostic Reading Tests, 1576
Public School Achievement Tests: Reading, 1590
Schrammel-Gray High School and College Reading Test, 1598
Standardized Oral Reading Check Tests, 1689
Standardized Oral Reading Paragraphs, 1690
Traxler High School Reading Test, 1610
Traxler Silent Reading Test, 1611
Williams Primary Reading Test, 1615
Williams Reading Test for Grades 4–9, 1616

Book Society of Canada Ltd. (The), 4386 Sheppard Ave. East, P.O. Box 200, Agincourt, Ont. M1S 3B6, Canada:
Watson Reading-Readiness Test, 1734

Brador Publications, Inc., Livonia, N.Y. 14487:
Reading Skills Diagnostic Test, 1644

Brigham Young University Press, 205 UPB, Provo, Utah 84601:
Sucher-Allred Reading Placement Inventory, 1604

Brown (Wm. C.) Co. Publishers, 2460 Kerper Blvd., Dubuque, Iowa 52001:
Classroom Reading Inventory, 1618

★Bureau of Educational Measurements, Kansas State Teachers College, 1200 Commercial, Emporia, Kan. 66802:
Emporia Reading Tests, 1549

CAL Press, Inc., 76 Madison Ave., New York, N.Y. 10016:
Reading/Everyday Activities in Life, 1744

★CTB/McGraw-Hill, Del Monte Research Park, Monterey, Calif. 93940:
California Achievement Tests: Reading, 1536
California Phonics Survey, 1617
Comprehensive Tests of Basic Skills
Reading, 1542
Study Skills, 1752
Diagnostic Reading Scales, 1624
Lee-Clark Reading Readiness Test, 1711
Lee-Clark Reading Test, 1563
Prescriptive Reading Inventory, 1639
Prescriptive Reading Inventory Interim Tests, 1640
Survey of Reading Achievement, 1606

CTB/McGraw-Hill Ryerson Ltd., 330 Progress Ave., Scarborough, Ont., Canada:
Pre-Reading Assessment Kit, 1719

Cal-State Bookstore, 25776 Hillary St., Hayward, Calif. 94542:
McHugh-McParland Reading Readiness Test, 1713

Committee on Diagnostic Reading Tests, Inc., Mountain Home, N.C. 28758:
Diagnostic Reading Tests, 1626

★Consulting Psychologists Press, Inc., 577 College Ave., Palo Alto, Calif. 94306:
School Readiness Survey, 1729
Study Habits Inventory, 1768

★Cooperative Tests and Services, Educational Testing Service, Princeton, N.J. 08540:
ANPA Foundation Newspaper Test, 1735
Cooperative English Tests: Reading Comprehension, 1583
Cooperative Primary Tests
  Reading, 1543
  Word Analysis, 1620
Sequential Tests of Educational Progress: Reading, 1599

Critical Thinking Project, 371 Education Bldg., University of Illinois, Urbana, Ill. 61801:
Cornell Class-Reasoning Test, 1753
Cornell Conditional-Reasoning Test, 1754
Cornell Critical Thinking Test, 1755

Croft Educational Services, Inc., 100 Garfield Ave., New London, Conn. 06320:
Cooper-McGuire Diagnostic Word-Analysis Test, 1619
McGuire-Bumpus Diagnostic Comprehension Test, 1635

Delaware County Reading Council, Delaware County Public Schools, Sixth and Olive Sts., Media, Pa. 19063:
Delaware County Silent Reading Test, 1547

Delco Readiness Test, 111 Linda Lane, Media, Pa. 19063:
Delco Readiness Test, 1701

Denver Public Schools, 414 Fourteenth St., Denver, Colo. 80202:
Denver Public Schools Reading Inventory, 1621

Department of Psychological Testing, De Paul University, 25 East Jackson Blvd., Chicago, Ill. 60604:
Commerce Reading Comprehension Test, 1538

De Paul University. *See* Department of Psychological Testing.

Developmental Reading Distributors (DRD Press), 1944 Sheridan Ave., Laramie, Wyo. 82070:
Maintaining Reading Efficiency Tests, 1566

Dreier Educational Systems, Inc., 320 Raritan Ave., Highland Park, N.J. 08904:
Group Phonics Analysis, 1632
Instant Word Recognition Test, 1664
Oral Reading Criterion Test, 1684
Phonics Criterion Test, 1636

Edcodyne Corporation, 1 City Blvd. West, Suite 935, Orange, Calif. 92668:
APELL Test, 1692

★Educational and Industrial Testing Service, P.O. Box 7234, San Diego, Calif. 92107:
Study Attitudes and Methods Survey, 1766

Educational Developmental Laboratories, 1221 Avenue of the Americas, New York, N.Y. 10020:
Flash-X Sight Vocabulary Test, 1678
Reader's Inventory, 1671
Reading Eye II, 1672
Reading Versatility Test, 1673

Educational Opportunities Division. *See* Follett Publishing Co.

Educational Performance Associates, Inc., 563 Westview Ave., Ridgefield, N.J. 07657:
Preschool and Kindergarten Performance Profile, 1722

Educational Stimuli, Telegram Bldg., Superior, Wis. 54880:
Nationwide Library Skills Examination, 1763

★Educational Testing Service, Princeton, N.J. 08540 (*See also* Cooperative Tests and Services, and Educational Testing Service [Berkeley Office]):
National Teacher Examinations: Reading Specialist—Elementary School, 1571

Educational Testing Service (Berkeley Office), 1947 Center St., Berkeley, Calif. 94704:
Survey of Primary Reading Development, 1605

Educators Publishing Service, Inc., 75 Moulton St., Cambridge, Mass. 02138:
Dyslexia Schedule, 1662
Gillingham-Childs Phonics Proficiency Scales, 1630

Pre-Reading Screening Procedures, 1721
Sipay Word Analysis Tests, 1648

Essay Press, Inc., P.O. Box 5, Planetarium Station, New York, N.Y. 10024:
Roswell-Chall Auditory Blending Test, 1674
Roswell-Chall Diagnostic Reading Test of Word Analysis Skills, 1643

Follett Publishing Co., 1010 West Washington Blvd., Chicago, Ill. 60607:
Adult Basic Education Student Survey: Reading, 1742
Basic Concept Inventory, 1697
Botel Reading Inventory, 1658
Individual Reading Placement Inventory, 1663

Garrard Publishing Co., 1607 North Market St., Champaign, Ill. 61820:
Basic Sight Word Test, 1657

Gibson (Robert) & Sons, Glasgow, Ltd., 17 Fitzroy Place, Glasgow G37SF, Scotland:
Kelvin Measurement of Reading Ability, 1561

★Ginn & Co. Ltd., Elsinore House, Buckingham St., Aylesbury, Bucks, England:
Reading Comprehension Test DE, 1585
Reading Test AD, 1591
Reading Tests A and BD, 1594
Reading Tests EH 1-3, 1595

★Guidance Centre, University of Toronto, 1000 Yonge St., Toronto, Ont. M4W 2K8, Canada:
Group Test of Reading Readiness, 1704
OISE Achievement Tests in Silent Reading, 1575
Reading Comprehension: Canadian English Achievement Test, 1582

Guidance Testing Associates, 6516 Shirley Ave., Austin, Tex. 78752:
Tests of Reading: Inter-American Series, 1609

★Harcourt Brace Jovanovich, Inc., 757 Third Ave., New York, N.Y. 10017:
Durrell Analysis of Reading Difficulty, 1628
Durrell Listening-Reading Series, 1660
Durrell-Sullivan Reading Capacity and Achievement Tests, 1661
Gilmore Oral Reading Test, 1679
Iowa Silent Reading Tests, 1560
Metropolitan Achievement Tests: Reading Tests, 1567
Metropolitan Readiness Tests, 1716
Murphy-Durrell Reading Readiness Analysis, 1717
Stanford Achievement Test: Reading Tests, 1603
Stanford Achievement Test: High School Reading Test, 1602
Stanford Diagnostic Reading Test, 1651
Watson-Glaser Critical Thinking Appraisal, 1775

Harper & Row, Publishers, Inc., 10 East 53rd St., New York, N.Y. 10022:
LRS Seriation Test, 1710
Test of Phonic Skills, 1654

★Harrap (George G.) & Co. Ltd., P.O. Box 70, 182/4 High Holborn, London WC1V 7AX, England:
Holborn Reading Scale, 1682
Kingston Test of Silent Reading, 1562

Hart-Davis Educational Ltd., Frogmore, St. Albans, Herts AL2 2NF, England:
Standard Reading Tests, 1650

Heinemann Educational Australia Pty Ltd., Box 173, South Yarra, Vic. 3141, Australia:
GAP Reading Comprehension Test, 1550a
GAPADOL, 1551

Heinemann Educational Books Ltd., 48 Charles St., London W1X 8AH, England:
GAP Reading Comprehension Test [Australia], 1550b

★Houghton Mifflin Co., 110 Tremont St., Boston, Mass. 02107:
Analysis of Readiness Skills: Reading and Mathematics, 1695
Harrison-Stroud Reading Readiness Profiles, 1705
Nelson-Denny Reading Test, 1572
Nelson Reading Test, 1573
Primary Reading Profiles, 1641
Reading Aptitude Tests, 1724
Tests of Academic Progress: Reading, 1608

★Human Sciences Research Council, Private Bag 41, Pretoria, Republic of South Africa:
N.B. Silent Reading Tests (Beginners), 1570
Silent Reading Tests, 1600

★Industrial Relations Center, University of Chicago, 1225 East 60th St., Chicago, Ill. 60637 (This publisher has not replied to our four requests to check the accuracy of the entry for the test listed below. The entry was, however, checked by the author.):
Understanding Communication (Verbal Comprehension), 1747

International Society for General Semantics, P.O. Box 2469, San Francisco, Calif. 94126:
Uncritical Inference Test, 1774

Kansas State Teachers College. *See* Bureau of Educational Measurements.

Klamath Printing Co., 320 Lowell St., Klamath Falls, Ore. 97601:
Standard Reading Inventory, 1649

Layton (Wilbur L.), 3604 Ross Road, Ames, Iowa 50010:
Study Performance Test, 1769

Lear Seigler, Inc./Fearon Publishers, 6 Davis Drive, Belmont, Calif. 94002:
Inventory of Primary Skills, 1707

Learning Research Associates, Inc., 1501 Broadway, New York, N.Y. 10036:
LRA Standard Mastery Tasks in Language, 1633

Learning to Learn School, Inc., 1936 San Marco Blvd., Jacksonville, Fla. 32207:
Sprigle School Readiness Screening Test, 1731

Lippincott (J. B.) Co., East Washington Square, Philadelphia, Pa. 19105:
Lippincott Reading Readiness Test, 1712

Lucas Brothers Publishers, 909 Lowry, Columbia, Mo. 65201:
Inventory of Teacher Knowledge of Reading, 1665

Lyons & Carnahan, 407 East 25th St., Chicago, Ill. 60616:
New Developmental Reading Tests, 1574
Silent Reading Diagnostic Tests, 1647

McCartney (William A.), P.O. Box 507, Kaneohe, Hawaii 96744:
Reading Comprehension Test, 1584

McGrath Publishing Co., P.O. Box 535, Whitmore Lake, Mich. 48189:
McGrath Test of Reading Skills, 1564

McGraw-Hill Book Co., Inc., 1221 Avenue of the Americas, New York, N.Y. 10020:
McGraw-Hill Basic Skills System
    Reading Test, 1593
    Study Skills Test, 1771

McMenemy (Richard A.), 3028 Northeast Brazee St., Portland, Ore. 97212:
McMenemy Measure of Reading Ability, 1565

Macmillan Education Ltd., Houndmills, Basingstoke, Hants RG21 2XS, England:
Neale Analysis of Reading Ability, 1683

Macmillan Publishing Co., Inc., 866 Third Ave., New York, N.Y. 10022:
Macmillan Reading Readiness Test, 1714
Reading Miscue Inventory, 1686

Miami University Alumni Association, Murstein Alumni Center, Miami University, Oxford, Ohio 45056:
Word Discrimination Test, 1675

Mills School (The), 1512 East Broward Blvd., Ft. Lauderdale, Fla. 33301:
Learning Methods Test, 1666

Montana Reading Publications, 419 Stapleton Bldg., Billings, Mont. 59101:
Contemporary School Readiness Test, 1700
Test of Individual Needs in Reading, 1653

NCS Interpretive Scoring Systems, 4401 West 76th St., Minneapolis, Minn. 55435:
Wisconsin Tests of Reading Skill Development
    Study Skills, 1776
    Word Attack, 1655

★NFER Publishing Co. Ltd., 2 Jennings Bldgs., Thames Ave., Windsor, Berks SL4 1QS, England:
Comprehension Test for Training College Students, 1539
Gates-MacGinitie Reading Tests: Primary A [United States], 1552a

National Council of Teachers of English, 1111 Kenyon Road, Urbana, Ill. 61801:
Cumulative Reading Record, 1659

★Nelson (Thomas) & Sons (Canada) Ltd., 81 Curlew Drive, Don Mills 400, Ont., Canada:
Informal Reading Assessment Tests, 1558

Nelson (Thomas) & Sons Ltd., Lincoln Way, Windmill Road, Sunbury-on-Thames, Middlesex TW16 7HP, England:
Bristol Achievement Tests: Study Skills, 1750
Wide-span Reading Test, 1614

Nevins (C. H.) Printing Co., 311 Bryn Mawr Island, Bayshore Gardens, Bradenton, Fla. 33507:
Group Diagnostic Reading Aptitude and Achievement Tests, 1631

New Dimensions in Education, Inc., 160 Dupont St., Plainview, N.Y. 11803:
SPIRE Individual Reading Evaluation, 1645

New Zealand Council for Educational Research, Education House, 178 Willis St., Wellington C.2, New Zealand:
A.C.E.R. Silent Reading Tests [Australia], 1531
Oral Word Reading Test, 1685
Progressive Achievement Tests of Reading, 1579

O'Connor Reading Clinic Publishing Co., 34555 Lytle Road, Farmington, Mich. 48024:
OC Diagnostic Dictionary Test, 1764
OC Diagnostic Syllabizing Test, 1668

Ohio State University. *See* University Publications Sales.

Oliver & Boyd, Croythorn House, 23 Ravelston Terrace, Edinburgh EH4 3TJ, Scotland:
Schonell Reading Tests, 1646

O'Rourke Publications, P.O. Box 1118, Lake Alfred, Fla. 33850:
Survey Tests of Reading, 1607

Perfection Form Co. (The), 214 West Eighth St., Logan, Iowa 51546:
Library Tests, 1760

Personal Growth Press, Inc., Box M, Berea, Ohio 44017:
College Adjustment and Study Skills Inventory, 1751

Personnel Press, Education Center, P.O. Box 2649, Columbus, Ohio 43216:
Clymer-Barrett Prereading Battery, 1699
McCullough Word-Analysis Tests, 1634

Personnel Research Associates, Inc., 701 Metropolitan Bldg., 1407 Main St., Dallas, Tex. 75202:
Reading Adequacy "READ" Test, 1741

Phonovisual Products, Inc., 12216 Parklawn Drive, Rockville, Md. 20852:
Phonovisual Diagnostic Test, 1638

Priority Innovations, Inc., P.O. Box 792, Skokie, Ill. 60076:
Parent Readiness Evaluation of Preschoolers, 1718
Primary Academic Sentiment Scale, 1723
Screening Test of Academic Readiness, 1730

Programs for Education, Lumberville, Pa. 18933:
Gesell Developmental Tests, 1703

★Psychological Corporation (The), 304 East 45th St., New York, N.Y. 10017:
Davis Reading Test, 1546
Survey of Study Habits and Attitudes, 1772

★Psychologists and Educators, Inc., Suite 212, 211 West State St., Jacksonville, Ill. 62650:
Cornell Learning and Study Skills Inventory, 1756
Prereading Expectancy Screening Scales, 1720

★Psychometric Affiliates, Box 3167, Munster, Ind. 46321:
Acorn Achievement Tests: Primary Reading Test, 1578
Binion-Beck Reading Readiness Test, 1698
Evaluation Aptitude Test, 1757
National Achievement Tests
    High School Reading Test, 1556
    Reading Comprehension Test [Crow, Kuhlmann, and Crow], 1586
    Reading Comprehension Test [Speer and Smith], 1587
    Reading Test (Comprehension and Speed), 1592

Reading Laboratory and Clinic, University of Florida, Gainesville, Fla. 32601:
Test on Use of the Dictionary, 1773

Research Concepts, 1368 East Airport Road, Muskegon, Mich. 49444:
ABC Inventory to Determine Kindergarten and School Readiness, 1691
School Readiness Checklist, 1728

Revrac Publications, 1535 Red Oak Drive, Silver Spring, Md. 20910:
Basic Reading Rate Scale, 1748
Carver-Darby Chunked Reading Test, 1537
Reading Progress Scale, 1589

★Richardson, Bellows, Henry & Co., Inc., 1140 Connecticut Ave. N.W., Washington, D.C. 20036:
RBH Basic Reading and Word Test, 1580
RBH Scientific Reading Test, 1740
RBH Test of Reading Comprehension, 1581

★Scholastic Testing Service, Inc., 480 Meyer Road, Bensenville, Ill. 60106:
Adult Basic Reading Inventory, 1736
Burnett Reading Series, 1535
Diagnostic Reading Test, 1625
Steinbach Test of Reading Readiness, 1732

★Science Research Associates, Inc., 259 East Erie St., Chicago, Ill. 60611:
Iowa Tests of Educational Development
    Ability to Interpret Reading Materials in the Natural Sciences, 1738
    Ability to Interpret Reading Materials in the Social Studies, 1737
    Use of Sources of Information, 1758
Reading for Understanding Placement Test, 1588
SRA Achievement Series
    Reading, 1596
    Work-Study Skills, 1765
SRA Reading Index, 1746
SRA Reading Record, 1597
Study Habits Checklist, 1767

Scott, Foresman & Co., 1900 East Lake Ave., Glenview, Ill. 60025:
Initial Survey Test, 1706
Inventory-Survey Tests, 1559
Primary Reading Survey Tests, 1577

★Sheridan Psychological Services, Inc., P.O. Box 6101, Orange, Calif. 92667:
Logical Reasoning, 1761

Skandinaviska Testförlaget, Box 461, S-126 04 Hägersten 4, Sweden:
Reversal Test, 1726

Slosson Educational Publications, Inc., 140 Pine St., East Aurora, N.Y. 14052:
Slosson Oral Reading Test, 1688

★Stoelting Co., 1350 South Kostner Ave., Chicago, Ill. 60623:
Diagnostic Reading Examination for Diagnosis of Special Difficulty in Reading, 1623

Teachers College Press, 1234 Amsterdam Ave., New York, N.Y. 10027:
Gates-MacGinitie Reading Tests, 1552
    Readiness Skills, 1702
    Survey F, 1553
Gates-McKillop Reading Diagnostic Tests, 1629
Library Orientation Test for College Freshmen, 1759
Phonics Knowledge Survey, 1637
Phonics Test for Teachers, 1669

Teaching and Testing Resources, P.O. Box 77, Fortitude Valley, Qld. 4006, Australia:
Concise Word Reading Tests, 1677
St. Lucia Graded Word Reading Test, 1687

★University Book Store, 360 State St., West Lafayette, Ind. 47906:
Purdue Reading Test for Industrial Supervisors, 1739

University of Chicago. *See* Industrial Relations Center.

★University of London Press Ltd., St. Paul's House, Warwick Lane, London EC4P 4AH, England:
Edinburgh Reading Tests, 1548
Graded Word Reading Test, 1680
Group Reading Assessment, 1554
Group Reading Test, 1555
Reading Comprehension Test for Personnel Selection, 1743
Southgate Group Reading Tests, 1601
Word Recognition Test, 1676

University of Minnesota Press, 2037 University Ave. S.E., Minneapolis, Minn. 55455:
Minnesota Reading Examination for College Students, 1568
Minnesota Speed of Reading Test for College Students, 1749

University of Toronto. *See* Guidance Centre.

University Publications Sales, Ohio State University, 20 Lord Hall, 124 West 17th Ave., Columbus, Ohio 43210:
Robinson-Hall Reading Tests, 1745

Van Wagenen Psycho-Educational Research Laboratories, 1729 Irving Ave. South, Minneapolis, Minn. 55403:
Comprehensive Primary Reading Scales, 1540
Comprehensive Reading Scales, 1541
Diagnostic Examination of Silent Reading Abilities, 1622
Van Wagenen Analytical Reading Scales, 1612
Van Wagenen Reading Readiness Scales, 1733

Wagner (Mazie Earle), 500 Klein Road, Buffalo, N.Y. 14221:
Buffalo Reading Test for Speed and Comprehension, 1534

Webster Division, McGraw-Hill Book Co., Inc., 1221 Avenue of the Americas, New York, N.Y. 10020:
Kindergarten Evaluation of Learning Potential, 1709

★Western Psychological Services, 12031 Wilshire Blvd., Los Angeles, Calif. 90025:
Anton Brenner Developmental Gestalt Test of School Readiness, 1696
Riley Preschool Developmental Screening Inventory, 1727
Study Skills Counseling Evaluation, 1770

INDEX OF TITLES

This cumulative index lists (*a*) reading tests in print as of February 1, 1974, and (*b*) reading tests out of print, status unknown, or reclassified since last listed in the 1968 *Reading Tests and Reviews* (RTR I) or in the reading section of *The Seventh Mental Measurements Yearbook* (7th MMY). Citations are to test entries, not to pages. Numbers without colons refer to in print tests listed in this volume; numbers with colons refer to tests out of print, status unknown, or reclassified. Unless preceded by the word "*consult*," all numbers containing colons refer either to tests in this volume (reprinted from the 7th MMY) or to tests in RTR I (reprinted from the first six MMY's or a new listing in RTR I). The guide numbers next to the outside margins in the running heads of the reprint sections should be used to locate a particular test. The first reprint section, from *Tests in Print II* (TIP II), has guide numbers ranging from 1529 to 1776; the second reprint section, from the 7th MMY, has guide numbers 7:682 to 7:783. Numbers with the letter R or any one of the digits 1 through 6 preceding the colon refer to tests in RTR I. To obtain the latest information on a test no longer classified with reading tests, the reader must consult either TIP II (if the test is in print) or an MMY (if the test is out of print). For example, "Lorimer Braille Recognition Test, R:212, 6:854; reclassified, *consult* T2:771" indicates that the *Lorimer Braille Recognition Test,* test 212 in RTR I and test 854 in the 6th MMY, has since been reclassified and for the latest information, test 771 in TIP II must be consulted. Superseded titles are listed with cross references to the current title. Tests which are part of a series are listed under their individual titles and also their series titles.

INDEX OF NAMES

This cumulative index covers both this volume (RTR II) and the 1968 monograph (RTR I), which, together, include the reading sections of the first seven *Mental Measurements Yearbooks* (MMY) and *Tests in Print II* (TIP II). It is an analytical index indicating authorship of a test, test review, excerpted review, or reference for a specific test. Citations are to test numbers, not to page numbers. In the reprint sections, the numbers of the first and last tests on facing pages are given in the running heads next to the outside margins. Numbers without colons refer to in print tests presented in the section reprinted from TIP II. Interpret abbreviations and numbers for in print tests as follows: "*test, 1603*" indicates authorship of test 1603; "*rev, 1702,*" authorship of a review of test 1702; "*exc, 1552,*" authorship of an excerpted review of test 1552; and "*ref, 1599,*" authorship of one or more references for test 1599. (The Cumulative Name Index for that test must be consulted to locate the references.) Numbers with colons (e.g., 3:507, test 507 in the 3rd MMY) refer to out of print tests listed either in this volume or RTR I, unless otherwise indicated. Out of print tests last listed in the 7th MMY will be found in this volume; out of print tests last listed in earlier yearbooks will be found in RTR I. For example, tests 1:1097, 2:1532, 3:484, 4:553, 5:620, 6:792, and R:238 are in RTR I; test 7:762 is in this volume. In the reprint sections, the yearbook digit preceding the colon is given in the running head only.

AARON, I. E.: *rev,* 1637, 1643, 1658, 1669, 1674
Abbott, R. F.: *ref,* 1716
Abell, A. P.: *ref,* 1583
Abell, E. L.: *exc,* 1610
Adair, N.: *test,* 1691
Adams, E. K.: *ref,* 1572
Adams, G. S.: *rev,* 1609
Adams, M.: *ref,* 1560
Adams, M. J. C.: *ref,* 1716
Adams, N. A.: *ref,* 1626
Adams, S.: *ref,* 1560
Adams, W. M.: *ref,* 1560
Adkins, D. C.: *rev,* 1746; *ref,* 3:535(13)
Afflerbach, J. G.: *rev,* 1559
Afflerbach, L. G.: *rev,* 1759
Ahmann, J. S.: *ref,* 1772
Ahr, A. E.: *test,* 1718, 1730; *ref,* 1730
Ainsworth, L. L.: *ref,* 1626, 1772
Akers, J. C.: *ref,* 1716
Alcorn, J. D.: *ref,* 1536
Alden, C. L.: *ref,* 1661
Alexakos, C. E.: *ref,* 1546, 1768, 1775
Allen, C. H.: *ref,* 1689
Allen, J.: *test,* 1776
Allen, J. E.: *ref,* 1552
Allen, L. W.: *test,* 1557

Allman, R. W.: *ref,* 1626
Allred, R. A.: *test,* 1604
Alodia, M.: *test,* 1673
Alpert, H.: *test,* 1645
Alshan, L. M.: *ref,* 1546, 1674
Alspaugh, C. A.: *ref,* 1775
Alston, D. N.: *ref,* 1775
Althouse, R. E.: *ref,* 1702, 1716
American Council on Education: *test,* R:221–2
Ames, L. B.: *test,* 1703; *ref,* 1703, 1724
Ames, W. S.: *ref,* 1681
Amstutz, W. S.: *ref,* 2:1544(7–8)
Anastasiow, N.: *rev,* 1731; *ref,* 1536, 1552, 1560, 1567, 1603, 1702, 1705, 1711, 1716–7
Anastasiow, N. J.: *ref,* 1596, 1599
Anderhalter, O. F.: *test,* 1625, 5:650, 6:850
Anderson, A. W.: *ref,* 1544, 1583
Anderson, H. E.: *ref,* 1536
Anderson, I. H.: *rev,* 1698, 1716, 1724, 1:1095, 1:1097, 1:1104, 3:521; *ref,* 1560, 1572, 3:507(3)
Anderson, J.: *test,* 1551; *ref,* 1550
Anderson, K. E.: *ref,* 1583
Anderson, M. R.: *ref,* 1598
Anderson, R. B.: *ref,* 1560
Anderson, R. P.: *ref,* 1628, 1772

Anderson, T. H.: *ref,* 1772
Anderson, V. L.: *ref,* 1560
Andrews, A. M.: *ref,* 1703, 1716
Andrews, R. J.: *test,* 1677, 1687; *ref,* 1646, 1683
Anthony, E. J.: *ref,* 1679
Apell, R. J.: *ref,* 1703
Armstrong, N. A.: *ref,* 1775
Arn, E. H. R.: *ref,* 1583
Arnold, R. D.: *ref,* 1567, 1609
Aronow, M. S.: *ref,* 1567
Artley, A. S.: *test,* 1665; *ref,* 1583
Ashburn, P. S.: *ref,* 1716
Ashford, Z. W.: *ref,* 1603
Ashworth, M. G.: *ref,* 1705
Askov, E.: *test,* 1655, 1776
Aspridy, C.: *ref,* 1716
Athey, I. J.: *ref,* 1603
Attea, M.: *ref,* 1624, 1628–9
Attwell, A. A.: *ref,* 1724
August, I.: *ref,* 1716
Aukerman, R. C.: *ref,* 1536, 1610
Austin, J. J.: *test,* 1728
Australian Council for Educational Research: *test,* 1613, 5:616, 6:782
Avakian, S. A.: *ref,* 1716
Avila, D.: *ref,* 1690
Avrill, D. V.: *ref,* 1711
Ayers, J. B.: *ref,* 1716

King, F. J.: *ref, 1772*
King, H. V.: *test, 4:547*
Kingston, A. J.: *rev, 1626, 1647, 1663, 1736; ref, 1546, 1716*
Kirby, B. J.: *ref, 1572*
Kirby, C. L.: *ref, 1679, 1681*
Kirby, C. L. L.: *ref, 1679, 1681*
Kirchner, W.: *ref, 1739*
Kirk, S. A.: *ref, 1724*
Kirkpatrick, M. S.: *test, 4:586*
Kirtley, D.: *ref, 1775*
Kittell, J. E.: *ref, 1536*
Klaeger, M. L. G.: *test, 1540, 1733*
Klausmeier, H. J.: *ref, 1761*
Kleyle, H. M.: *ref, 1560*
Klindienst, D. H.: *ref, 1546*
Kline, C. L.: *ref, 1631*
Kling, M.: *rev, 1662*
Knight, D.: *ref, 1536*
Knight, D. W.: *ref, 1703, 1724*
Knight, J.: *ref, 1772*
Knipe, C. S.: *ref, 1603*
Knoll, D. B.: *ref, 1691*
Koeninger, R. C.: *ref, 2:1544(8)*
Kolesnik, P. E.: *ref, 1536*
Kooker, E. W.: *ref, 1772, 1775*
Koontz, E. R.: *ref, 1716*
Kopel, D.: *rev, 1690, 1:1097, 1:1108, 2:1548*
Koppitz, E. M.: *ref, 1711, 1716*
Koskinen, P.: *ref, 1772*
Kottman, E. J.: *ref, 1774*
Kottmeyer, W.: *ref, 1716*
Kravitz, A.: *test, 1645*
Kress, R. A.: *rev, 1647, 1721*
Krippner, S.: *ref, 1536, 1628*
Krockover, G. H.: *ref, 1775*
Kropp, R. P.: *rev, 5:623, 5:636*
Krumboltz, J. D.: *rev, 6:857; ref, 1772*
Kuehn, J. A.: *ref, 1604*
Kuhlmann, M. J.: *test, 1586*
Kuhn, M. V.: *ref, 1716*
Kuntz, J. E.: *ref, 1772*
Kushinka, M.: *ref, 1560*

LaBUE, A. C.: *ref, 1583*
Ladd, E. M.: *ref, 1679*
Lafferty, J. C.: *test, 1728*
La Forest, J. R.: *ref, 1775*
Lamb, G. S.: *ref, 1574*
Lamb, P.: *ref, 1567*
Lambert, C. M.: *test, 4:548*
Lamberti, E.: *ref, 1536*
Lammi, E. H.: *ref, 1772*
Land, M.: *ref, 1775*
Landry, H.: *ref, 1560*
Landry, H. A.: *ref, 2:1539(5)*
Landsman, M.: *test, 7:747*
Lane, S. Z.: *ref, 1716*
Langford, W. S.: *ref, 1702*
Langmuir, C. R.: *rev, 1569, 1761*
Langsam, R. S.: *ref, 1560, 1568, 1572, 3:523(3)*
Lanier, J.: *ref, 1731*
Lanigan, M. A.: *ref, 1749*
Larsen, R. P.: *ref, 1560, 1572*
Larsen, S.: *ref, 1623*
Larsen, T. M.: *ref, 1583*
Larter, S. J.: *ref, 1775*
Laslett, H. R.: *ref, 1560*
Lawrence, W. A.: *ref, 1572*
Lawson, J. R.: *ref, 1690*
Lawson, J. W.: *ref, 2:1565(2)*

Layman, M. E.: *rev, 4:577*
Leaske, F.: *test, 1728*
Leavell, U. W.: *test, 5:664, 5:672*
Lebsack, J. R.: *ref, 1583, 1737-8*
Lee, C. H.: *ref, 1759*
Lee, D. M.: *ref, 1711*
Lee, J. M.: *test, 1563, 1711; ref, 1711*
Lee, N.: *ref, 1631*
Lee, R. E.: *ref, 1691, 1716*
Lee, S. E.: *ref, 1544*
Lee, Y. B.: *ref, 1536, 1766*
Lefever, D. W.: *test, 1596, 1765, 5:668*
Lemke, E. A.: *ref, 1761*
Lessler, K.: *ref, 1711*
Leton, D. A.: *ref, 1716*
Leutenegger, R. R.: *ref, 1626*
Levy, M.: *ref, 1772, 1775*
Levy, P.: *ref, 1683*
Lewis, D. G.: *ref, 1646*
Lewis, D. R.: *ref, 1775*
Lewis, F. D.: *ref, 1628*
Lewis, R. D.: *rev, 1772*
Lewis, R. W.: *ref, 1772*
Lichtman, M.: *test, 1744*
Liedtke, W.: *ref, 1603*
Light, L. L.: *ref, 1768*
Lin, Y. G.: *ref, 1772*
Lindley, M. R.: *ref, 1572*
Lindquist, E. F.: *test, 1737-8, 1758, 4:554, 4:588; ref, 1560, 1610, 1749*
Lindy, J.: *ref, 1711, 1716*
Linfoot, K. W.: *ref, 1646*
Lins, L. J.: *ref, 1583*
Liotti, A. R.: *ref, 1599*
Liske, R. E.: *ref, 1583*
Litterer, O. F.: *ref, 1560, 1568, 1749*
Littrell, J. H.: *ref, 1626*
Liveright, A. K.: *rev, 2:1549, 2:1565*
Livingston, H.: *ref, 1775*
Llewellyn, H. C.: *ref, 1626*
Lloyd, B. A.: *ref, 1711*
Lloyd, C. J.: *ref, 1567*
Lloyd, F. W.: *ref, 1716*
Lloyd, R.: *ref, 1711*
Locke, N. M.: *test, 2:1573; ref, 2:1573(1)*
Lockhart, H. M.: *ref, 1716*
Lockhart, H. S.: *ref, 1716*
Lockyer, L.: *ref, 1646*
Loflaud, W. T.: *ref, 1569*
Lohmann, V. L.: *test, 6:801*
Lohnes, P. R.: *rev, 1599, 1681*
Long, B. H.: *ref, 1716*
Long, D. J.: *ref, 1628*
Long, H. H.: *ref, 1603*
Long, J. A.: *ref, 1603*
Long, J. M.: *ref, 1626*
Long, J. R.: *ref, 1536*
Long, R. D.: *ref, 1666*
Loper, D. J.: *ref, 1702, 1716, 1733*
Lopez, D. C.: *ref, 1536*
Lore, S. W.: *test, 1533*
Lorge, I.: *test, 4:558; ref, 4:558(1)*
Lott, H. V.: *ref, 1572*
Lovell, K.: *ref, 1591, 1646, 1680*
Lovett, C. J.: *ref, 1536*
Lowe, A.: *ref, 1572, 1775*
Lowell, R. E.: *ref, 1711, 1716-7*
Lowery, D. W.: *ref, 1603*

Lowes, R.: *rev, 1563, 3:483, 3:494, 3:504*
Lowry, C. E.: *ref, 1583*
Lucas, D. G.: *test, 1720*
Luck, J. I.: *ref, 1775*
Lucker, W. G.: *ref, 1567*
Ludlow, H. G.: *ref, 4:581(17)*
Lum, M. K. M.: *ref, 1772*
Lund, K. W.: *test, 1567*
Lundstedt, V.: *ref, 1716*
Lundsteen, S. W.: *ref, 1599*
Luton, J. N.: *ref, 1775*
Luttgen, G.: *ref, 1696*
Lyder, W.: *ref, 1716*
Lysaught, J. P.: *ref, 1775*

McANDLESS, T.: *test, 2:1583.1*
McBee, G.: *ref, 1536*
McBride, J. F.: *test, 1548*
McBride, K. E.: *ref, 1690*
McBroom, M.: *test, 4:554, 4:588; ref, 1657*
McCall, R. A.: *ref, 1627, 1634, 1643, 1647, 1716*
McCall, R. B.: *ref, 1627, 1634, 1643, 1647, 1716*
McCall, R. J.: *test, 1538*
McCall, W. A.: *rev, 1768, 2:1580*
McCall, W. C.: *rev, 1568*
McCallister, J. M.: *rev, 1568, 1598, 3:505*
McCandless, B. R.: *rev, 1697*
McCarthy, J. J.: *rev, 1697, 7:746-7*
McCartney, W. A.: *test, 1584*
McCaul, R. L.: *rev, 1556, 1598, 1611, 2:1531, 3:506*
McClanahan, W. R.: *ref, 1572*
McClellan, D. A.: *ref, 1716*
McClusky, F. D.: *test, 2:1575; ref, 2:1575(1)*
McCollom, F. H.: *ref, 1560*
McCollum, C. G.: *ref, 1572*
McCormick, A. G.: *ref, 1572*
McCracken, R. A.: *test, 1649; ref, 1603, 1649-50, 1658*
McCranie, J.: *ref, 1609, 4:576(2), 4:577(2)*
McCreary, J. R.: *ref, 1531, 1685*
McCulloch, R. W.: *rev, 1557, 1646*
McCullough, C. M.: *rev, 1573, 1610, 1617, 3:501; test, 1634*
McCullough, R. O.: *ref, 1536*
McDonald, A. A.: *ref, 1583*
McDonald, A. S.: *rev, 1672; test, 1673; ref, 1673*
MacDonald, G. L.: *ref, 1572*
McGahan, C.: *test, 7:746*
McGahan, F. E.: *test, 7:746*
McGauvran, M. E.: *test, 1716*
MacGillivray, M. C.: *ref, 1599*
MacGinitie, W. H.: *test, 1552-3, 1702*
McGlade, C. A.: *ref, 1716*
McGlothlin, L. E.: *ref, 1711*
McGoldrick, D. T.: *ref, 1583*
McGowan, J. R.: *ref, 1716*
McGrath, J. E.: *test, 1564*
McGuire, C.: *ref, 1772*
McGuire, F. L.: *ref, 1546*
McGuire, M. L.: *test, 1619, 1635*
McHugh, W. J.: *test, 1713*
McKeachie, W. J.: *ref, 1772*
McKee, P.: *test, 1641*
McKillop, A. S.: *test, 1629*

READING
SCANNING INDEX

This scanning index is an expanded table of contents listing all tests in this volume. Foreign tests are identified by listing the country of origin in brackets immediately after the title. The population for which a test is intended is presented to facilitate the search for tests for use with a particular group. Stars indicate tests not previously listed in a *Mental Measurements Yearbook;* asterisks indicate tests revised or supplemented since last listed. Numbers refer to test entries, not to pages.

READING

DIAGNOSTIC

Stanford Diagnostic Reading Test, grades 2.5–8.5, see 1651

★*Swansea Test of Phonic Skills* [England], reading ages below 7.5, see 1652

Test of Individual Needs in Reading, grades 1–6, see 1653

★*Test of Phonic Skills,* reading level grades kgn–3, see 1654

★*Wisconsin Tests of Reading Skill Development: Word Attack,* grades kgn–6, see 1655

★*Woodcock Reading Mastery Tests,* grades kgn–12, see 1656

MISCELLANEOUS

Basic Sight Word Test, grades 1–2, see 1657
Botel Reading Inventory, grades 1–12, see 1658
Cumulative Reading Record, grades 9–12, see 1659
Durrell Listening-Reading Series, grades 1–9, see 1660
Durrell-Sullivan Reading Capacity and Achievement Tests, grades 2.5–6, see 1661
Dyslexia Schedule, children having reading difficulties and first grade entrants, see 1662
Individual Reading Placement Inventory, youth and adults with reading levels up to grade 7, see 1663
★*Instant Word Recognition Test,* reading level grades 1–4, see 1664
★*Inventory of Teacher Knowledge of Reading,* elementary school teachers and college students in methods courses, see 1665
Learning Methods Test, grades kgn–3, see 1666
★*National Test of Basic Words,* grades 1–5, see 1667
OC Diagnostic Syllabizing Test, grades 4–6, see 1668
Phonics Test for Teachers, reading methods courses, see 1669
Reader Rater With Self-Scoring Profile, ages 15 and over, see 1670
Reader's Inventory, entrants to a reading improvement course for secondary and college students and adults, see 1671
Reading Eye II, grades 1–16 and adults, see 1672
Reading Versatility Test, grades 5–16, see 1673
Roswell-Chall Auditory Blending Test, grades 1–4, see 1674
Word Discrimination Test, grades 1–8, see 1675
★*Word Recognition Test* [England], preschool to age 8.5, see 1676

ORAL

★*Concise Word Reading Tests* [Australia], ages 7–12, see 1677
Flash-X Sight Vocabulary Test, grades 1–2, see 1678
Gilmore Oral Reading Test, grades 1–8, see 1679
Graded Word Reading Test [England], ages 5 and over, see 1680
Gray Oral Reading Test, grades 1–16 and adults, see 1681
Holborn Reading Scale [England], ages 5.5–10, see 1682
Neale Analysis of Reading Ability [England], ages 6–13, see 1683
★*Oral Reading Criterion Test,* reading level grades 1–7, see 1684
Oral Word Reading Test [New Zealand], ages 7–11, see 1685
★*Reading Miscue Inventory,* grades 1–7, see 1686
★*St. Lucia Graded Word Reading Test* [Australia], grades 2–7, see 1687
Slosson Oral Reading Test, grades 1–8 and high school, see 1688
Standardized Oral Reading Check Tests, grades 1–8, see 1689

Standardized Oral Reading Paragraphs, grades 1–8, see 1690

READINESS

ABC Inventory to Determine Kindergarten and School Readiness, entrants to kgn and grade 1, see 1691
APELL Test, Assessment Program of Early Learning Levels, ages 4.5–7, see 1692
Academic Readiness and End of First Grade Progress Scales, grade 1, see 1693
American School Reading Readiness Test, first grade entrants, see 1694
★*Analysis of Readiness Skills: Reading and Mathematics,* grades kgn–1, see 1695
Anton Brenner Developmental Gestalt Test of School Readiness, ages 5–6, see 1696
Basic Concept Inventory, preschool and kgn, see 1697
Binion-Beck Reading Readiness Test for Kindergarten and First Grade, grades kgn–1, see 1698
Clymer-Barrett Prereading Battery, first grade entrants, see 1699
Contemporary School Readiness Test, first grade entrants, see 1700
★*Delco Readiness Test,* first grade entrants, see 1701
Gates-MacGinitie Reading Tests: Readiness Skills, grades kgn–1, see 1702
Gesell Developmental Tests, ages 5–10, see 1703
Group Test of Reading Readiness, grades kgn–1, see 1704
Harrison-Stroud Reading Readiness Profiles, grades kgn–1, see 1705
★*Initial Survey Test,* first grade entrants, see 1706
★*Inventory of Primary Skills,* grades kgn–1, see 1707
★*Kindergarten Behavioural Index* [Australia], grades kgn–1, see 1708
Kindergarten Evaluation of Learning Potential, kgn, see 1709
★*LRS Seriation Test,* ages 4–6, see 1710
Lee-Clark Reading Readiness Test, grades kgn–1, see 1711
Lippincott Reading Readiness Test, grades kgn–1, see 1712
McHugh-McParland Reading Readiness Test, grades kgn–1, see 1713
Macmillan Reading Readiness Test, first grade entrants, see 1714
Maturity Level for School Entrance and Reading Readiness, grades kgn–1, see 1715
Metropolitan Readiness Tests, grades kgn–1, see 1716
Murphy-Durrell Reading Readiness Analysis, first grade entrants, see 1717
Parent Readiness Evaluation of Preschoolers, ages 3–9 to 5–8, see 1718
★*Pre-Reading Assessment Kit* [Canada], grades kgn–1, see 1719
★*Prereading Expectancy Screening Scales,* first grade entrants, see 1720
Pre-Reading Screening Procedures, first grade entrants of average or superior intelligence, see 1721
★*Preschool and Kindergarten Performance Profile,* preschool and kgn, see 1722
Primary Academic Sentiment Scale, ages 4–4 to 7–3, see 1723
Reading Aptitude Tests, grades kgn–1, see 1724
★*Reading Inventory Probe 1,* grades 1–2, see 1725
Reversal Test [Sweden], grade 1 entrants, see 1726
Riley Preschool Developmental Screening Inventory, ages 3–5, see 1727
School Readiness Checklist, ages 5–6, see 1728
School Readiness Survey, ages 4–6, see 1729
Screening Test of Academic Readiness, ages 4–0 to 6–5, see 1730

SPECIAL FIELDS

SPEED

STUDY SKILLS